‹J P9-BYM-139

The Modern Language Association of America

Reviews of Research

The English Romantic Poets: A Review of Research and Criticism. Third revised edition. Edited by Frank Jordan. 1972.

Victorian Prose: A Guide to Research. Edited by David J. DeLaura. 1973.

Anglo-Irish Literature: A Review of Research. Edited by Richard J. Finneran. 1976.

Victorian Fiction: A Second Guide to Research. Edited by George H. Ford. 1978.

Victorian Periodicals: A Guide to Research. Edited by J. Donn Vann and Rosemary T. VanArsdel. 1978.

Victorian Fiction: A Guide to Research. Reprint of 1964 edition. Edited by Lionel Stevenson. 1980.

Recent Research on Anglo-Irish Writers: A Supplement to Anglo-Irish Literature: A Review of Research. Edited by Richard J. Finneran. 1983.

The Transcendentalists: A Review of Research and Criticism. Edited by Joel Myerson. 1984.

THE
TRANSCENDENTALISTS

---

*A Review of Research
and
Criticism*

Edited by
JOEL MYERSON

The Modern Language Association of America
NEW YORK
1984

Copyright © 1984 by The Modern Language Association of America

Library of Congress Cataloging in Publication Data
Main entry under title:

The transcendentalists.

Bibliography: p.
Includes index.
1. Transcendentalism (New England)—Bibliography.
I. Myerson, Joel. II. Modern Language Association
of America.
Z7128.T7T7   1984   [B905]   016.141'3'0973   83-19442
ISBN 0-87352-260-5
ISBN 0-87352-261-3 (pbk).

Published by the Modern Language Association of America
62 Fifth Avenue, New York, New York 10011

Contents

PREFACE   vii

ACRONYMS   ix

THE TRANSCENDENTALIST MOVEMENT   *Lawrence Buell*   1
TRANSCENDENTALISM: THE TIMES   *Joel Myerson*   37
UNITARIANISM AND TRANSCENDENTALISM   *Conrad Wright*   45
TRANSCENDENTALIST COMMUNITIES   *Carol Johnston*   56
TRANSCENDENTALIST PERIODICALS   *Donald F. Warders*   69

THE TRANSCENDENTALISTS

AMOS BRONSON ALCOTT   *Frederick C. Dahlstrand*   87
CYRUS AUGUSTUS BARTOL   *William G. Heath*   97
CHARLES TIMOTHY BROOKS   *Elizabeth R. McKinsey*   100
WILLIAM ELLERY CHANNING II   *Francis B. Dedmond*   102
WILLIAM HENRY CHANNING   *Elizabeth R. McKinsey*   108
JAMES FREEMAN CLARKE   *Leonard Neufeldt*   112
MONCURE DANIEL CONWAY   *Robert E. Burkholder*   117
CHRISTOPHER PEARSE CRANCH   *David Robinson*   123
JOHN SULLIVAN DWIGHT   *William G. Heath*   131
RALPH WALDO EMERSON   *Robert E. Burkholder and Joel Myerson*   135
CONVERS FRANCIS   *Guy R. Woodall*   167
OCTAVIUS BROOKS FROTHINGHAM   *J. Wade Caruthers*   171
MARGARET FULLER   *Robert N. Hudspeth*   175
FREDERIC HENRY HEDGE   *Leonard Neufeldt*   189
THOMAS WENTWORTH HIGGINSON   *Howard N. Meyer*   195
SAMUEL JOHNSON   *Roger C. Mueller*   204
SYLVESTER JUDD   *Francis B. Dedmond*   207
CHARLES LANE   *Joel Myerson*   211
CHARLES KING NEWCOMB   *Joel Myerson*   214
THEODORE PARKER   *Gary L. Collison*   216
ELIZABETH PALMER PEABODY   *Margaret Neussendorfer*   233

GEORGE RIPLEY   *Charles Crowe*   242
SOPHIA DANA RIPLEY   *Charles Crowe*   250
FRANKLIN BENJAMIN SANBORN   *Robert E. Burkholder*   253
HENRY DAVID THOREAU   *Michael Meyer*   260
JONES VERY   *David Robinson*   286
JOHN WEISS   *Robert E. Burkholder*   295
CHARLES STEARNS WHEELER   *Joel Myerson*   299

THE CONTEMPORARY REACTION

ORESTES AUGUSTUS BROWNSON   *Leonard Gilhooley*   303
WILLIAM ELLERY CHANNING   *David Robinson*   310
GEORGE WILLIAM CURTIS   *W. Gordon Milne*   317
EMILY DICKINSON   *Paul J. Ferlazzo*   320
NATHANIEL HAWTHORNE   *Joel Myerson*   328
JAMES RUSSELL LOWELL   *Thomas Wortham*   336
JAMES MARSH   *Douglas McCreary Greenwood*   343
HERMAN MELVILLE   *Brian Higgins*   348
EDGAR ALLAN POE   *Ottavio M. Casale*   362
SAMPSON REED   *Elizabeth A. Meese*   372
WALT WHITMAN   *Jerome Loving*   375

BIBLIOGRAPHY   385
CONTRIBUTORS   504
INDEX   507

Preface

The Transcendentalists: A Review of Research and Criticism is the first comprehensive bibliography of American Transcendentalism. Many of the Transcendentalists discussed here have not been covered in general bibliographies of American literature, and over half have not been favored by individual bibliographies of secondary works. This book rectifies these omissions and evaluates nearly a century and a half of writings by and about the Transcendentalists.

The first section of this volume contains five general essays surveying the Transcendentalist movement, its general historical context, its relationship to Unitarianism, and the communities and periodicals it helped bring into existence. The second section deals with individual Transcendentalists, their writings, and writings about them by contemporaries and later commentators. The third section discusses major contemporaries who influenced, were influenced by, or reacted against the Transcendentalists. A bibliography provides full citations for all items discussed in the text.

Readers will find much new information in this volume. Only six of the twenty-eight Transcendentalists discussed here have been the subjects of previous bibliographies. Nearly every one of the essays on individual Transcendentalists corrects existing information on locations of their manuscripts and adds new locations. All the essays in this book are particularly strong in discussing nineteenth-century criticism, master's theses, and doctoral dissertations. The essays on Emerson and Thoreau focus primarily on the Transcendentalist phase of their careers and thus provide a more thorough analysis of this aspect of their writings and the writings on them than other, more general essays have been able to do.

All items published through the end of 1981 have been consulted in preparing this book. Selected works appearing after 1981 have been added by individual contributors. The bibliography provides complete publication information for readers who wish to obtain individual volumes through interlibrary loan.

Thanks are due *Resources for American Literary Study* and *Studies in the American Renaissance* for permission to reproduce portions of essays. Robert E. Burkholder would like to thank Kaye Edwards and the Institute for the Arts and Humanistic Studies of the Pennsylvania State University. David Robinson is grateful for the support of the General Research Fund of Oregon State University and the National Endowment for the Humanities. I wish to thank the American Philosophical Society, the National Endowment for the Humanities (fellowships and research materials programs), the John Simon Guggenheim Foundation, and the University of South Carolina for supporting various projects out of which this book evolved.

Walter S. Achtert of the Modern Language Association has been a constant source of encouragement and help, and I am grateful for his continued support. Walter Harding and David B. Kesterson have improved the quality of the book by commenting upon an earlier version of it. Alan Seaburg and Wesley T. Mott graciously answered many queries. The University of South Carolina has provided much assistance, and I am particularly grateful to George L. Geckle, chairman of the department of English. I also wish to thank Robert E. Burkholder and Stephen Garrison for help during the early stages of this project, and Caroline Bokinsky for reading the manuscript and getting it ready for publication.

JOEL MYERSON

Acronyms

BOOKS

AAL	Leary, Lewis. *Articles in American Literature 1900–1950; 1950–1967; 1968–1975*. 3 vols. Durham: Duke Univ. Press, 1954, 1970, 1979.
ALM	Robbins, J. Albert, ed. *American Literary Manuscripts*. 2nd ed. Athens: Univ. of Georgia Press, 1977.
AmLS	Robbins, J. Albert, or James Woodress, ed. *American Literary Scholarship: An Annual*. Durham: Duke Univ. Press, 1965– .
BAL	Blanck, Jacob. *Bibliography of American Literature*. 6 vols. to date. New Haven: Yale Univ. Press, 1955– .
CHAL	Trent, William Petersfield, et al. *Cambridge History of American Literature*. 3 vols. New York: Putnam's, 1917–21.
DAB	*Dictionary of American Biography*. 20 vols. New York: Scribners, 1928–37.
FPAA	Bruccoli, Matthew J., et al., eds. *First Printings of American Authors*. 4 vols. Detroit: Gale Research, 1977–79.
NUC	*National Union Catalog of Pre-1956 Imprints*. 754 vols. London and Chicago: Mansell, 1968–81.
ULS	Titus, Edna Brown, ed. *Union List of Serials*. 3rd ed. 5 vols. New York: H. W. Wilson, 1965.

PERIODICALS

AAUWJ	*American Association of University Women Journal*
ABC	*American Book Collector*
ABiR	*American Biblical Repository*
ABR	*American Benedictine Review*
ACQR	*American Catholic Quarterly Review*
AEB	*Analytical and Enumerative Bibliography*
AGR	*American-German Review*
AH	*American Heritage*
AI	*American Imago*
AJP	*American Journal of Psychology*
AL	*American Literature*

AlB	*Alumni Bulletin* (Bangor Theological Seminary)
ALR	*American Literary Realism, 1870–1910*
AmA	*American Author*
AmerS	*American Studies*
AmerST	*American Studies* (Taiwan)
AMLA	*American Museum of Literature and the Arts*
AmM	*American Mercury*
AmR	*American Review*
AmS	*American Socialist*
Amst	*Amerikastudien/American Studies*
AnAA	*Annals of the American Academy*
AN&Q	*American Notes and Queries*
AndR	*Andover Review*
AnI	*Annals of Iowa*
AQ	*American Quarterly*
AR	*Antioch Review*
ArQ	*Arizona Quarterly*
ArtA	*Art in America*
ArtB	*Art Bulletin*
AS	*American Speech*
ASch	*American Scholar*
Ath	*Athenæum*
Atl	*Atlantic Monthly Magazine*
ATQ	*American Transcendental Quarterly*
BACH	*Bulletin de l'Association Canadienne des Humanités*
BapQR	*Baptist Quarterly Review*
BB	*Bulletin of Bibliography*
BBB	*Boston Book Bulletin*
BCP	*Book Collector's Packet*
BDA	*Boston Daily Advertiser*
BDE	*Brooklyn Daily Eagle*
BEI	*Bulletin of the Essex Institute*
BelMM	*Belford's Monthly Magazine*
BEM	*Blackwood's Edinburgh Magazine*
BET	*Boston Evening Transcript*
BGM	*Burton's Gentleman's Magazine*
BHJ	*Boston Home Journal*
BHPSO	*Bulletin of the Historic and Philosophical Society of Ohio*
BibS	*Bibliotheca Sacra*
BJ	*Broadway Journal*
BL	*Book-Lover*
BM	*Boston Miscellany*
BMMLA	*Bulletin of the Midwest Modern Language Association*
BNYPL	*Bulletin of the New York Public Library*
BoCom	*Boston Commonwealth*
BoH	*Boston Herald*
BoM	*Boston Magazine*
BoP	*Boston Post*

BoQR	Boston Quarterly Review
BPLQ	Boston Public Library Quarterly
BPP	Bengal: Past and Present
BQR	British Quarterly Review
BRH	Bulletin of Research in the Humanities
BRPR	Biblical Repertory and Princeton Review
BrQR	Brownson's Quarterly Review
BSUF	Ball State University Forum
BUK	Bulletin of the University of Kansas
BuR	Bucknell Review
BUS	Bucknell University Studies
CalR	Calcutta Review
Carrell	The Carrell: Journal of the Friends of the University of Miami (Fla.) Library
CathW	Catholic World
CAW	The Christian at Work
CCTEP	Conference of College Teachers of English (Texas) Proceedings
CE	College English
ChCent	Christian Century
ChEx	Christian Examiner
ChH	Church History
ChOb	Christian Observatory
CHR	Catholic Historical Review
ChReg	Christian Register
ChRev	Christian Review
ChT	Christian Thought
CKSHS	Collections of the Kansas State Historical Society
CL	Comparative Literature
CLAJ	College Language Association Journal
CLC	Columbia Library Columns
CLJ	Cornell Library Journal
CLQ	Colby Library Quarterly
CLS	Comparative Literature Studies
CM	Century Magazine
ColM	Columbian Magazine
ColQ	Colorado Quarterly
CoM	Continental Monthly
ComA	Coming Age
CoMag	Cornhill Magazine
ConnR	Connecticut Review
ContempR	Contemporary Review
CP	Collegium Proceedings
CraneR	Crane Review
CRevAS	Canadian Review of the American Studies
Crit	Critique: Studies in Modern Fiction
CriticE	Critic (England)
CriticNY	Critic (New York)
CritQ	Critical Quarterly

CS	Concord Saunterer (Thoreau Lyceum, Concord, Mass.)
CSR	Christian Scholar's Review
CSSH	Comparative Studies in Society and History
CSSJ	Central States Speech Journal
CuL	Current Literature
CWM	Continent Weekly Magazine
DAM	Dartmouth Alumni Magazine
DCLB	Dartmouth College Library Bulletin
DD	Double Dealer
DeltaES	Delta: Revue du Centre d'Etudes et de Recherche sur les Ecrivains du Sud aux Etats-Unis
DiA	Dickinson Alumnus
DicS	Dickinson Studies
DJSM	Douglas Jerrold's Shilling Magazine
DMM	Demorest's Monthly Magazine
DosP	Dos Pueblos
DR	Dalhousie Review
DuR	Dublin Review
EarlR	Earlham Review
EDB	Emily Dickinson Bulletin
EdF	Educational Forum
EdR	Edinburgh Review
EdT	Educational Theory
EIHC	Essex Institute Historical Collections
Éire	Éire-Ireland
EJ	English Journal
ELH	(Formerly Journal of English Literary History)
ELN	English Language Notes
ELWIU	Essays in Literature
EngRevL	English Review (London)
ESJ	Every Saturday Journal
ESQ	Emerson Society Quarterly (1955–71); ESQ: A Journal of the American Renaissance (1972–)
ESRS	Emporia State Research Studies
EthR	Ethical Record
EWR	East West Review
FoR	Fortnightly Review
ForumH	Forum (Houston, Texas)
FR	French Review
FrCR	Free Church Record
FrM	Fraser's Magazine
FurmS	Furman Studies
GaR	Georgia Review
GAS	Journal of German-American Studies
GentM	Gentleman's Magazine
GHQ	Georgia Historical Quarterly
GLB	Godey's Lady's Book
GMLB	Godey's Magazine and Lady's Book

GR	*Germanic Review*
GrJ	*Graduate Journal* (University of Texas)
GrM	*Granite Monthly*
GrMag	*Graham's Magazine*
HaAB	*Harvard Alumni Bulletin*
HAB	*Humanities Association Review/La Revue de l'Association des Humanités*
HAM	*Harvard Alumni Magazine*
H&H	*Hound and Horn*
Har	*Harper's New Monthly Magazine*
HaR	*Harvard Register*
HCB	*Howard College Bulletin*
HCQ	*History of Childhood Quarterly*
HDM	*Holden's Dollar Magazine*
HGM	*Harvard Graduates' Magazine*
HigJ	*Higginson Journal*
HJ	*Hibbert Journal*
HLB	*Harvard Library Bulletin*
HLQ	*Huntington Library Quarterly*
HM	*Harvard Magazine*
HMo	*Harvard Monthly*
HNH	*Historical New Hampshire*
HoJ	*Howitt's Journal*
HTR	*Harvard Theological Review*
HudR	*Hudson Review*
HuLB	*Huntington Library Bulletin*
HusR	*Husson Review*
IJAS	*Indian Journal of American Studies*
IJE	*International Journal of Ethics*
IJHP	*Iowa Journal of History and Politics*
IllQ	*Illinois Quarterly*
IM	*Irish Monthly*
Ind	*Independent*
IntQ	*International Quarterly*
IntR	*International Review*
IRNJM	*International Repository and New Jerusalem Magazine*
JA	*Jahrbuch für Amerikastudien*
JAAC	*Journal of Aesthetics and Art Criticism*
JAF	*Journal of American Folklore*
JAH	*Journal of American History*
JAmS	*Journal of American Studies*
JAMS	*Journal of the American Musicological Society*
JEGP	*Journal of English and Germanic Philology*
JHI	*Journal of the History of Ideas*
JHPER	*Journal of Health, Physical Education, Recreation*
JISHS	*Journal of the Illinois State Historical Society*
JLR	*Journal of Liberal Religion*
JMH	*Journal of Modern History*

JNH	Journal of Negro History
JNYES	Journal of the New York Entomological Society
JOFS	Journal of the Ohio Folklore Society
JP	Journal of Philosophy
JPC	Journal of Popular Culture
JR	Journal of Religion
JRH	Journal of Religious History
JSAH	Journal of the Society of Architectural Historians
JSP	Journal of Speculative Philosophy
JTP	Journal of Transpersonal Psychology
KAL	Kyushu American Literature
KindN	Kindergarten News
KindR	Kindergarten Review
Knick	Knickerbocker Magazine
L&WR	London and Westminster Review
Lang&S	Language and Style
LCrit	Literary Criterion
LE&W	Literature East and West
LitRev	Literary Review (New York)
LLA	Littell's Living Age
LMonog	Literary Monographs
LQR	London Quarterly Review
LW	Literary World (Boston)
LWNY	Literary World (New York)
MacM	Macmillan's Magazine
MASJ	Midcontinent American Studies Journal
MassQR	Massachusetts Quarterly Review
MB	More Books (Boston Public Library)
MeadJ	Meadville Journal
MEEJLR	Macphail's Edinburgh Ecclesiastical Journal and Literary Review
MethQR	Methodist Quarterly Review
MethR	Methodist Review
MFS	Modern Fiction Studies
MHSM	M. H. S. Miscellany (Massachusetts Historical Society)
MichA	Michigan Academician
MidM	Midland Monthly
MinnR	Minnesota Review
MissQ	Mississippi Quarterly
MLN	(Formerly Modern Language Notes)
MLQ	Modern Language Quarterly
MMRL	Monthly Miscellany of Religion and Letters
MoM	Monthly Magazine (England)
MonatDu	Monatshefte für Deutschen Unterricht, Deutsche Sprache und Literatur
MP	Modern Philology
MQ	Midwest Quarterly
MQR	Michigan Quarterly Review
MR	Massachusetts Review

MRM	Monthly Religious Magazine
MuQ	Musical Quarterly
MVHR	Mississippi Valley Historical Review
MWH	Magazine of Western History
N&Q	Notes and Queries
NAR	North American Review
NASS	National Anti-Slavery Standard
NBR	North British Review
NCent	Nineteenth Century
NCL	New-Church Life
NCM	New-Church Messenger
NCMag	New-Church Magazine
NConL	Notes on Contemporary Literature
NCR	New-Church Review
NDM	New Dominion Monthly
NDQ	North Dakota Quarterly
NEHGR	New England Historical and Genealogical Register
NEMag	New England Magazine
NEP	New England Palladium
NEPur	New England Puritan
NEQ	New England Quarterly
NewB	New Bulletin (Staten Island Institute of Arts and Sciences)
NewE	New Englander
NewP	New Philosophy
NHJ	Nathaniel Hawthorne Journal
NiagF	Niagara Frontier
NJM	New Jerusalem Magazine
NLH	New Literary History
NM	Neophilologische Mitteilungen
NMQ	New Mexico Quarterly
NNVHM	Northern Neck of Virginia Historical Magazine
NO	New Outlook
NOQ	Northwest Ohio Quarterly
NR	Nassau Review (Nassau Community College)
NRep	New Republic
NRev	National Review
NW	New World
NYA	New York Aurora
NYDT	New York Daily Tribune
NYH	New York History
NYHer	New York Herald
NYQ	New York Quarterly
NYR	New York Review
NYRB	New York Review of Books
NYTS	New York Tribune Supplement
OBW	Our Best Words
OC	Open Court
OhH	Ohio History

OJES	Osmania Journal of English Studies
OTNE	Old-Time New England
PAAAS	Proceedings of the American Academy of Arts and Sciences
PAAS	Proceedings of the American Antiquarian Society
PAH	Perspectives in American History
PAM	Potter's American Monthly
P&R	Philosophy and Rhetoric
PAPS	Proceedings of the American Philosophical Society
PBS	Proceedings of the Bostonian Society
PBSA	Papers of the Bibliographical Society of America
PCHS	Publications of the Cambridge Historical Society
PCP	Pacific Coast Philology
PCSM	Publications of the Colonial Society of Massachusetts
PE&W	Philosophy East and West
PeJ	People's Journal
Person	Personalist
PhR	Philosophical Review
PJE	Peabody Journal of Education
PMASAL	Papers of the Michigan Academy of Science, Arts, and Letters
PMG	Pall Mall Gazette
PMHS	Proceedings of the Massachusetts Historical Society
PMLA	PMLA: Publications of the Modern Language Association of America
PMM	Putnam's Monthly Magazine
PoeN	Poe Newsletter
PoeS	Poe Studies
PoL	Poet-Lore
PoR	Poetry Review
PoSM	Popular Science Monthly
PrI	Practical Ideals
PRIHS	Publications of the Rhode Island Historical Society
PrR	Princeton Review
PsyR	Psychoanalytic Review
PT	Papers for the Times
PUASAL	Proceedings of the Utah Academy of Sciences, Arts, and Letters
PUHS	Proceedings of the Unitarian Historical Society
PULC	Princeton University Library Chronicle
QCS	Quarterly Christian Spectator
QH	Quaker History
QJLC	Library of Congress Quarterly (Formerly Quarterly Journal of the Library of Congress)
QJS	Quarterly Journal of Speech
QQ	Queen's Quarterly
QRB	Quarterly Review of Biology
QRMECS	Quarterly Review of the Methodist Episcopal Church, South
RadfR	Radford Review
RadR	Radical Review
RALS	Resources for American Literary Study

RBUP	*Research Bulletin of the University of Punjab*
RDM	*Revue des Deux Mondes*
RecL	*Recovering Literature*
ReI	*Revue Indépendante*
RFEA	*Revue Française d'Etudes Américaines*
RHE	*Revue d'Histoire Ecclésiastique*
RIH	*Rhode Island History*
RinL	*Religion in Life*
RLC	*Revue de Littérature Comparée*
RLMC	*Revista di Letterature Moderne e Comparate*
RLV	*Revue des Langues Vivantes*
RMCM	*Randolph-Macon College Magazine*
RP	*Review of Politics*
RPhil	*Revue Philosophique*
RQR	*Reformed Quarterly Review*
RS	*Research Studies*
RSQ	*Rhetoric Society Quarterly*
RTR	*Religious and Theological Resources*
RUO	*Revue de l'Université d'Ottawa/University of Ottawa Quarterly*
SA	*Studi Americani*
SAB	*South Atlantic Bulletin*
SaN	*Satire Newsletter*
S&Map	*Surveying and Mapping*
SAQ	*South Atlantic Quarterly*
SAR	*Studies in the American Renaissance*
SB	*Studies in Bibliography*
ScAR	*Scottish Art Review*
SCB	*South Central Bulletin*
SchR	*School Review*
SchS	*School and Society*
ScR	*Scottish Review*
SCSH	*Smith College Studies in History*
SCUL	*Soundings: Collections of the University Library, University of California, Santa Barbara*
SEAL	*Studies in English and American Literature*
SEL	*Studies in English Literature*
SFQ	*Southern Folklore Quarterly*
SHR	*Southern Humanities Review*
Signs	*Signs: Journal of Women in Culture and Society*
SIR	*Studies in Romanticism*
SLitI	*Studies in the Literary Imagination*
SLM	*Southern Literary Messenger*
SLQ	*St. Louis Quarterly*
SM	*Scientific Monthly*
SMM	*Scribner's Monthly Magazine*
SN	*Studia Neophilologica*
SNPL	*Studies and Notes in Philology and Literature*
SocS	*Social Studies*

SoQ	Southern Quarterly
SoQR	Southern Quarterly Review
SoRes	Social Research
SoRose	Southern Rose
SP	Studies in Philology
SPJ	Southern Speech Journal
SPM	South Place Magazine
SpMonog	Speech Monographs
SpR	Springfield Republican
SR	Sewanee Review
SS	Scandinavian Studies
SSF	Studies in Short Fiction
SSR	Social Service Review
SST	Sunday School Times
StAH	Studies in American Humor
StJ	Stratford Journal
SUM	Sartain's Union Magazine
SWJ	Southwestern Journal
SWR	Southwest Review
TAUA	Transactions of the American Unitarian Association
TEM	Tait's Edinburgh Magazine
TH	Time and the Hour
TheosQ	Theosophical Quarterly
ThQ	Thoreau Quarterly
TJQ	Thoreau Journal Quarterly
TQ	Texas Quarterly
TR	Texas Review
TriQ	TriQuarterly
TSB	Thoreau Society Bulletin
TSE	Tulane Studies in English
TSL	Tennessee Studies in Literature
TSLL	Texas Studies in Literature and Language
TUM	Trumpet and Universalist Magazine
TWA	Transactions of the Wisconsin Academy of Sciences, Arts, and Letters
TxSE	Texas Studies in English
UBS	University of Buffalo Studies
UCPMP	University of California Publications in Modern Philology
UCQ	University College Quarterly
UCS	University of Colorado Studies
UIHS	University of Iowa Humanistic Studies
UISLL	University of Illinois Studies in Language and Literature
UKCR	University of Kansas City Review
UMB	University of Maine Bulletin
UnitR	Unitarian Review
UNSLLC	University of Nebraska Studies in Language, Literature, and Criticism

UR	Ulbandus Review
USMDR	United States Magazine, and Democratic Review
UTQ	University of Toronto Quarterly
UTSE	University of Texas Studies in English
UUC	Unitarian-Universalist Christian
UWR	University of Windsor Review
VMHB	Virginia Magazine of History and Biography
VQR	Virginia Quarterly Review
W&L	Women & Literature
WF	Western Folklore
WHR	Western Humanities Review
WJ	Woman's Journal
WJP	West Jersey Press
WM	Western Messenger
WMH	Wisconsin Magazine of History
WS	Women's Studies
WSL	Wisconsin Studies in Literature
WUS	Washington University Studies
WVUPP	West Virginia University Philological Papers
WWR	Walt Whitman Review
YC	Youth's Companion
YES	Yearbook of English Studies
YFS	Yale French Studies
YLM	Yale Literary Magazine
YR	Yale Review

THE
TRANSCENDENTALISTS
A Review of Research and Criticism

THE TRANSCENDENTALIST MOVEMENT

Lawrence Buell

INTRODUCTION

Few chapters in the history of American thought and writing have been discussed more thoroughly than the Transcendentalist movement, but its diversity and lack of structure have often baffled its most serious students. The activities of American Transcendentalism, as an organized movement, were mainly limited to a series of discussion groups, the most important being the so-called "Transcendental Club" (1836–40); some literary and miscellaneous journals, the most famous being the *Dial* (1840–44); reform agitation within the Unitarian church; and two utopian communities, Brook Farm (1841–47) and Fruitlands (1843–44). But the impact of American Transcendentalism extended far beyond these particular enterprises. Transcendentalism is best regarded as a certain state of mind, an intellectual ferment that began in the late 1820s, reached a peak during the next two decades, and gradually declined after the Civil War. Most of the major Transcendentalists were well-bred, well-educated, liberal Unitarians from eastern Massachusetts who knew each other socially as well as by reputation. But these bonds did not necessarily lead to collective action, for, if there was a central credo of Transcendentalism, it was a faith in the boundless possibilities of human nature. The majority of Transcendentalists held with Emerson, their greatest spokesman, that God exists within the individual soul. This doctrine led to individualism like Thoreau's more often than it led to joint enterprises, although some Transcendentalists used the doctrine of human divinity to argue that human community was superior to isolated individualism.

Although Transcendentalism might thus be described as essentially a religious orientation, it also had implications for epistemology, art, social reform, and the philosophy of nature. As a religion, it was the ultimate extension of the American Unitarian reaction against Calvinist doctrine, but it was directed against Unitarianism itself, in such a way as to reintroduce the mystical element that Unitarian rationalism had sought to discredit as superstition. In epistemology, Transcendentalism marked the first American manifestation of an international reaction against the constraints of John Locke's theory of the human mind, according to which the individual can know only what he or she learns empirically through sense experience—a position that, according to Locke's detractors, led to skepticism and atheism. As an aesthetic theory, Transcendentalism was a form of Romanticism that emphasized the analogy between the artist and God, glorifying the artist's creative and symbol-making powers but differentiating sharply between true "genius" and mere "talent." As a social reform movement, Transcendentalism lent varying degrees of support to the many crusades of the antebellum period, particularly religious and educational reform, abolitionism, and utopian socialism. Transcendentalist philosophy anticipated Darwin by viewing nature as organic and transitional rather than fixed and mechanistic, but the Transcendentalists remained prescientific in that they were finally interested in treating nature not as objective matter but as a manifestation of divine nature and teleology.

Among these various fields, Transcendentalism has had the most lasting impact on literature, partly because of the literary tastes and abilities of those associated with the movement and partly because many Transcendentalists preferred "inspired" to closely reasoned discourse. Not all Transcendentalists, however, felt as reverently about poetic genius as Ralph Waldo Emerson and Henry David Thoreau did. The minister-reformer William Henry Channing, for example, once accused Emerson of literary trifling. Indeed, Transcendentalists liked to boast that no two of them thought alike.

Because of these internal differences and the fact that Transcendentalist thought often reflected the spirit and ferment of its times, it is often difficult to distinguish Transcendentalists from non-Transcendentalists. Emerson, widely and justly regarded as the arch-Transcendentalist, preferred to speak of the Transcendentalists as "them," while, at the opposite extreme, the Christian perfectionism of an anti-Transcendentalist like the great evangelist Charles G. Finney had some affinities with Emersonianism. On the borderline are figures like the Episcopalian Caleb Sprague Henry and the moderate Unitarian Sylvester Judd who are conventionally ranked among the Transcendentalists but who would have been dismayed to find themselves so classed. Such problems of definition cause headaches for both novice and specialist, but they testify to the culturally representative quality of Transcendentalist thinking. Transcendentalism would not have endured to become the subject of this volume had it not been to a considerable extent the product of its age as well as a reaction against it.

Scholarship on Transcendentalism, like the movement itself, has been conducted for the most part in an irregular, piecemeal, heterogeneous fashion. Thousands of books and articles touch on the subject, and this chapter attempts to sort out only the best-known and most helpful works. An organized presentation like the following inevitably exaggerates the coherence of this sprawling body of knowledge, involving 150 years of accumulated material in a number of different disciplines. No one researcher is master of it all. One may hope, however, that such research tools as this may help future investigators to put together the authoritative history of Transcendentalism that has yet to be written.

BIBLIOGRAPHIES

PRIMARY

Most bibliographies of writings by Transcendentalists deal with individual authors and are therefore discussed in the second section of this book. Only works of general scope are mentioned here.

The Library of Congress' *NUC* and its supplements list, by author, basic publication data for virtually all editions of books and pamphlets written by the Transcendentalists, together with American libraries where the works are held. *FPAA* lists first American and English printings of works by several hundred writers, including many Transcendentalists. Likewise invaluable is *BAL*, a descriptive bibliography, still in progress, of the first book appearances and all first editions by approximately three hundred American writers. There is no comprehensive treatment of first magazine and newspaper appearances.

Clarence L. F. Gohdes, *The Periodicals of American Transcendentalism*, identifies each of the journals that served as forums of Transcendentalist opinion. Frank Luther Mott, *A History of American Magazines*, vols. 1–2, profiles some of these periodicals as well as others with which Transcendentalists associated or engaged in controversy. More comprehensive bibliographies of contemporary periodicals, including partial lists of contributors, are Jayne K. Kribbs, *An Annotated Bibliography of American Literary Periodicals, 1741–1850*, and *American Periodicals 1741–1900*, ed. Jean Hoornstra and Trudy Heath. Daniel A. Wells, *The Literary Index to American Magazines, 1815–1865*, indexes by selected authors and topics the contents of twenty-four major magazines of the period. For a virtually complete roster of nineteenth-century American magazines, together with major libraries of deposit, see the *Union List of Serials*. Winifred Gregory, *American Newspapers, 1821–1936*, provides similar information for newspapers. E. Bruce Kirkham and John M. Fink, *Indices to American Literary Annuals and Gift Books 1825–1865*, gives full tables of contents (including authors, where identified) of virtually all known productions of a popular antebellum genre to which many Transcendentalists contributed. Contributors to the *Dial*, Transcendentalism's most important magazine, are identified by Joel Myerson, *The New England Transcendentalists and the Dial*. *ALM* lists locations of known manuscript collections of many American authors, including a number of Transcendentalists. The following libraries are noted for their holdings of Transcendentalist manuscripts and memorabilia: Houghton Library (Harvard Univ.), Massachusetts Historical Society,

Boston Public Library, Andover-Harvard Theological Library, Pierpont Morgan Library (New York), New York Public Library (particularly the Berg Collection), Henry E. Huntington Library (San Marino, Cal.), Brown University Library, Concord Free Public Library, Fruitlands Museums (Harvard, Mass.), Clifton Waller Barrett Library (Univ. of Virginia), and Pilgrim Society (Plymouth). A catalog of the Transcendentalist holdings in this last collection, compiled by Kenneth Fuller, is in L. D. Geller, *Between Concord and Plymouth*. A similar compilation for Andover-Harvard has been done by Philip B. Eppard and Alan Seaburg.

Finally, Kenneth Walter Cameron, *Transcendentalism and American Renaissance Bibliography*, since reissued with supplements as *Bibliography on Transcendentalism or the American Renaissance*, catalogs most (though by no means all) of the items that Cameron has published at his press, Transcendental Books, in Hartford, Connecticut. These include manuscripts by Transcendentalists and their acquaintances, reprints of previously published writings by Transcendentalists, compendia of nineteenth-century newspaper and magazine accounts of the movement, New England lyceum proceedings, and obscure library lists, as well as scholarly monographs and essay collections (both original and reprinted). Some of this mountain of material is sheer trivia, but much of it can be helpful to the researcher if used selectively. Individual titles will be discussed later in this and other chapters.

SECONDARY

No comprehensive bibliography of scholarship on the Transcendentalist movement has been attempted on anything like the scale of the present volume. The first chapter of *AmLS*, an annual review of scholarship published since 1963, evaluates studies of Emerson, Thoreau, and Transcendentalism, providing an excellent running commentary on work in the field, particularly the aesthetic side of Transcendentalism. The annual *MLA International Bibliography* includes virtually all books and articles of a literary nature but generally lists items by author or genre rather than by movement.

The following sources provide useful selective bibliographies of nineteenth- and twentieth-century studies: *Literary History of the United States: Bibliography*, ed. Richard Ludwig; *American Transcendentalism: An Anthology of Criticism*, ed. Brian M. Barbour; Paul F. Boller, Jr., *American Transcendentalism, 1830–1860*; and especially *The American Renaissance in New England*, ed. Joel Myerson, which includes individual author bibliographies for all notable Transcendentalists and also a list of general scholarly works. See also Cameron's *Bibliography on Transcendentalism or the American Renaissance*.

Other bibliographical works that contain material of use to students of Transcendentalism are Charles H. Nilon, *Bibliography of Bibliographies in American Literaure*; Lewis Leary's *AAL*; James Woodress, *Dissertations in American Literature, 1891–1966*; and Lawrence Francis McNamee, *Dissertations in English and American Literature*. The last two works, however, are superseded (except for McNamee's European listings) by the *Comprehensive Dissertation Index, 1861–1972*. For more recent dissertations, consult the annual indexes of *Dissertation Abstracts International*.

All serious students of Transcendentalism should be aware of several current periodicals that publish heavily in the field. These include *ESQ: A Journal of the American Renaissance* (1972–   ), successor to *Emerson Society Quarterly* (1955–71); *American Transcendental Quarterly* (1969–   ); *Thoreau Quarterly* (1982–   ), successor to *Thoreau Journal Quarterly* (1969–81); *Thoreau Society Bulletin* (1941–   ); *Concord Saunterer* (1965–   ); and the annual *Studies in the American Renaissance* (1977–   ). All publish interpretative essays and bibliographical studies, some of them of considerable value. The first three decades of *TSB* bibliographies are collected in *A Bibliography of the Thoreau Society Bulletin Bibliographies, 1941–1969*, ed. Walter Harding and Jean Cameron Advena. The above periodicals range from strictly scholarly publications (*ESQ, SAR, ATQ*) to organs for the amateur as well as the specialist (*TSB, ThQ, CS*).

EDITIONS

PRIMARY

The most inclusive and balanced collection of writings by Transcendentalists (as well as some of their precursors and opponents) is *The Transcendentalists: An Anthology*, ed. Perry Miller. It is particularly valuable for its documentary presentation of the "miracles" controversy. Also excellent is Miller's shorter anthology, *The American Transcendentalists*, which overlaps with the former collection only in part and puts special emphasis on the literary aspects of Transcendentalism. A notable feature of both books is the editorial commentary: informative, often opinionated, always thought-provoking. Here and in his other writings, Miller views Transcendentalism condescendingly, as America's first youth movement, exciting but naive and dewy-eyed, but Miller's critical detachment makes his appraisals all the more discerning. After Miller, the most useful general collection is *Selected Writings of the American Transcendentalists*, ed. George Hochfield, which is notable for its balanced, objective overview of the movement. It is an inexpensive rival to Miller's first anthology.

The Poets of Transcendentalism, ed. George Willis Cooke, is the most complete collection of Transcendentalist verse. Among recent anthologies of American poetry, the Transcendentalists are best represented in *Poetry of the New England Renaissance, 1790–1890*, ed. George F. Whicher, which includes Emerson, Jones Very, C. P. Cranch, Thoreau, and Ellery Channing. *Singers and Songs of the Liberal Faith*, ed. Alfred P. Putnam, includes hymns and other devotional lyrics by a goodly number of Transcendentalists. No significant genre-oriented collections of Transcendentalist writing in forms other than poetry have yet appeared.

Liberal extracts from numerous important precursors of Transcendentalism, from the Cambridge Platonists through Goethe, appear in Kenneth Walter Cameron's *Emer-*

son the Essayist, a study of the backgrounds of Emerson's *Nature*. The first volume has been reprinted as *Young Emerson's Transcendental Vision*. Cameron's excerpts are too often snippets taken out of context, but his compendium of precursors is more complete than those of other anthologies. An even larger assemblage of background material is the fourteen-volume series *Specimens of Foreign Standard Literature*, consisting of translations from the French and German under the general editorship of George Ripley. The series includes *Philosophical Miscellanies* by Cousin, Jouffroy, and Constant, trans. Ripley; *Select Minor Poems* of Schiller and Goethe, trans. John Sullivan Dwight; Eckermann's *Conversations with Goethe*, trans. Margaret Fuller; Wolfgang Menzel's *German Literature*, trans. C. C. Felton; Théodore Jouffroy's *Introduction to Ethics*, trans. William H. Channing; Wilhelm M. L. De Wette's *Theodore; or, the Skeptic's Conversion*, trans. James Freeman Clarke; De Wette's *Human Life; or, Practical Ethics*, trans. Samuel Osgood; and *Songs and Ballads; Translated from Uhland, Körner, Bürger, and Other German Lyric Poets*, ed. Charles T. Brooks. Although some of these works might have had formative influences on certain Transcendentalists, they probably only corroborated ideas already formed. The series as a whole sought to increase public awareness of contemporary French and German writers, who were little known in New England, rather than to proselytize aggressively on behalf of Transcendentalism; witness the inclusion of the conservative Unitarian C. C. Felton among the contributors. The series is now being reprinted, with new introductions, under the general editorship of Walter Harding.

A number of later Transcendentalist manifestos, reminiscences, and miscellaneous memorabilia are gathered in Kenneth Walter Cameron's *Concord Harvest*. Cameron's *Massachusetts Lyceum during the American Renaissance* contains records (some previously unpublished) from Concord, Lincoln, Boston, Salem, and Marlborough. Cameron's *The Transcendentalists and Minerva*, *Transcendental Climate*, and *Transcendental Reading Patterns* are especially notable for describing Emerson, Thoreau, and Alcott and their circle in contemporary diaries and official documents, for reprinting their notebooks and juvenilia, and for borrowing lists and catalogues of small Massachusetts libraries used by the Transcendentalists.

SECONDARY

Transcendentalism and Its Legacy, ed. Myron Simon and Thornton H. Parsons, is a volume of original critical essays on various aspects of Transcendentalism, particularly its impact on later American writers and thinkers. The articles are too miscellaneous and specialized to be treated as a whole, but they are generally of high caliber and will be discussed under the appropriate chapter headings.

Two anthologies of previously published modern criticism are *The Transcendentalist Revolt against Materialism*, ed. George F. Whicher, and *American Transcendentalism*, ed. Brian M. Barbour. The latter is much broader in scope and its contributions superior in quality. The introductory overview and bibliography sections are particularly helpful, and nearly half the essays might be described as "classic" treatments of their subjects—among which religion gets the most attention. Both anthologies are superseded, however, by *Critical Essays on American Transcendentalism*, a more comprehensive and up-to-date collection edited by Philip F. Gura and Joel Myerson, reprinting sixty significant discussions from the early 1840s to 1981. The collection covers all major aspects of the movement and includes a number of previously overlooked nineteenth-century items as well as familiar early statements about Transcendentalism and significant modern scholarship.

Kenneth Walter Cameron has published a number of miscellaneous collections of criticism and reportage concerning the Transcendentalists. The following are symposia that originally appeared in *ESQ* or *ATQ*: *Themes, Tones and Motifs in the American Renaissance*, ed. Reginald Cook; *The Minor and Later Transcendentalists*, ed. Edwin Gittleman; *Critical Theory in the American Renaissance*, ed. Darrell Abel; *Style in the American Renaissance*, ed. Carl F. Strauch; and *Romanticism and the American Renaissance*, ed. Cameron. A series of other Cameron compilations assemble nineteenth-century newspaper and magazine accounts about the Transcendentalists: *Emerson, Thoreau, and Concord in Early Newspapers*, *Contemporary Dimension*, *Transcendental Log*, *Response to Transcendental Concord*, *Literary Comment in American Renaissance Newspapers*, and *Lowell, Whittier, Very and the Alcotts among Their Contemporaries*. These collections are especially rich in late nineteenth-century materials. Much is trivial, some illuminating, all necessary to peruse if one is to understand the whole history of Transcendentalism's impact.

OVERVIEWS OF THE TRANSCENDENTALIST MOVEMENT

GENERAL HISTORIES AND RECOMMENDED SHORT SURVEYS

No first-rate comprehensive general history of Transcendentalism exists. The first and most ambitious attempt, Octavius Brooks Frothingham, *Transcendentalism in New England* (1876), is dated and impressionistic, though still well worth perusing. Frothingham, himself a sometime Transcendentalist, is especially notable for his series of representative profiles (Emerson "the seer," Alcott "the mystic," Fuller "the critic," Theodore Parker "the preacher," Ripley "the man of letters," and several "minor prophets") and for his panoramic survey of Transcendentalism in Germany, France, and England as a backdrop for his discussion of the American strain. Such breadth of scope has been lost in our age of specialization. Since the rise of American literary studies in the 1920s, scholars have emphasized American Transcendentalism's indigenous roots at the expense of its European antecedents, or they have discussed the latter piecemeal in narrow-gauged studies of particular sources. Unfotunately, Frothingham's book is more a collection of vignettes, some brilliant and some merely garrulous, than a coherent sequential account. Frothingham's "Some Phases of Idealism in New England" and *Recollections and Impressions 1822-1890* supplement his *History* by adding profiles of other figures and by defining a little further the boundaries of the movement and its legacy.

Since Frothingham, several book-length surveys have been published, none of them fully satisfactory. Harold Clarke Goddard, *Studies in New England Transcendentalism* (1908), gives a careful but pedestrian and dated account of the Transcendentalist reaction against Unitarianism. It also provides intellectual profiles of five major figures (William Ellery Channing, Bronson Alcott, Emerson, Parker, Fuller), followed by an extended consideration of the relation, in each case, between "the Transcendentalists and Practical Life." Goddard predictably discovers a mixture of mystical-contemplative and practical-activist elements. The book is more systematic than Frothingham's but less urbane and discerning. Perhaps Goddard's most useful contribution is his attempt to pin down the essential connotations of the term "Transcendentalism," which Frothingham had left vague, and to place the movement in relation to the continuum of other "isms," from the respectable to the bizarre, that flourished during the antebellum period. A decade later Goddard summarized his revised outlook for the chapter on "Transcendentalism" in the *Cambridge History of American Literature*, the best essay-length summary of the movement written before 1950. Like Frothingham, Goddard describes New England Transcendentalism as "a late and local manifestation of that great movement for the liberation of humanity which . . . swept over Europe" at the turn of the nineteenth century, made distinctive by the local religious heritage.

Though simplistic, Goddard's diagnosis is still worth recalling as a corrective to the excesses of contemporary scholarship, which sometimes stresses Transcendentalism's indigenous roots at the expense of its international connections.

Two more recent books are Paul F. Boller, Jr., *American Transcendentalism, 1830-1860*, and Donald N. Koster, *Transcendentalism in America*. Both are passable introductions although not rigorous, profound, or precise by modern scholarly standards. Of the two, Boller is far superior in the areas he treats, namely the religious, philosophical, and reformist aspects of the movement. He barely mentions its aesthetic side. His final chapter thoughtfully appraises the continuing viability of Transcendentalist values, but on the whole, Boller's study is inferior to a still-unpublished work by Donald F. Warders, "'The Progress of the Hour and the Day': A Critical Study of the *Dial*." Though a little too committed to a summary-of-the-contents approach, Warders provides a remarkably wide-ranging and accurate survey of Transcendentalist religious, philosophical, social, and political attitudes. Altogether it is the best extended survey of Transcendentalist thinking on topics other than art. Koster's book is directed more toward the student of literature and is organized in terms of events (the Transcendental Club, the movement's periodicals) and people (individual chapters on Emerson, Thoreau, and others) rather than concepts. Unfortunately, the ninety-seven pages of text are skimpy and particularly inadequate on the nonliterary aspects of the movement.

More informative and discerning than either Boller or Koster is Alexander Kern's summary of "The Rise of Transcendentalism, 1835-1860." Kern refers to virtually all the dramatis personae of the movement, their leading works, and significant background influences; and he gives roughly equal time to all aspects of the movement. Kern's essay is too packed with names, dates, and titles to suit the taste of the beginning student, but as a model of comprehensiveness and conciseness it is unsurpassed. For student consumption, one of the following might be more appropriate: George Hochfield's introduction to his *Selected Writings of the American Transcendentalists* or, even better, his "New England Transcendentalism," in *American Literature to 1900*, ed. Marcus Cunliffe, and Frederic I. Carpenter, *Emerson Handbook* (124–36). These three overviews are informed and wide-ranging but written in a more essayistic style than Kern. Hochfield is particularly good at spelling out the religious, philosophical, and political implications of Transcendentalism and their historical context. Carpenter's essay is written in a similar style and organized in an easy-to-follow outline form, yet it manages to do justice to most of the movement's knottier issues.

Hochfield's and Carpenter's essays, like Goddard's chapter in *CHAL*, are merely superior examples of dozens of brief attempts to define the essence of Transcendentalism, starting almost with the first American usage of the term. These efforts can be divided into contemporary or near-contemporary accounts by friends, adversaries, participants, and distant observers and later, more systematic appraisals produced mostly by scholars. Frothingham's *Transcendentalism in New England* might be taken as a symbolic turning point, after which the literature of controversy and reminiscence begins to give way to more systematic, "objective" historical analysis. This analysis, in turn, increasingly reflects the commentator's particular field of specialization. Accordingly, after the next section on early discussions of Transcendentalism, the modern overviews are subdivided into four main types: literary, religious, philosophical, and social/political. This fourfold division is of course somewhat artificial, and the reader should be on the lookout for overlaps.

EARLY DEFINITIONS AND REMINISCENCES

Among descriptions of the Transcendentalist movement by its leading participants, the best-known documents are two lectures by Emerson: "The Transcendentalist" (1842), first collected in *Nature; Addresses, and Lectures* (1849), and "Historic Notes of Life and Letters in Massachusetts," written around 1867 but not published until 1883. The first of these contains the most quoted definition of Transcendentalism ("Idealism as it appears in 1842"), placing the movement in the context of post-Kantian philosophy (overstating the closeness of the linkage), and presenting an impressionistic portrait of the Transcendentalist mentality. The second lecture reminisces about some of the major people and events of the movement. Both are readable and illuminating, at times even brilliant, but written with too much ironic detachment to qualify as accurate, let alone sympathetic, accounts. In striking this tone, Emerson encouraged the conservative tradition of bracketing Transcendentalism as an amusing episode in romantic silliness. Some other prominent examples of this condescension are Nathaniel Hawthorne's novel *The Blithedale Romance* (1852), based partly on his experiences at Brook Farm; James Russell Lowell's preface to the notorious critique of *Letters to Various Persons* that helped ensure Thoreau's obscurity for several decades (1865); and Louisa May Alcott's fanciful account of Fruitlands, "Transcendental Wild Oats" (1873). This tendency of both insiders and outsiders to make light of Transcendentalism has provided welcome comic relief for generations of students but has also discouraged the study of certain aspects of the movement—notably its communitarian experiments—at least until quite recently. Perry Miller is a prime example of a modern scholar who has taken too seriously Emerson's self-deprecating irony concerning Transcendentalist ineffectiveness.

For descriptions of the movement by original participants that show greater fervor and commitment, as well as a better command of the facts, see William Henry Channing's section of *Memoirs of Margaret Fuller Ossoli* (1852, 2:12–15) and Theodore Parker, *Transcendentalism: A Lecture* (1876) and *Theodore Parker's Experience as a Minister* (1859). Also helpful are Christopher Pearse Cranch, "Transcendentalism"; George Ripley's 1840 letter of resignation to his congregation (published in 1841 as *A Farewell Discourse*) in Octavius Brooks Frothingham, *George Ripley* (84–86); and Ripley and George P. Bradford, "Philosophic Thought in Boston" (1881), which is particularly detailed on the subject of Brook Farm. It is symptomatic of the growing tolerance for Transcendentalism in the late nineteenth century that *The Memorial History of Boston*, a monumental scholarly work for its day, could accommodate Ripley and Bradford's chapter on philosophic thought devoted entirely to the rise of Transcendentalism. By the end of the century historians of Unitarianism had come to accept Transcendentalism as a renewal movement within the fold, initially threatening but fructifying in the long run. See Joseph Henry Allen, *Our Liberal Movement in Theology* (1882) and *Sequel to "Our Liberal Movement"* (1897); Francis Tiffany, "Transcendentalism: The New England Renaissance" (1889); and George Willis Cooke, *Unitarianism in America* (1902).

Also valuable are several other postwar accounts and retrospectives by individual Transcendentalists: Cyrus Bartol, "Transcendentalism" (1872), Samuel Johnson, "Transcendentalism" (1877), and Caroline H. Dall, *Transcendentalism in New England* (1897). The last of these is especially interesting as a feminist appraisal of the movement, identifying Anne Hutchinson as the original American precursor and stressing the contribution of Margaret Fuller.

The two first-generation Transcendentalists who commented most often on the movement's nature and history were Amos Bronson Alcott and Orestes A. Brownson. Alcott's *Journals*, ed. Odell Shepard (the much longer originals are in Houghton Library, Harvard Univ.), are more specific and circumstantial than the journals of Emerson and Thoreau. See also Alcott's "Reminiscences of the Transcendental Club" (1877–78) and "The Transcendental Club and the *Dial*" (1863). Brownson's transformation from a Transcendentalist reformer to a Catholic apologist is recorded in a number of his works, of which some of the most representative are the "Introductory Remarks" to his *Boston Quarterly Review* (1838), a Transcendentalist manifesto; "Protestantism Ends in Transcendentalism'' (1846); and a series of critiques of Theodore Parker elaborating this thesis (*BrQR*, 1845–46). See also Brownson's autobiography, *The Convert* (1857).

Several of the more revealing nineteenth-century accounts, like Brownson's at their best, came from ex-Transcendentalists or peripheral figures tinged for a season by its influence. The best of these is Charles Mayo Ellis, *An Essay on Transcendentalism* (1842), the most systematic attempt before Frothingham to define the movement. Written by an 1839 Harvard graduate and Emerson sympathizer who later became an abolitionist lawyer, the *Essay* clearly describes Transcendentalism's exaltation of spirit above form and matter, inspiration above rules of taste, religious sentiment above traditional theology and codes, conscience as opposed to self-interest as a guide to morals, and human nature as opposed to force or contract as the proper basis of social organization. In short, Ellis succeeds in pointing out, even at the height of controversy and misunderstanding, Transcendentalism's essential nature and most of its leading motifs. The *Essay* is too codified, too much of a treatise to be fully Transcendentalist in spirit, and it is not as specific about personalities and issues as one would wish, but it is an illuminating document nonetheless.

Other notable statements by Transcendentalist fellow-travelers and dropouts include J. A. Saxton, "Prophecy—Transcendentalism—Progress" (1841); Charles Lane, "Transatlantic Transcendentalism" (1842); William B. Greene, *Transcendentalism* (1849); Isaac Hecker, "The Transcendental Movement in New England" (1876); and Frederic Henry Hedge, "The Destinies of Ecclesiastical Religion" (1867). These essays are written from diverse viewpoints. Greene, for instance, likens Transcendentalism to Oriental religions, which he has studied in some depth but found dangerously solipsistic compared to Christianity; Hecker, disparagingly reviewing Frothingham, writes as an ex–Brook Farmer and Fruitlander who has converted to Catholicism and founded the Paulist Fathers; Hedge, a charter member of the Transcendental Club, has made his peace with conservative Unitarianism. All three agree, however, that Transcendentalism was doomed to transience by the very iconoclasm and free inquiry that attracted them to it initially, in contrast to Lane and Saxton, who write while under Transcendentalism's spell. Samuel Osgood, "Transcendentalism in New England" (1876), is, like Hedge's essay, a reminiscence by an 1830s liberal who became more conservative, but it summarizes Transcendentalism's history more generously, asserting that "the sect of Transcendentalists has disappeared, because their light has gone every where." Osgood suggestively compares Transcendentalism to the Broad Church movement in England, thereby hinting at his own conversion from Unitarianism to Episcopacy.

Like Brownson and Hecker after their conversions, most contemporary antagonists of the Transcendentalists opposed the movement largely on the ground that it lacked a principle of authority sufficient to curb its tendencies to intellectual, spiritual, and social anarchy. Critics also found the Transcendentalist style of expression nebulous and clogged with jargon. The best-known ''rebuttals'' by conservative Unitarians are Francis Bowen, "Locke and the Transcendentalists" and "Transcendentalism" (1837),

and Andrews Norton, *A Discourse on the Latest Form of Infidelity* (1839), an attempt
to refute Emerson's Divinity School Address. Also worth consulting are Alden Bradford, *An Address Delivered before the Society of Phi Beta Kappa in Bowdoin College*
(1841); C. C. Felton, "Emerson's *Essays*" (1843); William Silsbee, "The Transcendental Doctrine of Self-Reliance" (1844); George W. Burnap, "Transcendentalism"
(1846); and the passing remarks on Transcendentalism by Samuel Kirkland Lothrop
in *Some Reminiscences* (1888), the most forthright and critical of memoirs by conservative Unitarians.

The most discerning analysis of Transcendentalism by hostile contemporaries was,
however, produced by non-Unitarians. See especially Merrill Richardson, "A Plain
Discussion with a Transcendentalist" (1843), where Transcendentalist opinions are
given a full and surprisingly accurate airing and then criticized seriatim; Noah Porter,
"Transcendentalism" (1842); and a review of the first two volumes of the *Dial* by
Daniel K. Whitaker (1842).

The number of orthodox commentators that reacted to Transcendentalism mainly
with pious shock was, of course, far greater. For a cross section, see "Modern
Transcendentalism" in the Boston Calvinist *Christian Observatory* (1847); J. W. Alexander, A. Dod, and Charles Hodge, "Transcendentalism" (1839) ("Mr. Emerson is
an infidel and an atheist"); James Porter, *Three Lectures . . . on Come-out-ism*
(1844); Enoch Pond, "Pantheism" (1850); J. M. Manning, *Half Truths and the Truth*
(1872); as well as articles by Theophilus Parsons, a Swedenborgian who had previously
joined in the "miracles controversy" (1840–41).

Among contemporary accounts by outsiders, the following are of special interest.
James Kennard, Jr., "What Is Transcendentalism?" (1844), is a humorous dialogue
in which a sympathizer tries unsuccessfully to persuade a friend that he (and anyone
else) is in fact a Transcendentalist. James Murdock, "American Transcendentalism"
(1842), is remarkable as an ultraorthodox commentator's honest attempt to give an
objective working definition, in which (among other accomplishments) the discrepancy
between the New England and the Kantian senses of "Transcendentalism" is pointed
out. J. E. Snodgrass, "Transcendentalism. A Miniature Essay" (1842), exposes the
inconsistency of pious denunciations of another mode of thinking that holds that
ultimate truth surpasses rational understanding. Fredrika Bremer, *The Homes of the
New World* (1853), contains more interesting gossip about the Transcendentalists than
the work of any other mid-century foreign traveler, though Charles Dickens' remarks
in his *American Notes* (1842) are better known.

After the Civil War, despite new Transcendentalist departures like the Free
Religious Association, periodicals like the *Index* and the *Radical*, and the birth of
the Concord School of Philosophy, partisans on both sides increasingly adopt a tone
of reminiscence, conceding at least tacitly that the movement has either spent its force
or simply become respectable. Works mentioned above by Frothingham, Osgood, and
Ripley-Bradford exemplify this, as do John Orr, "The Transcendentalism of New
England" (1882), perhaps the best capsule summary of the movement before 1900;
Count Goblet d'Alviella, "The Transcendental Movement" (1886), one of the few

nineteenth-century accounts outside America and Britain (which leans heavily on Frothingham); Annie Wall, "Early Transcendentalism in New England" (1886), also much indebted to Frothingham; Giles Stebbins, "Transcendentalism" (1890), a western Massachusetts Unitarian's recollections of the social aspects of the movement; and Thomas Wentworth Higginson, "The Sunny Side of the Transcendental Period" (1904). Concomitantly, a number of sentimental pilgrimage essays began to appear, the most noteworthy being William Dean Howells, "My First Visit to New England, Fourth Part," which recounts visits in 1860 to Hawthorne, Emerson, and Thoreau (1894); Henry James, *The American Scene* (1907), which impressionistically reports a later Concord visit; and Henry A. Beers, "A Pilgrim in Concord" (1914).

The leading turn-of-the-century reminiscer was Franklin Benjamin Sanborn, a third-generation Transcendentalist notorious among scholars for his bowdlerized editions of the Concord group and for his overprotective and perhaps exploitative custodianship of their papers. Nonetheless, Sanborn is interesting and readable for gossip if not gospel. See his *Recollections of Seventy Years* (1909), and a series of compilations of his writings edited by Kenneth Walter Cameron: *Transcendental Epilogue*, vol. 3, *Memorabilia of Hawthorne, Alcott and Concord, Transcendental and Literary New England, Sixty Years of Concord, 1855–1915, Transcendental Writers and Heroes, Literary Studies and Criticism, The Transcendental Eye, Transcendental Youth and Age*, and *Table Talk*.

MODERN OVERVIEWS: LITERARY

The first histories of American literature treated Transcendentalism fumblingly or with condescension. John Nichol's *American Literature* (1882) is the work of an intelligent critic hampered by distaste for Transcendentalism's unsystematic and overly exuberant character, which Nichol considers typical of American faddishness. The first important native literary history by an American, Charles F. Richardson's *American Literature 1607–1885* (1887, 1889), defines Transcendentalism mainly with Britain in mind (as "the reaction from the utilitarianism of Jeremy Bentham") and does not attempt to trace the movement in detail. Barrett Wendell, in *A Literary History of America* (1900), is much more detailed than Richardson and more objective than Nichol, owing to Wendell's (qualified) respect for Emerson and for Transcendentalist moral seriousness as contrasted with Knickerbocker frivolity. Wendell probably deserves more credit than any other literary historian for giving prestige to the still-popular view (not original with him) that the Unitarian Transcendentalist ferment constituted the "New England Renaissance" and that the latter marked the real start of American literature. But Wendell is too fond of retailing anecdotes of Transcendentalist eccentricity to carry his discussion to any depth. A more pedestrian but less judgmental version of the same views is presented by Louis James Block (1897).

Fred Lewis Pattee devotes a long section of his textbook *A History of American Literature* (1896) to the Transcendentalists but merely provides capsule accounts of the lives and works of individual figures. His sketches are more objective but not a great deal more penetrating than the chatty profiles of Donald G. Mitchell, *American Lands and Letters* (1899), a late product of the prescholarly era of literary historicizing. Pattee's later, more rigorous *The First Century of American Literature* (1935) also lacks an extended discussion of Transcendentalism. Altogether the most satisfactory textbook summation of the movement before Goddard's *CHAL* essay is in William P. Trent's *A History of American Literature* (1903). Trent lacked Wendell's wit and polish but made up for it in accuracy, so far as the current state of knowledge permitted.

The most notable common denominator of the overviews just mentioned is that they are all *literary* histories. During the last century, studies of Transcendentalism have been undertaken, for better and for worse, mainly by literary specialists. Students of history, philosophy, and religion have made important contributions also, but by and large they have devoted less attention to Transcendentalism than have students of literature. Fortunately, most literary historians who write about the movement make some attempt to represent its interdisciplinary character, however rudimentary their knowledge may be about fields other than their own.

Since the *CHAL*, scholars have produced a great many literary history or guidebook chapters that follow a more or less "factual" approach, consolidating existing knowledge rather than attempting to be controversial or innovative. The essays of Kern, Carpenter, and Hochfield (see above) are the best efforts in this genre, which might be said to have reached a peak around 1950, after which the increasing specialization in American literary studies began to discourage the production of panoramic surveys except for beginning students. Other examples include William B. Cairns, *A History of American Literature* (1912); Bliss Perry, *The American Spirit in Literature* (1918); Ernest Leisy, *American Literature* (1929); Russell Blankenship, *American Literature as an Expression of the National Mind* (1931); Bernard Smith, *Forces in American Criticism* (1939); David Bowers, "Democratic Vistas," in *Literary History of the United States*, ed. Robert E. Spiller et al. (1948), vol. 1; Arthur Hobson Quinn, "Intuition and Independence," in *The Literature of the American People*, ed. Quinn (1951); Walter Fuller Taylor, *The Story of American Letters* (1956); Leon Howard, *Literature and the American Tradition* (1960); Chester E. Eisinger, "Transcendentalism," in *The American Renaissance*, ed. George Hendrick (1961); Rod W. Horton and Herbert W. Edwards, *Backgrounds of American Literary Thought* (1967); Jorge Luis Borges, *An Introduction to American Literature* (1971); and James T. Callow and Robert J. Reilly, *A Guide to American Literature from Its Beginnings through Walt Whitman* (1976). These discussions range from the generally solid (Eisinger) to the watered-down (Horton-Edwards) to the slapdash (Callow-Reilly) to the lamentably ill-informed (Borges).

MODERN OVERVIEWS: TRANSCENDENTALISM AS A RELIGIOUS MOVEMENT

Next to literary historians, students of American religion have understandably been most attracted to Transcendentalism. It is almost universally accepted that

Transcendentalism was essentially a religious movement, although it also made use of philosophical methodology, was at least fitfully committed to secular causes, and expressed itself most characteristically in literature. "The Transcendental Pattern of Religious Liberalism," in H. Shelton Smith, Robert T. Handy, and Lefferts A. Loetscher, *American Christianity* (vol. 2), gives a helpful account of the diversity of opinion among Transcendentalists on the nature of God, humanity, and Jesus, along with key primary documents. Two concise accounts of antebellum Transcendentalist religion in standard surveys are Winthrop S. Hudson, *Religion in America*, and particularly Sydney Ahlstrom, in the most ambitious and in many ways the best general survey of American religious history ever attempted, *A Religious History of the American People*, which concentrates on Emerson and Parker. Both Ahlstrom and Hudson tie Transcendentalism not only to Unitarianism but also to the romanticization of congregationalist orthodoxy represented in particular by Horace Bushnell. This approach should serve as a reminder that to most religious historians the Unitarian and Transcendentalist movements seem relatively minor and epiphenomenal compared with the ground swell of evangelicalism in the first half of the nineteenth century. William W. Sweet, for example, in his *Religion in the Development of American Culture 1765–1840*, devotes only three pages to Unitarianism and makes no mention of Transcendentalism at all. Likewise, the chapter on early nineteenth-century religion in Perry Miller's *The Life of the Mind in America from the Revolution to the Civil War* presents Transcendentalism as a peripheral analogue of Second Awakening revivalism personified by Charles G. Finney, whereas most literary histories would be apt to feature Transcendentalism as the only worthwhile literary result of that awakening.

Ironically, Miller himself, a literature professor, did more than any other scholar to perpetuate the Unitarian-Transcendental estimate of itself as a crucial stage in the history of American religion, despite his frequent categorization of the movement as parochial. In particular, see Miller's best-known essay, "From Edwards to Emerson." While disclaiming any direct genealogical link between Edwards and Transcendentalism, Miller argued that the latter was a reopening of "the mystical springs in the New England character" (in a pure but oversimplified form), a revolt against Unitarian negations that "rolled away the heavy stone of dogma" and released the enthusiasm that Puritan theology had kept in check. Miller's article was influential not because it was original (Miller's claim had been made in the nineteenth century) but because it was an articulate, vigorously argued presentation by the most brilliant scholar of New England intellectual history, uttered at the right historical moment, after years of overemphasis on the anti-Puritanism of Transcendentalism (see below). The rebirth of Puritan studies was just beginning, and the new field of American studies was struggling to be born. Coming at such a juncture, Miller's theory seemed to hold out exciting new possibilities for a synthetic overview of American culture.

As we shall see below, the Puritanism-Transcendentalism connection has appealed most to literary and intellectual historians who specialize in tracing themes and concepts. It has had a mixed reception among students of American religion. To specialists in denominational history and the evolution of American theology, Miller's leap across sects and eras seems irresponsible. At the opposite extreme, William A. Clebsch, *American Religious Thought*, follows Miller quite closely, favoring a "great minds" approach to its subject. Clebsch reduces his history to three seminal thinkers—Edwards, Emerson, and William James—discussing each competently but drawing perfunctory transitional links among them.

Among other overviews of Transcendentalism as a religion, passing mention should be made of Howard Mumford Jones' lucid and helpful lecture "Transcendentalism and Emerson"; Henry G. Fairbanks' overambitious and unreliable "Theocracy to Transcendentalism in America"; and Charles A. Ingraham's shoddy "Transcendentalism."

Most studies of the religious aspects of Transcendentalism consist of intensive examinations of the movement's Unitarian roots and evolution therefrom (see below and the chapter "Unitarianism and Transcendentalism").

MODERN OVERVIEWS: TRANSCENDENTALISM AS A PHILOSOPHY

Because of Transcendentalism's origins as a religious movement and because of the unsystematic character of Transcendentalist thought, students of American philosophy have often dismissed Transcendentalism as uninteresting and amateurish; see Bruce Kuklick, *The Rise of American Philosophy*. Perhaps for this reason, some of the standard histories of American philosophy have fallen below their usual level when dealing with Transcendentalism. Herbert W. Schneider, *A History of American Philosophy*, begins with a provocative if idiosyncratic presentation of the movement as the flowering of the Enlightenment in America but falls into a series of rather disconnected and superficial profiles of individual figures. Elizabeth Flower and Murray G. Murphey, in their chapter "Transcendentalism" in *A History of Philosophy in America*, begin with a succinct statement of the issues underlying the Transcendentalists' quarrel with Unitarianism but spend the rest of their essay tracing the careers of Emerson and Alcott through 1836, concluding with a prolix summary of Emerson's *Nature*.

Altogether the best philosophical overview is Morton White's "Transcendentalism: 'Hallelujah to the Reason Forevermore,'" which outlines the relationship of Unitarian, Kantian, Coleridgean, Edwardsean, and Scottish Realist thought to Transcendental intuitionism. White does full justice to the Transcendentalists' limited but genuine interest in philosophical ideas as distinct from religious faith, and he especially respects Ripley as a philosopher. The subsequent chapter "Emerson" is almost equally good. It and two other discussions are especially helpful in analyzing the links between Transcendentalism and Pragmatism, America's first (and perhaps only) indigenous philosophical movement. Along these lines, see also Paul K. Conkin, *Puritans and Pragmatists*, and Herbert W. Schneider, "American Transcendentalism's Escape from Phenomenology." Another solid general discussion of Transcendentalist philosophy is Joseph L. Blau, *Men and Movements in American Philosophy*, which includes detailed profiles of Emerson, Thoreau, and the elder Henry James. Like White, Blau gives primary emphasis to the intuitional, antirational character of Transcendentalism, but he is also concerned with its implications for social thought.

Other introductions to Transcendentalism as philosophy may be mentioned briefly. Woodbridge Riley, *American Thought from Puritanism to Pragmatism and Beyond*, too narrowly equates Transcendentalism with Emerson alone and Emerson with British Platonism. Frederick Mayer, *A History of American Thought*, is merely a series of capsule sketches of individual figures. Even more simplistic are W. H. Werkmeister, *A History of Philosophical Ideas in America*; Irving H. Bartlett, *The American Mind in the Mid-Nineteenth Century*; and Richard D. Mosier, *The American Temper*. Harvey Gates Townsend, *Philosophical Ideas in the United States*, was adequate for its day but has been superseded by Blau and White. Finally, Stow Persons, *American Minds*, is perhaps the best one-volume exposition of the main systems of thought in American intellectual history, but its discussion of Transcendentalism is too terse to be of much practical use as an introduction.

MODERN OVERVIEWS: TRANSCENDENTALISM AS A SOCIAL AND POLITICAL STANCE

Recent American social and political histories rarely include extended discussions of the Transcendentalists, who were only sporadically involved in social action. Transcendentalism is barely mentioned in the relevant volume of Daniel Boorstin's trilogy, *The Americans*, and if it receives a little more attention in Samuel Eliot Morison, *The Oxford History of the American People*, that is because Morison misleadingly stretches the term to denote the whole spirit of cultural renewal in New England during the antebellum period. (Morison here follows Barrett Wendell all too literally.) So far, the only good general social history is Anne C. Rose, *Transcendentalism as a Social Movement, 1830–1850*, an ambitious and generally perceptive analysis that uses the methods of the new social history in fairly sophisticated and often innovative ways. Rose appraises the social and economic bases of the Unitarian movement, the miracles controversy, Transcendentalist utopianism, and the Transcendentalist theory and practice of interpersonal relationships (see below for additional comments). Rose's study is a product of a long-standing scholarly side interest in the social ramifications of Transcendentalism that has lately begun to blossom.

The 1920s and 1930s saw the first serious scholarly attempts, undertaken by literary and intellectual historians, to portray Transcendentalism as preeminently a social protest movement against "Puritanism," "materialism," philistinism, narrow-mindedness, and the work ethic. The most powerful statement of this interpretation is Vernon Louis Parrington, *The Romantic Revolution in America 1800–1860*, which vigorously underscores the social responsibility of the Transcendentalists, despite their solipsistic tendencies, and curiously anticipates Perry Miller in tracing their philosophy back to "the original principle of Protestantism, the principle of individual responsibility."

Two other notable discussions in the Parringtonian vein of sociological-literary criticism are less sympathetic: Ludwig Lewisohn, in *Expression in America*, brings to bear a psychological approach in the course of criticizing the Transcendentalists for not advancing far enough beyond post-Puritan moralism, and V. F. Calverton's socialist critique, *The Liberation of American Literature*, indicts the Transcendentalists for being seduced by "the petty bourgeois individualism of the frontiersman." Lewisohn is provocative even when wrong; Calverton is simply crude.

After 1940 American literary studies became, at least until recently, markedly more belletristic. For Transcendentalism the symbolic turning point was F. O. Matthiessen's monumental *American Renaissance*, which attempted a fusion of social consciousness and aesthetic sensitivity but which influenced later scholars primarily through its groundbreaking application of "new critical" methodology to Emerson, Thoreau, and other writers. Most literary scholarship since Matthiessen (see below and the Emerson and Thoreau chapters) has occupied itself with Transcendentalist literary form and technique. But concurrently with Matthiessen, historians began intensive study of Jacksonian and antebellum era social ferment, in which the Transcendentalist movement was seen to play a symptomatic if not an actively influential part. Alice Felt Tyler, *Freedom's Ferment*, discusses Transcendentalism as part of the whole spectrum of "isms" and "ologies" that flourished in the first half of the nineteenth century. Arthur M. Schlesinger, Jr., *The Age of Jackson*, treated the Transcendentalists as an apolitical lot isolated in private dreamworlds. These two studies, both provocative and wide-ranging, both since challenged without having been superseded, in effect represent the opposite sides of two major interrelated questions concerning the Transcendentalists' social/political stance: To what extent did they value purely individual as opposed to collective action? And to what extent did they favor an activist posture as opposed to contemplative disengagment? Two thoughtful attempts to strike the correct balance between these poles are Boller's chapter "Social Reform" in his *American Transcendentalism* and Charles A. Barker, *American Convictions*, which compares and contrasts Transcendentalism with such other sectarian and perfectionist movements as the Mormons, the Shakers, and the Owenite socialists. But see particularly John L. Thomas, "Romantic Reform in America," an admirably concise general discussion of the contemporary climate of opinion that has much to say about the Transcendentalists.

A number of other penetrating essays address one or the other of the questions just mentioned. Concerning the issue of activism versus contemplation, Yves Carlet, "'Respectables Iniquités,'" argues that the "apolitical" Transcendentalists' sensitivity to social issues was shown precisely in their strategy of retreat from the world, communalism and Emersonian detachment being parallel forms of dissent. In taking this view, Carlet resembles Taylor Stoehr (see below). On the other hand, for Duane E. Smith, "Romanticism in America," and R. A. Yoder, "The Equilibrist Perspective," American Romanticism, with Transcendentalism as an example par excellence, is distinguished by its relative lack of radical dissent. Smith makes this point by contrasting the Transcendentalists' situation in the comparatively open society of the United

States with that of the German Romantics under a repressive regime. Comparatively speaking, the former can be seen as accepting their country's mainstream political philosophy, while the latter were driven to an ivory tower existence and to more outré forms of aesthetic and epistemological radicalism. Yoder bases his analysis on the relatively rapid shift of the major American Romantics from early moods of visionary affirmation or defiance to "a spirit of compromise or mediation." In effect, Yoder's essay takes a pattern that is evident in British Romanticism also—intellectual radicalism giving way to acquiescence—and finds the trend still more pronounced in America. Smith's analysis belongs in the company of other discussions that emphasize the essentially bourgeois, mainstream character of Transcendentalist thought, like Calverton's or (to take a much more discerning example) Jesse Bier, "Weberism, Franklin, and the Transcendental Style."

The extent to which Transcendentalism lent itself to a collectivist as well as an individualist ethos, to a theory of social order as well as personal liberation, has been treated in four solid essays that use Emerson or Thoreau and Brownson as exemplary figures respresenting the opposite poles. David Herreshoff, *American Disciples of Marx*, includes a thoughtful comparison of Emerson to Marx in the course of showing Brownson to be far the more important precursor of American Marxist thought. A. Robert Caponigri, "Brownson and Emerson: Nature and History," lucidly explains the sharp difference between Emerson's antihistoricism and Brownson's respect for the continuity of tradition in terms of Brownson's view that "the ascription of divinity must be made not in the first instance to the individual but to humanity." Caponigri's "Individual, Civil Society, and State in American Transcendentalism" shows Brownson as providing a solution to the anarchistic implications of Thoreau's social thought, which, Caponigri argues, were not fully intended even by Thoreau himself. Sam B. Girgus, "The Scholar as Prophet: Brownson vs. Emerson and the Modern Need for a Moral Humanism," follows Caponigri in noting the rift between Brownson's populist identification with society in the mass and Emerson's comparatively patrician individualism, but he also recognizes a significant dimension of social concern and responsibility in Emerson. Girgus' essay reflects, in part, recent scholarship by Sacvan Bercovitch and others on continuities between Puritanism and Transcendentalism, among which the concept of the interrelation of individual and society was very important. This body of scholarship is discussed below.

PARTICULAR ASPECTS OF THE TRANSCENDENTALIST MOVEMENT: A CLOSER LOOK

TRANSCENDENTALIST BIOGRAPHY

Short biographies of most of the active Transcendentalists can be found in *The American Renaissance in New England*, ed. Joel Myerson; *Dictionary of American Biography*; George Willis Cooke, *An Historical and Biographical Introduction to Ac-*

company the Dial, superseded by Myerson, *The New England Transcendentalists and the* Dial; *Heralds of a Liberal Faith,* ed. Samuel A. Eliot (vols. 2–3); and Alfred P. Putnam, *Singers and Songs of the Liberal Faith.*

Interpersonal relations among Transcendentalists have been dealt with in numerous scattered studies, most of which concentrate on two figures, Emerson usually being one. For details, see individual author chapters. One particularly searching discussion of general interest is Carl F. Strauch, "Hatred's Swift Repulsions: Emerson, Margaret Fuller, and Others." See also Anne C. Rose's chapter on human relationships in *Transcendentalism as a Social Movement.*

CLUBS AND DISCUSSION GROUPS

Joel Myerson has compiled an authoritative "Calendar of Transcendental Club Meetings" and a short but excellent "History of the Transcendental Club," the latter since condensed for inclusion in his *New England Transcendentalists and the* Dial. No official records were kept; both the above articles are based on examination of the participants' papers, among which the journals of Alcott and Emerson are most informative. Myerson's "Frederic Henry Hedge and the Failure of Transcendentalism" sheds additional light on the disintegration of the club and the first and major phase of the movement as a whole.

For the conversations of Fuller and Alcott, see the individual author chapters in this volume. The most detailed eyewitness account is Caroline H. Dall, *Margaret and Her Friends* (1895).

Louis L. Tucker, "The Semi-Colon Club of Cincinnati," recounts the history of a club to which a number of Transcendentalists belonged. Kenneth Walter Cameron gathers materials pertaining to "Emerson, Thoreau, and the Town and Country Club" of 1849–50. The history of *The Early Years of the Saturday Club 1855–1870,* a Brahmin-dominated Boston group joined by a few Transcendentalists, was laboriously compiled by Edward Waldo Emerson (1918). Mary E. Sargent published *Sketches and Reminiscences of the Radical Club* (1880), a postwar forum more congenial to younger Transcendentalists.

PERIODICALS

The only general study is Clarence L. F. Gohdes, *The Periodicals of American Transcendentalism,* which gives brief histories of all the major journals. For studies of individual magazines, see the chapter on periodicals in this volume.

RELIGIOUS REFORM AND VALUES

The story of those Transcendentalists who briefly engaged in Unitarian evangelism in the old Northwest is told by Frank R. Shivers, Jr., "A Western Chapter in the History of American Transcendentalism," and more fully in Elizabeth R. McKinsey's excellent monograph *The Western Experiment: New England Transcendentalists in the Ohio Valley*, which agrees with Shivers in its general findings. McKinsey concentrates on Clarke, Cranch, and W. H. Channing, whose dilemma as genteel idealists, unable to adjust to the rough-and-tumble west, McKinsey sees as prophetic of the course of Transcendentalism as a whole.

The so-called miracles controversy, which led to a rift between the Transcendentalists and conservative Unitarians, is documented in part 5 of Perry Miller's *The Transcendentalists*, which includes excerpts from all important primary sources as well as a running commentary. An authoritative history of that controversy is given in the best and most extensive study of Transcendentalist religion, William R. Hutchison's *The Transcendentalist Ministers*. Hutchison also surveys the entire history of Unitarian-Transcendentalist disagreement during the antebellum era, with special emphasis upon the church reform efforts of those Transcendentalist ministers (chiefly Parker and Clarke) who remained in the Unitarian ministry to challenge it from within. The dilemma of the conservative Unitarians, caught between Calvinism and Transcendentalism, is ably described in C. H. Faust, "The Background of the Unitarian Opposition to Transcendentalism."

The question of whether Transcendentalist values represented a sharp break from Unitarian thinking or a continuation thereof is much debated. The controversy centers on the problems of defining the allegiances of transitional figures (like William Ellery Channing) and evaluating the validity of Emerson's dismissal of Unitarianism as a corpse-cold shell. For a spectrum of opinions, see Conrad Wright, "The Rediscovery of Channing," which criticizes interpretations that erase the barrier between Channing and Transcendentalism; Mary W. Edrich, "The Rhetoric of Apostacy," which argues that Emerson's Divinity School Address departs from Unitarianism in rhetoric rather than in substance; Lawrence Buell, *Literary Transcendentalism*, which tries to take a middle position; and David Robinson, "Unitarian Historiography and the American Renaissance," which points out that the aggregate effect of recent studies has been "to call attention to previously neglected continuities" between Unitarianism and Transcendentalism.

A later and less widely known Transcendentalist protest against conservative Unitarianism was the founding of the Free Religious Association in 1865. For a manifesto by the Association, see its *Freedom and Fellowship in Religion* (1875). The rise and significance of the movement it inspired is recounted in memoir form by George Willis Cooke, "The Free Religious Association" (1903), and in a scholarly monograph by Stow Persons, *Free Religion*. For more details, including a critique of Persons, see the "Unitarianism and Transcendentalism" chapter in this volume.

Ronald Vale Wells, *Three Christian Transcendentalists*, studies Transcendentalism at its most conservative, personified by James Marsh, Caleb Sprague Henry, and Frederic Henry Hedge. Indeed, the first two figures were associated only tangentially with the movement, and Hedge became less Transcendentalist as he became more Christian. Wells is correct, however, in seeing them all as representing the right wing of the same philosphic current that led Emerson and Thoreau toward a more secularized idealism. The limits of Transcendentalist secularism, moreover, are pointed up in John B. Wilson, "Darwin and the Transcendentalists," which observes that although the Transcendentalists initially welcomed Darwin they resisted the late nineteenth-century alliance between evolutionary theory and logical positivism. As Persons says of the Free Religionists, "whether they were agnostics or liberal Unitarians," they "were bent on the preservation of religious values."

Catherine L. Albanese, *Corresponding Motion*, differs from the previous studies in approaching the movement less from the standpoint of intellectual or church history than from a phenomenological perspective. Basing her analysis on the Emersonian idea of mystical correspondence between the realms of nature and spirit, Albanese disassociates Transcendentalism from the linear, teleological, rationalistic thrust of Judaeo-Christian theology, which distinguishes sharply between the realms of sacred and profane, and aligns Transcendentalism with primitive and eastern religions that ignore this distinction, viewing the world of natural process as itself sacramental. The thesis breaks down when confronted with the increasingly kinetic, protoevolutionary element in Emerson's thought, which is obviously linear and teleological. Albanese regards this as a special variant of the ancient sacramental mentality, but that view makes less historical sense than the usual view of Transcendentalism as an eclectic late or post-Christian movement that assimilated nonwestern elements. Overall, however, the book is the most memorable attempt yet to come to terms with the nonwestern character of Transcendentalist thought. It largely incorporates Albanese's earlier article, "The Kinetic Revolution." Another East-West comparative study is Shôei Andô, *Zen and American Transcendentalism*, which compares the two as modes of achieving self-transcendence and concludes that "the goal of Transcendentalism—namely, to be conscious of the One at the bottom of the heart—abuts on the invisible barrier which obstinately obstructs our advancing to the goal of Zen," namely to get away from individuality altogether. The book has the formulaic quality of an elementary text, but this basic finding is plausible.

Far more prevalent than studies of Transcendentalism's non-Christian analogues has been scholarship, in the wake of Perry Miller's "From Edwards to Emerson," treating the idea of correspondence and other key themes in Transcendentalist writing as mutated forms of Puritan thought. Most of this work, however, falls mainly within the province of literary history and therefore will be treated below.

SECULAR ISSUES: THEORY AND PRACTICE

This section will review scholarship on the Transcendentalists and abolitionism, feminism, communitarianism, civil disobedience, and educational reform, with brief mention of reforms of lesser significance.

The relation between the Transcendentalist and feminist movements has not been satisfactorily charted except with reference to Margaret Fuller. Warders' study of the *Dial* provides the best general discussion to date. John B. Wilson, "The Transcendentalists and Women's Education," is slipshod. Anne C. Rose, *Transcendentalism as a Social Movement*, contains a groundbreaking discussion of Transcendentalist theory regarding sex roles in the contexts of their marriages, friendships, and utopian ventures.

Studies of Transcendentalist involvement in abolitionism have often been marred by misunderstanding. Stanley Elkins, *Slavery*, blames Transcendentalism for providing the primary impetus for abolitionism and, subsequently, the outbreak of the Civil War. Reversing Schlesinger's *Age of Jackson*, which treats the Transcendentalists as pathetically impotent in their refusal to enter the political arena, Elkins sees their anti-institutionalism as a social menace because it made a peaceful political solution to the slavery problem impossible. This argument is provocative but muddled. Elkins crudely equates "higher lawism" with Transcendentalism, largely disregarding the distinction between Yankee higher lawists in general and the particular group of Unitarian dissidents usually thought of as Transcendentalists. He thereby overemphasizes the role of Emerson and his circle as abolitionist instigators, although he is generally correct about their views and right in seeing their antiestablishmentarianism as symptomatic of the mentality that later prevented peaceful negotiation of the slavery issue. Most of Elkins' errors are corrected in Aileen S. Kraditor's excellent *Means and Ends in American Abolitionism* although she repeats the mistake of underplaying the Transcendentalists' (occasional) willingness to use institutional, organized means, and she overplays their vacillations of commitment. Like Schlesinger, Elkins and Kraditor are both too quick to equate Transcendentalism with disengagement from politics.

Douglas C. Stange, *Patterns of Antislavery Among American Unitarians, 1831-1860*, is a well-researched study that discusses Clarke, Parker, and Higginson, who represented diverse styles of antislavery commitment. The radicalization of Transcendentalist opinion, particularly Emerson's, on the slavery issue after 1850 is intelligently treated by George M. Fredrickson, *The Inner Civil War*. Daniel Aaron, *The Unwritten War*, and Robert C. Albrecht, "The Theological Response of the Transcendentalists to the Civil War," have some additional points to contribute. Leonard Neufeldt, "Emerson, Thoreau, and Daniel Webster," gives an accurate and lively picture of the comparative unfolding of the two Transcendentalists' views of slavery in terms of their disparate impressions of Webster. Warders' study of the *Dial* describes the state of Transcendentalist opinion on the slavery issue in the early 1840s.

Materials for the study of the two Transcendentalist ventures in utopian socialism, Brook Farm and Fruitlands, are listed in the chapter "Transcendentalist Communities" in this volume. The major books on each are readable but superficial and gossipy: Lindsay Swift, *Brook Farm*, Edith Roelker Curtis, *A Season in Utopia,* and Clara Endicott Sears, *Bronson Alcott's Fruitlands*. Of late the two enterprises have been taken more seriously. The section on the Brook Farm years in Charles Crowe, *George Ripley*, is excellent. The following essays are also indispensible: Richard Francis, "The Ideology of Brook Farm" and "Circumstances and Salvation"; and Taylor Stoehr, "Transcendentalist Attitudes toward Communitism and Individualism." Also illuminating on communitarian socioeconomic theory and practice is Rose, *Transcendentalism as a Social Movement*.

Stoehr's *Nay-Saying in Concord* deals also with two other forms of dissent associated with Transcendentalism: vegetarianism and civil disobedience, discussion of the latter drawing upon Stoehr's earlier " 'Eloquence Needs No Constable.' " In each of his three main sections, Stoehr focuses on Emerson, Alcott, and Thoreau, with side-glances at Charles Lane. In general Stoehr views Transcendentalism as the first important American affirmation of self-discipline and self-restraint in the modern "world as we know it—a world of *too much* . . . too many possessions and pleasures, too much complexity and ramification." Stoehr is consistently penetrating and provocative, especially on the subjects of communitarianism, Alcott, and Lane. A more simplistic description of Transcendentalist reform attitudes is Wilson Carey McWilliams, "Emerson and Thoreau" (in *The Idea of Fraternity in America*), which, despite some thoughtful passages, perpetuates an old false dichotomy between Thoreau as an activist and Emerson as an abettor of laissez-faire in the interest of giving elbow room to the autonomous individual. This prevents McWilliams from appreciating the similarities amid the differences between their views of friendship and community.

The issue of civil disobedience, discussed by both Stoehr and McWilliams, is also treated by Edward H. Madden, "The Transcendentalists" (in *Civil Disobedience and Moral Law in Nineteenth-Century American Philosophy*), a careful, fair-minded comparison of how Emerson, Parker, and Thoreau used higher law doctrine in formulating their ideas of civil disobedience, particularly in response to the Compromise of 1850. For more on civil disobedience scholarship, see the Thoreau and Parker chapters in this volume, as well as above.

Pedagogical reform was another high priority of a number of Transcendentalists, particularly Alcott, Elizabeth Palmer Peabody, and the Brook Farmers, whose school was the community's greatest acccomplishment. The one general study of early Transcendentalist educational attitudes and activities is Rüdiger C. Schlicht, *Die pädagogischen Ansätze amerikanischer Transzendentalisten*. Thoroughly researched and documented, it has the drawback of limiting itself to the decade of the 1830s and to three figures: Alcott, Emerson, and Thoreau. The later, postwar flowering of Transcendentalist-style pedagogy at Concord is recounted by Austin Warren, "The Concord School of Philosophy," and in Flower and Murphey's *History of Philosophy in America* (vol. 2). For a closer look at the curriculum, see *Concord Lectures on Philosophy*, ed. Raymond L. Bridgman (1883). Franklin B. Sanborn's reports of *Lectures on Literature and Philosophy* at the Concord School are edited by Kenneth Walter Cameron. Finally, John B. Wilson, "The Transcendentalists' 'Idea of a University,' " gives a digest of Transcendentalist opinion, centering on problems at Harvard College.

In "Phrenology and the Transcendentalists," Wilson discusses the Transcendentalists' ambivalence toward that pseudoscience. Russell M. Goldfarb and Clare R. Goldfarb note much the same attitude toward psychical research in *Spiritualism and Nineteenth-Century Letters*.

AESTHETIC THEORY AND PRACTICE

Of the many studies of Transcendentalist artistry and aesthetics, most have been devoted to either Emerson or Thoreau. The most detailed comparison of these two central figures is Joel Porte, *Emerson and Thoreau*, a provocative study that, however, exaggerates the differences between the two and is excessively biased against Emerson and in favor of Thoreau. More objective is Albert Gilman and Roger Brown, "Personality and Style in Concord," which correlates stylistic differences with personality differences using sample passages from each writer.

No extended general study of Transcendentalist aesthetics in relation to international Romanticism has ever been undertaken. The best short discussion is Tony Tanner, "Notes for a Comparison between American and European Romanticism." See also Yoder, "The Equilibrist Perspective," and the scholarship of Harold Bloom (below) for valuable comparisons between American and British Romantics. Michael J. Hoffman tries with limited success to assimilate Transcendentalism to Morse Peckham's theory of Romanticism in *The Subversive Vision*. The Transcendentalist contribution to *A History of Modern Criticism: 1750–1950* is briefly appraised by René Wellek, who describes Emerson as "the outstanding representative of romantic symbolism in the English-speaking world" but gives short shrift to the other figures discussed: Thoreau, Very, and Fuller. The analysis is good on the subject of Emerson's theory of symbolism but is not, overall, as well balanced or as well informed as one would expect a work of such authoritative pretensions to be.

Wellek's essay on Emerson is only one of many attempts to define the Transcendentalist theory of symbolism (using Emerson as the chief exhibit). The seminal modern discussion is F. O. Matthiessen, *American Renaissance*; the most brilliant is the Emerson chapter in Charles Feidelson, Jr., *Symbolism and American Literature*. The general conception of organic form underlying Transcendentalist symbolism is described extensively in Charles R. Metzger's two monographs, *Emerson and Greenough* and *Thoreau and Whitman*, but the analysis is somewhat superficial. For a short discussion, see Buell, *Literary Transcendentalism*. The metaphysical basis of Transcendentalist organicism, the idea of a mystical correspondence between nature and spirit, is most fully explored in Sherman Paul, *Emerson's Angle of Vision*. Albanese's *Corresponding Motion* supplements Paul somewhat. Elizabeth A. Meese, "Transcendentalism: The Metaphysics of the Theme," is a watered-down treatment. Christopher Collins, *The Uses of Observation: A Study of Correspondential Vision in the Writings of Emerson, Thoreau, and Whitman*, is a workmanlike essay that has little to add concerning the metaphysical or stylistic implications of correspondence. For more studies of symbolism, organicism, and correspondence, see the Emerson and Thoreau chapters in this volume.

Lucille Gafford, "Transcendentalist Attitudes toward Drama and the Theatre," the only general survey of the subject, argues its way carefully to the predictable conclusion that the Transcendentalists knew drama more through reading than through the stage but were excited by the possibilities of the latter, if not always enthusiastic about actual contemporary productions. Jeffrey Steinbrink's essay on Emerson's view of fiction, "Novels of Circumstance and Novels of Character," may be taken as representing Transcendentalist opinion in the absence of any more general study.

On the subject of Transcendentalist attitudes toward the fine arts, John B. Wilson, "The Aesthetics of Transcendentalism," ramblingly summarizes the artistic views of a number of figures. Two acceptable essays on Transcendentalist attitudes toward music are Irving Lowens, "Writings about Music in the Periodicals of American Transcendentalism (1850–50)," and Charmenz S. Lenhart, "Music and the Transcendentalists." But see especially Daniel Edgar Rider, "The Musical Thought and Activities of the New England Transcendentalists."

Analogies between Transcendentalist aesthetic theory and nineteenth-century American landscape painting, especially the luminist movement, are discussed in Barbara Novak, *American Painting of the Nineteenth Century* and *Nature and Culture: American Landscape Painting, 1825–1875*, as well as in Albert Gelpi, "White Light in the Wilderness." These are pioneer efforts—Gelpi is brief and Novak has a fuzzy understanding of what Transcendentalism is—but they point the way for more intensive studies, such as John Conron, " 'Bright American Rivers': The Luminist Landscapes of Thoreau's *A Week*."

Neil Harris also discusses "Art and Transcendentalism" in the course of *The Artist in American Society*, an important study of the growing practice and public acceptance of the arts in early nineteenth–century America. The chapter is interesting mainly for its attempt to define the Transcendentalist orientation as a highbrow aesthetic distinct, though not completely different, from the more utilitarian and commercial mainstream approach to art. The place of Transcendentalist aesthetics in the rise of literary nationalism is described in Benjamin T. Spencer, "The Spur of Transcendentalism" (in *The Quest for Nationality*). For additional studies of nineteenth-century American aesthetics that discuss the Transcendentalist contribution at least in passing, see the following chapter, "Transcendentalism: The Times."

The Transcendentalists' assumptions about their audience and the proper nature of rhetoric are examined in several studies. Irving Rein, "The New England Transcendentalists," is a challenging, provocative, but dubious effort to prove that the Transcendentalists' rhetorical tactics were self-defeating because they were not intended to persuade those outside the group. Philip K. Tompkins, "On 'Paradoxes' in the Rhetoric of the New England Transcendentalists," a comparatively pedestrian rebuttal, shows that the Transcendentalists *did* have a significant historical impact, but the main thrust of his argument—that the Transcendentalists did not intend to proselytize in the first place—is based on a too literal reading of their obiter dicta. The most detailed account of the Transcendentalists' awareness of their audience is given in Lawrence Charles Porter, "New England Transcendentalism." For the best description of that audience, see Jonathan Bishop, *Emerson on the Soul*. For the best discussion of the Transcendentalist philosophy of language in relation to nineteenth-century linguistics and theology, see Philip F. Gura, *The Wisdom of Words*.

The most extended study of Transcendentalist literary theory and practice is Lawrence Buell, *Literary Transcendentalism*. It puts special emphasis on the Unitarian

background of Transcendentalist aesthetics and on an analysis of a series of prominent Transcendentalist genres and techniques: conversation, moral essay (considered
as secular sermon), catalog rhetoric, the symbolic excursion (derived in part from travel
narrative tradition), and the autobiographical mode. Literary form in each case is considered as reflecting some aspect of Transcendentalist ideology. The book incorporates
portions of Buell's "Unitarian Aesthetics and Emerson's Poet-Priest" and—with a
marked shift of emphasis—"Transcendentalist Catalogue Rhetoric."

Most of the above topics, as well as others omitted by Buell (e.g., the lecture
as a genre) have been treated in more detail with reference to individual figures,
especially Emerson and Thoreau. Among general studies, see especially Gura, *The
Wisdom of Words*, on the Transcendentalist conception of symbolism; Philip Marshall Hicks, *The Development of the Natural History Essay in American Literature*,
which justly regards Transcendentalism (Thoreau in particular) as the crucial stage in
that development; and G. Thomas Couser, *American Autobiography*, which discusses
Emerson and Thoreau in the context of a general theory of prophetic autobiography.
Helen Hennessy (Vendler), "The *Dial*: Its Poetry and Poetic Criticism," gives a lively
and trenchant analysis of the gap between Transcendentalist idealization of the figure
of the poet on the one hand and the meager results (naive criticism, mediocre poetry)
on the other. Most literary historians, without going to the opposite extreme, are inclined to give Transcendentalist poetics a more serious hearing than this article does,
and all overviews of American poetry touch on Transcendentalism to some extent.
Donald B. Stauffer's "The Transcendentalists" (in *A Short History of American Poetry*)
is a competent and representative survey of this latter type. Less recent and less ob-
tainable, though more profound, is Stanley T. Williams, "The Poet of Philosophic
Thought" (in *The Beginnings of American Poetry*). Paul O. Williams, "The
Transcendental Movement in American Poetry," is far more thorough but long-winded.

In contrast to these last three studies, all essentially descriptive, most recent
treatments of Transcendentalist poetry and poetics are explicitly theoretical and describe
the movement as the first significant manifestation of the most distinctive American
poetic tradition. This claim is based on the theory that the Transcendentalists, particularly Emerson, were the first Americans to formulate the Romantic idea of the
poet as visionary seer. Though their own verse was a pale realization of this dream,
the Transcendentalists (and, again, Emerson particularly) inspired Whitman, possibly
Dickinson, and a whole tradition of antitraditional, experimental, visionary American
poetics. This thesis is presented succinctly in Edwin Fussell, "The Meter-Making Argument," which is anticipated to some extent by Roy Harvey Pearce, *The Continuity
of American Poetry*.

Among later developments of this thesis, three deserve special mention. Aaron
Kramer, *The Prophetic Tradition in American Poetry, 1835–1900*, is the least useful,
being organized in terms of poetic responses to particular public issues (the war with
Mexico, the fugitive slave controversy), rather than by writer, literary movement, or
stylistic motif. The result is a wide range of allusions to Transcendentalist poems
handled in obvious ways. More penetrating and influential have been Hyatt H. Wag-

goner, *American Poets from the Puritans to the Present*, and a series of studies by Harold Bloom dealing with the Transcendentalist (and especially the Emersonian) example and legacy: "Bacchus and Merlin: The Dialectic of Romantic Poetry in America," "Emerson and Influence," "In the Shadow of Emerson," "Emerson and Whitman," "Wallace Stevens: The Transcendental Strain," "Emerson: The Self-Reliance of American Romanticism," "The Native Strain," "The New Transcendentalism: The Visionary Strain in Merwin, Ashbery, and Ammons," and "American Poetic Stances: Emerson to Stevens."

Bloom and Waggoner differ greatly in their interpretations and methods. Waggoner is interested in the American poet as moral advocate; Bloom is interested in the poet as vatic seer. Waggoner generally treats his cast of characters in discrete, sequential order; Bloom constantly jumps backward and forward in time to catch subtle resonances and echoes that seem to establish interlinkage. Waggoner places the Transcendentalists in a general tradition of descent from the pietistic, utilitarian aesthetics of Puritanism, whereas Bloom, coming to American literature after having identified as a primary trait of British Romantic poetry its sense of anxiety and oppression under the weight of Milton's influence, finds the Transcendentalists (preeminently Emerson) strikingly different in their willful rejection of precursors. Bloom considers the Emersonian visionary spirit much more liberated and shamanistic than its British counterparts, except for Blake. Bloom believes that Emerson raised special problems that have been bequeathed to his descendants: for example, the problems of solipsism and an antinomian attitude toward one's literary forbears, the Americans being "uniquely open to influencings" in their desire to encompass all experience but "uniquely resistant to all *ideas* of influence."

When discussing Emerson, both Waggoner and Bloom tend to take a Carlylean "great heroes" approach to literary history that confuses the culturally symptomatic with the uniquely influential. On the whole, Waggoner is better grounded historically than Bloom, who largely ignores the American social and intellectual context and therefore overstates the differences between American Romantics and their intellectual precursors. Bloom is the more subtle analyst, however, always stimulating even when questionable; and he is fundamentally correct in emphasizing the importance, in Transcendentalist aesthetics, of breaking with the past for the sake of achieving a visionary immediacy.

Various other studies make a similar point. Tony Tanner, *The Reign of Wonder*, identifies the mood of visionary receptivity as a key theme in American writing, first manifested significantly in the Transcendentalists. Roger Asselineau, " 'Dreaming on the Grass'; or the Transcendentalist Constant in American Literature," builds thoughtfully on Tanner's insights. Richard Poirier, "Is There an I for an Eye?" and particularly A. D. Van Nostrand, *Everyman His Own Poet*, are two perceptive studies that discuss Transcendentalist (and particularly Emersonian) aesthetic theory and practice as pivotal instances of a distinctly American habit of constructing personal linguistic and literary universes.

The conception of Transcendentalism as representative of American culture by virtue of its visionary strain has also influenced another body of scholarship that concentrates less on the literary qualities of Transcendentalist writing than on how these reflect larger patterns in American thought. For example, R. W. B. Lewis, *The American Adam*, sees Transcendentalist enthusiasm as a prime example of the prevalent antebellum image of America as a new Eden and the American as a new kind of man. Emerson and Thoreau, in Lewis' view, are among the first memorable spokesmen of a still-vital American faith that "life and history" are "just beginning." Arguments of this kind, insofar as they appeal to historical evidence, are apt to be based on at least four points (of which Lewis touches on the first three): the rapid pace of material progress in nineteenth-century America; the heritage of American revolutionary thought, leading to the "second" or social revolution of the Jacksonian era; the importance of the frontier as a psychological fact; and the legacy of Protestantism descended from the New England Puritans. Partly because the more literary Transcendentalists were so interested in the themes of nature and spirit, the last two factors have been covered the most extensively by literary and cultural historians.

The thesis that Transcendentalism was a response to the frontier and westward expansion was first and most emphatically set forth in Lucy Lockwood Hazard, "The Golden Age of Transcendentalism" (in *The Frontier in American Literature*, 1927), a work that influenced the literary histories of Blankenship and Calverton, among others. Most scholars today would consider their arguments rudimentary while conceding some validity to the thesis. Joel Porte, for instance, thoughtfully discusses affinities between Transcendentalist rhetoric and frontier humor in "Transcendental Antics." Transcendentalist fascination with nature and wilderness (particularly in the work of Emerson and Thoreau) is explored in a series of studies, the most searching of which turn upon the perception that the Transcendentalists lived, emotionally speaking, somewhere between the city and the forest, not fully accepting or rejecting either untrammeled nature or the civilizing process. See especially Perry Miller, "Nature and the National Ego"; Roderick Nash, *Wilderness and the American Mind*; Edwin Fussell, *Frontier*; Richard Slotkin, *Regeneration through Violence*; and particularly Leo Marx, *The Machine in the Garden*. As a complement to these studies should be mentioned Bernard Rosenthal, *City of Nature*, which argues overzealously, but on the whole more resourcefully than previous commentators, that the major American Romantics were interested in a purely metaphorical rather than literal nature, following the predispositions of international Romanticism.

Studies of the relation between Transcendentalist writing and Puritan antecedents have tended to focus on three main subjects. The first and most specific is the comparative study of Transcendentalist and Puritan use of symbolism, inspired most particularly by the publication of Jonathan Edwards' notebook of natural symbols, *Images or Shadows of Divine Things* (1948), with an editorial introduction by Perry Miller that calls attention to Edwards' foreshadowing of American Romanticism. Charles Feidelson, in *Symbolism and American Literature*, was the first scholar to write extensively on the relevance of the Puritans' use of the traditional Christian pseudoscience of typology to later literary practice and the first to place Transcendentalist symbolism on a continuum somewhere between the Puritans and the moderns, although he exaggerated Emerson's anticipation of the latter. More recent commentators, most of them specialists in colonial literature, have redressed the balance and defined Transcendentalist symbolism more precisely as a partially secularized and liberated successor of the typological imagination, still grounded, however, in a perception of nature as a revelation of spirit. See especially Ursula Brumm, *American Thought and Religious Typology*; William Shurr, "Typology and Historical Criticism of the American Renaissance"; Karl Keller, "Alephs, Zahirs, and the Triumph of Ambiguity"; and Mason I. Lowance, Jr., *The Language of Canaan*, which draws on his article "From Edwards to Emerson to Thoreau." The studies by Lowance and Keller are particularly illuminating. Conrad Cherry, *Nature and Religious Imagination from Edwards to Bushnell*, describes the unfolding of the typological tradition within what used to be called "The New England Theology" (i.e., Edwardseanism), with sideglances at Transcendentalism.

A second perceived link between Puritan and Transcendentalist aesthetics is the conception of the writer as a secular prophet. The Transcendentalists took seriously Milton's vision of his muse as a kind of divine inspiration; see Phyllis Cole, "The Purity of Puritanism." More particular parallels between Transcendentalist and Puritan aesthetics have been traced in Waggoner, *American Poets*, and especially in Sacvan Bercovitch's impressive *The American Jeremiad*, which argues that the core conventions of the Puritan Fast Day sermon persisted in American literature down to the Transcendentalist era and beyond, constituting a social ritual that expressed not only communal guilt, chastisement, and fear of national extinction but also an underlying optimism about the nation's future based on their conviction that Americans were a chosen people.

The third and most fundamental question addressed by Puritan legacy scholarship concerns the nature of American (including Transcendentalist) individualism. On the one hand, Perry Miller, like Caroline Dall a half-century before and some of Transcendentalism's conservative critics a half-century before that, was inclined to stress the link between Transcendentalism and antinomianism. Roy Harvey Pearce, in *The Continuity of American Poetry*, bearing in mind the tradition of American literary iconoclasm already discussed, defines that tradition as essentially antinomian, latent during the Puritan era and coming to flower in the age of Emerson and Whitman. The antinomian theory, however, is vigorously disputed by Bercovitch in another brilliant book, *The Puritan Origins of the American Self*, which argues that American Romantic individualism, including Transcendentalism, is better understood in terms of the mainstream Puritan idea of the self as exemplary, of personal history as embodying patterns for communal history derived ultimately from scripture. The self Emerson sought, Bercovitch argues, "was not only his but America's, or rather his *as* America's, and therefore America's as his." This formulation overemphasizes the nationalist aspect of Emerson's thinking, but Bercovitch is correct in claiming that Emerson and most of the other Transcendentalists sought to ground their claims for the individual upon some sort of corporate correlative (usually the common divinity shared by all individuals) as a check on rampant individualism.

Scholarship on the continuities between Puritanism and Transcendentalism has opened up important vistas that will no doubt be explored for some time to come. As they are, the chief defect in the methodology will also become clearer: its inevitable tendency to ignore alternative genealogies, especially the distinctive influences of the Enlightenment. One recent study that makes excellent use of materials from that relatively neglected era is Robert D. Richardson, Jr., *Myth and Literature in the American Renaissance*, which examines how the Transcendentalists and other American Romantics reflect the two antithetical approaches of late eighteenth-century European mythography: a debunking tradition, equating myth with superstition, and an affirmative tradition, celebrating myth for its metaphorical validity. Parker, Alcott, Emerson, and Thoreau are discussed in detail.

SOURCE STUDIES

FOREIGN INFLUENCES IN GENERAL

New England Transcendentalism was so eclectic that almost any major religious, philosophical, or literary tradition in the history of the planet might plausibly be claimed as an influence. The problem is well illustrated by the rambling format of Nathaniel Kaplan and Thomas Katsaros, *Origins of American Transcendentalism in Philosophy and Mysticism*, which amounts simply to sixteen chapters of summary outlines of various philosophical traditions (Hinduism, Buddhism, Confucianism, Taoism, Neoplatonism, Gnosticism, Swedenborg, Kant, etc.) sandwiched between a brief definition of American Transcendentalism and a "reading" of Emerson's *Nature*. The result too faithfully mirrors the Transcendentalist habit of using source material superficially and allusively rather than systematically.

Concerning the general role of foreign influences, Perry Miller raises the basic question in his "New England's Transcendentalism: Native or Imported?" After emphasizing the "galvanizing effect of European ideas," Miller reaches the predictable conclusion that Transcendentalism was "after all, a peculiarly American phenomenon"—predictable because Miller habitually discusses the movement as an indigenous uprising and because other Americanists have, during the last half-century, increasingly stressed Transcendentalism's native backgrounds. "Beginnings of American Transcendentalism," by the Indian scholar S. P. Das, another attempt to give foreign influences their due, goes even further than Miller in emphasizing the movement's Americanness. Accordingly, Transcendentalism's international antecedents have not lately been given anything like the attention they received in Frothingham's extensive survey of German, French, and British precursors (see above). Yet many studies give at least a summary presentation of the international background; see especially Georg Friden, "Transcendental Idealism in New England," the best essay-length digest of foreign influences. See also Sydney Ahlstrom, "The Romantic Mood," in *A Religious History of the American People*, for a good short survey of the European religious background.

GERMANY

Although Transcendentalism takes its name from a word coined by Kant and can be classified as a form of post-Kantian epistemology, most commentators agree that the New England Transcendentalists received German thought more through French and British intermediaries than directly from the source. René Wellek is technically right in criticizing the limitations of Transcendentalist knowledge of German thought in his two essays "The Minor Transcendentalists and German Philosophy" and "Emerson and German Philosophy." The most intensive study of German sources, Stanley M. Vogel, *German Literary Influences on the American Transcendentalists*, is however also right in stressing Transcendentalist attentiveness to and respect for German writers and thinkers, particularly Goethe, whom the American Transcendentalists knew better than any other single figure. Vogel's outlook is generally in keeping with that of the other indispensible work on German influence, Henry A. Pochmann, *German Culture in America*, a magisterial study that in addition to describing the Germanic interests of some two dozen Transcendentalists, also gives an account of the transmission of German thought via England and France. For Transcendentalism's debt to the biblical criticism pioneered in Germany, see Robert Richardson, *Myth and Literature in the American Renaissance*, and Philip Gura, *The Wisdom of Words*. Gura also discusses Transcendentalist interest in Germanic philology, primarily through the agency of the Hungarian Charles Kraitsir, as does John B. Wilson in two articles entitled "Grimm's Law and the Brahmins." Altogether the German links with Transcendentalism have been more thoroughly researched than any other line of foreign influence.

FRANCE

The French backgrounds of Transcendentalism have only been traced in a preliminary way. Walter L. Leighton, *French Philosophers and New-England Transcendentalism* (1908), sketchily discusses the impact of Victor Cousin, Théodore Jouffroy, and Charles Fourier on Transcendentalist thinking and on Brook Farm. Also sketchy, but far more panoramic in scope, are William Girard's "Du Transcendentalism consideré essentiellement dans sa definition et ses origines françaises" (1916) and "Du Transcendentalism consideré sous son aspect social" (1918), which consider religious, philosophical, and social aspects of the movement, devoting special sections to the Transcendentalist response to Madame de Staël, Benjamin Constant, Baron de Gerando, Jean-Jacques Rousseau, George Sand, Saint-Simon, Cousin, Jouffroy, and Fourier. Despite exaggeration of the French contribution at the expense of the German (Pochmann does the reverse) and a tendency to equate frequency of citation with depth of impact, Girard's is a useful pioneering monograph. Georges J. Joyaux, "Victor Cousin and American Transcendentalism," documents American and particularly Transcendentalist interest in the leader of French Eclecticism with excerpts from magazine articles published in the first half of the nineteenth century. Howard Mumford Jones, *America and French Culture, 1750-1848*, anticipates Joyaux's view that Cousin attracted more notice among the Transcendentalists than did the other thinkers discussed by Girard. Altogether, Joyaux and Jones treat the French origins of Transcendentalism rather superficially, as does Henry Blumenthal's more recent and ambitious *American and French Culture, 1800-1900*. Historians today generally underestimate the role of French authors from de Staël (if not Rousseau) to Fourier in shaping Transcendentalist opinion, owing in part to Emerson's and Thoreau's apparent disregard of them; see Emerson R. Marks, "Victor Cousin and Emerson."

BRITAIN

Whereas French influences on Transcendentalism have been broadly surveyed yet not considered as important as they should be, the decisive impact of British authors on Transcendentalist thought is today taken for granted even though the subject has not been studied comprehensively since Frothingham and Edward Dowden's equally impressionistic and uneven "The Transcendentalist Movement and Literature" (1877). The influence of Coleridge, Carlyle, and Wordsworth, acknowledged to be crucial, has seldom been studied systematically except with reference to a few individual Transcendentalists: see "Transcendentalism: The Times" and individual author chapters, as well as Pochmann, *German Culture in America*. On Coleridge's influence, see also Noah Porter, "Coleridge and His American Disciples" (1847); Marjorie H. Nicholson, "James Marsh and the Vermont Transcendentalists"; and Alexander Kern, "Coleridge and American Romanticism." John H. Muirhead, *The Platonic Tradition in Anglo-Saxon Philosophy*, is a valuable but crotchety pioneering attempt to show that idealism is as Anglo-American as empiricism. Special chapters are devoted to the Cambridge Platonists (admired by the Transcendentalists), to Carlyle, and to American Transcendentalism but not, curiously, to Coleridge, though he is referred to throughout. George Mills Harper, "Thomas Taylor in America," discusses the impact of one of the Cambridge Platonists on Emerson and Alcott.

The bearing of Lockean and post-Lockean philosophy on Transcendentalism has been more carefully studied; see especially Cameron Thompson, "John Locke and New England Transcendentalism"; Merrell R. Davis, "Emerson's 'Reason' and the Scottish Philosophers"; and Edgeley W. Todd, "Philosophical Ideas at Harvard College, 1817-1837," which collectively demonstrate that Scottish common sense philosophy, originally conceived as a way of purging Locke's system of its skeptical tendencies and heavily relied upon by conservative Unitarians, also facilitated Transcendentalist acceptance of the crucial post-Kantian distinction between Reason and Understanding.

OTHER EUROPEAN SOURCES

Transcendentalism's grounding in the classics and in the Platonic tradition (from Plato through the Cambridge Platonists) has been carefully studied only with reference to Thoreau, Emerson, and Alcott. See also Muirhead below. The movement's debt to Swedenborg, his mysticism in general and his theory of correspondence in particular, has been studied mainly with reference to Emerson, but see also Frank Sewall, "The New Church and the New-England Transcendentalists," and Clarence Hotson's "Swedenborg's Influence in America to 1830." Unfortunately these articles are too pro-Swedenborgian and anti-Transcendentalist, and the current trend toward emphasizing the origins of Transcendentalist symbolism in Puritan typology has decreased scholarly interest in connections between the movement and Swedenborg, not to mention other European mystics such as Jacob Boehme. (See, however, the chapter on Sampson Reed in this volume.)

ORIENTAL INFLUENCES AND ANALOGUES

The still-indispensable pioneering work is Arthur Christy, *The Orient in American Transcendentalism*, a study of Emerson, Alcott, and Thoreau in relation to Hindu, Confucian, and Persian literature and thought. Also important are the sections of Frederic I. Carpenter, *Emerson and Asia*, that deal with Oriental influences. The best general survey, however, is Carl T. Jackson, *The Oriental Religions and American Thought*, more comprehensive and up-to-date than either Christy or Carpenter, although less detailed on the subjects they treat. Jackson lucidly summarizes the Transcendentalists' interest in Indian and East Asian religions in the larger context of the rise of American awareness of the East from colonial times to 1900, dwelling especially on Emerson but also taking note of a number of other figures from Alcott through Frothingham. Jackson credits the Transcendentalists with having been "unquestionably the first Americans to approach Asian thought sympathetically and to assimilate Oriental ideas into their world view." A more intensive survey of Trancendentalist use of Oriental materials, less broadly informed than Jackson's, is Roger Chester Mueller, "The Orient in American Transcendental Periodicals (1835–1886)," a descriptive account of Oriental references in the periodicals cited by Clarence Gohdes. A portion of this dissertation has been published in Mueller's "Transcendental Periodicals and the Orient," an article concentrating on the debate between Clarke, Johnson, and others over the superiority of Christianity to other world religions. J. P. Rao Rayapati, *Early American Interest in Vedanta*, another study of general scope, surveys "Early Vedic Readings by American Transcendentalists" but unaccountably stops short of the heyday of Transcendental Orientalism.

Several other studies, all mediocre, debate the influence of Oriental literature and thought on the Transcendentalists. John T. Reid, *Indian Influences in American Literature and Thought*, heavily indebted to Christy and Carpenter, takes a middle position, arguing that Hindu scriptures provided welcome corroboration rather than genuinely new light. W. E. Washburn, "The Oriental 'Roots' of American Transcendentalism," insists that they have been much exaggerated, and V. Krishnamachari argues with equal implausibility that "Transcendentalism without Orientalism is inconceivable" in "Transcendentalism in America."

Altogether, Transcendentalist interest in the Orient has not been studied exhaustively. Jackson's survey is likely to stand for some time as the standard reference work despite its relative brevity (some seventy-five pages devoted to the entire field of Transcendentalism) by virtue of its essential soundness and the dearth of serious scholarly interest in the subject.

THE TRANSCENDENTALIST LEGACY

Many American writers have at one time or another been diagnosed as tinged with Transcendentalism. The prevailing theory that American literature has a deeply "Romanticist" tradition suggests that Transcendentalism is the fountainhead of much that is distinctive in native writing. For studies that intelligently pursue this thesis in general terms, see particularly the works of Bloom, Tanner, and Asselineau cited above and Jesse Bier, "The Romantic Coordinates of American Literature."

Poets seen to fit (mayhap to their own surprise) in the Emerson or Whitman tradition have come under particular scrutiny as Transcendentalist legatees. See especially the studies of Bloom, Waggoner, and Pearce as well as James E. Miller, Jr., *The American Quest for a Supreme Fiction*. The two poets whose affinities with Transcendentalism have been examined most thoroughly are Wallace Stevens and Robert Frost. For two thoughtful and balanced discussions of Stevens' links with Transcendentalism, in addition to scholarship previously noted, see Nina Baym, "The Transcendentalism of Wallace Stevens," and Abbie F. Willard, *Wallace Stevens*, which includes a critique of Bloom's methodology. Robert Frost's ties with Transcendentalism are most fully discussed in Donald J. Greiner, *Robert Frost*, which reviews prior commentary.

Charles Child Walcutt, *American Literary Naturalism*, shows that Transcendentalism's mixture of idealist and naturalist elements prefigures a similar duality in literary naturalism. Marilyn Baldwin describes what with some stretching she calls "The Transcendental Phase of William Dean Howells." Frederic I. Carpenter strains to find links between "Eugene O'Neill, the Orient, and American Transcendentalism."

Turning to the other arts, Charles Ives, an avowed admirer of the Concord group, is pictured as their genuine disciple by Alfred F. Rosa; but Sam Girgus argues that he perverted Transcendentalism in the interest of insurance salesmanship (in *The Law of the Heart*). Raymond H. Geselbracht, "Transcendental Renaissance in the Arts: 1890–1920," briefly discusses Ives, Frank Lloyd Wright, and Isadora Duncan as Transcendentalist legatees by virtue of their belief in art and authenticity as "flowing from a union of soul with nature." Fred E. H. Schroeder aligns "Andrew Wyeth and the Transcendental Tradition."

For connections between Transcendentalism and subsequent American philosophy, see above, as well as Henry A. Pochmann, *New England Transcendentalism and St. Louis Hegelianism*, which describes the philosophical movement with which the Transcendentalists had the most direct ties. Frederic I. Carpenter, *American Literature and the Dream*, in the course of emphasizing the practical character of Transcendentalist idealism, links it with the Pragmatism of Peirce and William James.

For Transcendentalism's contribution to American liberal religion, see especially William R. Hutchison, *The Transcendentalist Ministers* (whose footnotes provide a good guide to further sources) and *The Modernist Impulse in American Protestantism*, which appraises the Transcendentalist contribution as part of the overall impact of the Unitarian movement. Some of the links that indirectly connect Transcendentalism with Christian Science and late nineteenth-century spiritualism are explored in Stewart W. Holmes, "Phineas Parkhurst Quimby," and Gail Thain Parker, *Mind Cure in New England*.

Several studies relate Trancendentalism to phases of 1960s radicalism: Herbert London, "American Romantics"; Paul H. Wild, "Flower Power"; and Martin Schiff, "Neo-Transcendentalism in the New Left Counter-Culture." The last is a searching and incisive comparison that criticizes the inadequacies of the counterculturists. The first two articles are ephemeral.

Three solid essays in *Transcendentalism and Its Legacy* discuss significant turn-of-the century interpreters of the movement: Joe Lee Davis, "Santayana as a Critic of Transcendentalism"; René Wellek, "Irving Babbitt, Paul More and Transcendentalism"; and Sherman Paul, "The Identities of John Jay Chapman."

Finally, Frederic I. Carpenter sketchily describes "American Transcendentalism in India," claiming that Nehru was influenced by Emerson and Gandhi by Thoreau. Joseph Jones detects traces of Transcendentalism in Australia and New Zealand in "Emerson and Whitman 'Down Under,'" extending his reflections in *Radical Cousins*.

CONCLUDING THOUGHTS

The huge quantity of printed matter on the subject of Transcendentalism might tempt one to demand a moratorium on all further scholarship, yet the fact is that this research has been uneven, leaving considerable gaps. Some of the areas in need of further study have been noted in this chapter: they include French and Oriental influences on and affinities with Transcendentalism; contributions of the Enlightenment to Transcendentalist ideology and aesthetics; Transcendentalism as a social movement and political force; Transcendentalist prose in lectures and essays; the boundaries, audience, and contemporary intellectual impact of the movement; and almost every aspect of Transcendentalism after the Civil War. Of course, the most interesting and influential future contributions to Transcendentalist scholarship may be precisely those of whose need one is presently unaware.

TRANSCENDENTALISM: THE TIMES

Joel Myerson

A common theme running through these first three introductory essays is that Transcendentalism did not exist in a vacuum; it was not, as Almira Barlow once told Emerson, *"A little beyond."* There was a definite context within which the Transcendentalists worked, thought, and wrote, and a number of studies by contemporaries and later writers deal with that milieu. Lawrence Buell's chapter "The Transcendentalist Movement" sets forth and evaluates the basic materials written about Transcendentalism; Conrad Wright's chapter "Unitarianism and Transcendentalism" challenges us to look on the Unitarian-Transcendentalist relationship in a more accurate historical context; and this chapter provides additional background material that places Transcendentalism within its immediate historical context.

One cannot truly understand Transcendentalism without reference to the histories of the 1830–60 period. Transcendentalism gained momentum in a period of American history marked by the rise of the "common man" and a general interest in reform. Good bibliographies of the period are in *The Harvard Guide to American History*, ed. Frank Freidel; Gerald N. Grob, *American Social History before 1860*; Donald F. Tingley, *Social History of the United States*; and Philip I. Mitterling, *U. S. Cultural History*.

Works that help modern readers to understand American life during the Transcendental period include Carl Russell Rish, *The Rise of the Common Man 1830-1850*; Gilbert Seldes, *The Stammering Century*; Van Wyck Brooks, *The Flowering of New England 1815-1865*; Ralph Henry Gabriel, *The Course of American Democratic Thought*; Alice Felt Tyler, *Freedom's Ferment*; Arthur M. Schlesinger,

Jr., *The Age of Jackson*; Robert E. Riegel, *Young America 1830–1840*; Harvey Wish, *Science and Thought in Early America*; Yehoshua Arieli, *Individualism and Nationalism in American Ideology*; Irving H. Bartlett, *The American Mind in the Mid-Nineteenth Century*; Fred Somkin, *Unquiet Eagle: Memory and Desire in the Idea of American Freedom, 1815–1860*; Jerome L. Clark, *1844*; Edward Pessen, *Jacksonian America*; Stow Persons, *The Decline of American Gentility*; Russel Blaine Nye, *Society and Culture in America 1830–1860*; Rush Welter, *The Mind of America 1820–1860*; and Herbert Hovenkamp, *Science and Religion in America 1800–1860*. Amusing anecdotal histories are Meade Minnegerode, *The Fabulous Forties 1840–1850*; E. Douglas Branch, *The Sentimental Years 1836–1850*; Fred Lewis Pattee, *The Feminine Fifties*; and Grace Adams and Edward Hutter, *The Mad Forties*. An interesting collection of documents is in *American Life in the 1840s*, ed. Carl Bode. A good sense of the reform impulse of the period can be gathered from Wendell Phillips Garrison, "The Isms of Forty Years Ago"; Lawrence Lader, *The Bold Brahmins: New England's War against Slavery 1831–1863*; *The Antislavery Argument*, ed. William H. Pease and Jane H. Pease; John L. Thomas, "Romantic Reform in America, 1815–1865"; C. S. Griffin, *The Ferment of Reform, 1830–1860*; Jane H. Pease and William H. Pease, *Bound with Them in Chains: A Biographical History of the Antislavery Movement*; Charles A. Barker, *American Convictions*; Gail Thain Parker, *Mind Cure in New England*; *The Perfectionists: Radical Social Thought in the North, 1815–1860*, ed. Laurence Veysey; Ann Douglas, *The Feminization of American Culture*; Ronald G. Walters, *American Reformers, 1815–1860*; and Stephen Nissenbaum, *Sex, Diet, and Debility in Jacksonian America: Sylvester Graham and Health Reform*. Other useful background studies are Arthur Hobson Quinn, "American Literature and American Politics"; Carl Bode, *The American Lyceum*; Russel Nye, *The Unembarrassed Muse: The Popular Arts in America*; and Donald S. Spencer, *Louis Kossuth and Young America: A Study of Sectionalism and Foreign Policy, 1848–1852*. The various Transcendentalist responses to this labyrinth of social and reform movements are outlined in the chapters by Buell and Wright, as well as in Carol Johnston's chapter "Transcendentalist Communities."

Because Transcendentalism was, in the broadest sense, a religious movement, special attention should be paid to Buell's and Wright's discussions of Unitarianism and Transcendentalism. One should also look at *Unitarianism: Its Origins and History* and Joseph Henry Allen and Richard Eddy, *A History of the Unitarians and Universalists in the United States*, especially pp. 195–246; both books are by contemporaries of the Transcendentalists. Unitarianism is placed within the context of contemporary religious reform in Ralph H. Gabriel, "Evangelical Religion and Popular Romanticism in Early Nineteenth-Century America," and Timothy L. Smith, *Revivalism and Social Reform in Mid-Nineteenth-Century America*. More specialized studies of Transcendentalism and religion are Henry G. Fairbanks, "The Transcendentalists and Theosophy," an interesting if all too brief comparison of the writings of the two groups; Harriet Elizabeth Knight, "Two Streams of Mysticism in America: Quakerism and Transcendentalism," and Stephanie Ann Reeck, "Transcendentalism and Quakerism";

Sister Mary Helena Sanfillippo, "The New England Transcendentalists' Opinions of the Catholic Church"; James R. Hodges, "Christian Science and Transcendentalism"; and Frank Sewall, "The New Church and the New England Transcendentalists," a skimpy treatment of Swedenborgianism.

The Transcendentalists' reaction to the temper of their time can be traced in their writings and in more recent studies of those writings. It is often useful to view these writings in the context of other studies, particularly those that give a sense of the state of native American literature and the influence of foreign literatures in America during this period.

A good picture of the American literary scene between 1830 and 1860 can be gleaned from Robert W. Flint, "The Boston Book Trade, 1835–1845: A Directory"; Frank Luther Mott, *A History of American Magazines 1741–1850* and *Golden Multitudes: A History of Best Sellers in the United States*; J. Albert Robbins, "Fees Paid to Authors by Certain American Periodicals, 1840–1850"; William Charvat, *Literary Publishing in America 1790–1850* and *The Profession of Authorship in America, 1800–1870*; Edward E. Chielens, *The Literary Journal in America to 1900*; Jayne K. Kribbs, *An Annotated Bibliography of American Literary Periodicals, 1741–1850*; and *American Periodicals 1741–1900*, ed. Jean Hoornstra and Trudy Heath. Only two publishers have been studied in depth for their connection with the movement: see Raymond L. Kilgour, *Messrs. Roberts Brothers, Publishers*, and Madeleine B. Stern, "James P. Walker and Horace B. Fuller."

Good general works on Anglo-American intellectual crosscurrents include George Stuart Gordon, *Anglo-American Literary Relations*; Clarence Gohdes, *American Literature in Nineteenth Century England*; James J. Barnes, *Authors, Publishers, and Politicians: The Quest for an Anglo-American Copyright Agreement, 1815–1854*; and Stephen Spender, *Love-Hate Relationships: English and American Sensibilities*. Also of value are these specialized studies: Samuel C. Chew, "Byron in America"; William Silas Vance, "Carlyle in America before *Sartor Resartus*" and "Carlyle and the American Transcendentalists"; Julia Power, *Shelley in America in the Nineteenth Century*; John Olin Eidson, *Tennyson in America*; Hyder Edward Rollins, *Keats' Reputation in America to 1848*; and Terrence Martin, *The Instructed Vision: Scottish Common Sense Philosophy and the Origins of American Fiction*. The influence of English philosophy on American writers of all sorts is discussed in Noah Porter, "Coleridge and His American Disciples"; William Charvat, *The Origins of American Critical Thought, 1810–1835*; Merle Curti, "The Great Mr. Locke: America's Philosopher, 1783–1861"; Wendell Glick, "Bishop Paley in America"; Sydney E. Ahlstrom, "The Scottish Philosophy and American Theology"; Richard J. Peterson, "Scottish Common Sense Philosophy in America, 1768–1850"; and George H. Daniels, "An American Defense of Bacon: A Study in the Relations of Scientific Thought, 1840–1855."

French sources of American thought are explored in these general studies: Woodbridge Riley, "La Philosophie française en Amérique"; Howard Mumford Jones, *America and French Culture 1750–1848* and "American Comment on George Sand,

1837–1848''; Leo Lemchen, "A Summary View of the Vogue of French Eclecticism in New England—1829–1844''; Georges Jules Joyaux, "French Thought in American Magazines 1800–1848''; C. M. Lombard, "The American Attitude towards the French Romantics (1800–1861)''; and Henry Blumenthal, *American and French Culture, 1800–1900*. For an interesting contemporary statement, see J. A. Heraud's four articles, under the general title of "Continental Philosophy in America.''

Studies of the German sources of American thought are particularly interested in the influences of Goethe and Kant. Good general background readings are James Murdock, "German Philosophy in America" (1842); Joseph Henry Allen, "The Contact of American Unitarianism and German Thought" (1890); and Philip Allison Shelley, "A German Art of Life in America: The American Reception of the Goethean Doctrine of Self-Culture.'' The essential work on the larger question of German literary influence is Henry A. Pochmann, *German Culture in America*, an encyclopedic and scrupulously annotated commentary. The American reception of particular authors is studied in Henry A. Brann, "Hegel and His New England Echo''; J. H. Muirhead, "How Hegel Came to America''; Edward V. Brewer, "The New England Interest in Jean Paul Friedrich Richter''; Joseph L. Blau, "Kant in America''; Siegfried B. Puknat, "De Wette in New England''; and *The American Hegelians*, ed. William H. Goetzmann. A useful examination of the reverse flow of ideas is Kaspar T. Locher, "The Reception of American Literature in German Literary Histories in the Nineteenth Century.''

Italian influences and responses are examined in Angelina La Piana, *Dante's American Pilgrimage*. Polish influences are traced in Francis J. Whitfield, "Mickiewicz and American Literature.''

The importance of Boston as the setting for Transcendentalism should not be underestimated. Interesting works in this respect are *The Memorial History of Boston*, ed. Justin Winsor; Helen M. Winslow, *Literary Boston of To-Day*; Lilian Whiting, *Boston Days*; M. A. DeWolfe Howe, "The Boston Religion" and "The 'Literary Centre'''; Cleveland Amory, *The Proper Bostonians*; Martin Green, *The Problem of Boston*; Paul Goodman, "Ethics and Enterprise: The Values of a Boston Elite, 1800–1860''; and Francis X. Blouin, Jr., *The Boston Region, 1810–1850*. Most of the Transcendentalists were educated at Harvard College and Harvard Divinity School, and these connections are examined in Andrew P. Peabody, *Harvard Reminiscences*; Edgeley Woodman Todd, "Philosophical Ideas at Harvard College, 1817–1837''; *The Harvard Divinity School*, ed. George Hunston Williams; Daniel Walker Howe, *The Unitarian Conscience*; and Ronald Story, *The Forging of an Aristocracy*.

Emerson and Thoreau lived most of their lives in Concord, and many of the Transcendentalists visited there, some dwelling in town for extended periods of time. Three good histories of the town are by Allen French, Townsend Scudder, and Ruth R. Wheeler. Reminiscences of Concord during the Transcendentalist period are in Julia R. Anagnos, *Philosophæ Quæstor; or, Days in Concord*, which is particularly good on the Concord School of Philosophy; Margaret Sidney, *Old Concord: Her Highways and Byways*; Frank Preston Stearns, "Concord Thirty-Odd Years Ago''; Mary Hosmer

Brown, *Memories of Concord*; L. D. Geller, *Between Concord and Plymouth*; and *Remembrances of Concord and the Thoreaus: Letters of Horace Hosmer to Dr. Samuel Arthur Jones*, ed. George Hendrick. Interesting group studies of the Concord authors are Randall Stewart, "The Concord Group," and Taylor Stoehr, *Nay-Saying in Concord*. A thought-provoking article is Robert A. Gross, " 'The Most Estimable Place in All the World': A Debate on Progress in Nineteenth-Century Concord."

The importance of Transcendentalism to the development of American literature has been much discussed. As an indigenous literary movement, Transcendentalism had much to do with the overall concerns that existed at the time for a truly American literature. In this latter respect, the following works provide a useful context: Benjamin T. Spencer, "A National Literature, 1837–1855" and *The Quest for Nationality*; John T. Frederick, "American Literary Nationalism"; Donald Vincent Gawronski, "Transcendentalism: An Ideological Basis for Manifest Destiny"; Robert Lemelin, *Pathway to the National Character 1830–1861*; and Larzer Ziff, *Literary Democracy*.

The Transcendentalists' connection with the New York-based "Young America" movement is discussed in John Stafford, *The Literary Criticism of "Young America"*; Perry Miller, *The Raven and the Whale*; Heyward Bruce Ehrlich, "A Study of the Literary Activity in New York City during the 1840 Decade"; and John Paul Pritchard, *Literary Wise Men of Gotham*. The standard study for the Southern reaction to Transcendentalism is Jay B. Hubbell, *The South in American Literature 1607–1900*. Transcendentalism in Salem is the subject of Alfred Rosa, *Salem, Transcendentalism, and Hawthorne*. Rhode Island Transcendentalism is discussed in Charles R. Crowe, "Transcendentalism and 'The Newness' in Rhode Island" and "Transcendentalism and the Providence Literati."

There are numerous published recollections by and studies of contemporaries of the Transcendentalists. The New York literary scene is discussed in Merle M. Hoover, *Park Benjamin*; *Memoirs of Anne C. L. Botta*, ed. Vincenzo Botta, and Madeleine B. Stern, "The House of Expanding Doors: Anne Lynch's Soirees, 1846"; Bette S. Weidman, "Charles Frederick Briggs"; Parke Godwin, *A Biography of William Cullen Bryant*, Charles H. Brown, *William Cullen Bryant*, *The Letters of William Cullen Bryant*, and E. Miller Budick, " 'Visible Images' and the 'Still Voices': Transcendental Vision in Bryant's 'Thanatopsis' "; George Edwin Mize, "The Contribution of Evert A. Duyckinck to the Cultural Development of Nineteenth-Century America"; Horace Greeley, *Recollections of a Busy Life*, and Glyndon G. Van Deusen, *Horace Greeley*; James Grant Wilson, *The Life and Letters of Fitz-Greene Halleck*, and Nelson Frederick Adkins, *Fitz-Greene Halleck*; Homer F. Barnes, *Charles Fenno Hoffman*; Donald Joseph Yanella, Jr., "Cornelius Mathews"; George Haven Putnam, *A Memoir of George Palmer Putnam*; John Sartain, *The Reminiscences of a Very Old Man 1808–1897*; Richard Henry Stoddard, *Recollections*; *The Diary of George Templeton Strong*; and Marie Hansen-Taylor and Horace Scudder, *The Life and Letters of Bayard Taylor*. A good reference work for the period is *Antebellum Writers in New York and the South*, ed. Joel Myerson.

Works by or about other contemporaries of the Transcendentalists, who are sometimes not associated with the movement, can shed light on the movement itself. For Washington Allston, whose ideas and paintings influenced the Transcendentalists, see E. P. Richardson, *Washington Allston*; George P. Winston, "Washington Allston and the Objective Correlative"; Doreen Hunter, "America's First Romantics"; and William H. Gerdts and Theodore E. Stebbins, Jr., *"A Man of Genius."* For George Bancroft, a historian who was friendly to Transcendentalist ideas, see Russel B. Nye, "The Religion of George Bancroft" and *George Bancroft*; and John W. Rathbun, "George Bancroft on Man and History." For John Burroughs, a naturalist and friend of the Transcendentalists, see Clara Barrus, *John Burroughs*; Margaret Ruth Lowery, "John Burroughs in Relation to the New England Transcendentalists"; Barrus, *The Life and Letters of John Burroughs*; and Perry D. Westbrook, *John Burroughs*. For Thomas Holley Chivers, a poet who often defended the Transcendentalists to his friend Edgar Allan Poe, see *The Correspondence of Thomas Holley Chivers*; Robert Marion Willingham, Jr., "The Poetic Theory of Thomas Holley Chivers and Its Relation to Transcendentalism"; and Charles M. Lombard, *Thomas Holley Chivers*. For James T. Fields, publisher of and friend to many of the Transcendentalists, see his *Yesterdays with Authors* and *Biographical Notes and Personal Sketches*; Annie Fields, *Memories of a Hostess*; and W. S. Tryon, *Parnassus Corner*. For Edward Everett Hale, an important contemporary of the Transcendentalists, see his *Memories of a Hundred Years* and "A Harvard Undergraduate in the Thirties"; Edward Everett Hale, Jr., *The Life and Letters of Edward Everett Hale*; and Jean Holloway, *Edward Everett Hale*. For Isaac Hecker, briefly a resident at Brook Farm and Fruitlands, see Vincent F. Holden, *The Early Years of Isaac Thomas Hecker* and *The Yankee Paul*. For the James family, friends of Emerson and acquaintances of other Transcendentalists, see F. O. Matthiessen, *The James Family*; Austin Warren, *The Elder Henry James*; Leon Edel, *Henry James: The Untried Years*; Ralph Barton Perry, *The Thought and Character of William James*; and Gay Wilson Allen, "James' *Varieties of Religious Experience* as Introduction to American Transcendentalism." For Henry Wadsworth Longfellow, a conservative contemporary of the Transcendentalists, see Samuel Longfellow, *Life of Henry Wadsworth Longfellow* and *Final Memorials of Henry Wadsworth Longfellow*; Lawrance Thompson, *Young Longfellow, 1807-1843*; and *The Letters of Henry Wadsworth Longfellow*.

Other works by or about the Transcendentalists' contemporaries that shed light on them and their time are *Memorial of Joseph and Lucy Clark Allen*, ed. E. W. Allen; Henry Greenleaf Pearson, *The Life of John A. Andrew*; Susan Hale, *Life and Letters of Thomas Gold Appleton*; Walter Donald Kring, *Henry Whitney Bellows*; Samuel Bradford, Jr., *Some Incidents in the Life of Samuel Bradford Senior*; Beman Brockway, *Fifty Years in Journalism*; Elbridge Streeter Brooks, *The Life-Work of Elbridge Gerry Brooks*; Sarah Theo. Brown, *Letters of Theo. Brown*; Joseph T. Buckingham, *Personal Memoirs and Recollections of Editorial Life*; Whitney W. Buck, Jr., "Warren Burton"; Nancy Craig Simmons, "The 'Autobiographical Sketch' of James Elliot Cabot"; Ida Gertrude Everson, *George Henry Calvert*; Robert M. York, "George B. Cheever"; George W. Childs, *Recollections*; John Thomas Codman, "The Men and

Thought That Made the Boston of the Forties Famous''; Charles T. Congdon, *Reminiscences of a Journalist*; J. C. Derby, *Fifty Years among Authors, Books and Publishers*; *Autobiography and Letters of Orville Dewey*; Charlotte C. Eliot, *Walter Greenleaf Eliot*; Maud Howe Elliott, *Three Generations*; Arthur B. Ellis, *Memoir of Rufus Ellis*; George B. Emerson, *Reminiscences of an Old Teacher*; Maunsell B. Field, *Memories of Many Men and of Some Women*; *Caleb and Mary Wilder Foote*, ed. Mary Wilder Tileston; S. G. Goodrich, *Recollections of a Lifetime*; *Passages from the Correspondence and Other Papers of Rufus W. Griswold* and Joy Bayless, *Rufus Wilmot Griswold*; Kurt F. Leidecker, *Yankee Teacher: The Life of William Torrey Harris*; Martha M. Pingel, *An American Utilitarian: Richard Hildreth as a Philosopher*; John T. Morse, Jr., *Life and Letters of Oliver Wendell Holmes*, and Eleanor M. Tilton, *Amiable Autocrat: A Biography of Oliver Wendell Holmes*; *Memorial of George Washington Hosmer*, ed. J. K. Hosmer; Julia Ward Howe, *Reminiscences 1819-1899*, and Laura E. Richards and Maud Howe Elliott, *Julia Ward Howe*; Arria S. Huntington, *Memoir and Letters of Frederic Dan Huntington*; Madeleine B. Stern, "Four Letters from George Keats"; Charles Godfrey Leland, *Memoirs*, and Elizabeth Robins Pennell, *Charles Godfrey Leland*; Thomas Sargent Perry, *The Life and Letters of Francis Lieber*; *Some Reminiscences of the Life of Samuel Kirkland Lothrop*, ed. Thornton Kirkland Lothrop; Susan I. Lesley, *Memoir of the Life of Mrs. Anne Jean Lyman*; *A Gentleman of Much Promise: The Diary of Isaac Mickle 1837-1845*; *Private Letters of William Minot*; *John Hopkins Morison: A Memoir*; *James and Lucretia Mott: Life and Letters*, ed. Anna Davis Hallowell; Benjamin Lease, *That Wild Fellow John Neal and the American Literary Revolution*; Thomas Low Nichols, *Forty Years of American Life 1821-1861*; Allen R. Clark, "Andrews Norton"; *Letters of Charles Eliot Norton* and Kermit Vanderbilt, *Charles Eliot Norton*; Frank Otto Gatell, *John Gorham Palfrey and the New England Conscience*; *Memorial of the Reverend George Putnam*; James B. Thayer, *Rev. Samuel Ripley of Waltham*; Nina Moore Tiffany, *Samuel E. Sewall*; M. E. W. Sherwood, *An Epistle to Posterity Being Rambling Recollections of Many Years of My Life* and *Here & There & Everywhere*; Edward Simmons, *From Seven to Seventy*; *The Letters of William Gilmore Simms*; *Selections from the Autobiography of Elizabeth Oakes Smith*; Denton J. Snider, *A Writer of Books in His Genesis*; Elizabeth Cady Stanton, *Eighty Years or More (1815-1897)*; Frank Preston Stearns, *The Life and Public Service of George Luther Stearns* and *Sketches from Concord and Appledore*; Laura Stedman and George M. Gould, *Life and Letters of Edmund Clarence Stedman*; Mary E. Phillips, *Reminiscences of William Wetmore Story*, and Henry James, *William Wetmore Story and His Friends*; Edward L. Pierce, *Memoir and Letters of Charles Sumner*; *Life, Letters, and Journals of George Ticknor*, ed. Anna Ticknor and G. S. Hillard, and David B. Tyack, *George Ticknor and the Boston Brahmins*; John Townsend Trowbridge, *My Own Story*; Maud Howe Elliott, *Uncle Sam Ward and His Circle*; John Ware, *Memoir of the Life of Henry Ware, Jr.*; Edward S. Hall, *Memoir of Mary L. Ware, Wife of Henry Ware, Jr.*; Joseph C. Grannis, "Henry Ware, Sr."; John G. Adams, *Memoir of Thomas Whittemore*; *The Letters of John Greenleaf Whittier*; Kate Douglas Wiggin, *My Garden of Memory*; and Sampson Reed, *A*

Biographical Sketch of Thomas Worcester.

There are, finally, a number of informative studies of the very minor Transcendentalists and of individuals who were briefly associated with the movement. A good reference work in this area is *The American Renaissance in New England*, ed. Joel Myerson. For the people associated with Brook Farm, see Lindsay Swift, *Brook Farm*, and Myerson, *Brook Farm: An Annotated Bibliography and Resources Guide*. All contributors to the *Dial* are discussed in Myerson, *The New England Transcendentalists and the* Dial. The Unitarian Transcendentalists are sketched in *Heralds of a Liberal Faith*, ed. Samuel A. Eliot. Studies of individuals associated with the Transcendentalist movement include Kenneth Walter Cameron, "Junius J. Alcott," on Bronson Alcott's brother; James M. Mathews, "George Partridge Bradford"; Charles S. Fobes, "Robert Bartlett"; *Reminiscences of Ednah Dow Cheney*; Lydia Maria Child, "Letter XIII.," in *Letters from New-York. Second Series, Letters of Lydia Maria Child*, superseded by *The Collected Correspondence of Lydia Maria Child*, and Helene G. Baer, *The Heart Is Like Heaven: The Biography of Lydia Maria Child*; Joel Myerson, " 'A True & High Minded Person': Transcendentalist Sarah Clarke"; Caroline Dall, *"Alongside": Being Notes Suggested by "A New England Boyhood" of Doctor Edward Everett Hale*, and Barbara Welter, "The Merchant's Daughter: A Tale from Life"; Richard Frederick Fuller, "The Younger Generation in 1840: From the Diary of a New England Boy," and *Recollections of Richard F. Fuller*; Richard F. Fuller, *Chaplain Fuller*; William C. Gannett, *Ezra Stiles Gannett*; Leo Stoller, "Christopher A. Greene"; *The Letters of Horatio Greenough*; Nina Moore Tiffany and Francis Tiffany, *Harm Jan Huidekoper*; Georgiana Bruce Kirby, *Years of Experience*; Samuel J. May, *Some Recollections of Our Antislavery Conflict*; Samuel Osgood, *Miles Stones in Our Life-Journey*; Stewart H. Holmes, "Phineas Parkhurst Quimby"; Elizabeth Hoar, *Mrs. Samuel Ripley*; Edward Waldo Emerson, "Samuel Gray Ward," *Ward Family Papers*, ed. Samuel Gray Ward, and David Baldwin, "Puritan Aristocrat in the Age of Emerson: A Study of Samuel Gray Ward"; *Beyond Concord: Selected Writings of David Atwood Wasson*; Charles William Wendte, *The Wider Fellowship*; E. P. Whipple, *Recollections of Eminent Men*, and Leishman A. Peacock, "Edwin Percy Whipple"; Caroline Ticknor, *Poe's Helen*, and John Grier Varner, "Sarah Helen Whitman."

UNITARIANISM AND TRANSCENDENTALISM

Conrad Wright

In 1950, when Perry Miller compiled his anthology of Transcendentalist writings, he insisted that New England Transcendentalism is best defined as "a religious demonstration." That proposition is simple enough, and some might think it obvious, but Miller was countering a tendency among scholars of American letters to treat Transcendentalism as a literary and philosophical movement and to neglect the religious impulse it embodied. Part of the problem, Miller thought, came from judging the whole movement by the familiar "but not always typical" works of Emerson and Thoreau. But, he added, students had also been misled by the tendency of Emerson, Thoreau, and others "to put their cause into the language of philosophy and literature rather than that of theology." In any event, his anthology aimed to provide a wider representation of Transcendentalist ideas and thinkers and thus emphasize "the inherently religious character" of the movement.

The interpretation of Transcendentalism that Miller was criticizing goes back at least as far as Octavius Brooks Frothingham's *Transcendentalism in New England* (1876). Frothingham introduced the movement by way of Kant and German philosophy and did not get to the topic "Religious Tendencies" until chapter 7. That chapter begins by noting that "the transcendental philosophy addressed itself at once to questions of religion"—which is not the same as saying that the movement was itself "a religious demonstration." Earlier in the book, Frothingham reviewed the controversies among Unitarians over Emerson's Divinity School Address, but he made a point of rejecting the "narrow" view that New England Transcendentalism "was a movement within the limits of 'liberal' Christianity or Unitarianism as it was called." Frothingham's chapter headings are revealing: he starts with "Beginnings in Germany," then moves to France and England, and only reaches New England on page

105. This scheme of organization almost programmatically excludes the liberal Christianity of 1805 to 1825 as an influence on Transcendentalism except by way of reaction.

Frothingham's book is regularly cited in bibliographies as the "standard" history, as though it were an objective and unbiased account. The extent to which it represents special pleading has hardly been recognized. Like Frothingham's autobiographical *Recollections and Impressions 1822-1890* and his quasiautobiographical attempt to come to terms with his father's memory in *Boston Unitarianism*, his history of Transcendentalism subtly denigrates the accomplishments and minimizes the influence of the older generation. In *Boston Unitarianism*, Frothingham effectively trivializes the achievements of that generation by praising it for amiable but secondary virtues. In *Transcendentalism in New England* he says, in effect, that the fresh vigor of the movement could not have sprung from the crabbed, rationalistic, and parochial religious culture of Boston Unitarianism; the only explanation for its revitalization of spiritual life is that it came from abroad. This bias, here and in the historical writings of his later years, was the residue of Frothingham's unresolved rebellion against his father and his father's generation.

A later version of the conventional interpretation of the origins of Transcendentalism may be found in Harold Clarke Goddard's *Studies in New England Transcendentalism* (1908). Goddard readily acknowledges that Transcendentalism flowered in soil the Unitarians had cultivated. As he puts it, it was "hard for others than Unitarians to become transcendentalists." Yet it was still an external influence, not some inner dynamic, that produced the transformation. The "widely accepted theory" that New England Transcendentalism was "a German importation" strikes Goddard as having "a large element of truth." He suggests that Unitarianism was important chiefly as a conduit for English thought anticipatory of Transcendentalism: "Into this perhaps relatively slender stream was turned the turbulent, but congenital volume of German and other continental waters, and into that united river the thought of former ages dropped—not, in the image of Emerson's poem, like ordinary rain, but like veritable cloudbursts."

Goddard finds it easy to emphasize the German origins of the movement because his definition of it is explicitly philosophical rather than religious. Transcendentalism, he states at the outset, was "first and foremost, a doctrine concerning the mind, its ways of acting and methods of getting knowledge." He therefore concentrates on the purely intellectual influences on four leading Transcendentalists, as revealed by the books they presumably read. This methodology eliminates from consideration a whole range of social and cultural forces shaping the early lives of his chosen figures. It makes Transcendentalism seem to be the solution to a problem in epistemology rather than—in Perry Miller's words—a "hunger of the spirit for values" lacking in the religious culture of that time and place.

But Miller's revisionism in *The Transcendentalists: An Anthology* (1950) went only halfway. He properly drew attention to the religious center of the movement, but he was still only able to see antagonism between the Unitarianism of the first generation and the Transcendentalism of the second. Far from sympathetic with liberal religion himself, he always took delight in criticizing the shortcomings of "liberal historians of the nineteenth century," particularly the filiopietism of writers like John Gorham Palfrey. The various adversaries of the Unitarians were therefore especially attractive to Miller. He was eager to take the part of Edwards against Chauncy in the eighteenth century and of Emerson against Andrews Norton in the nineteenth century. But if two people attack the same tradition, albeit from different angles, they must have something in common; hence the essay "From Edwards to Emerson."

Miller was chagrined to find that some readers were misinterpreting that essay to mean that there was an intellectual tradition whereby Emerson's ideas were derived, through some subterranean channel, from Edwards. The continuities Miller had in mind were cultural rather than explicitly intellectual; he wanted to suggest that an acceptance of ecstatic religious experience, which was half of the Puritan heritage, was still being carried in the culture, even when the mode of reason, sobriety, restraint, and convention seemed dominant. It was that way of being religious which Emerson and the Transcendentalists reasserted. But when Miller's later explanations of his thesis are taken into account, it is all the more evident that he was interested in underscoring the conflicts between Transcendentalism and Unitarianism rather than exploring the continuities between them.

If it is true that Transcendentalism was a reaction against early Unitarianism, it behooves scholars of the former to try to understand the latter on its own terms, from the inside. But students of Transcendentalism have usually been content with a second-hand textbook knowledge, itself the residue of conventional judgments transmitted from one secondary source to another, enlivened by Emersonian references to the "corpse-cold" Unitarianism of Brattle Street. (Most of them probably think the reference is to Brattle Street in Cambridge.)

One result is a persistent confusion into which scholars repeatedly stumble. For example, was Jones Very a Transcendentalist? If his religious doctrine did not quite square with Transcendentalist views, just what was it? And where did his piety come from? Some scholars assume that, if he was not a Transcendentalist, he must have been a "Calvinist." One of the few sensible treatments of this issue is by David Robinson, who has had the advantage of a theological component in his professional training. Robinson reminds us that Very identified himself as a "Channing Unitarian" and argues that "the roots of his piety are historically intelligible as a manifestation of Unitarian pietism" (*HTR*, 1975).

Sylvester Judd is another instance. His novel *Margaret* is often described as the only full-fledged Transcendentalist novel. Judd therefore gets listed among the Transcendentalists, despite his explicit disclaimer: "I am supremely a Christian, being neither pagan nor Jew, unbeliever nor transcendentalist," and beyond that, "I am, in all valuable and essential respects, an old-fashioned Unitarian." Such comments, coming from the author of a "Transcendental" novel, raise the question of how much of what we have been led to believe was peculiarly Transcendentalist, and therefore opposed to Unitarianism, was common to both. Unitarianism is therefore the obvious source for much that we have sought elsewhere, in Coleridge, Kant, or even Jonathan Edwards.

Most crucial of all is the relationship of William Ellery Channing to Transcendentalism. Emerson called him "our Bishop"; Elizabeth Peabody devotedly recorded his
sermons; he gave encouragement to Theodore Parker, even when he disagreed with
him. Turning to Miller's anthology, we find an excerpt from the sermon "Likeness
to God" (1828), in which Channing says, "We discern more and more of God in
every thing, from the frail flower to the everlasting stars." This may sound like
Transcendentalism rather than the Unitarianism of the day, until, a bit later, we find
Barzillai Frost saying, "We see God in nature as we see the soul of our friend in his
countenance." If all one knows about the Unitarianism of the first generation is Andrews Norton's *Discourse on the Latest Form of Infidelity* (1839), then Channing,
if a Unitarian at all, seems a most atypical one, as Goddard appeared to think. If,
on the other hand, one reads Channing's sermon in the context of Unitarian preaching
in general in 1828, and not simply by reference to the Divinity School Address a decade
later, it becomes apparent that Channing's "Transcendentalist" tendencies were no
aberration among the Unitarians, and the definition of Unitarianism must be broad
enough to include both Channing and Andrews Norton as members in good standing.

Such a reassessment of the Unitarianism of the first generation is now being conducted, especially by historians of American religion, with obvious implications for
literary scholarship. We are in the midst of what amounts to a revolution in American
Unitarian historiography, marked by a more refined and sympathetic appreciation of
first-generation Unitarianism. This revisionist approach struck Perry Miller with some
force as early as 1960, when he delivered an address at the Harvard Divinity School
commemorating the 150th anniversary of the birth of Theodore Parker. He noted a
new tendency "toward vindicating, or at least putting in a good word for, the hitherto
regularly berated opponents of Emerson and Theodore Parker." Interestingly enough,
he remarked, it was younger scholars who were beginning to suggest that the more
conservative Unitarians of that generation were not so bigoted, when they dissociated
themselves from the radicalism of Parker, as later historians had represented them.
"What a revolution in our historiography is adumbrated, let alone enacted," he ex-
claimed, "by the very raising of this consideration."

Two books in particular must have been fresh in Miller's mind. One was *The
Harvard Divinity School*, ed. George Huntston Williams, with chapters by Conrad
Wright and Sydney E. Ahlstrom; the other was William R. Hutchison, *The
Transcendentalist Ministers*. But also reflecting changing interpretations was Alexander
Kern, "The Rise of Transcendentalism, 1815–1860," which declared American
Transcendentalism to be "an essentially indigenous movement."

In any event, it is no longer possible to deal responsibly with the antecedents
of New England Transcendentalism by taking a hasty glance at selected passages from
Channing before concentrating on the *Aids to Reflection*. Too much good scholarly
work on Channing's contemporaries has already appeared, and more is on the way.
Scholars have pointed out the basic continuities between the older rationalistic
Unitarianism and the newer Transcendentalist Unitarianism and reminded us that the

two were not necessarily antagonistic. After all, James Walker is credited with having printed essays by the younger men in the *Christian Examiner*; most of the members of the Transcendental Club were, and continued to be, Unitarian ministers who exchanged regularly with colleagues doctrinally more conservative than they; and James Freeman Clarke served as Secretary of the American Unitarian Association.

Transcendentalism expanded far beyond the denominational boundaries of Unitarianism. Even as a "religious demonstration" it became something more than a subcategory of Unitarianism. But when one is defining the relation between Transcendentalism and Unitarianism, it makes sense to think of Transcendentalism as a phase of a changing and developing Unitarianism, subject, as all such movements are, to times of strain and tension. Indeed, the title assigned to this essay by the editor—"Unitarianism *and* Transcendentalism"—is really an artifact of an older tradition of scholarship. For Transcendentalism *was* Unitarianism in one of its historic manifestations, even if Andrews Norton was not very happy about it.

BIBLIOGRAPHIES

There has been an extraordinary increase of late in the number of scholarly articles and monographs relating to American Unitarianism. A bibliography of this material is being compiled, but how and when it might be published are uncertain. Meanwhile, a typescript is available for consultation at the Andover-Harvard Theological Library in Cambridge, Massachusetts. The manuscripts in that library are described in Alan Seaburg, "Some Unitarian Manuscripts at Andover-Harvard," and, with Philip B. Eppard, "American Literary Manuscripts in the Andover-Harvard Theological Library." An earlier bibliographical essay is Holley M. Shepherd, "Unitariana."

DENOMINATIONAL HISTORY

For further discussion of current revisionist historiography, see David Robinson, "Unitarian Historiography and the American Renaissance," a review essay of books by Lawrence Buell, Daniel Walker Howe, and Conrad Wright. Also see Wright, "In Search of a Usable Past."

The most recent general history of the denomination is *A Stream of Light: A Sesquicentennial History of American Unitarianism*, ed. Wright. This is a collaborative history, the nineteenth century being covered by chapters by Charles C. Forman (1805–35), Daniel Walker Howe (1835–65), and Wright (1865–98). Older general histories are still useful. Earl Morse Wilbur, *A History of Unitarianism in Transylvania, England, and America*, devotes three chapters to America, but by the time Wilbur arrived at that section of the book he was old, tired, and eager to get the manuscript off his hands. George Willis Cooke, *Unitarianism in America*, is still valuable for factual information on institutional developments. Of works by earlier participant-historians, those most worthy of mention are Joseph Henry Allen, *Our Liberal Movement in Theology* and *Sequel to "Our Liberal Movement,"* as well as the first and last chapters especially of John White Chadwick, *Old and New Unitarian Belief.* Chadwick's book seems to have been largely forgotten, but the last chapter is a particularly perceptive interpretation of the period after the Civil War.

THE UNITARIANISM OF THE OLDER GENERATION

The most important monograph dealing with the ideas of the older generation of Unitarians is Daniel Walker Howe, *The Unitarian Conscience: Harvard Moral Philosophy, 1805-1861.* Based on the writings of twelve intellectual leaders of the denomination, it ranges from philosophy proper to ethical theory, religion, aesthetics, politics, and reform. Written neither to discredit men like Andrews Norton or Francis Bowen nor to "rehabilitate"them, the book is absolutely essential for an understanding of the religious culture that produced Transcendentalism.

PHILOSOPHY

The underlying philosophy of the first generation was the sensational epistemology of John Locke, as modified by the Scottish philosophy of Common Sense Realism. Cameron Thompson, "John Locke and New England Transcendentalism," emphasizes the Lockean tradition but leaves the impression that the Unitarians were peculiar in their affinity for it. The widespread acceptance by the orthodox as well as liberals of the kind of Christian apologetics to which it gave rise ("Supernatural Rationalism") is discussed in Conrad Wright, "Rational Religion in Eighteenth-Century America." The prevalence of Scottish philosophy among Calvinists as well as Unitarians is demonstrated in Sydney E. Ahlstrom, "The Scottish Philosophy and American Theology." Wilson Smith, "John Locke in the Great Unitarian Controversy," seems somewhat out of focus. Howe's *The Unitarian Conscience* is well informed on the Scottish tradition. William Charvat, *The Origins of American Critical Thought, 1810-1835*, recognizes the importance of the Scottish school with respect to literary criticism but does not venture into theology or religion.

German influences began to be felt and assimilated by the liberals in the first decades of the century—positively with respect to biblical criticism and, at first, more negatively with respect to philosophy. For the experience of early Unitarians in Göttingen, see Orie William Long, *Literary Pioneers: Early American Explorers of European Culture.* Shorter works that pay more attention to the larger context are Henry A. Pochmann, *German Culture in America*, and Carl Diehl, *Americans and German Scholarship 1770-1870.* The interplay between the Scottish and German traditions in American religion is suggested in the early chapters of Jurgen Herbst, *The German Historical School in American Scholarship.*

BIBLICAL CRITICISM, THEOLOGY, AND THE RELIGIOUS LIFE

Liberal Christians believed in a correct understanding of Scripture as the basis for sound theology. They eagerly sought to master German biblical scholarship because they were confident that it would vindicate their rejection of Calvinism. This topic needs fresh treatment by a biblical scholar, perhaps in collaboration with a church historian; meanwhile see Jerry Wayne Brown, *The Rise of Biblical Criticism in America, 1800–1870: The New England Scholars*, and Eugene R. Chable, "A Study of the Interpretation of the New Testament in New England Unitarianism." A recent and rather brief treatment is in Herbert Hovenkamp, *Science and Religion in America 1800–1860*. The role of biblical criticism in the training of Unitarian ministers is stressed in *The Harvard Divinity School*, ed. Williams.

For religious doctrine and religious life, see Daniel Walker Howe, *The Unitarian Conscience*. Certain theological issues are treated in H. Shelton Smith, *Changing Conceptions of Original Sin*; Joseph Haroutunian, *Piety versus Moralism*; and Conrad Wright, *The Beginnings of Unitarianism in America*. Howe uses New England as a case study of "The Decline of Calvinism"; this article has the virtue of drawing on the varied perspectives of comparative history, sociology, and social psychology instead of confining the discussion to intellectual tendencies only.

Preaching style is discussed with particular reference to Joseph Stevens Buckminster, F. W. P. Greenwood, William Ellery Channing, and Orville Dewey in Lawrence Buell, "The Unitarian Movement and the Art of Preaching in 19th Century America."

INDIVIDUAL STUDIES

A number of Unitarian leaders have received individual attention, while others equally or more important await investigation. Of those neglected, one might mention both the Wares (especially the younger Henry Ware), Andrews Norton, Orville Dewey, and Ezra Stiles Gannett.

Joseph Stevens Buckminster has been of interest to literary scholars much more than to historians, doubtless because of his connection with the *Monthly Anthology* and his impact on preaching style; see especially Buell, "Joseph Stevens Buckminster," and Lewis P. Simpson, "Joseph Stevens Buckminster." On the *Monthly Anthology*, consult Simpson's *The Federalist Literary Mind* and "A Literary Adventure of the Early Republic." Buell has discovered sources for a more complete "Identification of Contributors to the *Monthly Anthology and Boston Review*, 1804–1811."

William Henry Furness is sometimes spoken of as a Transcendentalist, presumably because he was a friend of Emerson who questioned whether the miracles of Jesus represented an interruption in the regular order of Nature. It does not take much exploration of Furness' writings to discover that he was a pupil of Andrews Norton who sought to revise traditional Christian apologetics so as to disarm the freethinkers of the day. But miracles continued to be crucial in his view: "The rejection of the miracles is equivalent to a rejection of all that gives Christianity a peculiar value." Furness needs to be treated by someone who will do more than read two chapters of his *Remarks on the Four Gospels* (1836) out of context. Meanwhile, something of his career is interwoven with the history of the Philadelphia church in Elizabeth M. Geffen, *Philadelphia Unitarianism, 1796–1861*.

Samuel Gilman, author of "Fair Harvard" and husband of Caroline Howard Gilman, was the Unitarian minister in Charleston, South Carolina, for forty years. His public role in Charleston is discussed by Howe in two articles: "A Massachusetts Yankee in Senator Calhoun's Court" and "Samuel Gilman: Unitarian Minister and Public Man." Gilman's non-Transcendentalist theology is discussed, and its basis in Scottish philosophy indicated, in Conrad Wright, "The Theological World of Samuel Gilman."

James Walker is one of the figures analyzed in Howe's *The Unitarian Conscience*, but for separate treatment one must turn to a chapter in Wilson Smith, *Professors and Public Ethics: Studies of Northern Moral Philosophers before the Civil War*.

William Ware, brother of Henry Ware, Jr., was the first minister of the present All Souls Church in New York City, and that part of his professional career is described in Walter Donald Kring, *Liberals among the Orthodox*. He himself had doubts about his fitness for the ministry, and he will probably be remembered more for his historical novels of early Christian times; these are discussed in Curtis Dahl, "New England Unitarianism in Fictional Antiquity."

THE CULTURAL ENVIRONMENT: BOSTON AND HARVARD COLLEGE

New England Unitarianism in the nineteenth century can hardly be understood apart from its social and cultural setting, but one might easily be carried far afield in listing significant items on the history of Boston and Harvard College. The following, however, are especially relevant to the life of the mind. Lewis P. Simpson, " 'The Intercommunity of the Learned,' " sets the stage for Unitarian development. The interplay between Unitarian Boston and Harvard College is analyzed in some detail in Ronald Story, *The Forging of an Aristocracy*. George Ticknor is used as a sort of type figure for literary Boston both by Martin Green in *The Problem of Boston* and by David B. Tyack in *George Ticknor and the Boston Brahmins*.

THE TRANSCENDENTALIST PHASE OF UNITARIANISM

The single most important item here is William R. Hutchison, *The Transcendentalist Ministers*. The book recognizes the religious impulse at the core of Transcendentalism and its consequences for church polity. With his judicious and evenhanded treatment of the non-Transcendentalist and Transcendentalist Unitarians, Hutchison contributed significantly to revisionist historiography.

INDIVIDUAL STUDIES

We know far too little about the intellectual stance and development of non-Transcendentalist Unitarians who entered the ministry in the 1830s and 1840s. Some of those who should be studied more carefully are Joseph Henry Allen, George E. Ellis, Samuel K. Lothrop, Ephraim Peabody, Andrew Preston Peabody, George Putnam, and Oliver Stearns (five of whom were classmates at the Harvard Divinity School).

Francis Bowen is one figure whose importance has been in some measure recognized. Bruce Kuklick's discussion of him in *The Rise of American Philosophy* reminds us that non-Transcendentalist Unitarian thought was not static and fixed—that movement was not a monopoly of the Transcendentalists. (To be sure, Bowen was never able to come to terms with Darwinism.) Bowen also figures in Donald H. Meyer, *The Instructed Conscience*.

NON-CHRISTIAN RELIGIONS

Some Transcendentalists were much interested in non-Christian religions. This interest is related to the concerns of other Unitarians in George H. Williams, "The Attitude of Liberals in New England toward Non-Christian Religions, 1784–1885." Unitarians, both Transcendentalist and non-Transcendentalist, figure largely in Carl T. Jackson, *The Oriental Religions and American Thought*. The direct contacts of Rammohun Roy and the Brahmo Somaj with Henry Ware, Jr., Jared Sparks, and William Adam are discussed in Spencer Lavan, *Unitarians and India*. See also Lavan's articles: "Raja Rammohun Roy and the American Unitarians" and "Rammohun Roy and the Rev. Jared Sparks."

ANTISLAVERY AND SOCIAL REFORM

Unitarians—notably William Ellery Channing, Samuel J. May, and Theodore Parker—were involved in various phases of the antislavery movement, so many recent treatments of that movement have at least incidental references to them. For more concentrated focus, see Douglas C. Stange, *Patterns of Antislavery among American Unitarians, 1831–1860*. Stange has also published "The Making of an Abolitionist Martyr: Harvard Professor Charles Theodore Christian Follen (1796–1840)" and "Abolitionism as Treason."

Samuel J. May's abolitionism produced encounters with hostile public opinion, discussed in William H. Pease and Jane H. Pease, "Samuel J. May: Civil Libertarian." His problem in reconciling abolitionism and nonresistance is treated in the same authors' "Freedom and Peace." May is one of several Unitarians, both Transcendentalist and non-Transcendentalist, who figure in Peter Brock, *Pacifism in the United States from the Colonial Era to the First World War*.

FREE RELIGION

Free Religion, as a radical protest against mainstream Unitarianism, was a sort of post-Civil War equivalent of antebellum Transcendentalism. Like Transcendentalism, its leadership was largely made up of Unitarian ministers and it was in due course absorbed back into the mainstream of the denomination. Its leaders liked to think of themselves as the rightful heirs of the Transcendentalists and of Parker in particular. Some Transcendentalists, however, like James Freeman Clarke, were too much concerned with ensuring the institutional survival of the Christian Church to be more than tangentially involved in the Free Religious Association. Of the leaders of that association, Francis Ellingwood Abbot rejected Transcendentalism in the name of scientific theism, while Octavius Brooks Frothingham claimed to have gone beyond it. One should therefore not assume, as some scholars have done, that the postwar conflicts within the denomination, which ranged Abbot and Frothingham against the ecclesiasticism of Henry W. Bellows, were simply a late continuation of the earlier debate over Transcendentalism. The intellectual development of Unitarianism was more complicated than that.

For a general interpretation of post–Civil War Unitarianism, see chapter 3 of *A Stream of Light*, ed. Conrad Wright. Stow Persons, *Free Religion*, has often been cited as authoritative, but its findings have been much modified by later research. Persons' monograph draws on the writings, papers, and reminiscences of the "Radicals" and does not give adequate consideration to the other side of the debate. The extent to which revision is called for is suggested by a comparison of Persons' treatment of the New York convention of Unitarians in 1865 (in his opening chapter) with Wright, "Henry W. Bellows and the Organization of the National Conference." Compare also Persons' discussion of the Free Religious Association with Sydney E. Ahlstrom, "Francis Ellingwood Abbot and the Free Religious Association." Similarly, William H. Pease, "Doctrine and Fellowship: William Channing Gannett and the Unitarian Creedal Issue," sees events very much through Gannett's eyes. Use of the J. T. Sunderland papers now available at the Bentley Historical Library, University of Michigan, should make a more balanced view possible.

One important aspect of recent Unitarian historiography is the reemergence from obscurity of Henry W. Bellows, not only as the leading Unitarian denominational strategist and builder but also as a thinker of substance about institutions in general and the doctrine of the Church in particular. As the unrivaled leader of Unitarian ecclesiasticism from 1859 until his death in 1882, he was often the target of Radical protests, and thus he became a crucial figure in the history of Free Religion as well as mainstream Unitarianism. The external biography is generously treated in Walter Donald Kring, *Henry Whitney Bellows*. Aspects of Bellows' thought are discussed in Harry M. Stokes, "Henry W. Bellows's Vision of the Christian Church," and Clifford E. Clark, Jr., "Religious Beliefs and Social Reforms in the Gilded Age." A less than sympathetic treatment of Bellows' social thinking, as expressed in his leadership of the United States Sanitary Commission, may be found in George M. Fredrickson,

The Inner Civil War.

Free Religion had a scientific-empirical as well as a Transcendentalist component, as Francis Ellingwood Abbot made clear. This side of the movement is discussed in Charles D. Cashdollar, "European Positivism and the American Unitarians." Indeed, Cashdollar argues for Positivism as a significant factor, though not necessarily the most significant, in the extraordinary odyssey of Unitarianism from the static supernatural rationalism of the first generation to the developmentalism of the third.

Students of Transcendentalism have properly become wary of oversimplified characterizations of the movement. It was a complex phenomenon, not to be defined in terms of any one figure, not even Emerson. The same is true of the Unitarianism that gave it life, partly through continuities and partly by rebellion; it, too, is not to be defined by any one figure, certainly not by Andrews Norton. As for the problem of unraveling the lines of development that flowed from Transcendentalism and mingled with other, different influences in the period after the Civil War, the work is barely begun.

TRANSCENDENTALIST COMMUNITIES

Carol Johnston

BIBLIOGRAPHIES

George Ripley's Brook Farm (1841–47) and Bronson Alcott's Fruitlands (1843–44) were two of America's most famous communal experiments and, in their way, the best representations of the social aspects of Transcendentalism. Yet, with the exception of the relevant chapters in Charles Crowe, *George Ripley*, and Odell Shepard, *Pedlar's Progress*, there have been no sustained treatments of either community published in recent years. Of the two experiments, Brook Farm, a Transcendentalist and ultimately Fourierist community established by George and Sophia Ripley in a small valley on the banks of the Charles River between Dedham and West Roxbury, Massachusetts, is more completely documented. Joel Myerson, *Brook Farm*, a comprehensive and thoroughly annotated list of important manuscript and printed materials on the community, supersedes the piecemeal bibliographies appended to Lindsay Swift, *Brook Farm*, and *Autobiography of Brook Farm*, ed. Henry W. Sams. Myerson lists works on and by the Brook Farmers and their visitors, firsthand accounts of the community, writings in or about the *Harbinger* (the official paper of the community), and the contents of major manuscript collections. The material is topically ordered and indexed in detail. Also of bibliographic interest are Zoltán Haraszti, "Brook Farm Letters," and Arthur E. Bestor, Jr., *Brook Farm 1841–1847*. Haraszti surveys a collection of twenty-four letters in the John Sullivan Dwight Collection at the Boston Public Library written to Dwight by members of and visitors to the Brook Farm community (the Ripleys, Elizabeth Palmer Peabody, William Henry Channing, Albert Brisbane, Charles Dana, and others) and illustrates his survey with copious selections from these previously unpublished manuscripts. Still useful is Bestor's *Brook Farm 1841–1847*, a mimeographed checklist of books, periodicals, and illustrated materials on display in the Columbia University Libraries in the summer of 1941.

There is, unfortunately, no bibliography on Fruitlands comparable to Myerson's *Brook Farm*. The less successful of the two utopian ventures, Fruitlands was located on Prospect Hill on the outskirts of the small town of Harvard, Massachusetts. A chapter in *Literary History of the United States*, ed. Robert E. Spiller et al., treats both Brook Farm and Fruitlands briefly. Shirley W. Dinwiddie and Richard L. Herrnstadt's Alcott bibliography is a good source for material written by and about Alcott during the Fruitlands period, and Roger William Cummins' "The Second Eden" contains a valuable list of Charles Lane's writings. In addition, Fordyce Richard Bennett, "Sources for Alcott's Fruitlands," an attempt to modify the traditional view of Fruitlands as a "harebrained scheme," lists a substantial number of items relating Alcott's and Lane's beliefs and practices to "Essenian," "Pythagorean," and "Greavesian" thought.

MAJOR MANUSCRIPT COLLECTIONS

Myerson's *Brook Farm* lists and annotates the contents of the major Brook Farm manuscript collections at the Boston Public Library, the Kansas State Historical Society, the Massachusetts Historical Society (the most important collection), Middlebury College, and the University of Notre Dame. The Massachusetts Historical Society Collection has been published on microfilm. Less valuable, but still of interest, are the descriptions of the Communitarianism Collection in the Historical Library at the University of Illinois (mostly microfilms of the Boston area collections) and the Charles King Newcomb Collection in the John Hay Library at Brown University included in Lee Ash, *Subject Collections*.

The two most important collections of Fruitlands material are held at the library of the Fruitlands Museums at Harvard, Massachusetts, and the Alcott-Pratt Collection in the Houghton Library of Harvard University. Unlike the remnants of the Brook Farm community, which lie in ruins at the center of the Lutheran Gethsemane Cemetery in West Roxbury (see Neal Clark, "A Utopian Relic Worth Saving"), the reconstructed buildings of Fruitlands form the heart of a group of museums established by Clara Endicott Sears in 1914, nestled on the original Fruitlands property on Prospect Hill. Fruitlands Museums houses a large and well-cataloged collection of Alcott, Lane, "consociate family," and Transcendentalist material, much of which dates from the Fruitlands period. Two Alcott letters dealing with the experimental community and addressed to Alcott's brother, Junius J. Alcott, are included in the collection, as are a number of Charles Lane letters (written primarily to his fellow Greavesian, William Oldham) describing Lane's reception in America, his stay in Fruitlands, and his removal to the Shaker community nearby. The treasures of the collection are the eight extant pages of Louisa May Alcott's 1843 Fruitlands diary (all that remain of a manuscript that disappeared subsequent to Ednah D. Cheney's inclusion of selections from it in her *Louisa May Alcott*) and the original typescript of William Harry Harland's "Bronson Alcott's English Friends." The Harland typescript is based on papers relating to Alcott House in England (the Greavesian experiment that prompted Alcott, after a visit in the summer of 1842, to establish Fruitlands) and more than five hundred letters (most of which are now lost) written by Lane, James Pierrepont Greaves, and other followers of Greaves. The Fruitlands collection is not listed in *ALM* and, unfortunately, there is no published catalog of its contents. Clara Endicott Sears, *Revised Catalogue of "Fruitlands" at Harvard, Mass.*, a list of furniture, portraits, and ephemera in the museum, is outdated and a poor indicator of the materials accumulated there in the past decades. Harriet E. O'Brien, *Lost Utopias*, is a detailed description of the reconstructed buildings as they stand on the site of Fruitlands, noting displays of Lane, Ralph Waldo Emerson, and Bronson Alcott letters.

The Alcott-Pratt Collection of the Houghton Library at Harvard University is a major source of Alcott family material, much of which has been selectively printed in various editions. Unfortunately, its most interesting holding, the fifty-four volumes of Bronson Alcott's journal, is of little value to the student of Fruitlands: the volumes for 1841–44, as well as Alcott's "Fruitlands 1843" manuscript and letters dating from 1838–44, were reportedly lost by Alcott in the vicinity of Albany, New York, in the summer of 1844. This portion of Alcott's life can be at least partially reconstructed with the aid of two important manuscript documents also held in the Alcott-Pratt Collection, Bronson Alcott's "Autobiographical Index" and Abigail Alcott's Fruitlands Diary. The former, a list compiled by Alcott mostly from memory in 1851, details his visit to Alcott House in England, his meetings with Greaves's followers, Lane's purchase of the Wyman farm on Prospect Hill, and Alcott's visits to various other utopian communities upon leaving Fruitlands in mid-January 1844. Abigail Alcott's Fruitlands Diary, although parts have been excised by her family, is a valuable description of her day-to-day life with her husband at Fruitlands, hinting at the domestic dissension that led to the disbanding of the community. The Alcott-Pratt Collection also holds Bronson Alcott's 1844 letter to the keeper of the Railroad House at Albany inquiring after the loss of his books and documents, the manuscript list of the Fruitlands library printed in the *Dial* (1843), and Anna Alcott's Fruitlands Diary. The Fruitlands material in the Alcott-Pratt Collection is itself the subject of David Palmer Edgell, "The New Eden," which focuses on the historical importance of the documents and includes an index of the collection. Of additional interest are the diaries and letters of Isaac Hecker held in the Paulist Fathers Archives in New York. Hecker traveled freely between the Fruitlands and Brook Farm communities throughout the summer of 1843, comparing the two in an effort to determine which best served his needs.

Those interested in additional manuscript collections on Brook Farm or Fruitlands are referred, as well, to *ALM* and to the chapters in this volume on the individuals who participated in these communities.

EDITIONS

Several editions of letters and journals make notable contributions to our understanding of the communities. Letters of the two young Brook Farm idealists, George William Curtis and his brother Burrill, have been printed in *Early Letters of George Wm. Curtis to John S. Dwight: Brook Farm and Concord*, ed. George Willis Cooke, and in Joel Myerson, "James Burrill Curtis and Brook Farm." The subtitle of Cooke's unannotated edition is misleading; although many of the letters printed refer to Curtis' Brook Farm experience, none dates from the period of his residence. Myerson's well-annotated edition of seventeen letters written by Burrill Curtis is less ambiguously titled. Burrill's letters, along with those of Marianne Dwight (Orvis) (*Letters from Brook Farm 1844–1847*) and Elizabeth Curson (ed. Stephen Garrison and Myerson), remain the only extensive descriptions of the community in contemporary documents rather than in reminiscences. Burrill Curtis' letters, mostly financial accountings for inquisitive family members, are, on the whole, more introspective than Marianne Dwight's chatty missives, which record the stay of visitors and the daily activities at the community. Also of interest is a letter written by George P. Bradford in 1841, which James M. Mathews has edited. Nine of the *Love Letters of Nathaniel Hawthorne* to Sophia Peabody date from the Brook Farm period (13 April–22 Aug. 1841), as do about a dozen entries from his 1841 journal (*Passages from the American Note-books* and *The American Notebooks*). The notebook entries offer detailed descriptions of the Charles River valley where the community was located, and bear comparison to descriptive passages in Hawthorne's *The Blithedale Romance*. Ralph Waldo Emerson's impressions of the West Roxbury venture are documented in the second and third volumes of *The Letters of Ralph Waldo Emerson* and the eighth and ninth volumes of *The Journals and Miscellaneous Notebooks of Ralph Waldo Emerson*. The references are generally brief, but they reveal the genuine discomfort that Emerson felt in deciding not to join the community. Rusk includes as well the important 15 December 1840 letter from Emerson to Ripley declining Ripley's proposal of membership in the community, concluding that as Emerson perceived that Brook Farm might be of little value to him, so he might also be of little value to it.

Despite its casebook format, Henry W. Sams's well-researched and annotated anthology of primary materials, *Autobiography of Brook Farm*, is the most comprehensive treatment of the community available in a single volume. Sams includes extensive selections from the community's Articles of Association; from correspondence found in the Elijah P. Grant Papers at the University of Chicago, the Henry E. Huntington Library, and Middlebury College; from contemporary accounts of the community; and from reminiscences, journals, and notebooks. He reprints, as well, articles from the *Monthly Miscellany*, *Phalanx*, and *Harbinger*, in addition to appropriate selections from Thomas Wentworth Higginson, *Margaret Fuller Ossoli*; Octavius Brooks Frothingham, *George Ripley*; Georgiana Bruce Kirby, *Years of Experience*; John Thomas Codman, *Brook Farm*; George Willis Cooke, *John Sullivan Dwight*; *Early Letters of George Wm. Curtis to John S. Dwight*; John Van Der Zee Sears, *My Friends at Brook Farm*; Emerson, *Journals* and *Letters*; Marianne Dwight, *Letters from Brook Farm 1844-1847*; Zoltán Haraszti, *The Idyll of Brook Farm*; *The Journals of Bronson Alcott*, ed. Odell Shepard; and *The Correspondence of Henry David Thoreau*, ed. Walter Harding and Carl Bode. These selections are arranged chronologically and indexed. In addition, George Hochfield devotes a major section of his *Selected Writings of the American Transcendentalists* to Brook Farm, reprinting Ripley's letter to Emerson proposing membership in the Brook Farm Association, Emerson's response, an inquiry into membership by an unnamed minister, Ripley's response, Ripley's Letter on Association, and Elizabeth Palmer Peabody's "Plan of the West Roxbury Community."

None of the consociate family members of the Fruitlands community produced a history of the experiment, and much that has been written since has relied on legend and recollection. The most frequently reprinted account of the community is Louisa May Alcott's fictionalized reminiscence, "Transcendental Wild Oats." In 1975 the Harvard Common Press published the piece in booklet form, including eight extant pages from Louisa May Alcott's Fruitlands Diary, which resurfaced in Walpole, New Hampshire, in 1973. In 1981 the same press published an enlarged edition containing a letter by Alcott and Lane on "The Consociate Family Life" that had originally appeared as "Fruitlands" in the July 1843 *Dial*. The account, written over thirty years after the experiment, is an anecdotal but not unkind response to the whimsical eccentricities of the consociate family members. As the only account of the experiment to be published by a participant, "Transcendental Wild Oats" has had an influence on Fruitlands studies that is inappropriate to its fictional status. Louisa May Alcott's appraisal of Charles Lane as the villain of the experiment, for instance, has only recently been challenged by scholars.

With the exception of "Transcendental Wild Oats," all that is relevant to the Fruitlands experience is found in private manuscripts, selections from which have been culled for a variety of works. Ednah D. Cheney inserted sections from the Fruitlands Diary of Louisa May Alcott into her *Louisa May Alcott* prior to the loss of the manuscript document. These excerpts were apparently reprinted in Sears' *Bronson Alcott's Fruitlands* some twenty-five years later. Since there is evidence that the Cheney excerpts are, in at least one respect, inaccurate (the single overlapping entry between the extant pages at the Fruitlands Museums and Cheney's transcription do not coincide), both editions are suspect. Abigail Alcott's dissatisfaction with the community can be traced in her correspondence with Prudence Ward and in her diary. Two of Abigail Alcott's letters to Ward were published by Annie J. Ward in her 1895 article "Transcendental Wild Oats." The first of these letters, dated June 1843, describes the "blissful" nature of the community, whereas the second, an undated letter, sarcastically refers to Abigail's duties "among the higher intelligences." Shepard ingeniously bridges the gap left by the loss of the Fruitlands journals in *The Journals of Bronson Alcott* by printing selections from Abigail Alcott's diary. Of Abigail's loyalty to her husband there is no doubt; however, the exhaustion caused by the demands placed on her at Fruitlands is evident on nearly every page of the diary, in which she writes of the violation of her rights "as a woman and a mother." Shepard's well-chosen selections offer an alternative view of life at Fruitlands by one of its most overworked and least satisfied members. The Sears book, *Bronson Alcott's Fruitlands*, as outdated and undocumented as it is, remains the only full-length study of the community. Despite its unscholarly approach, it prints several well-chosen, firsthand accounts of the community that might otherwise be inaccessible to the general reading public, such as the Anna Alcott and Isaac Hecker diaries. Those parts of Hecker's diary dealing with Fruitlands and Brook Farm have been printed in Walter Elliott's *The Life of Father Hecker*, and his letters of the period are quoted in Vincent F. Holden's *The Early Years of Isaac Thomas Hecker (1819-1844)*.

The most important documents of the Fruitlands experience, however, are those edited by Alcott scholars. Two of Alcott's earliest biographers, F. B. Sanborn and William T. Harris, punctuate their treatment of the Fruitlands community (*A. Bronson Alcott: His Life and Philosophy*) with a series of excerpts from the published and private papers of interested contemporaries, including Emerson, Lane, Louisa May Alcott, and Lydia Maria Child. Several of these reveal the pathos of Alcott's venture: the jocose attitude taken by many contemporaries toward the community and Alcott's agonized response to its failure. Shepard, in his *Pedlar's Progress*, omits much of this material, choosing instead to focus on the Alcott family response to the community by quoting at length from Abigail Alcott's journal. The gap in the Alcott journals for the period is narrowed by David P. Edgell's edition of Bronson Alcott's "Autobiographical Index." The "Autobiographical Index" details Alcott's visit to England and his travels through New England, first to find a suitable site for Fruitlands and later, after the commune was abandoned, to find another community for himself and his family. Richard L. Herrnstadt prints a good selection of substantive correspondence from the Fruitlands period in *The Letters of A. Bronson Alcott*, identifying the owner of each letter but offering little else in the way of annotation. Frederick Wagner's well-annotated "Eighty-Six Letters (1814-1882) of A. Bronson Alcott" prints an 1848 Alcott letter to Charles Lane as well as Alcott's Albany inquiry into his missing manuscripts and diaries.

The English friends who inspired Alcott to found the community have received less attention. David Edgell was the first to suggest that Lane was something less than a villain when he published two of his Household-Post Office letters to Abigail Alcott ("Charles Lane at Fruitlands"). Both letters are complimentary missives. Of even greater value to an understanding of Lane is Joel Myerson's edition of "William Harry Harland's 'Bronson Alcott's English Friends,' " a thoroughly researched and annotated study of the Harland typescript with its treatment of James Pierrepont Greaves, William Oldham, Henry Gardiner Wright, and Lane. Harland's typescript (which was not available to Shepard before his publication of *Pedlar's Progress*) prints over a half dozen important letters from Charles Lane to William Oldham describing the Fruitlands community in detail.

HISTORIES AND CRITICISM

Much that has been written on Brook Farm and Fruitlands, like Emerson's description of clothespins dropping "plentifully" from the pockets of dancing Brook Farmers ("Historic Notes of Life and Letters in New England") or Annie M. L. Clark's bemused retrospection on the eccentric Harvard childhood she shared with the author of *Little Women* ("The Alcotts in Harvard"), is genial, anecdotal, and subjective reminiscence emphasizing either the self-indulgence of the first community or the eccentric irresponsibility of the second. More recent treatments, such as early discussions of Fourierism at Brook Farm and of Charles Lane's participation in Fruitlands, objectively discuss the communities in terms of broad social philosophies but tend to deemphasize the enthusiasms and aspirations of individual community members. Existing materials on Transcendentalist American utopias through 1960, then, do not generally provide a balanced treatment of the subjective ideals and the social realities of the communities. The past two decades, however, have produced a number of revisionary studies, such as Richard Francis' "The Ideology of Brook Farm" and "Circumstances and Salvation: The Ideology of the Fruitlands Utopia," that succeed in reconciling subjective and objective views of the two communities.

Because Joel Myerson's bibliography comprehensively lists the historical and critical material on Brook Farm, only a selection of articles on that community will be discussed in this essay. Brook Farm attracted a good deal of attention in its early years: Elizabeth Palmer Peabody, Orestes Brownson, and Lane all made their criticism and support of the community public. Nevertheless, the planning stages of the venture, Ripley's decision to establish the community, and the initial proposals made to prospective members remain largely undocumented, only hinted at in the correspondence and journals of those immediately involved. Emerson's *Journals* and *Letters* contain numerous entries on the venture. For instance, in a journal entry dated 17 October 1840, Emerson wrote that he, George and Sophia Ripley, Margaret Fuller, and Alcott had discussed the social plans: "I wish to be convinced, to be thawed, to be made nobly mad by the kindlings before my eye of a new dawn of human piety." He was not, however, as he concluded in a 15 December 1840 letter to Ripley refusing membership. Margaret Fuller's similar reluctance to join the community is dealt with by Higginson in *Margaret Fuller Ossoli*. Higginson draws on Fuller's letters to disprove the assertion that Hawthorne's Zenobia had been modeled on her; he also delineates Fuller's true relationship with the experiment. Similarly, Frothingham and Crowe, in their biographies of George Ripley, use his correspondence to cast light on the community. Frothingham prints Ripley's 9 November 1840 and 17 December 1841 missives to Emerson proposing membership in the community, as well as an early set of Articles of Association, yet his discussion of the community and Ripley's reasons for founding it lacks the depth of Crowe's more recent study, which treats Brook Farm in terms of the complex contradictions implicit in Transcendental and Fourierist thought.

Hawthorne decided to join the West Roxbury community after his resignation from the Boston Custom House in January 1841, probably with the practical intent of finding living quarters for him and his future wife, Sophia, as well as to find more time for writing. He was disappointed in both respects: Brook Farm offered neither the cozy hearth he sought nor the extended periods of idle time necessary for the writer. Documentation of his stay at the farm from 12 April to November 1841 can be found in his *Love Letters* and in *The American Notebooks*. The romance of the community provided him with the material for one of the most vivid fictional depictions of the experiment, *The Blithedale Romance*. Hawthorne's description of the community in his *American Notebooks* is the source of several descriptive passages in *The Blithedale Romance*, while several of his *Love Letters* to Sophia suggest the lack of esteem in which he held Emerson and Fuller.

It is, undoubtedly, dangerous to discuss Hawthorne's fictional characters in terms of possible prototypes. As Orestes Brownson wrote of the novel ("The Blithedale Romance"), "there has been no encroachment on the sanctity of private character, and pain has been given, we presume, to no private feeling." Yet it is safe to say that Hawthorne's treatment of the community did not endear him to the members and visitors who later perceived themselves as the targets of his humor. John Van Der Zee Sears, for instance, reduces most of his discussion of Hawthorne in *My Friends at Brook Farm* to the question of whether or not the "illustrious, poetic and romantic Hawthorne" did actually feed the pigs. Emerson, even thirty years after the publication of *The Blithedale Romance*, continued to speak of the book with some bitterness: "Hawthorne drew some sketches, not happily, as I think; I should say, quite unworthy of his genius. No friend who knew Margaret Fuller could recognize her rich and brilliant genius under the dismal mask which the public fancied was meant for her in that disagreeable story" ("Historic Notes of Life and Letters in New England"). Accounts of the relation of Brook Farm to Hawthorne's novel are Arlin Turner, "Autobiographical Elements in Hawthorne's *The Blithedale Romance*," and Joseph T. Gordon, "Nathaniel Hawthorne and Brook Farm."

Another novelist, Truman Nelson, some one hundred years later, attempted yet another romanticized novel on Brook Farm, entitled *The Passion by the Brook* (1953). His sentimentalized view of the community, unrelieved by the insight and creative genius that produced *The Blithedale Romance*, reduces the community to the mechanizations of a fictional love triangle.

The initial excitement about Brook Farm nearly enveloped Elizabeth Peabody's bookshop in Boston and the young reform-minded intellectuals who frequented it. Retrospective views of the community, in general, tend to lose sight of the genuine enthusiasm the plan inspired in contemporaries. Peabody published three articles in the *Dial* between 1841 and 1844 expressing both her hopes and her concerns. The first of these, "A Glimpse of Christ's Idea of Society," relates Christ's teachings to social organizations. Peabody suggests that the Christian churches set up by the apostles were initiatory institutions and that other socialistic communities would supersede them as the ultimate extensions of the visible church of Christ. The article is prefatory to Peabody's account of "The Plan of the West-Roxbury Community," in which she enthusiastically describes the venture as a communal attempt "to live a religious and moral life." She discusses possible obstacles to its success but predicts that "antagonism" and "coterie" will be overcome by the "common ground" of Transcendentalism. In "Fourierism" Peabody announced Brook Farm's decision to become a Fourierist establishment. In what is possibly the most intelligent contemporary response to the movement, Peabody suggests that Fourierism is to be the form and not the soul of the community and notes the possible dangers in confusing the two. "A tremendous tyranny," she writes, "is necessarily involved by constituting society itself the VISIBLE church of Christ. . . . We must be men before we are Christians, else we shall never be either Christians or men."

Brownson was similarly concerned with the viability of the experiment, in which individualism and social responsibility were inevitably at odds. His essay "Brook Farm," written prior to the Fourierist stage of the enterprise, focuses not only on the wisdom of the conception but also on possible obstacles to its success. In the first section of his essay, Brownson defines the liberalism of the community, comparing it favorably to the radicalism of unsuccessful Fourierist and Owenite communities. Brownson believed that the stability of the West Roxbury community lay in its family structure, which did not directly challenge or conflict with existing social or governmental institutions. The second half of his essay prints a letter in which an enthusiastic "friend" vividly describes the community to Brownson.

Yet it was this very "family" structure that bothered the founder of Fruitlands, Charles Lane. In his 1844 *Dial* article, "Brook Farm," he suggests that the community was not a true community but merely an aggregation of people lacking a "oneness of spirit": "If as we have been popularly led to believe, the individual or separate family is in the true order of Providence, then the associative life is a false effort. If the associative life is true, then is the separate family a false arrangement." His conclusions seem to have been more a projection of his frustration over the domestic controversies that assaulted the ill-favored Fruitlands community than a rational assessment of the actual problems facing Ripley's Brook Farm.

The late nineteenth century brought additional commentary on the community by two of its visitors. Thomas Wentworth Higginson, in "The Brook Farm Period in New England," describes the genuine air of excitement he found during his boyhood visits there, while in "Historic Notes of Life and Letters in New England," Emerson discusses the intellectual movements in mid-nineteenth-century New England that led to the development of the community.

The four most comprehensive treatments of Brook Farm vary in the approaches they take. John Thomas Codman's *Brook Farm* is the author's reminiscence of days spent at the community, Lindsay Swift's *Brook Farm* is the standard history of the venture, Marianne Dwight's *Letters from Brook Farm 1844–1847* is a series of eighty-four letters written by a young woman in residence at the community, Henry W. Sams's *Autobiography of Brook Farm* is an anthology of important primary materials tracing the development of the experiment. Swift and Sams provide the best general introductions, although the Codman and Dwight texts remain essential firsthand supplements for any study of the community.

Swift's well-researched and readable book is based primarily on previously published histories and recollections, and it successfully avoids the idealization of many earlier accounts. The study is structured around descriptions of the organization, buildings, grounds, industries, household work, amusements, and customs of the community; a discussion of the school and its scholars; and a series of chapters describing individual members and visitors.

Much of the raw material, both manuscript and published, from which Swift drew his conclusions is reprinted in Sams's *Autobiography of Brook Farm*, which anthologizes primary documents of the experiment, ranging from Peabody's "Plan of the West-Roxbury Community" to Hawthorne's *Love Letters*. The material is arranged chronologically. Each item is headed by a bibliographical note, and efforts have been made to retain the pagination of the original source.

Codman's *Brook Farm* details his impressions of the community, where he resided from 1843 to 1846, but it was written nearly fifty years after he left. The introductory chapters, in which he discusses the development of the community, are dull and tendentious, but the remainder of the book is a sprightly series of anecdotes describing the manner in which the Brook Farmers implemented their philosophy. The book's greatest weakness lies in a foggy lack of concern with dates. The author skips freely from one incident to another without following any explicit chronology. In addition to describing visits by Fuller and Theodore Parker, Codman reprints some important primary material: letters from Adin Ballou, Albert Brisbane, George Ripley, Minot Pratt, and Parker; the Brook Farm Articles of Association; and the prospectus for the *Harbinger*. Appended to the volume is a valuable selection of letters from persons interested in the community; responses by George Ripley; a reprint of Lane's "Brook Farm"; and writings by John Sullivan Dwight, Charles A. Dana, William Henry Channing, Horace Greeley, Fourier, and Brisbane.

Dwight's *Letters* is an even more valuable treatment of the community, since it offers contemporary documentation of the day-to-day affairs of the venture rather than retrospective anecdotes and analysis. Like Codman, Dwight arrived at the Brook Farm community in 1843; she stayed until 1847. The letters, written to her brother Frank and to a friend, Anna Q. T. Parsons, are breathless and detailed accounts of the activities of the community, visitors, and interpersonal relations. They reveal, better than any other single source, the actual workday of the Brook Farmers, their Fourierist scheme of industrialization involving the division of labor into smaller work units, their devotion to hard work, their social gatherings, and their aspirations. Dwight's attention to detail and careful reference to date and time make her letters an essential source for the study of Brook Farm.

In addition to these four works there are several general histories of the community that deserve mention or comment. George Willis Cooke, "Brook Farm," is a valuable account of the formation of the community, its physical appearance, its financial concerns, and its educational and religious theories. John Van Der Zee Sears, *My Friends at Brook Farm*, is, on the other hand, a highly subjective and anecdotal recollection of his boyhood days there. Sears was twelve when he arrived at Brook Farm, and most of his discussion centers on his reception as a "stranger in a strange land." Although he describes the West Roxbury neighbors as hostile and even suggests that they might have contaminated the community with smallpox and set the Phalanstery fire, his account probably reflects his own sense of alienation rather than any general feeling of paranoia at Brook Farm. Proper Bostonians might well have been horrified by the community, but most Brook Farmers disregarded respectable opinion: it was their own opinions that mattered most. Similarly suspect are Katherine Burton, *Paradise Planters*, and Edith Roelker Curtis, *A Season in Utopia*. The former, an apparently sincere attempt to create an accurate dramatization of the community, rapidly deteriorates into a dangerously misleading hodgepodge of fact and fiction. Burton errs not only in fact but also in technique: she culls written sources for material that she transforms into dialogue and then quotes out of context, with disastrous results. Curtis' study is less slipshod, but it too is based on a series of misconceptions, misapprehensions, and inaccuracies that limit its value.

The Brook Farm experiment is also the subject of several short sketches. The best of these appear in V. F. Calverton, *Where Angels Dared to Tread*, and Everett Webber, *Escape to Utopia*, both discussions of American utopian communities. Calverton builds his chapter on Brook Farm around a solid description of George Ripley and his dissatisfactions with society. His discussion of the wave of Fourierism that overcame the community in 1843 is based on the thesis that Fourierism, with its emphasis on communism, was essentially foreign to the original doctrines of the community, which had focused on regenerating rather than reforming society. Webber, on the other hand, explains the decline of the community in terms of the natural tendency for similar "phalanxes" to fail as the result of fire, peculation, mismanagement, or insolvency. Two years was, he suggests, a long time for a phalanx to survive. Brook Farm, which survived nearly four years after turning to Fourierism, was perhaps the most successful of the myriad utopian communities founded during the period.

Several important studies of Brook Farm remain unpublished: John Dillon Jones, "A Biographical Dictionary of Brook Farm"; Jane Maloney Johnson, "Moral Life at Brook Farm"; Marjorie Jean Menzi, "Women's Rights: An Aspect of Transcendentalism as Exhibited by Brook Farm"; and Charles Edward Alberti, "Brook Farm's Educational Philosophy." Jones's "Biographical Dictionary" is a valuable reference work that identifies members of the community, pupils at the school, and interested visitors and friends in a series of brief, alphabetically arranged entries. Johnson's study is an unreasonably hostile yet stimulating discussion of the "soft moralism" of the community that she sees Hawthorne condemning in *The Blithedale Romance*. Menzi argues that the Brook Farmers' Transcendentalist beliefs had as much impact on the crusade for women's rights as they did on theology and literature. Alberti recognizes the educational biases of the community and discusses the theories fostered there as anticipations of the work of John Dewey.

With the exception of Taylor Stoehr's "Transcendentalist Attitudes toward Communitism and Individualism," a perceptive study of the conflict between individual consciousness and "tribal" society that discouraged Emerson and Thoreau from joining the Ripley or Alcott communities, the best recent studies of the Brook Farm community are all concerned with its unnatural union of Transcendentalism and Fourierism. Arthur E. Bestor, Jr., initiated this discussion in 1940 in his "Fourierism in Northampton," which suggests that the relations between the Brook Farm and Northampton communities took a noticeably cool turn when the former turned to Fourierism. Charles Crowe, "Utopian Socialism in Rhode Island 1845–1850," describes the favorable impact that Fourierist lectures by Ripley, William Henry Channing, Horace Greeley, John Sullivan Dwight, John L. Clarke, and Joseph J. Cooke had on Providence audiences in the late 1840s. In "Transcendentalist Support of Brook Farm: A Paradox?" Crowe suggests that the communitarian drift of the Transcendentalists stemmed from the emotional coldness and isolation that so often characterized their personal lives rather than from any clearly defined commitment to communitism. Their individualistic philosophy, in Crowe's view, created a need for an antithetical "glow of communal life." In " 'This Unnatural Union of Phalansteries and Transcendentalists,' " Crowe argues that one of the more interesting aspects of the experiment was its attempt to reconcile Transcendental and Fourierist thought, an attempt that was neither a total success nor a total failure. And in "Fourierism and the Founding of Brook Farm," Crowe concludes that Fourierist principles were firmly established in Ripley's mind throughout the planning period of the community and that Brook Farm was from its beginning intensely collectivistic and equalitarian. By far the best recent treatment of the movement is Richard Francis' "The Ideology of Brook Farm." After carefully analyzing and evaluating most of the material written on the subject, Francis suggests that it was William Henry Channing's notion of "self sacrifice" that ultimately enabled Transcendentalism and Fourierism to coexist in the community.

The three most important published treatments of the Fruitlands community are F. B. Sanborn, *Bronson Alcott at Alcott House, England, and Fruitlands, New England (1842-1844)*, Clara Endicott Sears, *Bronson Alcott's Fruitlands*, and the Fruitlands account in Shepard, *Pedlar's Progress*. Although they are all conscientiously based on primary source materials, they do not entirely escape the realm of personal anecdote and reminiscence. Sanborn's is the earliest full-length treatment of the community. His history of Alcott's travels between England and New England and of the founding and dissolution of the community is based on (and somewhat biased by) Alcott family material. Sanborn provides an adequate treatment of the English backgrounds of the community, but he prints long quotations from Abigail and Louisa May Alcott's diaries implying that the community's problems resided largely in the person of Charles Lane. Despite its inaccuracies and omissions, Sears's book is a valuable collection of firsthand accounts of the experiment, correspondence, newspaper articles, and diaries. It is divided into a series of chapters centering on individual consociate family members, somewhat to the neglect of the community as a whole. Because his primary materials are less obtrusively worked into the text, Shepard is the most readable of the historians. His reconstruction of the Lane-Alcott conflict, based on a thorough reading of Alcott's letters and journals, is more complex and thought-provoking than Sears's, although his discussion of the Fruitlands experiment is necessarily peripheral to his interest in Alcott.

Several readily accessible treatments of the community can be found in works about American utopias, particularly Calverton, *Where Angels Dared to Tread*, and Webber, *Escape to Utopia*. Calverton's study touches briefly on the celibacy issue that divided Alcott and Lane, but, like many of the works on Fruitlands, focuses less on the failure of the enterprise than on its more illustrious founder. Webber, on the other hand, presents a balanced (though anecdotal) overview of the community, the individual members, and their daily activities.

The past two decades have seen a number of valuable studies that reveal the tentative inner logic on which Fruitlands was based by deemphasizing the eccentricities of the "consociate family" members and underscoring the philosophical stances assumed by Alcott and Lane. These works have reevaluated Lane's role in the community and reassessed the problems that led to its demise. The suggestion that the standard villainous portrayal of Lane might be inaccurate was first made in 1960 by David Edgell, who unearthed several conciliatory letters from Lane to Abigail Alcott ("Charles Lane at Fruitlands"). In 1966, John B. Wilson, in "Pythagoras Crosses the Merrimack (Fruitlands Revisited)," bolstered the philosophical reputation of the community by citing Pythagoras at Crotona as its probable prototype. Fordyce Richard Bennett further develops this theme in his "Sources for Alcott's Fruitlands." Roger William Cummins, "The Second Eden: Charles Lane and American Transcendentalism," and Robert Howard Walker, "Charles Lane and the Fruitlands Utopia," discuss the establishment of Alcott House and the English background to the experiment while focusing on the enigmatic Lane. Cummins contrasts Lane's fiscal responsibility to Alcott's fiscal irresponsibility, and, while not demeaning Abigail Alcott's burden, suggests that Lane should at least be given credit for paying the community's bills. Walker, dealing with much the same material, concludes that it is at best "unwise to assign the failure of the community to any individual." For Aurele Durocher ("The Story of Fruitlands") the spiritual assets of the community mitigated its practical debits. When set against the materialism of the post–Civil War period, the idealism of the consociate members—their visionary attempt to replenish spiritual reserves in a secular world—appears in a more favorable light. The most successful study of the community to date, however, is Richard Francis' brilliantly researched "Circumstances and Salvation." By showing how Lane and Alcott differed in their definition of the nature of family, Francis demonstrates the basic philosophical incompatibility that led to the demise of the community and suggests how easily Lane and Alcott could have overlooked this incompatibility in their early plans for the experiment. As in his "The Ideology of Brook Farm," much of the value of Francis' "Circumstances and Salvation" resides in his analytical approach to earlier critical arguments.

TRANSCENDENTALIST PERIODICALS

Donald F. Warders

INTRODUCTION

The Transcendentalist periodicals covered in this chapter are those identified by Clarence L. F. Gohdes in his important study, *The Periodicals of American Transcendentalism*: *Western Messenger* (1835–41), *Boston Quarterly Review* (1838–42), *Dial* (1840–44), *Present* (1843–44), *Harbinger* (1845–49), *Spirit of the Age* (1849–50), *Aesthetic Papers* (1849), *Massachusetts Quarterly Review* (1847–50), Cincinnati *Dial* (1860), *Radical* (1865–72), and *Index* (1870–86). Gohdes allots a full chapter to each journal with the exceptions of the *Western Messenger* and the *Dial*, which share a chapter. His purpose in discussing these two periodicals together is to show the similarities between them and the influence of the former on the latter. Gohdes has been criticized by William B. Cairns (1932) and Frederic I. Carpenter (1932), mainly for his inadequate treatment of the *Dial*, and he has been corrected (to the effect that Robert Owen never had any connection with the Workingmen's Party) by George K. Smart (1939). Clarence Hotson (1932) finds the study commendable, largely because it deals with issues of interest to the New Church, whose prophet is Swedenborg. On the whole, Gohdes' book is an excellent treatment of its subject, and every scholar must begin the study of Transcendentalist periodicals with this work.

Locations of sets of all the Transcendentalist periodicals except *Aesthetic Papers* are given in *ULS*. A new list of extant copies of the *Dial* is provided by Joel Myerson, "A Union List of the *Dial* (1840–1844) and Some Information about Its Sales." This list, in essentially the same format as *ULS*, corrects numerous errors in earlier lists and includes many locations of the journal not previously reported. Microfilm copies of eight of the journals are described in *American Periodicals 1741–1900*, ed. Jean Hoornstra and Trudy Heath, which omits the *Spirit of the Age*, *Aesthetic Papers*, and the

Index. Useful annotated listings of scholarship on all eleven Transcendentalist periodicals are available in Edward E. Chielens, *The Literary Journal in America to 1900*.

Jayne K. Kribbs, *An Annotated Bibliography of American Literary Periodicals, 1741-1850*, provides summary information about the *Western Messenger*, *Boston Quarterly Review*, *Dial*, and *Massachusetts Quarterly Review*. *The American Renaissance in New England*, ed. Myerson, contains brief sketches and bibliographies of the *Western Messenger*, *Boston Quarterly Review*, *Dial*, *Harbinger*, *Aesthetic Papers*, *Massachusetts Quarterly Review*, and the principal figures connected with them. This book is an indispensable reference work. *Index to Early American Periodical Literature 1728-1870* classifies the *Boston Quarterly Review*, *Dial*, *Present*, *Harbinger*, and *Massachusetts Quarterly Review* under four headings: "Edgar Allan Poe," "Walt Whitman," "Ralph Waldo Emerson," and "French Fiction." Daniel A. Wells, *The Literary Index to American Magazines, 1815-1865*, covers the *Boston Quarterly Review*, *Dial*, *Harbinger*, and *Massachusetts Quarterly Review*.

THE *WESTERN MESSENGER* (1835–41)

The *Western Messenger* was published monthly by liberal Unitarians in Cincinnati and Louisville, Ohio. Its principal editors were James Freeman Clarke, Christopher Pearse Cranch, Ephraim Peabody, and William Henry Channing. Beginning as a religious journal, it became essentially literary in emphasis. With the departure of its editors for New England, it came to an end.

Useful early accounts of the *Western Messenger* may be found in George Willis Cooke, *An Historical and Biographical Introduction to Accompany the* Dial, and in Algernon Tassin, *The Magazine in America*. A more substantial treatment is in Frank Luther Mott, *A History of American Magazines 1741-1850*. A study of lasting significance is Clarence L. F. Gohdes, "The *Western Messenger* and the *Dial*."

W. H. Venable, "Early Periodical Literature of the Ohio Valley: II," is a brief early treatment of the *Western Messenger*. A historical note about the periodical appears in Lawrence Mendenhall, "Early Literature of the Miami Valley." An account similar to Venable's, by a biographer of Emerson, is in Ralph Leslie Rusk, *The Literature of the Middle Western Frontier*. A study that, in addition to furnishing useful information about the journal, provides the names of as many as ten contributors (of nonreligious material only) not mentioned by Mott, Venable, or Rusk is Saul Hounchell, "The Principal Literary Magazines of the Ohio Valley to 1840." An article that has largely escaped notice is John G. Greene, "The *Western Messenger*," which briefly details the rise and fall of the periodical.

A factual history of the *Western Messenger* that presents fresh information and conclusions about its founding, editorship, publication, circulation, and demise is Charles E. Blackburn's dissertation, "James Freeman Clarke," partially condensed into a valuable article: "Some New Light on the *Western Messenger*." Blackburn's work is based on manuscript sources and study of the magazine's text. Historical details about the journal, its principal figures, and the Ohio Valley (particularly Cincinnati) in this period are provided in Frank R. Shivers, Jr., "A Western Chapter in the History of American Transcendentalism." A more recent, informative, and splendidly written short account of this same topic is Elizabeth R. McKinsey, *The Western Experiment: New England Transcendentalists in the Ohio Valley*. Essentially, it describes the failure of three editors of the periodical—Clarke, Cranch, and Channing—to adjust their Transcendentalist views to life in the West.

Judith A. Green, "Religion, Life, and Literature in the *Western Messenger*," deals with the religious background of the periodical. Green discusses three principal editors (Peabody, Clarke, and Channing), their work for the journal, and the principal contributors. The conclusion generalizes about the magazine in the context of its place and time. Green contends that the *Western Messenger* has been carelessly read, that it has often been quoted out of context, and that its Transcendentalism has been overemphasized; and she helps to clarify what the periodical did and did not stand for.

Robert David Habich, "The History and Achievement of the *Western Messenger*," explains the founding of the magazine within its religious context, its increasing radicalization, its demise, and its achievements. An appendix provides an annotated list of contributors and contributions. Habich aims to furnish a full history of the periodical in its context and an evaluation of its importance in American intellectual history, and he relies heavily on the text of the journal and on the papers of the principal figures connected with it. Like the work of Green, this study helps to fix the *Western Messenger*'s relation to Unitarianism and, later, to Transcendentalism.

The leading figure behind the *Western Messenger* was Clarke, and numerous references to his work with the journal appear in his *Autobiography, Diary and Correspondence* as well as in Blackburn's studies. A discussion of Clarke's involvement with the periodical from the perspective of German culture has been written by John Wesley Thomas. Arthur S. Bolster, Jr., "The Life of James Freeman Clarke," has numerous notes and identifies some of Clarke's contributions to the periodical. This dissertation is much more complete than Bolster's book, *James Freeman Clarke*. The contributions of Cranch, another major figure associated with the journal, are mentioned in a letter quoted in Leonora Cranch Scott, *The Life and Letters of Christopher Pearse Cranch*.

Kathleen Flynn has prepared a descriptive study of the literary content of the *Western Messenger*. The interest of the magazine in Orientalia is dealt with in Roger Chester Mueller's dissertation. An account of the substantial music criticism in the journal is furnished in Irving Lowens, "Writings about Music in the Periodicals of American Transcendentalism (1835–50)." This thorough article includes as an appendix "A Check-List of Writings about Music in the Periodicals of American Transcendentalism (1835–50)." French ideas reflected in the journal are dealt with in Georges Jules Joyaux, "French Thought in American Magazines 1800–1848." The attention paid to German writers is discussed in John Wesley Thomas, "The Western Messenger and German Culture" and in his later study of Clarke, as well as in Stanley

M. Vogel, *German Literary Influences on the American Transcendentalists*, and Henry
A. Pochmann, *German Culture in America*.

THE *BOSTON QUARTERLY REVIEW* (1838–42)

The *Boston Quarterly Review* was published primarily as a forum for its editor,
Orestes Brownson, and it vigorously addressed most of the important issues of the
day, Unitarians and Transcendentalists alike being targets of Brownson's criticism.
The periodical eventually merged with the *United States Magazine, and Democratic
Review*.

A brief note about the *Boston Quarterly Review* appears in Algernon Tassin, *The
Magazine in America*, and more detailed treatments are in Frank Luther Mott, *A History
of American Magazines 1741-1850*, and in Clarence L. F. Gohdes, *The Periodicals
of American Transcendentalism*. A much more recent and detailed analysis of the
contents of the periodical is in Leonard Gilhooley, *Contradiction and Dilemma: Orestes
Brownson and the American Idea*, which devotes two chapters to it.

An early biography of Brownson that provides information about his role as editor
in the form of letters from contributors is Henry F. Brownson, *Orestes A. Brownson's
Early Life*. A biographical study that treats the periodical in terms of the issues that
Brownson dealt with is Arthur M. Schlesinger, Jr., *Orestes A. Brownson*. A recent
work that devotes a chapter to the journal and two chapters to Brownson's article "The
Laboring Classes" is Thomas R. Ryan, *Orestes A. Brownson: A Definitive Biography*.
One indication of the high regard in which the periodical was held in its day is pro-
vided by an anonymous piece, "The Democratic Review and O. A. Brownson" (1843).
A chapter-long study of Brownson's response to the European political and social
upheavals of 1848 is included in Barbara Gans Gallant, "The New England
Transcendentalists and the European Revolutions of 1848." Although the *Boston
Quarterly Review* folded in 1842, this work sheds light on the years during which the
journal was published. The evaluation of European, English, and American literature
in the magazine is studied in Minda Ruth Dorn, "Literary Criticism in the *Boston
Quarterly Review*, the *Present*, and the *Massachusetts Quarterly Review*." The expression of French ideas in the periodical is considered in Georges Jules Joyaux, "French
Thought in American Magazines 1800-1848." The journal's interest in the French
novelist George Sand is touched on in Howard Mumford Jones, "American Comment on George Sand, 1837-1848"; a somewhat broader study of its coverage of French
novels is Albert L. Rabinovitz, "Criticism of French Novels in Boston Magazines,
1830-1860." German literature and thought in the *Boston Quarterly Review* is dealt
with in Stanley M. Vogel, *German Literary Influences on the American Transcendentalists*, and Henry A. Pochmann, *German Culture in America*. The slight interest of
the periodical in music is described by Irving Lowens.

THE *DIAL* (1840–44)

The *Dial*, a quarterly published in Boston, was the most important journal of the New England Transcendentalists. It was edited by Margaret Fuller during the first two years of its existence and by Ralph Waldo Emerson during the last two. Despite its broad and interesting contents and the talent of its contributors, the *Dial* never found the audience it deserved, and it died a premature death. The *Dial* has been reprinted in facsimile twice: once by the Rowfant Club in a limited printing in 1902 and again by Russell and Russell in 1961. The latter contains the "Prospectus" of the periodical, which appeared on the back cover of the July 1840 number.

The activities of the Transcendentalists at the time the *Dial* was launched are recorded by Bronson Alcott in Joel Myerson, "Bronson Alcott's 'Scripture for 1840.'" These selections from Alcott's journal for 1840, important parts of which had not been published before, are invaluable for understanding the historical context of the *Dial*. Information about the relationship in 1842 between the editor, Fuller, and the soon-to-be editor, Emerson, from the former's point of view is available in Myerson, "Margaret Fuller's 1842 Journal." Her journal begins with her arrival in Concord on 17 August 1842 and concludes with her departure on 25 September.

Numerous historical accounts of the *Dial* have been written. Perhaps the earliest of these, by one not connected with the venture, is F. B. Sanborn, "The *Dial*" (1855). This sketch of the *Dial*, written only a decade or so after its demise, is both informative about the journal and perceptive about its importance. More immediate is Alcott's account of the founding and contents of the *Dial* in the *Boston Commonwealth* (1863), a weekly newspaper edited by Sanborn. A useful though badly dated history of the Transcendentalist movement that deals briefly with the journal is Octavius Brooks Frothingham, *Transcendentalism in New England* (1876). An article about the *Dial* that appeared in one of its namesakes shortly before Emerson's death is Norman C. Perkins, "The Original *Dial*," which reviews facts about the journal and highlights the most important of its contents. Charles A. Cummings' "The Press and Literature of the Last Hundred Years" provides an overview of the period that focuses briefly on the magazine. A historical note in the form of a circular from Roberts Brothers, Publishers, dated 1 June 1882, seeking advance orders for a reprinting (eventually unsuccessful) of the journal, was published as "A Reprint of the *Dial*," together with a reprint of a brief sketch "Mr. Emerson and the *Dial*" by George William Curtis. That same circular, with minor changes, was also inserted in copies of Julia Ward Howe, *Margaret Fuller (Marchesa Ossoli)*. Emerson himself presented a brief but interesting recollection of the *Dial* in "Historic Notes of Life and Letters in New England."

The first substantial study of the *Dial*, and the most important work until the appearance of Joel Myerson's *The New England Transcendentalists and the* Dial, was George Willis Cooke, *An Historical and Biographical Introduction to Accompany the* Dial, which was sold with the Rowfant Club's reprint of the periodical. An earlier version of this study had appeared as "The *Dial*: An Historical and Biographical Introduction, with a List of the Contributors," along with Cooke's corrections to his article, "The *Dial* and Corrigenda." Cooke's book has been reprinted as *Memorabilia of the Transcendentalists in New England*. A part of the book—an index to the *Dial* listing titles and contributors—may also be found as "Emerson and Thoreau in the Index to the *Dial*."

J. F. A. Pyre, "The *Dial* of 1840–45," summarizes the brief life of the periodical with unusual perceptivity about its strengths and weaknesses. In Thomas Wentworth Higginson, "Old Cambridge in Three Literary Epochs," the appearance of the *Dial* begins the second epoch. Another standard history of Transcendentalism, every bit as durable and nearly as dated as Frothingham, that discusses the magazine briefly is Harold Clarke Goddard, *Studies in New England Transcendentalism*. The journal receives five pages of general but useful coverage in Algernon Tassin, *The Magazine in America*. A similar brief treatment is provided by Goddard in the *Cambridge History of American Literature*.

The first really important account of the *Dial* after the appearance of Cooke's book was Clarence L. F. Gohdes, "The *Western Messenger* and the *Dial*," which continues to be one of the essential works of scholarship on the magazine. Equally basic and useful is the sketch in Frank Luther Mott, *A History of American Magazines 1741–1850*, and a readable short history of the magazine is Helen E. Marshall, "The Story of the *Dial*." Completed nearly twenty-five years later, a little-known German work that furnishes a history of the journal as well as information about its contributors and their contributions is Wolfgang Rieger, "The *Dial*: Geschichte und Wertung einer Zeitschrift," available on microfilm from the Center for Research Libraries. A recent study of the Transcendentalists that includes a short sketch of the periodical and numerous references to it is Paul F. Boller, Jr., *American Transcendentalism*. Donald N. Koster, *Transcendentalism in America*, contains a chapter, "Transcendental Journals and the Transcendentalist Aesthetic," in which the *Dial* receives brief general treatment.

The most important work on the history of the *Dial* and its contributors is Joel Myerson, *The New England Transcendentalists and the* Dial, which furnishes a history of the journal and sketches of its contributors. An appendix provides a list of the contents for each number and an alphabetical arrangement of the contributors and their contributions. The notes and index are full and useful, and the bibliography is an invaluable list of scholarship bearing on the periodical. The bibliography in Myerson's dissertation is even more extensive, for it includes all the manuscripts and printed sources cited in the text. Any scholar seriously concerned with the *Dial* must start with Myerson's fine work, parts of which have also appeared as articles: the beginnings of the journal are described in "A Calendar of Transcendental Club Meetings," which lists, insofar as they are known, the dates and places of the meetings, the topics of discussion, and the names of those who attended; and "A History of the Transcendental Club" is a reliable account that fleshes out the earlier calendar of meetings.

An interesting and perceptive treatment of the source and significance of the periodical's name is Nicholas Joost, "The *Dial*: A Journalistic Emblem and Its Tradition," which, with only minor changes, is the introductory chapter in *Years of Tran-*

sition. The derivation of the name is also dealt with helpfully in Barbara Harrell Carson, "Proclus' Sunflower and the *Dial*."

The results of a collation of Cooke's list of contributors to the *Dial* and Emerson's attributions in the Harvard University and British Museum sets of the journal are presented and discussed by Burton R. Pollin, "Emerson's Annotations in the British Museum Copy of the *Dial*." A valuable authoritative list of contributors and their contributions to the periodical is provided in Myerson, "An Annotated List of Contributions to the Boston *Dial*." The contemporary popularity of the journal, based on the number of extant copies of each issue, is assessed in Myerson, "A Union List of the *Dial* (1840–1844) and Some Information about Its Sales," and the public response to the periodical as evidenced in journals and newspapers is traced in Myerson, "The Contemporary Reception of the Boston *Dial*." One item missed by Myerson, in the 2 June 1843 *Herald of Freedom*, is reprinted by Michael Meyer, "An Advertisement for the *Dial* and Obscurity for Thoreau."

The part that the *Dial* played in the Transcendental movement is reflected in *The Transcendentalists: An Anthology*, ed. Perry Miller, an excellent collection of Transcendentalist writings with annotations. A similar (though less comprehensive) collection with annotations is Miller's *The American Transcendentalists*. A short but useful introduction to the Transcendentalist movement and a small gathering of representative writings from the *Dial* may be found in *Selected Writings of the American Transcendentalists*, ed. George Hochfield.

Publications on Margaret Fuller's engagement with the journal are listed in Myerson, *Margaret Fuller: An Annotated Secondary Bibliography*. This full and nearly complete scholarly tool has an excellent index as well. Fuller's work on the periodical receives attention in the following works: Emerson, William Henry Channing, and James Freeman Clarke, *Memoirs of Margaret Fuller Ossoli*; Julia Ward Howe, *Margaret Fuller (Marchesa Ossoli)*; Thomas Wentworth Higginson, *Margaret Fuller Ossoli*; Katharine Anthony, *Margaret Fuller*; Mason Wade, *Margaret Fuller*; Madeleine B. Stern, *The Life of Margaret Fuller*; *Margaret Fuller: American Romantic*, ed. Perry Miller; Arthur W. Brown, *Margaret Fuller*; Paula Blanchard, *Margaret Fuller*; and Margaret Vanderhaar Allen, *The Achievement of Margaret Fuller*. Specific studies of Fuller's role in the *Dial* are Madeleine B. Stern, "Margaret Fuller and the *Dial*"; Mae Bernadine McKay, "Margaret Fuller (Ossoli), the Gnomon of the *Dial*"; Janice Elizabeth Wilson, "An Inquiry into Selected Writings of Margaret Fuller as They Appeared in the *Dial* Magazine 1840–44," which also draws conclusions about her religious, philosophical, social, artistic, cultural, and literary views and her significance in the Transcendentalist movement; Bernard Rosenthal, "The *Dial*, Transcendentalism, and Margaret Fuller"; and Aiko Moro-oka, "Margaret Fuller and the *Dial* of July, 1840," an article in Japanese. Two analyses of Fuller's critical principles—which were stated, in part, in the *Dial* and which guided her editorial policies—are Roland Crozier Burton, "Margaret Fuller's Criticism of the Fine Arts," and Wilma R. Ebbitt, "Margaret Fuller's Ideas on Criticism." The relationship between Fuller and her successor as editor is studied in Harry R. Warfel, "Margaret Fuller and Ralph Waldo Emerson."

The part George Ripley played in the *Dial* is dealt with in Charles Crowe, *George Ripley*, and Henry L. Golemba, *George Ripley*.

Emerson's work on the *Dial* has received a great deal of attention. A recent bibliography of secondary works on Emerson that is useful for locating information on this topic is Robert E. Burkholder and Myerson, *Ralph Waldo Emerson: An Annotated Secondary Bibliography*. A short account of Emerson's involvement with the journal appears in Frederic I. Carpenter, *Emerson Handbook*.

Biographies of Emerson that include material about his activities on behalf of the *Dial* are the following: George Willis Cooke, *Ralph Waldo Emerson*, which devotes a full chapter to a pioneering study of the *Dial*; Oliver Wendell Holmes, *Ralph Waldo Emerson*; James Elliot Cabot, *A Memoir of Ralph Waldo Emerson*; Elisabeth Luther Cary, *Emerson*, which devotes two chapters to the journal; O. W. Firkins, *Ralph Waldo Emerson*; Ralph L. Rusk, *The Life of Ralph Waldo Emerson*; and Gay Wilson Allen, *Waldo Emerson*. Of interest as well is an account of the relations between Emerson and the previous editor of the periodical, Margaret Fuller, in Harry R. Warfel, "Margaret Fuller and Ralph Waldo Emerson."

The correspondence of Emerson relating to the *Dial* is gathered in *The Letters of Ralph Waldo Emerson*. Emerson's discussion of the periodical with Thomas Carlyle is available in *The Correspondence of Emerson and Carlyle*, ed. Joseph Slater. An example of Emerson's correspondence with contributors to the journal is provided in William White, "Emerson as Editor." Also useful are *The Journals and Miscellaneous Notebooks of Ralph Waldo Emerson* (vols. 7–9, 12), and especially his "Dialling" Notebook published in vol. 8.

Individual treatments of the relationship of Emerson to the *Dial* are George William Curtis, "Mr. Emerson and the *Dial*"; Vishwa Mohan Mishra, "Ralph Waldo Emerson: The Leading Spirit of the *Dial*"; James Ray Blackwelder, "Ralph Waldo Emerson's Contributions to the *Dial*," which finds that Emerson's eighty articles in the journal reflect essentially literary interests; and Doris Morton, "Ralph Waldo Emerson and the *Dial*," which analyzes Emerson's critical theory as practiced in the journal.

Thoreau's contribution to the *Dial* is examined in the following studies: Roger C. Mueller, "Thoreau's Selections from *Chinese Four Books* for the *Dial*," discusses the excerpts that Thoreau edited for the October 1843 issue. Charles R. Anderson, "Thoreau and the *Dial*," concludes that the journal gave Emerson's protégé the opportunity to develop the themes and methods of his mature writing. Myerson, "Thoreau and the *Dial*," describes the reactions to Thoreau's contributions in contemporary reviews. Roger C. Mueller, "A Significant Buddhist Translation by Thoreau," deals with Thoreau's translation (the first into English) of a chapter from *Sutra of the Lotus Flower of the Wonderful Law* that appeared in the January 1844 number as one of the "Ethnical Scriptures." Of related interest is the notice about Thoreau's set of the *Dial*, with autograph letters and manuscripts inserted, in Kenneth Walter Cameron, "The Recent Sale of Thoreau Manuscripts." This set is now at Southern Illinois University.

There are several studies of minor figures connected with the *Dial*. The contemporary reception of the most notorious of Alcott's contributions to the journal is examined in Myerson, "'In the Transcendental Emporium': Bronson Alcott's 'Orphic Sayings' in the *Dial*." J. Wesley Thomas, "John Sullivan Dwight," touches on Dwight's music criticism. A nineteenth-century piece dealing with Ellery Channing, the *Dial*, and Transcendentalism is George William Curtis, "Editor's Easy Chair" (*Har*, Nov. 1871). Related to these studies is a note by Joan Macdonald about Burrill and George William Curtis, who originally owned seven numbers of the *Dial*.

A number of studies treating the Transcendentalist philosophy of the *Dial* have appeared. Kathryn Kides, "Transcendentalism as Reflected in the *Dial* Magazine," deals briefly with the history of the periodical, its editors, its religious, philosophical, and literary concerns, and its interest in reform. Ralph Emil Weber, "The *Dial*," contains a short history of the periodical, a statement about its purpose and contents, and brief discussions of its criticism of music, painting, sculpture, and literature. Lawrence C. Porter, "Transcendentalism," and an expanded version of this work, "New England Transcendentalism," point out the contributions of the journal to the definition of Transcendentalism. Gerald Ray Mathis, "The *Dial*," examines the contents of the periodical, dealing with the relationship of the oversoul, the individual, and nature. Chapter 3 of Wolfgang Rieger's "The *Dial*" is a more substantial discussion of the magazine's general critical articles, its literary criticism and book reviews, its critical essays about music, theater, and the plastic arts, and its key words.

A study that analyzes in detail the religious, philosophical, social, and political thought of the *Dial* is Donald F. Warders' dissertation, "'The Progress of the Hour and the Day.'" Chapter 1 reviews the historical background of the journal to show how the ideas of the Transcendentalists were formed and transmitted. Chapter 2, "Religious and Philosophical Thought," takes up five topics—"Religious Context," "Intuition," "Orientalism and Mysticism," "Nature," "Religious Heroes"—and concludes that New England Transcendentalism was primarily a reaction against Unitarianism and an attempt to purify and revitalize the Christianity of the day. Chapter 3, "Social and Political Thought," examines eight topics: "The Individual and Society," "Experimental Societies and the Dignity of Labor," "Fruitlands and Brook Farm," "Women's Rights," "Blacks and Abolitionism," "Education," "The Theory of Reform," and "Religious Reform." Some Transcendentalists advocated individualism in reform; others advocated associationism; but nearly all of them believed that politics should conform to the spirit and practice of Christianity. Chapter 4, "Conclusion," defines the Transcendentalism of the *Dial* as the persistent concern of the men and women associated with Emerson to identify the permanent content of Christianity, separate it from the transient, and then live it in their personal lives and apply it to society at large. The "Conclusion" also relates Transcendentalism to present-day attempts to find God.

The criticism of the arts that appeared in the *Dial* is investigated in Frank Martindale Webster, "Transcendental Points of View." Numerous references to the periodical's role in promoting Transcendentalist cultural aspirations may be found in John Byron Wilson, "Activities of the New England Transcendentalists in the

Dissemination of Culture," which focuses on major individuals rather than on Transcendentalist journals or the *Dial* in particular. Wilson deals with the *Dial*'s treatment of the fine arts in "The Aesthetics of Transcendentalism."

The significant and creative thinking about literature in the *Dial* is examined in Richard H. Fogle, "Organic Form in American Criticism." A useful investigation of the critical principles of the periodical is Sidney Poger, "The Critical Stance of the *Dial*."

The poetry and poetic criticism of the *Dial* have not received adequate attention, but one helpful study is Helen Hennessy (Vendler), "The *Dial*: Its Poetry and Poetic Criticism." The conspicuously small amount of fiction in the journal and the reasons why more was not published are the focus of Ann-Mari Peirce, "The Transcendentalists and Fiction." The interest of the periodical in drama is discussed in Lucile Gafford, "Transcendentalist Attitudes toward Drama and the Theatre." The musical articles that appeared in the journal are dealt with by Irving Lowens.

A detailed analysis of Orientalism in the *Dial* appears in Roger Chester Mueller, "The Orient in American Transcendental Periodicals." A summary of this work may be found in "Transcendental Periodicals and the Orient." The *Dial*'s interest in French culture is treated in Georges Jules Joyaux, "French Thought in American Magazines 1800–1848"; Howard Mumford Jones, "American Comment on George Sand, 1837–1848"; and Albert L. Rabinovitz, "Criticism of French Novels in Boston Magazines, 1830–1860." Coverage of German literature is recorded in Lillie V. Hathaway, *German Literature of the Mid-Nineteenth Century in England and America as Reflected in the Journals 1840–1914*, and, more fully, in Stanley M. Vogel, *German Literary Influences on the American Transcendentalists*, and Henry A. Pochmann, *German Culture in America*.

THE *PRESENT* (1843–44)

The *Present*, founded and edited by William Henry Channing, was published monthly in New York. Originally much like the *Dial*, it turned increasingly to matters of reform, especially the principles of Fourierism. The journal failed at least in part because Channing was unsuited for editorial work.

A useful early account of the *Present* may be found in George Willis Cooke, *An Historical and Biographical Introduction to Accompany the* Dial. The most substantial study of the journal is the chapter devoted to it in Clarence L. F. Gohdes, *The Periodicals of American Transcendentalism*. Literary theory and the evaluation of European, English, and American writers are studied in Minda Ruth Dorn, "Literary Criticism in the *Boston Quarterly Review*, the *Present*, and the *Massachusetts Quarterly Review*." The slight interest of the periodical in music is touched on by Irving Lowens.

THE *HARBINGER* (1845–49)

The *Harbinger*, a weekly journal, was the organ of Brook Farm and, when that experimental community dissolved, of the American Union of Associationists in New York. George Ripley served as principal editor. The periodical was primarily concerned with associationism, but it published a wide range of significant literary and cultural material. Scholarship about the *Harbinger* is listed in Joel Myerson, *Brook Farm: An Annotated Bibliography and Resources Guide*. The "Prospectus" for the journal and an appeal for aid appear in Ripley, "The *Harbinger*."

Edgar Allan Poe's ambivalent opinion of the *Harbinger*, based on its review of his *The Raven and Other Poems*, may be found in the *Broadway Journal* for 13 December 1845. An early history of the Transcendentalist movement that considers the contents of the *Harbinger* in passing is Octavius Brooks Frothingham, *Transcendentalism in New England*. A useful account of the journal may be found in George Willis Cooke, *An Historical and Biographical Introduction to Accompany the* Dial, and it receives very slight coverage in Algernon Tassin, *The Magazine in America*. The history of the *Harbinger*, its relation to Fourierism, and its cultural interests are treated by Janette Chilton Powell in "A Study of the *Harbinger*." A brief but reliable sketch appears in Frank Luther Mott, *A History of American Magazines 1741-1850*, and a more substantial treatment, as helpful today as when it was written, is the chapter in Clarence L. F. Gohdes, *The Periodicals of American Transcendentalism*. The most recent and the most complete study of the journal is Sterling F. Delano, "The *Harbinger*," which deals with its history, its advocacy of associationism, its treatment of social, political, and economic issues, and its literary criticism of American and European authors. This dissertation, the first full-scale study of the journal, also contains an extensive bibliography, and it will soon be published in a revised form. Delano, along with Rita Colanzi, has also indexed the eighth volume of the periodical.

Valuable information about Brook Farm, the *Harbinger*, and some of the important contributors to the periodical is available in John Thomas Codman, *Brook Farm*; Lindsay Swift, *Brook Farm*; and Edith Roelker Curtis, *A Season in Utopia*. The first biography of the principal editor of the journal is Octavius Brooks Frothingham, *George Ripley*, which includes the "Prospectus" of the paper. A fine work on Ripley in general and on his involvement with the *Harbinger* in particular is Charles Crowe, *George Ripley*. Ripley's contribution to the journal receives detailed coverage in a more recent work by Henry L. Golemba, *George Ripley*.

The *Harbinger*'s treatment of Eastern culture is discussed by Roger Chester Mueller (see above), and its substantial editorial commentary on European political upheavals is reviewed by Barbara Gans Gallant. The literary reviews of the periodical during its first two years express a philosophy based on the principles of Swedenborg, Fourier, and the American Union of Associationists, according to Marjorie Ruth Kaufman, "The Literary Reviews of the *Harbinger* during Its Brook Farm Period 1845-1847." The special interest of the journal in drama is discussed in Lucile Gafford, "Transcendentalist Attitudes toward Drama and the Theatre." The great importance of music to the periodical is demonstrated by Irving Lowens. The contributions of the journal's leading music critic are treated in Lorraine Donoghue, "The Musical Criticisms of John Sullivan Dwight in the *Harbinger* 1845–1849," and touched on in J. Wesley Thomas, "John Sullivan Dwight."

The *Harbinger*'s interest in French ideas is treated in Georges Jules Joyaux, "French Thought in American Magazines 1800–1848," and its defense of the French novelists George Sand and Eugène Sue is discussed in Howard Mumford Jones, "American Comment on George Sand, 1837–1848," Albert L. Rabinovitz, "Criticism of French Novels in Boston Magazines, 1830–1860," and Joyaux, "George Sand, Eugène Sue and the *Harbinger*." Its treatment of German literature and thought is covered in Stanley M. Vogel, *German Literary Influences on the American Transcendentalists*, and Henry A. Pochmann, *German Culture in America*.

THE *SPIRIT OF THE AGE* (1849–50)

The *Spirit of the Age* was another attempt by William Henry Channing to found and edit a journal, this one devoted to the principles of Christian Socialism and published weekly in New York. Even though he was aided by George Ripley, the periodical generally failed to deal with the social issues so important to Channing. Plagued by mental fatigue and financial problems, the editor allowed the journal to expire.

The *Spirit of the Age* receives a brief mention in Frank Luther Mott, *A History of American Magazines 1741–1850*, and there is a useful chapter in Clarence L. F. Gohdes, *The Periodicals of American Transcendentalism*. The interest of this journal in the Orient is studied by Roger Chester Mueller, its articles on revolution are examined by Barbara Gans Gallant, and its music criticism is dealt with by Irving Lowens. Channing's own copy of the *Spirit of the Age*, with his marginalia, is at the Newberry Library.

AESTHETIC PAPERS (1849)

Aesthetic Papers was a one-number journal edited and published by Elizabeth Palmer Peabody in Boston. Its impressive contents include Henry David Thoreau's "Resistance to Civil Government" and important pieces by Ralph Waldo Emerson and Nathaniel Hawthorne, as well as nine other articles and six poems. Poor sales ended the brief life of the periodical. *Aesthetic Papers* has been reprinted in a facsimile with an introduction by Joseph Jones, who provides an excellent short account of the times, the contributors, and the contents in order to show how the journal reflects both the strengths and weaknesses of New England Transcendentalism. This reprint also contains the "Prospectus."

A useful account of *Aesthetic Papers* may be found in George Willis Cooke, *An*

Historical and Biographical Introduction to Accompany the Dial, and in Clarence L. F. Gohdes, *The Periodicals of American Transcendentalism*. John Byron Wilson treats Peabody and her periodical in "Activities of the New England Transcendentalists in the Dissemination of Culture," and he discusses writings on the fine arts that appeared in the journal in "The Aesthetics of Transcendentalism." Music criticism is covered by Irving Lowens. The influence of an *Aesthetic Papers* article by Peabody on Thoreau's *Walden* is the subject of Joseph Jones, "Villages as Universities," which points out the similarity in idea and phraseology between the conclusion to "The Dorian Measure, with a Modern Application" and the conclusion to "Reading." The periodical is seen as a direct response to the European revolutions of 1848 by Barbara Gans Gallant.

THE *MASSACHUSETTS QUARTERLY REVIEW* (1847–50)

The *Massachusetts Quarterly Review* was edited by Theodore Parker, who hoped that it would be a mature *Dial*. It published the work of a number of well-known writers, such as Ralph Waldo Emerson and James Russell Lowell, and it dealt with significant religious and political issues. When its Boston publisher went bankrupt, the periodical ceased.

A helpful early account of the *Massachusetts Quarterly Review* is included in George Willis Cooke, *An Historical and Biographical Introduction to Accompany the* Dial. A very brief mention of the journal occurs in Algernon Tassin, *The Magazine in America*. A much more detailed sketch is in Frank Luther Mott, *A History of American Magazines 1741–1850*, and the most substantial study is the chapter in Clarence L. F. Gohdes, *The Periodicals of American Transcendentalism*. Parker's role in the venture is touched on in Octavius Brooks Frothingham, *Theodore Parker*, and in Henry Steele Commager, *Theodore Parker*.

The interest of the *Massachusetts Quarterly Review* in Oriental religion and literature is discussed by Roger Chester Mueller, and its response to European political upheaval is dealt with by Barbara Gans Gallant. Literary theory and the evaluation of European, English, and American literature are studied in Minda Ruth Dorn, "Literary Criticism in the *Boston Quarterly Review*, the *Present*, and the *Massachusetts Quarterly Review*." A survey of the periodical's interest in French ideas is Georges Jules Joyaux, "French Thought in American Magazines 1800–1848," and its articles on German literature are recorded in Lillie V. Hathaway, *German Literature of the Mid-Nineteenth Century in England and America as Reflected in the Journals 1840–1914*, and Henry A. Pochmann, *German Culture in America*. Of the eight Transcendentalist periodicals published through 1850, this was the only one that did not devote a piece to music, though it did present a brief discussion of singing in early New England, according to Irving Lowens.

THE CINCINNATI *DIAL* (1860)

The Cincinnati *Dial* was published and edited by Moncure Daniel Conway, who stood for the principle of freedom in every area of life. The journal appeared monthly, and much of the writing was done by Conway himself and Octavius Brooks Frothingham. Finding himself greatly overburdened and the pre–Civil War intellectual climate unfavorable, Conway let the enterprise lapse at the end of one year.

A brief early treatment of the Cincinnati *Dial* is included in W. H. Venable, "Early Periodical Literature of the Ohio Valley: VI." A useful account of the journal may be found in George Willis Cooke, *An Historical and Biographical Introduction to Accompany the* Dial. Another short but helpful sketch is available in Frank Luther Mott, *A History of American Magazines 1850-1865*, and the most substantial study is the chapter in Clarence L. F. Gohdes, *The Periodicals of American Transcendentalism*. Information about the *Dial* is furnished by its founder and editor in Conway, *Autobiography Memories and Experiences*. Short treatments of the journal are in Mary Elizabeth Burtis, *Moncure Conway 1832-1907*, and Loyd D. Easton, *Hegel's First American Followers*, and the interest of the magazine in Orientalia is studied by Roger Chester Mueller.

THE *RADICAL* (1865–72) AND THE *INDEX* (1870–86)

The *Radical*, a voice of the Free Religious Association, was a monthly journal edited and published in Boston by Sidney H. Morse. Its most important contributors were the later Transcendentalists Samuel Johnson, David Atwood Wasson, and John Weiss. The periodical was essentially religious in outlook, but by no means exclusively so. It ceased publication because of inadequate financial support.

The *Index*, a weekly journal, was published first in Toledo, Ohio, and then, after several years, in Boston, where it eventually became an organ of the Free Religious Association. Francis Ellingwood Abbot was its founder and, for ten years, its editor; Benjamin F. Underwood served as editor in its last years. The *Index* had much the same purpose and many of the same contributors as the *Radical*. Financial problems eventually brought it to an end.

Early accounts of both periodicals may be found in George Willis Cooke, *An Historical and Biographical Introduction to Accompany the* Dial. Brief sketches also appear in Frank Luther Mott, *A History of American Magazines 1865-1885*, and the most important treatment of the periodicals is in Clarence L. F. Gohdes, *The Periodicals of American Transcendentalism*. An anonymous notice for the *Radical* listing Emerson as a contributor was reprinted from the *National Anti-Slavery Standard* (1867) in Kenneth Walter Cameron, "The *Radical*." An account of the *Index* as an organ for the Free Religious Association is included in Stow Persons, *Free Religion*. The interest of both journals in the Orient is analyzed by Roger Chester Mueller.

SUGGESTIONS FOR FURTHER RESEARCH

The work done on the *Western Messenger*, *Dial*, and *Harbinger* suggests that similar studies of the other journals might profitably be carried out. But even the research that has been accomplished is not definitive: for example, a number of significant studies of the *Dial* have been done, but none of these has been sufficiently thorough to discourage other investigators. The field of research remains very much open.

Some individual periodicals could usefully be examined within the context of their sponsoring organizations, especially those affiliated with the Unitarians and the Free Religious Association. Of equal significance would be comparisons of Transcendentalist magazines with contemporary periodicals and with each other, such as Clarence Gohdes' work on the relation between the *Western Messenger* and the *Dial*. Also important would be analyses of contributions by individual writers, such as Doris Morton's study of Emerson's literary criticism in the *Dial*; assessments of the roles played by journal contributions in the professional careers of writers, such as Charles Anderson's article on Thoreau's apprentice years with the *Dial*; and comparisons of authors' contributions to Transcendentalist periodicals with their contributions to other journals—contrasting, say, Emerson's writings for the *Dial* with those for the *Atlantic Monthly*.

Two additional opportunities for scholarship may be mentioned in closing. It was dissatisfaction with existing periodicals that spurred the Transcendentalists to begin their own journals, particularly the *Dial*. A study of two of the important Unitarian periodicals against which the Transcendentalists were rebelling is Frank Luther Mott, "The *Christian Disciple* and the *Christian Examiner*," which later appeared, along with some additional information, in *A History of American Magazines 1741–1850*. Mott's work shows how to study journals contemporaneous with the Transcendentalist periodicals, and Paul Purushottam Reuben shows how to trace the influence of Transcendentalism on later magazines in "Dynamics of New England Transcendentalism in Benjamin Orange Flower's *Arena* (1889–1909)." Reuben's dissertation demonstrates that the *Arena*, published in Boston at the turn of the century, devoted itself to reviving interest in Transcendentalism. Unquestionably, much remains to be done in the way of scholarship and criticism on the Transcendentalist periodicals.

The Transcendentalists

AMOS BRONSON ALCOTT

Frederick C. Dahlstrand

BIBLIOGRAPHIES

The best bibliography of primary materials on Bronson Alcott is that compiled by Shirley W. Dinwiddie and Richard L. Herrnstadt, although it is only partially annotated and excludes manuscript materials. Other sources are generally inadequate. The entry in *BAL* (vol. 1) is too brief, as are those in the standard Alcott biographies. Helpful supplements to Dinwiddie and Herrnstadt are Dorothy McCuskey, *Bronson Alcott, Teacher*, which contains a thorough catalog of items related to Alcott's educational ideas and practices, and Fordyce Richard Bennett's "Sources for Alcott's Fruitlands."

The Dinwiddie-Herrnstadt bibliography is also the best for secondary materials, superseding Waldemar A. Thurow's "Amos Bronson Alcott, 1799–1888: An Annotated Bibliography," which is incomplete and sometimes inaccurate. Unfortunately, there is no comparable bibliography for materials produced or uncovered since 1954. A number of articles on Alcott, not covered in this essay, are listed in *AAL*.

MANUSCRIPTS

ALM lists forty-three institutions holding unpublished Alcott materials, although most of these repositories have fewer than five items. The largest and most important archive is the Alcott-Pratt Collection in the Houghton Library, Harvard University, which holds the fifty-four volumes of Alcott's journals, covering the years 1826 to 1882. The journals, as well as other documents in the collection, are generally well preserved, neatly bound, and legible; in his passion for neatness and order, Alcott recopied many of them from rougher versions. The journal volumes average six hundred pages in length, ranging from 152 pages (1830) to 1,338 pages (1851). Rarely did Alcott miss a daily entry, and the contents vary from mundane comments about everyday events to lengthy reflective analyses of the nature of the universe. Later volumes are far more concerned with the concrete details of day-to-day existence than earlier ones, and they include a large number of newspaper clippings and other scrapbook materials. Unfortunately, the journals for the critical Fruitlands years of 1841 through 1845 are missing. Alcott lost the volumes for 1842, 1843, and 1844 near Albany, New York, in the summer of 1844, when a stagecoach rumbled off with his baggage, and the whereabouts of the journals for 1841 and 1845 remain a mystery.

The Harvard collection also includes thirty-four bound volumes of correspondence. Alcott carefully saved letters to him and the members of his family and often made handwritten copies of letters he sent to others. He included some early letters as well as photographs, newspaper clippings, and other printed materials in ten volumes of "Autobiographical Collections" and five volumes of "Genealogical Collections," all of which are essential for piecing together the details of his early life and his family background. Also of importance are six volumes of Alcott's observations on his children, which are an excellent source for understanding the development of his transcendental philosophy and his educational theories. In addition, the Alcott-Pratt Collection contains the records of the Town and Country Club, three volumes of notes on Alcott's conversational tours of the 1870s, various letters and manuscripts written by members of his family, and an "Autobiographical Index." The "Index," though largely written from memory and thus possibly inaccurate in detail, is a valuable source for Alcott's early life and his Fruitlands years.

The Fruitlands Museums in Harvard, Massachusetts, owns several important documents and manuscripts, including the original typescript of William Harry Harland's "Bronson Alcott's English Friends," a major source for the Fruitlands experiment. The Concord Free Public Library has numerous letters and miscellaneous manuscripts, including Alcott's "Concord Book" and a microfilm copy of the journals and letter books. Other major manuscript collections listed in *ALM*, such as those at the New York Public Library, the University of Pennsylvania, Middlebury College, and the University of Virginia, consist mainly of letters, most of which have been published.

EDITIONS

There is no edition of Alcott's collected works, largely because his literary style lacked the attraction of other Transcendentalists, such as Emerson or Thoreau. He often expressed himself most beautifully in his unpublished manuscripts and his unrecorded conversations. Although Elizabeth Palmer Peabody's *Record of a School* and Alcott's *Conversations with Children on the Gospels, Tablets,* and *Concord Days* are available in reprints, many of his important early writings on education and culture are scattered in rare periodicals such as the *American Journal of Education* (1826–28) and the *American Annals of Education and Instruction*. Walter Harding has, however, made available several of Alcott's most significant educational writings in *Essays on Education*, including portions of the reports Alcott compiled as superintendent of the Concord schools and *The Doctrine and Discipline of Human Culture* (1836), which is one of his clearest published statements of Transcendentalism. George Hochfield has wisely included this latter pamphlet in *Selected Writings of the American Transcendentalists*. Alcott's "Orphic Sayings," published originally in the *Dial* and other Transcendentalist journals, have been reprinted with commentary in Perry Miller's two anthologies, *The Transcendentalists* and *The American Transcendentalists*, and in *Orphic Sayings*. George Willis Cooke's *The Poets of Transcendentalism* includes several of Alcott's poems, and his speeches and conversations at the Concord School of Philosophy from 1879 to 1882 are printed by Raymond L. Bridgman in *Concord Lectures on Philosophy*.

The essence of Alcott's thought is found in his manuscript journals, selections of which were edited by Odell Shepard as *The Journals of Bronson Alcott*. Shepard's edition is well done and the selections well chosen, but it is only about one twentieth of the manuscript, and it leaves out much that is important. Shepard includes nothing from the journal for 1840 and little concerning Alcott's western tours of 1874–75 and 1880–81. Joel Myerson has filled some of the gaps by publishing the full text of the journal for 1836 and part of the journal for 1840, key years in the history of Transcendentalism as well as in Alcott's own life, and Larry A. Carlson has done the same for the 1837 journal.

Most of Alcott's known letters have been published. Franklin B. Sanborn included some in the second edition of Alcott's *New Connecticut*, although his editorial work is suspect. The bulk of the letters are available in Richard L. Herrnstadt's *The Letters of A. Bronson Alcott*. Unfortunately, Herrnstadt missed many letters pasted or copied into Alcott's journals or autobiographical collections, and his annotations and index are weak. The edition's most serious flaw is the absence of nineteen letters to W. A. Alcott, dated from 1828 to 1833, that contain important clues to Bronson Alcott's early intellectual development. Frederick Wagner culled the journals and collections to find eighty-six additional letters but the nineteen key letters noted above, though also located in the Harvard collection, remain unpublished.

Other Alcott materials are scattered about in miscellaneous publications. Clara Endicott Sears included major letters and documents relating to Fruitlands in her *Bronson Alcott's Fruitlands* but without much editorial precision. "William Harry Harland's 'Bronson Alcott's English Friends' " has been edited and published by Joel Myerson. Selections from "Bronson Alcott's 'Autobiographical Index' " are printed with commentary by David P. Edgell; John C. Broderick describes and analyzes the contents of "Bronson Alcott's 'Concord Book' "; and Kenneth Walter Cameron has edited part of the Town and Country Club notebook ("Emerson, Thoreau, and the Town and Country Club"). Several previously unpublished letters and documents can be found in recent articles, such as Joel Myerson, "Additions to Bronson Alcott's Bibliography: Letters and 'Orphic Sayings' in the *Plain Speaker*," and Fordyce R. Bennett, "Alcott's Earliest Writings on Education." Only small portions of Alcott's manuscripts on childhood have been published. Cameron, *Emerson the Essayist*, contains parts of "Psyche," and Robert D. Richardson, Jr., includes a segment of "Psyche an Evangele" in *Myth and Literature in the American Renaissance*.

BIOGRAPHY

There are four major biographies of Alcott. The first, *A. Bronson Alcott: His Life and Philosophy*, is a memoir written by two of his closest friends and colleagues, F. B. Sanborn and William T. Harris. Though it is best treated as a primary source for sympathetic contemporary opinion rather than as a scholarly and critical study, it is thoroughly grounded in the manuscripts and in personal knowledge of Alcott and his contemporaries. Honoré Willsie Morrow, *The Father of Little Women*, is sentimental and lacking in scholarly restraint but is nevertheless a valiant effort to free Alcott's reputation from the grip of early twentieth-century literary scholars who had written him off as a useless visionary. Odell Shepard, *Pedlar's Progress*, long considered by scholars to be the standard biography, provides a solid description of events and a scholarly analysis of the early phases of Alcott's career. But the book is not documented, except for a brief bibliographical essay; the explanation of Alcott's intellectual evolution is weak and sketchy; and the discussion of his career after 1860 is far too brief. Shepard gives only brief glimpses of Alcott's latter-day religious transformation, his experiences with the St. Louis Hegelians, and his work in the Concord School of Philosophy. Frederick C. Dahlstrand's recent *Amos Bronson Alcott* strives to correct Shepard's deficiencies with full documentation based on a thorough study of the manuscripts and recent scholarship. Dahlstrand gives far greater attention to Alcott's later career than does Shepard and analyzes more completely the structure and the development of Alcott's thought. Madelon Bedell, *The Alcotts*, is rich in carefully researched biographical detail, but, because its focus is the Alcott family, it deals only in a general way with Bronson Alcott's ideas.

There are many shorter works that contain important biographical information. *Alcott Memoirs* is the personal recollection of Frederick L. H. Willis, who lived with the Alcotts as a young boy in the 1840s. Thomas Wentworth Higginson, a host of Alcott's conversations and an associate in the antislavery crusade, provides an illuminating glimpse of Alcott in *Contemporaries* and *Carlyle's Laugh and Other Surprises*. Ednah D. Cheney writes sympathetic yet dependable sketches of her longtime friend in *Reminiscences* and *Louisa May Alcott*. Emerson's only published critique of Alcott is in the *New American Cyclopædia*, and, though short, it is valuable, as is George Willis Cooke's sketch in *An Historical and Biographical Introduction to Accompany the* Dial. Among the more recent brief studies, the most important is Hubert Hoeltje's *Sheltering Tree*. Hoeltje maintains that Alcott, though a lesser figure than Emerson to be sure, was the one man who effectively could draw out Emerson's thought and creativity, thus making their friendship the most fruitful in American literary history. Alcott's role in the Transcendental Club and in the publication of the *Dial* is outlined in Joel Myerson, *The New England Transcendentalists and the* Dial, which gives additional insights into Alcott's relationship with Emerson and other Transcendentalists.

CRITICISM

GENERAL ESTIMATES

There has been an ongoing debate over the significance of Alcott as a literary and historical figure and over the merits of his character, a controversy detailed in Carol McIntyre Gay, "Bronson Alcott and 'His Little Critics.' " Nearly all of Alcott's contemporaries praised him as a person of the highest integrity and ideals, though a little short on common sense. They acknowledged his deficiencies as a writer and deplored his failure to support his family adequately, but they lauded him as a person of inspiration and insight whose creative brilliance, and hence his significance, lay in his unpreserved conversations and the example of his life. Octavius Brooks Frothingham (*Transcendentalism in New England*) portrays Alcott as the "mystic," who, though lacking in literary ability and versatility, had an uncompromising commitment to spiritual philosophy and intuitionism that made him, even more than Emerson, the central figure in the development of Transcendentalism in the 1830s. Nevertheless, historians and literary scholars of the early twentieth century, lacking concrete evidence of Alcott's ability or influence, either ignored him altogether or gave him short shrift. Barrett Wendell (*A Literary History of America*), Harold Clarke Goddard (*Cambridge History of American Literature*), and Russell Blankenship (*American Literature as an Expression of the National Mind*) all regard Alcott as an impractical visionary of little consequence other than as an example of the peculiar extremes to which Transcendentalism could lead. Thomas Beer, in a review of the Morrow biography, describes Alcott as a deluded and ineffective bore who offered nothing to modern thought or literature.

This trend was reversed in the early 1930s by the work of Van Wyck Brooks and Austin Warren. Brooks, in several works (*Emerson and Others*, *The Life of Emerson*, and *The Flowering of New England*), portrays Alcott as an important intellectual force who deserved more than notoriety about family irresponsibility. And Warren, in articles written in 1929 and 1931 ("The Concord School of Philosophy" and "The Orphic Sage"), praises Alcott as a representative Transcendentalist and respectable philosopher who taught Platonic and Neo-Platonic doctrines with perception and insight. Warren's conclusions were reaffirmed by Shepard's biography and the publication of Alcott's *Journals*, both of which stimulated a new interest in and awareness of Alcott materials. Thus came efforts to evaluate him in a more sophisticated way.

Frederic Ives Carpenter, "Bronson Alcott: Genteel Transcendentalist," recognizes Alcott's intellectual conflicts between radicalism and conservatism, between individualism and community solidarity, and between protestantism and orthodoxy, and he concludes that Alcott's impractical gentility made him unable to reconcile these opposites. Challenging Carpenter, David P. Edgell maintains, in "Bronson Alcott's 'Gentility,'" that Alcott effectively balanced a concern for tradition with a radical critique of society and that he offered far more practical means for realizing transcendental ideals than his more famous contemporaries, Emerson and Thoreau. Alcott's reputation was further enhanced by two lengthy studies of his educational work—George Haefner, *A Critical Estimate of the Educational Theories and Practices of A. Bronson Alcott*, and Dorothy McCuskey, *Bronson Alcott, Teacher*—which describe his contribution to American pedagogical thought.

As a result of this scholarship, more recent general literary surveys, such as *Literary History of the United States*, ed. Robert E. Spiller et al., give Alcott a far more serious treatment; and general histories of American philosophy, such as *Philosophy in America* by Paul Russell Anderson and Max Harold Fisch and *A History of American Philosophy* by Herbert W. Schneider, at least recognize Alcott's role in American thought. Indeed, Elizabeth Flower and Murray G. Murphey give him a lengthy analysis in *A History of Philosophy in America*. Recent studies of American Transcendentalism are also far more careful than their predecessors to examine the uniqueness and the complexity of Alcott's ideas. Paul F. Boller, Jr., *American Transcendentalism 1830–1860*, points to Alcott's peculiar view, held by no other Transcendentalist, that nature is a projection of human beings and notes his singular vision of Transcendentalist reform that set him apart from his contemporaries. Donald N. Koster's brief *Transcendentalism in America* describes Alcott as the quintessential Transcendentalist.

PHASES OF ALCOTT'S CAREER

As early as 1903, Annie Russell Marble tried to revive Alcott's reputation by describing him as an "American Pestalozzi" whose educational theories and reforms were slowly penetrating twentieth-century classrooms. Shepard and McCuskey reiterated this thesis, as have more recent scholars, such as Edmund G. Berry, Marjorie Stiem, and Rüdiger Schlicht, all of whom portray Alcott as a visionary who remodeled ordinary methods of instruction into "Progressive" patterns and thus became a forerunner of modern educational psychology. Not all writers have been so generous, however. Haefner blames Alcott's faulty philosophical idealism for his unsystematic, incomplete, and hence ineffective educational techniques. John B. Wilson believes that Alcott's mysticism had deleterious effects on his teaching ("Bronson Alcott, Platonist or Pestalozzian"). And Thomas P. Pietras charges that although Alcott's Transcendentalism glorified the goodness of human nature and the importance of intuitional, self-inspired acquisition of knowledge, his classroom practice involved guiding, directing, and even dictating the process of learning. However critical, these authors all recognize

Alcott's contributions to educational theory as further evidence of the richness of Transcendentalism.

Scholars have also analyzed Alcott's theories of child rearing as applied to his educational practices and to his transcendental philosophy. Sherman Paul, in "Alcott's Search for the Child," notes that Alcott saw the child as a symbol of the spiritual nature of human beings, a medium of spiritual revelation, and thus the key to the regeneration of society. According to Barbara Garlitz, Alcott's celebration of childhood was part of a trend in nineteenth-century Western thought ("The Immortality Ode: Its Cultural Progeny"). Charles Strickland, "A Transcendentalist Father," is the best study of Alcott's child-rearing theories. Strickland concludes that Alcott's work marked the beginning of child psychology in America, though it was a psychology wrapped in grandiose expectations about the possibilities of human regeneration. Such perfectionism placed enormous burdens on Alcott's family and thus may have had a damaging impact on Louisa, who, according to Martha Saxton (*Louisa May*), spent a lifetime desperately trying to please her demanding father.

Alcott's other reform efforts, especially the Fruitlands experiment, have also attracted much scholarly attention. Emerson, "English Reformers," and F. B. Sanborn, *Bronson Alcott at Alcott House, England, and Fruitlands, New England*, are descriptions by sympathetic yet skeptical friends. William A. Hinds, editor of the Oneida community's *American Socialist* and an Alcott correspondent, lauded Fruitlands as a sincere effort to found a new and glorious order of society. Hinds's enthusiasm was later reaffirmed by Clara Endicott Sears, who in her uncritical *Bronson Alcott's Fruitlands* praises Fruitlands as a noble experiment. Shepard's biography provides the first full analysis of Fruitlands but fails to explain satisfactorily its significance for Alcott's intellectual development or its overall historical importance. Captured by the mood of Louisa's fanciful "Transcendental Wild Oats" and Sanborn's account, Shepard blames the failure of Fruitlands on Charles Lane. He ignores Alcott's own unbending and tyrannical attitudes, which Taylor Stoehr describes in "Transcendental Attitudes toward Communitism and Individualism." Far less sympathetic is V. F. Calverton, who, in *Where Angels Dared to Tread*, describes Fruitlands as a quaint experiment doomed to failure by its fanaticism, tyrannical asceticism, and ideological confusion. Such doctrinal vagueness made Fruitlands ineffective and thus unimportant in the broad scheme of nineteenth-century reform, according to Alice Felt Tyler (*Freedom's Ferment*). David Palmer Edgell, "The New Eden," counters Calverton and Tyler by praising Fruitlands as an important and necessary effort to put Transcendentalist idealism into practice, one that failed largely because of the contradiction between Alcott's idealistic individualism and the fuzzy-minded associationism of his English friends. The importance of impractical asceticism both as a definition of Fruitlands and as an explanation of its failure are themes of John B. Wilson, "Pythagoras Crosses the Merrimack," and Aurele P. Durocher, "The Story of Fruitlands." The most thoughtful and carefully researched article on Fruitlands is Richard Francis, "Circumstances and Salvation," which focuses on the philosophical question of the connection between the spiritual world and the physical environment with which both

Alcott and Lane struggled. Dahlstrand's biography builds on Francis' analysis but takes issue with some of its key points, particularly the reasons for failure.

Other aspects of Alcott's career as a reformer have received scant attention aside from the biographies. John C. Broderick describes Alcott's civil disobedience in "Thoreau, Alcott and the Poll Tax." Taylor Stoehr analyzes Alcottian and Transcendentalist theories of reform in "Eloquence Needs No Constable." Lewis Perry discusses Alcott as a nonresistant in *Radical Abolitionism* and as an abolitionist in " 'We Have Had Conversation in the World.' " But there is still no full study of Alcott's role in the general stream of nineteenth-century reform, just as there is no satisfactory analysis of the relationship between Transcendentalism and reform in America.

Another important but neglected facet of Alcott's career is his work as an itinerant conversationalist and cultural messenger to the West. Contemporary descriptions of Alcott the conversationalist are largely anecdotal and often inaccurate, filled with sneering and uncritical condemnation, as in John Townsend Trowbridge, *My Own Story*, and Fredrika Bremer, *The Homes of the New World*. The best contemporary description, sympathetic yet critical, is Ednah D. Cheney, "Reminiscences of Mr. Alcott's Conversations." When interest in Alcott increased in the 1930s and 1940s, greater note was taken of Alcott's conversations and his western travels. Hubert H. Hoeltje describes Alcott's Iowa visits of the 1870s, and Clarence Gohdes, noting Alcott's success as a historian of Transcendentalism, reprints a transcript of Alcott's 1863 conversations on the Transcendental Club and the *Dial*. Brief descriptions of other western tours are provided by David Mead, C. Carroll Hollis, George L. Collie and Robert K. Richardson, and Louis A. Hasselmayer. But far more significant than these largely descriptive works is a recent recognition of the intellectual importance of Alcott's conversational tours. Alcott's relations with the St. Louis Hegelians in the 1860s and 1870s are analyzed by Henry A. Pochmann in "Plato and Hegel Contend for the West," which points out not only the idealistic harmony between Transcendentalism and Hegelianism but also the clash between Alcott's intuitionism and the Hegelian commitment to hard logic. Paul Russell Anderson (*Platonism in the Midwest*) and George Mills Harper ("Toward the Holy Land" and "Thomas Taylor in America") analyze Alcott's relationship with the midwestern Plato clubs of the 1870s; and Fordyce Richard Bennett ("Bronson Alcott and Free Religion") discusses a phase of Alcott's career largely ignored by other scholars. None of these works, however, fully evaluates the cultural and intellectual meaning of Alcott's tours. Conversation as a unique Transcendentalist art form was totally ignored until the publication of Lawrence Buell's excellent *Literary Transcendentalism*. Buell recognizes Alcott's legitimacy as an artist in a way that no previous critic has done by acknowledging conversation as the best realization of the Transcendentalist idea of the proper relation between art and life.

There is still no full history of the Concord School of Philosophy, even though it is essential to an understanding of the full meaning of Transcendentalism in American life. Contemporary anecdotal descriptions by participants and observers are plentiful, but only James McCosh's 1882 article in the *Princeton Review* provides useful critical analysis. There have been only a few recent treatments of the school. Austin Warren's

"The Concord School of Philosophy," is largely descriptive, and Kurt F. Leidecker's "Amos Bronson Alcott and the Concord School of Philosophy" is a preliminary study demanding further analysis. Dahlstrand's biography discusses the School in detail and attempts to establish its historical significance (along with that of Alcott's western tours) as a counterpoint to the evolutionary naturalism of the period. Teck-Young Kwon, in "A. Bronson Alcott's Literary Apprenticeship to Emerson: The Role of Harris's *Journal of Speculative Philosophy*," asserts the significance of Alcott's later career in the West and in the Concord School of Philosophy and agrees with Dahlstrand that Alcott's philosophical growth reflected important changes in American intellectual life generally.

SOURCE AND INFLUENCE STUDIES

Relatively little has been written about the sources of Alcott's thought. The best single work is Murray G. Murphey, "Amos Bronson Alcott: The Origin and Development of His Philosophy." Following Perry Miller's thesis about the ancestry of Transcendentalism ("From Edwards to Emerson"), Murphey traces Alcott's philosophy in part to Edwardsean Calvinism. Murphey's analysis is more thorough and satisfying than that of Shepard; and Dahlstrand, although he disagrees in part with Murphey, incorporates many of Murphey's insights into the 1982 biography along with additional comments about the socioeconomic context in which Alcott worked.

Other works treat the sources of Alcott's thought in only a fragmentary way. Arthur Christy (*The Orient in American Transcendentalism*) portrays Alcott as a great propagandist on behalf of the Orient but acknowledges that he was influenced by Eastern civilizations only after the broad contours of his thought had been formed. Carl T. Jackson (*The Oriental Religions and American Thought*) points out that Alcott's interest in Oriental thought, though often enthusiastic, was belated and tangential. René Wellek, in "The Minor Transcendentalists and German Philosophy," mistakenly concludes that Alcott neglected the greats in German thought and turned instead to lesser figures such as Boehme and Oken. Such neglect was true of Alcott's later years but not of his formative period. Of works with a narrower focus, the best are Barbara Garlitz, "The Immortality Ode," which analyzes the effect of Wordsworth's poem on Alcott's theories of childhood, and Barbara H. Carson, "Orpheus in New England," which discusses the ancient myth of Orpheus as transcendental imagery.

STUDIES IN STYLE AND GENRE

Even rarer than source studies are good analyses of Alcott's literary style, undoubtedly because of the common prejudice against Alcott as a writer. Ironically, "Orphic Sayings," which provoked more ridicule than any other of his works, has received the most critical attention as an attempt by Alcott to find a unique and personal mode of expression. The "Sayings" are included (with introductory comments) in all the major anthologies as well as in Randel's edition. Joel Myerson discusses contemporary reactions to the "Sayings" in " 'In the Transcendental Emporium.' " Alcott's poetry has received some cautious praise, but the only lengthy study of it, Elsie Furbush Brickett, "Studies in the Poets and Poetry of New England Transcendentalism," admits that Alcott's weaknesses as a writer make a psychological approach to his poetry more worthwhile than a literary one. Although Alcott's other works have largely been ignored by literary critics, recent scholars have seen significance and even merit in his use of imagery, especially of birth and growth, in the development of a unique transcendental symbolism (see Catherine Albanese, "The Kinetic Revolution"). Robert Richardson, Jr., in *Myth and Literature in the American Renaissance*, assigns Alcott a key role as a mythmaker though his pallid writing style and lack of concrete imagery made him relatively ineffective in conveying myths. And Lawrence Buell's analysis (*Literary Transcendentalism*) provides a new perspective on Alcott as a creative artist by treating seriously his use of conversation as a medium of expression. The works of Albanese, Richardson, and Buell, as well as the Dahlstrand biography, are evidence of the recent trend to treat Alcott as a serious intellect and literary figure rather than as a lightweight to whom Emerson and Thoreau inexplicably gave undue regard.

CYRUS AUGUSTUS BARTOL

William G. Heath

BIBLIOGRAPHIES

A prolific writer, Cyrus Bartol wrote ten books and numerous sermons, addresses, and journal articles. The most complete and accurate primary listing is by William G. Heath in his edition of selected Bartol writings, *On Spirit and Personality*. This list, which supersedes Heath's earlier bibliography in "Cyrus Bartol, Transcendentalist," contains approximately two hundred items, almost all of which are published works. The Heath listing also supersedes those by Charles G. Ames and Theresa Layton Hall. The Hall bibliography records five minor items omitted by Heath, but it is not comprehensive—only sixty titles are included—and some titles and dates are inaccurate. An additional six items not mentioned by Heath are included in the brief listing (19 items) in *Literary Writings in America*.

There is no definitive secondary bibliography. Numerous secondary items are, however, cited in Heath's dissertation. The lone Bartol entry in *AAL* is discussed in this chapter.

MANUSCRIPTS

The largest collection of Bartol's manuscripts is in the Library of Congress. The Hawthorne-Longfellow Library at Bowdoin College possesses a book of newspaper clippings covering the final three years of Bartol's ministry. The Massachusetts Historical Society has in its possession Bartol's "Memorandum Books, 1834–1848" in three volumes, which cover his activities and sermon topics over a fifteen-year period, as well as his extensive, fifty-year correspondence with Henry W. Bellows (in the Bellows Collection). The Houghton Library of Harvard University and the Boston Public Library possess additional Bartol letters. Bartol is not included in *ALM*.

EDITIONS

All Bartol's books are out of print, with the exception of a facsimile reprint by Arno Press of *Discourses on the Christian Spirit and Life* (1850), a collection of his early sermons. Since Bartol's flowering as a Transcendentalist and religious freethinker did not occur until the 1860s, it is his later writings that better represent his ideas and prose style. These writings deserve to be better known. Some of these are compiled in Heath's *On Spirit and Personality* (1977), which includes two review essays, a sermon, two addresses, and five essays from Bartol's last three books—*Radical Problems* (1872), *The Rising Faith* (1874), and *Principles and Portraits* (1880)—along with an introduction and notes. These selections are all relevant to Bartol's overriding theme, the Church of the Spirit, and to his belief in Personalism.

Kenneth Walter Cameron has reprinted two of Bartol's addresses to the Concord School of Philosophy—"Emerson's Religion" and "Goethe and Schiller"—in *Concord Harvest*. They first appeared in collections edited by F. B. Sanborn: *The Genius and Character of Emerson* and *The Life and Genius of Goethe*.

BIOGRAPHY

Published biographical material about Bartol is slight. Standard and reliable are Charles G. Ames's chapter on Bartol in *Heralds of a Liberal Faith*, and Samuel A. Eliot's article in the *DAB*. Also useful is an anonymous article in the *Harvard Graduate Magazine* (1901), and much valuable information can be found in *The West Church, Boston, Commemorative Services* (1887), published in observance of the fiftieth anniversary of Bartol's ministry. Two somewhat anecdotal profiles of Bartol published during his last years reveal something of the private, domestic side of the man (*BHJ*, Oct. 1895; *TH*, 13 May 1899). Finally, Bartol's own writings are filled with autobiographical references and constitute perhaps the best source of information about his life. Important unpublished biographical materials are included in the Bellows Collection at the Massachusetts Historical Society, as well as in Heath's dissertation.

CRITICISM

No book-length critical study of Bartol has been published. Heath's dissertation, however, provides a general introduction to Bartol's life and writings, with emphasis on his development as a Transcendentalist and on his religious ideas. Here and in his introduction to *On Spirit and Personality*, Heath presents Bartol as a Transcendentalist whose criticism of the movement, and of Emerson in particular, arose out of his strong personal theism.

William R. Hutchison has described Bartol's efforts to propagate a religion of Spirit in "To Heaven in a Swing." Placing Bartol in the context of church history and reform, Hutchison argues effectively that Bartol was "a thoroughly representative figure in the nineteenth-century Unitarian movement." Bartol is also cited in Hutchison's *The Transcendentalist Ministers*.

Two early commentators on Bartol's Transcendentalism are Octavius Brooks Frothingham, *Transcendentalism in New England*, and George Willis Cooke, *An Historical and Biographical Introducion to Accompany the* Dial.

Bartol has also been discussed in the context of the various organizations and activities with which he was affiliated. Clarence L. F. Gohdes, *The Periodicals of American Transcendentalism*, and Stow Persons, *Free Religion*, touch on Bartol's connection with the Free Religious movement. His response to the Civil War is discussed by Robert Albrecht, first in "The New England Transcendentalists' Response to the Civil War" and later in an article on that subject. Austin Warren, "The Concord School of Philosophy," cites Bartol as one of those responsible for the Transcendentalist element in the School.

Two considerations of Bartol that stress his literary interests are Henry A. Pochmann, *German Culture in America*, and Lawrence Buell, *Literary Transcendentalism*.

An interesting sideline in Bartol's career was his success as a speculator in real estate. The details of his transactions, along with an interpretation of the religious incentives that lay behind them, is found in William G. Heath's "Cyrus Bartol's Transcendental Capitalism."

Enough material exists for some enterprising scholar to put together a modest "life" of Bartol that would remain a standard work for years to come. Such a book would fill a need and would expand our understanding of New England Transcendentalism. In addition, one hopes that Bartol might benefit from the current proliferation of reprints. Facsimile editions of his final books of essays, with up-to-date scholarly introductions, would be valuable additions to the literature of Transcendentalism.

CHARLES TIMOTHY BROOKS

Elizabeth R. McKinsey

BIBLIOGRAPHIES

Brooks's published books and some articles are listed in *BAL*. His translations from the German published in American journals are in Martin Henry Haertel, *German Literature in American Magazines 1846 to 1880*. Because Haertel's volume lists items by year and journal rather than by translator it is awkward to use, but Brooks's name recurs frequently. A more specialized listing appears in Fannie Mae Elliott and Lucy Clark, *Charles Timothy Brooks: A Checklist of Printed and Manuscript Works of Charles Timothy Brooks in the Library of the University of Virginia*. Brooks is not listed in *AAL*.

MANUSCRIPTS

Major Brooks manuscript holdings are to be found at the Andover-Harvard Theological Library, Brown University, Houghton Library of Harvard University, and University of Virginia. *ALM* lists other smaller holdings, and *NUC* includes references to many poems and hymns in manuscript.

EDITIONS

Brooks published three small volumes of original verse during his lifetime: *Aquidneck* (1848), *Songs of Field and Flood* (1853), and *Roman Rhymes* (1869). His *Poems*, ed. W. P. Andrews (1885), is the most complete collection available, although *Singers and Songs of the Liberal Faith*, ed. Alfred P. Putnam (1875), should also be consulted, for it includes a number of other poems and hymns. *The Poets of Transcendentalism*, ed. George Willis Cooke (1903), reprints two poems.

Several of Brooks's sermons were collected in *The Simplicity of Christ's Teachings* (1859), and *NUC* lists several others published separately. Also of religious interest is *William Ellery Channing: A Centennial Memory* (1880). His *Remarks on Europe, Relating to Education, Peace, and Labor* (1846) is not included in *BAL*.

Brooks's principal translations include Schiller's *William Tell* (1838); *Songs and Ballads: Translations from Uhland, Körner, Bürger, and Other German Lyric Poets* (1842); Schiller's *Homage of the Arts* (1847); *German Lyrics* (1853); Goethe's *Faust*, pt. 1 (1856); and Jean Paul Richter's *Titan* (1862) and *Hesperus* (1865). A previously unpublished translation appears in Guy Stern, "Blücher, Brooks, and August Kopisch."

BIOGRAPHY

The standard biographical sketch is Charles W. Wendte, "Memoir," in *Poems*. Those by George Willis Cooke (in *An Historical and Biographical Introduction to Accompany the* Dial), Augustus P. Reccord, and Harris Elwood Starr (*DAB*) all derive from Wendte. Joel Myerson's sketch in *The New England Transcendentalists and the* Dial concludes in the early 1840s but is useful for relations with other Transcendentalists. E. B. Willson, C. W. Wendte, R. S. Rantoul, and W. P. Andrews, *Brooks Memorial*, includes elegies read before the Essex Institute.

CRITICISM

A poet and lifelong Unitarian minister in Newport, Rhode Island, Brooks is generally characterized as a man of childlike purity, impracticality, humor, and deep propriety. His major contribution to the Transcendentalist movement was as a translator of German literature, and this is the only aspect of his work that has received critical attention. He is mentioned in Stanley M. Vogel, *German Literary Influences on the American Transcendentalists*, and treated more extensively in Henry A. Pochmann, *German Culture in America*. Pochmann gives Brooks credit as "the most assiduous translator of German literature ever to appear on the American scene," but his criticism of both Brooks's choice of literature and his success in translating it is unsparing. Most of Pochmann's judgments echo Camillo von Klenze in the most complete treatment of Brooks and the only monograph devoted specifically to him, *Charles Timothy Brooks: Translator from the German and the Genteel Tradition*. Focusing on the affinity between the German works Brooks chose to translate and the tenets of what became known as the Genteel Tradition, von Klenze emphasizes their common predilection for sentiment, "poetic feeling," high moral tone, patriotism, and love of liberty (which appealed to Brooks's abolitionism), and a shared uncertainty in literary standards.

He presents Brooks as typical of the "facile serenity" of his generation in a study not only of Brooks's translations but also of the taste of the age. Arthur Schoenfeldt, "Charles Timothy Brooks, Translator of German Literature," is an uncritical appreciation focusing on *Faust* and the later translations of lighter works.

WILLIAM ELLERY CHANNING II

Francis B. Dedmond

BIBLIOGRAPHIES

Ellery Channing's published works are described in *BAL* (vol. 2) and works on him are listed in *AAL*. *Literary Writings in America* lists Channing's published volumes and several contemporary reviews of the various works, but beyond that (especially on Channing's periodical publications) it is woefully inaccurate and incomplete. Most of Channing's pieces in the *Dial* (1840–44), for instance, are attributed to Dr. William Ellery Channing, and few of his later fugitive pieces are listed at all. A fully documented and complete report of the *Dial*'s contents is in Joel Myerson, "An Annotated List of Contributions to the Boston *Dial*." Frederick T. McGill, Jr., *Channing of Concord*, mentions a number of collections that contain unpublished Channing material and provides a bibliography of published sources. Robert N. Hudspeth's bibliography in *Ellery Channing* lists Channing's books in order of publication, locates important manuscript sources, and contains a useful, annotated, selective secondary bibliography. Several articles on Channing listed in *AAL* are not discussed in this chapter.

MANUSCRIPTS

The Channing manuscripts are scattered, and anyone using the checklist in *ALM* should be forewarned to expect the usual confusion that occurs when two literary figures have similar names. The most important collections are the Ellery Channing Papers in the Houghton Library of Harvard University and the Channing Family Papers in the Massachusetts Historical Society. The Concord Free Public Library has more than a hundred letters written to or by Channing, in addition to the manuscripts of his autobiographical fiction, his lectures, and some of his poems. More than sixty Channing letters to Marston Watson and Mary Watson are in the Hillside Collection of the Pilgrim Society at Plymouth, Massachusetts (see L. D. Geller, *Between Concord and Plymouth*). Other letters from Channing and references to Channing are found at the Houghton Library in the Fuller Family Papers, Tappan Family Papers, Ward Papers, and Ralph Waldo Emerson Memorial Association Papers.

EDITIONS

In his lifetime, Channing published two volumes of prose—*Conversations in Rome: Between an Artist, a Catholic, and a Critic* (1847) and *Thoreau: The Poet-Naturalist* (1873)—and seven volumes of verse. In 1967, Walter Harding (*The Collected Poems of William Ellery Channing the Younger*) published in facsimile the books of poems—*Poems* (1843), *Poems: Second Series* (1847), *The Woodman, and Other Poems* (1849), *Near Home* (1858), *The Wanderer: A Colloquial Poem* (1871), *Eliot* (1885), and *John Brown, and the Heroes of Harper's Ferry* (1886). Harding also included the poems that appeared in *Conversations in Rome*, most of the memorial poems in *Thoreau*, the posthumously published verses in *Poems of Sixty-Five Years*, ed. F. B. Sanborn (1902), and several uncollected pieces that were published in the *Dial, Present, New York Daily Tribune, Boston Commonwealth*, giftbooks, and anthologies. But despite his effort "to include in the volume every poem of Channing's that has reached print," Harding missed a number of pieces, especially those appearing in the *Journal of Speculative Philosophy* and the *Independent* in the 1870s and 1880s. Channing's prose has not been collected, and only his *Thoreau* has gone through more than one edition.

Channing burned most of the letters written to him, and he often admonished those to whom he wrote to do the same. Fortunately, many ignored his admonitions. Francis B. Dedmond is collecting Channing's correspondence for publication. He will print all extant unpublished letters and all previously published letters to and from Channing. The correspondence reveals, better than any other source, the capriciousness of Channing, the nature of his friendships, and his haunting loneliness.

BIOGRAPHY

The correspondence, notebooks, journals, and biographies of Ralph Waldo Emerson, Henry David Thoreau, Bronson Alcott, Margaret Fuller, Nathaniel Hawthorne, and Daniel Ricketson all contain significant biographical material about Channing. Before Frederick T. McGill's *Channing of Concord*, the fullest biographical treatments of Channing were by F. B. Sanborn: "Biographical Introduction" to *Poems of Sixty-Five Years*, "Ellery Channing and His Table-Talk," "Thoreau and Ellery Channing," and the sketch of Channing in Sanborn's *Recollections of Seventy Years*. By far the best review of Channing's life through the *Dial* period is in Joel Myerson, *The New England Transcendentalists and the* Dial.

McGill's biography is an excellent treatment of Channing up to the death of Ellen Fuller Channing (1856), but it does not deal adequately with the resurgence of Channing's creative energies in the 1870s and 1880s, which produced three more volumes of verse and a number of poems. McGill also overlooks Channing's enduring friendship with the Watsons of Plymouth, for which see L. D. Geller's essay "Ellery Channing and the Watsons" in *Between Concord and Plymouth*. McGill might also have made use of the material found in Channing's pieces of thinly disguised autobiographical fiction. Francis B. Dedmond has published one of these—"Channing's Unfinished Autobiographical Novel." Channing's full-length autobiographical novel, entitled "Leviticus" (Concord Free Public Library), is as yet unpublished.

CRITICISM

Robert N. Hudspeth's *Ellery Channing* is the only full-length critical study of Channing. Hudspeth draws on the same manuscript sources for biographical information as McGill does, but he closely examines Channing's writing, "both prose and poetry, to understand the assumptions behind it and to show the implications of what he wrote." Hudspeth's treatments of Channing's published volumes are brief but critically perceptive and valuable. Also interesting are those sections of the book that focus on Channing's relationships with the best known of his Concord contemporaries.

A number of individual studies deal with those relationships. Emerson himself copied out extracts from his manuscript journals that Thomas Wentworth Higginson, with the blessings of the Emerson children, published as "Walks with Ellery Channing." The walks took place between 1841 and 1864. Although the topic of friendship runs continuously through the journals of Emerson and Thoreau, Hudspeth ("A Perennial Springtime") observes that neither had a theory of friendship. Perhaps the most attractive fruit of Channing's friendship for Emerson was found in conversation and for Thoreau in his friend's saving him from destructive isolation. Paul O. Williams ("Emerson Guided") shows that Emerson's walks with Channing were dominated by Channing's keen eye for beauty.

In "Nemesis and Nathaniel Hawthorne," Oscar Cargill explores the results of a misunderstanding between Hawthorne and Channing. Following Margaret Fuller's drowning on 19 July 1850, while the family was still in mourning, Hawthorne wrote in *The Blithedale Romance* his "devastating" satire on Fuller, Channing's sister-in-law. Hawthorne, says Cargill, resented Fuller's (Zenobia's) influence over Sophia Hawthorne (Priscilla), but William Peirce Randel, in "Hawthorne, Channing and Margaret Fuller," shows that the evidence presented by Cargill is often unsound and that there is no substantial proof that Hawthorne hated Fuller or felt any need to attack Channing. Francis B. Dedmond edited Channing's lengthy satire "Major Leviticus: His Three Days in Town," which pokes fun at Alcott's abject poverty, Thoreau's eccentricity, and Channing's own envy of the Boston aristocracy.

There are some excellent general studies of Channing's poetry. F. B. Sanborn, in "The Maintenance of a Poet," points out that, despite the memorable scenes Channing sketched from nature, few contemporaries recognized "the poetic radiance of Channing's genius." Paul O. Williams, "The Transcendental Movement in American Poetry," sees Channing, Emerson, Thoreau, Jones Very, and Christopher Pearse Cranch as radical experimenters who wrote on topics dear to the hearts of the Transcendentalists: isolation, friendship, love, and living in accord with natural law. Robert N. Hudspeth, in "Ellery Channing's Paradoxical Muse," comments on Channing's devotion to poetry, his admiration of nature, and his stubborn self-reliance, all of which identify Channing with the mainstream of Transcendentalism. Lawrence Buell, in *Literary Transcendentalism*, describes Channing as a conscious artist whose verse grappled with the issues of Transcendentalism as eloquently as the best poetry of Emerson and Thoreau.

William M. Moss, " 'So Many Promising Youths,' " reminds us that Emerson discovered five younger New England poets—Very, Thoreau, Cranch, Charles King Newcomb, and Channing—all within a four-year period (1838–42). Following something of a pattern, Emerson's initial enthusiasm for each promising youth eventually gave way to disappointment. In an essay of joyous discovery, Emerson in 1840 introduced Channing to the readers of the *Dial* ("New Poetry"). So taken was he with Channing's poems—a dozen of which he published in his essay—that he advocated that a new department of poetry be established for them and others like them to be called *Verses of the Portfolio*. Such verse, though lacking finish, would chant private griefs, "since Art is the noblest consolation of calamity."

Emerson ("Mr. Channing's Poems") continued his paean of praise when Channing's *Poems* (1843) appeared. He declared that Channing's verse was poetry for poets, even if the "genuine" imagery—"the form which the thought clothed itself in, and which required some courage to adopt"—was, at times, a little whimsical or surprising. Margaret Fuller ("American Literature") voiced her regret that Channing was unknown: "Some of the purest tones of the lyre are his, the finest inspiration as to feelings and passions of men, deep spiritual insight, and an entire originality in the use of his means." William Henry Channing, "Poems of William Ellery Channing," chided his cousin for being out of touch with his countrymen, since his *Poems* contained no indication that he was active in any of the social and political causes of the day. But it was left to Edgar Allan Poe ("Our Amateur Poets. No. III.—William Ellery Channing") to deal Channing a critical blow from which he never recovered. Channing's *Poems*, Poe said, ascribe sublimity to everything odd and profundity to everything meaningless, with nine-tenths of the book being "utter and irredeemable nonsense." An interesting comment on the reasons for Poe's dislike of Channing—as well as the reasons for his dislike of Fuller, Alcott, and Brownson—is found in Ottavio M. Casale, "Poe on Transcendentalism."

The year 1847 was a banner one for poets. Emerson's *Poems* and Channing's *Poems: Second Series* were among the outpourings of "Nine New Poets" that Francis Bowen treated in a review essay. Bowen called Channing "a feeble and diluted copy of Emerson," finding him not so mystical and incoherent but far more childish and insipid than his master. Both of them, according to Bowen, had inverted the poetical decalogue and were intent on committing literary suicide. In the same year, *Graham's Magazine* reviewed Channing's *Conversations in Rome*. The reviewer discerned only one voice in the book, which uttered some acute observations on painting, sculpture, poetry, manners, religion, and government, but he found Channing's tone presumptuous and impertinent.

In a belated but lengthy review (*BoCom*, 14 Aug. 1863) of Channing's *Near Home*, the critic—most likely F. B. Sanborn—promised to protect the identity of the author, who had "never publicly acknowledged his work." Admitting that the content and meter were often inconsistent and incongruous and that Channing often "stammers, creeps, and mars," the critic nonetheless discerned in the poet a loftiness of aim that never forsook him.

It was Sanborn who edited Channing's *The Wanderer* and asked Emerson to write the preface. Emerson declared that the poems in *The Wanderer* were original records of the poet's moods, fancies, and observations, but he admitted that they lacked the "conventional ornaments" and "correct finish" expected of poetry. And it was probably Sanborn who induced George William Curtis ("Editor's Easy Chair," 1871) to announce to his readers that Channing was about to publish, at long last, another volume of poems. Sanborn himself reviewed "Mr. Channing's Wanderer" in the *Independent*. In all honesty, Sanborn had to admit that the rhythms were halting and imperfect, but he and Curtis still believed that Channing possessed a rare poetic gift.

The reception of *Thoreau: The Poet-Naturalist* was mixed. The reviewer in the *Monthly Religious Magazine* deemed Channing's book as original as Thoreau's mode of living, but he felt that the work was written for a small circle and would only prove valuable for them. The reviewer in the *Nation* dubbed that circle the "Orphic School," and accused Emerson of being an enervating influence on the likes of Channing, plunging "them hopelessly into the slavery of an imitation at once grotesque, laughable, and painful." Thoreau, with his intellectual arrogance, unsocial intolerance, defective sympathies, and mock philanthropies, was the most conceited of the school, while Channing, the reviewer noted, was the most willful. In his *Atlantic* review, Sanborn may well have been answering the attack in the *Nation*. The Concord School, he said, was comparable to the Lake School of Poets in England, and Emerson was its founder and the root from which Thoreau, Hawthorne, Alcott, and Channing sprang. No one, Sanborn wrote, knew Thoreau as intimately as Channing did, and if the book were a little more methodical and a good deal clearer in style, it would be of greater worth than any recent literary biography. The *British Quarterly Review*, in a long, rambling piece in which large chunks of the book were quoted, called it "half biography and half criticism."

In 1902, Sanborn brought out his revision of Channing's *Thoreau*. The *Nation* now maintained that Thoreau's growing reputation gave the book an "inherent quality." The reviewer asserted that the volume "is a treasure-trove for those who care much for Thoreau and his Concord friends" and that "nothing written about Thoreau comes so close to his life and mind as this delightful and exasperating incoherency." Edith Kellogg Dunton, in "An Old and New Estimate of Thoreau," wrote that Sanborn had restored *Thoreau* to its "true form," working from "a copy marked with Channing's revisions and annotations"—or so Sanborn had maintained in the preface. According to Dunton, the book was erratic, irregular, rambling, often obscure, and repetitious, but it presented Thoreau with a vividness, an intimacy, and a completeness "equalled only by a few master biographies." Also in 1902, Thomas Wentworth Higginson reviewed *Poems of Sixty-Five Years* for the *Nation* and predicted that readers would be surprised at the strength, beauty, grace, and keen sympathy with nature and the human heart found in "the poems of this last of the Transcendentalists."

Future scholarship may well be directed toward producing a definitive critical biography of Channing. A psychoanalytical study of this capricious and enigmatic malcontent, with his compelling need for female sympathy and consolation, would also be an intriguing contribution to Channing studies.

WILLIAM HENRY CHANNING

Elizabeth R. McKinsey

BIBLIOGRAPHIES

NUC lists a number of addresses and pamphlets published during Channing's lifetime. There is no secondary bibliography available: Channing is not listed in *AAL*.

MANUSCRIPTS

Major manuscript holdings are in the Houghton Library of Harvard University, Andover-Harvard Theological Library, Massachusetts Historical Society, Boston Public Library, Countway Library of Harvard University, Rochester (New York) Unitarian Church, and New-York Historical Society; see *ALM* and *The National Union Catalogue of Manuscript Collections* for details and for lesser holdings. The manuscripts used to prepare Octavius Brooks Frothingham's *Memoir of William Henry Channing* apparently have not survived.

EDITIONS

Channing's works have not been collected. His best-known book is his biography of his famous uncle, *Memoir of William Ellery Channing* (1848). He also edited the elder Channing's discourses on *The Perfect Life* (1873), included in Dr. Channing's *Works* (1886). In 1851 Channing published *The Memoir and Writings of James Handasyd Perkins*, his cousin. He collaborated with Ralph Waldo Emerson and James Freeman Clarke in editing a tribute to a close friend in *Memoirs of Margaret Fuller*

Ossoli (1852), which includes his "Participant's Definition" of Transcendentalism, excerpted by Perry Miller in *The American Transcendentalists*.

Channing's translation of Théodore Jouffrey's *Introduction to Ethics* (1840–41) appeared as vols. 8 and 9 in George Ripley's series of *Specimens of Foreign Standard Literature*.

Most of Channing's periodical contributions appeared in the *Western Messenger*, *Present*, and *Spirit of the Age*, all of which he helped to edit, as well as in the *Dial* and *Harbinger*. Perry Miller reprints Channing's manifesto as the new editor of the *Messenger* as "An Ideal of Humanity" in *The Transcendentalists*. Another essay of note is a review of "Emerson's *Phi Beta Kappa* Oration" (1838).

BIOGRAPHY

The only full-length biography is Octavius Brooks Frothingham, *Memoir of William Henry Channing*. Brief sketches include the elegy given by his close friend James Freeman Clarke and short biographies by George Willis Cooke (in *An Historical and Biographical Introduction to Accompany the* Dial), Thomas Wentworth Higginson (in *Heralds of a Liberal Faith*), and Walter Samuel Swisher. Joel Myerson's sketch in *The New England Transcendentalists and the* Dial covers Channing's life only into the 1840s and his contributions to the *Dial*, but it is particularly good on his relations with other Transcendentalists.

CRITICISM

Channing's social philosophy and activism have received more critical attention than his writings. David Robinson, "The Political Odyssey of William Henry Channing," presents him as the "representative man" of the communal and social pole of Transcendentalism, with Emerson and Henry David Thoreau at the opposite pole of radical individualism. Robinson emphasizes Channing's crisis of 1841 as his crystallizing moment of commitment to Associationism. Channing's involvement in Brook Farm was the high point of his career; after his Utopian optimism waned, he turned from communal projects to work within society for women's rights and antislavery organizations. Although Robinson concludes that there was "a certain tragedy" of unfulfilled promise in his career, the article is a largely positive reevaluation of Channing's force and importance. William R. Hutchison's categorization of Channing's career in *The Transcendentalist Ministers* focuses specifically on experiments in religious organization, in which Channing was one of the seven most influential ministers until 1850, when he assumed a "conventional" pastorate in Rochester, New York. Hutchison's summary of Channing's social ideas—so often mere "half-expressed meanings," in Channing's own words—is particularly helpful.

Two general histories provide some useful information on Channing. George

Willis Cooke, *Unitarianism in America*, places him in the larger denominational context, whereas Octavius Brooks Frothingham, *Transcendentalism in New England*, terms him a "minor prophet" and emphasizes his literary achievement. More recently, Ann Douglas, *The Feminization of American Culture*, uses Channing as one of thirty northeastern liberal ministers on whom she bases her study. Although she does not discuss him individually, she generalizes about his group's status anxiety, their alliance with a comparable group of women and with "female" reform movements, their literary bent, and their role in the general sentimentalization of American cultural life during the middle decades of the nineteenth century.

The only studies of individual works by Channing also grow out of the recent historiographical interest in women. Madeleine B. Stern, "William Henry Channing's Letters on 'Woman in Her Social Relations,'" examines background documents for his address to the Woman's Rights Convention in Worcester, Massachusetts, in 1851—a speech that was never published and is now lost. Bell Gale Chevigny examines Channing's role in editing Margaret Fuller's *Memoirs* in "The Long Arm of Censorship" and finds him the worst culprit among the editors in suppressing political, moral, and social implications of her life and thought that violated his sense of propriety or the traditional norms of femininity. Newell Dwight Hillis, *Right Living as a Fine Art: A Study of Channing's Symphony as an Outline of the Ideal Life and Character*, is not really a study but a rhapsody on Channing's short credo, written to Fuller, and quoted by Frothingham in his *Memoir*.

Channing's abortive attempt to establish a Unitarian ministry-at-large in New York is detailed in Walter Donald Kring, *Liberals among the Orthodox*. His somewhat more fruitful years in Cincinnati are documented in Frank R. Shivers, Jr., "A Western Chapter in the History of American Transcendentalism." This is useful on the community of New Englanders in the West, but it is distorted by a too sanguine interpretation of Channing's experience there as a completion of his "education in idealism." Shivers virtually ignores his 1841 crisis of faith, which Frothingham depicts as deep religious doubt, and instead implies that it and his return to the East merely marked a shift in his thinking toward greater social concern. Elizabeth R. McKinsey, on the other hand, acknowledges the severity of the crisis and traces it to a clash of his Transcendentalist ideals with the social reality of the West in *The Western Experiment*. According to McKinsey, Channing had to return to the "safer," more familiar fold in Boston to regain his balance, although his subsequent wanderings indicate that he never achieved complete harmony. David Robinson's reading of the crisis is more positive, stressing the union of religious and social thought that directed Channing's energies into social reform.

Clarence L. F. Gohdes, *The Periodicals of American Transcendentalism*, is essential for Channing's various journal contributions. For the *Western Messenger*, see also McKinsey; W. H. Venable, *Beginnings of Literary Culture in the Ohio Valley*; Judith A. Green, "Religion, Life, and Literature in the *Western Messenger*," which analyzes all of Channing's contributions; and Robert David Habich, "The History and Achievement of the *Western Messenger*," which discusses Channing's roles as editor and contributor. For the *Dial*, see Cooke, *An Introduction*, and Joel Myerson. On the *Spirit of the Age*, see A. G. Thacher, Jr., "William Henry Channing and the *Spirit of the Age*." Channing's copy of the *Spirit of the Age*, with his marginalia, is at the Newberry Library.

Although Channing never formally joined Brook Farm, he played an important role there: see anecdotes in Lindsay Swift, *Brook Farm*, and Edith Roelker Curtis, *A Season in Utopia*. Richard Francis, "The Ideology of Brook Farm," considers Channing as second only to Albert Brisbane as a leader of American Fourierism and stresses the "moral dimension" he added. David Robinson also provides a helpful supplement on Fourierism. Charles Crowe, "Christian Socialism and the First Church of Humanity," focuses on Channing's Associationism as it grew out of Brook Farm and found expression in the Boston Religious Union of Associationists. It is the best source available on Channing's preaching and provides many details of the Union's services, creeds, and controversies.

Channing's activities in Washington, D.C., during the Civil War are emphasized in Walter Samuel Swisher's biographical sketch. George M. Fredrickson, *The Inner Civil War*, includes Channing as one of the "Prophets of Perfection" instrumental in founding the United States Sanitary Commission. Channing's final years in England have not been studied.

JAMES FREEMAN CLARKE

Leonard Neufeldt

BIBLIOGRAPHIES

Over the years there have been five attempts at compiling a comprehensive Clarke bibliography: Edward Everett Hale, in his edition of Clarke's *Autobiography, Diary and Correspondence*; Theresa Layton Hall, "A Bibliography of the New England Transcendentalist Movement"; Arthur S. Bolster, Jr., in his mammoth "The Life of James Freeman Clarke"; Joel Myerson, "James Freeman Clarke 1810–1888"; and Leonard Neufeldt, "James Freeman Clarke: Notes toward a Comprehensive Bibliography." Hale's list of primary works includes books, magazine articles, and a number of addresses, sermons, and articles in pamphlet form. Hall included fifteen books and pamphlets by Clarke omitted by Hale, but her list of secondary works overlooks many titles to 1929. Bolster attempted the first complete primary and secondary bibliography—an eighty-three-page inventory of manuscript collections, books, pamphlets, tracts, chapters in books, articles in periodicals, and secondary works. Myerson's checklist is considerably more complete than Bolster's record of first printings. Neufeldt surveys the known manuscripts (many of them still uncatalogued), identifies works by Clarke omitted in Bolster and Myerson, and furnishes an up-to-date list of secondary works. The present essay does not discuss a number of articles on Clarke listed in *AAL*.

MANUSCRIPTS

There is no reliable inventory of the enormous number of Clarke manuscripts scattered throughout the country. Many new documents have been deposited and some old collections have been broken up since Bolster completed his dissertation, so his information on manuscripts is now largely obsolete. Leonard Neufeldt briefly describes the major collections, the most important of which are at the Andover-Harvard Theological Library, Houghton Library of Harvard University, and Massachusetts Historical Society. *ALM* is silent on several major collections and inaccurate on most important holdings.

EDITIONS

Clarke's writings have not been collected partly because he was such a prolific writer. Those works most relevant to Transcendentalist studies are *Memoirs of Margaret Fuller Ossoli*, done with Ralph Waldo Emerson and William Henry Channing (1852); *Theodore Parker and His Theology* (1859); *A Look at the Life of Theodore Parker* (1860); "Memoir of Ralph Waldo Emerson, LL.D." (1885); *Autobiography, Diary and Correspondence* (1891); *The Letters of James Freeman Clarke to Margaret Fuller*, ed. John Wesley Thomas (1957); and Robert D. Habich, "James Freeman Clarke's 1833 Letter-journal for Margaret Fuller" (1981). Other significant titles include *Natural and Artificial Methods in Education* (1864), *Common-Sense in Religion* (1874), *Memorial and Biographical Sketches* (1878), and *Anti-Slavery Days* (1883). Unfortunately, many of Clarke's most revealing Transcendentalist pieces are scattered in various nineteenth-century periodicals or buried in manuscript collections. His verse appeared in four anthologies: *Selections from the Poetical Literature of the West*, ed. William D. Gallagher (1841); *The Poets and Poetry of America*, ed. Rufus W. Griswold (1842); *Singers and Songs of the Liberal Faith*, ed. Alfred P. Putnam (1875); and *The Poets of Transcendentalism*, ed. George Willis Cooke (1903).

BIOGRAPHY

Two full-length biographies have been published by John Wesley Thomas and Arthur S. Bolster, Jr. Thomas focuses on Clarke's intellectual development, particularly the influence of German literature, philosophy, and theology and his dissemination of German culture in America. Bolster's study, the preeminent scholarly work on Clarke to date, emphasizes his intellectual openness, catholicity of interests, dynamic religious views, "unshakeable optimism," diplomatic skills, and "middle-of-the-road" stance in ecclesiastical and social reform. This book is an abbreviated version of Bolster's doctoral dissertation, which contains significant biographical materials, annotations, and bibliographic information omitted in the book. A somewhat less satisfactory profile of Clarke as balanced man is Derek K. Colville, "James Freeman Clarke," which is useful especially for its commentary on Clarke's literary development and views. Essential to most of the substantial accounts of Clarke's life are his own words on the subject in *Autobiography, Diary and Correspondence*.

A myriad of brief biographical sketches appeared in the four decades following Clarke's death in 1888. Joseph Henry Allen, in *Sequel to "Our Liberal Movement,"* includes his recollection of a personal friendship with Clarke and notes his broad-church attitudes and interest in German culture. In *An Historical and Biographical Introduction to Accompany the* Dial, George Willis Cooke underscores that, although Clarke was strongly "influenced by the transcendental movement," he also "had more influence than any other person, except Emerson and Hedge, in shaping the Unitarianism of to-day." Cooke describes Clarke as a "reformer" who refused to be an "iconoclast" and who "approached all subjects from the poetical side." Clarke's daughter Lilian Freeman Clarke outlined the major events of his life in *Heralds of a Liberal Faith* and argued that he was most successful in the sermons, addresses, and literary writings of his later years. Francis G. Peabody, *Reminiscences of Present-Day Saints*, illuminates aspects of Clarke's personality through a chapter-length account of their personal friendship. A brief profile of Clarke by George F. Moore appears in *The Later Years of the Saturday Club 1870-1920*, ed. M. A. DeWolfe Howe.

Memorial literature from Clarke's congregation and admirers furnishes further information. Noteworthy are *Memorial of the Commemoration by the Church of the Disciples* (1860); *Church of the Disciples: Seventieth Birthday of James Freeman Clarke* (1880); the entire issue of *Christian Register* for 14 June 1888; the entire issue of *Our Best Words* for 15 July 1888; Andrew P. Peabody, "Memoir of James Freeman Clarke" (1889); Julia Ward Howe, "The Church of the Disciples" (1891); and *Treasures New and Old*, comp. Clara Bancroft Beasley (1910).

Other than the Thomas and Bolster books, there has been little biographical or historical scholarship on Clarke in recent years. Thomas published a slim article, "New Light on Margaret Fuller's Projected 'Life of Goethe,'" which describes Clarke as a disciple of Goethe ("more than a Prophet") who lent his forty-volume edition of Goethe so as to encourage her to write her projected biography. Derek Colville, "The Transcendental Friends: Clarke and Margaret Fuller," finds vicissitudes in their friendship by examining a few unpublished letters between them, all of which are collected in Thomas' edition of the Clarke-Fuller letters. Most substantial is Joel Myerson's chapter in his *The New England Transcendentalists and the* Dial, which surveys Clarke's early years and emphasizes his connection with the *Dial* in 1840-41.

Several biographical-historical studies on other subjects deal with Clarke tangentially: Margaret Fuller, *Summer on the Lakes*, a record of her travels in the Midwest in 1843 with Clarke and his sister; Samuel C. Clarke, *Records of Some of the Descendants of Thomas Clarke, Plymouth, 1623-1697* and *Records of Some of the Descendants of Richard Hull, New Haven, 1639-1662*; Octavius Brooks Frothingham, *Memoir of William Henry Channing*; Thomas Wentworth Higginson, *Margaret Fuller Ossoli*; George Batchelor, "Unitarianism: The Transcendental Period"; Edwin M. Bacon, *Literary Pilgrimages in New England*; Laura E. Richards and Maud Howe Elliott, *Julia Ward Howe, 1819-1910*; Randolph C. Randall, *James Hall*; Tilden G. Edelstein, *Strange Enthusiasm*; and Walter Donald Kring, *Henry Whitney Bellows*.

CRITICISM

SOURCES AND INFLUENCES

Although no general studies of Clarke have appeared, several scholars have examined Clarke's intellectual and literary development in terms of German influences. Within its biographical strictures, John Wesley Thomas, *James Freeman Clarke*, seeks to determine the extent to which Clarke "was influenced by the literature, philosophy, theology, and criticism of Germany, and to show how he, as editor, minister, and author, aided in the diffusion of German culture in America." Previously, Thomas had briefly assessed Clarke's efforts as a translator of German literature in "James Freeman Clarke as a Translator." In *German Literary Influences on the American Transcendentalists*, Stanley M. Vogel suggests that Clarke's interest in German literature and theology began at Harvard Divinity School but that his enthusiasm for German literature was awakened several years later by Margaret Fuller. Henry A. Pochmann, *German Culture in America*, offers a number of passing observations on Clarke as an enthusiast of German literature. Totally subsumed by the scholarship of recent decades is S. H. Goodnight's discussion of Clarke in *German Literature in American Magazines Prior to 1846* (1907).

SPECIAL AREAS OF INTEREST

The most thoroughly examined aspect of Clarke has been his western phase of Transcendentalism (1833–40), when he served as a Unitarian pastor and edited the *Western Messenger* in Louisville, Kentucky. In 1838, James H. Perkins, "The *Western Messenger*," alerted readers to Clarke's unique aims and accomplishments. The "remarkable career" of the *Western Messenger* is discussed by William H. Venable, *Beginnings of Literary Culture in the Ohio Valley*; Ralph Leslie Rusk, *The Literature of the Middle Western Frontier* (vol. 1); and Clarence L. F. Gohdes, "The *Western Messenger* and the *Dial*." Less pertinent studies are Frank R. Shivers, Jr., "A Western Chapter in the History of American Transcendentalism," and Louis L. Tucker, "The Semi-Colon Club of Cincinnati."

The most comprehensive examination of Clarke's Louisville phase is Charles E. Blackburn, "James Freeman Clarke: An Interpretation of the Western Years (1833–1840)," an illuminating study of Clarke as a preacher, a journalist, a literary artist, and especially as a disseminator of culture and Transcendentalist ideas. Some of Blackburn's findings were published in "Some New Light on the *Western Messenger*." Another important study is Elizabeth R. McKinsey, *The Western Experiment: New England Transcendentalists in the Ohio Valley*, which argues that Clarke's Transcendentalist idealism was too alien and genteel for the West and that his failure in the Ohio River Valley prefigured problems for Transcendentalism as a social movement.

There have been two recent and thorough studies of the *Western Messenger*. Judith A. Green, "Religion, Life, and Literature in the *Western Messenger*," spends ninety-three pages analyzing Clarke as a contributor and editor. Green's view of Clarke's role in the West—a broad-minded mainstream Unitarian, a promoter of the West, and a cautious editor with a balanced editorial policy—challenges some of McKinsey's conclusions. Robert David Habich, "The History and Achievement of the *Western Messenger*," traces the developing radicalism that alienated readers and led to the failure of the *Western Messenger*.

General theological and philosophical studies that touch on Clarke include Octavius Brooks Frothingham, *Transcendentalism in New England*; George Willis Cooke, *Unitarianism in America*; William R. Hutchison, *The Transcendentalist Ministers*; Paul F. Boller, Jr., *American Transcendentalism*; *A Stream of Light*, ed. Conrad Wright; and Catherine L. Albanese, *Corresponding Motion*. Frothingham credits Clarke with a "catholic mind," and Cooke identifies Clarke's views and activities as typical of a progressive Unitarian minister. Hutchison comments on Clarke's "Comprehensive Church" of the future—a universal, liberal, dynamically reforming body based on Transcendentalist principles. Boller weaves Clarke's religious and philosophical views into the fabric of Transcendentalism as a whole, whereas Wright channels Clarke's Transcendentalism into traditional Unitarian concerns. Albanese reminds one of Alfred North Whitehead when she focuses on Clarke's use of kinetic metaphors to define God, man, perception, and theological formulation as dynamic process.

Several other studies deserve mention here. In *A Review of a Lecture by Jas. Freeman Clarke on the Philosophy of Ralph Waldo Emerson*, Lizzie Doten castigated Clarke for his genteel ecclesiastical caveats concerning Emerson. (Clarke's later memoir of Emerson was more in keeping with the view Doten endorsed.) In Caroline H. Dall, *Margaret and Her Friends*, Clarke figures as a major and self-revealing participant in Fuller's "conversations." Robert C. Albrecht compares Clarke with other Transcendentalist ministers in "The Theological Response of Transcendentalists to the Civil War." In a cursory and less than accurate essay, Bell Gale Chevigny misses an important opportunity to explain the roles of Clarke, Emerson, and Channing in preparing their joint *Memoirs* of Fuller ("The Long Arm of Censorship: Mythmaking in Margaret Fuller's Time and Our Own"). Douglas C. Stange compares Clarke's theological assumptions and abolitionist activities to fellow Unitarian ministers in *Patterns of Antislavery among American Unitarians, 1831–1860*. Elsie Furbush Brickett makes a slight contribution to the study of Clarke as literary artist in "Studies in the Poets and Poetry of New England Transcendentalism." John B. Wilson, "Elizabeth Peabody and Other Transcendentalists on History and Historians," argues that, as a historian, Peabody was superior to Clarke. Finally, Kenneth Walter Cameron, in *Transcendental Reading Patterns*, lists over two thousand entries for library charges credited to Clarke. The absence of scholarship on Clarke as a literary artist and theorist is mute evidence of the principal need in the field.

MONCURE DANIEL CONWAY

Robert E. Burkholder

BIBLIOGRAPHIES

Although much of Conway's enormous body of work has been forgotten, there are several adequate primary bibliographies that at least provide a starting place for scholars. The best of these is Helen Gallaher, "Moncure Daniel Conway Author and Preacher." This work of only sixty-seven pages is most valuable for its lists of "Books by Conway," featuring brief annotations that explain the contents of each volume with, in many instances, annotated citations for reviews and an additional list of "Works Edited by Conway," including periodicals, also containing citations for reviews. Gallaher draws on the bibliography in Conway's *Addresses and Reprints 1850-1907*, in which more than seventy items written or edited by Conway are listed chronologically and, in most cases, briefly described. These basic sources are supplemented by the chronological "Selected Conway Bibliography" in Mary Elizabeth Burtis, *Moncure Conway 1832-1907*, which concentrates on books and pamphlets but also cites some reviews and provides limited information on Conway's periodical and newspaper publications.

Conway's work for newspapers and periodicals does pose some problems for the bibliographer. Because he began publishing at the age of fifteen and became increasingly prolific as time passed, many of his contributions remain unidentified. In her bibliography, Gallaher lists more than 280 newspaper and periodical contributions by Conway, annotated and arranged thematically, but she does not include later reprintings in books of newspaper and periodical contributions. A more complete catalog can be found in Ursula Wall Pitman, "Moncure Daniel Conway," which lists all known periodical publications by journal, as well as the newspapers to which Conway is known to have contributed.

There is no good bibliography of writings about Conway. Gallaher's list of secondary sources is valuable for its annotations, but it is woefully incomplete and outdated and must be used in conjunction with the more complete bibliography in Pitman's dissertation, to provide an adequate basis for research. Conway is also listed in both *AAL* and *Literary Writings in America*; however, because these sources contain spurious references and citations for inconsequential reviews, not all the items mentioned in them are discussed in this essay.

MANUSCRIPTS

The two major repositories for Conway's manuscripts are the Butler Library of Columbia University and the Boyd Lee Spahr Library of Dickinson College. The Columbia collection contains approximately five thousand items in more than thirty boxes, including letters of Conway and his family and letters to Conway (the list of correspondents runs into the hundreds); many manuscript sermons and addresses; miscellaneous material, including leases and contracts; a scrapbook with clippings of some of Conway's newspaper work; and notebooks and lists of sermons. The Dickinson collection, although not as extensive, is just as impressive, containing Conway's diaries, some letters to and from him, an extensive collection of his contributions to newspapers and periodicals, and a wealth of secondary material. Ursula Wall Pitman's dissertation provides a list of ancillary manuscript collections helpful in a study of Conway, as does *ALM*, which does not, however, list eight Conway letters at the Andover-Harvard Theological Library.

EDITIONS

There is no standard edition of Conway's writings. In fact, in the twentieth century, his reputation as a historian and biographer has rested almost completely on his book *The Life of Thomas Paine* (1892), which is still considered a standard biography. Of Conway's seventy-odd books and pamphlets, several are worthy of note: his two radical antislavery books, *The Rejected Stone* (1861) and *The Golden Hour* (1862); his two failed novels, *Pine and Palm* (1887) and *Prisons of Air* (1891); and the most important of his religious studies, *The Earthward Pilgrimage* (1870), an autobiographical allegory of his own religious development, *Demonology and Devil-Lore* (1879), *Solomon and Solomonic Literature* (1899), and *My Pilgrimage to the Wise Men of the East* (1906). Of particular interest are his literary biographies: *Thomas Carlyle* (1881), *Life of Nathaniel Hawthorne* (1890), *Emerson at Home and Abroad* (1882), which is still a valuable resource for studying Emerson's English connections, and the pamphlet, *Emerson and His Views of Nature* (1883). Only a few of Conway's pamphlets were reprinted in the memorial volume, *Addresses and Reprints 1850-1907* (1909), and his prodigious contributions to dozens of newspapers and periodicals, although important, remain unreprinted. His correspondence with the most important figures of his age exists only in manuscript or in scattered specialized studies. Some letters are printed in the *Autobiography Memories and Experiences of Moncure Daniel Conway* (1904), and six letters from him to Myron B. Benton can be found in *A Troutbeck Letter-Book (1861-1867)*, ed. George E. Woodberry.

BIOGRAPHY AND CRITICISM

All biographical study of Conway begins with a single source, his own *Autobiography*. This massive work is often rambling and uneven: the first volume is a sustained narrative but the second, written after the death of his wife in 1897, is a collection of anecdotes. Despite its defensiveness and inaccuracies, the *Autobiography* is still interesting today for its accounts of Conway's relationships with the great and near-great figures of his age. It is, above all, a marvelous exercise in name dropping. A slightly distilled version of Conway's life can be found in Mary Elizabeth Burtis, *Moncure Conway*, which is still the standard biography. Burtis' work is sympathetic to Conway and contains more discussion of his published work than any other single source.

Conway's most recent biographer is John d'Entremont, whose *Moncure Conway, 1832-1907* is the best brief biography. D'Entremont differs with Burtis over the emphasis that should be placed on certain influences and events in Conway's life. Specifically, he points out that the dual occupations of Conway's mother—house manager and homeopathic physician—might have inspired his later advocacy of women's rights and abolitionism. D'Entremont also stresses that Conway's liberal religious views may have grown out of his relation with the Hicksite Quakers at Sandy Spring, Maryland, and his appointment, at age twenty-two, to a Unitarian pulpit in Washington, D.C.

Most significantly, Burtis and d'Entremont ascribe different motives to the so-called Mason Affair. In early 1863, after a brief stint as editor of the antislavery weekly the *Boston Commonwealth*, Conway was asked to tour England to lecture on the justice of the Northern cause. On 10 June 1863, encouraged by Robert Browning, Conway drafted and sent a letter to John M. Mason, the Confederate envoy in England, proposing that if the South would free all its slaves, the abolitionists would drop their support of the war and work to have the Confederacy recognized as an independent nation. Before the end of June, Mason, who was fully aware that Conway had no authority to make such an offer, published this letter with other correspondence in the *London Times*. Conway was denounced by his fellow abolitionists and was briefly threatened with the charge of treason. Burtis presents a rather objective account of this incident, implying that Conway simply wanted to end the Civil War and abolish slavery even at the cost of the Union as did many abolitionists before the war. But d'Entremont suggests that Conway consciously or unconsciously committed this error in judgment to supply some rationale for remaining in exile in England, where he would soon be offered the pulpit of the liberal South Place Society and where he would be distanced from the prosecution of a war in which he did not believe. D'Entremont expands on this theory and others in his "Moncure Conway: The American Years."

Other biographical critiques of Conway generally fall into two categories: examinations of particular aspects of his life or general biographical sketches. Because Conway is an anomaly of sorts—a Southern abolitionist—his involvement in the antislavery movement has been the focus of several extended studies. Peter Walker's "Moncure Conway: Apostate Slave Master" attributes many of Conway's motives to an Oedipal relationship with his mother and father. Walker searches Conway's *Autobiography* and other sources, most notably the novel *Pine and Palm*, for the evidence that Conway was in many ways a "sacrificial rebel" to the religion and the slave system his father upheld. On the whole, this is a thought-provoking study and one of the few that attempts to explain all of Conway's multifarious activities.

Another fine source for the first thirty-five years of Conway's life is Ursula Wall Pitman's dissertation. Pitman expands her biographical account into areas passed over by others, notably Methodist and Quaker attitudes toward slavery, Conway's relationship with Ralph Waldo Emerson, Theodore Parker, and Henry David Thoreau, and his most active years in the antislavery movement. Here one can find details and references unavailable elsewhere, but Pitman's objectivity suffers in her attempt to portray Conway as "the conscience of Abolitionism." She glorifies the distinguished family that spawned him, and she naively explains away the Mason Affair by asserting that Conway, who was at the center of the abolitionist movement in the United States just months before, was unaware of his comrades' desire to fight the war to the end and save the Union.

Unlike Pitman, John Spencer Bassett, in "An Exile from the South," praises Conway's *Autobiography* for its portrait of "the great middle class of Southerners," where Bassett contends Conway's roots really were, and suggests that Conway was driven from Virginia because the society of the state opposed the pursuit of truth. Likewise, in his sketch of Conway's Southern years in *The South in American Literature 1607-1900*, Jay B. Hubbell claims that Conway was ostracized in Virginia for holding radical religious views that were "in a large measure those of the Revolutionary leaders of his native state." In "Moncure Daniel Conway: Radical Southern Intellectual," Richard Beale Davis attempts to "resurrect" Conway as a writer and historian particularly for Southern readers through a general discussion of his life and work.

Conway's involvement with Dickinson College is chronicled in several sources, including Edward N. Biddle's *Moncure Daniel Conway and Conway Hall*, which tells how Andrew Carnegie, whose acquaintance with Conway was slight, underwrote the construction of a building at Dickinson in Conway's name; it also supplies interesting details about the dedication ceremony that Conway attended in 1905. This information is expanded in Walter E. Beach, "The Hall and the Man: Conway," which also includes some anecdotes about Conway as a college student.

Conway's years as Unitarian minister in Washington, D.C., are discussed in Jennie W. Scudder, *A Century of Unitarianism in the National Capital, 1821-1921*, and in Laurence C. Staples, *Washington Unitarianism*.

Discussions of Conway's involvement with the Hegelians of Cincinnati while he was a minister there may be found in three works by Loyd D. Easton. "German Philosophy in Nineteenth-Century Cincinnati" discusses Conway's Hegelianism as it was manifested in his study of Strauss and his commemorative address, *David Friedrich Strauss* (1874). Easton's discussion of Conway in "Hegelianism in Nineteenth-Century Ohio" is much the same, but his "Religious Naturalism and Reform in the Thought of Moncure Conway" is much more informative.

Conway's London years, and particularly his association with and revitalization of South Place Chapel, are ably covered in Warren Sylvester Smith, *The London Heretics 1870-1914*. In a chapter entitled "Free-thought Congregations: South Place and Others," Smith gives a general biography of Conway that deals particularly well with two aspects of his religious development: the important influence of Roger Brooke and his settlement of Hicksite Quakers at Sandy Spring, Maryland, upon Conway when Conway was a circuit riding Methodist minister in 1851 and the evolution of Conway's theories of natural religion while he was minister at South Place. The information in this chapter can also be found in two articles by Smith, " 'The Imperceptible Arrows of Quakerism' " and "Moncure Daniel Conway at South Place Chapel," but Smith's book is important in placing Conway in the context of contemporary religious experimentalism. Another excellent source for the study of Conway's association with South Place is S. K. Ratcliffe, *The Story of South Place*, which is based primarily on the *Autobiography* but which does add some interesting details about Conway's ministry in England. A less sympathetic treatment of Conway's liberal ideas from a decidedly English point of view can be found in J. M. Davidson, *Eminent English Liberals in and out of Parliament*. Carl T. Jackson, "The Orient in Post-Bellum American Thought," examines Conway's religious ideas from a particularly American perspective. In his scrutiny of Samuel Johnson, James Freeman Clarke, and Conway, Jackson finds that Conway was the only "post-Transcendentalist" who actually tested his notions about the Far East by traveling there and facing its reality.

Conway was a noted critic and promoter of American literature in England, and it is surprising that more has not been done on this aspect of his career. Dennis Welland, in "Moncure Daniel Conway and Anglo-American Relations," summarizes the important role Conway played in establishing Emerson, Nathaniel Hawthorne, Mark Twain, and Walt Whitman in England. More information on the relationship between Conway and Whitman is available in J. V. Ridgely, "Whitman, Emerson and Friend," which includes discussions of Conway's meetings with Whitman, both in Brooklyn and in Washington, D.C., and his involvement with W. M. Rossetti's edition of Whitman's poems in England. Conway's relationship with Twain and the service he provided not only in selling *Tom Sawyer* to Andrew Chatto but also in writing a complimentary notice for the 24 June 1876 *Athenæum* is explained in Welland's *Mark Twain in England*. Literary politics is also the subject of Welland's "John Camden Hotten and Emerson's Uncollected Essays," which discusses Conway's part in a scheme to publish a volume of Emerson's fugitive essays from the *Dial* and *Atlantic* that eventually resulted in the English publication of *Letters and Social Aims* in 1876. Welland's scholarship is detailed and sound, and his portrait of Conway as a literary agent, dealing with high-powered manipulators like Hotten, shows a side of him rarely glimpsed in other studies. Olov M. Fryckstedt's "Howells and Conway in Venice" details Conway's visit with William Dean Howells in Venice shortly after the Mason Affair in July 1863. Much of the article deals with a dual publication by Howells and Conway, "Venice Come True," in the 28 August 1863 *Boston Commonwealth*; Conway's attempts to help Howells with the publication of his poetry; and their competition in trying to sell sketches of Venetian life to the *Atlantic*. In "Moncure D. Conway Looks at Edgar Poe—Through Dr. Griswold," Richard Beale Davis testifies to Conway's perspicacity as a literary critic, even as a young man, by printing a previously unpublished review by the eighteen-year-old Conway of *The Works of the Late Edgar Allan Poe*. Davis contends that Conway gave a better estimate of Poe as an artist than either James Russell Lowell or Rufus W. Griswold did.

Other general biographical studies that deserve some mention are Gayle T. Benton's "Moncure Daniel Conway of Stafford County," Richard Clements' "Moncure Daniel Conway," and Edwin C. Walker's *A Sketch in Appreciation of Moncure Daniel Conway*. An anonymous biographical sketch introduces *Addresses and Reprints 1850-1907*, and a special number of the *South Place Magazine* (1907) features a biographical sketch of Conway, statements of appreciation from thirteen of his English friends, and a discourse on Conway by J. M. Robertson.

Despite a promised biography of Conway by d'Entremont and a proposed study of Anglo-American literary relations by Dennis Welland that would feature Conway, there is still some significant work left to be done. Most notably, Conway's correspondence cries out to be published. Such an admittedly massive undertaking could provide a greater understanding of what Conway called his "earthward pilgrimage" and shed light on his relationships with the great figures of his age on both sides of the Atlantic. Additionally, work needs to be done on Conway as a literary critic, including identification of what he actually wrote. Welland has, to some extent, begun this task on the English side, but it is clear that a collection of Conway's articles on Transcendentalism alone would be a valuable resource.

CHRISTOPHER PEARSE CRANCH

David Robinson

BIBLIOGRAPHIES

The most comprehensive bibliography of Cranch's writings can be found in F. DeWolfe Miller's dissertation, "Christopher Pearse Cranch," which is especially valuable for its listing of Cranch's extensive contributions to periodicals. Publication of his books and contributions to gift books are recorded in *BAL* (vol. 2). Miller also offers an abbreviated bibliography of Cranch's books in *Christopher Pearse Cranch and His Caricatures of New England Transcendentalism*. David Robinson surveys "The Career and Reputation of Christopher Pearse Cranch"; this chapter revises and updates that essay.

Cranch's contributions to the *Dial* and the *Harbinger* can be found in works dealing with those periodicals. On the *Dial*, see Joel Myerson, "An Annotated List of Contributions to the Boston *Dial*" (which supplants George Willis Cooke, *An Historical and Biographical Introduction to Accompany the* Dial) and *The New England Transcendentalists and the* Dial. On the *Harbinger*, see Clarence L. F. Gohdes, *The Periodicals of American Transcendentalism*. All the articles on Cranch listed in *AAL* are discussed in this chapter.

MANUSCRIPTS

Cranch is included in *ALM*, where substantial holdings at Harvard University, the Boston Public Library, and the Massachusetts Historical Society are noted. In addition, the Andover-Harvard Theological Library has ten letters, and the University of Wyoming has a large collection of Cranch family papers and materials, including letters, drawings, sketches, and paintings by Cranch.

EDITIONS

Cranch published four volumes of verse in his lifetime: *Poems* (1844), *Satan: A Libretto* (1874), *The Bird and the Bell, with Other Poems* (1875), and *Ariel and Caliban with Other Poems* (1887). In addition, one earlier poem was published separately: *A Poem Delivered in the First Congregational Church in the Town of Quincy, May 25, 1840, the Two Hundredth Anniversary of the Incorporation of the Town* (1840). Portions of these writings are reprinted with an introduction in *Collected Poems of Christopher Pearse Cranch*, ed. Joseph M. DeFalco, although this collection is not comprehensive. Many poems published in periodicals are listed in the aforementioned bibliographies. In addition, "The Poetical Picnic" appears in Mary E. Sargent, *Sketches and Reminiscences of the Radical Club*; James E. Devlin edits and comments on a later poem; and, in his dissertation, Miller mentions thirty-six additional poems in manuscript that have "probably not been published."

Cranch's caricatures of Emerson, part of a collection of cartoons on the "New Philosophy," are his best-known works. They have been edited, with extensive and helpful commentary, by F. DeWolfe Miller in *Christopher Pearse Cranch and His Caricatures of New England Transcendentalism*. Three of the drawings that refer explicitly to passages in Emerson's *Nature* are reproduced in *Emerson's* Nature—*Origin, Growth, Meaning*, ed. Merton M. Sealts, Jr., and Alfred R. Ferguson.

Cranch also published two works of illustrated children's fiction: *The Last of the Huggermuggers, a Giant Story* (1856) and *Kobboltozo: A Sequel to the Last of the Huggermuggers* (1857). He later tried his hand at translating, publishing *The Aeneid of Virgil Translated into English Blank Verse* (1872).

A great many of Cranch's letters, as well as excerpts from an autobiography, are published in Leonora Cranch Scott, *The Life and Letters of Christopher Pearse Cranch* (1917), which is the primary source of information on him. K. Michael Olmert has edited a new text of one of Cranch's letters remarking on Emerson's Divinity School Address, and Joel Myerson has edited a previously unpublished letter from Cranch to John Sullivan Dwight, in which Cranch discusses his exclusion from the Unitarian pulpit because of his association with Emerson, Ripley, and other "corrupters of youth."

A good selection of Cranch's poems and his important early reviews of Emerson's addresses can be found in *The Transcendentalists: An Anthology*, ed. Perry Miller, and he is also included in *The Poets of Transcendentalism*, ed. George Willis Cooke. Cranch's prose, published primarily in the *Western Messenger*, *Dial*, *Harbinger*, *Dwight's Journal of Music*, and other periodicals, has not been collected or analyzed in any detail. His prose "Parables" for the *Western Messenger* carry distinct echoes of the New Testament and *The Pilgrim's Progress*, but they expound essentially Transcendentalist doctrine. The student of Cranch's prose should also consult his *Address Delivered before the Harvard Musical Association* (1845) and his memorial address on Robert Browning ("Personal Reminiscences," 1890).

BIOGRAPHY AND CRITICISM

Few if any of the Transcendentalists could claim either the variety of talents or the range of sensibility of Christopher Pearse Cranch. But to suggest, as we must, that he is important primarily as a literary personality is also to emphasize a certain lack of achievement that Cranch himself might have frankly but wistfully admitted. This survey will to some extent dull the edge of Perry Miller's charge that Cranch was "one of the most futile and wasted talents" among the Transcendentalists, but it will corroborate the sense of unfulfilled promise that many who knew Cranch or his works have felt.

CRANCH AS TRANSCENDENTALIST

Cranch assumed a place as one of the earliest exponents of Transcendentalism because of his association with the *Western Messenger*, the first periodical that could be labeled Transcendentalist. When he returned from the Ohio Valley to New England in 1839, he began to associate with Emerson and others in the Transcendentalist movement, contributing to the *Dial* from its first issue. Later, his close friendship with John Sullivan Dwight gave him a connection with Brook Farm and its journal, the *Harbinger*. Leonora Cranch Scott, *Life and Letters*, and F. DeWolfe Miller, *Christopher Pearse Cranch and His Caricatures of New England Transcendentalism*, are the best published sources of information, and there is more biographical detail in Miller's dissertation. There is a brief sketch in *The Library of Southern Literature*, ed. Edwin Anderson Alderman et al., and in more recent reference biographies by Frederick Coburn and Joel Myerson. Frank Preston Stearns (*Cambridge Sketches*) offers one of the most readable impressions of Cranch as a fascinating social figure.

In studies of the Transcendentalist movement, Cranch is usually given some mention. Octavius Brooks Frothingham, *Transcendentalism in New England*, notes his contributions to the *Dial* and the *Harbinger*. Harold Clarke Goddard, *Studies in New England Transcendentalism*, refers to Cranch as "one of the most picturesque figures of the period," and William R. Hutchison notes his "happy but relatively unproductive career as a painter and dilettante after leaving the ministry" (*The Transcendentalist Ministers*). Lawrence Buell, *Literary Transcendentalism*, sees Cranch, Dwight, and Ellery Channing as among those Transcendentalists whose temperaments were "closer to the purely artistic temperament than Emerson" and who were thus troubled by the demand for forceful prophecy that Emerson's aesthetics seemed to place on them. Cranch's German translations are discussed in Henry A. Pochmann's *German Culture in America* and in Stanley M. Vogel's *German Literary Influences on the American Transcendentalists*. Perry Miller's treatment of Cranch in *The Transcendentalists* is one of the most enlightening analyses of his career and his relation to the movement. Miller finds an early religious sensibility that attracted Cranch to Transcendentalism before it gave way to an "unabashed aestheticism." Lawrence Porter, "Transcendentalism," sees in Cranch a lack of clarity about Transcendentalist goals, and cites his satirical caricatures as evidence of his distance from the group.

Cranch's relationship with James Freeman Clarke and the *Western Messenger* is documented in Clarke's *Autobiography, Diary and Correspondence*. There is some discussion of the *Western Messenger* in W. H. Venable, *Beginnings of Literary Culture in the Ohio Valley*, and Ralph Leslie Rusk, *The Literature of the Middle Western Frontier*. Rusk singles out Cranch's poetical reference to Wordsworth ("To my Sister M., with Wordsworth's Poems," *WM*, 1838) as evidence of the growing presence of Romanticism in American literature. In *The Periodicals of American Transcendentalism*, Clarence Gohdes calls attention to Cranch's "Transcendentalism" and his early defense of Emerson's controversial addresses. More detailed information on Cranch's hand in editing the *Western Messenger* is contributed by Charles E. Blackburn. In her comprehensive study, "Religion, Life, and Literature in the *Western Messenger*," Judith A. Green discusses Cranch's role as editor and contributor and his merging of traditional Unitarianism, as he understood it, with Transcendentalism. Also useful is Robert David Habich, "The History and Achievement of the *Western Messenger*," which focuses on the editorial stance of the magazine in relation to the Transcendentalist controversy and includes information on the authorship of articles and biographical data on all the contributors.

The most thorough and suggestive study of the *Western Messenger* and those who founded and sustained it is Elizabeth R. McKinsey, *The Western Experiment*. This study treats not only the *Western Messenger* but also the larger attempt of several Unitarian ministers with decided Transcendentalist leanings—Clarke, Cranch, and William Henry Channing—to carry liberal religion to the Western frontier. McKinsey stresses the contrast between his graciously charming social presence and a private self that was tormented by feelings of isolation and a haunting fear of being unable to establish lasting relationships with others. Her analysis is thus a corrective to the temptation to regard Cranch's social reputation as evidence of superficiality in his dealings with others.

Further information on the "Western experiment" can be found in *The Memoir and Writings of James Handasyd Perkins*, ed. William Henry Channing, which recounts Perkins' life as one of the western missionaries; Frank R. Shivers, Jr., "A Western Chapter in the History of American Transcendentalism"; and Louis L. Tucker's account of "The Semi-Colon Club of Cincinnati."

After returning to New England from the West, Cranch found himself in the midst of a theological and social controversy centering on Emerson and his followers. His submission of poems to the *Dial* initiated a correspondence with Emerson, largely reprinted in Scott's biography. The full account of Cranch's relation to the *Dial* can be found in Joel Myerson, *The New England Transcendentalists and the* Dial. Myerson's study "The Contemporary Reception of the Boston *Dial*" notes reprints of several of Cranch's pieces in periodicals reviewing the *Dial*. Further information about the critical stance of the *Dial* can also be found in Donald F. Warders, " 'The Progress of the Hour and the Day.' " The most significant study of Cranch's personal dealings with Emerson is by Hazen C. Carpenter. Carpenter sketches the relationship from its beginnings to what he describes as a long barren period, in which Emerson's coolness toward Cranch was evident and the source of some pain for him. Carpenter's essay portrays Cranch as one more haunted by isolation than his reputation for social graces would suggest. William M. Moss puts Emerson's relations with Cranch into the larger context of his dealings with several other young poets who began in a promising fashion but who eventually disappointed Emerson in one way or another. For Cranch's view of Emerson, see his later essays, "Ralph Waldo Emerson" (1883) and "Emerson's Limitations as a Poet" (1892).

Cranch's other connection with Transcendentalism was his close friendship with John Sullivan Dwight and his resulting involvement with Brook Farm. His visits to Dwight, recorded in most histories of Brook Farm, established an image of Cranch as an "all-attractive entertainer," as Van Wyck Brooks described him in *The Flowering of New England*. Brooks and others derived this image partly from John Thomas Codman's *Brook Farm* (1894), which depicts Cranch as a musician (he always brought his flute when he visited Dwight) and notes that he delighted the children of the commune with his animal imitations. Much the same story is told in Katherine Burton, *Paradise Planters*, and Edith Roelker Curtis, *A Season in Utopia*. There is more detail on Cranch in Lindsay Swift, *Brook Farm*. Swift suggests that Cranch's versatility diluted his achievement, and thus he fosters the persistent argument that Cranch was a dilettante who never realized his full potential in any creative medium.

George William Curtis' graceful encomium in the "Editor's Easy Chair" (*Har*, April 1892) reflects the impression of a lifelong friend who first met Cranch at Brook Farm. For other glimpses of Cranch, see *Early Letters of George Wm. Curtis to John S. Dwight*, ed. George Willis Cooke.

CRANCH AS POET

Cranch won admirers for his poetry among his own circle of Transcendentalists, and even a degree of respect from the Transcendentalists' most bitter opponent, Edgar Allan Poe. Poe's notice and an early review by John Sullivan Dwight in the *Harbinger* (1845) stand as the most important and perceptive early critical assessments of Cranch's poetry. Poe ("The Literati of New York City.—No. III") refers to Cranch as "One of the least intolerable of the school of Boston Transcendentalists" and goes on to say that "I believe that he has at last 'come out from among them,' abandoned their doctrines (whatever they are) and given up their company in disgust." It is hard to tell whether Poe is writing for effect here, or whether he honestly suspects that Cranch's removal from the Boston area to New York indicates a falling away from Transcendentalism. But he goes on to note in *Poems* an "unusual vivacity of fancy and dexterity of expression." Cranch is also discussed in "The Rationale of Verse," where Poe calls him "one of our finest poets," and uses him as one of several examples in his development of a theory of scansion and rhythm.

There is praise in Dwight's review of *Poems*, as we might expect, given the close friendship of the two men and their shared philosophical outlook. There is also an honest recognition that Cranch's poetry is rather "passive," but Dwight is not entirely convinced that a lack of force is a fault: Cranch's passivity is preferable to misguided or clamorous force, and it bespeaks a corresponding receptivity to the central Transcendentalist vision of the unity of the universe. This early critique in some ways anticipated the development of Cranch's critical reputation: his "passive" voice has convinced some critics that he was a dilettante who never flowered into a mature poet, but others point to Cranch's fundamental perception of a monistic unity and praise him as a singularly direct translator of Transcendentalist philosophy into poetry. Cranch's ability to represent the poetic qualities of Transcendentalism also probably brought him the recognition of inclusion in the first edition of Rufus W. Griswold's *The Poets and Poetry of America* (1842).

When Cranch again began to publish volumes of verse in the 1870s, Transcendentalism was a waning movement. William Dean Howells greeted *Satan: A Libretto* with moderate praise, and George Parsons Lathrop called *The Bird and the Bell* representative of "a long term of artistic life with its successes and half-successes and its various endeavor in search of the ideal," a comment that seems to reflect respect for Cranch himself rather than for his poetry. George E. Woodberry later reviewed *Ariel and Caliban*.

After the comments of contemporary reviewers, there was little noteworthy analysis of Cranch's poetry until he began to attract occasional attention in academic criticism in the 1950s. Commentators in the early part of the century dealt largely with his life and his part in the Transcendentalist movement, and even recent criticism has tended to be heavily biographical. J. C. Levenson's essay remains one of the best treatments of Cranch's artistic career, emphasizing his small but well-deserved place as one of the sustaining secondary artists in the American tradition. Levenson sees Cranch's incomplete grasp of the nature of symbolism as his major weakness as a poet, especially when he is compared with his mentor Emerson. Perry Miller acknowledges the influence of Levenson on his anthology *The Transcendentalists*, in which he reprints a number of the *Dial* poems. The terms "inworld" and "outworld," used by Cranch in the poems thus titled in the *Dial*, are the focus of Marilyn R. Nicoson's dissertation and a related article. Nicoson argues for the importance of his later poetry, where he finally achieved a vision of harmony between the "inworld" and the "outworld." Nicoson's discussion of Cranch's personal confrontation with his admitted literary and artistic "failure" late in life is a moving and revealing glimpse of the inner man.

Cranch's early poetry receives some attention from Helen Hennessy, "The *Dial*," who finds it (and particularly the poem"Correspondences") representative of the Transcendentalist movement as a whole. His best-known poem, published as "Stanzas" in the July 1840 *Dial* and later entitled "Enosis," is the subject of two essays. Sidney E. Lind notes the persistent misspelling of the title as "Gnosis" (knowledge) rather than "Enosis" (unity). Paul O. Williams, "The Persistence of Cranch's 'Enosis,' " discusses Cranch's growing frustration over his persistent identification with that single poem, since he felt that its popularity with anthologists discouraged the reprinting and wider readership of his other poems. One of the later poems, "Veils," is the focal point for David Robinson's discussion of "Christopher Pearse Cranch, Robert Browning, and the Problem of Transcendental Friendship."

In *Musical Influence on American Poetry*, Charmenz S. Lenhart deals with the influence of music on Cranch's verse, noting his intention to merge musical and poetic forms in *Satan: A Libretto*. Donald B. Stauffer's survey, *A Short History of American Poetry*, briefly treats Cranch in the context of Transcendentalist poetry and suggests that his "Correspondences" anticipated Walt Whitman's overturning of the traditional poetic line.

CRANCH AS ARTIST

Cranch's turn from a career as a preacher and poet to that of a painter happened with remarkable quickness in 1841. Suffering from a debility that, he told Dwight, was "of a kind to depress and render unelastic both mind and will," he complained that "Thought, eloquence, and poetry desert me." He picked up painting as a diversion, having been forsaken by language, and found in it not only therapy for his illness but a life's work. His strength was as a landscape artist, and he devoted himself to landscapes of the Hudson Valley mode and to Italian scenes. His painting led him abroad, where he was associated with William Wetmore Story and other Americans living in France and Italy, and he is mentioned in Henry James's *William Wetmore Story and His Friends*. Like Dwight, James sees in Cranch's poetry and painting a certain lack of force about which he is ambivalently critical. Madeleine B. Stern also depicts, with interesting detail, the group of expatriate "New England Artists in Italy." The work of several members of the group, including that of Cranch, is also analyzed by Barbara Novak (*Nature and Culture*), who raises the question why so many American artists were so willingly "seduced" (to quote Henry James) by Italy. F. DeWolfe Miller's brief section on Cranch's career as a painter (*Christopher Pearse Cranch and His Caricatures*) makes a strong argument for Cranch's historical association with the Hudson River School. George Willis Cooke's book on the *Dial* lists and dates some of Cranch's individual paintings, and Frank Preston Stearns' discussion of Cranch's artistic career and tastes is also helpful. In "Return from Arcadia," Mabel Abbot and Gail K. Schneider describe an 1847–48 Italian sketch book of Cranch's that was originally given to George William Curtis and has since come into the possession of the Staten Island Institute of Arts and Sciences. Cranch's work as a painter and that of his brother

John are discussed in Willie Vale Oldham Quade, "Christopher Pearse Cranch and John Cranch," which includes a number of color photographs of Cranch's work. Cranch is briefly mentioned in Henry T. Tuckerman, *Book of the Artist*, and some records of his exhibitions of paintings are in Mabel Munson Swan, *The Athenæum Gallery*; the published exhibition catalog, *Travelers in Arcadia*; and the *National Academy of Design Exhibition Record, 1826-1861*. All in all, there has been little substantial discussion of Cranch's artistic accomplishment. This oversight may be corrected now that nineteenth-century American painting, and especially the landscape work of the Hudson River and Luminist schools, is attracting greater attention.

Cranch also maintained a lively interest in music and theater. Henry A. Pochmann (*German Culture in America*) notes that Cranch, John Sullivan Dwight, and Margaret Fuller formed an early Beethoven cult that took the lead in recognizing the composer. There is also passing mention of Cranch in George Willis Cooke, *John Sullivan Dwight*. Cranch's love for the theater is noted by Lucile Gafford.

Despite the general consensus that Cranch's literary career was damaged by his dabbling in other arts, it is hard to criticize or to regret his wide cultivation. Whether he was, as Emerson said, "a victim of [his] own various gifts," whether his artistic career robbed him of greater literary achievement, we cannot say, though the closer one examines the record, the more one believes that Cranch did not suppress his literary impulses in his turn to painting. It is clear, however, that art was both a psychological and an economic salvation for him, offering him deep personal satisfaction and a means of livelihood that could not have been obtained through letters alone.

Each phase of Cranch's career sheds light on the general cultural awakening of America in the middle nineteenth century. His early prose exemplifies the interplay of Unitarian sectarianism and Romanticism out of which Transcendentalism emerged, and Cranch's perspective on the controversy between Unitarians and Transcendentalists is a valuable one. The reconciliation of his spiritual goals and his aesthetic tastes typifies the merging of these two sensibilities in many other Transcendentalists. Cranch's later work, including his painting, which is still largely overlooked, suggests the delicate historical link between Transcendentalist moral concerns and the more purely aesthetic concerns of a later generation of Americans and furthers our understanding of the cultural environment that nurtured figures like Dwight, James Russell Lowell, Story, and even Henry James and William Dean Howells.

JOHN SULLIVAN DWIGHT

William G. Heath

BIBLIOGRAPHIES

Because there is no definitive bibliography of Dwight's writings, scholars must resort to various sources. The most complete listing appears in Walter L. Fertig's dissertation, "John Sullivan Dwight," which includes only works cited in the thesis. It compiles unpublished as well as published writings but not Dwight's numerous contributions to the *Harbinger* and his own *Dwight's Journal of Music*; scholars must consult the indexes of these periodicals. The *Harbinger* pieces on music are also listed in Irving Lowens, "Writings about Music in the Periodicals of American Transcendentalism." Dwight's books and sermons are listed in *NUC*.

The best secondary bibliography is also in Fertig's dissertation. With the appearance of new items about Dwight since 1952, however, the Fertig list needs updating. All the articles on Dwight listed in *AAL* are discussed in this chapter.

MANUSCRIPTS

ALM lists thirteen separate collections of Dwight materials, mostly of letters sent to Dwight. He received many more letters than he sent, and not all of those he received have survived. By far the largest collection is in the Boston Public Library. It contains three manuscripts by Dwight, several letters in his hand, 347 letters sent to him, and some miscellaneous personal documents. Thirty-two items in this collection relating to Brook Farm are described in Joel Myerson, *Brook Farm*. The other major collection is in the Houghton Library of Harvard University: twelve letters by Dwight, 144 sent to him.

Not mentioned in *ALM* but noted by Walter L. Fertig is a folder in the Harvard University Archives containing eleven themes written by Dwight in his senior year, in addition to some exercises in forensics. None of these items deals with music.

EDITIONS

George Willis Cooke, Dwight's first biographer, declared in 1898 that "a score of Dwight's essays on general topics connected with music . . . deserve a place alongside the best writings of Ruskin." A collection of Dwight's best essays in book form would make a valuable addition to American literature, but that need has not yet been fulfilled. Almost all Dwight's published writings remain scattered throughout the periodicals in which they originally appeared. Two of his essays have been anthologized, but only in excerpts. Perry Miller includes a selection from Dwight's essay "Music" in *The Transcendentalists*; the piece originally appeared in *Aesthetic Papers*, ed. Elizabeth Palmer Peabody (1849). George Hochfield includes almost all of Dwight's July 1840 *Dial* essay "The Religion of Beauty" in *Selected Writings of the American Transcendentalists*. It is also worth noting that the complete *Dwight's Journal of Music* has been reprinted in facsimile (1968).

BIOGRAPHY

The only book-length biography of Dwight we have is George Willis Cooke's affectionate memoir (1898). Although the study is reliable within the limits of what it sets out to do—present Dwight's career in broad outline and, as much as possible, in his own words—it lacks objectivity and scholarly apparatus, and it requires updating. Cooke's edition of *Early Letters of George Wm. Curtis to John S. Dwight* adds nothing to the biography and contains several errors. Information about Dwight's ancestry is contained in B. W. Dwight, *The History of the Descendants of John Dwight*.

Three items pertaining to Dwight fall under the heading of reminiscences rather than biographical studies. One of Dwight's musical disciples, W. S. B. Mathews, wrote a brief tribute and a review essay based on Cooke's biography. Another friend, C. H. Brittan, prints a letter he received from Dwight that describes Dwight's shaky financial situation in his later years.

Lindsay Swift's chapter on Dwight in *Brook Farm* is largely derived from Cooke. Cooke's own brief sketch of Dwight in *An Historical and Biographical Introduction to Accompany the Dial* distills the essential facts from his longer study. Objectivity, a quality missing from much that has been written about Dwight by his admirers, is a welcome virtue of Bliss Perry's chapter in Edward Waldo Emerson, *The Early Years of the Saturday Club 1855–1870*, which reviews Dwight's life in a genial but nonpartisan manner. Finally, *DAB* contains a short entry on Dwight by Eleanore Robinett Dobson but it adds nothing new to the record.

CRITICISM

No book-length critical study of Dwight has been published. Until one appears, the best alternative is Walter L. Fertig's dissertation. Although Fertig has not tried to write a definitive biography, his study surpasses Cooke's in depth and critical objectivity. Every facet of Dwight's life, particularly his writings, is examined in greater detail than one will find anywhere else. Fertig rejects the superficial notion that Dwight had two careers, one as a Transcendentalist and another as a music critic. Instead he views Dwight as an idealist and visionary whose goal in life was "the propagation of music for Transcendental reasons."

Fertig also discusses Dwight's prepublication notice of *Walden* to emphasize his ambivalence toward Transcendentalism. R. Baird Shuman's printing of a letter from Dwight to James Russell Lowell reveals that Dwight was already gathering material for the *Pioneer* by 1845, when he was still at Brook Farm.

Most of the existing commentary on Dwight deals with particular periods or phases of his life and can be divided into three general areas: studies connecting Dwight to Transcendentalism, studies connecting Dwight to American musical history, and studies that attempt to bridge these two areas.

In the first category, Joel Myerson surveys Dwight's three contributions to the *Dial*, along with the highlights of his life up to Brook Farm, in *The New England Transcendentalists and the* Dial. Clarence L. F. Gohdes, *The Periodicals of American Transcendentalism*, mentions Dwight's contributions to the *Harbinger*, of which he was an assistant editor under George Ripley. A more extended study of Dwight's work on the latter is Sterling F. Delano, "The *Harbinger*."

Dwight's interest in German Romanticism is treated most comprehensively in Henry A. Pochmann, *German Culture in America*. J. Wesley Thomas assesses Dwight's translations from German poetry, calling Dwight "the greatest influence in the assimilation of [German] Romanticism into American culture." A more moderate view is expressed by Stanley M. Vogel in *German Literary Influences on the American Transcendentalists*. Vogel rates Charles Timothy Brooks a superior translator to Dwight but acknowledges that "in belletristic forms of German culture Dwight's contributions are important." Kenneth Walter Cameron discusses "Dwight's Translation of Schiller's Bell Song before 1837."

Several essays deal specifically with Dwight's musical talents. William Apthorp's eulogy in the *Boston Evening Transcript* the day after Dwight's death is reprinted in *Musicians and Music-Lovers*. The best short assessment of Dwight's musical legacy is by Edward Waters. Honor McCusker deals anecdotally with this side of Dwight in "Fifty Years of Music in Boston." Irving Lowens discusses Dwight's Transcendentalist aesthetic as it applies to music and also includes a valuable checklist. Earl Walter Booth, "Beethoven and the American Transcendentalists," includes a chapter that argues that Dwight's enthusiasm for Beethoven contributed to the Transcendentalist element in his music criticism. Of greater interest is Douglas Allen Booth, "Words, Sounds, and the Over-Soul: A Study of the Aesthetic Philosophies of Ralph Waldo Emerson,

Henry David Thoreau, John Sullivan Dwight, and Charles Edward Ives.'' Booth sees affinities between Thoreau and Dwight and quotes the latter to show that his musical aesthetic was based on the concept of organic form.

FURTHER SCHOLARSHIP

There is still a need for a comprehensive primary bibliography to complete the work begun by Fertig. In addition, a published collection of Dwight's essays would enlarge our appreciation of Transcendentalist aesthetics. Lastly, the time has come to produce an up-to-date biography of Dwight, one that will build on Cooke and Fertig and incorporate the work done since 1952. Ideally, such a study would bring together the two prevailing lines of Dwight scholarship: the Transcendental and the musical. To ignore one or the other results in a half-portrait.

RALPH WALDO EMERSON

Robert E. Burkholder and Joel Myerson

BIBLIOGRAPHIES

The first separate primary bibliography of Emerson was George Willis Cooke, *A Bibliography of Ralph Waldo Emerson* (1908). Although excellent for its time, it is now outdated. The section on Emerson in *BAL* lists all first editions of Emerson's works, some reprintings, and some first-appearance contributions to books and pamphlets, but it does not attempt to be comprehensive. Robert E. Burkholder's list of first editions of Emerson's books (in *FPAA*, vol. 2) is also useful. The only comprehensive bibliography of Emerson's writings is Joel Myerson, *Ralph Waldo Emerson*, which lists all editions and printings of Emerson's works in English, all foreign-language editions of his works through 1882, all collected editions and collections of Emerson's works, all first-appearance contributions to books, pamphlets, newspapers, and magazines, all books edited by Emerson, all reprinted material in books and pamphlets through 1882, and material attributed to Emerson.

Cooke's book was also the first significant secondary bibliography of Emerson. Its listing of nineteenth-century works is supplemented by William J. Sowder's list of British reviews of Emerson's works. Also useful, though lacking in bibliographical documentation, are Kenneth Walter Cameron's several compilations, such as *Emerson, Thoreau and Concord in Early Newspapers*. Supplements to Cooke are provided by R. A. Booth and Roland Stromberg for 1908–20 and Jackson R. Bryer and Robert A. Rees for 1951–61. Jeanetta Boswell, *Ralph Waldo Emerson and the Critics*, adds a few titles for the period 1900–77 to those available in the earlier bibliographies, while perpetuating their errors and introducing new ones. Boswell clearly has not seen most of the items she lists, some of which do not exist, and she often provides false leads. An excellent annotated bibliography of criticism through 1976 on Emerson's prose has been done by Annette M. Woodleif. All these have been superseded by Robert E. Burkholder and Joel Myerson, *Ralph Waldo Emerson: An Annotated Secondary Bibliography*, a massive, fully annotated listing of some 5,500 works from 1816 through 1979.

There are a number of good bibliographical essays on Emerson. Carl F. Strauch's discussion "Emerson and the American Continuity," while weak on specific titles, ably describes the major themes in Emerson criticism. Burkholder's introduction to "Ralph Waldo Emerson's Reputation, 1831–1861" is an excellent (and the only) discussion of Emerson's reception in America during the years indicated. William J. Sowder, *Emerson's Impact on the British Isles and Canada*, covers the nineteenth-century response to Emerson, focusing more on his poetry than on his prose works. Although now outdated, Frederic Ives Carpenter's chapters on Emerson's biography, prose, poetry, ideas, and influence in world literature in his *Emerson Handbook* are still useful introductions to Emerson scholarship. The bibliographical essays by Floyd Stovall (*Eight American Authors*) are also useful overviews.

There are numerous general discussions of Emerson's critical reception in histories of American and world literatures. The American response can be traced in Burkholder's dissertation and in Richard Ruland, *The Rediscovery of American Literature*. Other studies deal with Emerson's foreign reception: for Australia and New Zealand, see Joseph Jones ("Emerson and Whitman 'Down Under' "); for England, see Clarence Gohdes (*American Literature in Nineteenth Century England*) and William J. Sowder; for France, see Maurice Chazin and Henry Blumenthal (*American and French Culture, 1800-1900*); for Germany, see Harvey W. Hewett-Thayer (*American Literature as Viewed in Germany*), Eugene F. Timpe (*American Literature in Germany*), Julius Simon (*Ralph Waldo Emerson in Deutschland*), Luther S. Luedtke, "German Reception and Criticism of Ralph Waldo Emerson," and Martin Christadler for recent work; for Greece, see James A. Notopoulos; for Italy, see Rolando Anzilotti and Maria Teresa de Majo for the period 1847–1963; for Japan, see Shunsuke Kamei for 1868–1912, Bunshō Jugaku, and, supplementing Jugaku, Kenneth Walter Cameron ("Notes on Emerson in Japan"); for Latin America, see John E. Englekirk; for Russia, see Valentina Libman; for Scandinavia, see Carl L. Anderson; for Spain, see John De Lancey Ferguson; and also see Luther S. Luedtke's survey "Emerson in Western Europe (1855-1975)."

Three concordances list Emerson's works in context. George Shelton Hubbell, *A Concordance to the Poems of Ralph Waldo Emerson*, is restricted to those poems published in vol. 9 of the Centenary Edition. Eugene F. Irey, *Concordance to Five Essays of Ralph Waldo Emerson*, arbitrarily (and despite its title) chooses *Nature*, "The American Scholar," the Divinity School Address, "Self-Reliance," and "Fate," and it uses the now-superseded Centenary Edition text. Mary Alice Ihrig, *Emerson's Transcendental Vocabulary*, lists all appearances of certain word clusters in the first seven volumes of the Centenary Edition. In addition, Walter Harding, *Emerson's Library*, lists all the books Emerson is known to have owned but not, as Harding acknowledges, all those he is known to have read or used.

MANUSCRIPTS

ALM lists 110 libraries and is still incomplete. The major collection of Emerson manuscripts is at the Houghton Library of Harvard University, where the Emerson family papers have been deposited. This collection includes sermons, letters to and from Emerson, journals, notebooks, family correspondence, and most of Emerson's library; various typed catalogs to most parts of the collection are available. Other significant collections are at Columbia University (where many of Ralph L. Rusk's working papers and photocopies of manuscripts are deposited), Henry E. Huntington Library, Massachusetts Historical Society, Pierpont Morgan Library, and University of Virginia. A valuable scholarly project would be a catalog of Emerson's scattered literary manuscripts, particularly those that have not been published or that need reediting.

EDITIONS

The standard edition of Emerson's works is *The Complete Works of Ralph Waldo Emerson*, ed. Edward Waldo Emerson (1903–04), referred to as the Centenary Edition (more information is available in Joel Myerson's introduction to the AMS Press reprint). Although the notes by Emerson's son are excellent, the texts were mangled in the process of editing them according to turn-of-the-century standards. This edition is slowly being superseded by *The Collected Works of Ralph Waldo Emerson*, ed. Alfred R. Ferguson et al. (1971–   ). Some works of Emerson's will not appear in either edition, most notably his college compositions (edited by Edward Everett Hale in *Two Unpublished Essays* [1896] and Kenneth Walter Cameron in *Indian Superstition* [1954]) and a number of periodical and gift-book contributions, some of which were slapped together by Charles C. Bigelow in *Uncollected Writings* (1912). Numerous periodical, gift-book, and pamphlet appearances still remain uncollected; for a listing, see Joel Myerson's bibliography. It is difficult to edit many of the works Emerson published in the last ten years of his life because they were pieced together with the help of his daughter Ellen and James Elliot Cabot, whose role in the publication of these works is not clear. Nancy Craig Simmons has done something to resolve this puzzle in her 1980 dissertation—a biography of Cabot with information on his activities as Emerson's literary executor—and in an article dealing specifically with Cabot's editorial work.

Some twenty-five of Emerson's 170 sermons have been edited and annotated with care by Arthur Cushman McGiffert, Jr., in *Young Emerson Speaks* (1938). A complete edition of Emerson's sermons is a prime desideratum. One step toward that end is William B. Barton, Jr., *A Calendar to the Complete Edition of the Sermons of Ralph Waldo Emerson*, which gives Emerson's title for each sermon, the text he took for the sermon, the dates on which he preached the sermon, a physical description of the manuscript, and the sermon argument (often in Emerson's own words).

Emerson's lectures have fared better. A number of early works, such as Clarence

Gohdes, *Uncollected Lectures* (1932), merely reprint newspaper reports. *The Early Lectures of Ralph Waldo Emerson*, ed. Robert E. Spiller, Stephen E. Whicher, and Wallace E. Williams (1959–72), is a masterful edition of Emerson's manuscripts for lectures delivered between 1833 and 1842. Supplemental annotations to the first volume were published by Kenneth Walter Cameron (*A Commentary on Emerson's Early Lectures (1833–1836) with an Index-Concordance*).

Editors have also done well by Emerson's journals. Edward Waldo Emerson and Waldo Emerson Forbes selected and annotated the *Journals of Ralph Waldo Emerson* (1909–14). This edition has been superseded by *The Journals and Miscellaneous Notebooks of Ralph Waldo Emerson*, ed. William H. Gilman et al. (1960–82), which is textually accurate (symbols allow the reader to follow the process of Emerson's writing) and fully annotated, including cross-references for journal passages that appeared in print. An excellent selection from this series is *Emerson in His Journals*, ed. Joel Porte. This edition will be followed by the publication of Emerson's poetry notebooks, under the general editorship of Ralph H. Orth. Emerson's account books, the day-to-day records of his financial dealings, have not been collected, and they remain a worthy project.

The Letters of Ralph Waldo Emerson, ed. Ralph L. Rusk (1939), is a brilliantly edited work. The texts are accurate, the annotations lengthy, and the index comprehensive. It is arguably the best edition of an American writer's letters. Still, for reasons of space and copyright, Rusk omitted most letters that had previously appeared in print, including those in "The Emerson-Thoreau Correspondence," ed. F. B. Sanborn (1892); *A Correspondence between John Sterling and Ralph Waldo Emerson*, ed. Edward Waldo Emerson (1897); *Letters from Ralph Waldo Emerson to a Friend* (Samuel Gray Ward), ed. Charles Eliot Norton (1899); *Correspondence between Ralph Waldo Emerson and Herman Grimm*, ed. Frederick William Holls (1903); *Records of a Lifelong Friendship* (correspondence with William Henry Furness), ed. Horace Howard Furness (1910); and *Emerson-Clough Letters*, ed. Howard F. Lowry and Rusk (1934). Emerson's correspondence with Thomas Carlyle, first published in 1883 with a supplementary volume in 1886, was also not included by Rusk, but *The Correspondence of Emerson and Carlyle*, ed. Joseph Slater (1964), presents it as well as Rusk would have. For other, uncollected letters, see Joel Myerson's bibliography. A supplemental edition of Emerson's letters, including all those known but not printed by Rusk and those that have come to light since 1939, is being completed by Eleanor M. Tilton.

Emerson's translation of Dante's *Vita nuova* has been edited with an introduction and annotations by J. Chesley Mathews (1957).

For classroom use, the best two anthologies are *Selections from Ralph Waldo Emerson*, ed. Stephen E. Whicher, which intersperses Emerson's writings with selections from his letters and journals to show the development of his thought, and *Selected Writings of Ralph Waldo Emerson*, ed. William H. Gilman. Both books have excellent introductions and notes, though Gilman's text is better (Whicher used the Centenary Edition).

BIOGRAPHY

Although all nineteenth-century biographies of Emerson have been superseded by the work of twentieth-century biographers, several of these early studies are still fruitful starting points for scholars today. George Willis Cooke's *Ralph Waldo Emerson* (1881) was the first full-scale biography, and its value today rests not only on Cooke's thorough knowledge of his subject but also on his mastery of the critical commentary on Emerson. Oliver Wendell Holmes's *Ralph Waldo Emerson* (1884) is perceptive and usually reverent, although Holmes applies his somewhat barbed wit to such topics as Emerson's genealogy, his unorthodox religious views, and his apparently weak stand against slavery. Cooke and Holmes had little or no recourse to Emerson's private papers and journals, but James Elliot Cabot, as Emerson's literary executor, enjoyed unlimited access; therefore, his two-volume *A Memoir of Ralph Waldo Emerson* (1887) is the most authoritative of these early works and was the standard biography until the publication of Ralph L. Rusk's *The Life of Ralph Waldo Emerson*. Of slightly less importance is Moncure D. Conway, *Emerson at Home and Abroad* (1882), which, like many of Conway's other books, suffers from being rushed and is not always reliable. Alexander Ireland raced Conway to press after Emerson's death with his *In Memoriam: Ralph Waldo Emerson* (1882) and later published an expanded version of that study, *Ralph Waldo Emerson: His Life, Genius, and Writings* (1882). Ireland's work remains one of the best sources for the study of Emerson's three visits to England. Of even less importance is Richard Garnett, *Life of Ralph Waldo Emerson* (1885), which has little to add to Cabot except some interesting opinions of Emerson and his work. Garnett's "Ralph Waldo Emerson" serves as a general summary of his earlier work.

Two reminiscences of Emerson that present a more human portrait of him than any of the nineteenth-century biographies, with the possible exception of Edward Waldo Emerson, *Emerson in Concord* (discussed below), are James B. Thayer, *A Western Journey with Mr. Emerson*, and Charles J. Woodbury, *Talks with Ralph Waldo Emerson*. Thayer's book relates his personal experiences while accompanying Emerson to California in 1871. A view of Emerson's visit to the Yosemite Valley from a different perspective can be found in John Muir, "The Forests of the Yosemite Park," which records the author's disappointment at not being allowed to take the sixty-eight-year-old Emerson on a camping trip in the mountains. Woodbury's volume, a greatly expanded version of his "Emerson Talks with a College Boy," publishes records of conversations the author had with Emerson between 1865 and 1870 that are arranged topically under such headings as "Criticism," "Concord," "Transcendentalism," and "Method." The line of biographical reminiscences by those who knew Emerson ended with books by John Albee (*Remembrances of Emerson*) and F. B. Sanborn (*Ralph Waldo Emerson* and *The Personality of Emerson*).

O. W. Firkins, *Ralph Waldo Emerson* (1915), is the best factual biography since Cabot's and convincingly evokes Emerson's character. Denton J. Snider, *A Biography of Ralph Waldo Emerson*, is an unjustly overlooked work that divides Emerson's life into three periods: his apprenticeship (1803–34), his revolutionary phase (1835–65), and the reconciled Emerson (1865–82). Although quirkily written, Snider's book does see the tensions in Emerson's life and art that were later discussed at length by such writers as Stephen E. Whicher (see below). Phillips Russell, *Emerson: The Wisest American*, a popular work stressing Emerson's Yankee shrewdness, in no way proves its title. Eulogistic approaches are taken by Régis Michaud, *Emerson: The Enraptured Yankee*, and Maurice Gonnaud, *Individu et société dans l'œuvre de Ralph Waldo Emerson*. Van Wyck Brooks tries an impressionistic approach, recreating scenes and dialogue, in *The Life of Emerson*, as does Townsend Scudder in *The Lonely Wayfaring Man*, a study of Emerson's first two trips to England. Unfortunately, both Brooks and Scudder effectively dilute their scholarship with their almost novelistic approaches. Ralph L. Rusk, *The Life of Ralph Waldo Emerson*, presents a brilliant synthesis of primary and secondary material and describes well the essential points of Emerson's philosophy and writings. The detailed documentation offers astute readers suggestions for further research. Some readers have criticized Rusk's failure to indulge in psychological speculations about Emerson; others complain of the flatness of Rusk's unenlivened portrait of Emerson as a man. Nevertheless, this is still the standard biography. Gay Wilson Allen, *Waldo Emerson*, does an excellent job of humanizing Emerson and restating his ideas in clear language, but for hard facts it does not supersede Rusk's biography; indeed, it contains numerous errors. H. L. Kleinfeld, "The Structure of Emerson's Death," is a masterful study of comments on Emerson from his death through the centennial observance of his birth in 1903. In addition, two useful compilations of biographical material have been published: Kenneth Walter Cameron, *The Transcendentalists and Minerva*, includes a number of short studies with new biographical information, and *Ralph Waldo Emerson: A Profile*, ed. Carl Bode, reprints a number of biographical studies, including Kleinfeld's.

Studies of the Emerson family are also useful in evaluating Emerson's life. *Diary and Letters of William Emerson 1743–1776*, ed. Amelia Forbes Emerson, provides good background on Emerson's grandfather. The women in Emerson's life have long fascinated biographers, beginning with David Green Haskins, *Ralph Waldo Emerson: His Maternal Ancestors*. Henry F. Pommer, *Emerson's First Marriage*, is the best study of Ellen Louisa Tucker and Emerson; it uses material not available to Rusk and complements Edith W. Gregg's introduction to her edition of *One First Love: The Letters of Ellen Louisa Tucker to Ralph Waldo Emerson*. Unfortunately, Emerson's letters to Ellen have not survived. The story of Emerson's second marriage is told by his daughter Ellen Tucker Emerson in *The Life of Lidian Jackson Emerson*, expertly edited and introduced by Delores Bird Carpenter, and *The Letters of Ellen Tucker Emerson*, ed. Edith E. W. Gregg. Two of Emerson's aunts have also received attention: Sarah Alden Bradford Ripley is studied by Frances W. Knickerbocker and Patricia Ann Carlson, and Mary Moody Emerson is the subject of a biographical pamphlet by George Tolman, and critical articles by Rosalie Feltenstein and Nancy Barcus. Elizabeth Hoar became like a sister to Emerson following the death of her fiancé, Emerson's brother Charles, in 1836, and her relationship with Emerson is discussed by Elizabeth Maxfield-Miller. Edith Emerson Webster Gregg has edited the fascinating childhood reminiscences of Emerson by his children. An interesting view of the Emerson household from the mid-1880s to 1909 is in Mary Miller Engel, *I Remember the Emersons*. Of little value is *The Letters and Journals of Waldo Emerson Forbes* (Emerson's grandson), ed. Amelia Forbes Thomas. We still need a good book on Emerson's relations and their influence on his life and thought.

The most important nineteenth-century study of Emerson's relationship with Concord is Edward Waldo Emerson's *Emerson in Concord: A Memoir*. This portrait by his son humanizes Emerson by concentrating on his relations with his Concord neighbors, something largely neglected by earlier biographers. Other contemporary writers who answered a public demand for information about Emerson's home life included George William Curtis, "Ralph Waldo Emerson"; M. D. Conway, "The Transcendentalists of Concord"; George B. Bartlett's much reprinted "Ralph Waldo Emerson"; F. B. Sanborn, "The Homes and Haunts of Emerson" and "Emerson and His Friends in Concord"; and George P. Lathrop, "Literary and Social Boston," who discusses Concord as a literary "ally" of Boston as well as Emerson's involvement in Concord's exclusive Social Circle. "Reminiscences of Ralph Waldo Emerson" by Louisa May Alcott presents, in its glimpses of Emerson's playing with the children of the town and his devastation at the death of Waldo, one of the most human portraits of the man available.

The description of *Concord: American Town* by Townsend Scudder is a good one. Hamilton Wright Mabie, "Concord and Emerson," gives a sense of the place, and Hubert H. Hoeltje, "Emerson, Citizen of Concord," provides a detailed description of Emerson's life there as drawn from town, parish, and church records. Emerson's interest in Concord libraries is discussed by Francis Dedmond, and his participation in the Concord Lyceum is examined in interesting articles by Colin Cuthbert Alexander and Alvah H. Low. The best study of Emerson in Concord, and a model for future works, is Leonard Neufeldt, " 'The Fields of My Fathers' and Emerson's Literary Vocation," which argues that Emerson attempted to find "a useable past in Concord's history." Joel Myerson has done a more general study of Emerson's comments on New England as a whole in *American Literature: The New England Heritage*, ed. James Nagel and Richard Astro.

Emerson also participated in a number of clubs. Joel Myerson has published "A Calendar of Transcendental Club Meetings" and "A History of the Transcendental Club." Interesting accounts of Emerson's involvement in the Town and Country Club appear in "What Is Talked About" (*LWNY*, 1849) and "A Pepysian Letter" (*HDM*, 1849), two articles by Thomas Wentworth Higginson (*Brains*, 1, 15 Dec. 1891), and a somewhat sketchy piece by Kenneth Walter Cameron, "Emerson, Thoreau, and the Town and Country Club." The Saturday Club is chronicled by George Willis Cooke (*NEMag*, 1898) and by Edward Waldo Emerson (*The Early Years of the Saturday Club*). Descriptions of a camping trip that some of the club's members took to the Adirondacks are provided by William J. Stillman and Paul F. Jamieson.

Finally, Emerson's stint as editor of the *Dial* is given detailed treatment in Joel Myerson, *The New England Transcendentalists and the* Dial, and incisive critical treatment in Donald F. Warders, " 'The Progress of the Hour and the Day.' " Emerson's editorship is contrasted with that of Margaret Fuller by Bernard Rosenthal, and his literary criticism in the *Dial* is surveyed by Doris Morton. Other works on the *Dial*, nearly all of which discuss Emerson, may be found in the chapter "Transcendentalist Periodicals."

CRITICISM

Perhaps the earliest general critical consideration of Emerson is that by the transplanted New Englander Samuel Gilman in the *Southern Rose* (24 Nov. 1838) of Charleston, South Carolina. Gilman notes the furor caused by Emerson's Divinity School Address but doubts it will do any permanent damage. Emerson, he argues, is less like a comet than like a shooting star; he may cause a momentary fuss, but ultimately his work will fizzle into unimportance.

Like other major American writers, Emerson first received serious attention abroad rather than at home. The most important critical assessment of Emerson in the first decade of his literary career is Richard Monckton Milnes, "American Philosophy— Emerson's Works," in the influential *London and Westminster Review*. Although most of Milnes' judgments of Emerson and American literature and culture in general are less than positive, his detailed analysis of Emerson's work and its cultural context suggests that the upstart American had enough substance to justify such analysis. Other, more positive early assessments of Emerson by Englishmen are John Heraud, "A Response from America," and George Gilfillan, "Ralph Waldo Emerson." Emerson's second visit to England in 1847–48 occasioned an outpouring of positive critical evaluations, including Goodwyn Barmby, "Emerson and His Writings," William Henry Smith, "Emerson," George Gilfillan, "Ralph Waldo Emerson; or, The 'Coming Man,' " George Cupples, "Emerson and His Visit to Scotland," and two anonymous essays, "Ralph Waldo Emerson" (*MEEJLR*, 1848) and "Letters from America: Ralph Waldo Emerson" (*PeJ*, 20 Nov. 1848). There were, of course, voices that dissented from the praise: in the *Dublin Review*, a writer named McCarthy criticizes Emerson's thought as "misdirected" and attacks the concept of self-reliance, and an anonymous critic of "The Emerson Mania" focuses attention on *Essays* and finds "more of paradox than of truth, and perhaps more of evil than of paradox." Other important foreign considerations of Emerson from this period include Daniel Stern (pseud. for the Comtesse D'Agoult), "Etudes contemporaines: Emerson"; Émile Montégut, "Avant-propos," and "Introduction" to his translation of Emerson's *Essais de philosophie américain*; and Herman Grimm, "Emerson." More references to foreign critical evaluations of Emerson may be found in Robert E. Burkholder and Joel Myerson's bibliography.

In his own country, Emerson fared less well during the early years of his literary career. In "Ralph Waldo Emerson" (1841), W. A. Jones is generally negative in his review of Emerson's ideas on philosophy and religion, and in "An Appendix of

Autographs" Edgar Allan Poe dismisses Emerson as one of the "mystics for mysticism's sake." Such unfavorable commentaries and a spate of bad reviews of *Essays: Second Series* prompted a writer identified only as "A Disciple" to defend Emerson against charges that he was obscure, aloof, and incoherent. This vindication was followed by two very different evaluations that contributed a great deal to the way Emerson and his work would be perceived through the rest of the nineteenth century. The first of these, Margaret Fuller's "American Literature," dubs Emerson "The Sage of Concord," discusses his profound thought and limited sphere of influence, and even suggests that although he is the best of American poets, his poems are too philosophical to be genuine poetry. The second, James Russell Lowell's satirical poem, *A Fable for Critics*, emphasizes Emerson's relationship with Carlyle and his lack of system. Lowell portrays him as a curious blend of idealistic dreamer and commonsense pragmatist, a "Plotinus-Montaigne," and this would be a standard characterization of Emerson for decades to come.

In the early 1850s, a number of generally positive assessments of Emerson's work appeared, including Thomas Powell, "Ralph Waldo Emerson," which argues that Emerson's prose is both "logical and consistent"; L. W. B., "Ralph Waldo Emerson"; and George Henry Calvert's general introduction to and defense of Emerson. There is evidence that the South was beginning to awaken to the potential of Emerson's thought in John Custis Darby, "Ralph Waldo Emerson," which argues that Emerson would debase Christianity in order to return to the paganism of ancient Greece, and J. B. H., "Ralph Waldo Emerson—History," which contends that in outlook and style Emerson is not American but European. There is also evidence in the *Critic* (1851) that Emerson's most enthusiastic promoter in England, Gilfillan, was rapidly turning against him. Gilfillan would reject Emerson completely by the latter half of the decade and attack his religious views in *The History of a Man* and *Christianity and Our Era*. But the 1850s would also see two milestones in the history of Emerson criticism: Theodore Parker's lucid and detailed examination of "The Writings of Ralph Waldo Emerson" and the first book-length study of Emerson's work, January Searle (pseud. for George Searle Phillips), *Emerson: His Life and Writings*. Both studies remain valuable documents for understanding the general critical attitude toward Emerson in America and England, respectively, during his most creative period.

From the Civil War until his death, Emerson enjoyed a nearly unassailable position at the head of American literature, as reflected in the general studies of him published during that period. Notable among these are essays by Delia M. Colton, George Stewart, Jr., John Francis Xavier O'Connor, and Francis H. Underwood. In particular, John Nichol, "Ralph Waldo Emerson," presents a comprehensive and balanced assessment of his life and work. Amos Bronson Alcott, "Fuller, Thoreau, Emerson," is a more substantive defense of Emerson's thought and literary style than one can find in Alcott's *Concord Days*, *Ralph Waldo Emerson: An Estimate of His Character and Genius in Prose and Verse*, or *Ralph Waldo Emerson: Philosopher and Seer*. Alfred Guernsey, *Ralph Waldo Emerson*, ostensibly a biography, is really more of a critical study, with considerations of Emerson's published works and a solid chapter on his philosophy.

Of course, the panegyrics that announced Emerson's unquestioned greatness at the time of his death number in the hundreds, or perhaps thousands, but as soon as 1884 the critical climate began to change. The first sign of this change was Matthew Arnold's lecture on Emerson, which was delivered in Boston in December 1883 and was published in 1884. When Arnold announced to a Boston audience that, measured against the highest standards—John Milton's poetry and Plato's philosophy—Emerson had no place among the greatest in either field, the subsequent outcry suggested that Boston was blinded by its longstanding habit of viewing Emerson as a symbol of its own position as a center of literary culture. No less revolutionary was John Morley's introduction to the Macmillan edition of *The Works of Ralph Waldo Emerson*, which criticizes the unpolished character of Emerson's prose, the purposelessness of his poetry, and the derivative nature of much of his thought. In their criticism, Arnold and Morley both aimed at a balanced treatment of Emerson from the perspective of literary and philosophic history, and they shattered his mythic image as "The Sage of Concord" so that his work could be discussed in a more impartial light. Notable among the general studies that benefited from this climate are those by Charles F. Johnson (in *Three Americans and Three Englishmen*), William R. Thayer (*The Influence of Emerson*), Henry James ("The Life of Emerson"), Coventry Patmore (in *Principle in Art*), and Joseph Forster ("Ralph Waldo Emerson"). John Jay Chapman, "Emerson, Sixty Years After," is a particularly valuable work because it places Emerson's work within the context of his time.

Certainly the best collection of essays on Emerson published in the nineteenth century is *The Genius and Character of Emerson: Lectures at the Concord School of Philosophy*, ed. F. B. Sanborn, which includes "Emerson and Boston" by Ednah D. Cheney, "Emerson as an American" by Julian Hawthorne, "A French View of Emerson" by René de Poyen Belleisle, "Emerson's Religion" by Cyrus A. Bartol, "Emerson as Preacher" by Elizabeth Palmer Peabody, "Emerson among the Poets" by F. B. Sanborn, "Emerson's Ethics" by Edwin D. Mead, "Emerson's Relation to Society" by Julia Ward Howe, "Emerson's View of Nationality" by George Willis Cooke, "Emerson's Philosophy of Nature," "Emerson's Orientalism," and "Emerson's Relationship to Goethe and Carlyle," all by William T. Harris, and "Emerson as Seen from India" by Protap Chunder Mozoomdar.

A number of critical studies appeared in connection with the Emerson centenary of 1903. *The Centenary of the Birth of Ralph Waldo Emerson*, in addition to describing the celebrations, contains interesting general criticism by such people as Thomas Wentworth Higginson and William James. Edwin D. Mead, *The Influence of Emerson*, contains chapters on Emerson's philosophy and his relations with Carlyle and Parker; none of the chapters is particularly useful. Also of little value is Elisabeth Luther Cary, *Emerson: Poet and Thinker*, which quotes Emerson instead of evaluating him.

George Edward Woodberry, *Ralph Waldo Emerson*, ostensibly a biography, is really a fine critical study of Emerson's writings, as opposed to his philosophy.

Woodberry is basically unsympathetic but evenhanded, saying, for example, that even though Emerson's works are failures "in the artistic sense," they "make their impression by their wholeness" very well. Like Woodberry, O. W. Firkins, *Ralph Waldo Emerson*, is more concerned with Emerson's writings than with his philosophy. Using the newly published *Journals*, Firkins presents sensitive and still useful readings of individual works.

The next group of books turned their attention to Emerson's philosophy. Henry David Gray, *Emerson: A Statement of New England Transcendentalism as Expressed in the Philosophy of Its Chief Exponent*, surveys Emerson's philosophical ideas on various topics. J. Arthur Hill, *Emerson and His Philosophy*, Samuel McChord Crothers, *Emerson: How to Know Him*, and Robert M. Gay, *Ralph Waldo Emerson: A Study of the Poet as Seer*, all use liberal quotations from Emerson's works to illustrate his inspirational greatness.

Books by Bliss Perry and Kenneth Walter Cameron next approach Emerson in different ways. In *Emerson Today*, Perry, in a published series of lectures, successfully evokes Emerson's personality, discusses the positive and negative assessments of him, and makes a case for Emerson's perduring value. Because Perry tries to convey the essential Emerson in readable prose, his book is still valuable today; indeed, it is one of the best short introductions to Emerson available. In *Emerson the Essayist*, Cameron "attempts to survey the chief influences upon Emerson's philosophy before the year 1837 and to set forth the available evidence." Vol. 1 discusses at length Emerson's years at Harvard, his sources and their influence on him, and *Nature*; vol. 2 reprints "Selected Documents of New England Transcendentalism." Like all of Cameron's works, this book is characterized by the virtue of detailed new information and the defect of having little selectivity exercised in bringing it forth.

In the 1950s, books on Emerson began to assume specific critical slants. Vivian C. Hopkins, *Spires of Form*, sees Emerson's aesthetic theory as "a cycle of three phases"—"the creative process," "the completed work of art," and "the reception of art by the observer"; its base is a "mystical" concept that there is "a sense of union between the subject and a larger source of spirit outside himself." In *Emerson's Angle of Vision*, Sherman Paul uses the idea of sympathetic correspondence (which "covered all the ways by which man came into relation with the world *outside* of himself, transformed the world *into* himself, and expressed the insight of the *experience* in words and character") to evaluate Emerson's writing. The major work of the decade was Stephen E. Whicher, *Freedom and Fate: An Inner Life of Ralph Waldo Emerson*. In this seminal work, Whicher argues that Emerson went from a loss of faith in traditional Christianity to a view of the infinitude of man by God's working directly through him to a more restricted view of man's potential as bounded by the facts of experience. By thus humanizing and demystifying Emerson, Whicher reveals a creative artist pulled in opposite directions by the tensions of his art, a far cry from the portrait of an "enraptured Yankee" or "wisest American" that had been presented by others. Nearly all subsequent criticism of Emerson argues for or against Whicher's position.

Jonathan Bishop, *Emerson on the Soul*, begins the 1960s with an excellent discussion of Emerson as a literary artist. Most of the original essays on *Transcendentalism and Its Legacy*, ed. Myron Simon and Thornton H. Parsons, deal with Emerson: Kenneth Burke on *Nature*, Harry Hayden Clark on "Conservative and Mediatory Emphases in Emerson's Thought," Emerson R. Marks on "Victor Cousin and Emerson," Albert Gilman and Roger Brown on the stylistic differences between Emerson and Thoreau, Joe Lee Davis on Santayana's criticism of Emerson, and René Wellek on Irving Babbitt's and Paul Elmer More's criticism of Emerson (some of these articles will be discussed later in this chapter). In *City of the West*, Michael H. Cowan subjects Emerson to an American studies approach.

In the 1970s, the number of critical books on Emerson increased markedly. William A. Huggard, *The Religious Teachings of Ralph Waldo Emerson*, merely arranges Emerson's writings on religion under various topics. By examining Emerson's "concept of polarity," Jeffrey L. Duncan, *The Power and Form of Emerson's Thought*, argues that, contra Whicher, Emerson did not reject optimism in his later years. Warren Staebler, *Ralph Waldo Emerson*, attempts nothing more than to accurately summarize Emerson's ideas and writings, and he succeeds. In an odd and sometimes flamboyant work, *The Universal Autobiography of Ralph Waldo Emerson*, Erik Ingvar Thurin examines Emerson's bipolar vision of the dichotomy between the sexes, and later, in *Emerson as Priest of Pan*, he discusses Emerson's "metaphysics of sex." In a more traditional vein, Edward Wagenknecht, *Ralph Waldo Emerson: Portrait of a Balanced Soul*, presents a general discussion of Emerson's character and personality.

The second half of the 1970s saw the publication of books as important as those published between 1949 and 1953. *Emerson: Prophecy, Metamorphosis, Influence*, ed. David Levin, contains original essays by Daniel B. Shea on Emerson and metamorphosis, James M. Cox on Emerson's visionary imagery, Phyllis Cole on "Emerson, England, and Fate," and Maurice Gonnaud on Quentin Anderson's *The Imperial Self*; it also reprints parts of books by Sacvan Bercovitch, Harold Bloom, and Albert Gelpi. In *Emerson and Literary Change*, David Porter argues that Emerson's poems are stylistic constructs that clearly place him in the modernist tradition. William J. Scheick, *The Slender Human Word*, presents a detailed stylistic analysis of Emerson's writing. The last two books of the 1970s are major contributions to Emerson scholarship. R. A. Yoder, *Emerson and the Orphic Poet in America*, argues that the Orphic poet he described in *Nature* (a "seer and builder") gradually changed over the years, becoming a resident of "a middle region where poetry is a limited power and the poet a man of common size or less." In *Representative Man*, Joel Porte focuses "not so much on . . . the finished thinker as on Emerson in the act of thinking," and presents a fresh and often exciting view of Emerson's literary artistry.

The first book of the 1980s, Lewis Leary, *Ralph Waldo Emerson: An Interpretive Essay*, began the decade on a good note. Leary, carefully avoiding particular themes, presents a solid overview of Emerson's ideas and writings. Eric Cheyfitz, *The Trans-Parent: Sexual Politics in the Language of Emerson*, is a psychoanalytic study of the conflict between masculine and feminine identities that Cheyfitz sees in Emerson's writings. In *Apostle of Culture: Emerson as Preacher and Lecturer*, David Robinson produces a major work on Emerson that traces "the shape that his oratorical ambition gave to his career, the corresponding dependence of that career on his Unitarian background, and the nature of the inherent paradox of self-culture that he discovered in following Unitarian assumptions to their logical conclusions." Two other important books are B. L. Packer's *Emerson's Fall*, which presents a discussion of the "four chief fables or formulas" that Emerson invented for explaining the Fall of Man and offers these fables as keys to understanding Emerson's work from *Nature* through *Representative Men*, and Leonard Neufeldt, *The House of Emerson*, which is especially good on Emerson's epistemology and use of metaphor. In *Emerson Centenary Essays*, ed. Joel Myerson, there are discussions of Emerson's early illness by Evelyn Barish, his sermons by Wesley T. Mott, "Emerson's Foreground" by Jerome Loving, his "Problem of Professionalism" by Glen M. Johnson, *The Method of Nature* by David Robinson, *Essays: Second Series* by Richard Lee Francis, "Experience" by David W. Hill, his views on Shakespeare by Sanford E. Marovitz, the contemporary reception of *English Traits* by Robert E. Burkholder, "The Adirondacks" by Ronald A. Sudol, and "Emerson as Teacher" by Merton M. Sealts, Jr.

Over the years a number of good, short, general critical essays on Emerson have appeared, the best of which are by Paul Elmer More (*CHAL*, vol. 1); Bliss Perry (*The American Spirit in Literature*); Frederic I. Carpenter (in his introduction to *Ralph Waldo Emerson: Representative Selections*); Robert E. Spiller (in *Literary History of the United States*); Arthur Hobson Quinn (*The Literature of the American People*); Josephine Miles (*Ralph Waldo Emerson*); Joel Porte ("The Problem of Emerson"); and Lawrence Buell (in *The American Renaissance in New England*, ed. Joel Myerson).

Collections of original or reprinted essays on Emerson dealing with particular aspects of his life or works are discussed in the appropriate sections of this chapter. These general collections of reprinted essays are useful: *Emerson: A Collection of Critical Essays*, ed. Milton R. Konvitz and Stephen E. Whicher; *Emerson's Relevance Today*, ed. Eric W. Carlson and J. Lasley Dameron; *The Recognition of Ralph Waldo Emerson*, ed. Milton R. Konvitz; *American Transcendentalism*, ed. Brian M. Barbour; and *Critics on Emerson*, ed. Thomas J. Roundtree, the only collection presenting snippets from the critics rather than whole essays. The most comprehensive collection is *Critical Essays on Ralph Waldo Emerson*, ed. Robert E. Burkholder and Joel Myerson.

Emerson has also been examined by the following types of criticism: depth psychology (J. Russell Reaver, *Emerson as Mythmaker*), Eriksonian (Joel Porte, *ForumH*, 1976, and Richard Lebeaux), existential (Mary Edrich Redding), Freudian (Ludwig Lewisohn; Vivian C. Hopkins, *ATQ*, 1971; John Clendenning; Robert A. Hutch; and Oscar Salinas), gay (Jonathan Katz), Jungian (Gloria Young and Martin Bickman), Marxist (V. F. Calverton, *The Liberation of American Literature*, and David Herreshoff), psychosexual (Evelyn Barish, *ATQ*, 1976), and psychotherapy (William E. Bridges).

SOURCES

Because of the sheer volume of Emerson's published works (when all the modern editions are completed, there will be nearly forty volumes of his letters, journals, and works available), the information on sources is staggering. Nevertheless, scholars have risen to the challenge. Kenneth Walter Cameron's *Ralph Waldo Emerson's Reading* and "Emerson's Early Reading List," among other of his publications, list Emerson's borrowings from Boston-area libraries. Walter Harding, *Emerson's Library*, is also useful as a starting point.

Among the general sources for Emerson's works, scholars have pointed to the Bible (Harriet Rodgers Zink), metaphysical poets (Norman A. Brittin), seventeenth-century authors (J. Russell Roberts), the English Romantics (Sheldon W. Liebman), and, as a group, *Three Children of the Universe: Emerson's View of Shakespeare, Bacon, and Milton*, by William M. Wynkoop.

Among the writers on Emerson's sources in world literature, the most useful are: on Chinese literature, Donald M. Murray; on French literature, Walter L. Leighton and Hans Keller (*Emerson in Frankreich: Wirkungen und Parallelen*); on German literature, Kuno Francke, Paul Sakmann (*Ralph Waldo Emerson's Geisteswelt*), Fred B. Wahr, René Wellek (*NEQ*, 1943), Stanley M. Vogel, who prints a list of German books in Emerson's library, and especially Henry A. Pochmann (*German Culture in America*), the best and most comprehensive study of the subject; on Italian literature, J. P. Brawner; on Oriental literature, W. T. Harris (in *The Genius and Character of Emerson*), Swami Paramananda, Frederic Ives Carpenter (*Emerson and Asia*), Arthur Christy, Kenneth Walter Cameron's introduction to his edition of *Indian Superstition*, Andrew M. McLean, Elamanamadathil V. Francis, and J. P. Rao Rayapati; on Persian literature, J. D. Yohannan and Mansur Ekhtiar; and on Spanish literature, Stanley T. Williams.

Numerous writers and schools of writing are seen to have influenced Emerson. Because many critics believe Emerson learned about Immanuel Kant from reading Samuel Taylor Coleridge, the English poet is often discussed as a source of Emerson's ideas: see Frank T. Thompson (*SP*, 1926), Clarence Paul Hotson (*NCMag*, 1934), Joseph Warren Beach (*The Concept of Nature in Nineteenth-Century English Poetry*), Kenneth Walter Cameron (*PQ*, 1951), Frank Lentricchia, and Barry Wood. The influence of Goethe, a great favorite of the Transcendentalists, is studied by Henry A. Brann ("Hegel and His New England Echo"), Frederic B. Wahr (*Emerson and Goethe*), Frederick A. Braun (*JEGP*, 1916), Vivian C. Hopkins (*PQ*, 1948), Phillip Allison Shelley, Mary A. Wyman, Joel Porte (*NEQ*, 1968), and Rüdiger Els (*Ralph Waldo Emerson und "Die Natur" in Goethes Werken*). Montaigne is believed to be a major source of Emerson's skepticism: see W. Lee Ustick, Charles Lowell Young's excellent *Emerson's Montaigne*, and Joseph Lawrence Basile. The source for much of Emerson's idealistic thought is seen as being in Plato and the Neoplatonists; see Orestes A. Brownson ("Emerson and Plato"), John S. Harrison (*The Teachers of Emerson*), Stuart Gerry Brown, Ray Benoit, George Mills Harper ("Thomas Taylor in America"),

Arlene J. Hansen, and Stanley Brodwin. Emerson's sense of an inner voice may have been derived from his acquaintance with the Quakers: see Frederick B. Tolles, Howard W. Hintz, Marcy C. Turpie, and Yukio Irie (*Emerson and Quakerism*). His ambivalent feelings toward the Shakers are discussed by Priscilla J. Brewer. The basis for Emerson's distinction between Reason and Understanding, when not seen as resting in Coleridge, is often seen in the Scottish philosophers, such as Dugald Stewart, who were required reading when Emerson was an undergraduate at Harvard: see Merrell R. Davis, J. Edward Schamberger, and Sheldon W. Liebman (*AL*, 1973).

Those who see mystical elements in Emerson feel he derived at least some of them from Emanuel Swedenborg: see John Goddard, Kenneth Walter Cameron ("Emerson and Swedenborg"), George Hendrick (*ATQ*, 1978), and a series of articles by Clarence Paul Hotson (all derived from his 1929 Harvard Univ. dissertation on Emerson and Swedenborg) on such subjects as Emerson's lecture on Swedenborg (*NewP*, 1928; *SP*, 1929; *NCL*, 1929; two in *NCM*, 1930, 1932; three in *NCMag*, 1931–32; *NEQ*, 1938), Sampson Reed's influence on Emerson (*NEQ*, 1929), "Emerson and the Swedenborgians," George Bush's influence on Emerson (two in *NCMag* 1931, 1932; *PQ*, 1931), and "Emerson and the 'New-Church Quarterly Review.'" Much of Hotson's work is based on the writings of a vocal group of nineteenth-century Swedenborgians in this country and in England, most of whom protested against what they recognized as Emerson's misrepresentation of their master. This group included a reviewer in the *Intellectual Repository and New Jerusalem Magazine* (1837) and John Westall, both of whom reviewed *Nature*, George Bush (*Prof. Bush's Reply to Ralph Waldo Emerson on Swedenborg*), R. M'Cully, and W. J. Underwood (*Emerson and Swedenborg*). A positive treatment of Emerson by a nineteenth-century British Swedenborgian is that by David George Goyder (in *The Biblical Assistant and Book of Practical Piety*), and an early study of the influence of Sampson Reed upon Emerson is Alexander H. Japp, "A Gift from Emerson."

For articles tracing sources for Emerson's ideas to such widely disparate individuals as Francis Bacon, Pierre Bayle, Beethoven, Jacob Boehme, Byron, Victor Cousin, Ralph Cudworth, Dante, Baron Gerando, George Herbert, David Hume, Thomas Jefferson, John Keats, Lucretius, Michelangelo, Milton, Isaac Newton, Plutarch, Schelling, Walter Scott, Shakespeare, Vico, William Wordsworth, and Edward Young, see Burkholder and Myerson's bibliography.

THOUGHT

PHILOSOPHY

Among the most significant general considerations of Emerson's philosophy in the nineteenth century is George Ripley and George P. Bradford, "Philosophical Thought in Boston," which discusses Emerson as the single most important force in the Transcendentalist movement; Emanuel Cohen, "The Philosophy of Emerson," which states that the two major tenets of Emerson's thought are "the dignity of character'' and the idea that there is something beyond the individual soul that governs human will; the anonymous ''The Philosophy of Emerson,'' which argues that optimism, nature, and simplicity are the chief features of Emerson's thought; and W. L. Courtney, ''Emerson's Philosophy,'' which examines the importance of optimism, idealism, and the concept of self-cultivation in Emerson's work. A valuable general assessment of Emerson's thought is by John M. Robertson, *Modern Humanists*, who presents a valuable and balanced evaluation of Emerson's philosophy that is particularly critical of Emerson's method (which is described as ''booking'' ''every generalization that occurred to him day-to-day'') and of his failure to arrange his inspirations into coherent statements. Robertson ultimately argues, in anticipation of many later critics, that Emerson's poetic inspiration cannot be mistaken for philosophy in an age of science. This essay is more substantative and harsher in its criticism than Robertson's earlier *Ralph Waldo Emerson: Man and Teacher*. More polemic critics of Emerson's thought are H. N. Holland, ''Mr. Emerson's Philosophy,'' who outlines Emerson's Transcendentalism only to argue that it has been superseded by Positivism; Vernon Lee (pseud. for Violet Paget), ''Emerson: Transcendentalist and Utilitarian,'' who concludes that the final products of Emerson's philosophy are a realization of nothingness and a failure to differentiate good and evil; and James Lindsey, ''Emerson as a Thinker,'' who seems either unable or unwilling to decide Emerson's ultimate worth as a philosopher.

Emerson's idealism is a major concern of Octavius Brooks Frothingham, *Transcendentalism in New England*. J. C. Allen, in ''The Two Phases of Emerson's Thought,'' examines both Emerson's idealism and his sense of the practical; Walter Lewin, ''Emerson and the Transcendentalists,'' suggests that this idealism represented a revival of spirituality preferable to the alternatives, worship of science or blind acquiescence to fundamentalist religions; and Henry Norman, ''Ralph Waldo Emerson: An Ethical Study,'' argues that it was through ''the most sweeping idealism'' that Emerson managed to bridge the gap between empirical ethics and transcendental ethics. Ethics is also the concern of William J. Potter, ''Emerson's View of Ethics,'' who describes ethical considerations as a dominating influence upon Emerson's work, and of Frederick May Holland, ''Emerson as a Moralist,'' and Edwin D. Mead (in *The Genius and Character of Emerson*). The ''Sources of Emerson's Optimism'' are discussed by Frederic J. Dutton, but William F. Dana, *The Optimism of Ralph Waldo Emerson*, is a discussion of Emerson's thought as an ameliorating force on the pessimism of his age that is generally outshone by George Santayana, ''The Optimism of Emerson,'' an unsuccessful and unpublished submission for the 1885–86 Bowdoin Prize that Dana won. Epistemology is the subject of Cyrus A. Bartol's eulogistic but often valuable ''The Nature of Knowledge: Emerson's Way.'' The relation of Emerson's thought to the systems of Herbert Spencer and James Martineau is treated by William R. Alger. Emerson's major role, with Jonathan Edwards, in the rise of ''Free Thought in New England'' is described by Henry A. Brann.

Beginning with Henry David Gray (1917), a number of writers have tried to discern a coherent general philosophy in Emerson's writings. Indeed, nearly every history of

American philosophy has a section on Emerson, albeit a skimpy one that oversimplifies. Three general studies are of note: William B. Barton's discussion "Emerson's Method as a Philosopher," Leonard Neufeldt's examination of Emerson's epistemology, and Richard Lee Francis, " 'Morn at Mid Noon': The Emerging Emersonian Method." Most studies have tried to place Emerson's philosophy within the context of a particular movement: Stanley Cavell puts Emerson in the Hegel-Heidegger camp (*NLH*, 1979), Virginia Moran allies him only with Hegel, and Russell Kirk places Emerson in the conservative tradition (*The Conservative Mind from Burke to Santayana*). Overall, though, most studies try to classify Emerson as an inheritor of English Romanticism, a propounder of Transcendentalism, or a transitional link in the development of pragmatism.

G. Harrison Orians provides an excellent overview of Emerson's role in "The Rise of Romanticism, 1805–1855." A shorter study along the same lines has been done by Robert N. Hertz. See also "Emerson: The Glory and Sorrows of American Romanticism," by Harold Bloom. Two specific studies are worth noting: Joseph Baim's discussion of Emerson's use of the child motif and Edward Halsey Foster's self-explanatory *The Civilized Wilderness: Backgrounds to American Romantic Literature*.

Every book on Transcendentalism naturally devotes a major section to Emerson. A list of the better books may be found in Lawrence Buell's chapter in this volume. Since scholars cannot agree on a definition of Transcendentalism and since the Transcendentalists refused this general appellation themselves, studies of Emerson and Transcendentalism are usually doomed from the start, but a number of them are worth consulting. A good starting point is Alexander Kern, "The Rise of Transcendentalism, 1815–1860." Some individual works of note are those by George Willis Cooke (*NEMag*, 1903), Henry A. Beers (*BL*, 1903), Harold Clarke Goddard (*Studies in New England Transcendentalism*), Régis Michaud (*AJP*, 1919), Howard Mumford Jones (*Belief and Disbelief in American Literature*), Elizabeth A. Meese (*AL*, 1975), James E. Mulqueen (*TSL*, 1976), and the chapter on Transcendentalism in volume 1 of Elizabeth Flower and Murray G. Murphey, *A History of Philosophy in America*.

A negative comment on Emerson's unpragmatic philosophy is Henry Bamford Parkes, but a more positive view is expressed by Eduard C. Lindeman. A number of studies see Emerson as either a forerunner of pragmatism or a part of the pragmatic tradition: Eduard Baumgarten (*Der Pragmatismus*), Alfred S. Reid, who groups Emerson with Horace Bushnell, and Paul K. Conkin, who places Emerson at the center of American thought, between Puritanism and pragmatism.

Emerson's relation to other movements of his time has been studied in less detail. Some good general studies are Lewis Mumford, *The Golden Day*, Gilbert Seldes, *The Stammering Century*, Perry Miller, *The Raven and the Whale*, and Jay Martin, *Harvests of Change*. Special studies have examined Emerson's comments on literary nationalism (Benjamin T. Spencer, *The Quest for Nationality*, and John Stephen Martin), feminism (Adapa Ramakrishna Rao, *IJAS*, 1974), phrenology (Stephen S. Conroy), theosophy (F. S. Darrow), and spiritualism (John B. Wilson, *NEQ*, 1968, and Russell M. Goldfarb and Clare R. Goldfarb).

AESTHETICS

Emerson's place in *A History of Literary Aesthetics in America* is discussed by Max I. Baym. Vivian C. Hopkins, *Spires of Form*, is the best single work. Among the better shorter studies are Donald MacRae, "Emerson and the Arts," Charles R. Metzger, "Emerson's Religious Conception of Beauty," Theodore M. Brown on the organic Aesthetic, Percy W. Brown, "Emerson's Philosophy of Aesthetics," and Wendell Glick, "The Moral and Ethical Dimensions of Emerson's Aesthetics."

NATURE

When one's first book is called *Nature*, that subject naturally gets much attention from critics. General discussions of Emerson's philosophy of nature are found in Woodbridge Riley (*American Thought from Puritanism to Pragmatism and Beyond*) and Norman Foerster (*Nature in American Literature*). W. T. Harris suggests that Emerson was able to discover spiritual correspondence in nature through a combination of poetic insight and scientific theory ("Emerson's Philosophy of Nature"). Philip Marshall Hicks describes Emerson as the most important influence in *The Development of the Natural History Essay in American Literature*. Douglas C. Stenerson discusses "Emerson and the Agrarian Tradition," R. W. B. Lewis places Emerson in the Adamic tradition (*The American Adam*), and William L. Hedges sees nothing original in Emerson's ideas about nature (*TWA*, 1955). Leo Marx explores Emerson's reaction to technology's advance over nature (*The Machine in the Garden*); Joel Porte, in "Nature as Symbol," sees Emerson's "temperament and attitudes," not his philosophy, as the primary basis upon which he developed his views of nature. David Robinson has done a perceptive study of "Emerson's Natural Theology and the Paris Naturalists."

Closely allied to Emerson's theories of nature are his theories of organicism. Good general studies are by W. T. Harris, "The Dialectic Unity of Emerson's Prose"; Norman Foerster, "Emerson on the Organic Principle in Art"; Richard P. Adams, "Emerson and the Organic Metaphor"; and Carl F. Strauch, "Emerson's Use of the Organic Method," which argues that Emerson's attempt to control "the chaotic flux of existence" was itself a contradiction. Emerson's application of the organic theory to architecture is discussed by Robert B. Shaffer and James Early. Studies of Emerson's use of the organic principle in his writings are discussed below.

SCIENCE

Nineteenth-century commentators tended to view Emerson's association with science almost exclusively in relation to Darwin. As early as *The Conduct of Life*, critics pointed out similarities between Emerson's concept of fate and the theory of evolution, but it remained for Moncure D. Conway (*Emerson and His Views on Nature*) to argue without reservation that all Emerson's work was built upon a theory of development that resembled Darwinian evolution. In a similar fashion, Thomas Wentworth Higginson, in his address to the sixteenth annual meeting of the Free Religious Association (*Index*, 14 June 1883), discusses parallels in the lives and thought of Darwin and Emerson, but such comparisons are rejected by J. B. Thomas in "Darwin, Emerson and the Gospel." The anonymous author of "Emerson" (1899) suggests that Emerson's concept of evolution was poetic rather than scientific, and Harriet C. B. Alexander argues in "Emerson and Evolution" that Emerson's evolutionary ideas probably came from his reading of Goethe rather than from any knowledge of science.

In the twentieth century, Harry Hayden Clark, " Emerson and Science," traces Emerson's interest in science through 1838, arguing that it led him to break with "ecclesiasticism." Emerson's comments on evolution are studied by Joseph Warren Beach (1934), and Robert L. Haig pinpoints his acceptance of evolution in 1859. Carl F. Strauch, "Emerson's Sacred Science," relates evolution to Emerson's "Beautiful Necessity," whereas Peter A. Obuchowski relates it to Emerson's "lifelong avowal of monism." Other studies deal with Emerson's views on science as he expressed them in particular works: Carl F. Strauch on "Song of Nature," Gay Wilson Allen on the early lectures (in *Literature and Ideas in America*, ed. Robert Falk), Philip L. Nicoloff on racial science in *English Traits*, and Leonard Neufeldt on "Works and Days" (*JHI*, 1977).

RELIGION

Emerson's religious beliefs were criticized as early as 1833, when a writer signed "G." attacked Dr. William Ellery Channing and his disciple, "an Unitarian minister in the north part of Boston, [who] has lately declared that the Lord's Supper is of no validity," in the pages of the *New-England Magazine*. The Divinity School Address and the commotion it spawned only served to provoke Emerson's opponents, notably Andrews Norton ("The New School of Religion and Literature") and the Princetonians J. W. Alexander, Albert Dod, and Charles Hodge. These attacks inspired eloquent defenses of Emerson by men like Orestes A. Brownson ("Mr. Emerson's Address"), James Freeman Clarke ("R. W. Emerson and the New School"), and Emerson's successor in the pulpit of the Second Church, Chandler Robbins, who as editor of the *Christian Register* defended Emerson as often and as forcefully as he could in an official publication of the Unitarian Church during the fall of 1838.

Ironically, Emerson's religious beliefs would never be upheld as vehemently as they were when they were under heaviest attack. With the exception of Cyrus A. Bartol (*Radical Problems*) and John Savary, both of whom provide background for understanding the controversy of the late 1830s, critics in the 1860s and 1870s generally disliked Emerson's treatment of religion. In "Phases of American Liberal Theology,"

A. F. Spaulding argues that Emerson's work represents philosophy with a patronizing air; Orestes Brownson suggests that it "unchristianizes Christianity" ("Free Religion"); and Henry Hemming, "A Few Notes on Emerson and the Pantheists," criticizes his attempt "to make all things under heaven bend to a preconceived pantheistic theory." The one bright spot in this morass of negative criticism is John Beattie Crozier, "Emerson," a detailed elaboration of Emerson's philosophy and religious ideas that, among other things, compares them to those of Carlyle.

Confusion about Emerson's rumored turn to religious orthodoxy near the end of his life resulted in elaborate explanations of Emerson's firm stand behind Free Religion, such as George Willis Cooke, "Emerson's Attitude toward Religion." Also see Joseph Cook, "Emerson's Theism," and Bronson Alcott, "Has Mr. Emerson Changed His Views?" Emerson's death brought even more religious controversy. Robert Ingersoll's pronouncement that "If Christianity be true, Longfellow and Emerson are in Hell tonight" (see "Creed vs. Character") was followed by two controversial blasts from the pen of Frederic Dan Huntington. In the first (*Ind*, 18, 25 May 1882), Huntington criticizes Emerson's theory of sin as a "grave fault" and suggests that his aberrant religious notions were the result of an "inaptitude for thinking consecutively." In the second (*SST*, 20 May 1882), Huntington denounces Emerson as the one who did the most "to unsettle the Faith of educated young men of our age and country," and he is incredulous that Christian ministers extol Emerson's contribution to religion. Because of the unpropitious timing of Huntington's remarks, a number of defenses of Emerson's religious position appeared, including those by Samuel J. Barrows, J. H. Clifford, G. W. Gallagher (*Were Emerson and Longfellow Christians?*), and Minot J. Savage (*Bishop Huntington and Mr. Emerson* and *Ralph Waldo Emerson*). In "Emerson's Religion," Cyrus A. Bartol argues that, despite the popular assumption that Emerson was against religion, he was "preeminently religious," a view that was also advanced by John M. Robertson (*Ralph Waldo Emerson*). In her consideration of "Emerson as Preacher" (in *The Genius and Character of Emerson*), Elizabeth Palmer Peabody claims that Emerson's religion was in his poetry.

Negative assessments of Emerson's religious views may be found in C. S. Walker, "Emerson's Relation to Christ and Christianity"; Maud Petre, "The Emersonian Creed"; Isaac T. Hecker, "Two Prophets of This Age," which condemns Emerson and Matthew Arnold for attempting to replace God with human reason as an object of worship; and S. Law, "The Theology of Emerson." Positive assessments include William Salter, "The Christian Idealism of Ralph Waldo Emerson," Lewis G. Janes, "Emerson, the Believer," and W. H. Savage, "The Religion of Emerson." Of course there were also those who refused to play by the rules: Henry C. Badger, in "Emerson's Agnosticism," suggests that Emerson's religious notions only sound radical because he did not know what he was saying and that his doctrines are simply old-fashioned Christianity.

Emerson's religious views—or lack thereof—have continued to claim the attention of twentieth-century commentators. The best William James could do was to refer to Emerson's "transcendental idealism" (*The Varieties of Religious Experience*). Other writers have vaguely described Emerson as a mystic, including Yvor Winters (*AmR*, 1936), Patrick F. Quinn (*AL*, 1950), Lester Mondale, and Edith Mettke (*Der Dichter Ralph Waldo Emerson*). Mentor L. Williams has linked Emerson with the occult.

More traditional (and more valuable) studies have placed Emerson securely within the American Unitarian tradition. Especially good in this light are C. H. Faust, Conrad Wright (in *The Harvard Divinity School*, ed. George Huntston Williams), William R. Hutchison's excellent *The Transcendentalist Ministers*, and Lawrence Buell's valuable "Unitarian Aesthetics and Emerson's Poet-Priest." Discussions of the Divinity School Address are listed below. Emerson's relations with the western Unitarians are discussed in Charles H. Lyttle, *Freedom Moves West*. Emerson's involvement with the Free Religious Association is examined by George Willis Cooke and Stow Persons (*Free Religion*).

Emerson's essential Christian virtues are discussed by Robert C. Pollock, and James Wiseman praises Emerson for reconciling the "transcendence" and "immanence" of God. Carl Dennis (*ATQ*, 1975) sees the biblical concept of the poet as "a revealer of holy truth" at the heart of Emerson's poetics. Sheldon W. Liebman (*AL*, 1968) sees Emerson in the 1820s as changing from a Unitarian to a Transcendentalist, whereas Karl Keller (*AL*, 1967) argues that Emerson reconciled Unitarianism and Transcendentalism. Stephen Donadio writes that Emerson translated "all experience into Christian experience," but Harold Fromm believes that, like Kierkegaard, Emerson rejected Historical Christianity. Randall Stewart (*TSL*, 1957) protests that Emerson's doctrine is "radically anti-Christian, and has done more than any other to undermine Christian orthodoxy in America"; for a rebuttal, see Robert Stafford Ward. According to Richard D. Birdsall, Emerson definitely rejected Catholicism.

Unfortunately, further scholarship on Emerson and religion must wait for his sermons to be edited. Those who have worked with the manuscript sermons have produced useful studies: Arthur Cushman McGiffert's introduction to *Young Emerson Speaks* provides an excellent overview of Emerson's early religious thought, Kenneth Walter Cameron generalizes about "History and Biography in Emerson's Unpublished Sermons," and Wesley T. Mott gives an excellent discussion of "Emerson and Antinomianism" and a fine detailed study of the sermon "Christ Crucified" (in *Emerson Centenary Essays*).

Closely allied to Emerson's religious thought are his ideas concerning good and evil. Emerson the optimist is described by Floyd Stovall (*CE*, 1942), Charles Howell Foster (*NEQ*, 1943), Frederick W. Conner (*Cosmic Optimism*), Howard Mumford Jones (*The Pursuit of Happiness*), Robert E. Spiller ("The Four Faces of Emerson"), Everett Carter (*The American Idea*), and David Robinson (*PQ*, 1978). Martin Green (*Re-Appraisals*) goes so far as to argue for a return to Emerson's optimism in place of the vogue of such "dark" writers as William Faulkner. Opposed to these are articles by Charles Gray Shaw on "Emerson, the Nihilist," John Lydenberg on Emerson's "darkness," Louis B. Salomon, and Richard Tuerk (*ATQ*, 1975). Less extreme are articles on Emerson and skepticism by Carl F. Strauch (*HLB*, 1957) and Margaret Wiley Marshall.

Many of the better articles on the topic of religion recognize a tension between optimism and a lack of optimism (pessimism is perhaps too strong a word) in Emerson's writings. Some, like A. D. Van Nostrand (*Everyman His Own Poet*), simply see Emerson as progressing from idealism to determinism, whereas others, like Zacharias Thundyil, claim that Emerson bridged this gap by a leap of faith. Others are less sure of a solution. Chester Eugene Jorgenson argues that Emerson believed in a "beneficent Deity whose unchanging laws lead to happiness if obeyed, and whose laws if transgressed bring immediate retribution, that evil results from a disproportion of passion in life, private and public, and thus is fragmentary and privative, and that man has free will to choose between the life of reason and the lure of the senses." Carl F. Strauch (*Person*, 1952) writes that while Emerson "abundantly acknowledged that raw energy of the daemonic and its perilous attractions, he was not bound by his philosophy to sacrifice himself, like an automaton, to that energy and those attractions." In "Emerson's Tragic Sense," Stephen E. Whicher argues that each time Emerson's "inner promise of ideal power came up against the narrow limits of his experience, the response could only be the same—the renewed surrender to the Power that planned it that way." Newton Arvin feels that Emerson acknowledged a "tragic sense of life"; however, "he rejected tragedy not because he was by temperament wholly incapable of tragic insight but because it seemed to him that . . . [it] belongs . . . in the world of appearance, of the relative, of illusion; not in the realm of transcendent reality and truth in which Emerson's faith was complete." Emerson is seen by Loren Baritz as embodying "many of the contradictions and tensions" of America: "He could sustain an optimism that had a demon, could speak of the good of the universe in a nation of slavery, could justify actual evil in the name of a higher good, could defend spiritual equality but long for heroes, could speak for abstract democracy and find most actual men offensive." According to Joseph F. Doherty, Emerson's loneliness—his "solipsistic entrapment . . . that gods can only know themselves"—is often overlooked by readers, because whenever Emerson "manages to wrestle his horrors back under control at those moments when they erupt into full consciousness, readers lulled by his confident tones have missed the precariousness by which he maintains his apparent equilibrium. We have mistaken equilibrium for equanimity."

SOCIAL AND POLITICAL REFORM

An informative general study of Emerson's involvement in various reform movements is William Salter, "Emerson's Views on Reform," which concludes that he was primarily concerned with inward reform. "Emerson's Social Philosophy" (1883) uses Emerson to support the anonymous critic's argument against materialism.

Specific studies of Emerson's contribution to the campaign for women's rights are by Thomas Wentworth Higginson, "Tested by Time," who discusses Emerson's role in the first National Woman's Rights Convention in 1850, and Julia Ward Howe, "Ralph Waldo Emerson," who hails Emerson's work on the behalf of woman suffrage.

C. C. Hazewell, "Emerson as a Politician," and John W. Chadwick, "Emerson: The Patriot," discuss the conventional ways that Emerson performed his role as a citizen. Chadwick emphasizes his participation in the antislavery movement, as does Moncure D. Conway, "Ralph Waldo Emerson." In his biography, Oliver Wendell Holmes questioned whether Emerson had much sympathy for the abolitionists, arousing a brief debate in the *Index* in November and December 1885 that was finally quieted by Elizabeth Palmer Peabody's assurances in "Emerson and the Abolitionists" that Emerson was "uncompromisingly an abolitionist," even before his second marriage.

Emerson's failure to understand the importance of Brook Farm, and religious and social unity in general, is discussed briefly in John Humphrey Noyes, *History of American Socialisms*. Emerson's relation to Brook Farm is discussed by Lindsay Swift in an excellent study, *Brook Farm*, and an interesting defense of Emerson's decision not to join the utopian community is in Richard Garnett, *Life of Ralph Waldo Emerson*. See also John T. Flanagan, "Emerson and Communism." Other works on this topic may be found in Joel Myerson, *Brook Farm: An Annotated Bibliography and Resources Guide*, and in the chapter "Transcendentalist Communities" in this volume.

For studies relating Emerson to the major social and political questions of the day, see Raymer McQuiston on public affairs; Alfred Taylor Odell, *La Doctrine sociale d'Emerson*; William Allen Huggard, "Ralph Waldo Emerson and the Problem of War and Peace"; Ernest E. Sandeen, "Emerson's Americanism"; Alexander C. Kern, "Emerson and Economics"; John C. Gerber, "Emerson and the Political Economists"; John Q. Anderson, "Emerson on Texas and the Mexican War"; R. Jackson Wilson, *In Quest of Community*; and Edward H. Madden, *Civil Disobedience and Moral Law in Nineteenth Century American Philosophy*. An overview of the subject is provided in Adapa Ramakrishna Rao, *Emerson and Social Reform*.

Emerson's politics are the subject of a number of articles: Arthur I. Ladu, "Emerson: Whig or Democrat," sees him as dissatisfied with both parties. Arthur Hobson Quinn (*PAAS*, 1944) finds Emerson's basic principles at odds with his party ties to the Whigs. Otis B. Wheeler views "Emerson's Political Quandary" as the conflict between a philosopher's long view of history and an individual's involvement with contemporary events in the real world. George F. Carter places Emerson in the conservative Whig camp. In an odd article, Irene P. McKeehan compares Emerson's politics with those of Carlyle and Adolf Hitler and fortunately places Emerson closer to Carlyle in her conclusion to this no-win situation.

Most writers like to define Emerson as a democrat without reference to political party. An excellent discussion of how Emerson's democratic tendencies separated him from his aristocratic contemporaries is Perry Miller, "Emersonian Genius and American Democracy." Pure admiration for Emerson's democracy is in works by John Dewey (*IJE*, 1903), Stuart P. Sherman (in his edition of *Essays and Poems of Emerson*), Vernon Louis Parrington (*The Romantic Revolution in America 1800–1860*), Ralph Henry Gabriel (*The Course of American Democratic Thought*), Edwin Harrison Cady (*The*

Gentleman in America), and John G. Cawelti (*Apostles of the Self-Made Man*). Others are not so sure: John O. McCormick argues that Emerson had a "profound distrust of people in the mass"; Alfred J. Kloeckner believes that Emerson lacked faith in the majority of men; Anthony Hilbrunner calls Emerson antiequalitarian; and Wilson Carey McWilliams (*The Idea of Fraternity in America*) sees a tension between Emerson's favorable published comments on fraternity and his personal distrust of friendships.

Scholars also debate Emerson's view of progress. Arthur Alphonse Ekirch (*The Idea of Progress in America*) and Daniel Aaron (*Men of Good Hope*) see Emerson as forward-looking, whereas Mildred Silver feels that he questioned every advance. Nearly all critics agree that Emerson viewed the western frontier in a positive light: see Lucy Lockwood Hazard (*The Frontier in American Literature*), Ernest Marchand, R. T. Flewelling, and Arthur Cushman McGiffert, Jr. But when this expansion led to civil strife, as in the Mexican and Civil Wars, Emerson recoiled.

A fine article on "Emerson and the Civil War" is by Leonard Neufeldt. Also useful are "Emerson's Philosophy of War and Peace" by William A. Huggard; studies of Emerson and abolitionism by Len Gougeon (*NEQ*, 1981; *SAR*, 1981), Marjory M. Moody, Adapa Ramakrishna Rao (*OJES*, 1971), and Satya S. Pachori; and "Emerson and John Brown" by John J. McDonald. Emerson's changing views on the South are chronicled by Jay B. Hubbell (*The South in American Literature*), Philip Butcher, and Howard R. Floan (*The South in Northern Eyes*).

Emerson's views of education and educational reform are given in *Emerson on Education*, ed. Howard Mumford Jones, and are discussed in works by Charles W. Thwing, Philip Magnus, Ada E. Davis, Hazen C. Carpenter (*NEQ*, 1951), J. A. Ward, and Rüdiger C. Schlicht (*Die pädagogischen Ansätze amerikanischer Transzendentalisten*).

A few critics have tried to generalize about Emerson's responses to reform movements. Theodore L. Gross (*BuR*, 1969) feels that Emerson's early faith in freedom yielded to a belief in fate in his later years. Quentin Anderson, *The Imperial Self*, argues that Emerson eventually judged society "irrevelant"; for a rejoinder, see Maurice Gonnaud (in *Emerson: Prophecy, Metamorphosis, Influence*). According to Gay Wilson Allen (*UWR*, 1973), Emerson resolved that the structure of society needed to be changed. Mary K. Cayton agrees, contending that Emerson reached this conclusion around 1823–25, when he was in Roxbury before entering divinity school. Taylor Stoehr (*CRevAS*, 1974) argues that Emerson believed his lectures and essays were a more effective vehicle for reform than was his active participation in the political movements of the day. Emerson's "Ode Inscribed to W. H. Channing" is probably his best expression of this view; see articles by George Arms and Carl F. Strauch. Phyllis Cole (in *Emerson: Prophecy, Metamorphosis, Influence*) argues that Emerson was caught between "the individual's need for incarnation into the world and the danger of being engulfed by it." Gustaaf Van Cromphout (*PMLA*, 1976) concludes that Emerson viewed history first as "a conflict between hero and society" and later as "a synthesis of hero and society."

SPECIFIC IDEAS

Compensation. John Beattie Crozier (*ContempR*, 1917) argues against the idea of compensation, as does Maria Moravsky, who calls it "untrue and pitiless." On the other hand, an anonymous reviewer of "Emerson's Essays" in the *Trumpet and Universalist Magazine* (1841) is surprisingly taken with the concept because he sees it as closely related to the Universalist doctrine of present retribution. Perhaps the best discussion of compensation is by Henry F. Pommer. Roland F. Lee sees affinities to existential thought, but William K. Bottorff finds it contradicts all of Emerson's philosophy.

Correspondence. The basis of the doctrine of correspondence in Swedenborgian thought is exhaustively treated in four articles by Clarence Paul Hotson (*NCR*, 1929) and its influence on later writers of the "New Thought" school is treated by Gail Thain Parker (*Mind Cure in New England*). Emerson's literary uses of correspondence are examined in Christopher Collins, *The Uses of Observation*, and Catherine L. Albanese, *Corresponding Motion*.

Friendship. Emerson's friendships with many of his younger contemporaries are surveyed by William M. Moss. The ways in which these relations were transformed into art are examined by John Bard McNulty and by Carl F. Strauch, whose article "Hatred's Swift Repulsions" is original and often provocative.

Over-Soul. Kathryn Whitford makes some general comments on this topic. Of more use is Robert Detweiler, "The Over-Rated 'Over-Soul,' " which shows that Emerson's commentators, not Emerson, are enamored of the term.

Self-Reliance. Early reviews of Emerson's work often indicted the idea of self-reliance as either inherently antisocial (see the review of *Essays*, *NYR*, 1841) or harmful because it contradicted Christian humility and self-renunciation (see "Emerson's Addresses," *LWNY*, 1849). Later in the nineteenth century, however, Frederick May Holland (*Liberty in the Nineteenth Century*) would discuss self-reliance as Emerson's most useful doctrine, and F. L. Pattee would present a flattering analysis (*Chautauquan*, 1900). A number of twentieth-century essays give general discussions of this idea: Ralph L. Rusk (*CE*, 1953), Wilson O. Clough, Charles A. Barker, Ellwood Johnson, Raymond Gardella, and William K. Bottorff (*ESQ*, 1972).

Key Words. A number of articles are wholly devoted to explaining one or two terms used by Emerson: On "truth" and "nature," see Paul Lauter. On "Emerson and the Double Consciousness," see Frank Davidson. On "Emerson and the 'Moral Sentiment,' " see John Q. Anderson. On "Emersonian Virtue," see James A. Emanuel.

On "Emerson and the Doctrine of Sympathy," see Carl F. Strauch. On "Emerson's Each and All," see Norman Miller.

WRITINGS

LITERARY EXPRESSION

Although reviewers of Emerson's works paid a great deal of attention to stylistic considerations, few specialized studies of Emerson's style appeared during his lifetime. One notable exception is John Burroughs, "A Word or Two on Emerson," which suggests that the unique quality in Emerson's writing is analogous to electricity and that his chief weapon as a writer is surprise. Oliver Wendell Holmes was later to make a similar observation in his biography of Emerson, that the "point and surprise" Emerson uses to characterize Plutarch's style "belong eminently to his own." Other evaluations may be found in T. W. Hunt, "Emerson's English Style"; Charles H. Lerch, "Emerson's Prose"; W. J. Dawson, "Emerson"; and George C. Hirst, "Emerson's Style in His Essays."

The ways in which Emerson's method of composition affected his style are dealt with by George Santayana (in *American Prose*, ed. George Rice Carpenter) and W. L. Courtney, both of whom speculate on the possible effect that Emerson's composition for the lecture halls may have had on his prose.

Among those concerned with the method of organization used by Emerson in his essays are W. T. Harris, who, in "The Dialectic Unity of Emerson's Prose," argues that Emerson's essays are structured according to an organic principle that "begins with the simplest and most obvious phase of the subject and discovers by investigation the next phase that naturally follows." Patrick Dillon, in "The Non-Sequaciousness of Ralph Waldo Emerson," frets that the use of Emerson's essays as literary models for those just learning to write could result in an underdeveloped reasoning faculty.

The problem of how to judge Emerson's prose style—or lack thereof—continued well into the twentieth century. For example, Hall Frye praises Emerson's fragmentary style; W. C. Brownell admires Emerson's colloquial style but complains of his lack of organization. Good arguments for Emerson's conscious literary artistry are made by William J. Scheick (*The Slender Human Word*), Lawrence Buell (*QJS*, 1972), and David W. Hill (in *Emerson Centenary Essays*).

A number of general works contain solid comment on Emerson's writing abilities. F. O. Matthiessen, *American Renaissance*, examines Emerson in the context of his time and, through an examination of individual works, shows how he organized his writings to effectively convey his ideas. Emerson's proximity to "modern notions of symbolic reality" and his central role in American symbolic literature are noted in Charles Feidelson, Jr., *Symbolism and American Literature*. Tony Tanner, *The Reign of Wonder*, is perhaps the best examination of Emerson's use of visionary imagery, but the best study of Emerson as a writer is Lawrence Buell, *Literary Transcendentalism*, a brilliant work that firmly roots Emerson's writings in their time and the literary genres to be found then. In *The Wisdom of Words*, Philip F. Gura masterfully relates Emerson's use of language to that of other nineteenth-century authors, beginning with the Unitarians. Some useful general studies are those by Andre Celieres (*The Prose Style of Emerson*), Clark Griffith (*MLQ*, 1961), David F. Finnigan, Richard Poirier (*A World Elsewhere*), Jesse Bier (*NEQ*, 1970), Laurence Stapleton (*The Elected Circle*), Brian M. Barbour (*MLQ*, 1974), James M. Cox (in *Emerson: Prophecy, Metamorphosis, Influence*), Catherine Albanese (*NEQ*, 1975), and Gayle L. Smith.

Various studies have focused on aspects of Emerson's literary expression. Emerson Grant Sutcliffe shows how Emerson's style evolved from a ministerial one to a symbolic one. Similarly, Mason I. Lowance (*The Language of Canaan*) notes that Emerson replaced the biblical symbolism of the Puritans with Platonic and mystical allusions. "Emerson's Literary Method," according to Walter Blair and Clarence Faust, was based on Plato's twice-bisected line. Roland F. Lee feels that Emerson's writings can best be understood by applying Kierkegaard's theory of communication. In an excellent and straightforward discussion, Robert Spiller shows how Emerson revised "From Lecture to Essay." R. A. Yoder ("Emerson's Dialectic") contends that, as Emerson got older, his style changed from a series of parallel paragraphs to a series of contrasting paragraphs. "The Development of Emerson's Theory of Rhetoric, 1821–1836" is ably discussed by Sheldon W. Liebman. Barbara Packer (*GaR*, 1977) argues that Emerson "deliberately made his own texts hard to understand."

Individual stylistic techniques of Emerson's have also been studied. His use of mythology is covered by J. Russell Reaver (*ESQ*, 1965), John Q. Anderson (*ATQ*, 1975), and, in the best study of the subject, Robert D. Richardson, Jr., *Myth and Literature in the American Renaissance*. Metamorphosis as a stylistic element in Emerson is examined by Daniel B. Shea (in *Emerson: Prophecy, Metamorphosis, Influence*), Michael H. Cowan (*ATQ*, 1975), and Brian R. Harding (*ATQ*, 1976). Other topics have been studied in less detail, including analogy (Sidney P. Moss, *ESQ*, 1965), autobiographical style (Lawrence Buell, *ATQ*, 1971), epiphanies (Gene Bluestein), hieroglyphics (John T. Irwin; William J. Scheick, *The Slender Human Word*), image transformation (Leonard Neufeldt, *ATQ*, 1974), and type and symbol (Ursula Brumm, *American Thought and Religious Typology*). "Composition as a Stylistic Feature" is studied by Donald Ross, Jr., and Richard H. Dillman has compiled a bibliography of resources for the study of Emerson's rhetoric.

Emerson's comments on language are surveyed by Albert Lewis and Jeffrey L. Duncan (*BMMLA*, 1976). John Q. Anderson discusses Emerson's use of "folk speech" (in *Folk Travelers*, ed. Mody C. Boatright et al.); and Emerson's use of proverbs is explored by C. Grant Loomis, J. Russell Reaver (*SFQ*, 1963), and, in the best study of the subject, Ralph C. LaRosa (*LMonog*, 1976).

Surprisingly, few studies have examined Emerson's use of humor. See Lawrence F. Abbott, Joseph Jones (*CL*, 1949), Arthur M. Cory on humor in the *Journals*, V.

L. O. Chittick on Emerson and frontier humor, Reginald L. Cook (*ESQ*, 1969), and Joel Porte's masterful "Transcendental Antics."

Emerson's literary criticism has been explored by Norman Foerster (*American Criticism*), Bernard Smith (*Forces in American Criticism*), John Paul Pritchard (*Return to the Fountains*), John Stafford (*The Literary Criticism of "Young America"*), Richard H. Fogle, John Paul Pritchard (*Criticism in America*), René Wellek ("Emerson's Literary Theory and Criticism"), Therman B. O'Daniel, and John W. Rathbun (*American Literary Criticism*). An excellent collection of *Emerson's Literary Criticism* has been edited with an informative introduction by Eric W. Carlson. For Emerson's specific comments on fiction, see John T. Flanagan, Paul Hourihan, Jeffrey Steinbrink, and J. A. Magat.

LECTURES

Early general considerations of Emerson as a lecturer tended to be either paeans or denunciations. A good example of the former is an anonymous essay in the *Boston Post* (25 Jan. 1849), which is full of overblown praise and overwrought metaphors: "He drops nectar—he chips out sparks—he exhales odors—he lets off mental skyrockets and fireworks—he spouts fire," and on and on. Needless to say, this account drew a lot of unfavorable attention. The opposite extreme is best represented by an anonymous article entitled "Emerson's Queer Movements in Literature" (*NYHer*, 24 March 1850), which compares his lecture tours to the migrations of infectious diseases. The notion that Emerson was corrupting the young with his lectures and destroying the Lyceums of America is the theme of a series of articles in the *New England Puritan* (5, 12, 19, 26 Feb., 5 March 1846). Other negative reviews of Emerson as lecturer include George Searle Phillips' "An Etching of Emerson" and the anonymous "Mr. Ralph Waldo Emerson as a Lecturer." The latter criticism is answered by George Lunt in his *A Reviewer Reviewed* and "Ralph Waldo Emerson."

Later considerations of Emerson as lecturer include George William Curtis, "Editor's Easy Chair" (*Har*, Feb. 1865); M. D. Conway, "Recent Lectures and Writings of Emerson"; James Russell Lowell, "Mr. Emerson's New Course of Lectures"; Annie Fields, "Mr. Emerson in the Lecture Room"; and Henry James's brief but unrestrained praise of Emerson's lectures in his *Hawthorne*.

General discussions of Emerson as a public speaker are by Theodore T. Stenberg (in *Studies in Rhetoric and Public Speaking in Honor of John Albert Winans*), Herbert A. Wichelns (in *A History and Criticism of American Public Address*, ed. William Norwood Brigance), Robert T. Oliver (*History of Public Speaking in America*), John H. Sloan, Roberta K. Ray, and Gay Wilson Allen (*Ariel*, 1976). A. M. Baumgartner (*AL*, 1963) has studied homiletics in Emerson's early lectures, and Ralph C. LaRosa has examined Bacon's influence (*ELN*, 1970) and Emerson's use of commonplace sentences or *sententiae* (*AL*, 1972) in the early lectures. Valuable lists of Emerson's lecture schedules have been compiled for "Emerson's British Lecture Tour, 1847–1848" by Townsend Scudder and for all Emerson's American lectures by William Charvat, supplemented and corrected by Eleanor M. Tilton. For the numerous articles describing particular lectures or lecture tours, see Robert E. Burkholder and Joel Myerson's bibliography.

POETRY

Before the publication of *Poems* in 1847, Emerson's poetry was not widely noticed. One of the earliest serious considerations of Emerson as a poet is to be found in Orestes A. Brownson's review of the July and October 1840 *Dials* (1841). The publication of *Poems* was greeted with particular skepticism, especially in England, where one reviewer speculated that the volume was not "calculated to increase the fame" Emerson had "acquired from his essays" (*Daguerreotype*, 4 Sept. 1847). Except for an anonymous review in the *United States Magazine, and Democratic Review* (1847), which proclaimed Emerson the "most original . . . of living writers," few American reviewers admired his poetry: John Sullivan Dwight (*Harbinger*, 23, 30 Jan. 1847) mixes praise with criticism of Emerson's coldness and lack of humanity; Cyrus A. Bartol (*ChEx*, 1847) likens Emerson to Shakespeare and Milton but criticizes his disregard of traditional Christianity; Francis Bowen (*NAR*, 1847) calls the poems "prosaic, unintelligible stuff"; and Brownson (*BrQR*, 1847) suggests that they are "hymns to the devil." As a measure of how Emerson's reputation as a poet changed in twenty years, one need only consult reviews of *May-Day and Other Pieces*, especially two anonymous essays in the *Nation* and *North American Review* and David A. Wasson's notice in the *Radical*, all of which not only praise Emerson's poetry unreservedly but also suggest that the later volume far exceeds *Poems* in quality.

The first important general consideration of Emerson as a poet appeared in the *Harvard Magazine* (1855), and an outpouring of critical studies began with Joel Benton's useful *Emerson as a Poet*, which is augmented by his comments in the *Continent Weekly Magazine* (1884). Benton was followed by useful studies by Edmund C. Stedman (*CM*, 1883, and *The Poets of America*), C. C. Everett, Edmund Gosse, Coulson Kernahan, Frank Preston Stearns (*UnitR*, 1891), Christopher Pearse Cranch (*CriticNY*, 27 Feb. 1892), William Sloane Kennedy (*PoL*, 1899–1900); and a series of articles by Charles Malloy (*ComA*, 1899–1900; *PrI*, 1903; *PoL*, 1903; *Arena*, 1904–05). Other good general studies of Emerson's verse are by Augustus Hopkins Strong (*American Poets and Their Theology*), Elmer James Bailey (*Religious Thought in the Greater American Poets*), Norman Foerster (*PMLA*, 1922), Frank T. Thompson (*PMLA*, 1928), Jean Gorely, Gay Wilson Allen (*American Prosody*), Nelson F. Adkins, Kathryn Anderson McEuen, Stanley T. Williams (*The Beginnings of American Poetry*), Andrew Schiller (*PMASAL*, 1955), Seymour L. Gross, Josephine Miles (*MinnR*, 1962), Epifanio San Juan, Jr., Richard Lee Francis (*ELH*, 1966), Bernard Duffy (*Poetry in America*), Aaron Kramer (*The Prophetic Tradition in American Poetry*), Carl Dennis (*ESQ*, 1970), Albert Gelpi (*The Tenth Muse*), and Louise Schleiner. Albert J. von Frank has edited Emerson's boyhood and collegiate verse.

Of the books published on Emerson's poetry, the best ones are by Hyatt H. Waggoner, *Emerson as Poet*, and R. A. Yoder, *Emerson and the Orphic Poet in America*, which includes his article "Toward the 'Titmouse Dimension': The Development of Emerson's Poetic Style." Waggoner's book, particularly valuable for its history of the criticism of Emerson's poetry and for its readings of individual poems, complements his earlier *American Poets from the Puritans to the Present*, which argues that Emerson was a central figure in the American poetic tradition. The latter point has also been argued, often at tiresome length, by Harold Bloom in a series of articles that are all listed, with their myriad reprintings, in Robert E. Burkholder and Joel Myerson's bibliography. Two other books are less successful: Charles Howell Foster, *Emerson's Theory of Poetry*, puts together extracts from Emerson's writings on poetry, and John Q. Anderson, *The Liberating Gods*, surveys many of the same comments. The work of Carl F. Strauch, beginning with his 1946 dissertation, "A Critical and Variorum Edition of the Poems of Ralph Waldo Emerson," has added much to our understanding of the composition and meaning of the poems; his many articles are listed in Burkholder and Myerson's bibliography. Strauch has also edited *Characteristics of Emerson, Transcendental Poet*, a good collection of original essays.

INDIVIDUAL WORKS

Of the numerous reviews and critical studies of individual works listed in Robert E. Burkholder and Joel Myerson's bibliography, a few stand out as being particularly useful for an understanding of Emerson's Transcendentalism.

Good general introductions to *Nature* are in editions by Kenneth Walter Cameron and Warner Berthoff. An excellent study of "The Architectonics of Emerson's *Nature*" is by Richard Lee Francis. *Emerson's* Nature—*Origin, Growth, Meaning*, ed. Merton M. Sealts, Jr., and Alfred R. Ferguson, is an edited text of *Nature*; it presents those parts of Emerson's journals, letters, and lectures that deal with the planning of *Nature* or were actually used in *Nature*, and it reprints an excellent selection of contemporary reviews and later critical commentary on the book. In a second edition, two original essays are added: a masterful discussion of the composition of *Nature* by Sealts, and a study of Emerson's cosmogony by Barbara Packer.

"The American Scholar" is seen as central to an understanding of Emerson's search for a vocation by Henry Nash Smith. In a series of instructive articles (*PMLA*, 1970; in *Literature and Ideas in America*; *Ariel*, 1976), Sealts traces Emerson's views on the scholar. *"The American Scholar" Today: Emerson's Essay and Some Critical Views*, ed. C. David Mead, is a weak collection.

The Divinity School Address is placed in historical context by D. Elton Trueblood, who shows how little effect it had on the students who heard it, and William R. Hutchison, *The Transcendentalist Ministers*, who traces its influence on ministers. Conrad Wright (*HTR*, 1956) provides an informed discussion of the composition of the address, and Mary Worden Edrich (*TSLL*, 1967) perceptively examines its rhetorical flourishes.

Although individual essays have received much attention, *Essays* as a book has not. Morton Cronin discusses prose diction in the work; Paul Lauter examines "Emerson's Revisions of *Essays: First Series*"; and Lewis Leary (*Prospects*, 1977) sees a unified structure in the book. Recently, Glen M. Johnson has studied the composition and revisions of *Essays* in depth.

Finally, Emerson's *Journals* have received little attention as literature. "C." (1912) criticizes them as Theosophical literature. John Burroughs (*The Last Harvest*) and G. R. Elliott discuss the problems of editing and omission in the 1909–14 *Journals*. Two recent critical studies, though, have approached the *Journals* as literature: Ralph C. LaRosa sees the journals as part of "Emerson's Search for Literary Form," and Evelyn Barish Greenberger has done a psychological reading of various journal entries.

INFLUENCE

A number of writers have seen Emerson as part of a continuum in American literary history, bridging a gap between different movements. Percy H. Boynton, Marshall Van Deusen (*A Metaphor for the History of American Criticism*), and William A. Clebsch (*American Religious Thought*) all see Emerson as revolting against Puritanism, whereas Perry Miller, in an important essay "From Edwards to Emerson," perceives Emerson's roots in orthodox Calvinism. When he revised and reprinted his essay (*Errand into the Wilderness*), Miller warned that he was not arguing "a direct line of intellectual descent," only suggesting that "continuities persist in a culture," a view shared by Mason I. Lowance, Jr. (*ATQ*, 1973). Others who see Emerson as heir to the Puritan mantle include Arnold Smithline (*Natural Religion in American Literature*), who connects Emerson with Cotton Mather; Hyatt H. Waggoner (*ESQ*, 1969), who sees similarities between Emerson and Edwards; and William L. Hedges, who sees Franklin, "the practical side of Puritanism," as Emerson's source.

Emerson's relations with Thoreau have long been studied, and references to the scholarship may be found in Robert E. Burkholder and Joel Myerson's bibliography and in the chapter on Thoreau in this volume. Emerson's major statement on the subject is his essay "Thoreau," which has been edited from manuscript, with a description of its composition, by Myerson. Thoreau's work was linked to Emerson's even in the 1850s: a writer in the *Athenæum* (27 May 1854) suggests that Emerson's failure to publish his long-awaited *English Traits* might be partially compensated for by the "early utterance of one of his disciples"—that is, Thoreau's *Walden*—and Lucian Paul, writing in the *Critic* (1851), includes a fairly detailed biographical sketch of Thoreau as part of an article on Emerson's circle. Certainly the two essays most influential in arguing Thoreau's dependence on and inferiority to Emerson are James Russell Lowell, "Thoreau's Letters," and Robert Louis Stevenson, "Henry D. Thoreau." In "Thoreau and Emerson," F. B. Sanborn claims that heredity produced the differences of manner in the two men, much to the detriment of Thoreau.

To the studies listed in the chapter on Thoreau in this book, a number of other works of interest should be added. Books by Emerson that Thoreau is known to have owned or read are listed by Kenneth Walter Cameron ("Thoreau Discovers Emerson: A College Reading Record") and Walter Harding, *Thoreau's Library*, supplemented by Myerson (*CS*, 1978). Percy Whiting Brown (*Middlesex Monographs*) and Julia Wendell argue that Thoreau entirely rejected Emerson. John Newell Sanborn discusses a possible portrait of Thoreau in Emerson's poem "Forbearance."

A particularly interesting subject is Emerson and Zen: see Van Meter Ames, *Zen and American Thought*, Donald D. Eulert, Shôei Andô, *Zen and American Transcendentalism*, and Robert Detweiler, "Emerson and Zen."

Emerson's pervasive influence on American Literature has been noted by Sherman Hill Adams; Paul Elmer More ("The Influence of Emerson"); David Lee Maulsby (*The Contribution of Emerson to Literature*); Carl F. Strauch ("Emerson as Literary Middleman"); Luther S. Mansfield ("The Emersonian Idiom and the Romantic Period in American Literature"); Alfred S. Reid ("Emersonian Ideas in the Youth Movement of the 1960s"); and Morton White (*Science and Sentiment in America*). For Emerson's influence on his contemporaries, see Burkholder and Myerson's bibliography and the other chapters in this book, particularly that on Whitman. For Emerson's influence on such diverse figures as Conrad Aiken, Sherwood Anderson, Matthew Arnold, Irving Babbitt, Charles Baudelaire, Jorge Luis Borges, Bliss Carman, Jimmy Carter, John Jay Chapman, Robert Duncan, T. S. Eliot, Ralph Ellison, William Faulkner, Robert Frost, Mahatma Gandhi, Bret Harte, Rutherford B. Hayes, Ernest Hemingway, Robert Henri, Charles Ives, Henry James, William James, Sidney Lanier, D. H. Lawrence, Denise Levertov, Marshall McLuhan, Jose Marti, Henry Miller, John Muir, Friedrich Nietzsche, Ezra Pound, Marcel Proust, Rainer Maria Rilke, E. A. Robinson, John Ruskin, J. D. Salinger, George Santayana, Jean-Paul Sartre, Wallace Stevens, Algernon Swinburne, Lev Tolstoy, Lewis Turco, John Tyndall, Miguel de Unamuno, John Updike, Alfred North Whitehead, and Thomas Wolfe, as well as comments by these and other writers on Emerson, see Burkholder and Myerson's bibliography.

CONVERS FRANCIS

Guy R. Woodall

BIBLIOGRAPHIES

There is no complete primary or secondary bibliography of Convers Francis. Two in-complete lists of his publications appeared not long after his death: in an anonymous notice in the *Christian Register* (2 May 1863) and in William Newell, "Memoir of the Rev. Convers Francis, D.D." Francis is not listed in *AAL*.

MANUSCRIPTS

ALM reports that Francis' papers are scattered about in thirteen locations and include forty-eight letters by Francis, 120 letters to him, six documents, and two general manuscripts. Most of these materials are held in three libraries. The Boston Public Library has five letters by Francis, 110 to him, and three documents; the Houghton Library of Harvard University has twenty-two letters by Francis, one to him, one docu-ment, and one general manuscript; and the Massachusetts Historical Society has eighty letters by Francis (considerably more than the eleven letters listed in *ALM*), two documents, and one manuscript. The ten remaining libraries listed in *ALM* average two manuscripts apiece.

There are, however, some significant deposits of Francis' manuscripts that do not appear in *ALM*. Twenty-four letters, for example, are at the Andover-Harvard Theological Library. Most of these are from Francis to the secretary of the American Unitarian Association. In the institutional records in the Harvard University Archives at the Pusey Library, there are about fifty letters or official copies of letters written by and to Francis, most of them on routine matters of Divinity College business. Francis bequeathed his large library to Harvard; in the University Archives and at the Andover-

Harvard Library, there are two separate inventories of his books, mostly on divinity and the classics, which after his death passed into the divinity collection and the general library. Many of these books are generously annotated. The notes are, for the most part, neither highly personal nor critical in nature but are explanations of or additions to the text.

Not accounted for in *ALM* are some significant holdings at the Watertown, Massachusetts, Free Public Library. Among these is a Sunday diary, mainly a record of Francis' preaching, that he kept between 1819 and 1827, published by Guy R. Woodall. Also at Watertown are several hundred of Francis' sermons and his church records. As pastor and scribe for the First Parish Congregational (Unitarian) Church between 1819 and 1842, Francis kept a record of invitations and acceptances to attend ordinations, changes in congregational worship, and everyday business matters in the parish.

EDITIONS

The bibliographies list twenty journal articles on miscellaneous subjects, seventeen sermons, ten public addresses, four religious tracts, three memorial essays, three obituaries, two extended biographies, and one book of history. The journal articles include lessons in religion, explications of scriptures, reviews of books, and translations of sermons and biblical criticism; they appeared in the *American Monthly Review*, *Christian Disciple*, *Christian Examiner*, *Juvenile Miscellany*, *Scriptural Interpreter*, *Liberal Preacher*, and *Unitarian Advocate*. The public addresses, mostly on historical and educational subjects and delivered on holidays and ceremonial occasions, were privately printed. The printed sermons were occasioned by ordinations, dedications, and funerals. Francis' few religious tracts were widely circulated as a part of the American Unitarian Association Tract series. Francis' obituaries were of close friends, and all appeared in Boston newspapers. The three memorial essays were written to honor deceased members of the Massachusetts Historical Society, of which Francis was an active member, and were published in the *Collections of the Massachusetts Historical Society*. The two extended critical biographies that Francis wrote were a part of Jared Sparks' *Library of American Biography*. Francis' single long book, published in 1830, was a history of Watertown, Massachusetts, where he was for a long time parish minister.

The only modern edition of any of Francis' writings is Guy R. Woodall's "The Journals of Convers Francis."

BIOGRAPHY

There is no good biography of Francis. The longest and best sketches of Francis' life are John Weiss, *Discourse Occasioned by the Death of Convers Francis, D.D.*; William Newell, "Memoir of the Rev. Convers Francis, D.D."; and Mosetta I.

Vaughan, *Sketch of the Life and Work of Convers Francis, D.D.* Weiss and Newell, close friends and colleagues of Francis, made extensive use of his personal journals, and Vaughan provides a useful appreciation that derives much from Weiss and Newell. Other important details about Francis may be found in necrologies, the most factual of which are Frederic Henry Hedge, "The Late Rev. Convers Francis, D.D.," "The Death of Dr. Francis" (*Ch Reg*, 1863), and "Obituaries" (*BDA*, 15 July 1863). Two well-written and readily accessible sketches of Francis' life are those by Edward Hale in *Heralds of a Liberal Faith* and Harris Elwood Starr in *DAB*.

A wealth of biographical information is scattered throughout the correspondence and journals of Francis' literary friends and acquaintances. His close relationship with Ralph Waldo Emerson is evident throughout *The Journals and Miscellaneous Notebooks of Ralph Waldo Emerson* and *The Letters of Ralph Waldo Emerson*, ed. Ralph L. Rusk. The friendship between Francis and Theodore Parker may be studied in thirty letters and excerpts in John Weiss, *The Life and Correspondence of Theodore Parker*. Since the letters in Weiss' book were often selectively edited, one ought to use it in conjunction with Gary L. Collison, "A Critical Edition of the Correspondence of Theodore Parker and Convers Francis." One letter from Francis to Parker has been published by Jesse Ishikawa. Some of the most personal biographical information on Francis is located in the published letters of his sister, Lydia Maria Child, the famous author and reformer. Thirty-seven of her letters to Francis and twenty-six dealing substantially with him are in *The Collected Correspondence of Lydia Maria Child*. Vignettes of Francis as a professor of divinity at Harvard have been left in the personal recollections of three of his students: Octavius Brooks Frothingham, *Boston Unitarianism 1820-1850*; Thomas Wentworth Higginson, *Contemporaries*; and Moncure Daniel Conway, *Autobiography Memories and Experiences*. Francis' long tenure with the First Parish Congregational (Unitarian) Church at Watertown, Massachusetts, has been treated in George Frederick Robinson and Ruth Robinson Wheeler, *Great Little Watertown*; Solon F. Whitney, *Historical Sketches of Watertown, Massachusetts*; and Maud de Leigh Hodges, *Crossroads on the Charles*. A profile of Francis as the eldest and one of the most active members of the Transcendental Club is Joel Myerson, "A Calendar of Transcendental Club Meetings" and "A History of the Transcendental Club." Francis' professorship at Harvard has been touched on in *The Harvard Divinity School*, ed. George Huntston Williams.

CRITICISM

Joel Myerson, "Convers Francis and Emerson," illuminates the friendship of the two members of the Transcendental Club. Based mainly on previously unpublished extracts from Francis' journals, which his daughter had copied for Edward Waldo Emerson, the article treats particularly Francis' reaction to Emerson's lectures. A significant unpublished study is Gary L. Collison's edition of the Francis-Parker cor-

respondence. Using 129 letters exchanged between them, Collison traces the friendship of two of the most erudite members of the Unitarian and Transcendentalist
communities.

Francis' relation to the various divisions within the Unitarian church and to the
Transcendentalist movement has been broached significantly by several authors but
never explored in great detail. In his *Transcendentalism in New England*, Octavius
Brooks Frothingham places Francis among the minor prophets of the New England
Transcendentalist movement. In another of his books, *Boston Unitarianism 1820–1850*,
Frothingham presents Francis as a man of vast erudition, absolutely free from
dogmatism, modest and self-effacing, a natural eclectic who was noncommittal on
most controversial matters except such humanitarian issues as the slavery question.
Francis' preoccupation with Transcendentalist thought is revealed in three letters from
Hedge to Francis in Ronald Vale Wells, *Three Christian Transcendentalists*. In *The
Transcendentalist Ministers*, William R. Hutchison identifies Francis as one of the
Unitarian ministers who was active in the early stages of the Transcendentalist move-
ment but whose influence is difficult to assess because of his "all-sided" opinions.
In *Corresponding Motion*, Catherine L. Albanese concludes from a few of Francis'
published sermons that he, like other ministers in the Transcendental Club, preached
a gospel of motion.

There is a need for a complete biography of Francis. He is one of the few major
members of the Transcendental Club who has not been the subject of a book-length
biography or critical investigation. In addition, articles could be written on Francis'
Transcendentalist influence on his students at the Harvard Divinity School and his
peculiar theological stance among the liberal Christians of his time.

OCTAVIUS BROOKS FROTHINGHAM

J. Wade Caruthers

BIBLIOGRAPHIES

The most complete list of secondary works and primary sources is in J. Wade Caruthers, *Octavius Brooks Frothingham*. Additional items will be found in the *NUC*. Frothingham is not listed in *AAL*.

MANUSCRIPTS

Locations of manuscripts by Frothingham are listed in *ALM*, but it is incomplete. Additional Frothingham material may be found at the Andover-Harvard Theological School, Boston Athenæum, Essex Institute, New York Public Library, North Church (Salem, Mass.), and the Unitarian Universalist Association (Boston). Information on these collections is in Caruthers, *Octavius Brooks Frothingham*.

EDITIONS

Octavius Brooks Frothingham grew to maturity and into the Unitarian ministry during the golden age of Transcendentalism (1830–50). In the course of his career, he went full circle from Transcendentalism to disillusionment and back again. He left behind no fewer than seventeen literary works dealing with the members and ideas of the movement.

His two biographies of leading Transcendentalists Theodore Parker (1874) and George Ripley (1882) are superseded by modern scholarship, yet they reveal Frothingham's insight into the careers of these men and helped preserve their papers for posterity. Written for America's centennial, *Transcendentalism in New England* (1876) is still a useful work, both for the brilliant analysis of the German and English backgrounds of American Transcendentalism and for commentary on Transcendentalist thinkers and their impact on American intellectual history. Likewise, Frothingham's *Memoir of William Henry Channing* (1886), his "Memoir" of David Wasson in the latter's *Essays: Religious, Social, Political* (1889), and his introduction to Samuel Johnson's *Oriental Religions and Their Relation to Universal Religions. Persia* (1885) give a contemporary view of Transcendentalism and its links with the Free Religious Association.

The formative and active period of Transcendentalism spanned the same years as Frothingham's study of his father's generation, *Boston Unitarianism 1820–1850: A Study of the Life and Work of Nathaniel Langdon Frothingham* (1890). The son remembers the father as representing the middle-ground Unitarians who were influenced by Transcendentalist thinkers but "offish" toward Ralph Waldo Emerson's invitation to attend meetings of the Transcendental Club, who stood between the conservative Dr. William Ellery Channing and the "abrasive," "shallow" thinking of Parker. This book, written mostly from memory, seems to indicate that Frothingham had recanted his Transcendentalist philosophy, yet he is critical of his father's generation for their inaction and unwillingness to face social and theological controversy. It is not clear whether Frothingham had repudiated the influences of his earlier years or had acquired a mature respect for his father's generation, which had broken the religious ground so that Frothingham could go beyond Transcendentalism. These ambiguities are somewhat clarified in Frothingham's memoirs, *Recollections and Impressions 1822–1890.*

In his old age, Frothingham acknowledged the early direct influence of Parker, from whom he had borrowed books, yet rejected Parker's theology, describing his own as based on the Transcendentalism of Emerson and Thomas Carlyle, not Christian but theistic in a broad humanistic sense. In a chapter of *Recollections and Impressions* entitled "Progress of Religious Thought," Frothingham states that Transcendentalism had been a "balm and elixir" to him, but speculation had been superseded by science. In his recollections, he sees the dual roles of the Transcendentalists and theologians influenced by them, revealing his own transition from Transcendentalism to the theories of Charles Darwin.

Frothingham delivered and published approximately three hundred sermons, of which three are especially relevant to his Transcendentalist views. *Theodore Parker: A Sermon* (1860), read in observance of his death, is a coldly objective criticism of Parker's theology that is not dealt with in Henry Steele Commager's *Theodore Parker. The Ministry of Reconciliation* (1868), a Divinity School address delivered thirty years after Emerson's, is Frothingham's statement of radical Christianity, valuable for revealing the break between Transcendentalism and Unitarianism. *Duties and Dreams* (1877), delivered before the Ethical Culture Society in New York, reflects the Transcendentalist theme of the indwelling divinity that unites the human and the divine and goes beyond the five senses in probing the secrets of existence. In addition, Frothingham's articles in the *Christian Examiner, Atlantic Monthly Magazine,* and *North American Review* reflect his Transcendentalist views as modified by Darwinism and his own natural skepticism; see, for example, "Imagination in Theology"

(1859), "Mill's Review of Hamilton" and "Drift Period in Theology" (1865), "Some Phases of Idealism in New England" (1883), "The Philosophy of Conversion" (1884), and "Why I Am A Free Religionist" (1887).

Of minor importance in discussing Frothingham as a Transcendentalist are an article and two comments on papers or lectures delivered at the Radical Club, probably in the late 1860s. He attacks both a paper by Nathan Shaler on Darwinism and a presentation by Frederic Henry Hedge on pantheism. Darwinism, states Frothingham, does not destroy moral categories and pantheism weakens conscience, eliminating the tension between good and evil. These items do not survive, but they are described in Mary E. Sargent's *Sketches and Reminiscences of the Radical Club*.

In one of his last writings, "Memoir of Rev. James Walker" (1891), his former Divinity School professor, Frothingham again delves into the beliefs of his father's generation. Walker, according to Frothingham, was a "mild Transcendentalist," familiar with the English and German sources of that philosophy. A conservative Unitarian, Walker is given credit for stimulating Frothingham's generation to avoid shallow skepticism and to act on their beliefs.

BIOGRAPHY AND CRITICISM

The problem of Frothingham as a Transcendentalist involves two questions: when and from where did he derive his radical religious views? and did he recant in later life? The writings of his contemporaries and recent scholarship present contradictory evidence and reflect the ambiguities characteristic of Frothingham's own intellectual style. The record of Sunday School lectures delivered by Frothingham while a divinity school student reveal him as a religious radical in the Transcendentalist tradition before his direct contact with Parker. These notes might modify the impression of Frothingham as a conservative presented by Commager, Ralph Henry Gabriel, and Stow Persons (see below), but they may not be reliable, as they were compiled by a credulous young woman who was shocked by Frothingham's radicalism (manuscript notes of Sunday School lectures delivered on the gospels of Matthew and John, the book of David, and the Apocalypse [1846–47], comp. Eliza David Bradlee, 4 vols., Andover-Harvard Theological School).

Colleagues who wrote in defense of Frothingham pointed out his similarity to Emerson, his broad Transcendentalist views, his extension of Parker's theology, and his bold radicalism. Their writings, based on personal contacts and readings of his published works, were prepared not only for reasons of personal affection but also to balance criticism of Frothingham's career. Although they add little to our knowledge of Frothingham as a Transcendentalist, they provide a useful insight into some of the details of his life. The articles in the *Index* by William J. Potter and M. J. Savage (1881) are relevant to Frothingham's supposed recantation, but no conclusions can be drawn from this controversy. Also of use are Edmund C. Stedman, *Octavius Brooks Frothingham and the New Faith* and *Proceedings at a Reception Given in Honor of the Rev. O. B. Frothingham*.

More critical than the comments of Frothingham's friends is his own cousin's review of *Transcendentalism in New England*. Henry Adams' unfavorable assessment of the book as history is one that most modern historians would agree with, yet he brought out a strength of the author not generally noticed today—Frothingham's ability to synthesize German philosophy and use it in a comprehensive context. Henry A. Brann, a conservative clergyman, presents a typical criticism of Transcendentalism when he accuses Frothingham of preaching a dangerous individualism that destroys social organization ("The Rationalism of O. B. Frothingham and Felix Adler"). Robert Buchanan, a writer and literary critic, gives Frothingham credit for harmonizing Transcendentalist faith with modern science to attack old creeds, but he equates Frothingham's Free Religion with Transcendentalism, and he criticizes both for a lack of clarity, warmth, and concrete dogma ("Free Thought in America"; "Octavius Frothingham").

After Frothingham's death in 1895, his younger colleagues wrote a number of eulogies and memorial essays, none of which added to his stature as a Transcendentalist. These essays portray him as a leading figure in radical religion—an evolutionist, a believer, a skeptic, yet one who never recanted his Transcendentalism. Typical of these eulogies are John White Chadwick, "Funeral Address for Octavius Brooks Frothingham"; Josiah P. Quincy, "Memoir of Octavius B. Frothingham"; Edward Young, "Remarks [on the Death of O. B. Frothingham]"; the memorial address in the Free Religious Association's *Prophets of Liberalism*; and Paul Revere Frothingham's memoir in *Heralds of a Liberal Faith*, ed. Samuel A. Eliot.

As for modern scholarship, Gabriel first revived the memory of the Free Religious Association and recalled its Transcendentalist-Unitarian connection in short biographical sketches of its principal figures (*The Course of American Democratic Thought*). Gabriel gives more credit to Frothingham and other older Transcendentalists and less to Francis Ellingwood Abbot than does Stow Persons' later study of the Free Religious Association, *Free Religion*. Persons argues that Transcendentalism split the Unitarians and that the younger generation formed the Free Religious Association.

Frothingham is generally depicted as the popularizer of Free Religion (not a great scholar) and Parker's devoted disciple, whereas Abbot is portrayed as its chief organizer and philosopher. These assumptions have come under serious scrutiny in the only biography of Frothingham, Caruthers, *Octavius Brooks Frothingham*. In contrast to Persons, Caruthers argues that Abbot was a dogmatist who was held in check while Frothingham's influence kept the Free Religious Association moving in a broad creedless direction in the Transcendentalist tradition. As for Frothingham's alleged recantation, no conclusions can be reached. Two accounts of Frothingham's Transcendentalism and its connection with Free Religion are available: Sydney Ahlstrom's introduction to the 1959 reprinting of *Transcendentalism in New England* and Caruthers' "Who Was Octavius Brooks Frothingham?"

No further research on Frothingham is likely to be produced until his papers are located, but the relation of Transcendentalism to the Free Religious Association might be more thoroughly explored. It may be possible to trace the philosophic threads of twentieth-century humanism back to Free Religion and from there to its Transcendentalist roots.

MARGARET FULLER

Robert N. Hudspeth

BIBLIOGRAPHIES

The list of Margaret Fuller's writings in *BAL* has been completely superseded by Joel Myerson, *Margaret Fuller: A Descriptive Bibliography*, which fully describes all her works. Section C, "Writings in Newspapers, Magazines, and Journals," is especially useful for following Fuller's career as a practicing critic. Myerson, *Margaret Fuller: An Annotated Secondary Bibliography*, lists and annotates everything written on Fuller from 1834 to 1975, including all the articles listed in *AAL*. With its topical and name index, this bibliography provides a ready guide to scholarship.

MANUSCRIPTS

Margaret Fuller's manuscripts are listed under "Ossoli" in *ALM*. The two largest collections, those at the Boston Public Library and at the Houghton Library of Harvard University, have typewritten guides available in the reading rooms. The Houghton collection begins with the Fuller Family Papers in seventeen bound volumes, four copybooks, and three boxes of loose manuscripts and other papers. In addition, Fuller manuscripts are to be found in the Clarke, Tappan, Ward, and Emerson family papers at the Houghton Library. The Emerson collection has a few uncataloged Fuller manuscripts. At the Boston Public Library, the Margaret Fuller papers are divided into two groups: one (a gift from Thomas Wentworth Higginson) contains many of the mutilated manuscripts left from the *Memoirs*; the other includes the letters to James Nathan used in *Love-Letters*. The Boston Public Library also has a collection of Richard Fuller papers and two Margaret Fuller letters in the Dwight and Weston collections. The Fruitlands Museums has Fuller letters and a portion of her 1844 journal. The Massachusetts Historical Society has the majority of the 1844 journal in the Perry-Clarke papers as well as other manuscripts, including one letter in the Channing family collection. Two Margaret Fuller letters have recently been given to the Andover-Harvard Theological Library and placed in the Hedge collection. Both Virginia and Princeton have small collections of Fuller letters, and each library has miscataloged one letter. A letter cataloged as Margaret Fuller's at Kansas is her mother's. Robert N. Hudspeth, "A Calendar of the Letters of Margaret Fuller," lists and locates the letters Fuller is known to have written. No significant Fuller holdings are known to exist in private collections.

EDITIONS

The lack of well-edited, authoritative texts has always hampered Fuller scholarship. Beginning in 1855, her brother Arthur issued a series of editions: *Woman in the Nineteenth Century, and Kindred Papers* (1855); *At Home and Abroad* (1856), which incorporates *Summer on the Lakes, in 1843* (1844); *Art, Literature, and the Drama* (1860), which incorporates *Papers on Literature and Art* (1846); and *Life Without and Life Within* (1860). These volumes contain Fuller's published work, to which Arthur Fuller added material from her unpublished manuscripts. Unfortunately, these editions were created with an eye toward "improving" his sister's work. Although none of the volumes has any textual authority, each has been repeatedly used by later scholars. These books, together with the *Memoirs of Margaret Fuller Ossoli*, were issued in 1860 as a uniform edition of *Margaret Fuller's Works*. Since then, only *Woman in the Nineteenth Century* has been reprinted in a usable text, a 1980 facsimile of the 1845 edition, edited by Joel Myerson with a fine introduction by Madeleine B. Stern.

The largest anthology of Fuller's writing, the one most often used and the least trustworthy, was the first: *Memoirs of Margaret Fuller Ossoli* (1852), edited by Ralph Waldo Emerson, William Henry Channing, and James Freeman Clarke. This "life and letters" has been the foundation for all subsequent Fuller scholarship. The three editors were close friends of Fuller; each possessed many of her letters; each enjoyed the confidence of her family and friends; each had unmatched access to her manuscripts. Given their interest in Fuller's literary work, the three editors chose well: they quote from interesting letters and from thoughtful journals. The *Memoirs* is chronologically comprehensive, spanning Fuller's career from her childhood to her death. But we have known for many years that the editors meddled with the text to the point of rendering it unreliable. They rewrote freely: Fuller's phrasing and punctuation were repeatedly altered; almost nothing is presented in its entirety; personal names are often omitted; the chronology of her writing is often muddled; letters, journals, and published essays are often silently spliced together. The results are appalling: the nature of Fuller's writing is changed, her tone is falsified, her ideas are modified (sometimes drastically so), and it becomes hard to understand the context for much of the writing. The damage can be partly repaired by modern, scrupulous texts, but not all of the original can be recovered, for when the editors finished the *Memoirs*, they destroyed many of Fuller's manuscripts and obliterated much of what was left. A good summary of the damage can be found in Bell Gale Chevigny, "The Long Arm of Censorship." Anyone who writes on Fuller must carefully assess this problem: given a corrupt text, what valid biographical or critical conclusions can we draw? It is painful to confront the fact that almost all nineteenth-century work on Fuller and far too much in the twentieth century rests on the *Memoirs* texts. Obviously, in some cases we must proceed with caution with what we have, but in other instances the opportunity of consulting manuscript material was not taken advantage of.

After the *Memoirs*, the next significant new text was the *Love-Letters of Margaret Fuller 1845-1846* (1903), containing the fifty letters she wrote to James Nathan. As far as we can tell, none of the early biographers knew anything about Nathan and his "affair" with Fuller. Unfortunately, the unnamed editor (not, I believe, Julia Ward Howe, as many assume) deleted or otherwise altered a number of sentences in the letters.

Not until almost forty years later did another selection of Fuller's writing appear, when Mason Wade edited *The Writings of Margaret Fuller* (1941), a volume still used owing to its ready availability in most libraries. Wade, however, not only used Arthur Fuller's corrupt text for *Summer on the Lakes*, but he further altered it himself. His version of *Woman in the Nineteenth Century* was also taken from Arthur Fuller's text, as was the section "Italy and the Roman Revolution," which reprints Fuller's *New-York Tribune* letters from Europe. Wade did, however, use original texts of the thirteen critical essays of Fuller's that he published, and he printed twenty-five of her letters, using mostly manuscript sources except for the letters to Emerson. Wilma Robb Ebbitt edited "The Critical Essays of Margaret Fuller from the New York *Tribune*," the only edition of all the literary essays in the *Tribune*. Ebbitt and Robert N. Hudspeth are now completing an edition of Fuller's *Tribune* essays. Perry Miller printed excerpts from six of Fuller's works in *The Transcendentalists*.

Later, in *Margaret Fuller: American Romantic* (1963), Miller wrote his own version of the *Memoirs*. He used letters, journals, critical writings, and excerpts from Fuller's books to trace her life from beginning to end. Although Miller returned to the manuscript sources for some of the letters and journals, he reprinted much from the *Memoirs* and used the Rusk text for letters to Emerson and the *Love-Letters* text for letters to Nathan, even though the originals were available in Boston-area libraries. Finally, in the interest of concentrating on her biography, Miller printed little of what she wrote in its entirety.

An even more ambitious biographical anthology is Bell Gale Chevigny, *The Woman and the Myth: Margaret Fuller's Life and Writings* (1976). Chevigny reprints a large number of excerpts from Fuller's writings, often—but not always—using original manuscripts. Unfortunately, the choice of texts is erratic. She uses Arthur Fuller's versions of *Life Without and Life Within* and *Woman in the Nineteenth Century*; she uses the *Love-Letters* for the letters to Nathan; and she even uses Wade's text for a *Tribune* essay.

The only anthology with reliable texts is *Margaret Fuller: Essays on American Life and Letters*, ed. Joel Myerson (1978). Myerson prints thirty-three essays, a part of *Summer on the Lakes*, and the entire text of *Woman in the Nineteenth Century*. The anthology has an introduction that traces Fuller's career, a useful bibliography, and textual notes that clearly identify the original texts, which are fully annotated. Also, three portions of Fuller's journals have been published, each giving important biographical data: Robert N. Hudspeth, "Margaret Fuller's 1839 Journal," Myerson, "Margaret Fuller's 1842 Journal," and Leona Rostenberg, "Margaret Fuller's Roman Diary." Hudspeth is editing Fuller's letters for publication by Cornell University Press.

Biography

Most writing on Fuller has been biographical. The first biography, the *Memoirs*, has been viewed ambivalently from the beginning. Thomas Wentworth Higginson, in justifying his own biography of Fuller, put it well: "the prevalent tone of the 'Memoirs' leaves her a little too much in the clouds, and gives us too little of that vigorous executive side which was always prominent in her aspirations for herself." More recent Fuller biographers have pointed out the severe limitations the *Memoirs* editors placed on themselves in making the best they could of Fuller's marriage and motherhood. Inevitably, Emerson, Henry Channing, and Clarke have emerged as neurotic Victorians who strove manfully to protect Fuller's reputation. We have now become as suspicious of their biographical judgments as we have of their editorial practices. Still, for all its limitations, the *Memoirs* gives us the most complete contemporary record of Fuller's personality.

In her *Margaret Fuller (Marchesa Ossoli)*, Julia Ward Howe could have given a similar contemporary account, for she met Fuller in early adulthood. Instead, she relies on the *Memoirs* and other published writing. While she says that she intends to defend Fuller's personality, which, Howe believes, is misunderstood, she fails to draw on her own experiences with Fuller.

Higginson's *Margaret Fuller Ossoli* is by far the best nineteenth-century biography and one of the best overall. Higginson had new material to draw on (as well as the manuscript remains from the *Memoirs*), and he put that material to good use. Not only does he quote liberally from manuscript sources, but he goes on to develop his own critical point of view. Higginson laments the fact that he sees Fuller as primarily a social thinker, although the American Men of Letters series for which he wrote demanded a literary approach. He freely acknowledges Fuller's want of tact, but he goes on to make her into a more warm-blooded woman than did the earlier biographers.

Katharine Anthony, *Margaret Fuller*, is the only Freudian work on Fuller. The book contends that Fuller showed "manifestations of hysteria, and [she] had long been known to have a neurotic constitution"; but Anthony does little with this theory. She contents herself with retelling Fuller's story, as does Margaret Bell in *Margaret*

Fuller. Bell attempts to recreate dialogue between her characters and assiduously invokes details to make the narrative "immediate," but the effect is strained.

In *Margaret Fuller*, Mason Wade paints a detailed, balanced portrait, but his discussion is not annotated and he makes only rudimentary literary judgments. The worst limitation is Wade's simplistic idea of "womanhood." Toward the conclusion of his book, he says that Fuller's "subjugation of herself to a man in the marriage act, and the bearing and rearing of a child, had made her nature soft and gentle and feminine at last. The psychological change is clearly evident in her writing." Both the theory and the alleged fact are erroneous. In 1942, Madeleine B. Stern published *The Life of Margaret Fuller*, a biography grounded in thorough research. It is written, however, in a way that many readers (such as this one) find distracting. Stern dramatizes conversations and scenes so that the biography reads much like a novel, but the unmodified written sources simply make poor dialogue. There is also a problem of chronology and setting, for conversations are used out of context according to the needs of the biographer. Stern, however, did an exhaustive search of manuscripts and printed sources; her bibliography remains a rich source for anyone working on Fuller or her times. Stern makes good judgments about Fuller's writing, corrects the foolishness of Wade's "gentle and feminine" portrait, and gives the best account we have of the question about Fuller's marriage date.

Emma Detti, *Margaret Fuller Ossoli*, focuses on the European years; she includes a valuable appendix that prints letters to Fuller from Mazzini, Costanza Arconati, Adam Mickiewicz, Lewis Cass, and others. Faith Chipperfield's *In Quest of Love* badly romanticizes and oversimplifies. Arthur W. Brown, *Margaret Fuller*, is a fine work, full of insight and, despite its brevity, a thorough account of her life. It is the best introduction to Fuller, a mature work of scholarship, and one of the few Fuller biographies that is close to being adequately annotated.

Joseph Jay Deiss, *The Roman Years of Margaret Fuller*, is important for its focus on her sojourn in Italy. Deiss gives more information on the Ossoli family than any other biographer, and his familiarity with Italian sources affords a more complete account of Fuller's life in the Italian states. Unfortunately, the callow literary judgments, the skimpy annotation, and the lapses of fact (he has the Ellery Channings separating during Fuller's lifetime, and Samuel Gray Ward is confused with the Washington lobbyist) create problems for the reader.

In a format quite similar to the *Memoirs*, Bell Gale Chevigny's *The Woman and the Myth* presents seven biographical chapters, combined with writings by and on Fuller, "designed to trace the struggle to conceive and act out of free womanhood, by showing how Margaret Fuller construed her problem and by examining, one at a time, the various identities she assumed in an effort to resolve the struggle." The resulting discussion is sophisticated and provocative. Chevigny bases her interpretation on two premises: that Fuller moved from "idealism to a critical or radical realism" and that her "unusual" qualities are most interesting "for what they reveal about the feelings of ordinary American women of her class: their restlessness, ambitions, and frustrations." Chevigny has little to say about Fuller's writings except insofar as they provide biographical insight. Chevigny presents a forceful case for her reading, but she, in common with a number of recent critics, transforms Emerson into a timid dreamer.

The most recent Fuller biography is now the "standard" life: Paula Blanchard, *Margaret Fuller*, a study well grounded in original source material. Blanchard has written a straightforward book, but one that does not closely examine any of Fuller's works except *Woman in the Nineteenth Century*. This study clearly develops Fuller's life, but it lacks a comprehensive analysis of her personality. If Blanchard errs, she errs on the side of modesty; the reader comes away looking for a stronger assessment of Fuller. Like most other Fuller biographies, Blanchard's is inadequately annotated, making it hard for a reader to find her sources.

Although the major documents for a study of Fuller's life are in manuscript, a number of printed sources are important. Part of Richard Fuller's journal was published as "The Younger Generation in 1840," and his autobiography was privately printed as *Recollections of Richard F. Fuller*. Richard's *Chaplain Fuller*, a biography of Arthur B. Fuller, has valuable comments on Margaret Fuller and the family. A major biographical source is *The Letters of Ralph Waldo Emerson*, ed. Ralph L. Rusk, which prints many letters from Fuller to Emerson in the notes. *The Journals and Miscellaneous Notebooks of Ralph Waldo Emerson* has scattered Emerson comments on Fuller. Vol. 11 is especially noteworthy, for it prints the entire "Margaret Fuller Ossoli" notebook that Emerson produced in 1851 as he worked on the *Memoirs*. Fuller is also dealt with in *The Correspondence of Emerson and Carlyle*, ed. Joseph Slater. Responses to Fuller appear in *The Letters of A. Bronson Alcott*, *The Journals of Bronson Alcott*, and Larry A. Carlson, "Bronson Alcott's 'Journal for 1837.'" Joel Myerson, in "Bronson Alcott's 'Journal for 1836'" and "Bronson Alcott's 'Scripture for 1840,'" publishes Alcott's references to Fuller during those years. Hawthorne mentions Fuller in his *American Notebooks*, which now exists in two editions: the one edited by Randall Stewart has more complete notes, and the one by Claude M. Simpson is the authoritative text. James Freeman Clarke's *Autobiography, Diary and Correspondence* has a number of comments on Fuller. *The Letters of James Freeman Clarke to Margaret Fuller*, ed. John Wesley Thomas, has few (and often erroneous) notes and lacks an index, but the letters are of great value. Robert D. Habich, "James Freeman Clarke's 1833 Letter-journal for Margaret Fuller," adds more detail to the Clarke-Fuller friendship. Several of Fuller's other friends published reminiscences of her. *Letters and Journals of Thomas Wentworth Higginson*, ed. Mary Thacher Higginson, contains William H. Hurlbut's account of Fuller. Julia Ward Howe's recollection is in Laura E. Richards and Maud Howe Elliott, *Julia Ward Howe*, William Story's memoir is in *Reminiscences of William Wetmore Story*, ed. Mary E. Phillips, and Emelyn Story's diary is partly reprinted in Henry James, *William Wetmore Story and His Friends*. Other significant sources are Horace Greeley, *Recollections of a Busy Life*; Oliver Wendell Holmes, "Cinders from the Ashes"; George Willis Cooke, *John Sullivan Dwight*; Georgiana Bruce Kirby, *Years of Experience*; and Ednah Dow Cheney, *Reminiscences*. Leopold Wellisz, *The Friendship of Margaret Fuller D'Ossoli and Adam Mickiewicz*, prints letters from the poet to Fuller and recounts the details of their friendship.

Margaret and Her Friends, ed. Caroline Healey Dall, remains the single most important account of the Conversations. Dall wrote often about Fuller, most importantly in "The Late Lawsuit" and "Margaret Fuller Ossoli." Joel Myerson, "Caroline Dall's Reminiscences of Margaret Fuller," prints a portion of Dall's journal discussing Fuller. Dall's comments are vigorous, but they say more perhaps about her than about Fuller. Myerson has also published "Mrs. Dall Edits Miss Fuller," an article tracing the history of Dall's book.

Madeleine B. Stern, "Margaret Fuller and the Phrenologist-Publishers," describes Fuller's interest in phrenology, her meeting with Orson Fowler, and her relations with various phrenologist publishers, including the *American Phrenological Journal* and the house of Fowler and Wells. Two essays by Joel Myerson give important details of Fuller's friendships: "Frederic Henry Hedge and the Failure of Transcendentalism" and "'A True & High Minded Person,'" which deals with Sarah Clarke. Alexander E. Jones, "Margaret Fuller's Attempt to Write Fiction," marshals all the facts we have about Fuller's "Lost and Won," her fictional account of George and Harriet Davis. Henry L. Greene, "The Greene-St. School, of Providence, and Its Teachers," is by far the best account of the school and of Fuller's part in it. Charles R. Crowe, "Transcendentalism and the Providence Literati," and Edward A. Hoyt and Loriman S. Brigham, "Glimpses of Margaret Fuller," both discuss the Providence days in useful detail. Accounts of Fuller's life as a teacher are given in Annie Russell Marble, "Margaret Fuller as Teacher," and Harriet Hall Johnson, "Margaret Fuller as Known by Her Scholars." Richard V. Carpenter, "Margaret Fuller in Northern Illinois," has little new to add on Fuller but gives a detailed commentary on the people she met on her trip. Finally, Joel Myerson, "A Calendar of Transcendental Club Meetings," records Fuller's attendance at the club.

Fuller's career on the *Dial* has been carefully treated. The original work, George Willis Cooke, *An Historical and Biographical Introduction to Accompany the* Dial, thorough as it was, has now been wholly superseded by Joel Myerson, *The New England Transcendentalists and the* Dial. Myerson, working from original manuscript sources, carefully reconstructs the journal's inception and history. He has individual chapters on the editorships of Fuller and Emerson and full alphabetical lists of contributors and their contributions. Myerson previously published a more detailed "Annotated List of Contributions to the Boston *Dial*."

All the serious biographies of Fuller's closest friends discuss her in detail. Especially noteworthy are Ralph L. Rusk, *The Life of Ralph Waldo Emerson*, Walter Harding, *The Days of Henry Thoreau*, John Wesley Thomas, *James Freeman Clarke*, Arthur S. Bolster, Jr., *James Freeman Clarke*, and Charles E. Blackburn, "James Freeman Clarke," a work that draws heavily on manuscript sources. Charles Crowe, *George Ripley*, Edwin Gittleman, *Jones Very*, Frederick T. McGill, Jr., *Channing of Concord*, and Robert N. Hudspeth, *Ellery Channing*, all explore Fuller's relationships with other Transcendentalists.

Since the publication of the *Love-Letters*, little new information has been discovered about Fuller; we have been in possession of what facts we have for almost eighty years. As a result, the large number of biographies written in this century mostly retell the story of her life. Only the interpretations are new: Fuller is now seen less as a literary figure—and especially as one in the orbit of Emerson—and more as a representative woman living in a society hostile to her sex. One must assume that this point of view will be developed, especially as we come to understand better the conditions that faced all women in the nineteenth century. Studies like Carrol Smith-Rosenberg's "The Female World of Love and Ritual"—an essay that is valuable for suggesting ways to view Fuller's friendships—will help us come to terms with the complexities of her personality and experiences.

It is, however, depressing to contend with the scholarly ineptitude of so many Fuller biographies. Dates are often wrong, people are misidentified (surely by now we can distinguish Samuel Gray Ward of Boston from Sam Ward of Washington), titles of books come out garbled, and almost no one publishes a set of notes worth the effort. Of the nine biographies written in this century, only Brown's, and his only partially, is annotated well enough for a reader to pursue the original sources.

CRITICISM

Joel Myerson has edited a good selection of *Critical Essays on Margaret Fuller*. Myerson collects fifty-three essays, beginning with William J. Pabodie's review of the *Dial* in 1840 and concluding with Marie Mitchell Olesen Urbanski on *Woman in the Nineteenth Century*. Myerson also includes a succinct account of Fuller's publishing career and the critical reaction to her. In addition, four critical books on Fuller have appeared: Frederick Augustus Braun, *Margaret Fuller and Goethe*; Russell F. Durning, *Margaret Fuller, Citizen of the World: An Intermediary between European and American Literature*; Margaret Vanderhaar Allen, *The Achievement of Margaret Fuller*; and Marie Urbanski, *Margaret Fuller's* Woman in the Nineteenth Century: *A Literary Study of Form and Content, of Sources and Influence*. Of these, Allen's is the most ambitious and comprehensive; her "concern is with Fuller's ideas and where they led her." Allen admirably concentrates on what Fuller wrote (though too much of the discussion relies on the *Memoirs*), and the chapter on Emerson is quite illuminating. Unfortunately, much of what Allen says is marred by reductive statements: "In fleeing New England, [Fuller] escaped that religiosity"; "Margaret Fuller struggled against the bondage of her Puritan heritage"; and T. S. Eliot becomes "the arch-Puritan." Durning's best work is on Fuller's study of German letters (see below), though he too often merely summarizes what Fuller wrote and fails to pursue a critical analysis of his own. Nevertheless, Durning's work is valuable for its examination of all of Fuller's writing on foreign literature. Urbanski examines several possible influences on *Woman in the Nineteenth Century* and advances the not wholly convincing thesis that the book has the form of a sermon oration. Although Urbanski's notion is interesting, it is undercut by the frequent use of "seems" to qualify the discussion: "The structure of *Woman* does seem to fit loosely the sermon-oration form." Since Urbanski recognizes the meddling hand of Arthur Fuller in his editions of Fuller, it is dismaying that she should use his text for this book. Niggling errors distract the reader: Healey is misspelled, and the conjecture that Hawthorne answered Fuller's "Brutus" essay is given as fact.

The most ambitious discussion of Fuller and German literature is Braun's. After summarizing her comments on Goethe printed in the *Memoirs*, Braun emphasizes the degree to which Goethe "re-educated" Fuller: "Her whole life in America, and later in Italy, was in conformity to the great principles which she had learned from Goethe." Braun then strenuously disassociated Fuller from the Transcendentalists in order to defend her practical, critical ability. The book concludes with a chapter on Fuller's defense of Goethe, but Braun offers no commentary, preferring instead to quote at great length from Fuller's published writings. In "Margaret Fuller's Translation and Criticism of Goethe's *Tasso*," Braun compares parallel German and English passages to show how Fuller handled the original. Arthur R. Schultz, "Margaret Fuller—Transcendentalist Interpreter of German Literature," adds little to what Braun demonstrated, for the essay mostly summarizes Fuller's comments. Equally slight is René Wellek, "The Minor Transcendentalists and German Philosophy." Wellek briefly notes Fuller's confusion about German philosophy (as distinct from literature) and concludes that she "cared nothing for what she thought were German technicalities and had only vaguely understood that German philosophy from Jacobi to Hegel justified the religion of the heart." Stanley M. Vogel does not add much to what a reader of the *Memoirs* would know in *German Literary Influences on the American Transcendentalists*. Even though he uses manuscript versions of letters from Clarke to Fuller, Vogel does little more than tell the chronological story of her interest in German letters. J. Wesley Thomas, "New Light on Margaret Fuller's Projected 'Life of Goethe,'" quotes Clarke's letters to Fuller and her replies while she was planning the biography. A more ambitious and accomplished essay is Harry Slochower's "Margaret Fuller and Goethe," which argues that Fuller could not reconcile the Platonic idealism and Baconian realism of her time, a duality she found most clearly expressed in Goethe. What she distrusted in Goethe—his coldness—she feared most in her own divided self. Slochower concludes that "Goethe's life-work represented the strongest indictment of her own [and] exposed the pathetic futility of her discordant quests." In a thorough, illuminating discussion, Hildegard Platzer Collins and Philip Allison Shelley, "The Reception in England and America of Bettina von Arnim's *Goethe's Correspondence with a Child*," place Fuller's reaction in the context of the harshly negative British response to Bettina's book.

The two best studies of Fuller's interest in German literature are Henry A. Pochmann, *German Culture in America*, and Russell F. Durning, *Margaret Fuller, Citizen of the World*. Pochmann explains what German literature (especially Goethe) meant to Fuller and concludes that "there was no personality, either in books or among her acquaintances, who did more to emancipate her soul from the limitations of New England morality and the restrictions of femininity." Though short, Pochmann's discussion is useful and suggestive. His notes give a running summary of Fuller's writings on Germany and are as valuable as his criticism. Durning's chapter on Fuller and the Germans, our most detailed account of her long interest in that literature, examines each of her essays and reviews and concludes with a thorough discussion of her translations. In a separate essay, "Margaret Fuller's Translation of Goethe's 'Prometheus,'" Durning examines a translation Fuller included in a letter to Caroline Sturgis.

Octavius Brooks Frothingham, in *Transcendentalism in New England*, pays tribute to Fuller as a critic, even though she was only marginally a "Transcendentalist." Frothingham does little more than collect lengthy quotations from the *Memoirs*. This rather breathless paean has little that would help a modern reader. Helen Neill McMaster, in "Margaret Fuller as a Literary Critic," writes with more spirit and recognizes the problems created by bad editing and subjective biographies. Having noted the problems, however, she goes on to base her monograph on Arthur Fuller's editions and on the *Memoirs*. Like Frothingham, McMaster rarely ventures beyond summary and quotation.

Roland Crozier Burton, "Margaret Fuller's Literary Criticism of the Fine Arts," convincingly analyzes Fuller's attitude toward nonliterary art. Using original sources, Burton explores the sources of Fuller's aesthetics and surveys all she wrote on the subject. His conclusion, that hers were the "adventures of an active and intelligent but essentially unspeculative mind in a strange field," seems all too accurate. A thorough exploration of Fuller's approach to criticism is to be found in Henry L. Golemba, "The Balanced View in Margaret Fuller's Literary Criticism." A sound discussion of Fuller's role as a critic is Wilma R. Ebbitt, "Margaret Fuller's Ideas on Criticism." Ebbitt uses the original *Dial* and *Tribune* essays and the first edition of *Papers on Literature and Art* to develop Fuller's "theory of criticism and to indicate the consequences of this theory for her critical method." Ebbitt then discusses the "Short Essay on Critics" Fuller published in the *Dial* and shows how her later "Dialogues" modified her theory of criticism. Ebbitt concludes that Fuller knew the difference between morals and aesthetics and wanted to bridge the two but that she was not always successful. Albert J. von Frank has written a sophisticated, quite rewarding discussion of Fuller's view of art and criticism, "Life as Art in America," which contends that "of all the circumstances that contributed to the shaping of Margaret Fuller's mind and career, perhaps none was more fatally decisive than the provinciality of her environment." His essay explores Fuller's Cambridge life and connects her surroundings and education with her conception of criticism. Von Frank's conclusion is that Fuller achieved her goal of becoming a hero but that, given the conditions of her culture, hers was "the life of a frontier hero." Von Frank admirably pursues a fresh line of inquiry, though he probably overstates the provinciality of the Boston area and Fuller's isolation from her youthful contemporaries. Karen Ann Szymanski, "Margaret Fuller: The New York Years," contends that "Fuller sets forth a notion of wholeness which departs significantly from the transcendental model and leads her to change her definitions of the other terms she uses and her view of the world." This is our most thorough account of Fuller's stay in New York and the changes she underwent there.

Of the other individual essays, not much need be said. John Paul Pritchard, *Criticism in America*, notes that Fuller was not really a Transcendentalist, that she was well equipped to be a critic, and that she was interested in American literature. With meager annotation, this essay is mostly descriptive. Benjamin T. Spencer, *The Quest for Nationality*, provides no annotation at all. His chapter on the Transcendentalists mentions Fuller slightly, usually in contrast to Emerson. Vivian C. Hopkins, in "Margaret Fuller," presents a well-documented discussion but develops little criticism of her own. John B. Wilson, "The Aesthetics of Transcendentalism," concludes that Fuller "often lost herself in sentimentalism" when discussing art and sculpture. In effect, Wilson accepts Emerson's verdict in the *Memoirs* and goes on to say that Fuller believed that America would develop a genuine art.

On Fuller's relationship with the *Dial*, both Cooke and Myerson have much to say. The latter's work especially supersedes Helen E. Marshall, "The Story of the *Dial*." Helen Hennessy (Vendler), "The *Dial*," has little on Fuller, but the essay is a good summary of the journal's place in American Romanticism. Hennessy notes that both Fuller and Emerson "stated and restated their two cardinal principles: that contemplative activity is valuable as an end in itself, and that literature must be judged on aesthetic, not moral, grounds." The most ambitious single essay on Fuller and the *Dial* is Bernard Rosenthal, "The *Dial*, Transcendentalism, and Margaret Fuller," which claims that "from 1840 to 1842 *The Dial* was more the journal of Margaret Fuller than it was the journal of American transcendentalists." Rosenthal goes on to discuss Fuller's interest in German literature.

Scholarly interest in Fuller's social criticism is limited but growing. Charles R. Crowe, "Transcendentalist Support of Brook Farm," has little on Fuller, and H. Leland Taylor, "Margaret Fuller: Commitment in Italy," is trivial, doing little more than reprinting sections from Fuller's reports from Italy. By far the best work is Francis E. Kearns, "Margaret Fuller's Social Criticism," and an essay derived from it, "Margaret Fuller and the Abolition Movement." Kearns concludes that Fuller's aloofness from the abolitionists has been exaggerated: her misgivings were based mostly on the fact that they did not have an equal interest in the freedom of women.

David M. Robinson, "Margaret Fuller and the Transcendental Ethos: *Woman in the Nineteenth Century*," argues that Fuller's book "remains both compelling and historically important, not only as a major feminist document, as recent criticism of it has stressed, but also as a key expression of the values of American transcendentalism." Robinson focuses on Fuller's insistence on "self-culture," tracing the idea in Transcendentalist thought from Dr. William Ellery Channing to *Woman*. Fuller "discovered that self-culture as an end required social reform as a means, that the fulfillment of woman necessitated the concerted action of women. *Woman in the Nineteenth Century* is her monument to that discovery." In passing, Robinson makes the interesting assertion that Transcendentalism was linked to American millennial thought. Robinson successfully brings together several themes in Fuller's work (self-culture, feminism, and social reform) and sets this synthesis off against the larger pattern of Transcendentalism.

Fuller's friendships with other writers as an intellectual (rather than purely biographical) question have concerned Ralph L. Rusk, Robert N. Hudspeth, and Perry Miller (all discussed above). Helene G. Baer, "Mrs. Child and Miss Fuller," is an undocumented summary of what could have been a rewarding topic. Baer claims that "their influence on each other was significant, their association intimate," without demonstrating either assertion. Derek Colville, "The Transcendental Friends: Clarke and Margaret Fuller," quotes from the correspondence of the two without adding a cogent commentary. (The Clarke letters Colville uses are printed in John Wesley Thomas' edition discussed above.) Marie Urbanski, "Henry David Thoreau and Margaret Fuller," claims that *Summer on the Lakes* "influenced" Thoreau's *A Week*, but the discussion merely isolates common themes in the two books, hardly a demonstration of influence.

On Emerson and Fuller much has been published, especially by Fuller's recent biographers, Chevigny and Blanchard, and by Allen, Urbanski, and Douglas (below) in their critical books. John Bard McNulty, "Emerson's Friends and the Essay on Friendship," marshals the facts of the friendship and shows which passages about Fuller in Emerson's journals wound up in his essay. Harry R. Warfel, "Margaret Fuller and Ralph Waldo Emerson," tries to plumb the topic without recourse to the original letters of either writer. The result is disappointing: Warfel concludes merely that Fuller grew beyond Emerson after 1844, but he does not explain how or why. By far the best single essay on the topic is Carl F. Strauch, "Hatred's Swift Repulsions." Working from the original manuscripts, Strauch first traces the discussions of friendship in the letters of Emerson, Fuller, and Caroline Sturgis, and then shows how the two women and Samuel Gray Ward influenced the poetry Emerson was then writing. Some of the poems, Strauch claims very convincingly, are "verse commentary on a critical moment in Emerson's life." Strauch is especially good on the crucial period from August to October 1840. Marie Urbanski, "The Ambivalence of Ralph Waldo Emerson towards Margaret Fuller," shows that Emerson first felt a strongly, even sexual attraction to Fuller and found in her the inspiration he needed for all his writing from 1835 to 1844. Later, he was wounded by her aloofness and cruelly created a "Margaret myth" after her death. Urbanski finds little but neurotic defensiveness in Emerson, as do a number of recent critics.

For the bitter controversy surrounding Hawthorne's hostile comments on Fuller, the reader should consult the Hawthorne chapter of this research guide, as well as Myerson's secondary bibliography.

Another critical discussion of note is Lawrence Buell, *Literary Transcendentalism*, especially the chapter "From Conversation to Essay." Robert D. Richardson, Jr., "Margaret Fuller and Myth," presents a lively and convincing discussion of Fuller's attitude toward mythology. Richardson claims that "the increasingly active side of the last ten years of her short life was not so much a reaction against her earlier beliefs as it was in important ways a natural outgrowth of them." He goes on to make several points: Fuller was widely read in myths outside the Greek-Roman-Christian traditions;

it was "the relation of Greek mythic values to modern values that interested her"; and the Greeks "provided her with a cultural paradigm that was an alternative to the threadbare Christian one." Unfortunately, Richardson uses less than adequate texts and muddles a few facts—he has Hawthorne engaged too soon and mistakenly places Fuller in Egypt.

Currently, the most vigorous critiques of Fuller come from a school one may loosely term "feminist," and by far the best of these is Bell Gale Chevigny's *The Woman and the Myth*. Chevigny has also published "Growing out of New England," an essay that covers some of the ground she previously worked in the anthology. Here, Chevigny says, her interest "is in asking how [Fuller's] childhood and young womanhood in New England made her strong and showed her that her field of action lay beyond it." Her conclusion is that Fuller's Conversations gave her the strength to accept herself and that *Summer on the Lakes* and *Woman in the Nineteenth Century* were her means of making the transition from Transcendentalist aloofness to "social realism." The concluding chapter in Barbara Welter's *Dimity Convictions* is an exploration of Fuller's life. "Her interest in women was a vital part of her, perhaps her core. . . . All women were part of the woman she was, and she was part of them." This, says Welter, "was the mystical element of her feminism." As a result, "Helping women help themselves was her true vocation, for which her mysticism and her feminism had long been preparing her." Welter's discussion of Fuller is sound, though it all but ignores the Nathan episode and is scanty about the European years. Oddly, the Fuller chapter has no annotations whatsoever, the only such chapter in Welter's otherwise carefully documented book.

Two other books have polemical essays on Fuller that provoke and disturb, but disturb for the wrong reasons: each is marked by sloppy scholarship and is thus hard to take seriously. "'The Beauty of a Stricter Method,'" in Susan P. Conrad, *Perish the Thought*, attempts to set Fuller in the context of American Romanticism, something that needs doing. The term "Romantic," however, is not clearly defined, nor is "Transcendental," which seems to mean anti-Romantic in Conrad's discussion. Although the essay has insights worth having ("To teach others to make demands upon literature was an act of social redemption that required her to maintain a public intellectual stance"), some of her judgments are bizarre: she describes *Woman in the Nineteenth Century* as "perhaps the most romantic nonfictional document America produced in that century." Furthermore, Conrad makes factual errors (she calls Timothy Fuller "clearly a persuaded Jacksonian"); she misses information readily available (Ellen Kilshaw is "unfortunately unnamed"); she often strains to shock ("Almost every sentence [Fuller] ever wrote is fraught with active, assertive, dynamic, sexual imagery that is intensely phallic"). Finally, the writing is embarrassingly loaded with such phrases as "having chained the mind to the hearth or literally swept it under the rug" and Fuller's mother was "literally only a symbol."

Equally frustrating is "Margaret Fuller and the Disavowal of Fiction," in Ann Douglas, *The Feminization of American Culture*. Douglas advances the thesis that Fuller was unfortunately under the spell of "rhetoric." Having escaped her father's "dictatorial rule," she indulged her "fascination with rhetoric and talk" when she came under Emerson's influence. Fuller, claims Douglas, was able to "attack the metaphorical life," represented by Emerson, "which depended on the substitution of 'eloquence' for experience." Douglas goes on to posit a "crippling narcissism" that Fuller finally escaped only by becoming a journalist and then a historian in Italy. She did so because she "clearly believed that 'art' was increasingly functioning in American culture as a diversion from the pressing problem of socio-economic order, and that 'history' suggested active participation in the revolutionary changes necessary to transform and better that order. For distinctions more complex and more profound than these, she had no time." Douglas' thesis is challenging, but it often rests on questionable premises, such as the negative quality of public talk or Fuller's "crippling narcissism." Also, this work, extensively annotated though it is, is badly compromised by factual mistakes: Dr. Channing's death date is incorrect; Dr. John Park becomes "Dr. Parks"; Henry Hedge emerges as "Frederick Hedges"; Chipperfield is consistently rendered "Chippenfield"; Braun is "Brown"; *Papers on Literature and Art* is labeled "New York, 1832"; *At Home and Abroad* is "Boston and London, 1836"; *Life Without and Life Within* is "Boston, 1960." Each of these is a niggling error, the sort anyone can (and almost all of us do) make. Still, a book purporting to be a serious scholarly work must convince by its care and precision as well as by its energy.

Both Urbanski and Allen address Fuller's feminism, the former in the last chapter of her book, where she traces the reputation of *Woman in the Nineteenth Century* among later feminists. Allen covers much of the same ground in her chapter "Feminism."

FURTHER RESEARCH

Clear lines of future Fuller scholarship now suggest themselves. The single greatest need is for an edition, fully reported and annotated, of the journal fragments that survive. This task is complicated by the state of the manuscripts, which are often fragments or copies of dubious authenticity scattered among several repositories, with the largest portions in the Boston Public Library and the Houghton Library. Only by a painfully laborious matching of ink and paper can the job be done at all, but it must be done. Beyond this, we need reliable texts of *Summer on the Lakes*, of the *Western Messenger* and *Dial* articles, and particularly of the essays written from Italy. The field of criticism is wholly open: no single topic has been exhausted for anyone who brings a sharp critical intelligence to Fuller's writing. We still need critics who will take Fuller's language and ideas seriously and place her in the context of intellectual history. Above all, we must tackle the problem of unreliable texts and be scrupulous in using the sentences she actually wrote, as she wrote them. Otherwise, we only perpetuate the distortions that were first created by her contemporaries.

FREDERIC HENRY HEDGE

Leonard Neufeldt

BIBLIOGRAPHIES

No comprehensive and reliable bibliography of Hedge is available as yet, a fact that reflects the scant critical attention devoted to him over the years. Two useful features of O. W. Long, *Frederic Henry Hedge: A Cosmopolitan Scholar*, are his extensive inventory of early biographical profiles and information on first printings of Hedge's major essays. Unquestionably, the most comprehensive and accurate bibliography of primary works is Joel Myerson, "Frederic Henry Hedge" (in *FPAA*, vol. 3); the format of this checklist, however, does not allow for an inventory of Hedge's many publications in journals, magazines, and newspapers, an inventory that is badly needed. As for secondary works, Ronald Vale Wells's list in his *Three Christian Transcendentalists* is both highly selective and out-of-date, but it remains the best available. All the articles on Hedge listed in *AAL* are discussed in this essay.

MANUSCRIPTS

Manuscript information is equally unsatisfactory. *ALM* overlooks important collections such as those at the Andover-Harvard Theological Library and the Bangor Historical Society. Included in the Andover-Harvard collection are Hedge letters to various secretaries of the American Unitarian Association; these letters are bound in the AUA letter books, for which the library's index is helpful but incomplete. *ALM* statistics reflect faulty information in card catalogs, inaccurate reports by library staffs on their cataloged materials, and silence on uncataloged holdings. Important recent deposits of manuscripts at Andover-Harvard and the prospect of additional deposits elsewhere by Hedge descendants make the *ALM* census almost useless.

EDITIONS

There is no complete or partial edition of Hedge's works. For students of Transcendentalism the most important works by Hedge are "Coleridge" (1833), *Conservatism and Reform* (1843), *Prose Writers of Germany* (1848), his manuscript "Lecture on Natural Religion" (1851, located at the Houghton Library of Harvard Univ.), *Recent Inquiries in Theology* (1860), *Reason in Religion* (1865), *Sermons* (1891), and a collection he coauthored with Annis Lee Wister, *Metrical Translations and Poems* (1888). Three well-known and highly partial poetry anthologies featured original verse by Hedge: *War Songs for Freemen*, ed. Francis J. Child; *Singers and Songs of the Liberal Faith*, ed. Alfred P. Putman; and *The Poets of Transcendentalism*, ed. George Willis Cooke. Hedge's 1849 Harvard Divinity School address, "The Broad Church," and "The Religion of the Resurrection" (the latter two from *Sermons*) have been reprinted in a special Hedge number of the *Unitarian Universalist Christian* (1981).

BIOGRAPHY

Hedge's lifelong loyalty to the Unitarian ministry, his stature as minister and spokesman, his efforts to introduce German literature and Romanticism to America, and his association with Transcendentalism inspired a number of profiles that began with George Cressey's twelve-page career survey, *Sketch of Frederic Henry Hedge*, and his *Frederic Henry Hedge: Pastor of the Society*. Upon Hedge's death in August 1890, scores of obituary notices appeared, including sketches by Cyrus Bartol, Joseph Henry Allen, Howard N. Brown, and John White Chadwick. In 1891, Chadwick published his *Frederic Henry Hedge: A Sermon*; in 1897, Allen published *Sequel to "Our Liberal Movement,"* which included a "personal memoir" of Hedge and incorporated Allen's profiles from the *Unitarian Review*; and in 1910 Brown wrote a chapter on Hedge for *Heralds of a Liberal Faith*, ed. Samuel A. Eliot. Most of these portraits reveal as much about the authors as about Hedge. Chadwick underscores Hedge's "ecclesiastical conservatism"; Allen and Brown portray an erudite and loyal Unitarian (Brown's anti-Transcendentalism distinguishes him from Allen); and the radical Bartol admires Hedge's catholicity of thought, persistently fresh and independent theological views, interest in German literature, literary talents, and critical aptitude. Allen and Brown seem to have influenced each other, and Bartol and Allen clearly influenced O. W. Long's monograph *Frederic Henry Hedge*, which provides an account of Hedge's career with particular attention to his interest in German literature and his connection with Transcendentalism. His role in American intellectual history is described as major.

Several other studies of biographical-historical interest warrant notice here: Stillman F. Kneeland, *Seven Centuries in the Kneeland Family*; William H. Lyon, *The First Parish in Brookline* and *Frederic Henry Hedge: A Sermon*; George Willis Cooke's chapter on Hedge in his *An Historical and Biographical Introduction to Accompany the* Dial; Bliss Perry's chapter on Hedge in *The Early Years of the Saturday Club 1855–1870*; Martha Ilona Tuomi, "Dr. Frederic Henry Hedge"; Peter Carley, "The Early Life and Thought of Frederic Henry Hedge"; James R. McGovern, *Yankee Family*; and the chapter on Hedge in Joel Myerson, *The New England Transcendentalists and the* Dial. Lyon and Cooke hold views similar to Allen's, whereas Perry's tribute is to a liberal spirit, a competent if testy and unsuccessful professor, and a quiet club member. Hedge's eczema, according to Perry, "caused him to reexamine his philosophical tenets . . . and forced him to the conclusion that the Devil had a much larger share in the government of the world than he had previously supposed. But he did not commit these views to writing." Tuomi's stylistically insecure thesis is nonanalytic but useful in tracing Hedge's lineage and noting the major events in the first half of his life. Carley also limits his study to this period but is more analytical and more aware of Hedge's liberalism and his influence on other liberal Transcendentalists. Myerson expertly surveys Hedge's role in the *Dial* and his uneasy relationship with the Transcendentalists in the late 1830s and early 1840s.

Valuable biographical information on Hedge may be found in the newspapers of Cambridge, Boston, Bangor, Providence, and Brookline; the journals and magazines to which he contributed and those that he edited; correspondence, journals, diaries, and memoirs of acquaintances, friends, and associates; and records and studies of the parishes in which Hedge served. One should also consult general studies of Transcendentalism, the Transcendental Club, and nineteenth-century Unitarians, especially Caroline H. Dall, *Transcendentalism in New England*; George Willis Cooke, *Unitarianism in America*; Kenneth Walter Cameron, *Transcendental Reading Patterns*; Joel Myerson, "A Calendar of Transcendental Club Meetings" and "A History of the Transcendental Club"; and *A Stream of Light*, ed. Conrad Wright. Some autobiographies and biographies of Hedge's contemporaries are particularly relevant: Thomas Wentworth Higginson, *Margaret Fuller Ossoli*; James Elliot Cabot, *A Memoir of Ralph Waldo Emerson*; James Freeman Clarke, *Autobiography, Diary and Correspondence*; and Walter Donald Kring, *Henry Whitney Bellows*.

Although Hedge has benefited from the resurgence in Transcendentalist scholarship, most recent histories and surveys of Transcendentalism pay him little or no attention, which suggests the staying power of a tradition begun by Octavius Brooks Frothingham. Out of strong personal, philosophical, and political differences with Hedge, he treated him with two inconsequential references in *Transcendentalism in New England*. One can expect that Hedge scholarship will be significantly advanced by the ambitious biographical study recently undertaken by Charles Grady, pastor of the Unitarian-Universalist parish in which Hedge began his ministry. A preview of this study is "Frederic Henry Hedge: A Forgotten Transcendentalist."

CRITICISM

GENERAL STUDIES

Three essays in *Unitarianism: Its Origins and History* explain Hedge's importance in American intellectual history. Joseph Henry Allen recognizes his mythic interpretation of the Bible and his liberal religion; Francis Tiffany characterizes Hedge as one who "for better or worse" disseminated German thought throughout America but who developed a largely homegrown Transcendentalism; and Francis Hornbrooke presents him as an example of the fusion of theology and literature. Add to these observations Stanley M. Vogel's declaration in *German Literary Influences on the American Transcendentalists* that Hedge "has never been given sufficient credit for his leadership in the Transcendental movement," and contrast it with Herbert W. Schneider's conclusion in *A History of American Philosophy* that "Hedge clearly did not share the transcendental temper," and we have the range of views expressed thus far in critical studies of Hedge.

Cyrus Bartol produced the first general position statement on Hedge. In "Sermons by Frederic Henry Hedge," Bartol uses the posthumous appearance of a collection of Hedge's sermons as an opportunity to praise "the Goethe of our time" and explain aspects of Hedge's theological and philosophical thought, literary contributions, methods of composition and argumentation, catholicity of thought, "reserved strength," and "rhetorical charm." Joseph Henry Allen, in *Sequel to "Our Liberal Movement,"* focuses on "the character, the spiritual endowment, and the mental habit" of Hedge, describing him as a liberal Unitarian, a rare and independent intellect, and an artist and literary scholar attracted to the "higher uses" of art and the "atmosphere of German thought." Unlike Allen, George Willis Cooke, in his book on the *Dial*, emphasizes Hedge's tie to Transcendentalism: "He was a transcendentalist, but not of the extreme type. . . . Nor did he keep pace with Emerson in his individualism." Howard N. Brown, in *Heralds of a Liberal Faith*, concedes Hedge's Transcendentalist inclinations but cites his removal to Bangor as the act that fortunately saved him for the Unitarian church and allowed him to develop a philosophically "broader and saner position."

Between 1910 and 1975 only one general study of Hedge appeared, Ronald Vale Wells's *Three Christian Transcendentalists*. The fifty pages Wells devotes to Hedge constitute the most comprehensive and influential appraisal to date. According to Wells, Hedge, an embodiment of Christian Transcendentalism (with the emphasis on Christian), attempted to rethink fundamental Christian tenets by conducting them through German idealism, especially the philosophies of Kant and Schelling. The discussion is most useful in its brief exposition of Hedge's thoughts on progress and change, nature and spirit, evil, politics and social ethics, moral sense and moral law, personality and individuality, science and religion, higher criticism, aesthetics, "Broad Church" tolerance, and "negative theology."

Recently, two important studies have appeared: Joel Myerson, "Frederic Henry

Hedge and the Failure of Transcendentalism," and Doreen Hunter, " 'Frederic Henry Hedge, What Say You?' " Myerson examines the "immediate consequences of the Transcendental rebellion" on Hedge, a founder of the Transcendental Club who fell from favor because of his "enlightened conservatism" and who withdrew his approval from mainstream Transcendentalism. In short, "the New England Transcendentalists failed to convince him of the worth of their movement for paradoxically the same reasons which attracted so many others: an opposition to existing institutions, a distrust of the past, an intense reliance upon individual intuition, and a non-acceptance of the miracles of the New Testament." Hedge regarded himself not as an exemplar of failed Transcendentalism but as an intellectual who critically defined the failures of Transcendentalism. Hunter forcefully counters Myerson, and by extension Wells and Brown, by depicting Hedge as a moderate (in the mold of the dialectical and skeptical Emerson) who "neither betrayed his earlier convictions nor grew more conservative" when he moved to Bangor. To some extent both Myerson and Hunter are confirmed by Charles Grady's "Frederic Henry Hedge," a brief biographical-critical profile well versed in the bitter controversies of Hedge's West Cambridge parish, the bristling resistance of the Boston Unitarian leadership to Transcendentalist ministers, and the largely untold story of Hedge's quasi banishment to Bangor by that Boston leadership. When one considers the evidence of the unpublished and largely untouched Hedge manuscripts, the American Unitarian Association records and letter books, the Bangor congregation's unflinchingly tough moratorium on anything remotely Transcendentalist or German, Hedge's energetically progressive leadership in Providence and Brookline, and his strong friendship with Emerson in their late years, Hunter's article is a significant departure.

SOURCES AND INFLUENCES

Four studies are noteworthy. Sister Mary Eleanor, "Hedge's *Prose Writers of Germany* as a Source of Whitman's Knowledge of German Philosophy," is followed closely by Henry A. Pochmann in *German Culture in America*, who also goes far beyond her in his extensive examination of German philosophical and literary influences on Hedge. Alexander Kern, "The Rise of Transcendentalism, 1815–1860," devotes special attention to Hedge's Coleridge essay and the Kant-Coleridge influence on him. Vernon R. Lindquist, "Emerson and Bangor," discusses Hedge's role in exposing Bangor to Emerson and Emerson and his group to Bangor. Lindquist's Bangor is more congenial than Hunter's or Grady's.

SPECIAL AREAS OF CONCERN

William T. Harris was the first scholar to examine Hedge as philosopher, an attribution he extended to several other Transcendentalists as well. In "Frederic Henry

Hedge, D.D.,'' Hedge is described as a proponent of German philosophy in America and the first to acquaint Americans with Schopenhauer. René Wellek accords Hedge a small role among the "Minor Transcendentalists and German Philosophy." In the chapter "Spirituality among Christians" in *A History of American Philosophy*, Herbert W. Schneider takes all his cues from Wells in describing the theological conservatism and philosophical idealism of Hedge and fellow ministers James Marsh and Caleb Sprague Henry. Bryan F. LeBeau, in "Frederic Henry Hedge: Portrait of an Enlightened Conservative," not surprisingly characterizes Hedge as an enlightened conservative in philosophy and theology.

Only five treatises have dealt principally with Hedge's theology: James Freeman Clarke, "Dr. Hedge and His Critics"; Howard N. Brown, *Frederic Henry Hedge*; George H. Williams, *Rethinking the Unitarian Relationship with Protestantism*; William R. Hutchison, *The Transcendentalist Ministers*; and Catherine L. Albanese, *Corresponding Motion*. Always a virtuoso diplomat, Clarke used the publication of Hedge's *Reason in Religion* as occasion to endorse a thoroughly liberal religion by means of ingeniously ambiguous and pleasing pieties. Reappraisals of Hedge's religious views should begin with Williams but should also take note of Hutchison, whose recurrent references to Hedge describe an "ecclesiastically conservative, though intellectually radical" minister (a combination Hedge believed to be compatible) as well as a "mediator between Transcendentalism and the traditional faith." Hedge is one of six figures Albanese uses to demonstrate her thesis that "some part of the meaning of Transcendental community as an American religious group can be understood by studying the language . . . the community spoke and wrote." Her passing analyses of Hedge often conflict with her characterization of him as a conservative who became "almost a reactionary."

Hedge's literary contributions have also attracted little scholarly attention. The debate in Hedge's lifetime and after his death over the quality of his work in German literature notwithstanding, Stanley M. Vogel's *German Literary Influences* and Henry A. Pochmann's *German Culture in America* are starting points for a study of the subject. Aside from Bartol's, the only other literary discussion of consequence is Sterling Delano, "A Rediscovered Transcendental Poem by Frederic Hedge."

FURTHER RESEARCH

The current needs in Hedge scholarship are clear: the deposit of all Hedge manuscripts in libraries that will make them available to scholars; plenary primary and secondary bibliographies; an authoritative biographical study; and literary analyses of Hedge's sermons, poetry, literary theory, and criticism.

THOMAS WENTWORTH HIGGINSON

Howard N. Meyer

BIBLIOGRAPHIES

The most complete listing of Higginson's publications is in *BAL* (vol. 4). Although it covers books, broadsides, manifestos, pamphlets, sermons, reports to library and school trustees, and other miscellaneous works by Higginson, *BAL* "does not pretend" to include all appearances in the publications of "many civic, religious and other groups, which he supported." Nor are Higginson's many periodical contributions or published reports of his frequent formal and informal talks included. Still useful, because they include material in categories omitted by *BAL*, are Winifred Mather, *A Bibliography of Thomas Wentworth Higginson* (1906), compiled for the Cambridge Public Library, and the bibliographical appendix to Mary Thacher Higginson's *Thomas Wentworth Higginson* (1914), which incorporates and updates the 1906 list but lacks its index. Higginson's significant relations with the *Atlantic Monthly Magazine* are the subject of a 1968 dissertation by Leonard Brill.

Secondary references may be found in the Cambridge Public Library pamphlet. There is no secondary bibliography of Higginson, but the published abstract of the Hintz dissertation and the other dissertations referred to below are helpful. Other sources useful for both primary and secondary references are Francis I. Buck, "Thomas Wentworth Higginson 1823–1911: A Selected Bibliography," which was specifically prepared to be "used with" the bibliography to Mary Higginson's biography of her husband; Theresa Layton Hall, "A Bibliography of the New England Transcendentalist Movement"; the sixteen-page "Notes and Sources" in Anna Mary Wells, *Dear Preceptor*; the notes in Tilden G. Edelstein, *Strange Enthusiasm*; and Howard N.

Meyer, "Disciple of the Newness," an extended bibliographical essay. A number of articles on Higginson listed in *AAL* are not discussed in this essay.

EDITIONS

Higginson published at least thirty books and edited several more. The best seller during his lifetime was *The Young Folks' History of the United States*, a pioneer in young adult popularizations that first appeared in 1875 and was used by school systems for many decades afterward. Higginson's work was out of print by 1961, when a resurgence of interest began with three reprintings of his classic *Army Life in a Black Regiment* (1870). Other works, including those that contain his accounts of Transcendentalism, were soon reprinted, such as his nature book, *Out-Door Papers* (1863); his pioneer and avant-garde (for a male writer) essays on feminist advocacy, *Women and the Alphabet* (1900), itself a rearrangement of an 1882 work, *Common Sense about Women*; his biography of *Margaret Fuller Ossoli* (1884); *A Reader's History of American Literature* (1903), written with Henry Walcott Boynton; and his autobiographical (in whole or part) works, *Cheerful Yesterdays* (1898), *Comtemporaries* (1899), *Old Cambridge* (1899), *Studies in History and Letters* (1900), *Part of a Man's Life* (1905), and *Carlyle's Laugh and Other Surprises* (1909). By 1980, eighteen of his books were in print, including six of the seven volumes he had selected for republication in 1900 as his *Works: Definitive Edition*.

Excerpts from Higginson's correspondence with Emily Dickinson appear in several works about her (see below). His *Letters and Journals* (1921), edited by his widow, Mary Thacher Higginson, is so fragmentary and assumes so much knowledge of the subject that it is not useful except as a companion work or research book.

MANUSCRIPTS

ALM lists a staggering number of libraries with one or more Higginson manuscripts. The most important is the Houghton Library of Harvard University, with over 1,300 letters and fifty volumes of journals. The Boston Public Library has a significant collection, and there are a handful of others that cannot be ignored if a comprehensive study is being made: American Antiquarian Society, Yale University, Henry E. Huntington Library, Massachusetts Historical Society, and University of Virginia. Not included in *ALM* are the Marston Watson Papers at the Pilgrim Society library; these are described in L. D. Geller, *Between Concord and Plymouth*.

BIOGRAPHY

Shortly after Higginson's death in 1911, his widow published what was to be the sole biography until 1963. *Thomas Wentworth Higginson* is a straightforward, uncritical narrative, interspersed with selections from journals and numerous letters. This work hardly touches on Transcendentalism as such, and it only deals with Higginson as a Transcendentalist to the extent that his letters and diaries express yearnings that reflect the impact of the movement on one who was seventeen years old when the *Dial* was launched in 1840. Until recently, this book, *Letters and Journals*, and Higginson's own autobiographical writings (which Howard Mumford Jones has called exemplars of "autobiography as an art form") were our only sources for studying his life. Th. Bentzon (pseud. for Marie Thérèsa Blanc), *A Typical American*, is nothing more than an extremely lengthy summary and review essay of Higginson's own autobiographical publications with a few idiosyncratic comments by an author who had met Higginson personally on a few occasions.

The first of the modern biographies was Anna Mary Wells, *Dear Preceptor*, whose title reflects its central emphasis, the relationship between Higginson and Emily Dickinson, who addressed him as "preceptor" in part of her correspondence. This work appeared at a time when the few references to Higginson consisted of snide or hostile comments in studies of Dickinson, and Wells' work can be seen in retrospect as a pioneer revisionist interpretation. (It was preceded many years before by her essay, "Early Criticism of Emily Dickinson.") In dealing with Transcendentalism, however, this admirable work is of limited scope. Since its focus on Higginson's career is elsewhere, there is but passing reference to Transcendentalism. That young Higginson was affected by the spirit of the age is made evident, and that spirit is lightly and not unsympathetically sketched.

Howard N. Meyer's *Colonel of the Black Regiment* is designed for a general audience and, although enlightening and readable, is short on scholarly apparatus. It emphasizes Higginson's career as an abolitionist, a feminist, an antiimperialist, and a combatant in the Civil War. Higginson's relations with Ralph Waldo Emerson, Henry David Thoreau, and Theodore Parker are covered. Due respect is paid, also, to the role of Transcendentalism, as depicted in Higginson's own writings, as constituting the initiating impulse in the emergence of literary nationalism in the United States.

The most scholarly of the modern biographies is Tilden G. Edelstein, *Strange Enthusiasm*. Somewhat marred by the author's too neat assertion that Higginson never avoided a good fight before the Civil War and never joined in one afterward, the book is nevertheless a solid study. Edelstein thoroughly explores the impact of Transcendentalism on Higginson's growth and development and, to a limited extent, on his role in later life as a preacher and practitioner of the ideas of the 1840s. The book deals with Higginson's participation in the Radical Club, a "Latter-day Transcendentalist circle," and the Free Religious Association, proponents of the ecumenical nondenominationalism to which Transcendentalism might logically have led had it not ultimately been swallowed up by Unitarianism. The word "strange" in the book's title was a curious choice, lifted expressly from Daniel Webster, with seeming acquiescence in his hostility to abolitionism. Edelstein does cite in contrast Amos Bronson Alcott's orphic statement in the *Dial*, "Let the flame of enthusiasm

fire alway your bosom . . . it has wrought all miracles since the beginning of time."
Edelstein defends Higginson the literary critic and insists that he cannot be written
off as a specimen of the "genteel" tradition, for he was quite unlike "the reigning
genteel writers and critics who sought to avoid major social problems." A complement to this book is Edelstein's "Thomas Wentworth Higginson: The Ante-Bellum
Years," which deals sympathetically with his career as an abolitionist reformer.

Rounding out the modern biographies is James W. Tuttleton, *Thomas Wentworth Higginson*, in Twayne's United States Authors Series. Its publication in such
a series completes the resurrection of Higginson as at least a minor literary figure instead of the unperson he had become prior to 1960. Tuttleton's biographical sections
are frankly derivative; its main value is as a work of criticism, and it will be discussed
below.

Higginson's support of Emily Dickinson has always been slighted in studies of
her life. In "Emily Dickinson and Thomas Wentworth Higginson," Theodora V. W.
Ward presents a straightforward study of the Higginson-Dickinson correspondence,
an always available and often ignored primary source. Higginson still needs to be
defended against the derogations of Dickinson's partisans: regrettably, neither this
article nor the Wells biography (nor, one may add, the facts) has prevented such recent attacks as those contained in the popular play by William Luce, *The Belle of
Amherst*, in Karl Keller's *The Only Kangaroo among the Beauty*, and even in Cynthia Griffin Wolff's "The Reality of Emily Dickinson." These distortions are definitively
refuted in three papers (scheduled for later publication) read by Wells, Edelstein, and
Meyer at a November 1980 Hofstra University Conference on Nineteenth-Century
Woman Writers. In a brief earlier paper, Jonathan Morse shows that Luce misuses
the term "spasmodic," disregarding the literary significance it had in Higginson's time.

CRITICISM

Higginson died in 1911 at the age of eighty-seven, and his pen was busy up to
the moment of his passing. Even before the turn of the century, he had become a
living legend. Early in his writing career, he was introduced to Moses Coit Tyler's class
in English at the University of Michigan as "the best writer of the English language,"
and his reputation continued at this level for many years. His literary productions,
however, inspired no critical studies; his continuing career as a progressive reformer,
lacking some of the militant activism of his antebellum years and rendered more respectable by his military record, stirred up no personal attacks. Numerous sketches and
vignettes appeared about him in encyclopedias, periodicals, and miscellaneous compilations, but these contain little more than the known facts of his life. The best list
of these sketches, up to 1906, is in the Cambridge Public Library pamphlet.

Two representative longer essays written during Higginson's lifetime are George
Willis Cooke's chapter in *Authors at Home* and A. W. Jackson's more comprehensive essay. Cooke offers some data on Higginson's ongoing civic activities as he entered

his long senior citizenship. Jackson's article contains a serious literary appreciation by one who, as a subordinate officer in Higginson's black regiment, was stunned not merely to meet a man who had "really written a book . . . but to receive a volume from its author's hand."

The immediate postmortem comments were marked by a sustained note of high regard. Their character is reflected in the title of a *Current Literature* essay in 1911: "The Last Eminent Survivor of the Great New England Age." The essay quotes copiously from Edwin W. Mead's admiring article published that same year. Other laudatory works were published by Andrew McFarland Davis, Bliss Perry (in *The Praise of Folly and Other Papers*), and M. A. DeWolfe Howe (*DAB*). The Chicago *Dial* promptly memorialized Higginson's passing by declaring that his "place in American literature is high and altogether honorable" (16 May 1911).

The *Dial*'s opinion was universal, shared by highbrow and lowbrow alike, for Higginson led a popularity poll taken at the turn of the century. Fifty years later, he was a forgotten man, with none of his books in print—not even his masterpiece, *Army Life in a Black Regiment*. He had coined a metaphor with which his widow closed his posthumous *Letters and Journals*—he had eaten the "wrong leaves": "To a literary fame, death comes like the leaves in Alice's Adventures, by eating which one suddenly grew tall or short. How instantly Bayard Taylor's shrunk when he died . . . on the other hand, Hawthorne, Thoreau, and even Poe suddenly rose in dimensions."

What signaled (if anything did) the negative consensus that lasted from the 1920s to the 1960s was the review written by Van Wyck Brooks of the 1921 *Letters and Journals*, later reprinted in his *Sketches in Criticism*. The book, Brooks concluded, "did not explain the decline of New England," but it did "certainly reflect it." He pigeonholed Higginson as one of those "writers of the New England decadence" who had "too little of the intense in his own composition." Brooks's blast was followed by a reaction against the genteel tradition in general and many hostile and superficial commentaries on Higginson's relations with Emily Dickinson in particular.

Obscurity verging on obliteration can be attributed as well to the aspect of his life and work held in high regard by such as Mead, who wrote in 1911: "But who shall say what his greatest work was? Many hold it to be the work done in command of the South Carolina regiment of colored troops."

It may be suggested that the decline in the literary establishment's regard for Higginson stemmed not only from his supposed "gentility" but also from the self-consciousness about our nation's racism during the decades in which the abolitionists were generally treated with hostility and the antiracist traditions of the Transcendentalists were severely undermined.

One work of this period bucked the tide: Howard W. Hintz, "Thomas Wentworth Higginson: Disciple of the Newness." Writing at a time when interest in Higginson was heading for its nadir, Hintz paid his respects to the context of Transcendentalism from which he emerged. Hintz ranges over Higginson's entire life and work and covers considerable manuscript material. He argues, with much conviction, against

the prevailing view that Higginson "is thoroughly typical of, and chiefly to be identified with, the completely conservative, debilitated, outgrown, and self-complacent
aspects of the later New England tradition." Yet Hintz is by no means blandly sympathetic and offers some severely objective commentary on (for example) Higginson's
social criticism, finding it "sporadic, trivial and superficial." Hintz's published abstract
(1939) can stand with little amendment as the best single short study of Higginson
as a writer.

In 1940 Brooks wholly revised and reversed his earlier estimate of Higginson.
By then he had found Higginson an invaluable source and frequently cited him
(sometimes without credit) in his *Makers and Finders* series, particularly *The Flowering of New England* and *New England: Indian Summer*. In the latter work he has
high praise for Higginson, particularly for his abolitionism, *Army Life*, and his support of feminism and of many woman writers. Also in the 1940s, Stow Persons, in
Free Religion, acknowledges Higginson's "important" and "tangible" Transcendentalist contributions to "subsequent religious thought." Persons described Higginson's
tract, *The Sympathy of Religions*, written in 1855, as "the most widely distributed
document of free religion" and says very accurately of its writer:

> The Transcendental atmosphere that encircled the Harvard yard, where he was brought
> up, caused Higginson to pass over a law career for the humanities, and to become an
> ardent disciple of the new spirituality.

The 1950s began with Edgar L. McCormick, "Thomas Wentworth Higginson
as a Literary Critic." It surveys the hostile views of the 1920s and of Dickinson scholars
in particular, and it argues for a serious reevaluation of Higginson's literary criticism.
Another dissertation, Sister Thomas C. Brennan, "Thomas Wentworth Higginson:
Reformer and Man of Letters," concentrates, as its abstract states, on Higginson's
"political views, his anti-slavery activity, his service in the Civil War, his woman suffrage activities, and his writings on these subjects." The full text demonstrates that
"woman suffrage" is hardly adequate to describe Higginson's support of a wide spectrum of feminist causes. Although Brennan does not deal with Transcendentalism
as such, she remarks aptly that, in "his own life, Higginson endorsed the ideals and
principles of the Transcendentalists in a practical way."

Interest in Higginson was renewed in the 1960s with the many reprintings of
Army Life and the publication of three book-length biographies. The revival of in-
terest in a commander and chronicler of a black regiment was hailed by a number
of black literary and political publications. As a by-product of his dissertation, E. L.
McCormick published a favorable assessment "Thomas Wentworth Higginson, Poetry
Critic for the *Nation*, 1877–1903," noting his perceptive intuitions rooted in the sur-
viving but "muted liberal and humanitarian influence of the Transcendentalists."
John A. Lucas portrayed Higginson as an "early apostle of health and fitness," and
appreciative sketches were written by John T. Bethell and J. Wade Caruthers (in *The
American Renaisssance in New England*, ed. Joel Myerson).

James W. Tuttleton, *Thomas Wentworth Higginson*, treats the Transcendentalist influence on Higginson with care and sensitivity, even if, as a volume in Twayne's United States Authors Series, it is limited in scope. The roles and works of Parker and Emerson (in that order, for a change) are summarized with aphoristic quotations chosen to carry the overall narrative. In an original suggestion that is plausible as well, Tuttleton theorizes that Higginson sensed in Transcendentalism a failure to perceive the reality of evil, and the need for an aggressive "great man" to lead the fight against it; as an adolescent, Higginson fantasized that he might be that man. The book finds Higginson's "first principles" in the "spiritual and ethical base" provided by the "Newness," which enabled him "to move out in various directions through the Sisterhood of Reforms into the literary life." Tuttleton treats the pioneer ecumenical essay, Higginson's oft-reprinted and now forgotten *The Sympathy of Religions*, which was practically a manifesto of the Free Religious Association, as a statement of Higginson's creed. He then offers a fairly accurate summary of Higginson's viewpoint, perhaps the best in such short compass:

> Out of the views expressed in his creed and in "The Sympathy of Religions" derived his belief in the brotherhood of man, his love of philanthropy, and his hatred of slavery as a violation of human equality before God. From such beliefs also sprang his moral indignation at the legal and cultural subordination of women. His condemnation of materialism and his liberal labor views, his sympathy with immigrants and oppressed minorities like Catholics and Jews, his opposition to political imperialism, and his quasi-socialistic political views all derived from these first principles of religious and ethical belief. These beliefs, however, required Higginson to act, to be at the center of dissent and political activism . . . and out of these beliefs grew his passion for a democratic American literature—of, by, and for the people, reflecting American themes, the American character, and American values.

All in all, Tuttleton's work is a few notches above the average Twayne product.

In an ultimate tribute, Frederick L. Morey publishes the *Higginson Journal* (a companion to the *Emily Dickinson Bulletin*), which in 1980 printed an essay pointedly titled "The *Atlantic*'s Mr. Higginson" by Anna Mary Wells and Howard N. Meyer, setting the record straight on his connection with the *Atlantic Monthly* and his role in the life and work of Dickinson. Leonard Brill's dissertation also discusses Higginson's many contributions to the *Atlantic*, some of which deserve to have been included in anthologies of the magazine.

It is ironic, given Higginson's many writings on Transcendentalism and the Transcendentalists, that this aspect of his life has generated virtually no critical studies. Higginson is mentioned in passing in Octavius Brooks Frothingham, *Transcendentalism in New England*; in Clarence L. F. Gohdes, *The Periodicals of American Transcendentalism*, which is also useful for bibliographical references (Higginson contributed to every publication, subsequent to the *Dial*, mentioned in this work); and in Alexander Kern, "The Rise of Transcendentalism, 1815–1860."

Perhaps one reason for this gap is Higginson's own late-in-life ambivalence toward

Transcendentalism. He developed a habit of referring to the Transcendentalists in the third person: they were not "us" but "them." He wrote that the *Dial* "revealed literally some of the follies of the movement it represented" (*Contemporaries* 12), that "the effect of Transcendentalism on certain characters, a minority of its adherents, was seemingly disastrous" (*Part of a Man's Life* 16), and that one could "not speak of understanding it, for it hardly understood itself" (*Reader's History* 166). These derogatory remarks contrast with the proud assertion that "I am perhaps the last among even the rejected contributors" to the *Dial* (*Outlook*, 23 May 1903) and the wistful recollection that "those whose youthful enthusiasm created this periodical kindled much life in the hearts of those still younger" (*Margaret Fuller Ossoli* 172), the "younger" unmistakably meaning the writer. There is likewise a marked inconsistency in his treatment of Alcott: immediately after his death, Higginson wrote that the "Orphic Sayings" "were held to be the worst shibboleth of that new bugbear Transcendentalism"; twenty years later, quoting several of the sayings as "fine," Higginson expresses "his astonishment at their more than contemptuous reception." Higginson's disassociation from Transcendentalism appears inconsistent with his postwar association with many ex-Transcendentalists and with Boston's Radical Club (1867–80), although the latter had neither the reverberating impact nor the antiestablishment radicalism of the 1840s, despite its bold title. It also does not seem to fit in with his persistent advocacy of theological principles spawned by Transcendentalism or with his lifelong activism in the Free Religious Association.

However his retrospective mood fluctuated, Higginson did not turn his back on the rich store of raw material that Transcendentalism afforded a professional writer. He had chosen a literary career by the late 1850s and left his radical ministry at Worcester, where he had led a congregation that "the influence of Theodore Parker had brought into existence," according to his wife's biography, "composed of radicals of all description." In the October 1860 *Atlantic* Higginson published an essay on Parker's life, work, and character, which was to be the first of numerous such pieces dealing with his contemporaries. Many of these were reprinted in *Contemporaries*, *Carlyle's Laugh*, and *Part of a Man's Life*, and others appeared in his *Reader's History* and in his autobiography, *Cheerful Yesterdays*, which is really an episodic collection of recollections.

These short studies of individual Transcendentalists do not attempt any serious discussion of their ideas as such. Typically there is a warm, intimate, anecdotal sketch of the person but little of the "movement," perhaps because Higginson was so ambivalent toward Transcendentalism. His essay on Parker provides more information than an encyclopedia would (and less than a full-length book); and, like all of his work, it is not merely factual but gracefully written. But it contains no substantial reference to Transcendentalism in Parker's life beyond the cryptic concession: "Not an original thinker in the same sense as Emerson, Parker yet transplanted for tens of thousands that which Emerson spoke to hundreds only."

Besides the numerous essays and lengthy passages contained in the books listed above, Higginson wrote about Alcott (*Brains*, 1 Jan. 1892), Ellery Channing (1902),

Emerson (*Brains*, 1 Dec. 1891; *Outlook*, 23 May 1903), Frothingham (1896), Fuller (in *Eminent Women of the Age*, 1868), Samuel Johnson (in *Samuel Johnson: A Memorial*, ed. Augustus Mellen Haskell, 1882), and Thoreau (*Brains*, 1 Dec. 1891). Of these works, only that on Thoreau has been studied in detail, in Howard N. Meyer, "Higginson, Thoreau, and the Equation of Fame." Nevertheless, these sketches have been an indispensable resource for biographers and critics. Also of use is Higginson's "The Brook Farm Period in New England" (1882).

Higginson's most complete statements on Transcendentalism are in his biography of Fuller, the chapter on the *Dial* in *Old Cambridge*, and "The Sunny Side of the Transcendental Period" in *Part of a Man's Life*, which can be supplemented by the chapters "The Birth of a Literature" in *Cheerful Yesterdays* and "The Concord Group" in *Reader's History*. These works reflect Higginson's personal view of the historical significance and legacy of Transcendentalism. He downplays its socioeconomic radicalism and its important contributions to Free Religion (although he was a leader of that later movement) for the sake of emphasizing what he viewed as most significant: that Transcendentalism was the harbinger of a distinctively American literary tradition that threw off the British yoke and enriched itself eclectically from the Continent. Indeed, he argues that the literary nationalism of the movement began not with Emerson but with an 1839 Master of Arts oration at Harvard by Robert Bartlett. Higginson was a pioneer in discerning what some literary critics and historians claim to have first discovered half a century later.

Higginson was the outstanding memoirist and informal biographer of the Transcendentalist movement and the individuals it comprised. Although not as prolific as F. B. Sanborn, he was more perceptive and honest. To say that he was the historian of the movement would be inaccurate; he did not pretend to write any complete, coherent narrative. Rather, he produced a wealth of anecdotes, commentaries, miscellaneous facts, random insights, and episodic descriptions, that, when woven together, present a more comprehensive picture of the lives and times of the various personalities whom we collectively identify as Transcendentalists than can be found in the works of any other writer or in any other single source.

SAMUEL JOHNSON

Roger C. Mueller

BIBLIOGRAPHIES

Samuel Longfellow, Samuel Johnson's friend and collaborator on a number of hymnals, published a brief list of his works in *Lectures, Essays, and Sermons* (1883). That bibliography has been updated and enlarged in Roger C. Mueller, "Samuel Johnson, American Transcendentalist." Joel Myerson contributed the entry on Johnson to *FPAA* (vol. 3). Johnson is not listed in *AAL*.

MANUSCRIPTS

The Essex Institute in Salem, Massachusetts, has most of Johnson's published works and is the repository for his papers. Letters to and from Johnson, sermons, diaries, and juvenalia are contained in the twenty cartons of this collection. Libraries holding a few other letters are noted in *ALM*.

EDITIONS

The Samuel Longfellow–Johnson hymnals are *A Book of Hymns for Public and Private Devotion* (1846) and *Hymns of the Spirit* (1864). *Hymns* (1899) is by Johnson alone.

Lectures, Essays, and Sermons provides a sampling of Johnson's writings on American religion, labor reform, suffrage, Transcendentalism, and the symbolism of nature. The selections for this posthumous volume reflect Longfellow's view of Johnson as a churchman and social reformer. Therefore, there are no extracts from Johnson's Oriental books (*Oriental Religions and Their Relation to Universal Religion. India*, 1872; *China*, 1877; and *Persia*, 1885). The only other collection is *Selected Writings of Samuel Johnson*, ed. Roger C. Mueller (1977), which reprints selections from the India and China volumes of *Oriental Religions*, the essay on Transcendentalism (1877), the final sermon to his Free Church, and three articles from the *Radical* setting out Johnson's religious creed (Natural Religion or Naturalism) and distinguishing it from Unitarianism.

BIOGRAPHY

Besides the entry by Harris Elwood Starr in *DAB*, there are Samuel Longfellow's "Memoir" in *Lectures, Essays, and Sermons*, valuable because of his close association with Johnson, and Roger C. Mueller's article. The latter is an illustrated biography that treats Johnson's life in and around Salem; his relation to Unitarianism, Transcendentalism, and the Free Religious Association; and the production of his Oriental books.

CRITICISM

Johnson's contributions to the Transcendentalist movement grew out of his speculations on religion. Like Ralph Waldo Emerson and Henry David Thoreau, he held that religious beliefs are not only intensely personal, growing out of intuitive knowledge, but also universal, part of a plan that transcends temporal and spatial barriers. Johnson's major writings articulate his Transcendentalist view of religion, distinguishing it from Unitarianism on one hand and demonstrating the links between Christianity and the religions of Asia on the other. He was also a hymn writer, a supporter of various reform movements, and minister to the nondenominational Free Church in Lynn, Massachusetts, for seventeen years.

Johnson, like Emerson, Thoreau, James Freeman Clarke, and Moncure D. Conway, tried to find a common thread uniting the world's religions. His Oriental books are an attempt to undergird the intuitive notions of world religious unity first expressed by Emerson and Thoreau in the "Ethnical Scriptures" series they published in the *Dial*. Johnson built a theoretical model based on evolutionary theory and contemporary scholarship, contending that all the world's religions were developing along evolutionary lines toward a single universal religion.

Unfortunately, this intriguing hypothesis was supported only by facts gleaned from secondary sources. Because Johnson knew no Asian languages and had never visited the Orient, he was forced to depend on the work of French, German, and English scholars, and his work suffered accordingly. In the words of the Orientalist Max Müller, "There are few things in his volume on the 'Religions of India' for which, at all events, he could not give chapter and verse, though chapter and verse may not always have come from the right book" (see *Samuel Johnson: A Memorial*, ed. Augustus Mellen Haskell). Attacked by the popular press as ponderous and anti-Christian (e.g., *Nation*, 21 Nov. 1872), the books did not sell well. As Carl T. Jackson notes: "Perhaps the major problem was the failure to find a suitable audience. If too scholarly for the general reader, the volumes were not sufficiently so for the professional in the field" (see "The Orient in Post-Bellum American Thought"). Jackson further assesses Johnson's contributions in "Oriental Ideas in American Thought" and in *The Oriental Religions and American Thought*.

Johnson's "Transcendentalism" deserves further study. Octavius Brooks Frothingham, in *Transcendentalism in New England*, praises Johnson's "calm, lofty, reasonable interpretation" of the movement. The essay outlines the origins of Transcendentalist thought, argues that its metaphysics are universal, and reconciles Transcendentalism with scientific thought. It is one of the most readable, comprehensive, and carefully argued defenses of Transcendentalism to emerge from the movement.

SYLVESTER JUDD

Francis B. Dedmond

BIBLIOGRAPHIES

Bibliographies of Judd's published works appear in *BAL* (vol. 5); Francis B. Dedmond, *Sylvester Judd*; and Richard D. Hathaway, *Sylvester Judd's New England*. Dedmond's study also contains an annotated bibliography of selected secondary sources, and Hathaway's critical biography lists memoirs, reminiscences, published letters and journals, reviews, and critical articles and books useful in a study of Judd and his work. A number of articles on Judd listed in *AAL* are not discussed in this essay.

MANUSCRIPTS

Judd is listed in *ALM*, but the information is both inaccurate and incomplete. Some, for example, confuse the manuscripts of Sylvester Judd the novelist with those of his father, Sylvester Judd the antiquary. More important, the Judd papers in the Houghton Library of Harvard University are not listed at all in *ALM*. These uncataloged manuscripts and documents—the most extensive Judd collection—are stored in eighteen boxes. Two boxes of papers (55M-1)—originally owned by Mrs. Sylvester Judd Beach—contain letters by various members of the Judd family, other personal papers, a journal of the elder Judd, and such manuscripts as Arethusa Hall's "Sathurea: The Story of a Life." The remaining sixteen boxes (55M-2)—collected by the Kennebec Historical Society and deposited in the Houghton—contain manuscript letters, notes, student papers, plays in manuscript, manuscript poems, a scrapbook of clippings, parts of the *Margaret* manuscript, a hundred or more neatly stitched handwritten sermons, a number of pocket diaries, and books from Judd's library. Other Judd manuscripts,

scattered in a number of libraries, are located, listed, and described in Francis B. Dedmond, *Sylvester Judd*. Recently, nine new letters have been found at the Andover-
Harvard Theological Library.

EDITIONS

In 1845, Jordan and Wiley published anonymously Judd's first novel, *Margaret:
A Tale of the Real and Ideal, Blight and Bloom; Including Sketches of a Place Not
Before Described, Called Mons Christi*. Five years later, Judd brought out his long
narrative poem, *Philo: An Evangeliad*, and his second novel, *Richard Edney and the
Governor's Family. A Rus-Urban Tale, Simple and Popular, Yet Cultured and Noble, of Morals, Sentiment, and Life, Practically Treated and Pleasantly Illustrated Containing, Also, Hints on Being Good and Doing Good*. After Judd's death, two volumes
of his sermons—*The Birthright Church: A Discourse* (1853) and *The Church: In a
Series of Discourses* (1854)—were published. Only one of Judd's works, *Margaret*,
has gone through more than one edition. A revised edition in two volumes was published in 1851, and in 1871 a new one-volume edition of the 1851 revision was published. Judd omitted from the 1851 revised edition many of the passages that critics
found vulgar in the 1845 edition.

BIOGRAPHY

In the year following Judd's death, his adoring aunt Arethusa Hall published
her *Life and Character of the Rev. Sylvester Judd*. In this 531-page biography—Hall
preferred to call it a compilation—she included the Judd manuscripts, letters, and
journals she had carefully collected, obviously with Judd's cooperation. These
manuscripts have since disappeared. Hall insists that, with Judd, "religion
was . . . the first thing and the last; . . . it was to him all in all"; and readers
should be warned that she is careful to omit anything not in keeping with that theme.
A more balanced, scholarly, and critical biography is Richard D. Hathaway, *Sylvester
Judd's New England*, which is particularly valuable for its description of the intellectual milieu Judd worked in. Hathaway traces Judd's intellectual development in the
context of his New England heritage and *Margaret*.

CRITICISM

The first full-length critical study of Judd to appear after Arethusa Hall's compilation was Phillip Judd Brockway, *Sylvester Judd* (1941), which argues that Judd
derived his greatest inspiration from the ideals of Ralph Waldo Emerson's Transcendentalist philosophy. Brockway admits, however, that after *Margaret* Emersonian

Transcendentalism began "to exhaust its inspiration" for Judd. Francis B. Dedmond, in *Sylvester Judd*, concludes that, although Judd shared with "the most ardent of the Transcendentalists and indeed with Emerson some of their most cherished views," his particular kind of liberal Christianity, his Christology, his view of the church as a vital and necessary spiritual institution, and his concept of the Christian ministry place him closer to Dr. William Ellery Channing than to Emerson.

Judd was thought of in his day (and even in ours) as a man of one book: *Margaret*. Positive responses to that novel from Emerson, Margaret Fuller, Theodore Parker, and others are recorded by Dedmond, but reviews written by Judd's fellow Unitarian ministers, from whom Judd expected understanding and acceptance, almost invariably charged the work with vulgarity. Frederic Dan Huntington found *Margaret* encumbered with dialogue from low life, although he did appreciate the eloquence and power with which Judd set forth the truths of Christianity, while W. B. O. Peabody attacked Judd for making New England seem "so desperately vulgar" and treating weighty theological doctrines in a novel. Dexter Clapp, a New Orleans Unitarian minister, pointed to what he regarded as bad taste, ludicrous excesses, and caricatures in *Margaret*, yet he echoed Fuller's contention (*NYDT*, 1 Sept. 1845) that *Margaret* "leads us to believe in the possibility of a distinctive American literature," and he anticipated James Russell Lowell's observation (*A Fable for Critics*, 1848) that *Margaret* "will be called the Yankee novel."

Later, Fuller, in her essay "American Literature" (1846), called *Margaret* a work of great power and richness and asserted that "Of books like this, as good and still better, our new literature shall be full." Lowell, in his review of Henry Wadsworth Longfellow's *Kavanagh* (1849), reiterated his view that *Margaret* was "the most emphatically American book ever written." Despite its slovenliness of construction, Lowell praised Judd's handling of scenery, characters, and dialect. In the decade following Judd's death in 1853, critics like Edward Everett Hale and John Hopkins Morison pointed, like Lowell, to Judd's skill in depicting the New England character and the New England scene. Samuel Osgood ("The Real and Ideal in New England") agreed with Hale and Morison, but he did not find in Judd *the* American novelist he and others had been looking for.

Even twentieth-century literary historians have eyes only for *Margaret*. An excellent study of Judd's memorable scenes, his narrative use of folklore, and his native idioms in *Margaret* is C. Grant Loomis, "Sylvester Judd's New England Lore." Van Wyck Brooks (*The Flowering of New England*) says that Judd's utopian romance has scenes so vividly picturesque as to rival the best work of Hawthorne, and Carl Van Doren (*The American Novel, 1789–1939*) also finds the novel's genuine merit in its depiction of New England scenes, not in any demonstration of Judd's narrative skills.

Only three nineteenth-century critics—Orestes A. Brownson ("Protestantism Ends in Transcendentalism"), Moncure D. Conway ("Sylvester Judd"), and Octavius Brooks Frothingham (*Transcendentalism in New England*)—argued that Judd was a Transcendentalist, something that twentieth-century critics have generally assumed without question. But several recent scholars have insisted that, even in *Margaret*,

Judd's Transcendentalism is, at best, a curious ecumenical blend. For instance, Sacvan Bercovitch, *The Puritan Origins of the American Self*, finds a startling similarity between Judd's Theopolis Americana in *Margaret* and Cotton Mather's Theopolis Americana. Kenneth Walter Cameron, "The Episcopal Church in the Romanticism of Sylvester Judd," discovers in *Margaret* echoes of the ecclesiastical vocabulary of Anglicanism and the liturgical year. In an especially perceptive article ("Sylvester Judd's *Margaret* ") Bruce Ronda admits that Judd was influenced by Transcendentalism, but he insists that Judd never completely abandoned the Calvinistic doctrines of conversion and regeneration and never resolved the question of inherent goodness versus the necessity of divine grace for salvation.

Unlike the publication of *Margaret*, the publication of *Philo* and of *Richard Edney* in 1850 was generally ignored by the leading journals of the day. Only the *North American Review* noticed the two works. Andrew Preston Peabody acknowledged that *Philo*—Judd's poem on the coming of the millennial age—was an original work but stated that it lacked the common "canons of good taste"; and A. W. Abbott was disturbed by the many dramatic absurdities in *Richard Edney*, a novel that anticipated Horatio Alger. No other individual critical studies of these works have since appeared.

Additional research on Judd might well center on Judd's millennialism, his writing in relation to the outpouring of millenarian writing in the 1840s and 1850s, and the similarity of Judd's views with those of the postmillennial Edwardsian revivalists who, with Judd, shared Jonathan Edwards' conviction that sacred history was reaching its climax in the New World. Such studies might clarify the true nature of Judd's Transcendentalism.

CHARLES LANE

Joel Myerson

BIBLIOGRAPHIES

The best bibliography of Lane's writings is in Roger William Cummins, "The Second Eden: Charles Lane and American Transcendentalism," although it is incomplete for Lane's numerous newspaper and periodical contributions. Cummins' secondary bibliography lists the major works on Lane, who is not included in *AAL*.

MANUSCRIPTS

Lane is not listed in *ALM*. His letters (about thirty) to Ralph Waldo Emerson and Amos Bronson Alcott are at the Houghton Library of Harvard University, and those to Isaac Hecker at the Paulist Fathers Archives. The Fruitlands Museums has a major collection of Lane's correspondence and materials concerning him. Most of Lane's manuscripts were sent to him when he returned to England and have since disappeared.

EDITIONS

Lane's works have not been collected. His articles of interest to students of Transcendentalism include "Transatlantic Transcendentalism" (1842), a review of works by Emerson, Alcott, and Elizabeth Palmer Peabody; "Literature" (1842), a review of the *Dial*; "A. Bronson Alcott's Works" (1843), probably the best contemporary evaluation of Alcott's educational practices; "Social Tendencies" (1843); "A

Voluntary Political Government" (1843); "The Consociate Family Life" (1843); "The Third Dispensation" (1843); "Interior or Hidden Life" (1844); "Brook Farm" (1844); and "Life in the Woods" (1844), which is considered by some to have influenced Thoreau in the writing of *Walden* (see, for example, Sherman Paul, *The Shores of America*).

Lane's letters to Thoreau have been published in *The Correspondence of Henry David Thoreau*, ed. Walter Harding and Carl Bode, and those he wrote from Fruitlands are in Clara Endicott Sears, *Bronson Alcott's Fruitlands*, and Joel Myerson, "William Harry Harland's 'Bronson Alcott's English Friends.'" His published letters on "A Voluntary Political Government" have been edited, with an introduction stressing Lane's libertarianism, by Carl Watner.

BIOGRAPHY AND CRITICISM

All biographies of Lane derive from two main sources: Bronson Alcott's manuscript journals and William Harry Harland's essay. Selections from the former are in *The Journals of Bronson Alcott*, ed. Odell Shepard, and all of the latter was published by Joel Myerson.

The best biography of Lane is Cummins, "Charles Lane and American Transcendentalism," a thorough examination and evaluation of the available material. Lane's relations with the *Dial* are examined by George Willis Cooke, *An Historical and Biographical Introduction to Accompany the* Dial, and, in more detail, in Joel Myerson, *The New England Transcendentalists and the* Dial. Three biographies of Alcott deal extensively with Lane: Odell Shepard, *Pedlar's Progress*, Madelon Bedell, *The Alcotts*, and Frederick C. Dahlstrand, *Amos Bronson Alcott*. Emerson's *Journals and Miscellaneous Notebooks*, ed. William H. Gilman et al., contains valuable comments on Lane, as does his "English Reformers" (1842).

Of the many studies of Fruitlands (discussed in the chapter "Transcendentalist Communities"), those containing the best material on Lane are F. B. Sanborn, *Bronson Alcott at Alcott House, England, and Fruitlands, New England*; Clara Endicott Sears, *Bronson Alcott's Fruitlands*; David Palmer Edgell, "The New Eden" and "Charles Lane at Fruitlands"; and Robert Howard Walker, "Charles Lane and the Fruitlands Utopia." Mrs. Alcott's Fruitlands diary is partially printed in Shepard's edition of her husband's journals, and sections of Louisa May Alcott's Fruitlands diary are in Ednah D. Cheney, *Louisa May Alcott*, and Alcott's *Transcendental Wild Oats and Excerpts from the Fruitlands Diary*. Lane's relations with Brook Farm are documented in Joel Myerson, *Brook Farm*.

Fictional portraits of Lane were drawn by Louisa May Alcott ("Transcendental Wild Oats") and, as "Mr. Lang," by Mary Gove Nichols in *Mary Lyndon*.

Nearly all studies of Alcott and Fruitlands have cast Lane as a sinister figure, partially to exonerate Alcott himself from a fair share of blame in the failure of the community. The most balanced view of the Alcott-Lane relationship is by Richard Francis. In "Circumstances and Salvation," he shows how Lane "was able to complement and extend" certain of Alcott's principles and how their vast differences in defining the "nature of the family" led inevitably to their philosophical and personal separation. Taylor Stoehr, "Transcendentalist Attitudes toward Communitism and Individualism," includes a good piece on Lane's social philosophy that treats him more seriously than do most other studies. Priscilla J. Brewer also gives Lane his due, showing how he first embraced and then strayed from the Shakers.

Further research on Lane should reevaluate his relations with Alcott and his role in the Fruitlands community. On both subjects the manuscript material is available but has not been used as effectively as it might.

CHARLES KING NEWCOMB

Joel Myerson

BIBLIOGRAPHIES

A brief listing of books in which Newcomb is mentioned is *The Journals of Charles King Newcomb*, ed. Judith Kennedy Johnson. Newcomb is not listed in *AAL*. There is no primary bibliography.

MANUSCRIPTS

There are two depositories of Newcomb's papers, both listed in *ALM*. Brown University has the Newcomb family papers, including Newcomb's letters to his family and his journals, and the Houghton Library of Harvard University has his letters to Ralph Waldo Emerson and Caroline Sturgis.

EDITIONS

Newcomb's only publication was "The Two Dolons" in the July 1842 *Dial*; it has not been reprinted. *The Journals of Charles King Newcomb* prints selections arranged under the topics "Arts and Letters," "Nature," "Society and Government," and "Man and Morals." Unfortunately, Newcomb did not comment on his contemporaries in his journals. An unimportant letter is printed in F. B. Sanborn, "Thoreau, Newcomb, Brook Farm."

BIOGRAPHY AND CRITICISM

The best biography of Newcomb is Judith Kennedy Johnson's introduction to her edition of Newcomb's *Journals*. Using manuscript sources, Johnson provides a detailed description of Newcomb's life during the period he was most involved with the Transcendentalists. Information on Newcomb's life at Brook Farm can be found in most histories of the community (discussed in the "Transcendentalist Communities" chapter); a handy guide to the material is Joel Myerson, *Brook Farm*. Newcomb's relations with Emerson, Margaret Fuller, and the *Dial* are discussed in George Willis Cooke, *An Historical and Biographical Introduction to Accompany the* Dial, and, in more detail, in Joel Myerson, *The New England Transcendentalists and the* Dial. Also of interest are Van Wyck Brooks's comments in *The Flowering of New England*.

Newcomb's contemporaries left some interesting impressions of him. Hawthorne portrayed him "in a deep mist of metaphysical fantasies" in "The Hall of Fantasy" (1843) and in still less favorable terms in his *American Notebooks*. Emerson's initial praise of Newcomb, to be found in his *Journals and Miscellaneous Notebooks*, ed. William H. Gilman et al., and *Letters*, ed. Ralph L. Rusk, was later tempered by disappointment: see his portrayal of Newcomb as a youth of "invalid habit, which had infected in some degree the tone of his mind" (*Memoirs of Margaret Fuller Ossoli*), as Benedict in the "Worship" chapter of *The Conduct of Life*, and as a "youth of the subtlest mind . . . puny in body and habit as a girl" in "Historic Notes of Life and Letters in New England." Comments on Newcomb by Fuller, Marianne Dwight, and Georgia Bruce Kirby may be found in their letters and in their articles on Brook Farm.

Two critical articles dealing with Newcomb have been published: Richard Lee Francis provides an Eriksonian analysis of Newcomb's later years, in particular the impact of the death of his mother and his readings in Shakespeare. William M. Moss, in discussing Emerson's support of younger poets in the 1830s and 1840s, adds little to our knowledge of Newcomb.

Future scholarship on Newcomb might reevaluate his relations with Emerson and Fuller, explore more thoroughly the psychological crisis he underwent before and during his years at Brook Farm, or examine his nearly one thousand erotic poems in manuscript at the Brown University Library (Newcomb is alone among the Transcendentalists in having created a significant body of erotic literature).

THEODORE PARKER

Gary L. Collison

BIBLIOGRAPHIES

The first comprehensive bibliography of Parker, covering both primary and secondary sources, appeared in John White Chadwick, *Theodore Parker*. Charles W. Wendte added more than 150 items to Chadwick's list in the bibliography in vol. 15 of the Centenary Edition of Parker's works (see below). The section on Parker in Theresa Layton Hall, "A Bibliography of the New England Transcendentalist Movement," adds only a few items and is marred by incomplete and inaccurate citations. There is an excellent bibliographic essay, mostly on secondary sources, at the end of Henry Steele Commager's biography, *Theodore Parker*. Scholarly and nonscholarly materials published between 1936 and 1960, the centennial of Parker's death, have been reviewed by Herbert E. Hudson in a special Parker issue of *PUHS*. Joel Myerson's listing of Parker's separately printed works in *FPAA* (vol. 4) has been superseded by his *Theodore Parker*, which lists and describes all editions and printings of Parker's separately published works in English. This chapter discusses all the articles listed in *AAL* with the exception of a few minor pieces.

MANUSCRIPTS

Parker's papers, bequeathed at his death to his wife and, on her death in 1881, to F. B. Sanborn, have remained largely together in a few collections. *ALM* lists holdings in fifty libraries but misses several important collections. Parker's private papers are described in Carol Johnston's dissertation, "The Journals of Theodore Parker: July–December 1840," and Gary L. Collison, "A Calendar of the Letters of Theodore

Parker." Johnston's list of extant journals, notebooks, and journal fragments supersedes an earlier listing at the end of Herbert E. Hudson's review of scholarship. Collison's calendar, with an index of correspondents and libraries, lists over 1,800 extant letters and announces the compiler's intention of editing the complete correspondence.

Four libraries in the Boston area hold the bulk of Parker's papers and related materials. The Boston Public Library has almost all of Parker's enormous library of books and pamphlets as well as memorabilia, several valuable scrapbooks, and over a hundred holograph letters. For Parker's library, see the two-volume manuscript catalog at the Boston Public Library and Thomas Wentworth Higginson's brief description ("Report on the Parker Library"). In addition to more than one hundred manuscript letters in various collections, the Massachusetts Historical Society has seventeen bound volumes of Parker's papers deposited by F. B. Sanborn in 1916 (reproduced in a recent microfilm edition), including two manuscript journals, two slim volumes of manuscript letters mostly to Parker, and several notebooks. Unfortunately, only the volumes of copies of letters (five volumes from Parker, six to him) are included in the society's *Catalog Guide to the Microfilm Edition of the Theodore Parker Papers*. At Harvard, the Houghton Library holds many letters, notably those to Ralph Waldo Emerson, Charles Sumner, and Wendell Phillips (the latter in the recently acquired Blagden Collection), but the largest body of Parker materials is several blocks away in the Andover-Harvard Theological Library, a repository not surveyed in *ALM*. The main collection, inventoried in Hudson's typescript catalog at the library, consists of hundreds of manuscript sermons, several copybooks of letters, four manuscript journal volumes, and several notebooks as well as drafts and copies of *Theodore Parker's Experience as a Minister* (1859). Outside the Boston area there are several significant smaller collections: letters and miscellaneous materials at the Library of Congress, correspondence with Thomas Wentworth Higginson and Frances Power Cobbe at the Henry E. Huntington Library, correspondence with William Henry Seward at the University of Rochester, and letters to John Parker Hale at the New Hampshire Historical Society and Dartmouth College.

EDITIONS

During Parker's lifetime, no collected edition of his works appeared in English, though a five-volume edition was printed in German (trans. Johannes Ziethen, 1854–61). Three collected editions have been published in English since his death. The first, *The Collected Works* (ed. Frances Power Cobbe, 14 vols., 1863–71), is still useful as it contains pieces not collected elsewhere. Many small changes were made in the texts, however, and there are no notes. Between 1864 and 1871 the printer Horace B. Fuller of Boston issued ten volumes of "Theodore Parker's Works," all reprinted from the plates of earlier editions with the exception of *Historic Americans* (1870), which first appeared in this edition. The Centenary Edition (15 vols., 1907–12) was sponsored by the American Unitarian Association to commemorate the centennial of Parker's birth and atone for earlier neglect. Although it promised to be a substantial improvement on the two earlier editions, the expectation was not entirely fulfilled. Some of the volumes contain extensive notes, amounting to seventy pages in one volume, yet others have few or no notes at all; moreover, some texts were taken from the unreliable Cobbe edition. Few previously uncollected or unpublished writings were added to the edition, and other published works were unaccountably left out. The fifteenth and final volume, which contains Charles W. Wendte's bibliography, Higginson's sketch of Parker's library, and an extensive index, numbers the previous volumes and refers to the collection for the first time as the "Works of Theodore Parker." Previous volumes contained only the words "Centenary Edition" on the half-title page. Because of the scarcity of both editions, many scholars will find it easiest to use the microfiche reprints of the Cobbe edition (Lost Cause Press, 1966) and the Centenary Edition (Microbook Library of American Civilization, LAC 23062-69).

Major works not in the collected editions are the pseudonymous Levi Blodgett letter on Andrews Norton (1840), reprinted in John Edward Dirks, *The Critical Theology of Theodore Parker*; Parker's translation of Wilhelm M. L. De Wette's *A Critical and Historical Introduction to the Canonical Scriptures of the Old Testament* (1843); *West Roxbury Sermons 1837-1848*, ed. Samuel J. Barrows (1892); and *The Trial of Theodore Parker, for the "Misdemeanor" of a Speech in Faneuil Hall against Kidnapping . . . with the Defence, April 3, 1855* (1855). The original printed version of Parker's South Boston Sermon, "The Transient and Permanent in Christianity" (1841), is reprinted in *Three Prophets of Religious Liberalism*, ed. Conrad Wright. Parker's sermon *The Revival of Religion Which We Need* (1858), collected only in a highly edited form, has been reprinted as originally published but without commentary or notes. Both George Hochfield (*Selected Writings of the American Transcendentalists*) and Perry Miller (*The Transcendentalists*) print scant portions of Parker's important works. Much more useful is Henry Steele Commager, *Theodore Parker: An Anthology* (1960), a rich selection of the most significant and revealing essays, sermons, addresses, and letters. In *Theodore Parker: American Transcendentalist* (1973), Robert E. Collins reprints six major essays and sermons, but all the works are taken directly from the collected editions without additional editorial work or notes.

Although Parker's letters have long been recognized as an important historical resource, there has been no modern attempt to collect them until recently. Consequently, historical and literary scholars have had to depend on the often incomplete and unreliable texts in the two earliest biographies and the few letters that have appeared elsewhere. Thomas Wentworth Higginson (*Radical*, 1871) printed all or part of nine letters from Parker, mostly revealing details of his personal life. The *Radical* of the same year also printed John T. Sargent's selection of four of "some forty or fifty" of Parker's letters to him, all chosen to show that Parker had "a rare tenderness of heart." Another group of letters, apparently to Rebecca L. Duncan, appeared in "Theodore Parker's Bettine" (1897). For the identification of Duncan, see *The Letters of Ralph Waldo Emerson*, ed. Ralph L. Rusk. An ample selection of Parker's letters to William Herndon, Abraham Lincoln's law partner in Springfield, Illinois, was printed in Joseph Fort Newton, *Lincoln and Herndon*. These fascinating letters about political maneuvering in the years before the Civil War make a substantial contribution to our understanding of Parker's political views in the later phase of the antislavery movement.

In addition to the few letters published in Rusk's edition of Emerson's letters, other correspondence has been published in more or less reliable form in the last seventy years. Granville Hicks offers one very brief letter from Parker to William Francis Channing that is interesting for its reference to the Boston Vigilance Committee. C. Carroll Hollis adds six letters that describe Parker's arrangements for a speaking tour of Ohio in 1854, his publication difficulties, and his attempts to help foreign exiles. Emile A. Freniere publishes an insignificant letter to R. M. S. Jackson, a physician who cared for Charles Summer in 1856. The forty letters in the Dartmouth College Library from Parker to John P. Hale, the first antislavery senator, have been edited by George E. Carter, but the work fails to include letters to Hale in the nearby collection of the New Hampshire Historical Society and makes frequent errors in transcription. Some of these letters to Hale were previously published in Richard H. Sewell, *John P. Hale and Politics of Abolition*. Gary L. Collison has edited Parker's correspondence with Convers Francis. These 129 letters are especially important for the period between 1838 and 1845.

Until Carol Johnston's dissertation, Parker's nearly impenetrable journals had been known almost exclusively through the fragments scattered among the early biographies and in F. B. Sanborn's carelessly edited version of Parker's account of his confrontation with the Boston Asssociation of Ministers in 1843 ("Theodore Parker's Ecclesiastical Relations"). The usefulness of Johnston's work can hardly be overestimated. Never before has there been a reliable edition of any part of Parker's journals, and the portion she edits in an unmodernized text covers the crucial months when Parker assumed the role of the principal dissenter within Unitarianism after the voluntary removal of Emerson and George Ripley.

BIOGRAPHY

Five American biographies based on original research have appeared in the 120 years since Parker's death. The first, John Weiss's *Life and Correspondence of Theodore Parker*, makes a wealth of letters and journal passages so conveniently available that it continues to be a major resource for the study of Parker and his time. The publication date (1864) and the fact that Parker's widow, Lydia, supervised this authorized account after thwarting an effort by F. B. Sanborn, Parker's own choice, suggest some dangers confirmed by the text. Not only are Parker's own interpretations of events too often uncritically accepted, but the letters, carefully selected to present him in a favorable light, are sometimes badly distorted by detectable and undetectable deletions. A few excised fragments of Parker's more biting comments are restored on bound-in slips in the English printing of the work. Octavius Brooks Frothingham,

Theodore Parker, remedied some of the disorder and weaknesses of Weiss's effort by restoring letters, sections of letters, journal passages, and proper names omitted by Weiss. The result is a fuller picture, though by no means a complete one. Like Weiss, Frothingham is too close to his subject to place him accurately in context, and Frothingham strangely underplays the links between Parker and the radical group of third-generation Unitarians to which Frothingham himself belonged. In *Theodore Parker*, John White Chadwick concentrates on Parker's work as a minister, consequently slighting his work as a reformer. Nevertheless, Chadwick, the last biographer who could consult with any of Parker's contemporaries, adds much useful new information. In *Theodore Parker*, Henry Steele Commager sacrifices some overview in favor of sustaining the narrative interest. Commager, however, had ransacked secondary sources for information about Parker and his friends, and the result is a deeper and more intimate portrait than any previous work. Particularly good are the later chapters dealing with the reform and antislavery movements. The usefulness of the bibliographic essays for each chapter is balanced by the frustrating absence of footnotes. Two chapters had been published in earlier versions (*NEQ*, 1933; *ASch*, 1934). John H. Martin, "Theodore Parker," adds little new information, but a variety of secondary sources are used intelligently.

The foreign biographies, all derived from the major American biographies, are listed in Charles W. Wendte's bibliography, with the exception of a study by Jean Schorer, *Deux Grands Américains: T. Parker, W. Channing*. The short, accurate biographical sketch by Francis A. Christie (*DAB*, vol. 14) has been superseded by Conrad Wright's sketch in *The American Renaissance in New England*, ed. Joel Myerson. Frances E. Cooke, *The Story of Theodore Parker*, is a popularized account for young readers.

The major biographies, none of which can be considered complete or authoritative, need to be supplemented by a handful of books and articles. For genealogical and biographical material on Parker and his family, see the account by another Theodore Parker (b. 1869), *Genealogy and Biographical Notes of John Parker of Lexington*. Charles Hudson, *History of the Town of Lexington*, is still useful for background. Abram English Brown, *Beneath Old Roof Trees*, provides some vivid memories of Parker in Lexington by his boyhood companion. An excellent though brief reminiscence of Parker as a student at the Harvard Divinity School is by George E. Ellis ("Parker at Cambridge"), who remembers Parker as full of a "rollicking geniality" not often noticed. Revealing too is the admission that some of Ellis' letters from Parker were kept back from the biographers because of caustic remarks not "tempered with a prevailing kindness." John Haynes Holmes, "The Education of Theodore Parker," adds no new facts, and the claim that Parker had to gain his real education as a humanitarian outside Cambridge draws too much on a stereotype of Harvard and the Divinity School popularized by Emerson and Parker himself. For the West Roxbury years, the best account is in Carol Johnston's introduction to her dissertation. She depends too heavily on a few journal passages for her conclusion that, in the years between graduation and the South Boston Sermon, Parker was an "angry young man" dissatisfied with his career and his domestic relations, but she nevertheless provides a useful corrective to entirely sanguine views elsewhere. Her theory is supported somewhat by John C. Broderick in "The Problems of the Literary Executor," which reproduces the text of some journal passages inked out by Lydia Parker but preserved in copies. Besides printing Parker's vague complaints about his wife, her relatives, and a general sense of melancholy, Broderick tells the story of Lydia Parker's heavy-handed control of Parker's literary estate. Also useful for the West Roxbury years are Charles G. Mackintosh, *Some Recollections of the Pastors and People of the Second Church of Old Roxbury*; John H. Applebee, "The First Parish of West Roxbury"; and Helen D. Orvis, "First Parish, West Roxbury."

Parker's involvement in the Transcendentalist movement, particularly in the controversy with Unitarian conservatives, is probably the most fully studied portion of his life. Far and away the best study is the fourth chapter of William R. Hutchison, *The Transcendentalist Ministers*. In telling the story simply, using documents from both sides of the controversy, Hutchison manages to write an objective, unflattering, and accurate history of Parker's role in the Unitarian controversy. The following chapter traces the development of Parker's Twenty-Eighth Congregational Society, which, Hutchison concludes, was less successful than some other ventures in forming a durable "church of the future." For Parker and the Transcendental Club, see Joel Myerson's "A Calendar of Transcendental Club Meetings" and "A History of the Transcendental Club." *Three Prophets of Religious Liberalism: Channing, Emerson, Parker*, ed. Conrad Wright, contains a good, succinct description of the South Boston ordination and its aftermath. Accounts of Parker's work with the *Dial* by George Willis Cooke (*An Historical and Biographical Introduction to Accompany the* Dial) and Clarence L. F. Gohdes (*The Periodicals of American Transcendentalism*) have been superseded by Joel Myerson's detailed work, *The New England Transcendentalists and the* Dial.

Two aspects of Parker's career in the neglected period between 1845 and 1850 have received careful attention. The history of Parker's *Massachusetts Quarterly Review* (1847–50) is admirably summarized in a separate chapter in Gohdes, which includes a list of contributors (taken largely from Parker's annotations in his own copy) and an account of his relationship with Emerson. An equally valuable study of a little-known aspect of Parker's life is David Mead's summary of two lecture tours of Ohio in the 1850s. Drawing on contemporary newspaper advertisements and reviews, Mead follows Parker's conquest of somewhat skeptical western audiences. The appended list of engagements and subjects reveals that Parker left his most controversial lectures and sermons at home.

The role played by Parker in several fugitive slave cases has been treated in a handful of studies. The affair of the fugitive Thomas Sims is ably discussed by Leonard W. Levy, who recounts the legal and political maneuvering skillfully but only incidentally mentions Parker's part in the proceedings. In "Fugitive Slave Days in Old Boston," Harold Schwartz reconstructs both the Sims case and the later case of Anthony Burns from Parker's unpublished letters and journal as well as other sources. Schwartz assigns Parker a prominent role in both cases and in the effective nullification of the Fugitive

Slave Law in Boston and New England. But Samuel Shapiro, "The Rendition of Anthony Burns," which makes excellent use of primary resources, indirectly questions Schwartz's interpretation by noting that attitudes toward the antislavery movement had been growing warmer across a broad cross section of Northern society long before the Burns case. In a more recent article on that case, David R. Maginnes draws on some research not previously available to recreate the events in a way that supports Schwartz's argument. One glaring weakness of Maginnes' article is that he apparently accepts as legitimate history Truman Nelson's *The Sin of the Prophet*, a fictional account of the events with Parker as the prophet of the title. John E. Talmadge, "Georgia Tests the Fugitive Slave Law," sheds some additional light on Parker and William and Ellen Craft, fugitives whom Parker helped to escape from Boston to England. John T. Horton, "Millard Fillmore and the Things of God and Caesar," locates Parker's original letter to President Fillmore and some other documents in the Fillmore papers, but otherwise adds little to Talmadge's history. There are a few significant references to Parker in Wilbur H. Siebert, "The Underground Railroad in Massachusetts," in a shorter version of the same article (1936), and in his "The Vigilance Committee of Boston."

Lawrence Lader's discussion of Parker in *The Bold Brahmins* is a pious but accurate history of Parker's antislavery career. Oscar Sherwin, "Of Martyr Built," based on third-hand sources, is both pious and inaccurate. The history of Parker's membership in the Secret Six, John Brown's financial backers, has been often told in biographies of Brown, most recently in Stephen B. Oates, *To Purge This Land with Blood*. Although too disparaging toward Parker and his friends, Oates's work is generally reliable and informative. Nevertheless, F. B. Sanborn, *The Life and Letters of John Brown*, must still be consulted for some details of Parker's relationship with the antislavery martyr. Otto J. Scott's history of the conspirators, *The Secret Six*, is based entirely on published sources.

The history of Parker's relationship with his Twentieth-Eighth Congregational Society of Boston is traced in Hutchison (see above), in A. A. Burrage, "Theodore Parker's Society," in the anonymous *The Twenty-Eighth Congregational Society of Boston* (1883), and in Ednah D. Cheney's more personal "Theodore Parker, the Pastor." Also valuable is Charles W. Wendte, *The Wider Fellowship*.

Kenneth Walter Cameron has added two sources of biographical information. His *Transcendental Reading Patterns* lists nearly one thousand books Parker borrowed from Harvard and the Boston Athenæum beginning in 1834. Cameron's edition of F. B. Sanborn's diary for 1854-55 (in *Transcendental Climate*) contains numerous references to Parker, suggesting that Sanborn's other diaries and his voluminous correspondence are a rich mine of information about Parker in the 1850s, when Sanborn was a frequent companion.

Charles Kassel, "Theodore Parker—A Study from the Life of Edwin Miller Wheelock," argues that Parker "stirred deeply" the younger abolitionist minister, but Wheelock's rather conventional eulogy, which Kassel prints in its entirety, is the only evidence offered. Helen P. Trimpi, "Three of Melville's Confidence Men," tries to see Parker satirized in the person of Melville's "Seminole Widow and Orphan Society" agent, but her argument depends on a few vague similarities.

CRITICISM

GENERAL ESTIMATES

Many early critiques of Parker combined genuine attempts to assess his merits with bigoted denunciations of his theology and character, and the questions they raised have yet to be satisfactorily answered. Still important for its criticism is a comprehensive evaluation by D. P. Noyes that not only gives Parker exceedingly low marks for accuracy and thoroughness of scholarship but also judges his reform work deficient in depth and seriousness of effort. G. Prentiss' lengthy three-part evaluation follows Noyes in casting suspicion on Parker's claims to linguistic and scholarly accomplishments, attributing to him a "disposition to exaggerate" that was "the fundamental vice of his nature." For two severe criticisms of Parker's accuracy as a scholar, see the review of the posthumous *Historic Americans* by Edmund Quincy (1871) and the anonymous review of Parker's translation of De Wette (1847) with its scathing comments on the translator's command of German. Equally vituperative but far shallower than any of the criticisms just mentioned are Joseph Cook's smug attacks on Parker in six different lectures from his popular "Monday Night" series (*Transcendentalism, with Preludes on Current Events* and *Orthodoxy, with Preludes on Current Events*). Of the more moderate early evaluations, two stand out: Samuel Johnson, *Theodore Parker*, ed. John H. Clifford and Horace L. Traubel, and an 1867 review in the *Pall Mall Gazette* only recently attributed to Matthew Arnold. Johnson's lecture, delivered many times between 1860 and its publication in 1890, calls Parker a great spiritual leader but faults him for failing to imagine a truly universal religion. Arnold's striking criticism pairs Parker and Walt Whitman to praise their vigorous and bold (though flawed) American writing. While noting lapses of taste in Parker's writings, Arnold finds the main weakness to be a "spiritual construction" that was "not of the first order," lacking the "full and harmonious development" that is also missing from Puritanism.

Among the positive estimates, Octavius Brooks Frothingham's biography is perceptive, but his discussion of Parker in *Transcendentalism in New England* is far too general and undiscriminating to be of use. The section on Parker in Harold Clarke Goddard, *Studies in New England Transcendentalism*, is superficial, as is Edwin D. Mead's treatment in *The Influence of Emerson*. In an odd article, Charles Angoff dresses Parker in shining armor and recruits him to lead an attack on the timid "tenth-rate Channings" of the twentieth century. An effusive, somewhat inaccurate estimate by Vernon Louis Parrington (*The Romantic Revolution in America*) elevates Parker to something like sainthood. In Parrington's hands all of Parker's sins are washed away and he enters heaven as "the greatest scholar of his generation among New England ministers," along with other titles of questionable merit. Parrington's enthusiasm is matched in Herbert Edson Hudson's recent estimate, "The Paradox of Theodore Parker," an apparently unretouched sermon that fails to find any real paradox. Far more judicious but almost as conventional is the very brief estimate by Donald N. Koster in *Transcendentalism in America*.

Other studies clearly show the revisionist influence of William R. Hutchison. A fresh air stirs in the analysis of Parker in Paul F. Boller, Jr., *American Transcendentalism, 1830–1860*. Boller notes provocatively that Parker "lacked the social perceptions of Brownson at his best, and he remained essentially a moralist," but this conclusion lacks the weight of careful analysis and calls for further study. In stating that the views of Emerson and Parker on the divinity of human beings were essentially the same, Boller glosses over what seem to be significant differences. Part of Carl R. Scovel's "Theodore Parker" is a suggestive and well-documented criticism of Parker's sarcastic and dogmatic tendencies, but the accompanying psychological analysis tends to get out of hand, as when Scovel offers Parker's "terrific sense of obligation and guilt" and his dissatisfaction with himself, his career, and his wife to explain his "great activity and early death." Robert C. Albrecht, *Theodore Parker*, is a solidly researched study that is both a biography and the only extended study of the growth of Parker's thought. Albrecht brings new evidence from Parker's unpublished writings to bear on an informed reading of the published works, but his treatment of Parker's early Transcendentalist phase is not original and sometimes reveals a limited familiarity with the background.

POLITICAL AND SOCIAL THOUGHT

From 1845 on, Parker and several of his friends tried unsuccessfully to coordinate the work of various social reform movements, and their failure has obscured Parker's role in contemporary social reform. John Haynes Holmes ("Theodore Parker and the Work of Social Reform") casts Parker as a prophet of enlightened understanding of the environmental causes of crime, poverty, and other social diseases, but he goes far beyond the evidence in attributing to Parker original ideas about legal aid to the poor, prison reform, and similar subjects. Holmes's claim that Parker "plainly" supported the elimination of all disparity between rich and poor is not plain at all. The very brief, incomplete, and not wholly accurate discussion of Parker in Alice Felt Tyler, *Freedom's Ferment*, makes him only a supporter, not a leader, of a few reform movements. More comprehensive and useful but still inadequate is William Riback's review of Parker's "total social service platform." Though based on both published and unpublished sources, Riback's list of fourteen reforms espoused by Parker makes a flimsy platform, and his speculation that Parker, inaccurately identified as a "Brook Farmer," may have been influenced by Karl Marx rests on the thinnest tissue of coincidence. In a formidable attempt to place Parker among the first rank of nineteenth-century reformers, Daniel Aaron (in *Men of Good Hope*) identifies him as "the link" between Emerson and post–Civil War progressives like Henry George. Aaron argues persuasively that Parker was "among the first of the middle-class radicals" to recognize the dangers of industrialism, and he finds some interesting foreshadowings of later progressive thought in Parker's writings, but his case for Parker's importance ultimately rests on not much more than chronological accident. Herbert London, "American Romantics, Old and New," is a vague and weak attempt to turn a few similarities between Parker and the folksinger Bob Dylan into an empty hymn to iconoclasm laced with phrases like "martyrdom was Theodore Parker's 'bag.'"

A simple but significant study of Parker in Carl Siracusa, *A Mechanical People: Perceptions of the Industrial Order in Massachusetts, 1815–1880*, shows just what can be accomplished with a narrowly defined field. Concentrating on Parker's defense of the poor in an industrial society, Siracusa finds that Parker was more realistic than some other reformers but that, along with William Lloyd Garrison and Wendell Phillips, he "accepted blithely" the notion that the worker was free to choose his opportunities and to negotiate his wages in a system dominated by large industries. Siracusa attributes Parker's nearsighted view of the economics of industrialism to his moralism and his disappointment with labor for failing to rally beneath the banner of abolitionism.

Two very different studies approach Parker's social and political ideas from other directions. In "Theodore Parker: The Minister as Revolutionary," Louis B. Weeks III claims that Parker made his most important contribution to humanitarian movements not as a writer or an activist but as a minister. Weeks adds Lucretia Mott and several other well-known reformers to the list of those who testified to Parker's influence, but his argument ultimately amounts to a clever strategy to get around the charge that Parker was really a minor figure because he did not lead any movement, found any lasting organization, or leave any coherent system of thought to guide succeeding generations. Despite the weakness of this central argument, Weeks's study still is useful for its thorough survey of Parker's opinions on reforms. Arthur I. Ladu, "The Political Ideas of Theodore Parker," attempts to show that Parker "based his political theory squarely on his transcendentalist philosophy," in that he placed "supreme value" on the individual personality and the authority of the conscience in social and political affairs. This survey is helpful but myopic: it fails to identify ideas that were not just Parker's but were part of the shared beliefs of Transcendentalists and reformers.

Surprisingly little had been written on Parker's role in the antislavery movement until recently. This seems partly the result of a longstanding failure of professional historians to take the Transcendentalists seriously and to treat them as something more than satellites of Emerson. Even as late as 1969, Aileen S. Kraditor, in her otherwise distinguished *Means and Ends in American Abolitionism*, could dismiss the Transcendentalists in a lump because, according to her, they lacked a commitment to action. Louis Filler, *The Crusade against Slavery*, is more discriminating, granting

Parker a place among the "literary preachers" who aided the cause, but Filler over-simplifies in naming Parker as Dr. William Ellery Channing's successor to the leader-ship of the Unitarian abolitionists. In *Slavery*, Stanley Elkins criticizes Parker, other Transcendentalists, and New England abolitionists for seeing slavery as a moral abstrac-tion, not as a social institution. Parker was especially irresponsible, according to Elkins, because he had made a thorough study of other systems of slavery, some much more humane, but refused to champion reforms of the most offensive aspects of the American institution, such as the disregard of marriage bonds. George M. Fredrickson, *The In-ner Civil War*, concludes that a combination of moralism and emotionalism led Parker to view the slavery issue exclusively in terms of violent confrontation. Douglas C. Stange, *Patterns of Antislavery among American Unitarians*, places Parker precisely within the context of denominational antislavery, showing that he had not complete-ly abandoned his formal Unitarian ties, as is sometimes assumed.

Several studies consider Parker's opposition to the Mexican War. "Theodore Parker and the Triumph of Optimism," a chapter in William Clough Jones, "The New England Transcendentalists and the Mexican War," describes Parker as the "best in-formed war critic in New England," but Jones's real interest is in the philosophical underpinnings that sustained Parker's optimism when the war drove his Transcenden-talist friends George Ripley, William Henry Channing, and John Sullivan Dwight (all then writing for the *Harbinger*) into a deep pessimism. Jones believes that the deciding difference was Parker's romantic notion of the progressive development of the human race, which was opposed to the Adamic mythology of the *Harbinger* group. John H. Schroeder, *Mr. Polk's War*, singles out Parker for his eloquent opposition to the Mexican War and usefully places him in the context of national dissent. Charles J. Beirne, "The Theology of Theodore Parker and the War with Mexico," obscures that eloquence in a poor recounting of Parker's life accompanied by mere summary of three antiwar "sermons," one of which turns out to be a speech.

Perhaps the most challenging and original of all the works dealing with Parker's abolitionism is Michael Fellman, "Theodore Parker and the Abolitionist Role in the 1850's." This is the first study to confront Parker's speculations about racial qualities and a supposed hierarchy of races, themes he adopted with increasing conviction in his last decade. Fellman draws on recent scholarship about racial prejudices before the Civil War to show that Parker was not immune to the careless racial theories and fantasies particularly attractive to the Know-Nothings, with whom Fellman finds Parker in surprising agreement on several points.

WRITER AND LECTURER

Given the almost universal agreement that Parker's influence arose largely from his power as a writer and speaker, it was inevitable that his literary and rhetorical skills would eventually become the subject of close study. What is remarkable is that Parker was paid so little attention when other major Transcendentalists were being analyzed to a hair. One valuable and neglected contribution is Roy C. McCall's study of Parker's habits of composition, rhetorical devices, and manner of delivery (in *A History and Criticism of American Public Address*, ed. William Norwood Brigance), an adaptation of his dissertation. Among McCall's findings are that Parker preferred Anglo-Saxon words and concrete language, used metaphors sometimes to excess, and was in general "effective but inelegant, rhetorical but not literary." Especially welcome parts of this original study are the gleanings from contemporary newspaper reports of Parker's public speaking and the analysis of his manuscripts, which show, according to McCall, that he wrote hastily and revised little. In a narrower rhetorical study, "Parker's Assessment of Webster," Valerie Schneider declares that Parker created a powerful effect with the "unusual persuasive strategy" of likening Webster's life to a classical tragedy. Robert T. Oliver's brief account of Parker in his *History of Public Speaking in America* is largely a summary of McCall and Commager.

The assessments just mentioned are worlds apart from two related and overly ambitious studies, Charles H. Nichols, "Theodore Parker and the Transcendental Rhetoric," and William E. Coleman, Jr., "The Role of the Prophet in the Abolition Rhetoric of the Reverend Theodore Parker." According to Nichols, Parker "created a tradition" of "idealistic rhetoric" that was to nourish both Abraham Lincoln and John F. Kennedy, among others. The essay contains many such sweeping and empty statements. Coleman's work dwells too slavishly on the concept of the prophet, producing along the way a good deal of jargon about "role analysis," but Coleman adds to our knowledge of Parker's effectiveness by drawing on contemporary newspaper reports and criticism. Robert H. Ramsey discusses Abraham Lincoln and Parker's earlier versions of the famous "of the people" phrase in "Theodore Parker and the Gettysburg Phrase."

Lawrence Buell, *Literary Transcendentalism*, gives Parker's writings perhaps the most sensitive and sympathetic reading they have ever received and presents the most provocative modern interpretation. Buell finds "a truly prophetic sweep and intensity, combined with aphoristic bite" in the South Boston Sermon, which many commentators have slighted following Parker's own disparaging remarks. An altogether expected conclusion of the analysis is that Parker's rhetoric is "much tighter" and his arguments more rigorous than Emerson's. More surprising is the conclusion that Parker used the sermon form "more flexibly than any of his colleagues" and that the didactic form of the sermon ultimately frustrated his aesthetic sensibility and his Transcendentalism. To support these conclusions, Buell turns to a descriptive passage in Parker's later letters "worthy of Whitman," but the single suggestive passage hardly proves the point. Buell's line of reasoning leads him to argue that Parker was not really the empiricist he often seems but was "driven by his sense of mission into a rigor which he simultaneously distrusted." Buell's analysis of Parker's writings is, unfortunately, quite brief. It remains for others to follow his leads and to test his arguments.

CRITICAL THOUGHT

Far and away the most ambitious assessment of Parker as a critic is Perry Miller's magisterial "Theodore Parker: Apostasy within Liberalism," which dismisses the persistent popular image of Parker as a saint of liberalism and free expression who was martyred in battle with the forces of conservatism, conformity, and narrow-mindedness. Parker's significant legacy, according to Miller, was his insistence on raising the act of criticism to a position of authority in arbitrating all matters: Parker "faced up to the problem of criticism as no one else in America did." Some of Parker's writings might seem to present problems for Miller's thesis, but as yet it has not been seriously and directly challenged.

Two studies come close to the ground where Miller issued his challenge. One is a long-needed, splendid discussion of Parker's attitude toward mythology in a chapter of Robert D. Richardson, Jr., *Myth and Literature in the American Renaissance*. In naming Parker as the chief American example of "an historical-minded critic who found the mythical view essentially negative and destructive," a position completely opposite to that held by Amos Bronson Alcott and Emerson, Richardson establishes new ground for our understanding of Parker in relation to his times and to other Transcendentalists and illuminates an area of Parker's thought little understood or appreciated previously. Richardson's analysis of the "two traditions" of mythography provides a far more effective test for distinguishing Parker from his Transcendentalist colleagues than do most of the methods applied before. Russel B. Nye, "The Literary Theory of Theodore Parker," though more concerned with Parker's historiography than with his literary theory, offers a view of his internal conflicts similar to Buell's. Parker's attachment to both rationalism and Transcendentalism, Nye argues, created the fundamental inconsistency whereby Parker could demand a scientific and objective criticism on one hand and, on the other, scourge historians like William Hickling Prescott for failing to write democratic history from the point of view of the "welfare of the people."

One reason Richardson's study is so welcome is that it breaks down the unnatural barriers placed between biblical criticism and purely "literary" concerns. To understand Parker and his place in the intellectual world of the nineteenth century, these two related subjects had to be reunited. A number of studies of Parker's biblical criticism, long considered unimportant by the literary scholar of the Transcendentalist movement, have begun to make a more complex understanding of Parker possible. The most significant of these studies is Jerry Wayne Brown, *The Rise of Biblical Criticism in America*. Brown traces Parker's biblical scholarship from his moderate views as a divinity student and contributing editor to the *Scriptural Interpreter* through the time when he stood as the most radical biblical critic in America. The comparison of De Wette's original work with Parker's "expanded" translation shows, according to Brown, that Parker's actual additions to the work were far less significant than he claimed. A much briefer survey of Parker's scientific criticism of the Bible is included in Herbert Hovenkamp, *Science and Religion in America*, which can serve as a good introduction to Parker's views in the context of a broader perspective than Brown's. William Adler, "Theodore Parker and D. F. Strauss's *Das Leben Jesu*," which covers some of the same ground as Hovenkamp and Brown, attempts to explain why Parker adopted Strauss's conclusions about the mythological features of the New Testament but rejected Strauss's Hegelian methodology. The explanation is that Parker used Strauss's conclusions only insofar as they confirmed his own notions of intuition and of the progressive evolution of the "intellectual grasp" of God.

Two other studies that consider Parker's biblical criticism are a chapter in Eugene R. Chable's "A Study of the Interpretation of the New Testament in New England Unitarianism" and Siegfried B. Puknat, "De Wette in New England." Chable attempts to cover all Parker's New Testament criticism too hastily, and his theological jargon is liable to prove a stumbling block to the literary scholar. Nevertheless, some passages in which Chable brings modern New Testament criticism tc bear on Parker's writings make an important first step toward understanding the full range of his biblical criticism. Puknat, on the other hand, adds nothing in his three pages devoted to Parker.

THEOLOGY AND PHILOSOPHY

Studies of Parker's religious and philosophical ideas often lack fine discrimination. This is especially true of James Eells, "Theodore Parker and the Naturalization of Religion," and, more recently, Arnold Smithline's chapter on Parker in his *Natural Religion in American Literature*, where Parker is made a "transitional figure between Deism and transcendentalism" because he was "less mystical than Emerson or Alcott." "Theodore Parker and Modern Theology," Francis A. Christie's attempt to get beyond the obvious, places Parker in the humanist tradition of Johann Gottfried von Herder. Christie concludes vaguely, however, that Parker is not a Transcendentalist but a "philosophic Realist" who "asserts the objectivity of more than spatially extended things, of subsistences as well as existences."

Two modern works see in Parker's theology common Transcendentalist elements. In *The Critical Theology of Theodore Parker*, John E. Dirks places Parker among the other Transcendentalists on the basis of his theological and critical writings. Like Christie, Dirks finds Parker's thought resting on a foundation of humanism, but he inconsistently puts Parker "near, not within" Transcendentalism at one point and "nearer evolutionism" at another. In a brilliant and provocative chapter comparing Parker and Orestes Brownson, R. W. B. Lewis (*The America Adam*) argues that Parker's theology, amounting to a mere "mouse of doctrine," was entirely "Adamic," as it was all contained in his absolute separation of religion and history. Yet Lewis claims that Parker originated the idea that man could recover the Adamic condition, ignoring similar views among Transcendentalists and other thinkers.

Other studies concentrate more directly on taking Parker's Transcendentalist measure. Henry Steele Commager, both in his biography and in "The Dilemma of Theodore Parker," sees in Parker's belief in both intuition and experimentation a fundamental American dualism. In *A History of American Philosophy*, Herbert W. Schneider identifies the same dualism, though he concludes that Parker's rationalism completely overshadowed his Transcendentalism, which was "more critical than romantic." George F. Newbrough, "Reason and Understanding in the Works of Theodore Parker," argues convincingly that an empirical approach to truth "is not—as charged by Commager, for instance—inconsistent with a primary reliance on intuition." H. Shelton Smith, "Was Theodore Parker a Transcendentalist?," attempts to settle this question by arguing that Parker's reliance on intuition for his knowledge of God, of moral law, and of immortality aligned him with his Transcendentalist contemporaries. According to Smith, Parker always kept his fundamental core of intuitionist beliefs separate and inviolate, even when he seemed to be following the empirical road exclusively. In the most recent contribution to the debate, Peter White finds provocative but vague connections between Parker and the "rational strain of New England thought" going back to Charles Chauncy in the eighteenth century.

Studies that compare Parker directly with other Transcendentalists, usually Emerson, generally avoid the problem of defining Transcendentalism. In "Channing, Emerson, and Parker," John White Chadwick finds that the significant differences between Parker and his spiritual mentors arose from Parker's rural middle-class upbringing, a conclusion echoed in Alexander Kern, "The Rise of Transcendentalism, 1815–1860." For Kern, the lower-middle-class origins of Parker and Orestes Brownson help explain their social and political consciousness. Robert E. Collins' introduction to his collection of Parker's writings contains a suggestive but thin and mechanical series of comparisons of four pairs of similar essays by Parker and Emerson. Collins finds, for example, that Parker's South Boston Sermon covers the same "general points" as Emerson's Divinity School Address but "with greater order, detail, and comprehensiveness." In this and other similar comments exalting Parker over Emerson, Collins proves mainly that he is insensitive to the power of Emerson's rhetoric. F. B. Sanborn, "Theodore Parker and R. W. Emerson," prints some interesting observations of Emerson drawn from Parker's journals but provides no real comparison.

Analyses of Parker's specific theological and religious views are rare and, in general, disappointing. John Wallace Laws identifies some important questions that need to be asked about Parker's religious writings, but his discussion is superficial and unreliable. For example, Laws carelessly disregards chronology and genre in treating Parker's most successful hymn, "O Thou Great Friend," as a mature statement of theology. A study with a promising title, Anthony P. Johnson's "Friend, Brother, Teacher: Images of Jesus of Nazareth in the Preaching of Theodore Parker," proves similarly disappointing not only in its argument but in the poor quality of its writing. An absence of references to other contemporary views of Jesus, together with a disregard for chronology, makes the analysis feeble. A closely related study, Prescott Browning Wintersteen's chapter on Parker and Emerson in his *Christology in American Unitarianism*, provides some summary and a handful of quotations but little of the commentary and almost none of the background promised in the title. Much wider-ranging is William Rosenfeld, "The Divided Burden: Common Elements in the Search for a Religious Synthesis in the Works of Theodore Parker, Horace Bushnell, Nathaniel Hawthorne, and Herman Melville," but the common elements hardly turn out to be unique to this strange grouping, which Rosenfeld finds impossible to justify. More useful is Robert E. Ireland, "The Concept of Providence in the Thought of William Ellery Channing, Ralph Waldo Emerson, Theodore Parker, and Orestes Brownson," which traces the idea of "higher law." The title of Truman Nelson's "Theodore Parker as Revolutionary Moralist" is misleading: it is not a treatise on revolutionizing morals but an entirely conventional paean to Parker as a radical and a moralist.

German influences on Parker's thought have been considered in a few works. Stanley M. Vogel, *German Literary Influences on the American Transcendentalists*, finds Parker "without any doubt the most learned" of the Transcendentalists in German literature and philosophy, though Vogel admits that Parker's grasp of the German language was inferior to Frederic Henry Hedge's. In another useful survey, Henry A. Pochmann, *German Culture in America*, concludes that Parker's practical contribution was to apply German critical thought and scholarship to the American religious problems of his time. Like the other Transcendentalists, Parker misinterpreted Kant and was not much concerned with technical philosophy, according to René Wellek ("The Minor Transcendentalists and German Philosophy"). Wellek finds Parker indebted to Friedrich Schleiermacher, Friedrich Jacobi, and the French eclectics and concludes that though his grasp of the Germans was uneven, it was sometimes profound. In "European Positivism and the American Unitarians," Charles D. Cashdollar finds that Parker had only a partial understanding of Auguste Comte but nevertheless was "an important link in the transmission of positivism to the American Unitarians," notably to O. B. Frothingham and Francis Ellingwood Abbot.

There is no agreement on Parker's influence on succeeding generations of Unitarians. Samuel Barrett Stewart (in *Unitarianism*) ends his summary of Parker's career by attributing to him the original impulse for the study of comparative religion "in which many of our clergymen have distinguished themselves." Joseph Henry Allen, *Our Liberal Movement in Theology*, though critical of Parker's "scorn and sarcasm," argues that his "heresies" saved "hundreds . . . from a reckless and blank atheism." Similar claims are recorded in *Theodore Parker: Anniversaries of Birth and Death Celebrated in Chicago*, a summary of the most lavish of the Parker centennial celebrations, presided over by Jane Addams and others. See also the Free Religious Association, *Proceedings of the Forty-Third Annual Meeting*, for additional reflections on Parker's place in the development of liberal religion.

In religious histories that focus on denominational growth, Parker is usually given little space and virtually no importance beyond the negative one of forcing the Unitarians to clarify and set down their beliefs. Even George Willis Cooke, *Unitarianism in America*, a standard denominational history, gives Parker and the Transcendentalist controversy only a supporting role in the drama of the "Denominational Awakening." William W. Fenn's condescending appraisal (in *Heralds of the Liberal Faith*, ed. Samuel A. Eliot) treats Parker not as a glorious herald but as an annoyingly crude forerunner whose once radical views have become "conservative commonplaces" upon which it would be "unprofitable to dwell." Parker is, however, given a central role in the transition from Transcendentalism to later phases of Unitarian radicalism in Stow Persons, *Free Religion*. According to Persons, Parker's failure to abandon his intuitionist belief in the immortality of the soul and in an afterlife prevented him from leading the modern movement more forcefully.

Aside from a few remarks that can be gleaned from the foreign biographies, there is little evidence that Parker had any lasting influence abroad. Count Goblet d'Alviella, *The Contemporary Evolution of Religious Thought in England, America, and India*, takes previous accounts of Transcendentalism at face value, adding nothing. F. C. DeVries, "The Influence of Parker on European Thought," is a slight affair that neither advances substantial evidence nor names any specific influences.

CONCLUSION

No longer do students of Transcendentalism and Unitarianism look only at Parker's early career, and historians no longer dismiss him because of the "literary" character of his career. The growth of interdisciplinary studies, of intellectual and social history in particular, and the explosion of abolitionist historiography have changed all that. Still, many aspects of Parker's life and work need more thorough examination. New works along the lines of Richardson's study of mythology and Brown's study of biblical criticism, an edition of Parker's letters and journals, and a complete Parker bibliography are required before there can be a new, comprehensive appraisal of the man and his legacy.

ELIZABETH PALMER PEABODY

Margaret Neussendorfer

BIBLIOGRAPHIES

No complete and accurate bibliography of the published works of Elizabeth Palmer Peabody exists at present; her writings have, in general, been overlooked in favor of her activities and her relations with more widely known contemporaries. *NUC* omits four books: *The Visitor of the Poor* (1832), one of her two translations from the French of Joseph Marie de Gerando; *The Hebrews* (1833), part 2 of her series *Key to History*; and two short works that appeared as separate publications, *Memorial of Mad. Susanne Kossuth Meszlenyi* (1856) and *Kindergarten Culture* (1870). *First Lessons in Grammar, on the Plan of Pestalozzi* (1830) is listed under the name of her father, who entered the copyright. Joel Myerson (*FPAA*, vol. 3), while making no claim to completeness, omits only *Visitor of the Poor* and several pedagogical works, providing reproductions of seventeen title pages.

The only comprehensive published bibliography that includes short works appears in Ruth M. Baylor, *Elizabeth Palmer Peabody*. Although useful, it is far from complete and not entirely accurate. Books and short works are listed together, with separate sections for Peabody's work as an author, translator, editor, reviewer, and publisher. The author list of 154 items omits some eighty-five known works and includes eight misattributions. The five anonymous poems from *Aesthetic Papers* (1849), *Edward's First Lessons in Grammar* (1843), and "The Kindergarten of Germany" (*ChEx*, 1859) are not by Peabody, and her essay "Exhibition of Allston's Paintings in Boston in 1839" is confused with that by Margaret Fuller in the *Dial* (1840). Noteworthy omissions from the "Translator" section are *The Water-Spirit* (1833), a free rendition of La Motte-Fouqué's *Undine*, and "The Preaching of Buddha," one in the series of "Ethnical Scriptures" in the *Dial* (1844), which has consistently been attributed to Thoreau. Numerous review essays are omitted or not identified as such. One of particular interest to Transcendentalist scholars is Peabody's anonymous early review of Emerson, "Nature—A Prose Poem" (1838), which is listed as appearing in the *Atlantic Monthly Magazine* nineteen years before that journal was founded. This confusion and others in Baylor's list can be explained by the fact that it relies without adequate verification (and without specific acknowledgment) on a working bibliography compiled by Robert Lincoln Straker, the typescript of which is at Antioch College. Some book chapters are listed even when not separately published, and the eighteen additional items in Josephine Elizabeth Roberts, "A New England Family" (see below), are not incorporated, although the dissertation itself is included in the secondary bibliography.

The bibliography of secondary materials in Baylor's volume is too broad to be useful, since it includes the many studies of early childhood education that serve the purposes of her book. Scattered throughout this list are some forty-five books—twenty-five by contemporaries—that make reference to Peabody, and twenty articles, most of which are memoirs by former students and colleagues, with only four dated after 1900. Essentially the same references appear in the Roberts dissertation, but in a more homogeneous list and with thirty-five additional short works. More recent references can be found in the selected bibliography in Hersha Sue Fisher, "The Education of Elizabeth Peabody." A number of articles on Peabody listed in *AAL* are not discussed in this essay.

MANUSCRIPTS

Lists of manuscripts are likewise incomplete. The Peabody letters and journals are widely scattered, with holdings in at least fifty repositories from Maine to California and in some foreign countries. Of the thirty-eight entries listed in *ALM*, that for Miami University is in error, since the E. Peabody whose correspondence is held there is male. Lists from the *National Union Catalogue of Manuscript Collections* and from *Women's History Sources*, ed. Andrea Hinding et al., provide information on holdings in eight additional repositories, the most important of which are the Ralph Waldo Emerson, Nathaniel Hawthorne, Samuel Johnson, and Peabody Collections of the Essex Institute. Collections not covered by these combined lists include the Boston Athenæum, with several letters to Charles Folsom about Peabody's library of Polish books and the disposition of Charles Kraitsir's library; the Fales Library of New York University, with Peabody correspondence in the Henry Barnard Papers; and the Concord Free Public Library, with fifteen letters from Peabody to William Torrey Harris, as well as other correspondence. The Chapin Library of Williams College has ten letters in the Samuel Gridley Howe Papers and two Peabody holographs relating to the Argentine revolution. The Library of Congress holdings are listed only in part in *Women's History Sources*. The Manuscript Division has scattered Peabody letters in the Bancroft-Bliss Papers and the papers of Charlotte Cushman, Henry Dawes, Frederick Douglass,

Whitelaw Reid, Carl Schurz, Reinhold Solger, and others. The Fields and Garrison Collections contain letters to her. In the National Archives there are extensive Peabody materials in the records of the Bureau of Indian Affairs and in a special file on Sarah Winnemucca Hopkins, the Piute teacher who was one of Peabody's protégés during the 1880s. The records of the Office of Education include documents dating from Peabody's 1871 experience as a special consultant to the Commissioner of Education, John Eaton. There are also eight letters in the Wordsworth Museum in Grasmere, England, and several in the archives of the Domingo Faustino Sarmiento Museum in Buenos Aires.

Of the collections listed in *ALM*, several should be described briefly. The Sophia Smith Collection at Smith College contains Elizabeth Peabody's correspondence with her girlhood friend Maria Chase of Salem, and the New England Hospital Papers, which date from her later years. Spanning her life but clustering in the 1820s and 1830s are the seventy-four letters from Peabody to her sister Sophia (Mrs. Nathaniel Hawthorne) in the Berg Collection of the New York Public Library. Most of the 105 letters to her sister Mary (Mrs. Horace Mann) are from the "Cuba Journal" letters written seriatim from December 1833 until the summer of 1835, when the two younger sisters returned from their stay on a Cuban plantation. There are also two sections of Elizabeth Peabody's journals and notebooks by Sophia. All told, the combined Peabody-Hawthorne-Mann holdings in the Berg Collection occupy roughly two thousand catalog cards—a formidable resource. The Massachusetts Historical Society holds more than seventy Elizabeth Peabody letters, including ten written to Governor Long and Senator Dawes on behalf of Indian rights, fourteen to Caroline Healey Dall about education, publishing, and woman's place in society, and (among the Perry-Clarke Papers) several letters to James Freeman Clarke. The Theodore Parker letters include twenty-five to Peabody.

In the Harvard-Radcliffe complex, the Schlesinger Library holds twenty-four letters from the 1880s to Harriet Lothrop and her publisher husband, Daniel Lothrop. The Houghton Library, among more than sixty items, includes several letters each to Amos Bronson Alcott, Henry Wadsworth Longfellow, Charles Kraitsir, Charles Eliot Norton, Dorothea Dix, and Mr. and Mrs. Samuel Gray Ward. Of letters to Peabody, those from Lidian Emerson discussing religious beliefs may be of special interest. Theological and political concerns are also expressed in the six letters to John Sullivan Dwight at Vassar College and those at the Boston Public Library. The latter holds some four hundred family letters, with twenty-three by Elizabeth Peabody.

Noteworthy recent acquisitions include 140 pages of letters from Sophia Hawthorne to Elizabeth Peabody (1865–70), which came to the Pierpont Morgan Library from the estate of Rose Hawthorne Lathrop, and the Gage Family Papers deposited in the American Antiquarian Society, both in 1980. The Gage correspondence includes an exchange between Peabody and Mary Moody Emerson and Ann Brewer Sargent Gage (friends in Waterford, Maine), with twenty-five letters by Elizabeth Peabody.

Finally, there is perhaps the most valuable collection of all for the beginning

Peabody researcher, the chronologically organized, indexed set of 3,500 pages of Peabody family typescripts assembled by Robert Lincoln Straker in the 1940s and placed in the Olive Kettering Library of Antioch College. The manuscript collection—the bulk of which had been in the hands of Peabody's literary executor and nephew Benjamin Pickman Mann before coming to Straker via the Washington bookseller W. H. Lowdermilk—numbers over three hundred items, including a hundred letters received by Elizabeth Peabody from her mother and forty-two written by her.

EDITIONS

Of Peabody's books, few need concern us in the matter of revisions and editions. Her anonymous translation of Gerando's *Self-Education*, encouraged by William Ellery Channing and serving as a text for the "self-culture" emphasized by the Transcendentalists, went through three early editions (1830, 1832, 1833). It was reissued ("Third Edition, with Additions") in 1860, with a new preface and with Peabody identified as the translator. The anonymous *Record of a School* appeared in 1835. The appendix, "General Principles of Education," an attempt to explain Alcott's theories, is considered one of the characteristic documents of Transcendentalism. The 1836 second edition contains an "Explanatory Preface," which Peabody substituted for the appendix in the interests of clarity. This was published anonymously in the same year as a forty-three page pamphlet with the title *Method of Spiritual Culture*. When Roberts Brothers of Boston reissued the book in 1874 and 1878, in the wake of Louisa May Alcott's popular success, the title was clarified to read *Record of Mr. Alcott's School*. Peabody signed her new "Preface to the Third Edition," which pays tribute to Alcott's effectiveness as an educator while disclaiming his emphasis on introspection. The "Explanatory Preface" is relegated to the end as chapter 5, and those paragraphs that contradict Peabody's 1870 Froebel-oriented empirical approach to education are deleted. The world history text, *The Polish-American System of Chronology*, went through separate printings in 1850, 1851, and 1852. It was reissued in a revised edition as *Universal History* (1859). Peabody's *Moral Culture of Infancy and Kindergarten Guide*, coauthored with her sister Mrs. Horace Mann, appeared in at least six successive editions with three different publishers from 1863 to 1877, being revised in 1870 to reflect Peabody's eighteen-month study of the kindergartens of Europe. *Lectures in the Training Schools for Kindergartners* (1886) was reprinted in 1888, 1893, 1897, and 1906, and it appeared in an English edition under the title *Education in the Home, the Kindergarten, and the Primary School* (1887).

Last Evening with Allston, and Other Papers (1886) reprints fifteen of Peabody's essays and two poems, dating from 1830 to 1881. It includes three articles on the life and work of Washington Allston, the peculiarly Transcendentalist "A Vision" from James Russell Lowell's *Pioneer*, and "The Dorian Measure," which Emerson admired as among her most original works. "Brook Farm Interpretation of Christ's Idea of Society" was considered by George Ripley as the best theoretical statement of the ideals underlying that experiment when the essay appeared in the *Dial* (1841), and although Peabody omitted her second article, which dealt with more practical aspects of the community, she reprinted from the 1844 *Dial* her interpretation of "Fourierism" as the final stage of Brook Farm.

BIOGRAPHY AND CRITICISM

In spite of the considerable resources available, scholars have been slow to establish the facts of Peabody's life and work. She is dealt with in a few group or movement studies, but no complete biography has yet been published. The most useful short references are the entries by Charles H. Foster in *Notable American Women*, ed. Edward T. James et al., and by Margaret Neussendorfer in *The American Renaissance in New England*, ed. Joel Myerson. Ruth M. Baylor, *Elizabeth Palmer Peabody*, includes several well-annotated chapers on her life, but they are interspersed with historical chapters on the kindergarten movement, and they are too condensed to answer the need for a biography. Gladys Brooks, *Three Wise Virgins*, devotes a seventy-page chapter to an enthusiastic account designed for popular audiences, without documentation. She relies on the equally sentimentalized and partially fictionalized work of Louise Hall Tharp, *The Peabody Sisters of Salem*. Although that book represents extensive research in the manuscripts and a command of the available scholarship, the notes do not clearly indicate what has been drawn from the sources and what has been supplied by imaginative conjecture. If read with the aid of corrective notes ("A Gloss upon Glosses") by Robert Lincoln Straker (typescript at Antioch Coll., Boston Public Library, and several other locations), it can be a pleasant and useful introduction to the three Peabody women and their world.

Some of the earliest and best critical work is found in unpublished theses and dissertations. Only twenty-four years after her subject's death, Doris Louise McCart wrote "Elizabeth Peabody: A Biographical Study" as her M.A. thesis at the University of Chicago. A work of sixty-five pages, it emphasizes Peabody's association with Channing, Hawthorne, and the Boston Transcendentalists, relying entirely on published sources. Aside from several egregious historical errors at the outset, McCart's presentation serves well to establish the lines for future studies. Queenie Bilbo, "Elizabeth Palmer Peabody, Transcendentalist," follows McCart in concluding that "the history of [Peabody's] development is . . . in miniature the progress of the movement as a whole." Her impressive original contribution is her discovery and use of the manuscript materials in possession of Horace Mann III, W. H. Lowdermilk, and W. T. H. Howe before they were donated to the Massachusetts Historical Society, Antioch College, and Berg Collection, respectively. She also identifies thirty-seven books and thirty-two periodical publications by Peabody and provides ample footnotes on members of the Transcendentalist circle. Mabel Flick Alstetter's largely anecdotal "The Life and Work of Elizabeth Palmer Peabody" rings a change in that it divides the study into "Elizabeth Palmer Peabody—The Woman" and "Elizabeth

Palmer Peabody—The Educator." Josephine Elizabeth Roberts, "A New England Family," a chronological account relying almost entirely on personal reading and interpretation of manuscripts, describes the interwoven lives of Elizabeth Peabody and her two sisters. It makes a conscious effort to exploit the inherent interest of the subject while providing continuous and specific scholarly references. The result is a highly readable text, with attention to both personal data and sociocultural contexts.

Peabody occupies only one of ten chapters in John Byron Wilson, "Activities of the New England Transcendentalists in the Dissemination of Culture," and that segment is wholly concerned with her thought, her aesthetic theory, and (relevant to these) her relation with other Transcendentalists. Robert James Saunders, "The Contributions of Horace Mann, Mary Peabody Mann, and Elizabeth Peabody to Art Education in the United States," throws light on Peabody's relationships with the artists Washington Allston and Francis Graeter, analyzes her writings on aesthetics, and details the art manual and essays that came from her publishing house. Mary Stroube Adams turns to what seems an inevitable comparison: "Two Women Transcendentalists: Margaret Fuller and Elizabeth Palmer Peabody." Influenced in part by Wilson, it presents Peabody as combining the Greek aesthetic sense with the moral tradition of New England orthodoxy.

Bruce A. Ronda, "The Transcendental Child," includes a chapter based on seven selected books by Peabody and a few key manuscripts from the Berg Collection. Unfortunately, the Yale library's misattribution of Anna Cabot Jackson Lowell's *Theory of Teaching* (1841) to Elizabeth Peabody has crept into this chapter to distort some of the conclusions. Aside from this, Ronda's subject is a highly significant one, for the concept of childhood's primal innocence is a touchstone of Transcendentalist philosophy and forms the basis for all of Peabody's work as a teacher. Louise Swiniarski, "A Comparative Study of Elizabeth Palmer Peabody and Susan Blow," traces the kindergarten theory of Froebel to its basis in German idealism, indirectly demonstrating that the central interest of the last three decades of Peabody's life was an application of attitudes retained from her high Transcendentalist years. Hersha Sue Fisher, "The Education of Elizabeth Peabody," is among the best studies to date. She takes "education" in the broad sense of self-development, which was the meaning Peabody herself consistently gave it. Fisher presents a rounded portrait of a strong, self-directed woman, an emphatic contrast to the caricatures of a dependent, ill-organized do-gooder all too often repeated in previous references to Peabody. Her relationships with Channing, Emerson, Alcott, Kraitsir, and others are illustrated by judiciously chosen passages from the documents, and her public activities are treated in balance with her personal and family life.

Taken as a group, these unpublished studies provide an impressive source of information whose scope has not been equaled in the published works.

A thorough canvas of comments on Elizabeth Palmer Peabody in works published by her contemporaries must await the appearance of a complete bibliography. In general, it can be said that she was in more than casual contact with many of her fellow Transcendentalists. Alcott wrote a sonnet to her and quoted her in his journals; William Henry Channing gave the New England Women's Club a charming vignette of her fresh loveliness at the age of sixteen; Moncure D. Conway, James Freeman Clarke, Thomas Wentworth Higginson, Theodore Parker, F. B. Sanborn, and Emerson left striking anecdotes and brief tributes to her in their journals and autobiographies. Yet, there is no volume of memoirs from these friends, most of whom she outlived. Sanborn and Ednah Dow Cheney spoke at her memorial service, but the written records come from those who inherited the practical fruits of her Transcendentalist ideals: her colleagues and pupils in kindergartens.

The February 1894 issue of *Kindergarten News* and the May 1904 issue of the *Kindergarten Review* commemorate her death and the centennial of her birth in a series of memoirs and critiques. Other testimonials include Mary Garland's pamphlet biography printed for the Elizabeth Peabody House Association, Jane Marsh Parker's vivid reminiscence of Peabody's personal style, Maria S. Porter's comments on her intellectual life and friendships, Lucy Wheelock's remembrance of her former teacher in *Education* (1894) and in *Pioneers of the Kindergarten in America*, and Kate Douglas Wiggin's account of the eighty-three-year-old Peabody sharing her unflagging enthusiasms in *My Garden of Memory*.

Peabody's earliest extended involvement with Transcendentalist ideas took place in 1835–36, when she helped Bronson Alcott to establish the Temple School and kept her daily account of that experiment. Although *Record of a School* aroused enthusiastic public interest, a similar account of Alcott's *Conversations with Children on the Gospels*, which Alcott published despite her warnings, offended both theological and moral proprieties sacred to conservative Bostonians. Peabody withdrew from the school and public sentiment forced the premature termination of this most promising application of Transcendentalist ideals. The story is told in Odell Shepard, *Pedlar's Progress*, Josephine Elizabeth Roberts, "Elizabeth Peabody and the Temple School," and Madelon Bedell, *The Alcotts*.

Elizabeth Peabody's part in Margaret Fuller's Conversations is treated in Caroline H. Dall, *Margaret and Her Friends*, while the bookshop where some of these took place is the subject of Leona Rostenberg, "Number Thirteen West Street," and Madeleine B. Stern, "Elizabeth Peabody's Foreign Library." Her work for the *Dial* is discussed by George Willis Cooke (*JSP*, 1885), who attests to Elizabeth Peabody's translation of Buddha in the "Corrigenda" at the end of the issue. In the two-volume expansion of this work, *An Historical and Biographical Introduction to Accompany the* Dial, Cooke curiously forgets his own correction and credits Peabody only with the series of Brook Farm essays. An update is provided by Joel Myerson's articles (*RALS*, 1973; *SB*, 1973) and his *The New England Transcendentalists and the* Dial, which presents a concrete portrait of Peabody in relation to the *Dial* and its circle.

For her relationship with Hawthorne, the sources most often relied on are the books by Elizabeth Peabody's niece and nephew, which contain significant but somewhat biased accounts of "Aunt Lizzie" and her doings: Rose Hawthorne Lathrop, *Memories of Hawthorne*, and Julian Hawthorne, *Nathaniel Hawthorne and His Wife* and *Hawthorne and His Circle*. Norman Holmes Pearson, however, has gone behind these to the unpublished sources in his several works: "Elizabeth Peabody on Hawthorne" makes available the significant portions of Julian Hawthorne's manuscript journal at the Pierpont Morgan Library; "A 'Good Thing' for Hawthorne" discusses her agency in producing the Custom House appointment for her brother-in-law through George Bancroft; and *Hawthorne's Two "Engagements"* adduces the evidence against the persistent rumor that Hawthorne was engaged to Peabody before his choice was fixed on her sister Sophia. Finally, several articles in the *Nathaniel Hawthorne Journal* have dealt with Peabody: C. E. Frazer Clark, Jr., "Elizabeth Peabody Identifies the 'Original' Judge Pyncheon" and "Elizabeth Peabody to Mrs. Harriet K. Lothrop"; Joel Myerson, "Sarah Clarke's Reminiscences of the Peabodys and Hawthorne"; Arlin Turner, "Elizabeth Peabody Reviews *Twice-Told Tales*"; and Wayne Allen Jones, "Sometimes Things Don't Work Out: Hawthorne's Income from *Twice-Told Tales* (1837), and Another 'Good Thing' for Hawthorne."

The single issue of *Aesthetic Papers* is discussed in Clarence L. F. Gohdes, *The Periodicals of American Transcendentalism*, and in the thoroughly researched introduction supplied by Joseph Jones for the 1957 reprint of the work, where (among other things) he identifies by author almost all of the anonymous poetry. Jones also discusses "Villages as Universities: *Aesthetic Papers* and a Passage in *Walden*." Peabody's introduction to *Aesthetic Papers* furnishes a springboard for John B. Wilson, "The Aesthetics of Transcendentalism."

Wilson's series of original and informative essays also includes "Elizabeth Peabody and Other Transcendentalists on History and Historians," in which he concludes that Parker, Clarke, and George Ripley were dilettante historians in comparison with Peabody. His "A Transcendental Minority Report" also marks him as a partisan of Peabody when he credits her with a broader Christian humanism and a more balanced view of humankind than is to be found among others in the movement. Finally, his two articles on "Grimm's Law and the Brahmins" identify a topic central to the epistemology of Transcendentalism.

Peabody's analytical approach to language is peripherally treated in John O. Rees, "Elizabeth Peabody and the Very ABC." It becomes the focal point of Philip F. Gura, "Elizabeth Peabody and the Philosophy of Language," and is more briefly treated in his *The Wisdom of Words*. Both discussions place Peabody's works in the broad context of the theological-cultural milieu from which they sprang and show how her publication of Oegger's *The True Messiah* (1842), her dissemination of Kraitsir's theories of language, and her early essays following Herder's interpretation of scriptural exegesis served to bring European philosophies of language to the attention of her contemporaries.

The last public contacts Elizabeth Peabody had with her Transcendentalist friends were at the Concord School of Philosophy in the years 1879–87. Julia R. Anagnos, *Philosophiæ Quæstor*, describes her as the sage and honored "Nestoria" who provided the living link with the great ones who were gone. Her 1882 lecture "Childhood" was printed in *Concord Lectures on Philosophy*, ed. Raymond L. Bridgman, and her memorial lecture "Emerson as Preacher" appeared in *The Genius and Character of*

Emerson, ed. F. B. Sanborn. Florence Whiting Brown, *Alcott and the Concord School of Philosophy*, Sarah A. Underwood, "Sketches of Concord Philosophers," and Augusta Larned, "Impressions of Concord," all present vivid sketches of the "old woman eloquent," whose entry never failed to cause a stir and to arouse awe at the historical past she represented.

Elizabeth Palmer Peabody's life and work offer numerous avenues for further exploration. Several new studies are in progress: Bruce A. Ronda is preparing a selection of her letters, Claire Badaracco is editing the "Cuba Journal," Leslie P. Wilson has physically collected and indexed the more than four hundred volumes extant in Peabody's bequest to the Concord Free Public Library, and Margaret Neussendorfer is writing a comprehensive study of her life and thought and assembling a primary and secondary bibliography.

The criteria put forth in Gura's study on language need to be applied to Peabody's theological writings, her theory of history, and her essays on educational psychology: they should be studied in the context of their times and the European sources that fed into them. Other topics that require more extensive examination include Peabody's relation with other men and women of note (especially with the Transcendentalists), her involvement with reform movements, and her status and career as a single professional woman. As Emerson once commented, Elizabeth Palmer Peabody's personal and public writings afford "a complete literary and philosophical history of New England in her time"—a time of great ferment in which she played so important a role.

GEORGE RIPLEY

Charles Crowe

BIBLIOGRAPHIES

George Ripley, Transcendentalist and the founder of the Brook Farm community, served as a Unitarian minister between 1826 and 1841 and became the most popular and prolific literary critic in America during the last thirty-three years of his life. Although Joel Myerson lists first book publications in *FPAA* (vol. 3), Charles Crowe, *George Ripley*, provides the most complete bibliography. Myerson, *Brook Farm*, is a model bibliography for Ripley and his associates, friends, and allies in relation to Brook Farm, with judicious and helpful comments on publications, manuscripts, and persons. The four volumes of Ripley scrapbooks in the Houghton Library of Harvard University contain the best lists of Ripley's publications as a literary critic. The best bibliography of writings about Ripley is in Crowe's book. All the articles on Ripley listed in *AAL*, except one useless popular essay, are discussed in this chapter.

MANUSCRIPTS

Aside from a small number of items in private hands, *ALM* has a comprehensive list of the several libraries that own at least a few Ripley manuscripts. The most important collections of letters from and to Ripley are in the Boston area, except for ten letters at the Fruitlands Museums, twenty-five in the State Historical Society of Wisconsin, and 105 items (most of secondary importance from the later years) in the old *New York Herald Tribune* files, now located at the Queens Borough Public Library. The three central libraries are the Boston Public Library, with thirty-seven items in the John Sullivan Dwight Collection and seventy-eight in other collections; the Massachusetts Historical Society, with seventy-two letters in the Bancroft and Frothingham papers and thirty-nine in other collections; and the Houghton Library, with twenty-seven letters in the Emerson papers and the Ripley scrapbooks and eleven items in other collections. The Houghton has Ripley's memoranda and commonplace books and his manuscript Bowdoin Prize essay. The Massachusetts Historical Society has the Brook Farm constitution drafts, labor books, and minutes and resolutions book; and, from the New York years, Ripley's notebook of philosophical speculations, notes entitled "Books and Men," and five important sermon manuscripts—"Jesus Christ the Same, Yesterday, Today, and Forever" (14 May 1834), given at Orestes A. Brownson's ordination, "Christianity and the Evolution of Religion" (1834), "Commonsense in the Affairs of Religion" (1837), "Sermon Extending the Right Hand of Fellowship" (27 May 1839), and "Prayer for the Celebration at the Odeon" (4 July 1839). Also, the Andover-Harvard Theological Library has seven letters by Ripley.

EDITIONS

EARLY WRITINGS

As a student at Harvard Divinity School and as a young minister at Purchase Street Church in Boston, Ripley between 1824 and 1826 published his first works, mainly brief items of Unitarian religious news, in the *Observer and Religious Intelligencer* of Boston. For several years from about 1825 he helped edit the Boston *Christian Register* and contributed to that journal a number of items that indicate his progress away from congregational religious orthodoxy and social conservatism and toward intellectual and religious liberation. Under the signature "C" some of the more interesting items appeared in the issues of 26 August, 2 September, 28 October, and 11 November 1826; 4 August 1827; 19 December 1829; 23 January 1833; 16 and 25 August 1834; 28 May 1836; and 3 June and 11 November 1837. After 1837, Ripley and the journal parted company by mutual consent, as Ripley moved into intellectual and social ventures too radical for the *Register*.

UNITARIAN WRITINGS

As a Unitarian, Ripley, in *The Divinity of Jesus Christ* (1831), attributes divinity only to the "message" and "character" and not to the "person" of Christ. "A Letter to a Trinitarian Friend" (1833) argues that Congregational ideas about the Trinity invited the same charges of irrationality and inconsistency that all Protestants made against the Catholic "dogma" of transubstantiation, and the *Report on a Union of Churches for Benevolent Purposes* (1834), drafted by Ripley, makes an ecumenical plea for all Protestants to unite in fighting major moral and social evils. *Discourses on the Philosophy of Religion. Addressed to Doubters Who Wish to Believe* (1836), an important pamphlet and a preliminary statement on intuitional ethical philosophy, places a strong stress on ethics over dogma in religion and argues that only the most liberal and thoughtful religious creed can allay the skepticism aroused by the irrational elements of traditional Christianity. Ripley expresses both Transcendentalist themes and a growing social conscience in *The Temptations of the Times* (1837) and *The Claims of the Age on the Work of the Evangelist* (1840), the latter preached at the ordination of John Sullivan Dwight. The most radical of the religious pamphlets, *A Letter Addressed to the Congregational Church in Purchase Street* (1840) on Ripley's resignation and *A Farewell Discourse, Delivered to the Congregational Church in Purchase Street* (1841), raise troubling questions about all organized religion. Here Ripley, much like Theodore Parker, describes religion as relativistic and evolving. He also registers a strong social protest, bidding farewell not only to his own church but to all churches of "the past."

TRANSCENDENTALIST WRITINGS

Ripley's developing Transcendentalist thought appeared in thirteen articles written for the *Christian Examiner* between 1830 and 1837 and in a curious, final item of 1847. Essays on the French educational philosopher, "Degerando on Self-Education" (1830), and on the innovative practice of the Swiss educator, "Pestalozzi" (1832), express a Transcendentalist faith in self-knowledge, self-development, and nonauthoritarian education. In his essays "Religion in France" (1831), "Benjamin Constant on Religion" (1834), "Cousin's Philosophy" (1836), and "Jouffroy's Contributions to Philosophy" (1837), Ripley argues that post-Revolutionary French philosophy and Romantic letters, and particularly the eclectic school of Victor Cousin, helped to provide an effective antidote to the "sensual" and presumably antireligious empiricism and skepticism of John Locke and David Hume. "Martineau's Rationale" (1832) and "Martineau" (1836) provide an occasion to praise English cultural forces that avoid both theological obscurantism and piety-denying rationalism and sustain a religion of "the heart." The impact of German Romantic idealism in letters, philosophy, and theology can be seen in "Professor Marsh's Translation of Herder" (1835) and "Schleiermacher as a Theologian" (1836). "Professor Follen's Inaugural" (1832), "Mackintosh's Ethical Philosophy" (1833), and "Theological Aphorisms" (1837) all give witness to Ripley's developing intuitionist philosophy. The final item, published after a ten-year silence in the *Examiner*, the poem "The Angels of the Past" (1847), seems to represent a lament for the dying idealism of Brook Farm and the Transcendentalist years.

Other important Transcendentalist literary efforts by Ripley include articles written in contention with Andrews Norton, translations of European writers and thinkers, and essays and reviews for the *Dial*. The public debate with Norton, the would-be "Unitarian Pope of Boston," sprang from Ripley's assaults on pulpit authoritarianism and the use of miracles to prove the truth of Christianity, as well as from Ralph Waldo Emerson's Divinity School Address, which denounced the word "Miracle" as "Monster . . . not one with the blowing clover and the falling rain." Ripley defends freedom of inquiry and the Transcendentalist cultural movement in a long communiqué to the *Boston Daily Advertiser* (9 Nov. 1836), *"The Latest Form of Infidelity" Examined: A Letter to Mr. Andrews Norton* . . . (1839), *Defence of "The Latest Form of Infidelity" Examined: A Second Letter to Mr. Andrews Norton* . . . (1840), and *Defence of "The Latest Form of Infidelity: A Third Letter to Mr. Andrews Norton* (1840). Meanwhile, the Specimens of Foreign Standard Literature series edited by Ripley (14 vols., 1838–42) represented an attempt to acquaint American intellectuals with major European writers, philosophers, poets, and theologians whose work might serve not as "standard literature" but as manifestos of revolt. The first two volumes, *Philosophical Miscellanies* (1839), personally translated by Ripley, consisted largely of selections from Cousin, Théodore Jouffroy, and Constant.

Ripley also wrote eight essays for the first volume of the *Dial* in 1840–41, served as chief business manager for more than a year, and acted as one of three editors until Brook Farm claimed all of his time. "Cousin's Plato" enables Ripley both to praise Cousin's philosophy and to trace the roots of intuitionist thought to classical sources. Brief comments on "Channing's Works" and "Professor Walker's Vindication of Philosophy" suggest that the best of a still much respected Dr. William Ellery Channing survived and progressed, even at Harvard. Three other items, "Brownson's Writings," "Letter to a Theological Student," and "Harwood's Materialism in Religion" also focus on religious thought. Praising Brownson for eschewing "art for art's sake," Ripley declares that his old friend tried to advance true religion, "spiritual philosophy," and social progress in his letters. In discussions of "Harwood" and the "Theological Student," Ripley, denouncing "Bibliolatry" and the tendency of the churches to bury the "Christian spirit" in "formalism and materialism," sharply criticizes "church rulers," and particularly self-styled Unitarian rulers, for trying to perpetuate "a worm-eaten, stereotyped system of theology." Ripley strikes a stronger note of social criticism in praising the "heroic" actions of the author of "Two Sermons on the Kind Treatment and on the Emancipation of Slaves," a man who had been driven from his Southern pulpit by the slavocracy. In "Edward Palmer's 'A Letter to Those Who Think,' " Ripley sympathizes with the author's religious communism but finds him too quick to tie all religions to social oppression and to dismiss all of Christianity as completely obsolete.

BROOK FARM WRITINGS

The task of organizing Brook Farm left Ripley with little time to write anything other than letters, records, and public documents such as the "Articles of Association of the Subscribers to the Brook Farm Institute of Agriculture and Education" (1841), *Constitution of the Brook Farm Association for Industry and Education* (1844), and

Constitution of the Brook Farm Phalanx (1845). When the community converted to Fourierist socialism in 1845, Ripley became a national leader in the communitarian and labor movements, reaching an extensive audience as editor and chief contributor to the *Harbinger*. Among the several hundred articles that he wrote on the evils of competition and American capitalism, the need for socialism, and the thought and activities of "Associationists" were these representative essays: in 1845, "Introductory Notice," "Infidelity of Modern Society," "Influence of Machinery," "What Do You Propose?" "Tendencies of Modern Civilization," "Our Predicament," "War to the Knife," "Where Are We?"; in 1846, "Influence of Social Circumstances" and "Waste! Waste!" David A. Zonderman has edited a lecture on Charles Fourier which Ripley often delivered during this period.

LATER WRITINGS

After the collapse of Brook Farm, Ripley devoted his life mainly to a prolific career in literary criticism and journalism. A mainstay of the *New-York Tribune* whose work was reprinted in newspapers from Boston to San Francisco, he wrote for other northeastern journals as well as for the *Atlantic Monthly Magazine*, *Harper's Magazine*, and *Putnam's Monthly Magazine*. He edited reference works such as the *Hand-Book of Literature and the Fine Arts* with Bayard Taylor (1852) and *The New American Cyclopædia* with Charles A. Dana (16 vols., 1858–63), and he contributed a retrospective essay, finished by George P. Bradford, "Philosophic Thought in Boston" (in *The Memorial History of Boston*, 1881). A few representative examples of the several thousand articles, reviews, and brief items Ripley wrote between 1847 and 1880 are "Hawthorne's *Scarlet Letter*" (1850), "Hawthorne's *House of the Seven Gables*" (1851), "Thackeray's *History of Pendennis*" (1851), "Melville's *Moby Dick*" (1851), "Heine's Work" (1856), "Cobb on Slavery" (1858), "Greeley's American Conflict" (1864), "The Philosophy of Herbert Spencer" (1869), "The War in Europe" (1870), and "Fitzgerald's Rubaiyat" (1877). (Michael Meyer has convincingly argued that the review of Thoreau's *A Week* in the 12 June 1849 *Tribune*, traditionally attributed to Ripley, is in fact by Horace Greeley.)

None of Ripley's New York work has been reprinted. From the Brook Farm years, three *Harbinger* articles, part of the first community constitution, and scattered letters appear in *Autobiography of Brook Farm*, ed. Henry W. Sams. Octavius Brooks Frothingham, *George Ripley*, includes a rich collection of documents, excerpts from articles, and several dozen letters. George Hochfield includes in *Selected Writings of the American Transcendentalists* two pamphlet excerpts, one article, part of the first Brook Farm constitution, and a few letters. Although Perry Miller strangely ignores Ripley in *The American Transcendentalists*, he prints in *The Transcendentalists* thirteen items, including the introduction to the Specimens of Foreign Standard Literature series and the *Harbinger*, portions of four pamphlets, and seven articles (the latter mainly from the *Christian Examiner*).

BIOGRAPHY AND CRITICISM

The only published book-length works on Ripley are Octavius Brooks Frothingham, *George Ripley*, a useful but hastily prepared memoir; Charles Crowe, *George Ripley*, the standard biography; and Henry L. Golemba's brief, superficial, and sometimes erroneous *George Ripley*. Among unpublished studies, " 'Arise and Depart; For This Is Not Your Rest': A Study of the Resignation of George Ripley from the Ministry of the Unitarian Church on Purchase Street, in Boston, in the Year 1841," the Bowdoin Prize winner at Harvard in 1941 by Arthur Kinoy (pseud. for Channing Edwards), adds only marginally to Frothingham. Howard Wilson, "George Ripley, Social and Literary Critic," is a promising introduction to Ripley's criticism but is weak on the pre-1847 years and inadequately based on manuscripts. Lisette Riggs (Isely), "George and Sophia Ripley," is stronger on manuscripts and includes an account of Sophia's thought while neglecting George's. Charles Crowe, "George Ripley," the most comprehensive study, was later published in a substantially revised and expanded book version. Caroline Smith Rittenhouse, by concentrating on intuitionist philosophy and the 1830s, produced a more detailed dissertation on "The Testimony of Man's Inward Nature."

The first sketches of Ripley tended to portray him as a national pillar of genteel letters with a distant and "colorful" reform past: William P. Trent, *A History of American Literature*, and Barrett Wendell, *A Literary History of America*. George Willis Cooke (in *Heralds of a Liberal Faith*, ed. Samuel A. Eliot) sees Ripley as an heroic pioneer of liberal religion. Vernon Louis Parrington, *The Romantic Revolution in America 1800-1860*, in an influential (and sometimes badly mistaken) interpretation, describes Ripley as a man of "mechanical views, the least individualistic and most prosaic" Transcendentalist, and a dreamer who fled both individualism and industrialism at Brook Farm. Ripley's associates, according to Parrington, "balked at task allotment" in the name of individualism, and with the coming of Fourierism they "lost faith in the experiment." Arthur M. Schlesinger, Jr., in a slashing attack in *The Age of Jackson* on "the worst, the pure transcendentalists, incapable of effective human relations, terrified of responsibility and given to transforming evasion into a moral triumph," exonerates Ripley of complete "purity" but blames him for having "no conception at all" of the difficult and persistent work in mainstream politics essential to real social change and for fleeing to the "escapist" enterprise of Brook Farm. Paul F. Boller, Jr., *American Transcendentalism, 1830-1860*, describes Ripley as an authentic religious liberal defending freedom of inquiry and speech, and he portrays Brook Farm as a serious reform enterprise, but he sees Fourierism as an enemy of "free inquiry, natural tolerance and joyous spontaneity." Donald N. Koster has some scattered remarks on Ripley in his brief and sketchy *Transcendentalism in America*.

Among the essayists who deal with Ripley's work of the 1830s, Arthur R. Schultz and Henry A. Pochmann explore the connections between his liberal religion and his Transcendentalism ("George Ripley: Unitarian, Transcendentalist, or Infidel?"); Joseph

Slater describes Ripley's debt to English Romanticism ("George Ripley and Thomas Carlyle"); Kenneth Walter Cameron provides insight into Ripley's intellectual development ("The Library of George Ripley"); Crowe attempts to explain the transformation of an orthodox and conservative youth into a cultural and social rebel ("The Genesis of a Nineteenth Century Reformer"); Jeter A. Isely and Elizabeth R. Isely find several of Ripley's mature ideas in his early Unitarianism; John J. Duffy supplies data on the influence of Coleridge on Ripley ("Transcendental Letters from George Ripley to James Marsh"); and Sheldon P. Peterfreund argues for Ripley's modern philosophical relevance.

Important essays on Ripley and Brook Farm include two early items by Clarence L. F. Gohdes, "The *Harbinger*" (in *The Periodicals of American Transcendentalism*) and "Getting Ready for Brook Farm." Crowe explores tensions between Ripley's reformism and the ultraindividualists in "Transcendentalist Support of Brook Farm," discusses tensions among individualists and collectivists and elements of class conflict in " 'This Unnatural Union of Phalansteries and Transcendentalists,' " gives an account of friends and supporters in a neighboring state in "Utopian Socialism in Rhode Island 1845–1850," and shows that Ripley and his associates had been influenced by Fourier as early as 1840 in "Fourierism and the Founding of Brook Farm." Barbara Gans Gallant adds several minor points in a section on Ripley and the *Harbinger* in "The New England Transcendentalists and the European Revolutions of 1848." Finally, Crowe casts some light on Ripley's religious views during the 1840s in "Christian Socialism and the First Church of Humanity."

No bibliographical account of Ripley and Brook Farm would be complete without a listing of the best accounts of the men and women who knew him personally. On Ripley's departure from the ministry for the community, see "Rev. George Ripley" (1841). For aspirations and community life, see Orestes A. Brownson, "Brook Farm"; Elizabeth Palmer Peabody, "A Glimpse of Christ's Idea of Society," "Plan of the West Roxbury Community," and "Fourierism"; Charles Lane, "Brook Farm"; and Marianne Dwight, *Letters from Brook Farm 1844–1847*, ed. Amy L. Reed. See also Ralph Waldo Emerson's recollections in "Historic Notes of Life and Letters in New England"; "George Ripley and the Brook Farm Association" (1860); and Octavius Brooks Frothingham, *Recollections and Impressions*. Volumes containing both recollections and efforts at systematic historiography are John Thomas Codman, *Brook Farm*, Lindsay Swift, *Brook Farm*, and John Van Der Zee Sears, *My Friends at Brook Farm*.

Among the large volume of literature that bears on Ripley in relation to Transcendentalism and Unitarianism, it is possible to list only the most important books and articles. Essential background for Ripley's education and early thought can be found in Samuel Eliot Morison, "The Great Rebellion in Harvard," Edgeley Woodman Todd, "Philosophical Ideas at Harvard College," and Sydney Ahlstrom, "The Scottish Philosophy and American Theology." On the relation of Unitarianism to Transcendentalism in Ripley's thought, see the dated but still useful Octavius Brooks Frothingham, *Transcendentalism in New England*, C. H. Faust, "The Background of the Unitarian Opposition to Transcendentalism," Conrad Wright, *The Beginnings of Unitarianism in America*, William R. Hutchison, *The Transcendentalist Ministers*, and Catherine L. Albanese, *Corresponding Motion*. On Ripley, the Transcendental Club, and the *Dial*, see George Willis Cooke, *An Historical and Biographical Introduction to Accompany the* Dial, and Joel Myerson, "A Calendar of Transcendental Club Meetings," "A History of the Transcendental Club," and *The New England Transcendentalists and the* Dial. On French and German influences on Ripley, see William Girard, "Du Transcendentalism considéré essentiellement dans sa définition et ses origines français," René Wellek, "The Minor Transcendentalists and German Philosophy," Stanley M. Vogel, *German Literary Influences on the American Transcendentalists*, Walter L. Leighton, *French Philosophers and New-England Transcendentalism*, and Henry A. Pochmann, *German Culture in America*. Also of value is Michael J. Colacurcio, "A Better Mode of Evidence—The Transcendental Problem of Faith and Spirit."

SOPHIA DANA RIPLEY

Charles Crowe

BIBLIOGRAPHIES

There are no published bibliographies of Sophia Ripley, but there is information on her work in Charles Crowe, *George Ripley*, and Joel Myerson, *The New England Transcendentalists and the* Dial. She is not listed in *AAL*.

MANUSCRIPTS

About forty surviving letters of Sophia Ripley written between 1838 and 1847 are in the Boston Public Library, Massachusetts Historical Society, and Houghton Library of Harvard University, with many of the most important ones in the John Sullivan Dwight Collection at the first and the Margaret Fuller papers at the third. Letters to or about her by Ralph Waldo Emerson, Fuller, Amos Bronson Alcott, Elizabeth Palmer Peabody, and several members of the Dana Family can be found in the same libraries; letters by Theodore Parker are at the Andover-Harvard Theological Library. The Schlesinger Library of Radcliffe College has documents of importance in the Dana papers. On the New York years, see the several dozen letters written by her to Charlotte Dana in the Massachusetts Historical Society. She is not listed in *ALM*.

EDITIONS

The offspring of two Boston Brahmin families (the Danas and the Willards) and the daughter of a charming, irresponsible, and often impecunious father, Sophia Ripley taught modern languages in the 1820s and in the late 1840s, and during the interval between she participated with her husband George in nearly every major Transcendentalist activity. Aside from the lost translations of several religious tracts from her later, Catholic years, her publications consist of three articles that appeared in the *Dial* during 1841. Her "Letter" from Zoar, Ohio, a sympathetic account of a pietistic Christian communitarian society, displays an emotional responsiveness to nature, a limited but genuine gift for narration, and considerable skill in depicting character and human relations. "Painting and Sculpture" speculates on the connections between the two arts and provides an interesting cultural document on the decline of the old Puritan doubts about too much devotion to the arts and on the transfer of moral earnestness to the fine arts. The third essay, "Woman," a perceptive account of the dilemmas of New England's female intellectuals, expresses the problems of women tied to a passionate ideology of self-development and fulfillment but trapped in social and sexual roles that denied them higher education, self-expression, and equal cultural opportunities. Complicating Sophia Ripley's life was a hunger for absolute values and cosmic assurance that made her a Catholic, privately, in 1846, and a public convert in 1847, after the collapse of the Brook Farm Phalanx.

Perry Miller reprints "Painting and Sculpture" in *The Transcendentalists*. Octavius Brooks Frothingham, *George Ripley*, Zoltán Haraszti, *The Idyll of Brook Farm*, and *Autobiography of Brook Farm*, ed. Henry W. Sams, include excerpts and letters by her.

BIOGRAPHY AND CRITICISM

Despite the brevity of her publications list, Sophia Ripley played a significant role in the Transcendentalist movement. One of the best-educated women of her generation, she taught James Russell Lowell and various Higginsons, Parkmans, and Tuckermans of note in the Cambridge school operated by the Dana women in the 1820s. She provided substantial assistance to her husband George in the writing of Unitarian sermons and the translation of French philosophy for the Specimens of Foreign Standard Literature series. She served as an important leader in the formation and development of Brook Farm, where she taught one of the first courses in America on Dante. She was a mainstay of Fuller's Conversations, participated in meetings of the Transcendental Club, assisted Emerson in preparing several important essays for publication, did editorial and business chores for the *Dial*, and became a key member of that fascinating group of Boston-Concord women that included Fuller and Elizabeth Peabody. She may also have influenced the conception of Zenobia in Nathaniel Hawthorne's *The Blithedale Romance* (1852) and several aspects of Henry James's *The Bostonians* (1886).

The record of her Transcendentalist activities must be gleaned largely from unpublished letters to, from, and about her. Among published works, the fullest account of Sophia Ripley can be found in Charles Crowe, *George Ripley*, and a few general facts about her can be found in Henry W. L. Dana, *The Dana Saga*. The most informative unpublished narratives are Lisette Riggs (Isely), "George and Sophia Ripley," Henrietta Dana Raymond, "Sophia Willard Dana Ripley," and Sue Ellen Green, "Women in Fourierist Theory and Associationist Practice." Standard biographies and published journals and letters of Emerson, Hawthorne, Alcott, Parker, and especially Fuller mention or briefly discuss Sophia Ripley. For example, see Thomas Wentworth Higginson, *Margaret Fuller Ossoli*, Madeleine B. Stern, *The Life of Margaret Fuller*, Paula Blanchard, *Margaret Fuller*, and Granville Hicks, "A Conversation in Boston." Many accounts of Brook Farm by former members and students contain information on her: in particular, see John Thomas Codman, *Brook Farm*, Lindsay Swift, *Brook Farm*, Georgiana Bruce Kirby, *Years of Experience*, and Marianne Dwight, *Letters from Brook Farm 1844-1847*, ed. Amy L. Reed.

Sophia Ripley belonged to an interesting group of Catholic converts that included Orestes A. Brownson, Isaac Hecker, Charles King Newcomb, and Sarah Stearns. Her conversion has attracted considerable attention, inasmuch as it involved the apostasy from liberal Protestantism of a prominent intellectual and a Boston Brahmin (with a signer of the Declaration of Independence, a Revolutionary War hero, and a president of Harvard among her many distinguished ancestors) to a church then consisting largely of Irish immigrants and struggling for a stronger foothold in America. For interesting if not very scholarly accounts, see Caryl Coleman, "A Forgotten Convert," Katherine Burton, "Sophia Dana Ripley," and Georgianna Pell Curtis, *Some Roads to Rome in America*. On her considerable efforts to establish a convent in New York, see Katherine E. Conway, *In the Footprints of the Good Shepherd*. Some of the works on Brownson and Hecker that touch on Sophia Ripley are Walter Elliott, *The Life of Father Hecker*, Henry F. Brownson, *Orestes A. Brownson's Life*, and *The Brownson-Hecker Correspondence*, ed. Richard F. Gower and Richard M. Leliaert.

FRANKLIN BENJAMIN SANBORN

Robert E. Burkholder

BIBLIOGRAPHIES

Franklin Benjamin Sanborn probably never gave a thought to those who someday might wish to catalog his work, and if he did it was surely a mean one. An active contributor to newspapers and periodicals from 1848 until his death in 1917, Sanborn presents problems for the bibliographer: he often published the same article in two or three serials, erratically signing one version and not another, and he often collected and bound several serial articles in one volume, titling this patchwork as though it were a separate publication and sending it off for copyright. As a result, there are many ghosts in Sanborn's bibliography

There is no comprehensive inventory of works by or about Sanborn, but two valuable lists go a long way toward fulfilling the scholar's needs. The first of these, and by far the more ambitious, is at the end of Benjamin Blakely Hickock's "The Political and Literary Careers of F. B. Sanborn." Besides providing a detailed description of major collections of Sanborn manuscripts, Hickock lists more than forty books and pamphlets, over twenty-five publications that were "Edited, Prefaced, or Introduced by Sanborn or Contain Memoirs or Notes by Him," and approximately 275 contributions to some thirty-five periodicals or newspapers—not including "Our Boston Literary Letter" or "Our Weekly Boston Letter," two columns Sanborn wrote for nearly every weekly edition of the *Springfield Republican* for more than half a century, beginning in 1856. Unfortunately, there is no index or complete study of Sanborn's work for the *Republican* as resident editor from 1868 to 1872 or as a columnist. Neither is there a complete list of his writings for the antislavery weekly *Boston*

Commonwealth, which he edited from 1863 to 1867; the Boston newspapers the *Adver-tiser* and *Journal*; or the *Concord Freeman*, all of which he contributed to regularly at various periods during his life. A more accessible and usable list than Hickock's is John W. Clarkson, Jr., "A Bibliography of Franklin Benjamin Sanborn," which lists 158 original and edited works published by Sanborn (that number includes separate publications as well as serial appearances) and forty-six "Unpublished Works," most of which are in manuscript collections at the Concord Free Public Library or the American Antiquarian Society. The most useful and reliable source for determining Sanborn's first book publications is Joel Myerson's list in *FPAA* (vol. 4).

There is no good list of writings about Sanborn. Compilations of such articles in *AAL*, not all of which are discussed in this essay, are too skimpy to be represen-tative. Although *Literary Writings in America* lists approximately thirty contemporary reviews, it contains no references to biography or criticism. Only the secondary bibliography at the end of Hickock's dissertation, with nearly 250 items, pretends completeness, but it is out of date, and it includes some items that deal with Sanborn only in the most ephemeral way.

MANUSCRIPTS

Upon Sanborn's death, many of his manuscripts were burned by his sons Francis and Victor. Those papers that escaped the flames were subsequently sold by Francis and are, therefore, widely scattered. The manuscripts that were sold are listed in a 1917 auction catalog that Kenneth Walter Cameron has reprinted as "American and British Authors in F. B. Sanborn's Papers."

All of the major Sanborn manuscript collections are listed in *ALM*, but a few of them deserve special notice here. The Concord Free Public Library owns the largest cache of letters by and to Sanborn, including a number of valuable letters from San-born to Theodore Parker. The American Antiquarian Society also has a large sam-pling of correspondence as well as Sanborn's journal and a portion of the manuscript of *Recollections of Seventy Years* (1909), Sanborn's autobiography. The Houghton Library of Harvard University holds some 160 Sanborn letters, materials compiled by Sanborn for a memoir of Parker, and a box of papers relating to Sanborn's association with John Brown. Perhaps the most valuable collection of manuscripts on Sanborn and Brown is in the Thomas Wentworth Higginson Collection of John Brown letters at the Boston Public Library. Other important manuscript repositories include the Historical Society of Pennsylvania, Kansas State Historical Society, Watkinson Library of Trinity College, Massachusetts Historical Society, Henry E. Huntington Library, and the private collections of Walter Harding (Geneseo, New York) and Boyd B. Stutler (Charleston, West Virginia). Other information on the holdings of various libraries can be gleaned from John W. Clarkson, Jr.'s dissertation, to be discussed below.

Two series of letters that will not be found in any of these collections are Sanborn's love letters to his first wife, Ariana Walker, which are rumored to be sealed in the chimney of the home Sanborn built on Elm Street in Concord in 1880, and Sanborn's exchange with Ralph Waldo Emerson's eldest daughter, Edith, which apparently contains his proposal of marriage and his response to Edith's rebuke, a response that caused her father to intercede forcefully in the matter. Some of this latter correspondence is held by a resident of Concord who, perhaps with good cause, does not wish it to be published.

EDITIONS

Sanborn was an indefatigable chronicler of the social, political, and literary currents that swirled around him. As the youngest member of the group of Concord literati, he seems to have inherited the biographical and editorial work of his talented friends—Amos Bronson Alcott, Ellery Channing, Emerson, and Henry David Thoreau—when that work might have been accomplished more ably by others. Inexplicably, Sanborn devoted a disproportionate amount of his energies to Thoreau, producing three biographies—*Henry D. Thoreau* (1882), *The Personality of Thoreau* (1901), and *The Life of Henry David Thoreau* (1917)—and a number of editions of his letters, poems, and other writings. Of the biographies the last is generally considered Sanborn's best work on Thoreau and his finest literary accomplishment, despite its numerous editorial problems. Similar difficulties characterize Sanborn's editions of the *Familiar Letters of Henry David Thoreau* (1894) and Thoreau's *Poems of Nature* (1895), edited with Henry S. Salt and distinguished by its excellent introduction to Thoreau as a poet. The work that has permanently established Sanborn's notoriety as an editor is his two-volume version of *Walden* (1909), which Raymond Adams once referred to as a "monument to editorial stupidity." The biographies *Ralph Waldo Emerson* (1901) and *The Personality of Emerson* (1903) are of little value except for Sanborn's personal reminiscences of his close friend, but *The Genius and Character of Emerson* (1885), edited by Sanborn and featuring essays and poems read at a special session of the Concord School of Philosophy in the summer of 1884, is perhaps the most substantial single volume of criticism produced on Emerson in the nineteenth century. *A. Bronson Alcott: His Life and Philosophy* (1893), written with William T. Harris, is flawed by Sanborn's unwillingness to use Alcott's journals, even though he had unrestricted access to them, and his *Bronson Alcott at Alcott House, England, and Fruitlands, New England (1842-1844)* (1908) is little more than an attempt to fill in details missing from his earlier biography. Among many other projects, Sanborn edited Ellery Channing's *Poems of Sixty-Five Years* (1902) and wrote a valuable biographical-critical introduction to the volume, edited and enlarged Channing's *Thoreau: The Poet-Naturalist* (1902), and, rather curiously, wrote a book on Hawthorne, whom he apparently did not much care for (*Hawthorne and His Friends: Reminiscence and Tribute*, 1908). Some of these works are reprinted in Kenneth Walter Cameron, *Memorabilia of Hawthorne, Alcott, and Concord* (1970). Despite all this

work, a myriad of other editions, and hundreds of serial articles, Sanborn still had
more to say, and he said it in the second volume of his autobiography, *Recollections
of Seventy Years*.

Many of Sanborn's books and articles have been reprinted in the last thirty years.
Kenneth Walter Cameron is responsible for resurrecting hundreds of Sanborn's valuable
serial essays from the obscurity of nineteenth-century periodicals and newspapers by
reprinting them in facsimile in a series of massive volumes that includes *Sixty Years
of Concord 1855-1915: Life, People, Institutions and Transcendental Philosophy in
Massachusetts—With Memories of Emerson, Thoreau, Alcott, Channing and Others*
(1978); *Literary Studies and Criticism: Evaluations of the Writers of the American
Renaissance—With Fresh Approaches to Transcendentalism, Literary Influences, New
England Cultural Patterns and the Creative Experience* (1980); *The Transcendental
Eye: Historical Papers Concerning New England and Other Points on a Great Circle*
(1980); *Transcendental Youth and Age: Chapters in Biography and Autobiography*
(1980); and *Table Talk: A Transcendentalist's Opinions on American Life, Literature,
Art and People from the Mid-Nineteenth Century through the First Decade of the
Twentieth* (1981). These impressively titled tomes reproduce more than five hundred
serial publications (mostly newspaper articles) by Sanborn but should be used with
some caution; they are, despite their titles, merely chronologically arranged reprintings selected with little attention to quality or ultimate value. Cameron has also
gathered together papers relating to Sanborn's association with the Concord School
of Philosophy and published them as *Lectures on Literature and Philosophy: Reports
of Transcendental, Biographical, and Historical Papers Read before the Concord School
1881-1888* (1975), and Joel Myerson has published Sanborn's marvelous lecture
"Reminiscences of Brook Farm and Its Founders," originally delivered in 1900, in
"An Ungathered Sanborn Lecture on Brook Farm."

Sanborn's poetry, which even those most favorably disposed toward him con-
sider mediocre at best, has been ably edited and collected by John Michael Moran,
Jr., in *Collected Poems of Franklin Benjamin Sanborn of Transcendental Concord*
(1964). Moran later attributed eight poems in the 1871 *Radical* to Sanborn in "More
F. B. Sanborn Poems"; however, as Alfred R. Ferguson points out in "Sill's Poems
Wrongly Ascribed to Sanborn," five of the eight poems are actually by Edward Rowland
Sill. Cameron published a sheaf of manuscript poems that were unavailable to Moran,
as well as a considerable number of additional periodical and newspaper articles, in
Ungathered Poems and Transcendental Papers (1981).

Parts of Sanborn's now-lost college journal are reprinted in George Sidney
Hellman's "An Unpublished Concord Journal," and in Cameron's *Transcendental
Climate*, vol. 1. A diary from Sanborn's early Concord years is published along with
seventy-nine more newspaper and periodical contributions in Cameron's *Transcendental
and Literary New England* (1975). Some of Sanborn's letters have been printed in
his biographies and memoirs, and two specifically relating to Thoreau were published
by Walter Harding as "Two F. B. Sanborn Letters," but most of his valuable correspondence remains in manuscript. John W. Clarkson, Jr., provides an indispensable

key to that correspondence in "An Annotated Checklist of the Letters of F. B. Sanborn (1831–1917)." Clarkson's work lists 1,449 letters by Sanborn, and each entry supplies information on the date and place of writing, the name of the correspondent, the location of the manuscript, publication (if any), and a brief summary of the contents of the letter. This format is also used in Clarkson's "Mentions of Emerson and Thoreau in the Letters of Franklin Benjamin Sanborn," which lists 183 letters. It is prefaced by the best short biographical-critical introduction to Sanborn available, which also serves as the introduction to Clarkson's dissertation. Cameron has contributed two additional checklists of Sanborn letters: *The Correspondence of Franklin Benjamin Sanborn the Transcendentalist* (1982), which lists several hundred letters not in Clarkson's dissertation, and *The Young Reporter of Concord: Extracts from Sanborn's Letters to Benjamin Smith Lyman, 1853–1867* (1978).

BIOGRAPHY AND CRITICISM

Undoubtedly the best introduction to Sanborn is his two-volume autobiography, *Recollections of Seventy Years*, the first installment of a proposed four-volume memoir that he was working on at the time of his death. The first volume is devoted to his political career, specifically his activities as secretary of the Massachusetts Free-Soil Party, and his close association with John Brown. The second volume tells the story of Sanborn's literary life, his ill-fated courtship of and marriage to Ariana Walker, and (as one comes to expect from Sanborn) a seemingly endless string of genealogies and personal reminiscences of Alcott, Emerson, Thoreau, and other New England authors. But the autobiography is really valuable as a revelation of Sanborn's personality; one finds in it all the intelligence and magnanimity as well as the flashes of pettiness and downright meanness that make Sanborn's ultimate contribution to American literature difficult to estimate. Consequently, anyone who reads Sanborn's *Recollections* must also read Benjamin Blakely Hickock's dissertation for balance, thoroughness, and the perspective it provides on Sanborn's life and work.

Given Sanborn's relatively interesting life, it is surprising that Hickock's work or another authoritative biography has not yet been published. If Sanborn's life is in his letters, then we must also consult Clarkson's dissertation (with its valuable annotations), which includes an excellent biographical introduction (see *SAR*, 1978) that is particularly valuable for summarizing Sanborn's relations with Emerson and Thoreau. D. R. Wilmes, "F. B. Sanborn and the Lost New England World of Transcendentalism," also recounts Sanborn's life and briefly examines some of his poetry to prove that "the process by which the forces of Transcendental energy and creativity were redirected and dispersed during the second half of the nineteenth century is in fact archetypally figured in Sanborn's life and mind." Wilmes argues that, by remaining in Concord, Sanborn participated in "a regionalist contraction of Transcendentalism" while he also translated Emersonian thought into the larger context of American optimism, specifically by accepting the tone of Emerson's optimism as a rationale for social and political action.

Other biographical sketches include two anonymous articles, "Franklin Benjamin Sanborn" (*GrM*, 1895) and "Famous People at Home. VIII. Franklin Benjamin Sanborn," as well as Edward Stanwood, "Memoir of Franklin Benjamin Sanborn." General biographical essays about Sanborn by his son, Victor Channing Sanborn, are "Franklin Benjamin Sanborn, A. B.," which contains some interesting reminiscences by Sanborn himself; "Franklin Benjamin Sanborn"; and "Memoir of Franklin Benjamin Sanborn, A. B." In "F. B. Sanborn, The Last of the Abolitionists," Harold D. Carew focuses on Sanborn's activities as a member of John Brown's Secret Six (those who had prior knowledge of the plans for the Harper's Ferry raid) and the subsequent unsuccessful attempt to kidnap Sanborn from his Concord home to testify before a United States Senate Committee. (Nearly all studies of John Brown discuss this episode; see the chapter on Theodore Parker for some representative titles.) Alexander Johnson, "An Appreciation of Frank B. Sanborn," concentrates on Sanborn's significant contributions to the fledgling field of social science. Wallace B. Conant, *Paper on Franklin Benjamin Sanborn*, is a valuable general consideration of Sanborn's life and multifarious activities from the perspective of a Concord neighbor whom Sanborn helped to start a newspaper. In "Personal Reminiscences of F. B. Sanborn," William E. Connelley discusses his several visits with Sanborn in Kansas and Boston from 1900 to 1913, as well as Sanborn's dabbling in Kansas politics. One tribute notable for its tone is that by Lindsay Swift (*PMHS*, 1917). Apparently Sanborn attacked Swift for biographical work he had done on William Lloyd Garrison and Alcott because Swift did not know his subjects personally. The restraint Swift exercises in his tribute is sometimes not enough to contain his bitterness, and the entire incident serves to highlight Sanborn's wounding and often irrational critical judgments and the manner in which he laid claim to the lives and work of those he had known.

All of the above essays are reprinted in Cameron's *Transcendental Youth and Age*. Two general studies that are not reprinted are Victor Channing Sanborn's brief tribute, "Franklin Benjamin Sanborn, A.B. 1831-1917," and Raymond Baldwin, "Franklin B. Sanborn," which is particularly useful as a guide to Sanborn's often stormy relations with the exclusive social club that twice removed his name from its rolls. For a clue to Sanborn's tastes as a reader and book collector, the best source is George H. Sargent's description of his library, "Frank B. Sanborn's Jewels and Junk."

It is not surprising that nearly all the critical work done on Sanborn, who has been the object of exceptional disfavor among bibliographers, critics, and especially editors of texts since his death, has been devoted to his editorial work. The one notable exception is the consideration of Sanborn's literary career in Hickock's dissertation. Not only does Hickock ably comment on Sanborn's many editorial projects and summarize the views of other critics, he also discusses the value of Sanborn's poetry and biographical work, and he is the only critic that does so. One of the earliest and most scathing attacks on Sanborn's edition of *Walden* is Maude Ethel Cryder, "An Examination of the Bibliophile Edition of Thoreau's *Walden*." By comparing Sanborn's work with an earlier edition of *Walden*, Cryder finds evidence of one editorial atrocity after another, and she indicts Sanborn for his inconsistent use of notes, his omission of material in previous editions, his unexplainable interpolations of "new" material, his rearrangement of chapters, and, perhaps most significantly, his failure to realize that the twelve thousand words of manuscript material he so cavalierly added to *Walden* were actually taken from drafts of the book and were not parts of Thoreau's final text (an amazingly accurate hypothesis that Cryder arrived at exclusively through her study of Sanborn's editorial additions). Francis H. Allen is considerably kinder to Sanborn in *Thoreau's Editors*, although he does admit that he was never tempted to read the "Sanbornized *Walden*." Walter Harding's "Franklin B. Sanborn and Thoreau's Letters," an examination of Sanborn's editorial work in *Familiar Letters of Henry David Thoreau*, compares the editor's transcriptions with the author's manuscripts to show that Sanborn not only took liberties with the text but also edited carelessly. The most valuable discussion of Sanborn as an editor of Thoreau's poems is found in Carl Bode's introduction to *Collected Poems of Henry Thoreau*, which examines Sanborn and Salt's edition of *Poems of Nature* and also calls into question Sanborn's editing of several of Thoreau's poems in the *Boston Commonwealth*.

HENRY DAVID THOREAU

Michael Meyer

BIBLIOGRAPHIES

The most comprehensive primary bibliography of Thoreau's writings is Raymond R. Borst, *Henry David Thoreau*, which lists separate publications of Thoreau's works, collections, and collected editions, and first-appearance contributions to books, pamphlets, magazines, and newspapers. Also included are illustrations of Thoreau's first edition title pages, bindings, and dust jackets. Borst's excellent work supersedes all previous efforts to establish a primary bibliography for Thoreau.

Secondary bibliographies have been largely successful in keeping track of the vast amount of material written about Thoreau. There is, however, no single comprehensive secondary bibliography available. The most useful work covering the nineteenth century is Francis H. Allen, *A Bibliography of Henry David Thoreau*, and a worthwhile project would be to incorporate Allen's listings into a comprehensive bibliography of nineteenth-century items. William White extends Allen's list in "A Henry David Thoreau Bibliography, 1908–37," as does J. S. Wade, who covers the period 1909 to 1936. The period 1938 to 1945 is inventoried by Philip E. Burnham and Carvel Collins. Since 1941, each quarterly issue of the *Thoreau Society Bulletin* includes an important continuing bibliography of popular and scholarly responses to Thoreau. Walter Harding and Jean Cameron Advena have compiled most of them in *A Bibliography of the Thoreau Society Bulletin Bibliographies, 1941–1969*, retaining many of the helpful brief annotations; unfortunately, the lack of an index limits the work's usefulness. Christopher A. Hildenbrand provides a more selective list along with a brief index in *A Bibliography of Scholarship about Henry David Thoreau: 1940-1967*. Jeanetta Boswell and Sarah Crouch draw on and add to these bibliographies in *Henry David Thoreau and the Critics*, a listing of 2,150 selected items published between 1900 and 1978, accompanied by a limited subject index and an index of coauthors, editors, and translators. Though not always reliable, this list supplements previous bibliographies, particularly for the years 1969-78. Annette M. Woodlief has compiled a useful annotated checklist of *Walden* criticism published through 1973.

A few bibliographical essays serve as helpful guides to the several hundred books and dissertations and several thousand articles written about Thoreau. Lewis Leary offers a succinct but detailed overview in *Eight American Authors*. Leary is especially strong on the development and direction of Thoreau scholarship and criticism over the years; in about forty pages he provides plenty of bibliographic information while describing Thoreau's growing reputation. The most complete guide to Thoreau scholarship and criticism is Walter Harding and Michael Meyer, *The New Thoreau Handbook*, which examines in six chapters his life, works, sources, ideas, literary art, and reputation. Each chapter is followed by a bibliographic essay that lists and comments on the sources that inform the chapter discussion. This is an expanded and updated revision of Harding, *A Thoreau Handbook*, which attempted to be comprehensive, an effort that makes the latter book still useful, particularly for studies that have been superseded and for ephemeral material, such as Elbert Hubbard's writings on Thoreau. Readers should also be aware of the reviews that have appeared in *Thoreau Society Bulletin*, *Concord Saunterer*, *Thoreau Journal Quarterly* (no longer published), and the *Thoreau Quarterly* (begun in 1982).

Several specialized bibliographies are also available. Among those that have not been superseded are three by Harding: "A Bibliography of Thoreau in Poetry, Fiction, and Drama"; "A Check List of Thoreau's Lectures"; and *Thoreau's Library*, a list and description of the books Thoreau owned (revised and updated in *SAR*, 1983). One other useful source for locating important or obscure items is Harding, *A Catalog of the Thoreau Society Archives in the Concord Free Public Library*. The Concord library houses copies of many of the doctoral dissertations written on Thoreau. A number of them are cited in the sections below, because dissertations often provide convenient and valuable bibliographic sources for specific topics.

Detailed discussion and sources concerning Thoreau's reception in the United States will be found in Michael Meyer, *Several More Lives to Live: Thoreau's Political Reputation in America*; the notes constitute a bibliography of trends in Thoreau criticism since the 1920s. Thoreau's foreign reception is surveyed in *Thoreau Abroad*, ed. Eugene F. Timpe, which includes studies on Britain, France, the Netherlands, Germany, Switzerland, Italy, Bohemia, Russia, Israel, India, Japan, and Australia. Also useful are James F. Lacey, "Henry David Thoreau in German Criticism 1881-1965"; Justo Garate, *Thoreau and the Spanish Language*; Nikita Pokravosky, "Basic Bibliography of Russian Translations, Publications and Studies of Thoreau"; and William Condry, "Thoreau's Influence in Britain."

MANUSCRIPTS

As the entry in *ALM* indicates, Thoreau's manuscripts are scattered throughout the United States. William L. Howarth, *The Literary Manuscripts of Henry David Thoreau*, lists, describes, and locates all known papers in public and private collections. Although Thoreau's manuscripts are housed in numerous libraries and collections, there are several major collections. The Henry E. Huntington Library includes various manuscript versions of *Walden* as well as many poems, letters, and journal material. The Berg Collection at the New York Public Library houses the largest collection of letters. At Harvard University, the Houghton Library holds many letters and the drafts of some essays. These three collections are cataloged by Francis B. Dedmond, and Alexander C. Kern has produced a list of "Thoreau Manuscripts at Harvard." Most of Thoreau's journals, in addition to his Indian and Canadian notebooks, are in the Pierpont Morgan Library (see Walter Harding, *TSB*, 1947). The Abernethy Library of Middlebury College also holds many important miscellaneous items (see Viola C. White, *Check List: Abernethy Library of American Literature*). Catalogs of other collections are cited in Harding and Meyer, *The New Thoreau Handbook*. Carolyn Kappes et al., "A Calendar of the Correspondence of Henry David Thoreau," lists locations for all letters to and from Thoreau.

EDITIONS

Until recently, *The Writings of Henry David Thoreau* (1906) was generally regarded as the standard edition of Thoreau's works. These twenty volumes (fourteen of which consist of Thoreau's journal) were first published as the Manuscript Edition because a manuscript page was tipped into the first volume of each numbered set. Later, less expensive sets, known as the Walden Edition, were printed from the same plates with very minor revisions. Most of the first six volumes of the 1906 edition (*A Week on the Concord and Merrimack Rivers*, *Walden*, *The Maine Woods*, *Cape Cod and Miscellanies*, *Excursions and Poems*, and *Familiar Letters*) have been superseded by several later editions and, most important, by *The Writings of Henry D. Thoreau* (1971–   ), published by the Princeton University Press. Of the approximately twenty-five projected volumes in the Princeton Edition, six are in print at this writing. This edition attempts to provide the most authoritative version possible by using modern textual principles. Each volume includes introductory sections and appendixes explaining the editorial choices that were made in order to come as close as possible to Thoreau's original intentions.

The Princeton editions of *A Week on the Concord and Merrimack Rivers*, ed. Carl F. Hovde et al., *Walden*, ed. J. Lyndon Shanley, and *The Maine Woods*, ed.

Joseph J. Moldenhauer, supersede the 1906 editions of those titles. *Early Essays and Miscellanies*, ed. Moldenhauer, collects Thoreau's college essays along with a dozen other pieces, including "Sir Walter Raleigh" and "Thomas Carlyle and His Works." *Reform Papers*, ed. Wendell Glick, supersedes "The Service" and the political essays in the 1906 *Cape Cod and Miscellanies*. For the controversy concerning Glick's use of "Resistance to Civil Government" as the title for "Civil Disobedience," see articles by Thomas Woodson (*BRH*, 1978) and Glick (*AEB*, 1978). Still to be published by Princeton are the journals from 1844 to 1862, *Excursions*, *Cape Cod*, *Correspondence*, *Poems*, *Translations*, and *Nature Essays*.

Princeton has also published Thoreau's *Journal, Volume 1: 1837-1844*, ed. John C. Broderick et al., which includes previously unpublished material and supersedes most of the first volume of the 1906 edition (1837–47) as well as material printed in *The First and Last Journeys of Thoreau*, ed. Franklin Benjamin Sanborn (1905), and Perry Miller, *Consciousness in Concord: The Text of Thoreau's Hitherto "Lost Journal" (1840-41), Together with Notes and a Commentary* (1958). In addition to the editorial apparatus included in the other volumes of the Princeton edition, *Journal 1* also provides helpful annotations. Unfortunately, the textual apparatus does not allow the reader to reconstruct all of Thoreau's revisions in those journal passages later used in his published writings. Until Princeton publishes the rest of the journal, the remaining 1906 volumes are standard. A handy, unabridged two-volume reprint of the 1906 *Journal*, which was edited by Bradford Torrey and Francis H. Allen, is available from Dover Publications.

The Correspondence of Henry David Thoreau, ed. Walter Harding and Carl Bode (1958), supersedes the badly edited *Familiar Letters* (1906). For annotations and more letters, see Kenneth Walter Cameron, *Companion to Thoreau's Correspondence* and *Over Thoreau's Desk*. Additional stray unpublished letters that have turned up are listed in bibliographies. Harding is currently working on the new Princeton edition that will include letters discovered since 1958.

The best available edition of Thoreau's poetry is *Collected Poems of Henry Thoreau*, ed. Carl Bode (1943; enl. ed., 1964). Until Elizabeth Hall Witherell's edition of Thoreau's poems is published in the Princeton Edition, see her dissertation, a selected critical edition of the poems, which is both a textual and critical analysis of the poems Thoreau published during his life for which manuscripts survive.

The Princeton Edition will not be completed for a number of years. Until all its projected volumes are in print, readers should consult Harding and Meyer's bibliography for reliable texts.

Photographs by Herbert W. Gleason, a landscape photographer of the nineteenth and early twentieth century, were used in the 1906 edition of the *Journal* and in two Princeton volumes, *The Illustrated Walden* and *The Illustrated Maine Woods*. Unfortunately, these and the other standard editions are too expensive for use in most classrooms. The problems associated with choosing a reliable classroom text of *Walden* are described by Joseph R. McElrath, Jr., who compares and evaluates college texts.

BIOGRAPHY

A close study of Thoreau might well begin by looking at the man himself. Thomas Blanding and Walter Harding, "A Thoreau Iconography," reproduce the handful of known authentic likenesses of him in photographs, drawings, caricatures, sculpture, and a portrait. For some 250 "daguerreotypes, photographs, paintings, drawings, cartoons, broadsides, news clippings, maps, and charts" of Thoreau and his times, see Milton Meltzer and Harding, *A Thoreau Profile*, which, with its accompanying text, is an effective introduction. To better understand Thoreau's life it is important to have a sense of that other major character in his writings—the town of Concord. Townsend Scudder, *Concord*, and Ruth R. Wheeler, *Concord*, provide that valuable context. A more personal view by a student of Thoreau's will be found in the fascinating anecdotes supplied in *Remembrances of Concord and the Thoreaus*, ed. George Hendrick. Another helpful source for seeing Thoreauvian landscapes more clearly is Robert F. Stowell, *A Thoreau Gazeteer*, which provides maps, photographs, and reproductions of paintings and engravings of the places described in Thoreau's writings. Given the details and factual texture of Thoreau's work, it makes sense to pay attention to these matters whether one is reading him literally or metaphorically. Also useful are Cameron's numerous collections related to Thoreau, Concord, and his contemporaries. Though there are too many to cite here, Cameron has listed and briefly described most of the collections of primary and secondary materials he has published; see *Transcendentalism and American Renaissance Bibliography*, published with supplements as *Bibliography on Transcendentalism or the American Renaissance*.

Ralph Waldo Emerson's revised and expanded eulogy for the *Atlantic Monthly Magazine* was the first significant attempt to create a biographical portrait of Thoreau. Joel Myerson's new and authoritative edition of "Thoreau" from manuscript shows what the revisions reveal about the relationship between Emerson and Thoreau, a relationship that is fundamental to understanding Thoreau's growth and development. Excerpts from scores of contemporary commentaries on Thoreau are collected in *Thoreau: Man of Concord*, ed. Harding, including assessments by Emerson, Hawthorne, Walt Whitman, Amos Bronson Alcott, Louisa May Alcott, Margaret Fuller, Horace Greeley, Isaac Hecker, William Dean Howells, Henry James, Thomas Wentworth Higginson, James Russell Lowell, Daniel Ricketson, and Ezra Ripley. For Thoreau's relations with other contemporaries, see the indexes to the biographies cited below and the biographies of individual figures.

William Ellery Channing, *Thoreau: The Poet-Naturalist*, is a friend's labor of love and the first biography of Thoreau, but it is more a source of anecdotes than a full biographical portrait. It was later revised by F. B. Sanborn, whose notorious editing rendered the book less trustworthy. The Englishman H. A. Page (pseudonym for A. H. Japp) offered a more socially conscious thinker in *Thoreau: His Life and Aims*, but it too provided little information about his life. Not until Sanborn's *Henry D. Thoreau* did readers have a better sense of some of the details of Thoreau's life. That book includes many previously unpublished manuscripts, but these texts have since been superseded. Sanborn's best effort is *The Life of Henry David Thoreau*, which is rich in detailed information.

The most successful early biography is *The Life of Henry David Thoreau* by Henry S. Salt, who never knew Thoreau or Concord but who managed to write the first comprehensive account of his life from the information available to him. It is still worth reading. Two sympathetic treatments (rather than biographies) are Annie Russell Marble, *Thoreau: His Home, Friends, and Books*, and Edward Waldo Emerson (Ralph Waldo's son), *Henry Thoreau as Remembered by a Young Friend*, both useful for the reminiscences they supply. Mark Van Doren, *Henry David Thoreau*, is sympathetic with the writings rather than with the unhappy "deluded" man Van Doren describes, an assessment similar in tone to *Henry Thoreau: The Cosmic Yankee* by Brooks Atkinson, who clearly prefers Thoreau the nature writer to Thoreau the social critic.

Aside from Salt's study, the first full-scale biography was Henry Seidel Canby, *Thoreau*. Canby incorporates newly available materials from Thoreau's contemporaries; unfortunately, he also includes a thin and fashionable Freudian reading of Thoreau's sex life that is neither useful nor convincing. Several later psychological studies are very much worth reading, however; they are based on conjecture but are nevertheless provocative. Raymond Gozzi, "Tropes and Figures," is a detailed Freudian reading of his life and writings that opens up an intriguing perspective. Two revised chapters appear in *Henry David Thoreau: A Profile*, ed. Harding. Earlier, Carl Bode drew on and developed Gozzi's work ("The Half-Hidden Thoreau").

Walter Harding, *The Days of Henry Thoreau*, is the standard work on which other biographical and critical studies can build. Its purpose is to present the facts of Thoreau's life rather than to interpret them from a particular point of view. Harding provides the day-to-day activities and contexts (as well as valuable footnotes) that have been indispensable to countless readers and scholars. A Dover reprint restores those notes Harding originally had to drop for reasons of space; it also includes a new afterword.

Richard Lebeaux, *Young Man Thoreau*, is the first book-length biography that attempts to interpret the facts available in Harding's biography. Lebeaux restricts himself to the years 1837 to 1845, the period between Thoreau's graduation from Harvard College and his departure for Walden Pond. Where Gozzi's emphasis is Freudian, Lebeaux uses Eriksonian principles to describe Thoreau's struggle to create a satisfying identity for himself. Along the way Lebeaux discusses Thoreau's problematic relations with Emerson, his family (particularly his brother John), and the people of Concord in order to reveal the roots of *A Week* and *Walden*. The reader may find some of Lebeaux's hypotheses and assertions difficult to accept, but they might provoke alternative theories that will help us to understand Thoreau better. Lebeaux extends his psychobiographical study to other periods of Thoreau's life in " 'Sugar Maple Man': Middle-Aged Thoreau's Generativity Crisis." Here the emphasis is on Thoreau's anxieties about becoming stagnant after publishing *Walden*, which, as Lebeaux puts it, was "a hard creative act to follow."

Nearly twenty years after Harding's *The Days of Henry Thoreau*, there is still no comprehensive full-length biography that brings together the accumulated facts of Thoreau's life and the critical insights about his writings that have developed alongside those facts. We need that book.

CRITICISM

Over the years there have been discernible trends in Thoreau criticism. As detailed information and unpublished manuscripts were made available to critics, Thoreau was gradually perceived as more than simply an imitator of Emerson and a verbal illustrator of nature. Not until the 1930s was he widely read as a serious social critic, and not until the 1940s were his writings afforded close critical analyses. These trends in criticism are surveyed by Lewis Leary and Meyer and in Wendell Glick's introduction to *The Recognition of Henry David Thoreau*, which reprints selected criticism from 1848 through the mid-1960s. For developments up through 1980, consult Harding and Meyer's *New Thoreau Handbook*.

The following collections of reprinted or original essays also suggest the range of criticism: *Pertaining to Thoreau*, ed. Samuel A. Jones; *Thoreau: A Century of Criticism*, ed. Harding; *Thoreau: A Collection of Critical Essays*, ed. Sherman Paul; *The Western Thoreau Centenary*, ed. J. Golden Taylor; *The Thoreau Centennial*, ed. Harding; *Thoreau in Our Season*, ed. John Hicks; *New Approaches to Thoreau*, ed. William Bysshe Stein; *Henry David Thoreau: Studies and Commentaries*, ed. Harding, George Brenner, and Paul A. Doyle; and *Henry David Thoreau: A Profile*, ed. Harding. Three collections are devoted entirely to *Walden*: *Approaches to* Walden, ed. Lauriat Lane, Jr., *Twentieth Century Interpretations of* Walden, ed. Richard Ruland, and *The Merrill Studies in* Walden, ed. Joseph J. Moldenhauer.

SOURCES

Thoreau was not shy about borrowing—whether it was land to live on for two years or words to live by provisionally. "The highest law," he wrote in his journal for 9 November 1855, "gives a thing to him who can use it." His frequently noted eclectic tastes and sensibilities are apparent in the variety of allusions that appear in his writings. An overview of source studies suggests the intellectual background that informs his writing.

Much of Thoreau's reading—the books he borrowed from libraries, took notes on, or owned—is listed in several works by Kenneth Walter Cameron: *Transcendental Apprenticeship: Notes on Young Henry Thoreau's Reading: A Contexture with a Researcher's Index*; *The Transcendentalists and Minerva*; and *Thoreau's Literary Notebooks in the Library of Congress*. See also Walter Harding, *Thoreau's Library* and *Emerson's Library*, which Thoreau had access to. John Aldrich Christie, *Thoreau as World Traveler*, identifies the travel books Thoreau read and used to create a microcosm in Concord. Thoreau's use of his reading is discussed in many of the biographical and critical book-length studies, but see also assessments by Norman Foerster (*TR*, 1917), Wendell Glick (*NEQ*, 1971), Douglas A. Noverr's reply to Glick, and E. Earle Stibitz.

Thoreau's secondary education is surveyed by Hubert H. Hoeltje ("Thoreau and the Concord Academy"). "The Education of Henry Thoreau, Harvard 1833–37" by Christian Gruber is the most complete examination of his college experiences; see also Cameron's *Thoreau's Harvard Years*. Philosophical ideas current at Harvard are considered by Edgeley Woodman Todd and Joseph Kwiat. Richard Whately's *The Elements of Rhetoric*, one of Thoreau's Harvard texts, is discussed in Annette M. Woodlief, "The Influence of Theories of Rhetoric on Thoreau." Whately is also included in Richard H. Dillman, "Thoreau's Psychological Rhetoric," a portion of which has been published (*ESQ*, 1979).

Within the past decade scholars have attempted to determine how Thoreau's writings were influenced by nineteenth-century language theorists. Michael West discusses the influences of Charles Kraitsir and Walter Whiter, but the most sustained and significant study of the impact of language theory on Thoreau (as well as on other writers) is Philip F. Gura, *The Wisdom of Words*. Gura shows "how the terms of theological debate, particularly with regard to the accuracy and implication of scriptural revelation, when coupled with the influence of Continental romanticism, were transformed into premises with deep reverberations in epistemology, theology, education and literary form." Thoreau's fascination with language is placed in this context to suggest the influence language theorists had on his use of language and his perennial search for truth. (The chapter on Thoreau is an expanded and revised version of an earlier piece in *NEQ*, 1979.) Gura further develops this theme by connecting the competing ideas of Alexander Bryan Johnson and Horace Bushnell to the literary art of Thoreau and Melville (*AL*, 1981).

Thoreau's relationship with Emerson has attracted considerable attention. In addition to Joel Myerson's study of Emerson's eulogy, there are three other useful analyses: Leonard Neufeldt offers a close reading of the text in order to describe the tensions between Emerson and Thoreau (*ESQ*, 1970); Gabrielle Fitzgerald discusses it in the context of the Civil War; and Hubert H. Hoeltje, in contrast to many commentators, argues that it did not damage Thoreau's reputation (*PQ*, 1968). In an extended study, Joel Porte, *Emerson and Thoreau*, emphasizes the philosophical differences and the rift between the two; Porte further explores Emerson's ambivalent response to Thoreau in *Representative Man*. Paul Hourihan examines "The Inner Dynamics of the Emerson-Thoreau Relationship," and William M. Moss connects Thoreau to Emerson's relationships with other promising young men of the time such as Jones Very, William Ellery Channing, Christopher Pearse Cranch, and Walt Whitman. Thoreau is discussed as Emerson's "American Scholar Incarnate" by Edward J. Rose and as Emerson's poet by Charles Berryman. What is known about Thoreau's brief stay with Orestes Brownson is described by Cameron (*ESQ*, 1968). A concise and valuable essay that places Thoreau in a Transcendentalist context is Alexander C. Kern's "The Rise of Transcendentalism,

1815–1860," which, together with Emerson's published lecture "The Transcendentalist" (1849), helps to explain the sources of many of Thoreau's ideas as well as his temperament.

Thoreau read hardly any fiction. In American literature he was primarily interested in travel narratives and local histories. Lawrence Willson, "The Influence of Early North American History and Legend on the Writings of Henry David Thoreau," remains the fullest study of Thoreau's reading of early American literature. The significance of John Josselyn's exploration and travel narrative is argued by Philip F. Gura (*NEQ*, 1975). Helpful studies of Thoreau's use of local history and folklore are Lonnie Willis, "Folklore in the Published Writings of Henry David Thoreau," and Richard F. Fleck, "Henry David Thoreau's Interest in Myth, Fable, and Legend."

The Willson, Willis, and Fleck studies also include sections on Thoreau's readings about native Americans. Fleck presents "Evidence for Thoreau's 'Indian' Notebooks as Being a Source for His Journal" and offers a brief "representative sampling" of excerpts from the notebooks in *The Indians of Thoreau* (1974). The richest study of the twelve unpublished "Indian Books"—in which Thoreau copied information and quotations from travelers, missionaries, and ethnographers—is Robert F. Sayre, *Thoreau and the American Indians*, which traces Thoreau's "fascination with Indian life, his attempts to learn about it and imitate it, and also some of the differences between Indians as he read and wrote about them and as they were." Linck C. Johnson, "Into History: Thoreau's Earliest 'Indian Book' and His First Trip to Cape Cod," discusses when Thoreau began to compile the notebooks as well as their purpose and their relationship to his other writings.

The influence of American Protestantism on Thoreau's beliefs and personality is explored in Alexander C. Kern, "Church, Scripture, Nature and Ethics in Henry Thoreau's Religious Thought." A revision of Perry Miller's work is argued by Mason I. Lowance, Jr., "From Edwards to Emerson to Thoreau." Thoreau's affinities with Puritan moral and aesthetic sensibilities have been discussed in several good studies: Sacvan Bercovitch, *The American Jeremiad*, places *Walden* within "the tradition of the jeremiad"; Egbert S. Oliver, "Thoreau and the Puritan Tradition," finds Thoreau's defense of John Brown similar to the "form, measure, and language" of seventeenth-century English Puritans; Wesley T. Mott describes "Emerson and Thoreau as Heirs to the Tradition of New England Puritanism"; and Errol M. McGuire places Thoreau in a "native religious tradition" in "The Art of Growing Pure." Gordon V. Boudreau compares Thoreau and St. Augustine.

"Thoreau's Use of the Bible" is discussed by John R. Burns, who also lists biblical references, allusions, and texts in his writings. Larry R. Long's study of "The Bible and the Composition of *Walden*" includes an extensive listing of the biblical sources Thoreau used in different stages of writing *Walden*; Long also describes "Thoreau's Portmanteau Biblical Allusions." Hugh Cook focuses on "Thoreau and the King James Bible."

Thoreau's reading in British literature was uneven. Anne Whaling, "Studies in Thoreau's Reading of English Poetry and Prose," examines the quotations he copied into his commonplace books. Robert Sattelmeyer (*SAR*, 1980) makes a convincing case that Thoreau, in the early 1840s, worked on "an appreciative and critical collection of English poetry" that he never finished. Few studies have explored Thoreau's interest in British literature, partly because that interest was limited. Although alluded to in other studies of Thoreau, his reading of English authors has been treated mostly in a piecemeal way: on Francis Bacon, see George W. Smith; on Chaucer, see Caroline Spurgeon, *Five Hundred Years of Chaucer Criticism and Allusion*; on Samuel Taylor Coleridge, see Alexander Kern in *New Approaches to Coleridge*, ed. Donald Sultana; on Samuel Daniel, see Raymond Himelick; on Daniel Defoe, see Willard H. Bonner and Mary Alice Budge; on William Gilpin, see William Templeman and James G. Southworth; on Bishop Hall, see Walter Gierasch; on John Milton, see Buford Jones; on Ossian, see Ernest Leisy; on Francis Quarles, see Leisy; on Shakespeare, see Esther Cloudman Dunn, *Shakespeare in America*; on John Smith, see Darlene Unrue; and on Isaak Walton, see Thomas Blanding. The only two lengthy treatments of nineteenth-century British figures are Laraine R. Fergenson, "Wordsworth and Thoreau," a portion of which has been published (*TJQ*, 1973), and Michael Touloumtzis, "Thoroughly Saxon: The Influence of Thomas Carlyle on Henry D. Thoreau's Art and Thought." This list of particular figures reflects not so much the range of Thoreau's reading—Sir Walter Raleigh is, for example, conspicuously absent—as the range of the separate studies available.

European literature had little appeal for Thoreau. References to his reading of some European writers are scattered throughout Thoreau scholarship, but there are few specific studies that claim either an influence or an affinity. For Rousseau, see M. J. Temmer and L. Gray Lambert; for Voltaire, see Edith Peairs; and for "Thoreau's Notes from Dubuat's *Principles*," Cameron. On Italian literature, see J. Chesley Mathews for Dante and John C. Broderick for Pellico (*BPLQ*, 1955). On Scandinavian literature, see Adolph B. Benson, and on Swedenborg, see Brian R. Harding. For German literature, see Stanley M. Vogel, *German Literary Influences on the American Transcendentalists*, and Paul Elmer More, "Thoreau's Journal."

Thoreau's reading in Greek and Latin classics runs deep in his writings, because he found myth provided archetypal truths relevant to his own experiences. Cameron (*ATQ*, 1977) describes Thoreau's reading of the classics at Concord Academy and reproduces in facsimile some of the texts he used there. Ethel Seybold, in *Thoreau: The Quest and the Classics*, argues that the classics were central to his Transcendentalist search for reality; she lists the editions he used and compiles quotations from and references to the classics found in his writings. Kevin P. Van Anglen corrects Seybold's identification of "The Sources for Thoreau's Greek Translations" in order to determine the quality of those translations, and he finds them more literal and accurate than previously supposed. Anthony John Harding discusses Thoreau's interest in Homer and the Greek language. Thoreau's use of myth (along with Whitman's, Hawthorne's, and Melville's) is placed in a helpful context and admirably clarified by Robert D. Richardson, Jr., *Myth and Literature in the American Renaissance*, which builds on some of Sherman Paul's insights in *The Shores of America*. Richardson explains that "What Thoreau found most impressive in myth was the *process* by which myth universalizes and generalizes personal or individual experience, giving it general significance and narrative shape. Thoreau learned from myth how to mythicize his own perceptions and experiences." Thoreau's use of pastoral traditions is discussed by John Seelye (*TriQ*, 1972) and Gordon E. Slethhaug. Plato's shadow is discerned in *Walden* by Joseph R. Millichap, who finds patterns of imagery suggestive of the allegory of the cave.

Thoreau's use of, interest in, and affinity with Oriental literature has attracted considerable attention. For general background information on the effects of Asian religious thought on Thoreau and his contemporaries, see Carl T. Jackson, *The Oriental Religions and American Thought*. Arthur Christy's chapter on Thoreau in *The Orient in American Transcendentalism* was the first significant study of his interest in Eastern literature and philosophy. For comments on and additions to Christy's work, see Sreekrishna Sarma and Stephen D. Strachner. William Bysshe Stein, "A Bibliography of Hindu and Buddhist Literature Available to Thoreau through 1854," is preliminary to source study work. For the volumes Thoreau was actually given by Thomas Cholmondeley, see Mohan Lal Sharma. Miriam A. Jeswine, "Henry David Thoreau: Apprentice to the Hindu Sages," is the longest study of its kind. Parallels between Thoreau's writing and Eastern literature and thought are discussed in Karmala Bhata, *The Mysticism of Thoreau and Its Affinity with Indian Thought*; David G. Hoch, "Annals and Perennials"; David T. Y. Chen, "Thoreau and Taoism"; Roger C. Mueller, "Thoreau's Selections from *Chinese Four Books* for the *Dial*"; and Kichung Kim, "On Chuang Tzu and Thoreau." Specific studies of *A Week* include Stein, "Thoreau's First Book" and "Thoreau's *A Week* and Om Cosmography"; and Ellen Raghavan and Barry Wood on the Hindu quotations in the book. For *Walden*, see Lyman V. Cady on quotations from the Confucian books; Stein on the *Bhagavad Gita* and on Yogic elements (*LE&W*, 1969; *CL*, 1970; *TSLL*, 1971); and additional discussions of Yoga by Frank MacShane, David C. Hoch, and Michael Gates.

IDEAS

GENERAL STUDIES

Most studies of Thoreau's ideas focus on specific topics, such as his attitudes toward nature, science, religion, society, economics, education, government, and reform. There are, however, several broader approaches that provide useful overviews. Joseph Wood Krutch, *Henry David Thoreau*, brings together the naturalist, the individualist, and the Transcendentalist by describing and explaining Thoreau's lifelong attempt to "simplify." Sherman Paul further articulates Thoreau's attempts to live deliberately in *The Shores of America*, the most detailed critical study of his ideas. It is remarkable that in the twenty-five years since publication of Paul's book no critic has attempted a study as comprehensive. Paul's chronological treatment of Thoreau's life covers his minor works as well as the major ones (though there is little on the political essays) and charts his philosophical and artistic development in order to determine "what it meant to live a transcendental life." Paul's purpose is not to recount Thoreau's life but to write "a spiritual biography or a biography of vocation." There is, to date, no fuller portrait of Thoreau's inner life and literary art. For a broad yet detailed understanding of "the direction transcendental ideas took in Thoreau's life," Paul's book is indispensable.

Several critics, including Paul, Mark Van Doren, and Perry Miller (*Consciousness in Concord*), have argued that Thoreau lost his Transcendentalist faith in the 1850s, but J. Lyndon Shanley, "Thoreau: Years of Decay and Disappointment?," follows Henry Seidel Canby and Joseph Wood Krutch in asserting that Thoreau was essentially happy and satisfied with his life to the end. Using different kinds of evidence, however, and working from a psychological perspective, Richard Lebeaux (see the Biography section above) seems to have opened up the question yet again.

The best recent overview is Edward Wagenknecht, *Henry David Thoreau: What Manner of Man?*, "a study of Thoreau's character and personality" organized primarily around his ideas. Wagenknecht manages to discuss a wide range of topics and evaluate a considerable amount of recent scholarship without being reductive; hence, this survey is useful for beginning students as well as those familiar with Thoreau. Two other general studies are far inferior to Wagenknecht's work: James G. Murray, *Henry David Thoreau*, is mostly a paraphrase of Thoreau's thought, and Leon Edel, *Henry D. Thoreau*, is a pamphlet too many undergraduates use as evidence that Thoreau was little more than a nasty grump. To see how simple it is to distort Thoreau's ideas by quoting him selectively, read Wade Thompson's reply to Louis B. Salomon (*CE*, 1956); Thompson's main point is that Thoreau, on a "literal residual level, is virtually amorphous."

NATURE

Thoreau's responses to nature were both poetic and scientific. Critics have debated whether he sustained a lifelong Transcendentalist view or whether he stumbled over a mass of dead facts that yielded no spiritual meaning to him. Reginald L. Cook, *Passage to* Walden, notes Thoreau's interest in scientific data and his attempts "to penetrate the essential quality and evoke the richness of his correspondence with nature." Later studies tend to see more ambivalence and often argue that Thoreau's chilling experience on Mount Ktaadn made him take a different view of nature: see John G. Blair, Lewis Leary (*SLitI*, 1974), and John Jacques. Jonathan Fairbanks supplies a good summary of this controversy and the views of earlier critics in "Thoreau: Speaker for Wildness." More recently, Ronald Hoag has argued that Thoreau's contact with Ktaadn finally confirmed rather than challenged his Transcendentalist faith. William Howarth provides a convenient collection, with commentary, of Thoreau's accounts of his various climbs in *Thoreau in the Mountains*. James McIntosh, *Thoreau as Romantic Naturalist*, compares Thoreau with Wordsworth and Goethe and calls "attention to his divided attitudes toward nature." Though Thoreau "wants to be involved in nature," he also "feels that he is apart from it, either because he values the distinctiveness of his human state, or because he distrusts the nature he confronts, or both." According to McIntosh, Thoreau did not abandon one view of nature for another but entertained both at once. Like McIntosh, Frederick Garber, in *Thoreau's Redemptive Imagination*, explores analogies between Thoreau and Anglo-European Romantics, but his main purpose is to "illuminate the ways in which the order of his mind tried continually to adjust itself, but to retain its essential duties, as the world changed for him." Garber describes how Thoreau attempted to use his imagination to transform nature into consciousness and "to make a place for the self in American nature." Also useful on Thoreau's imaginative response to nature is Joel Porte (*NEQ*, 1968), who discusses Emerson as well. Several relevant dissertations include analyses and bibliographic information that provide helpful background: William P. Michaels, "The Good and the Wild"; Robert Dupree, "From Analogy to Metaphor to Wordplay"; Mary G. Bernath, "Substance and Process in Thoreau's Universe"; Richard J. Schneider, "The Balanced Vision"; and Robert K. Thomas, "The Tree and the Stone."

Thoreau's abilities as a naturalist are challenged by John Burroughs, *The Last Harvest*; Francis H. Allen, *Thoreau's Bird-Lore*; W. L. McAtee; and Fanny Hardy Eckstorm. But these challenges have not gone unanswered: see Alec Lucas; R. H. Welker, *Birds and Men*; and Mary P. Sherwood on "Fanny Eckstorm's Bias." There are fewer questions about his accuracy as a surveyor, which placed him squarely in nature but was a curious profession for one who insisted on the importance of seeing the landscape rather than owning it. Marcia Moss has compiled *A Catalog of Thoreau's Surveys in the Concord Free Public Library*, which includes an informative introduction and reproduces selected surveys. For other discussions, see those by Harry Chase and Albert McLean, who connect Thoreau's surveying to revisions in *Walden*.

Thoreau is presented as a pioneer ecologist and conservationist by Philip Whitford and Kathryn Whitford and by William J. Wolf, *Thoreau: Mystic, Prophet, Ecologist*. Cecelia Tichi supplies valuable contexts in *New World, New Earth*, as does Roderick Nash in *Wilderness and the American Mind*. For Thoreau's "Transcendentalist View of the West," see Lawrence Willson; also relevant are portions of Edwin Fussell, *Frontier*, and Richard Slotkin, *Regeneration through Violence*. Gay Wilson Allen compares Thoreau, Emerson, and Whitman on the frontier in *Toward a New Literary History*, ed. Louis J. Budd et al., and Robert C. Deamer connects Thoreau's West with England in *The Westering Experience in American Literature*.

SCIENCE

Related to Thoreau's ecological concerns is the larger question of his attitude toward science and his work in natural history. Walter Harding (*VQR*, 1981) summarizes both, keeping in mind the state of science in Thoreau's time as he discusses Thoreau's inaccuracies, his Transcendentalist attitudes, his use of details, his record keeping, and his contributions to meteorology, documentation of species, plant succession, limnology, phenology, and ecology. For more detail, see Joseph Wade for Thoreau's entomology, Edward S. Deevey, Jr., for science at Walden Pond, Raymond Adams for a general overview of "Thoreau's Science," Kathryn Whitford for "Succession of Forest Trees," Leo Stoller for phenology, Lawrence Willson on "Thoreau and New England's Weather," Nina Baym for Thoreau's "anti-scientific bias," Donald G. Quick for limnology, and Arthur G. Volkman and Richard J. Schneider (*ESQ*, 1975) for physics. For a connection with Transcendentalism that develops further Schneider's discussion of Thoreau's knowledge of physics, see Valerie S. Neal, "Transcendental Optics."

Thoreau is related to other early naturalists—such as Louis Agassiz, John James Audubon, William Bartrum, and Charles Darwin—by Kichung Kim, "Thoreau's Involvement with Nature," a portion of which has been published (*ESQ*, 1972). John B. Wilson (*JHI*, 1965) provides some background on Transcendentalist responses to evolutionary theories, and comparisons between Darwin and Thoreau are made by Loren Eiseley (*The Unexpected Universe*) and Herbert Uhlig.

RELIGION

Thoreau was baptized by a Unitarian minister and buried from a Unitarian church, but that was the extent of his involvement with that church or any other. Although he signed off from all organized religions, he did have a religious attitude toward life and because of his eclecticism, there have been many discussions relating him to a variety of religious beliefs. Christian and oriental influences are cited in the Sources section above. The final chapter of Edward Wagenknecht, *Henry David Thoreau: What Manner of Man?*, offers a succinct overview of Thoreau's religious attitudes. His rejection of institutionalized Christianity is discussed by Robert Treat and Betty Treat; see also Joel Porte (*TSB*, 1978) and C. A. Rogers, "God, Nature and Personhood." See Lawrence Wilson on "Thoreau and Roman Catholicism" and Theron E. Coffin on "Henry D. Thoreau—Quaker?" Raymond Adams finds evidence that Thoreau believed in immortality (*SP*, 1929), but Mary Elkins Moller (*ESQ*, 1977) argues that he entertained ambivalent ideas about death.

Thoreau has been placed in various traditions of mysticism, depending upon the critic's particular conception of what constitutes a mystic. For an extensive study of Christian, Hindu, and Buddhist mysticism in Thoreau's writings, see Charles C. Kopp, "The Mysticism of Henry David Thoreau." William J. Wolf, *Thoreau: Mystic, Prophet, Ecologist*, attempts to show how Thoreau's mysticism is relevant to modern readers. Michael Kelley describes three stages in Thoreau's mysticism in the most detailed published study on the topic.

SOCIAL AND POLITICAL REFORMS

An oblique but interesting way to approach the social and political issues that Thoreau addressed is to explore first how he responded to the people immediately around him. There are several specialized studies that examine Thoreau's attitudes toward friendship, love, and sex. Mary Elkins Moller's purpose in *Thoreau and the Human Community* is "to explore and analyze those passages in Thoreau's writings which reveal his varying attitudes toward other persons and toward Humanity, which reveal his need for communication and intimate relationships—for some means of reaching beyond the Self—and his varying degrees of success and failure." In his relationships with the Emersons, Ellery Channing, H. G. O. Blake, Bronson Alcott, and others, Moller finds Thoreau ambivalent but not the brooding stoic and misanthropic nature-lover described by Perry Miller (*Consciousness in Concord*). Robert D. Richardson, Jr., also softens the image of Thoreau as "A Perfect Piece of Stoicism" by discussing stoicism not as a personality stereotype but as a body of ideas; see also Peter Buitenhuis's essay in *The Stoic Strain in American Literature*, ed. Duane J. MacMillan. Useful in understanding the emotions that inform Thoreau's social views are Joel Porte, "Thoreau on Love," and James Armstrong, "Thoreau as Philosopher of Love." Jonathan Katz claims Thoreau for his *Gay American History*.

Thoreau's distance from society was not measured in miles but in sensibilities. Winfield E. Nagley finds an Oriental flavor in "Thoreau on Attachment, Detachment, and Non-Attachment." See also Joel Porte, "Henry Thoreau: Society and Solitude." For a comparison with Emerson, see Wilson Carey McWilliams, *The Idea of Fraternity in America*. A witty but unsympathetic assessment of Thoreau's ideas about solitude is offered by Leon Edel (*ASch*, 1975), who elicits rejoinders two issues later. Leonard Neufeldt emphasizes Thoreau's private identity in "The Wild Apple Tree," in contrast to Gerald J. Galgan, who describes a growing social orientation in "The Self and Society in the Thought of Henry David Thoreau."

To sustain his individualism Thoreau had to create his own self-reliant economy, a subject for which there is no paucity of studies. "Economic Protest in Thoreau's Journal" is surveyed by Francis B. Dedmond. Leo Stoller argues in *After* Walden that Thoreau eventually accommodated himself to social, economic, and political realities by becoming more aware of community needs and less insistent on absolute independence, although he never went so far as to participate in any institutionalized reform movements. Robin Linstromberg and James Ballowe compare Thoreau's earlier views of economic reform with J. A. Etzler's *The Paradise within the Reach of All Men*, which Thoreau reviewed in 1843. In "The Idea and Significance of 'Economy' before *Walden*," Thomas Werge describes the religious significances of that term, and Judith Saunders explains how Thoreau uses the language of commerce for his own ends, as does M. Claire Kolbenschlag. Comparisons with Benjamin Franklin are made by Reginald Cook (*TJQ*, 1976), Charles Brashers (see accompanying comments by Gerald J. Butler), and Jesse Bier, who also discusses Max Weber. Elsa Nettels describes principles of economy that suggest similarities with Henry James. Herbert

F. Smith links Thomas Robert Malthus, David Ricardo, and Adam Smith to the first chapter of *Walden*; Richard H. Dillman (*ESQ*, 1979) sees Jean-Baptiste Say's economic philosophy reflected in Thoreau's; and John P. Diggins compares Karl Marx with Thoreau. For a study that emphasizes the daily integrity of Thoreau's economies at Walden, both mental and physical, see Harold Hellenbrand.

Walden Pond was not only an experiment in economic living but also a pastoral alternative to an increasingly mechanized society. Leo Marx, *The Machine in the Garden*, argues that Thoreau ultimately locates his pastoral ideal "in literature, which is to say, in his own consciousness, in his craft, in *Walden*," rather than in history, where it is impossible to sustain. John Seelye, "Some Green Thoughts on a Green Theme," goes well beyond Marx to explore the literary antecedents and political significance of Thoreau's pastoralism. James Tillman clearly describes "The Transcendental Georgic in *Walden*." Thoreau's response to the railroad is linked to Emerson's and Hawthorne's by G. Ferris Cronkhite, and his treatment of telegraphy is described by Lewis H. Miller, Jr. Thoreau's attitudes toward technology are compared with the Southern Agrarians by Joseph L. Basile (*SoR*, 1976) and with Marshall McLuhan by Sam B. Girgus. Also see Basile on "Technology and the Artist in *A Week*" and "Man and Machine in Thoreau." Thoreau's views on progress are compared with those of a Concord contemporary, Dr. Edward Jarvis, by Robert A. Gross, who shows that their differing perspectives "constitute a provocative dialog on progress that anticipates modern approaches to the history of industrialization in America."

Thoreau's interest in the pastoral included a fascination with the wilds, so it was inevitable that he would look to the Indian as a source of values for a revitalized life. Robert Sayre, *Thoreau and the American Indians*, points out that Thoreau "did not study Indians, in all their variety and social relationships; he studied 'the Indian,' the ideal solitary figure that was the white American's symbol of the wilderness and history," a product of romantic notions of "savagism." Thoreau, according to Sayre, rid himself of much of this "savagist prejudice" by reading about Indians and acquiring firsthand knowledge of them. Sayre argues less convincingly that Thoreau's use of Indian life in *A Week* and *Walden* were important unifying principles for each. Another detailed study is Joan S. Gimlin, "Henry Thoreau and the American Indian." Focusing on Joe Polis, Philip F. Gura ("Thoreau's Maine Woods Indians") explains how Thoreau's attempts to understand what the Indians could teach him about nature were related to Emerson's efforts to find a representative genius. For "Thoreau's Indians and His Developing Art of Characterization" in *The Maine Woods*, see Donald M. Murray; for "Thoreau's Autumnal Indians," see Lauriat Lane, Jr. Leslie A. Fiedler, *The Return of the Vanishing American*, includes comments on *A Week*. For Thoreau's reading about Indians, see the Sources section above.

Thoreau's progressive views on education are discussed by Louis B. Salomon (*AQ*, 1962), Kevin Ryan, and Abraham Blinderman (*American Writers on Education before 1865*). His teaching practices are described by Walter Harding (*EdF*, 1964). The most extensive survey is Anton M. Huffert, "Thoreau as a Teacher, Lecturer, and Educational Thinker." For his work with the Concord Lyceum, see Harding, "Thoreau on

the Lecture Platform." "A Checklist of Thoreau's Lectures" has been compiled by
Harding, and the Concord Lyceum's surviving records are reprinted in Kenneth Walter
Cameron, *Massachusetts Lyceum during the American Renaissance*.

Among the discussions of Thoreau's concept of the proper role of government,
William A. Herr's is the most succinct. Eunice M. Schuster's description of Thoreau's
anarchism has been qualified by John C. Broderick, who points out "Thoreau's Proposals for Legislation." The difficulty in labeling Thoreau an anarchist is considered
by Richard Drinnon. Taylor Stoehr, *Nay-Saying in Concord*, compares Thoreau, Emerson, and Alcott on slavery, war, and individual reform, arguing that they were more
aware of the social evils of their day than has been previously acknowledged, and
Leonard Neufeldt contrasts "Emerson, Thoreau, and Daniel Webster." Although there
is no book-length study of Thoreau's political views, there are several dissertations,
among them two written for political science degrees by Charles M. Evans and Glen
W. McKay.

Of the numerous attacks on Thoreau's political posture, two are particularly strong:
Heinz Eulau and Vincent Buranelli. Eulau sees Thoreau as "dangerous" because his
"whole political philosophy was based on the theoretical premise of individual conscience as the only true criterion of what is politically right and just." According to
Eulau, Thoreau's rejection of all compromise and adjustment made him essentially
"unpolitical" and not part of the Jeffersonian political tradition in which Vernon Louis
Parrington (*The Romantic Revolution in America 1800–1860*) placed him. Buranelli
also finds Thoreau "politically scarifying," self-righteous, and solipsistic "in subor-
dinating law to conscience" and "denigrating majority rule to institutional checks."
This objection to the primacy of individual conscience over law is at the heart of scores
of attacks on Thoreau's politics, but just as there are Creons to condemn Thoreau
so are there Antigones to defend him. This dialog is fully scripted in Michael Meyer,
Several More Lives to Live. There is also the kind of argument made in Stanley Edgar
Hyman's often reprinted essay that Thoreau's politics are important only for understanding him as a writer, not as a thinker. Lawrence Bowling, for example, reads
"Thoreau's Social Criticism as Poetry." Nevertheless, detailed studies of his political
attitudes continue to appear.

Thoreau's response to slavery, the most pressing issue of his time, is described
in Wendell Glick, "Thoreau and Radical Abolitionism." Glick refutes Nick Aaron
Ford's contention that Thoreau was always sympathetic to the abolitionists even though
he did not join them. Glick acknowledges Thoreau's hatred of slavery but argues that
his turning away from the power of Moral Law and supporting John Brown's violent
means to end slavery amounted to a rejection of abolitionist principles. Kerry Ahearn
and James Goodwin see no radical movement away from Transcendentalist principles
in Thoreau's support of Brown, a position argued in Harding, *The Days of Henry
Thoreau*. Truman Nelson (in *Thoreau in Our Season*, ed. John Hicks) disagrees and
asserts that Thoreau rejected passive resistance. Joseph DeFalco assesses Thoreau's acceptance of Brown's violence as a practical, realistic form of direct social action, but
C. Roland Wagner (in *Thoreau in Our Season*), using a psychoanalytic perspective,

finds that Thoreau's politics represented little more than "infantile wishes." For valuable details on Thoreau's relationship to Brown, see Gilman Ostrander, but compare Michael Meyer (*SAR*, 1980), who argues that Thoreau knew about Brown's role in the Pottawatomie massacre of 1856 and that Thoreau's selective Transcendentalist vision allowed him to ignore or disbelieve Brown's brutality. Meyer (*AL*, 1981) also contends that, after Brown's failure at Harper's Ferry, Thoreau briefly entertained the idea that black emigration could be the solution to the slavery issue, because he believed blacks were too vulnerable to white dominance and exploitation in America. For a richly detailed overview of Thoreau's mixed reactions toward another ethnic group, see George E. Ryan, "Shanties and Shiftlessness: The Immigrant Irish of Henry Thoreau." Specific political essays by Thoreau are covered in the section on his writings below.

WRITINGS

LITERARY EXPRESSION

Since F. O. Matthiessen's discussion of the organic symbolic structure of *Walden* (in *American Renaissance*), critics have closely examined and analyzed Thoreau's style, particularly his use of wit, humor, imagery, symbol, and myth. Many of Thoreau's own comments about writing and his method of composition are collected by Laurence Stapleton in *H. D. Thoreau: A Writer's Journal* (1960) and Franklin W. Hamilton in *Thoreau on the Art of Writing* (1967). William Howarth, *The Book of Concord: Thoreau's Life as a Writer*, examines "How he wrote, what he thought about writing, and how the two affected each other." Howarth particularly stresses Thoreau's journal as central to an understanding of his achievements as a literary artist.

As Wendell Glick (*ESQ*, 1973) points out, Thoreau took seriously his vocation as a writer, believing his task was to transform experience into literary art so that life was inseparable from art. But he did not articulate a consistent theory of writing, and he wrote little literary criticism. Consequently, there are few studies of his aesthetics or criticism beyond scattered comments within discussions of individual works. The few specific studies that attempt to treat the subject in depth are all unpublished: see Raymond Adams, "Henry Thoreau's Literary Theory and Criticism," George D. Craig, "Literary Criticism in the Works of Henry David Thoreau," and Robert J. DeMott, " 'The Eccentric Orbit.' " Charles R. Metzger offers a helpful if brief discussion of Thoreau's Transcendentalist aesthetics in *Thoreau and Whitman*; see also Andrew Schiller's discussion of "Thoreau and Whitman."

Thoreau's preference for organic forms—natural forms that grow from within outward—extended to architecture and music as well as life and literature. Theodore M. Brown argues that "Thoreau's Prophetic Architectural Program" anticipated the work of modern architects such as Frank Lloyd Wright and Louis Sullivan; see also William J. Griffin for Thoreau's response to Horatio Greenough. The Transcendentalist nature and function of music for Thoreau is carefully explained by Kenneth W. Rhoads, and Sherman Paul (*NEQ*, 1949) shows how sound serves as an agency of Transcendentalist correspondence in Thoreau's writings, an idea that is explored further by James V. Kavanaugh, "Music and American Transcendentalism." For Thoreau's favorite popular song, see Caroline Moseley.

Unlike Matthiessen and the many critics who followed the insights of his *American Renaissance*, early commentators tended to see Thoreau's "organic" writing as relatively formless. Fred W. Lorch, for example, argues that Thoreau suffered from the "formlessness inherent in romantic doctrine," and that "structural unity" was "a distinctly secondary interest" for him. Many later critics, however, have found unifying elements in his writing by closely analyzing his style. The most ambitious stylistic study is Sherman Paul, *The Shores of America*, which examines Thoreau's works chronologically and relates his Transcendentalist principles to his developing art. Herman L. Eisenlohr, "The Development of Thoreau's Prose," is a chronological exploration of Thoreau's use of organic principles in his writings. John C. Broderick discusses "The Movement of Thoreau's Prose" from "the mundane known to the transcendent knowable and back again." Joseph J. Liggera, "Thoreau's Heroic Language," describes Thoreau's efforts to create language commensurate to the spirituality he discovered in nature. Thoreau's "concrete vision" is stressed by Laurence Stapleton, *The Elected Circle*; Stapleton's emphasis is anticipated in a comparison of Thoreau's and Emerson's styles by Albert Gilman and Roger Brown (in *Transcendentalism and Its Legacy*, ed. Myron Simon and Thornton H. Parsons). Employing structural linguistics and word-class-distribution statistics, Donald Ross (*Lang&S*, 1973) finds that Thoreau's style is more "idiosyncratic" than Emerson's. Francis E. B. Evans, "The Genuine Word, the Unfolding Sentence," provides a study of Thoreau's vocabulary and syntax. "Americanisms in Thoreau's Journal" not already included in historical dictionaries are listed by Lee H. Pederson.

In addition to examining Thoreau's vocabulary and sentence structure, critics have listened carefully for the tone of his prose, an especially important approach to the writings given Thoreau's use of irony, satire, paradox, parody, understatement, and exaggeration. A good many readers have agreed with James Russell Lowell ("Thoreau's Letters") that "Thoreau had no humor," but that assessment misreads Thoreau's rhetorical strategies. James P. Brawner specifically refutes Lowell by discussing "Thoreau as Wit and Humorist." See also Harold N. Guthrie, "The Humor of Thoreau," and Charles F. Gruenert, "Henry David Thoreau's Humor in Theory and Practice." Many of the book-length studies on Thoreau comment on his humor; see particularly for Thoreau's wit, Charles R. Anderson, *The Magic Circle of* Walden. More focused approaches, primarily limited to *Walden*, follow. J. Golden Taylor, *Neighbor Thoreau's Critical Humor*, shows how humor saves his social criticism from being too didactic or sentimental, and M. Thomas Inge adds that humor also saves Thoreau from fanaticism and misanthropy. Ralph C. LaRosa writes on "David Henry Thoreau: His American Humor," and Edward L. Galligan characterizes the narrator of *Walden* as a comic hero whose strategies measure the "ludicrous disparities of life in Concord."

For "Thoreau's Mock-Heroics" in *Walden*, see Raymond Adams; for the absurd, see Harold F. Mosher, Jr.; for the witty positioning of several of its chapters, see Alan Holder; and for the satire in the "Brute Neighbors" chapter, see Robert R. Hodges.

David Skwire provides "A Checklist of Wordplays in *Walden*," but Joseph J. Moldenhauer, "The Rhetoric of *Walden*," includes a more comprehensive list along with proverbs and commonplaces. Published portions of Moldenhauer's dissertation appear as "Paradox in *Walden*," a particularly valuable essay on Thoreau's rhetorical strategies, and "The Rhetorical Function of Proverbs in *Walden*." Skwire's list is complemented and analyzed into linguistic categories by Donald Ross, Jr. (*ATQ*, 1971). More generally, the shifting tones in Thoreau's prose are examined by William Donald Payne, "Pressing the Seed," and Richard Dillman has put together an extensive and useful bibliography on rhetorical strategies in "Resources for the Study of Transcendental Rhetoric."

One of the major purposes of Thoreau's writing was to evoke the spiritual truths he found latent in nature, and there are numerous studies of the symbolic imagery he used to accomplish this. Charles Feidelson, Jr., *Symbolism and American Literature*, compares Thoreau with Emerson in the context of major writers contemporary to them. Melvin E. Lyon sees Walden Pond as the chief symbol in *Walden*. Among the many readings of the railroad cut passage, Michael Orth's is one of the most detailed; the most revealing analysis of its language is Philip F. Gura's in *The Wisdom of Words*; and John T. Irwin (*American Hieroglyphics*) bases his discussion on Thoreau's reference to Champollion in the "Spring" chapter. Several of the many interpretations of the hound, bay horse, and turtle dove passage are summarized in Walter Harding's *The Variorum Walden*. Thoreau's symbolic use of colors is charted by Richard Colyer and his symbolic views of the West are described by C. A. Tillinghast. For discussions of circle imagery in Thoreau's writings, see Richard Tuerk, *Central Still*, which further develops the insights in Joseph J. Moldenhauer, "Images of Circularity in Thoreau's Prose," J. J. Boies, "Circular Imagery in Thoreau's *Week*," and Charles R. Anderson, *The Magic Circle of Walden*. Water imagery is examined by Nina Baym (*SIR*, 1966) and Willard H. Bonner (*AL*, 1963). Bonner also presents an analysis of sailing images (*NEQ*, 1966), to which Edwin Stockton, Jr., replies. Other symbolic image studies include J. Golden Taylor on "Thoreau's Sour Grapes," Michael West on "Scatology and Eschatology," Theodore Haddin on fire, and Mary L. Kaiser on celestial bodies. Richard C. Cook's work adds up to an interesting quantitative analysis of images in *Walden*. Longer studies include Howard R. Houston's fine analysis of "Metaphors in *Walden*" and Gloria J. Stansberry's study of bird imagery. Other studies of symbolic imagery are Walter L. Shear, "Thoreau's Imagery and Symbolism," William Drake, "The Depth of *Walden*: Thoreau's Symbolism of the Divine in Nature," and Brian R. Harding, "Transcendental Symbolism in the Works of Emerson, Thoreau, and Whitman."

The purpose and technique of Thoreau's myth-making is richly explained in Sherman Paul, *The Shores of America*, and Robert D. Richardson, Jr., *Myth and Literature in the American Renaissance*. Richard Fleck reads "Thoreau as a Mythologist," and a structuralist perspective is provided by Louise C. Kerstesz, "A Study of Thoreau as Myth Theorist and Myth Maker."

Of all the studies dealing with images, symbols, myths, and the structural unity of Thoreau's writings, one of the most satisfying and tactful readings is offered by Lawrence Buell, *Literary Transcendentalism*. Buell approaches Thoreau's writing with an awareness of its "descriptive, peripatetic, and miscellaneous or hybrid character: part sketch, part information, part narrative, part wit, part philosophy." Buell urges readers not to impose too rigid a set of "literary architectonics" on Thoreau's writing because it "is to be more appreciated as process than as product, more for its irregular flow than for any patterns which can be abstracted from it, although the awareness of such patterns naturally enhances one's pleasure in the work." James McIntosh, *Thoreau as Romantic Naturalist*, largely agrees, pointing out that Thoreau's works are not "masterpieces of Byzantine ingenuity." For an earlier and briefer appreciation of Thoreau's "sauntering eye," a vision that favors putting down impressions in "random order," see Tony Tanner, *The Reign of Wonder*.

In contrast to most commentators, Richard Bridgman (*Dark Thoreau*) finds many opaque and obscure passages in the writing that undercut Thoreau's effectiveness as a writer. Bridgman argues that these passages are symptoms of Thoreau's fundamental morbidity, pessimism, and aggression, qualities often overlooked by readers who read Thoreau selectively in order to use him as a spokesman for individualism, a champion of nature, or a social critic. Though Bridgman consciously exaggerates the darker elements of Thoreau's writings, he raises important questions that may draw forth a more balanced study that connects Thoreau's prose style with his personality and ideas.

LITERARY WORKS

POETRY

Henry Wells provides "An Evaluation of Thoreau's Poetry," and Hyatt H. Waggoner places that poetry in the context of *American Poets from the Puritans to the Present*. The most extensive published study is Arthur Lewis Ford, Jr., "The Poetry of Henry David Thoreau." Donovan L. Welch provides "A Chronological Study of the Poetry of Henry David Thoreau," and Elizabeth Hall Witherell has produced a new edition of the poems that will be the basis of the Princeton Edition of Thoreau's poetry. Critics have been careful not to claim too much for Thoreau's poetry, but for two extremes, see Frederick P. Lenz III, who argues that Thoreau was a major American poet, and Richard C. Gurney, who regards the poetry as "The Worst of Thoreau." Lauriat Lane, Jr. (*ESQ*, 1970), explains why Thoreau stopped writing poetry, but Paul O. Williams describes "Thoreau's Growth as a Transcendental Poet"; Williams also explains "The Concept of Inspiration in Thoreau's Poetry." For "Correspondence in Thoreau's Nature Poetry," see Carl Dennis; for poetics, see Betsy F. Colquitt; for a metaphysical poetic tradition, see H. Grant Sampson; and for the function of the poetry in the prose works, see Raymond Gozzi (*ESQ*, 1964) and Robert O. Evans.

Thoreau's poetry (as well as his prose) in the *Dial* is discussed in Joel Myerson, *The New England Transcendentalists and the* Dial; Donald F. Warders, " 'The Progress of the Hour and the Day' "; and Charles R. Anderson, "Thoreau and the *Dial*."

INDIVIDUAL WORKS

The following review of scholarship includes separate studies of Thoreau's individual works that help shed light on ideas and techniques useful for understanding his Transcendentalism. Individual works for which no separate relevant studies exist are not listed.

Among the earliest of Thoreau's writings that suggest Transcendentalist influences is "The Service," for which Kenneth E. Harris surveys the scholarship. Thoreau's emblematic technique in "The Landlord" is discussed by Joseph DeFalco; see also Sherman Paul's analysis. For Thoreau's "walking" essays, see Lauriat Lane, Jr., on the four versions of the essay (*BNYPL*, 1965) and "A Walk to Wachusett" as a "transcendental allegory" contrasted with "A Winter Walk" (*TSB*, 1969). See also Richard Tuerk on "A Walk to Wachusett" and "Natural History of Massachusetts" as archetypal myths of withdrawal from society and return; James M. Marshall on heroic adventure in "A Winter Walk"; Frederick Garber on "Unity and Diversity in 'Walking' "; and David L. James on "Movement and Growth in 'Walking.' " Thoreau's alternative views of economic reform in "Paradise (to Be) Regained" are described by Robin Linstromberg and James Ballowe; and for its mythic quality, see Frederic I. Carpenter (*PMLA*, 1959). Wendell Glick includes important background information on Thoreau's relationship to the abolitionists in "Thoreau and the 'Herald of Freedom.' "

Some of the sources for "Civil Disobedience," also known as "Resistance to Civil Government," are suggested by Martin Doudna and Raymond Adams (*SP*, 1945), who also describes its printing history (*TSB*, 1949). Walter Harding (*AH*, 1975) points out that Thoreau's arrest was illegal, thereby qualifying the otherwise valuable background information by John C. Broderick on "Thoreau, Alcott and the Poll Tax." Wendell Glick writes on " 'Civil Disobedience': Thoreau's Attack upon Relativism." For rhetorical strategies, see Michael Erlich, and for narrative art, see Barry Wood (*PQ*, 1981). John Beaver discusses Thoreau's frequent use of negative constructions in the essay as compared with *Walden*. For an unfavorable view of the essay, see Alfred Kazin, "Thoreau and American Power," and for a reasoned empathetic view, see John A. Christie. Laraine Fergenson discusses "Thoreau, Daniel Berrigan, and the Problem of Transcendental Politics."

There are several useful tools for studying *A Week*: James Karabatsos, "Word-Index to *A Week*"; Ted Billy's checklist of wordplays; and William Brennan's index to quotations, keyed to the Princeton Edition. For "The Bibliographical History of

Thoreau's *A Week*," see Raymond Adams. Carl Hovde has described Thoreau's use of his journals in *A Week* and has also examined the literary materials Thoreau quotes. In his dissertation, Linck C. Johnson shows how Thoreau wrote *A Week* and presents a text of the first draft. See also Jonathan Bishop on "The Experience of the Sacred in Thoreau's *Week*"; Paul David Johnson on the theme of self-liberation; Jamie Hutchinson on Thoreau's historical vision; Eric Sundquist (*Home as Found*) on Thoreau's difficulty in finding the Edenic in nature; John C. Rowe on the trip as "a metaphor for poetic composition"; and Steven Fink on the "multiplicity of voices" Thoreau used to articulate his Transcendentalist vision. A number of dissertations reflect the increased interest in finding patterns in *A Week*; see, for example, Gail Baker on *A Week*'s organic unity, Rosemary Whitaker on the book as an experiment in the communication of the transcendental experience, and Mary Suzanne Carroll on symbolic patterns in *A Week*. For a study of the book as travel literature, see Robert Sattelmeyer, Jr., "Away from Concord." For a Marxist reading, see Edwin Fussell (*RLV*, 1976).

Comparatively little has been written about "An Excursion to Canada." Edmund Berry criticizes Thoreau's narrow views of the Canadians, a topic further developed by Lawrence Willson (*RUQ*, 1959). Barrie Davies relates this essay to Thoreau's other writings and finds similarities between them; Sidney Poger (*ATQ*, 1972) discusses the satire in the narrative; and Stephen Adams argues that the cold Thoreau caught on the trip has a symbolic meaning.

"Slavery in Massachusetts" has also attracted little critical attention. The only separate article-length discussion of the essay is by Robert C. Albrecht (*ESQ*, 1973), who provides historical background and sees Thoreau arguing that hope should be placed in the permanent values of nature rather than in the corrupt institutions of men. Richard Tuerk discusses "Man and Nature in 'Slavery in Massachusetts.' "

Readers interested in critical studies of *Walden* should be familiar with Annette M. Woodlief's annotated checklist from 1854 through 1973, a selected listing of 334 items. Additional listings are available in Walter Harding and Michael Meyer, *The New Thoreau Handbook*. Studies of humor, symbolic imagery, and myth in *Walden* are cited in the previous section, and collections of critical essays on it are listed in the Criticism section. J. Lyndon Shanley, *The Making of* Walden, and Ronald Clapper, "The Development of *Walden*," are the most extensive studies of the various drafts of *Walden*; see also Thomas Woodson, "The Two Beginnings of *Walden*." A useful tool is J. S. Sherwin and R. C. Reynolds, *A Word Index to* Walden; also helpful are the annotations in Harding's *The Variorum Walden* and Philip Van Doren Stern's *The Annotated Walden*. The most sustained reading of the work is by Charles R. Anderson, *The Magic Circle of* Walden, who reads it "as if it were a poem." Anderson's method is to comb Thoreau's journals "for everything relevant" to his close examination of the book. Stanley Cavell, *The Senses of* Walden, speculates that *Walden* "is itself about a book, about its own writing and reading." This compact philosophical approach to the language of *Walden* is densely textured, but there are interesting insights along the way. The 1972 version, with two new chapters on Emerson, has been republished as *The Senses of* Walden: *An Expanded Edition.*

Among the studies published since Woodlief's checklist are two that relate Thoreau to other writers of autobiography: Mutlu K. Blasing, *The Art of Life*, and G. Thomas Couser, *American Autobiography*. The structure of *Walden* is found to be an "organized refutation" of Emerson's "American Scholar" by Charles Child Walcutt. Walcutt's fresh interpretation should be read in conjunction with Edward J. Rose, who sees Thoreau as "Emerson's American Scholar Incarnate." "*Walden*'s False Bottoms" are the subject of Walter B. Michaels, who argues that Thoreau wrote into the book a "principle of uncertainty" that makes it impossible to find a single central meaning. Joseph Allen Boone traces images of delving and diving for truth in *Walden* and sees "a pattern of kinetic energy suggestive of penetrating or breaking through surfaces in order to near the greater reality beneath." Both Michaels and Boone emphasize the process of finding meaning in *Walden* rather than any particular meaning. For three articles devoted to specific chapters, see Jim Springer Borck and Herbert B. Rothschild, Jr., on "The Pond in Winter" as a summation of *Walden*; Judy Schaaf Anhorn on the language of "The Beanfield"; and Neill R. Joy on "Two Possible Analogies for 'The Ponds' in *Walden*: Jonathan Carver and Wordsworth." Eugene Green treats *Walden* as "local history" and compares it with Lemuel Shattuck's *A History of the Town of Concord* and Emerson's *Historical Discourse*. *Walden* is related to the economic changes that transformed Concord society in the mid-nineteenth century by Robert Gross (*JAH*, 1982) and Philip Yannella.

Thoreau's experiences on Ktaadn in *The Maine Woods* are cited in studies in the Nature section above. J. Parker Huber retraces Thoreau's Maine woods travels in *The Wildest Country: A Guide to Thoreau's Maine*. For the composition of the "Ktaadn" portion of *The Maine Woods*, see Robert Cosebey and Robert C. Sattelmeyer, "Away from Concord," who discusses the composition of each of the book's three sections. Thoreau's response to Indians is discussed in the Ideas section above. For an appreciation, see Vesta M. Parsons. Fanny Hardy Eckstorm's essay is still useful.

"Thoreau's Use of Sources in *Cape Cod*" is discussed by Suzanne S. Lewis, who also provides a useful listing of sources for allusions and quotations in "Thoreau and His Sources." Comments on the humor, descriptions, and character sketches in the book are made by Martin L. Pops. John J. McAleer analyzes "Thoreau's Epic *Cape Cod*." Richard J. Schneider carefully examines Thoreau's view of hostile nature in the book; see also Mario D'Avanzo ("Fortitude and Nature in Thoreau's *Cape Cod*"). Lauriat Lane, Jr., writes on "*Cape Cod*—Thoreau's Sandy Pastoral"; Mitchell R. Breitwiesser explores the meanings of the shipwrecks Thoreau encounters; and G. Thomas Couser describes "Thoreau's Cape Cod Pilgrimage" for "self-fulfillment."

Analyses of Thoreau's later prose have centered primarily on the John Brown essays. Wendell Glick discusses these in "Thoreau and Radical Abolitionism," which is cited along with other secondary works in the Social and Political Reforms section above. Robert C. Albrecht (*AL*, 1961) describes the changes Thoreau made when he used his journal entries to prepare "A Plea for Captain John Brown." Thomas Woodson (*PMLA*, 1970) compares Thoreau's characterization of Brown with Melville's and finds

Thoreau's art more limited and less satisfactory. According to Lauriat Lane, Jr. (*Ariel*, 1975), Thoreau described Brown's death in "ritual autumnal terms" and saw him as "a dying god bringing renewal to his world." For discussion of other later essays, see Bernard Rosenthal (*ESQ*, 1969) on "Autumnal Tints," as well as Willard H. Bonner, "The Harvest of Thought in Thoreau's 'Autumnal Tints' "; Kevin P. Van Anglen on the Adamic myth in "Wild Apples"; R. N. Stromberg's comparison of "Life without Principle" with the *Communist Manifesto*; Kenneth Walter Cameron on "Thoreau's Lecture on 'Misspent Lives' and the Evolution of 'Life without Principle' "; and William L. Howarth on "Moonlight" as a possible course of lectures that Thoreau was planning in 1854. Thoreau's journals are related to his use of Concord in his writings by William Howarth (*The Book of Concord*), who argues that in the pages of his journals Thoreau had come to see Concord "as a metaphor for the world."

INFLUENCE

Michael Meyer's study of Thoreau's political reputation in America and Eugene F. Timpe's collection of bibliographic essays on Thoreau abroad are cited in the Bibliography section above. Also useful is the final chapter in Walter Harding and Meyer, *The New Thoreau Handbook*, which is accompanied by a bibliographic essay. See also Meyer on "The 1970s: The Question of Thoreau's Declining Reputation." For Thoreau's reputation in the nineteenth century, see *The Making of Thoreau's Modern Reputation*, ed. Fritz Oehlschlaeger and George Hendrick, which includes a lengthy and valuable introduction that provides a rich context for understanding the negative assessments of Thoreau by such writers as Robert Louis Stevenson and James Russell Lowell.

"The Influence of Thoreau on the American Nature Essay" is described by Paul O. Williams. See also Philip Marshall Hicks, *The Development of the Natural History Essay in American Literature*; Reginald Cook, *Passage to* Walden; and James M. Aton, " 'Sons and Daughters of Thoreau,' " which examines Thoreau's influence on Edward Abbey, Annie Dillard, and Peter Matthessen. Thoreau's affinities with luminist landscape painting of the nineteenth century are fruitfully explored by Barbara Novak, *Nature and Culture*, John Conron, and Barton Levi St. Armand (*CRevAS*, 1980).

Separate studies that describe Thoreau's influence on and affinities with subsequent writers include Brad Hayden on Richard Brautigan; Walter Gierasch on Willa Cather; Rufus Mathewson, Jr., on Anton Chekhov; Thomas Ford and Rhoda Nathan on Emily Dickinson; Owen W. Gilman, Jr., on John Dos Passos; Shyamal Bagchee on T. S. Eliot; Mario L. D'Avanzo, Lyle Domina, Lauriat Lane, Jr. ("Mountain Gloom and Yankee Poetry"), Thornton H. Parsons, and Michael West ("Versifying Thoreau") on Robert Frost; George Hendrick on Mahatma Gandhi; Richard Predmore on Hawthorne; Donald M. Murray on Ernest Hemingway; George E. Carter on Martin Luther King, Jr.; Barry A. Marks on Norman Mailer; William S. Thomas on José Martí; Michael Delizia on Vladimir Nabokov; Roger C. Mueller (*TJQ*, 1977) on Robert M.

Pirsig; Kenneth T. Reed on Harriet Beecher Stowe; Richard Predmore on Miguel de Unamuno; and Wendell Glick, Sidney Poger, and J. Lyndon Shanley on William Butler Yeats. Other comments on Thoreau by his contemporaries will be found in the individual author chapters of this book.

JONES VERY

David Robinson

BIBLIOGRAPHIES

The most complete listing of writings by and about Very is in William Irving Bartlett, *Jones Very*. Bartlett's bibliography, which includes Very's poems published in *Harvardiana*, the *Salem Observer*, and the *Western Messenger*, is especially important because all the editions of Very's poetry are unreliable or incomplete. Bartlett also provides a list of major anthologies containing Very's poetry, a list of the locations of Very's manuscripts, and a listing of secondary material through 1942. Edwin Gittleman's "Selected Bibliography" in *Jones Very* both updates and expands Bartlett's listing of secondary criticism. The first printings of Very's works have been compiled by Joel Myerson (*FPAA*, vol. 3). "Jones Very: An Essay in Bibliography" by David Robinson is revised and expanded in this chapter, which does not discuss a number of articles on Very listed in *AAL*.

MANUSCRIPTS

William Irving Bartlett and Edwin Gittleman include major unpublished manuscripts in their bibliographies, and a brief listing of material at the Houghton Library of Harvard University is in Ernest Kurtz and William R. Hutchison, "Boston Area Resources for the Study of American Religious History." A nearly complete listing of the locations of Very manuscripts can be found in *ALM*. Major repositories of Very material are the Houghton Library for poems and 105 unpublished sermons, the Harris Collection of American Poetry at Brown University and the Essex Institute for other poems, and the Wellesley College Library for a series of prose "epistles" (letters to Ralph Waldo Emerson) and materials relating to Very. Not listed in *ALM* are three Very letters at the Andover-Harvard Theological Library.

EDITIONS

Very's somewhat extravagant claim that the Holy Spirit dictated his verse, and that it therefore should not be altered, has not been respected by his editors. Emerson made a number of editorial revisions in his edition of Very's *Essays and Poems* (1839). Although Very resented the changes, we are obliged to admit that without Emerson's continued interest, Very's poetry would probably not have been published in one volume in his lifetime, and perhaps not afterward. Emerson's volume was a selection of sixty-five poems preceded by three essays, "Epic Poetry," "Shakespeare," and "Hamlet." For a detailed history of the genesis, editing, and publication of the volume, see Edwin Gittleman, *Jones Very*.

After his death in 1880, two other collections of Very's poetry were published. *Poems by Jones Very with an Introductory Memoir by William P. Andrews* (1883) added seventy-three new poems to the ones published by Emerson, with the general intention of emphasizing Very's "remarkable religious experience." Andrews' edition was followed shortly by *Poems and Essays by Jones Very: Complete and Revised Edition*, ed. James Freeman Clarke (1886), which, though not complete as it purports to be, is the "standard" and most thorough edition of Very's verse. Clarke also reprints the three essays included in Emerson's edition. Unfortunately, both Andrews and Clarke persisted in the editorial liberties taken by Emerson—sometimes returning to manuscripts or earlier printed editions, sometimes perpetuating previous changes, and sometimes making editorial changes of their own. A brief but pointed analysis of the editorial problems of these three editions has been published by Byrne R. S. Fone.

The incompleteness of Clarke's edition is remedied somewhat by William Irving Bartlett's biography of Very, which prints the poems found in the two major collections of Very manuscripts. These include eleven poems and hymns that Bartlett erroneously lists as having been preserved at Andover Theological Seminary, Cambridge, Massachusetts; they were actually given to the Harvard Divinity School in Cambridge and placed in the Andover-Harvard Theological Library, and they have since been transferred to the Houghton Library. Bartlett also reproduces poems now located at Brown University, sixteen poems published in the *Salem Observer* but not included in any edition of Very's works, twenty poems published in the *Western Messenger* but not collected, one uncollected poem from the *Dial*, and another from the *National Anti-Slavery Standard*. To these, one should add "A College Poem by Jones Very" (*ESQ*, 1956), first published by Kenneth Walter Cameron. Four poems from Very's college days, which were among the papers of Charles Stearns Wheeler, are in David Robinson, "Four Early Poems of Jones Very." The manuscript "Spiritual Navigation," which includes an untitled prose prayer, is in the Yale University Library. The only published translation of Very's poetry is Albert Ritter's 1903 German translation of ninety-two poems.

Two recent editions of Very's poetry have proved useful in some respects, but they are either incomplete or unreliable. The profusion of editions, not to mention anthology selections, complicates the task of choosing the proper text for reading and citing Very's poetry. *Poems by Jones Very: James Freeman Clarke's Enlarged Collection of 1886 Re-edited with a Thematic and Topical Index* (1965) reprints Clarke's collection of poems (with the additions published earlier in *ESQ*), omitting the essays and Clarke's "Biographical Notice of Jones Very." This edition carries over Clarke's errors and his arbitrary and somewhat confusing organization. Cameron's index is a welcome tool, however, and the volume serves the important function of making the 1886 edition more readily available to scholars and libraries. *Jones Very: Selected Poems*, ed. Nathan Lyons (1966), is the most recent and certainly the most carefully edited collection of Very's poetry, relying upon "the last manuscript version" for a text when possible. Lyons selects seventy-five poems grouped under three headings to illustrate the thesis of his introductory essay: that Very is best understood as part of the quietist tradition of Christianity. Lyons' notes to the poems, giving locations of manuscripts and dates of publication, are thorough and useful. The limitation of the edition, however, is that it is a selection. Even though Lyons' introductory essay is a valuable addition to Very criticism, many poems of lasting value are omitted from the collection.

Two modern anthologies deserve special note for their large and representative selection of Very's poems. Perry Miller's *The Transcendentalists* includes eighteen Very poems with selections from the three essays included in Emerson's and Clarke's editions. *American Poetry*, ed. Gay Wilson Allen, Walter B. Rideout, and James K. Robinson, reprints twenty-five of Very's poems, including several lesser-known verses from the period after 1840, along with a thorough and helpful section of notes.

Very's literary productions included essays and sermons as well as poems. It was, in fact, his essay "Epic Poetry" that first attracted Emerson's attention before he knew of Very's poetic gifts. The essay began as Very's Bowdoin Prize essay at Harvard on the question, "What Reasons Are There for Not Expecting Another Great Epic Poem?" (published by Kenneth Walter Cameron, *ESQ*, 1958). Very revised the essay and published it in the *Christian Examiner* (1838). Cameron also reprints two earlier college essays by Very, "The Heroic Character" and "Individuality," in "Two Harvard Essays by Jones Very." His sermons remain unpublished.

One manuscript work of considerable importance, a prose work that borders upon the poetic, should also be noted. Very's "To the Unborn," consisting of "An Epistle on Birth," "An Epistle on Prayer," and "An Epistle on Miracles," was composed in the spring of 1839 and intended as an introduction to his *Essays and Poems*. These "epistles" show Very at the height of his mystical fervor of the later 1830s. Throughout these works he constantly exploits the technique of merging his personal voice with that of the spirit in a striking but disturbing way—disturbing enough to make Emerson exclude them from the volume. Edwin Gittleman discusses these epistles, quoting portions of them at length, and they have been edited in full by Phyllis Cole, who also provides a useful commentary. Another of Very's literary curiosities, entitled "The Morning—A Dialogue," was sent by Very on 4 December 1839 to Amos Bronson Alcott, who recorded it in his journal for 5-6 December 1839; it is reprinted by Gittleman.

BIOGRAPHY

Very has been far luckier in his biographers than in the editors of his poems, perhaps because his personality was so fascinating and puzzling. It was his unique character that won him a place among the Transcendentalists despite some obvious philosophical and theological differences with the group. The only biography of Very's entire life is William Irving Bartlett's *Jones Very*, which incorporates Bartlett's earlier essays. This book concentrates on the relationship of Emerson and Very that developed in the late 1830s and was so influential for both men. This relationship has continued to be the focal point for many biographical and critical studies of Very, not only because of Emerson's stature but also because Very produced most of his finest poetry while they were friends. Bartlett also offers a description of Very's childhood and early student days at Harvard and a particularly valuable discussion of his long and quiet retirement from the literary scene from 1840 to 1880. As noted previously, this volume makes available many unpublished manuscript poems.

Edwin Gittleman's *Jones Very: The Effective Years, 1833-1840* is, as the title implies, a more restricted study of the most interesting and important phase of Very's life. Gittleman traces in detail Very's intellectual development from his last years as a Harvard undergraduate, through his intense but troubling religious conversion, his short bout with "insanity" at the McLean Asylum in 1838, and his disappointing attempts to convert Emerson and his Concord associates. Gittleman also makes impressive use of the poems as signposts of the development of Very's unique theological system, and he brings to bear a wealth of manuscript resources in constructing his portrait of Very. It should be noted that Gittleman's thesis rests heavily on his interpretation of certain psychological pressures of Very's childhood, particularly those relating to his mother. This is always tenuous ground for a critic, but Gittleman's argument is well documented, cogent, and convincing, if not conclusive.

Although Gittleman does not consider Very's life after 1840, Bartlett's chapter "Last Years" is a starting point for consideration of Very's later life. More recently, Paschal Reeves has provided additional analysis of that period ("The Making of a Mystic"). Reeves's depiction of Very's domestic life and his career as a supply preacher for Unitarian pulpits helps to balance Gittleman's picture. Reeves stresses a continuity in Very's life centering on the term *mystic*, which suggests a link between his turbulent earlier years and his quiet, pious retirement. Nathan Lyons' short biographical sketch in his edition of Very's poems complements Reeves by emphasizing Very's reading of George Fox, Thomas Upham, and other "quietist" philosophers in the 1840s. Lyons makes Very's last years seem less a puzzling retirement and more a conscious, willed retreat into pious self-examination. Another interesting (though not entirely unbiased) account of his late years is a letter of Very's sister Lydia to the *Boston Herald* of 6 June 1880, responding to that paper's obituary of 16 May 1880 (the obituary is reprinted in Cameron, "Jones Very's Academic Standing at Harvard"). She denies suggestions that he failed as a preacher and reports that he "had opportunities of being settled" in a pastorate but turned them down because "he did not wish to leave his home." She also blames "narrow-minded clergymen" for placing "obstacles" in the way of his preaching.

Students of Very inevitably return to the issue of his religious conversion and the subsequent "insanity" that caused his confinement in 1838. Very's letter to Emerson two days before his confinement, with Very's letter to Henry W. Bellows explaining the incident, have been published by Harry L. Jones ("The Very Madness"). James Freeman Clarke's introduction to a group of sonnets in the March 1839 *Western Messenger* defends Very's sanity and uses the sonnets to prove that his thoughts were "deeply important and vital." Samuel Gray Ward's account of a visit from Very in 1839, edited by L. H. Butterfield, gives a sense of Very's odd intensity as a proselytizer for his version of the new birth. For an analysis of the effect of Very's religious fervor on his literary career, especially as it was perceived by others associated with the Transcendentalist group, see Joel Myerson, *The New England Transcendentalists and the* Dial.

Other useful recent information can be found in Kenneth Walter Cameron's "Sophomore Thoreau and Religious Improvement," on Very's religious activities at Harvard; Robert D. Arner's discussion of Very's strained relations with Hawthorne (compare Arner with Gittleman); Carlos Baker's analysis of the relationship between "Emerson and Jones Very"; Joel Myerson's "A Calendar of Transcendental Club Meetings," which catalogs Very's participation in the group; references to Very's breakdown at Harvard in John Olin Eidson, *Charles Stearns Wheeler*; and George Willis Cooke's brief sketch of Very in *An Historical and Biographical Introduction to Accompany the* Dial.

The most important of the earlier biographers of Very is William P. Andrews. His short articles "An Inspired Life" and "Jones Very" and his biographical sketch in the 1883 edition of Very's poetry stress the "benign and gentle spirit of his personality." Andrews' brief discussion of Very's idea of "will-less existence" is one of the earliest considerations of this important theme in his intellectual development. G. M. Hammell's encomium, "Jones Very—A Son of the Spirit," adds little new information but provides an interesting example of the view of Very's almost mythical "saintliness." Percy P. Burns makes use of Emerson's journal entries on Very and gives an account of his failure as a preacher.

For a sense of Very's impact on his contemporaries, one should read "The Life and Services to Literature of Jones Very" (1881). Most interesting are the letters of reminiscence and tribute read at the end of the memorial meeting, but there is also a biographical sketch by William P. Andrews and a literary appraisal by Edward A. Silsbee. Very himself researched and wrote a detailed genealogy of his family, "The Very Family." For brief reference, see the biographies by Carlos Baker (*DAB*) and David Robinson (in *The American Renaissance in New England*, ed. Joel Myerson).

CRITICISM

Of the lesser-known Transcendentalists (all, in other words, but Emerson and Thoreau), Very has increasingly come to be seen as one of the more important literary contributors to the movement. There is a certain irony in this, since scholars do not agree that he should in fact be considered a Transcendentalist. That question hinges finally on how wide a definition one is willing to give to the movement and whether one insists that the label "Transcendentalist" covers the entire literary and intellectual work of any author. It certainly does not cover all of Very's work, but his growing reputation as a poet and his presence in Concord and Cambridge at the height of the Transcendentalist ferment warrant a consideration of his career in conjunction with the Transcendentalists, whether or not he passes the strictest tests for inclusion in the group.

Significant critical appraisal of Very's poetry begins, appropriately, with Emerson—a man who knew Very's strengths well enough to publish his poems, at some cost of time and effort, but who also knew his limitations. Emerson's review of *Essays and Poems* in the *Dial* (1841) succinctly identifies a source of Very's appeal: "The genius of this book is religious, and reaches an extraordinary depth of sentiment." Emerson goes so far as to argue that Very's shortcomings in technique ("no *composition*, no elaboration, no artifice . . . no variety . . . no pretension to literary merit") only amplify the purity and singleness of his insight: verses "flow through him rather than from him," and attention to form would only detract from the vision. Emerson's critique of Very, therefore, anticipates his conception of "The Poet"—a communicator of insight rather than an artificer. Very's weakness, however, one which twentieth-century readers have certainly perceived, is his reliance on "popular religious language," a medium that Emerson had come to see as inadequate to the fresh insights a poet must communicate. Emerson's initial warmth and eventual coolness toward Very is traced by William M. Moss, who perceptively notes that this pattern also marked Emerson's relations with several other younger poets—Whitman, Henry David Thoreau, Ellery Channing, Christopher Pearse Cranch, and Charles King Newcomb.

Margaret Fuller had reviewed Very's book earlier in the *Boston Quarterly Review* (1840), noting "an unsought nobleness and Purity" but complaining that it was "unfinished in style." This view sets her apart from Emerson, who valued the book's lack of "style" and emphasis on vision. Nathaniel Hawthorne, somewhat later in "A Virtuoso's Collection" (1842), mentioned Very as "a poet whose voice is scarcely heard among us, by reason of his depth."

Emerson and other early critics recognized the importance of vision and belief in Very's poetry and stressed its power to communicate a mystical or quietist religious experience. Rufus W. Griswold reveals some discomfort over Very's religious "enthusiasm," labeling his poetry "mystical" but valuable nevertheless (a grudging admission that Very's importance is chiefly spiritual), in *The Poets and Poetry of America* (1842). Evert and George Duyckinck point more approvingly to Very's religious qualities—which link him, they feel, to the seventeenth-century meditative poets—in the *Cyclopædia of American Literature* (1855). In his study of comparative religion, *Events and Epochs in Religious History* (1881), James Freeman Clarke places Very in a tradition of mysticism common to all faiths.

The appearance, in the 1880s, of two editions of Very's poetry following his death renewed critical interest. In this period the focus changed from Very's religion to his skill as a nature poet. Edward A. Silsbee's estimation of "Very's literary excellence and place" for the Essex Institute memorial observance stressed America's lack of a truly great nature poet and Very's partial fulfillment of that role. Very is here compared not with the meditative poets, but with Wordsworth. The same comparison is made in George Batchelor's early review of Andrews' edition of the poetry ("A Poet of Transcendentalism," 1883), and Gamaliel Bradford's review of Clarke's edition (1887). Bradford's article, revised and expanded into a chapter of *Biography and the Human Heart*, is the fullest and most suggestive early appraisal of Very after Emerson's.

Yvor Winters' attempt to "rediscover" Very as a neglected major figure in American literature marks a turning point in critical appraisal of the poet. His essay "Jones Very: A New England Mystic" extols Very as a "genuine" religious mystic, and uses him to accentuate what Winters considers to be the inadequacies of Ralph Waldo Emerson. In his foreword to N. Scott Momaday's edition of *The Complete Poems of Frederick Goddard Tuckerman*, Winters calls Very, with Tuckerman and Emily Dickinson, one of the three "most remarkable American poets of the nineteenth century." His judgment is questioned by Lewis Turco, who labels the poetic "rediscoveries" of Very, Tuckerman, and Edward Taylor "graveyard raiding." Yet the value of Winters' essay is not in its somewhat self-conscious "discovery" of Very but in its attempt to place the poet in a proper historical context. Here, Winters follows Emerson in stressing Very's religious vision, but he argues that the poet is a Calvinist, wrongly linked with Transcendentalism. The key term in the essay is "will," and Winters reads Very's belief in a "will-less existence" as a restatement of Calvinist determinism. Carlos Baker ("Emerson and Jones Very") also discusses Very's views on the will, seeing them, however, as a personal and poetic defect, the cause of his break with Emerson. That break, for Baker, suggests Very's failure; for Winters, it establishes Very's success.

Perry Miller's analysis of Very in *The Transcendentalists* persuasively argues that Very's place is indeed with the Transcendentalists. Aware of Very's conflicts with individuals in the group, Miller reads those conflicts as symptoms of an unwillingness on the part of the Transcendentalists to recognize the logical consequences of their doctrines. Very was, in Miller's eyes, "a welcome and a trying recruit to Transcendentalism" in his embodiment of the doctrine of poetic inspiration: "The Transcendental theory of genius practically demanded one or two mad poets; most Transcendentalists were not quite prepared to sacrifice themselves, and Very vindicated the theory by proving a willing victim."

Warner Berthoff, "Jones Very: New England Mystic," also feels that Very's religion is the basis for continuing interest in the poet. Although he stresses Very's theological differences with Emerson and the Transcendentalists, as does Winters, he attributes that difference to Unitarianism rather than to Calvinism. Berthoff also offers a brief but valuable analysis of Very's essays and sermons, which have received little critical attention. Berthoff's thesis has been expanded more recently by David Robinson ("Jones Very, the Transcendentalists, and the Unitarian Tradition"), who argues that Unitarianism, especially the strain of Unitarian pietism described by Daniel Walker Howe (*The Unitarian Conscience*), more accurately describes the intense piety and stress on conversion and rebirth in Very's poetry.

Recent critics of Very have attempted to answer the unresolved question of the poet's historical context through a much closer analysis of his poems. Gittleman's biography is indispensable in providing the background of many of the poems, along with some notable (though brief) analyses. Among studies of Very in recent unpublished doctoral dissertations, see those by Paul O. Williams, Harry L. Jones, Charles T. Summerlin, Bruce A. Ronda, and Colette Gerbaud. Very's relation with the *Dial* is discussed by Donald F. Warders.

In the introduction to his edition of the poems, Nathan Lyons applies the quietist terminology he introduced in his biographical essay to the poems themselves. The introduction is notable not only for its thematic approach to Very's Christian quietism but also for its analysis of his poetic technique, certainly the fullest such discussion to date. Lyons stresses Very's use of paradox and his intentionally sparse imagery and economy of statement. Lyons also assigns far greater importance to the religious sonnets than to the "prosaic" and "stale" nature poems—a remarkable dissent in light of the interest that Very's nature poems have recently generated.

Hyatt H. Waggoner, in *American Poets from the Puritans to the Present*, also describes Very as a man who was "with them [the Transcendentalists] but not really of them." Waggoner sees instead an intellectual affinity between Very and Hawthorne in that both men saw clearly the darker side of both nature and the human soul. The essay comes full circle by arguing that Very "most completely embodied the quality the Transcendentalists valued highest, absolute trust of the inner vision." The theory that Very was not really "of" the Transcendentalists but embodied their doctrines raises serious questions about the movement itself. If one accepts Waggoner's argument, one is forced to question either the sincerity of the Transcendentalists (which Waggoner certainly does not) or the consistency with which they carried out the logic of their doctrines. One is also reminded, in considering this question, of the limits of a logical inquiry into a movement founded upon intuition.

The nature poems are the focus of Anthony Herbold, who argues that Very held two "mutually incompatible" concepts of nature, seeing it as finite and infinite simultaneously. The contradiction is based on the conflicting claims of Calvinist dualism and Romantic monism. When the Calvinist claims held precedence, Herbold feels, Very was the better poet. James A. Levernier extends the perspective of Winters and Herbold by finding Calvinism principally in Very's insistent dualism, a vision that incorporated the essentially monistic idealism of Transcendentalism.

Lawrence Buell's comparison of Very and Whitman in the final chapter of *Literary Transcendentalism* concentrates on a group of sonnets in which Very speaks not as a man or a poet, but as God or the Holy Spirit. Buell argues that such a stylistic innovation, even if somewhat unconsciously adopted, was the logical extension of the Transcendentalist faith in the divinity of the individual soul. In this light, Very's haunting exercises in egotism are also profound poetic experiments that make him a participant in the Transcendentalist quest for newness. Buell's insight is extended by David Robinson ("The Exemplary Self and the Transcendent Self in the Poetry of Jones Very"), who reveals textual evidence of a more conscious manipulation of voice by Very. On that basis, he groups Very's devotional verse into two broad categories: in poems of the "exemplary" self, Very offers his persona as an example to his readers; in poems of the "transcendent" self, that persona is subsumed in the direct voice of God.

In other various studies, Paschal Reeves ("Jones Very as Preacher") surveys the major themes, sources, and influences of Very's manuscript sermons, finding Calvinism, Unitarianism, and Transcendentalism to be the major influences on Very. Very's study of and sympathy for the American Indian is described by Richard Fleck. Phyllis Cole traces his attitude toward Milton as expressed in his essays on "Epic Poetry" and "Shakespeare" ("The Purity of Puritanism"), and there is also mention of the "Epic Poetry" essay by David Porter as an example of the internal direction of modern poetry (*Emerson and Literary Change*). In the history of Shakespeare criticism, however, Very figures, according to S. Schoenbaum (*Shakespeare's Lives*), only as an "obscure American cleric" whose essays promoted a kind of biographical criticism best exemplified by Emerson's *Representative Men*.

Very's appearance on the Concord scene in the midst of the Transcendentalist ferment was a mixed blessing for him. If his contact with Emerson and his associates gave him the hope or promise necessary for the development of his unique theology of "will-less existence," his failure to proselyte Concord also played a large role in his eventual frustrated retirement. Very's reputation has been perpetuated by his friendship with Emerson, but that association has often clouded an objective historical assessment of Very's Transcendentalist credentials, which have been either too uncritically accepted or too vigorously rejected.

JOHN WEISS

Robert E. Burkholder

BIBLIOGRAPHIES

There is no adequate bibliography of works by John Weiss. *NUC* provides the most complete list of separate publications, with citations for twenty-five pamphlets, four books, two edited works, and five periodical publications. This basic list is somewhat supplemented by Theresa Layton Hall, "A Bibliography of the New England Transcendental Movement." Although Hall's list is less complete than that of *NUC*, it does contain some items that the latter does not. One should be warned, however, that Hall's listing is confusing because she includes book publications under the rubric "Addresses and Sermons." It should also be noted that together Hall and *NUC* account for only approximately twenty-five published sermons, addresses, and lectures by Weiss, whereas his obituary in the 10 March 1879 *Boston Daily Advertiser* states that "from 1845 to 1874 he published forty sermons and lectures." In his journal Weiss lists thirty-eight separate sermon publications and another sixty-five lectures and addresses, including some that were separate publications, some that appeared in periodicals or as part of his books, and some that remained in manuscript.

Unfortunately, the *Daily Advertiser* obituary is the best published source for discovering Weiss's contribution to periodicals. It states that he published eleven articles or poems in the *Christian Examiner* between 1846 and 1856, sixteen in the *Atlantic Monthly Magazine*, fourteen in the *Radical*, and two in the *Galaxy*. It does not mention contributions to the *Massachusetts Quarterly Review*, *Brownson's Quarterly Review*, *Christian Register*, and several other periodicals, all identified by Weiss in his journal.

The only worthwhile sources for material about Weiss are the brief lists that conclude Minot J. Savage, "John Weiss" (in *Heralds of the Liberal Faith*, ed. Samuel
A. Eliot), and George Harvey Genzmer (*DAB*). All items cited in these lists are discussed in this essay. Weiss is not listed in either *AAL* or *Literary Writings in America*.

MANUSCRIPTS

Weiss is not represented in *ALM*, and the best available evidence indicates that
his manuscripts were scattered after his death. The Houghton Library of Harvard
University owns approximately forty-six letters by Weiss, and the Boston Public Library
owns nine. The public libraries of New Bedford and Watertown, where Weiss spent
most of his professional life, do not own any of his manuscripts. The most valuable
single source for the study of Weiss is his manuscript journal (in four volumes covering the period from 1843 to 1876) and his theological commonplace book, a storehouse
of ideas for sermons, articles, and books, both of which are available at the
Massachusetts Historical Society.

EDITIONS

Weiss's most valuable contribution to the study of American Transcendentalism,
The Life and Correspondence of Theodore Parker (1864), is the only work by him
that is readily available today in numerous reprints. It is, in fact, still a standard work
on Parker's life, owing to Weiss's familiarity with his subject, his eye for detail, and
an objectivity that is unusual in a biographer so close to his subject.

Weiss also enjoyed a reputation among his contemporaries as a poet and wit,
but except for reprintings of a few of his poems in *The Poets of Transcendentalism*,
ed. George Willis Cooke, and *Singers and Songs of the Liberal Faith*, ed. Alfred P.
Putnam, his poetry remains scattered in periodicals and nearly forgotten. The same
is largely true of his translations of works by Novalis and Schiller, his edition of William
Smith's *Memoir of J. G. Fichte* (1846), and his other book publications—*American
Religion* (1871), *Wit, Humor, and Shakspeare. Twelve Essays* (1876), and *The Immortal Life* (1880).

BIOGRAPHY AND CRITICISM

Weiss's manuscript journal is invaluable to those wishing to study his life and
work today. It is a combination diary, poetry notebook, and clipping collection containing first drafts of many of his poems, insights into his relationships with Amos
Bronson Alcott, Ralph Waldo Emerson, Thomas Wentworth Higginson, and Parker,
and information on his involvement in the antislavery movement, the Free Religious

Association, and the Radical Club. It also includes a biographical sketch that apparently so affected Weiss that he clipped it, pasted it in his journal, and jotted his comments on the criticism alongside it. This article, "Twelve Apostles of Heresy" (*Ind*, 20 Jan. 1870), was attributed by Weiss to F. B. Sanborn, with whom Weiss had apparently had a run-in, perhaps over the publication of some Parker material (Sanborn's reservations about Weiss's *The Life and Correspondence of Theodore Parker* are mentioned in his *Recollections of Seventy Years*). Sanborn presents a generally balanced criticism of Weiss but describes him as "short, dark, and weird-looking."

The previously mentioned obituary in the *Boston Daily Advertiser* serves as the basis for a number of later sketches of Weiss, including those in Alfred P. Putnam's *Singers and Songs of the Liberal Faith* and Henry Williams' "John Weiss" (in *Memorials of the Class of 1837 of Harvard University*). The latter is most interesting for its emphasis on Weiss's sense of humor as a Harvard student. Much of the information in the *Daily Advertiser* obituary is repeated in the 29 March 1879 *Christian Register*, and a very brief outline of Weiss's life can be found in the "Notes" section of Cooke's *The Poets of Transcendentalism*.

Of the more substantive memorials to Weiss, perhaps the best is Octavius B. Frothingham, "John Weiss." Frothingham discusses at length Weiss's theology (which he believes to be untenable), Weiss's sympathy with science, the poetry that pervades all his writing, and his sharp wit, which Frothingham describes as a "wicked wit" that was "barbed and poisoned." Frothingham pays Weiss the one compliment he would have most appreciated by claiming that although he followed Parker in his ideas on reform, he "went far beyond him in subtlety and accuracy of mental delineation." This essay is far more exhaustive in its treatment of Weiss's life and work than Frothingham's earlier consideration of him in *Transcendentalism in New England*. Cyrus A. Bartol's tribute, "John Weiss" (*BDA*, 10 March 1879), anticipates his article in the *Unitarian Review* (1879), which is overly sentimental but valuable for the anecdotes Bartol chooses to include. Bartol's later essay, "The Genius of Weiss" (in *Principles and Portraits*), is a more balanced and less sentimental treatment of Weiss that suffers from being too general in both its praise and its criticism. Edwin Stanton Hodgin is surprisingly critical in "John Weiss, Genius of the Pulpit." Hodgin devotes nearly half of his essay to background information on the points of disagreement between orthodox Unitarians and the New School, represented in this case by Weiss. When he finally turns his full attention to Weiss, Hodgin tempers his praise of Weiss's learning by noting that Weiss was often obscure and undercuts his acknowledgment of Weiss's genius by suggesting that his brilliance caused him to be "critical, sometimes captious, and on rare occasions bitingly bitter."

Two brief but valuable sketches of Weiss by men who knew him are by Minot J. Savage (in *Heralds of a Liberal Faith*) and Joseph Henry Allen (*Sequel to "Our Liberal Movement"*). Weiss's life is also outlined by George Harvey Genzmer (*DAB*) and J. Wade Caruthers (in *The American Renaissance in New England*, ed. Joel Myerson).

Those who wish to gauge the critical response to Weiss's *The Life and Cor-*

respondence of Theodore Parker should see the lengthy and important reviews of that work by Joseph Henry Allen ("Weiss's Transcendentalism") and Octavius Brooks Frothingham ("Theodore Parker"). For more information on Weiss's association with the Radical Club and the *Radical* magazine, the best sources are Mary E. Sargent, *Sketches and Reminiscences of the Radical Club*, and Clarence L. F. Gohdes, *The Periodicals of American Transcendentalism*. Another important biographical source and a key to Weiss's diverse scholarly tastes is the fifty-page *Catalogue of the Private Library of the Late John Weiss* . . . (1879).

A recent note by W. Keith Kraus, "An Uncited Reply to Twain's Letter on the Foster Case with a Note on John Weiss," seeks to prove that Weiss's theory of humor as developed in *Wit, Humor, and Shakspeare* was a precursor of and perhaps an influence on the theories Mark Twain advanced in "How to Tell a Story." But even with this slight resurgence of interest in Weiss's work, awareness of him is certainly less today than it was in 1888, when Frothingham stated that, with his death, Weiss and his work "simply disappeared from view."

CHARLES STEARNS WHEELER

Joel Myerson

BIBLIOGRAPHIES

A complete list of Wheeler's writings is in John Olin Eidson, *Charles Stearns Wheeler*. All the articles on Wheeler listed in *AAL* are discussed in this essay.

MANUSCRIPTS

Wheeler is not listed in *ALM*. In the later 1940s, Wheeler's manuscripts were nearly all in the possession of his descendants. This collection was used by John Olin Eidson, who also lists in his book Wheeler's letters (written mostly to Ralph Waldo Emerson) located at the Houghton Library of Harvard University. After 1951, the Wheeler family papers were dispersed into at least three groups: one collection, containing family correspondence and documents relating to Wheeler's undergraduate years at Harvard, is at the Lincoln, Massachusetts, Public Library; a second collection, consisting mostly of Wheeler's correspondence, was purchased and given to Harvard by Kenneth Walter Cameron; the third collection, which contains Wheeler's manuscript journal, has not been located.

EDITIONS

Wheeler's writings have not been collected. Of particular interest to students of Transcendentalism are Wheeler's review of James Russell Lowell's *A Year's Life* (1841), two installments of "Literary Intelligence" from Germany in the *Dial* (1843), some "Letters from Germany" (*Pioneer*, 1843), and "What Reasons Are There for Not Expecting Another Great Epic Poem?" a Bowdoin Prize essay edited by Kenneth Walter Cameron. Wheeler's correspondence has been partially edited by Cameron, who has published a selection from the manuscripts he has given to Harvard ("Emerson, Transcendentalism, and Literary Notes in the Stearns Wheeler Papers").

BIOGRAPHY AND CRITICISM

John Olin Eidson's *Charles Stearns Wheeler* is an excellent biography, fully documenting his Harvard years (both as student and tutor), his relations with contemporaries, and his trip to Germany. It is especially valuable since many of the manuscripts Eidson used are now apparently lost. Also useful is Eidson's "Charles Stearns Wheeler: Emerson's 'Good Grecian,'" a summing up of his biography with new information. William Augustus Davis, *Biographical Notice of Charles Stearns Wheeler*, a eulogistic work, was reprinted with other "Notices of Mr. Wheeler" by C. C. Felton (1843). A minor point about Wheeler's Harvard years is made by Kenneth Walter Cameron ("Harvard Rules and Certificates of Thoreau's Day"). Descriptions of Wheeler at Harvard are printed in Henry Williams, *Memorial of the Class of 1837 at Harvard University*. New information on Wheeler's death, from a letter by James Elliot Cabot describing his deathbed vigil, is given by Joel Myerson.

Everyone agrees that Wheeler's death in Germany at age twenty-six cut short a promising life. He helped edit and introduce Alfred Lord Tennyson and Thomas Carlyle to America, prepared Greek texts for use at Harvard, contributed to the *Dial* and *Pioneer*, and was a good friend of Henry David Thoreau, whose Walden sojourn is said to have been influenced by Wheeler's similar stay at a shanty at Flint's Pond a decade before Thoreau's more famous retreat. Information on Wheeler's publishing activities is in John Olin Eidson, *Tennyson in America*, and *The Correspondence of Emerson and Carlyle*, ed. Joseph Slater. On the *Pioneer*, see Sculley Bradley, "Lowell, Emerson, and the *Pioneer*." On the *Dial*, see George Willis Cooke, *An Historical and Biographical Introduction to Accompany the* Dial, superseded by Myerson, *The New England Transcendentalists and the* Dial. Wheeler's friendship with Thoreau can be traced in *The Correspondence of Henry David Thoreau*, ed. Walter Harding and Carl Bode; Harding, *The Days of Henry Thoreau*; and Cameron, "Thoreau and Stearns Wheeler: Four Letters and a Reading Record," which also lists Wheeler's charges from the Harvard College Library.

Further significant work on Wheeler must remain undone until the remainder of his manuscripts, including his journal, are located.

The Contemporary Reaction

ORESTES AUGUSTUS BROWNSON

Leonard Gilhooley

WORKS

Orestes Brownson's vigorous mind and questing spirit drew his early allegiance to Transcendentalism. From the beginnings of the Transcendental Club through 1840 he was, in his thorny way, a Transcendentalist. He thought enough of Brook Farm, for instance, to send Orestes, Jr., there for nearly two years, even though the father had reservations about some of the assumptions of that group, as, indeed, had Ralph Waldo Emerson and Nathaniel Hawthorne. By 1842, however, Brownson was edging away from the Transcendentalist movement itself. Certainly by 1845 he had developed, with "implacable fluency" (in Arthur M. Schlesinger, Jr.'s phrase), not only into a rigorous critic of the movement but, as some believe, into its most percipient, especially on social, philosophical, and religious grounds. Thus, Brownson is important because he was both a quondam Transcendentalist and a part of the "contemporary reaction" against Transcendentalism.

Brownson never produced a complete book on Transcendentalism, but he did write specific essays in his *Boston Quarterly Review* (1838–42). Yet his attitudes toward that movement, which themselves constituted a signal involvement of his intellectual life, colored much of his writing; see, for example, *New Views of Christianity, Society, and the Church* (1836); *The Mediatorial Life of Jesus* (1842); *The Spirit-Rapper: An Autobiography* (1854); and *The Convert; or, Leaves from My Experience* (1857), the last containing surprisingly little specific comment on the Transcendentalists. Even his master work, *The American Republic: Its Constitution, Tendencies, and Destiny* (1865), seems, at first glance, only tangentially related to Transcendentalism. A rereading of each may prove otherwise. Listings of Brownson's published work have been compiled by Joel Myerson (in *FPAA*, vol. 4) and by Leonard Gilhooley (*The American Renaissance in New England*, ed. Myerson).

A major problem in Brownson scholarship surfaces here. His work is presently best known through Henry F. Brownson's twenty-volume edition of his father's essays and books: *The Works of Orestes A. Brownson* (1882–87). Yet this impressive filial undertaking includes considerably less than half of Brownson's total work. Although this edition is much more accessible than Brownson's two *Reviews* (which have also been reprinted), none is as readily available as it might be. Some early articles of Brownson's appeared in periodicals that he edited (e.g., *Gospel Advocate and Impartial Observer, Genesee Republican and Herald of Reform, Free Enquirer, Philanthropist, Christian Examiner,* and *Boston Reformer,* among others prior to 1838); in 1843 he wrote for the *United States Magazine, and Democratic Review.* From 1865 until 1872 his essays appeared (often unsigned) in many places, especially in Isaac Hecker's *Catholic World* and in *Ave Maria.*

The earliest published biography of any value is a three-volume work by his son Henry F. Brownson, which includes a generous sampling of his letters. A truly seminal study, especially of the years up to 1844, is Arthur M. Schlesinger, Jr., *Orestes A. Brownson.* Theodore Maynard's *Orestes Brownson* is helpful, particularly after 1844, and includes an interesting discussion of Brownson's genealogy. The most complete biography is Thomas R. Ryan, *Orestes A. Brownson,* an enormous book crammed with Brownsoniana, especially key letters, though hampered somewhat by an inadequate index. A brief, trenchant work is Americo D. LaPati, *Orestes Brownson.*

A full edition of Brownson's letters is being prepared by Daniel Barnes and William J. Gilmore. Joseph F. Gower and Richard M. Leliaert have edited *The Brownson-Hecker Correspondence,* a book of especial interest for the mutually interactive comments on Transcendentalism by the correspondents. See also Daniel Barnes' dissertation, "An Edition of the Early Letters of Orestes Brownson." Many of Brownson's letters, as well as other manuscript and printed materials, are available in the *Microfilm Edition of the Orestes Augustus Brownson Papers* at the University of Notre Dame, which is described in a guide by Lawrence Bradley.

THOUGHT

Perry Miller has termed 1836 the American annus mirabilis, since five works central to the development of Transcendentalism were published in that year: Bronson Alcott's *Conversations with Children on the Gospels,* William Henry Furness' *Remarks on the Four Gospels,* George Ripley's *Discourses on the Philosophy of Religion,* Ralph Waldo Emerson's *Nature,* and Brownson's *New Views.* The last of these represented a kind of resting place on Brownson's journey toward Transcendentalism and, as he saw it later, beyond. Progress, the nineteenth-century's "evangel," was upward and a "kindling doctrine" to Brownson during his early years. He supported the "Movement Party" (the party of "Hope" or of the "Hopeful") against the "Stationary Party" (that of "Memory" or of the "Fearful"). There had developed in his autodidactic, spiral course through social, philosophical, and theological matters an insight that forced a rejection of Calvinism (especially the rigidity of the Synod of Dort) and a Unitarianism slowly being garroted by Lockean method. Brownson was moving toward an individual "religious sentiment" (see his articles in the *Christian Examiner* in 1834 and 1836) under the influence of Benjamin Constant's *De la religion*, Saint-Simon, Victor Cousin, and others. The "sentiment" was an intuitive agent able to grasp truth directly; this true power had perdured, lively and questing, through the generations of men. The ultimate defeat would be to support transient religious *institutions*, ossified by their own impermanence. In *New Views* Brownson made clear his espousal of "eclecticism": in the constant polar movement between "spiritualism" and "materialism,"the Christian church had arrived at Protestantism, which itself, as he thought, had lost its force in the French Revolution. What was now needed was the corrective, vital agency of a "New Church" capable of assimilating the best features of past institutional systems. This "Church of the Future" would embody a vastly improved version of the earlier historical amalgamation of Christian inspiration and Alexandrian syncretism.

Not surprisingly, Harriet Martineau considered Brownson an oak among Boston daisies. Having attended the early meetings of the Transcendental Club, he founded the *Boston Quarterly Review* (1838). During the first two years of the magazine he often gave qualified acceptance to the loosely-joined principles of the loosely-associated Transcendentalists, but always with some reservations. It was hardly enough, Brownson thought, to perfect an individual spiritually and solely; character is not uninfluenced by the social order: "All is not fate, nor yet is all freedom." Then the edge appears: "We hold, therefore, that one of the means of perfecting individuals is the melioration of man's external condition; that is, the progress of society . . . man and society go onward to their lofty destiny, not by means of any single power, but by the combined action of all outward and inward influences."

Here he seems to stand apart from the Transcendentalists, certainly from Emerson and Thoreau. Total freedom for an individual had the odor of license; when the need or duty of one impinged upon the rights of another, what was Solomon to do? Democracy needed an outward binding, an agreed-on ligature, a society based on the assent of equals. Transcendentalism, a social, political, philosophical, and theological movement (as Brownson regarded it in 1840), was, to be sure, for liberty, yet it seemed to accept no authority save the individual human sensibility (informed by the "religious sentiment"). It claimed to know the truth of religion and to be the hope of progress. Brownson therefore wrote that he "accepted the name Transcendentalism although it is not one of our own choosing, nor the one we approve." He approved reluctantly since Transcendentalism posited that man *can* know intuitively an order of existence of which sense and experience may be ignorant. When, however, feeling is assumed to be superior to reason, dreaming to reflection, "instinctive intimation [to] scientific exposition, lawless fancy [to] enlightened understanding as we apprehend it is understood in our neighborhood . . . we must disown it, and deny we are Transcendentalists." Hint had grown to theme.

Further, Brownson did not think man to be the sole well of wisdom, either in theology (man was *not* God), philosophy (pantheism was the result), nor society (man could not lift himself "by his own waistband"). The Other, who touched man for the True (intelligence), the Good (will), the Beautiful (imagination) was, bluntly put, the other. *Gratia naturam supponit.*

The thrust of Brownson's thought from 1840 to 1843 was to base social reform (man's freedom to recognize fate and, much more gradually, providence) on Christianity as it had developed in history and tradition. However, fairness demands acknowledgment that he had raised that possibility earlier. The climax came in his "The Mediatorial Life of Jesus," dedicated to his "spiritual father," William Ellery Channing. In this period, there is also praise for Emerson's "The Problem" and a lukewarm review of the *Dial* (1841), a full review of Emerson's *Essays* (1841), articles on Theodore Parker's *Discourse on the Transient and Permanent in Christianity* (1841), and reviews of Margaret Fuller's *Summer on the Lakes* (1844) and her *Woman in the Nineteenth Century* ("Miss Fuller and Reformers," 1845).

At this time Brownson seemed unsure of the notion of "Providential Men," although he had already written of "God-patented nobles" and would write of the "Optimates." The latter idea seems to have been derived from Jaime Balmes, Donoso Cortés, and Vincenzo Gioberti.

His first full discussion of Pierre Leroux came in July 1842 ("Leroux on Humanity"), together with *The Mediatorial Life of Jesus.* Leroux's theory of "Communion" encompassed the individual "communing" with family, and, ultimately, with the state (through individuals and, with God, through the Church). The last points up the importance of history and tradition, since it places the Incarnation at the center of history and underscores the necessary love of humanity through love of God. The famous "The Laboring Classes" essays (1840), those "horrible doctrines" that have earned Schlesinger's characterization of Brownson as an "American Marxist before Marx," were now two years in the past.

Brownson suspended his *Review* in December 1842 and spent 1843 with John O'Sullivan's *United States Magazine, and Democratic Review.* His writing there, often unclear, sometimes turgid, concerns the notion of providence, its relation to progress, and the static-dynamic quandaries raised by philosophy. In January 1844 he launched *Brownson's Quarterly Review*, and in October he joined the Catholic church. The opening numbers of his new review had three long, critical articles on Transcendentalism; later (July 1846), he wrote "Protestantism Ends in Transcendentalism." The rupture with the New England group was complete.

In these articles his argument is often with Parker; Brownson isolated and vehemently denied "Three fundamental propositions" of the Transcendentalists: "1. Man is the measure of truth and goodness; 2. Religion is a fact or principle of human nature; 3. All religious institutions, which have been or are, have their principle and cause in human nature."

Thereafter, Brownson's formal attitude toward Transcendentalism (if not toward individual Transcendentalists) was an adversary one. Yet his work never lost the resonances of that unique intellectual, religious, and historical experience; indeed, he was to hear the echoes, sometimes faintly, sometimes quite clearly, in the ensuing years.

SCHOLARSHIP

Harvard University has contributed mightily to a restimulation of Brownson studies. Arthur M. Schlesinger, Sr., Perry Miller, Kenneth Murdock, F. O. Matthiessen, Howard Mumford Jones, and Arthur M. Schlesinger, Jr., have all put honest sweat into scholarly reevaluation; the admirable but myopic study by Octavius Brooks Frothingham, *Transcendentalism in New England*, is no longer the sole key to nineteenth-century thought in America. The younger Schlesinger believes that Brownson's Transcendentalism was "verbal," that his rigorous philosophical mind rejected "die-hard" devotees, and that, if he was a Transcendentalist at all, his sentiments were with Victor Cousin rather more than they were with Emerson. To Perry Miller, the movement was more "religious" than literary. It tried to make "literature a substitute for religion, and religion . . . for philosophy"—thus Brownson's "nay." To Miller, in his indispensable book, Brownson was "in many respects the most powerful of the Transcendentalists," a point that is arguable but provocative and meant as a counterweight to prior neglect. Alexander Kern, "The Rise of Transcendentalism, 1815–1860," sees Brownson as Transcendentalism's best philosopher, as does René Wellek ("The Minor Transcendentalists and German Philosophy"). One may also read with profit A. Robert Caponigri, "European Influences on the Thought of Orestes Brownson." Alvan S. Ryan, in what may be the best short account of the matter ("Orestes Brownson: The Critique of Transcendentalism"), believes that Brownson found a "gentile rationalism" to avoid gnosticism in New England's attempt at autotelic theology and feared a religion-sponsored disaster for what Gilhooley has termed Brownson's version of the American Idea (*Contradiction and Dilemma*). Brownson, according to Ryan, believed that Transcendentalism raised "the most fundamental religious and philosophical problems of his time," a thesis further amplified in Ryan, "Brownson's Significance for American Democracy Today."

Among articles that compare Brownson and Emerson one should remark especially A. Robert Caponigri's "Brownson and Emerson." In another study, Caponigri contrasts the differing social attitudes of Brownson, Emerson, and Thoreau ("Individual, Civil Society, and State in American Transcendentalism"). Russell Kirk, "Two Facets of the New England Mind: Emerson and Brownson," should be read together with his *The Conservative Mind* and *The Roots of American Order*. Further, one might profitably examine Duane E. Smith's "Romanticism in America" and Quentin Anderson's important *The Imperial Self*. A carefully wrought (if possibly dated) study is that by Matthew A. Fitzsimmons, "Brownson's Search for the Kingdom of God." Lawrence Roemer, *Brownson, Democracy and the Trend toward Socialism*, seems to scant Brownson's earlier period but is, withal, a rewarding work. Per Sveino, under the influence of Perry Miller and Kenneth Murdock, has published the only book yet done by a European, *Orestes A. Brownson's Road to Catholicism*. Two other substantive non-American contributions are by Bernard Aspinwall and Armand Maurer. Sveino finds in Brownson an "ingrained sense of tradition" and terms his "Catholicity" "a 'transfigured' Transcendentalism." In an extremely useful chapter in *The American Adam*, R. W. B. Lewis studies the basic theological differences between Brownson and Parker and sees the former as a member of the "Party of Irony," a third force in New England that could find rest neither in the "Party of Hope" nor in the "Party of Memory." Lewis' point had been anticipated by C. Carroll Hollis in a work cited below; Paul F. Boller, Jr., *American Transcendentalism, 1830-1860*, takes a similar view.

Brownson's literary propensities, criticism, and style, seldom first-rate, are best examined in the works of C. Carroll Hollis: "The Literary Criticism of Orestes Brownson" and "Orestes Brownson, Jacksonian Literary Critic." Chester Soleta, "The Literary Criticism of O. A. Brownson," should be read together with Leonard McCarthy, "Rhetoric in the Works of Orestes Brownson." Worthwhile comments on the *Boston Quarterly Review* can be found in George Ripley, "Brownson's Writings," Clarence L. F. Gohdes, *The Periodicals of American Transcendentalism*, Harold Laski, *The American Democracy*, and Minda Ruth Dorn, "Literary Criticism in the *Boston Quarterly Review*, the *Present*, and the *Massachusetts Quarterly Review*."

A good many substantial doctoral dissertations have recently been written on Brownson. A partial list includes John E. Daly on Brownson and Transcendentalism, William J. Gilmore on the early Brownson and New England religious culture, Josephine K. Newman on Brownson's philosophical thought and Aquinas, Robert E. Ireland on Brownson, Channing, Emerson, and Parker and the concept of providence, Robert E. Moffit on Brownson's philosophical and political theory, Joseph L. Quinn on the crucial January–September 1842 period in Brownson's life, and Richard M. Leliaert on Brownson's theology.

FUTURE RESEARCH

Opportunities for future work on Brownson abound, though they will require a great deal of interdisciplinary research. No proper study has been done on his economic theory or on his revolutionary attitudes before and after the "Laboring Classes" essays. A useful effort might be made to compare Alexis de Tocqueville's work with that of Brownson, as the latter's ideas developed before, during, and after his Transcendentalist phase. What, if any, relationship is there between Orestes A.

Brownson and the "social pragmatists" (Charles Sanders Peirce, the elder Henry James, Oliver Wendell Holmes, Jr.) or the "new humanists" (Irving Babbitt, Paul Elmer More) or George Santayana? Is there any connection between Transcendentalism and gnosticism (diluted or direct), as Brownson saw the matter? Further, a difficult but important task would be to ferret out the writing Brownson produced during his "lost years" (1866–73) and to assess the value of the final years of *Brownson's Quarterly Review* (1873–75).

At the vestibule of death Brownson wrote (*BrQR*, 1875): "Were we not trained in Boston, 'the Hub of the Universe,' at a time when it was really the focus of all sorts of modern ideas, good, bad, and indifferent? What have any of you to teach one who participated in the Boston intellectual movement from 1830 to 1844? We Bostonians were a generation ahead of you."

The memory, it seems, yet held a pleasant seat in that aging, weathered globe.

WILLIAM ELLERY CHANNING

David Robinson

BIBLIOGRAPHIES

A bibliography of Channing's works can be found in Madeleine Hooke Rice, *Federal Street Pastor*. Joel Myerson has compiled a listing of first printings of his works (*FPAA*, vol. 4) . For critical studies, "A Channing Bibliography: 1929–1959" has been compiled by Conrad Wright. Most of the articles on Channing in *AAL* are discussed in the essay.

MANUSCRIPTS

A listing of the locations of Channing manuscripts can be found in *ALM*. Important repositories of these manuscripts include the Andover-Harvard Theological Library, where drafts of "Unitarian Christianity" (1819) are preserved, the Houghton Library of Harvard University, the Massachusetts Historical Society, and the Meadville Theological School. John White Chadwick reported that many of Channing's papers were destroyed in an accident at the turn of the century.

EDITIONS

A six-volume edition of Channing's *Works*, published partially under his supervision, was issued between 1841 and 1843. In 1875 a one-volume edition, sponsored by the American Unitarian Association, was published; it was expanded to include a late work, *The Perfect Life* (1873), in 1886. Much important material, including correspondence and sermon extracts, is printed in William Henry Channing, *Memoir of William Ellery Channing* (1848). Extracts from Channing's journal were published in Grace Ellery Channing, *Dr. Channing's Notebook* (1887). Also useful is Anna Letitia Le Breton's edition of the *Correspondence of William Ellery Channing, D. D., and Lucy Aiken* (1874). At his death, Channing left unfinished a major work, *Treatise on Man*, upon which he had been working for some years. The manuscript, at Meadville Theological School, has been edited and introduced by Morton deCorcey Nachlas, "A Study and Transcription of William Ellery Channing's Unfinished Treatise on Man." The most recent addition to the Channing texts is Richard E. Myers' edition of two sermons from manuscripts at Meadville.

BIOGRAPHY AND CRITICISM

Although the Transcendentalists undertook much of their reform in what they felt was Channing's spirit, he was content to be adviser and inspirer to the movement, and he therefore remained uncommitted, or at least selectively committed, to it. Nevertheless, his career is almost always discussed with Transcendentalism not very far in the background. In assessing Channing criticism, we must first examine the general biographical estimates and then trace the commentary on his theological speculation, his literary example, and his political activism, all of which had an impact on Transcendentalism. Finally, we must assess his personal influence on individual members of the movement.

The richest source of information concerning his intellectual development is William Henry Channing's *Memoir*, despite its poor organization. Elizabeth Palmer Peabody, *Reminiscences of Rev. Wm. Ellery Channing, D. D.*, is an invaluable record of Channing's remarks on key issues, if one allows for the fact that Peabody was at pains to minimize the differences between Channing and her own Transcendentalist friends. John White Chadwick, *William Ellery Channing*, is "a minor classic" in American biography, to quote Sydney Ahlstrom. Chadwick is a fine stylist, and he presents Channing in a theological context, which is where Channing himself focused his concern.

Almost half a century passed before another important book-length study appeared, but in the 1950s a Channing revival began with two biographies, Arthur W. Brown's *Always Young for Liberty* and Madeleine Hooke Rice's *Federal Street Pastor*, and two critical analyses of his thought, Robert Leet Patterson's *The Philosophy of William Ellery Channing* and David P. Edgell's *William Ellery Channing: An Intellectual Portrait*. Brown wants to "re-define" Channing by correcting the prevalent tendency to associate him with "other, more familiar names"—to alter, in other words, the frequent tendency to see Channing as a Unitarian who almost but never quite made it to Transcendentalism. Brown succeeds in showing not only how important

Channing's inspiration was to the Transcendentalists, but also how he supported them as individuals while maintaining his distance from the movement. Rice's biography is a straightforward chronological record, valuable for its stress on Channing's exercise of his social and political influence. Patterson claims for Channing a unique place in the Christian tradition by virtue of his insistence that God can be known directly by humanity, a "*Via Affirmativa*" strongly contrasting with the Calvinist and Thomistic traditions. What he says of Channing seems relevant to Ralph Waldo Emerson, Theodore Parker, and others, for it was Channing's doctrine of the immediate availability of God in human experience that became a favorite Transcendentalist theme. Edgell's study is not restricted to theological issues: it draws a more rounded "intellectual portrait" of Channing, considering his literary career, his political commitments, his theological development, and his relation to the Transcendentalists. Although this approach inevitably sacrifices some depth, it reminds us of Channing's broad interests. Moreover, Edgell sees Channing as more in agreement with the Transcendentalists than most other critics, emphasizing parallels between his thought and Emerson's—a somewhat controversial position, as we will see.

These works confirmed Channing's importance. Jack Mendelsohn, *Channing,* goes on to investigate "the basis of Channing's claim on people." Mendelsohn's Channing is "a prophet and reformer of the moral life," a more political Channing than one usually encounters. Mendelsohn takes his direction partly from Ahlstrom ("The Interpretation of Channing"), who labels Channing's remarkable ability to inspire diverse followers "the mystery of Channing." Ahlstrom finds the answer to the mystery in both the man and his milieu and thus points toward broader social and cultural analyses. Andrew Delbanco, *William Ellery Channing*, takes this direction by approaching Channing as the founder, and in many senses the exemplar, of American "liberalism," a thesis that leads him into a detailed interpretation of Channing's politics.

These books reflect the trends in Channing's reputation, but in many ways the landmark studies of Channing have been a handful of briefer essays. Robert E. Spiller, "A Case for W. E. Channing," Van Wyck Brooks, *The Flowering of New England*, Herbert W. Schneider, "The Intellectual Background of William Ellery Channing," and Conrad Wright, "The Rediscovery of Channing," are notable not so much as definitive studies but as suggestive forays whose implications have yet to be completely assimilated into the emerging portrait of Channing. The essays by Spiller and Brooks concern the literary Channing. Schneider's essay deals with his philosophy and is an important corrective to Vernon Louis Parrington's engaging but misleading attempt to make Channing a New England Jefferson altered completely by his reading of the French Enlightenment (*The Romantic Revolution in America*). Schneider gives appropriate weight to "republicanism," "rationalism," and "pietism" as three factors from which Channing wove a synthesis that was "the turning point from the Enlightenment to transcendentalism." But if, for Schneider, Channing was a bridge to Transcendentalism, he did not himself make that crossing, and he was "repelled by much of it." The conservative older Channing is consistent with Schneider's younger one, influenced by the Calvinist Samuel Hopkins. Even Channing's philosophical idealism is attributed ultimately to "Calvinistic pietism." In the wake of Schneider's essay came Arthur I. Ladu's more limited argument against Channing's association with Transcendentalism, refuting earlier studies such as Harold Clarke Goddard, *Studies in New England Transcendentalism*. Ladu focuses his case on Channing's critique of Parker and his reservations about the doctrine of intuition; he even finds some coolness among the Transcendentalists themselves towards Channing. Both Edgell's biography and his publication of a letter to Channing from Andrews Norton intimating Channing's Transcendentalist sympathies ("A Note on Channing's Transcendentalism") respond to Ladu's thesis.

The essays by Ahlstrom and Wright review the Channing revival of the fifties; Ahlstrom outlines what remains to be done, Wright corrects what has been done. Ahlstrom calls for a reconstruction of Channing's milieu emphasizing his vocation as minister, a corrective to the history of ideas method of Parrington and Schneider. Wright attempts to save Channing from Hopkinsian Calvinism (Schneider) and from Transcendentalism (Edgell) by arguing that Hopkins was a late and minor footnote to Channing's real affinity with Francis Hutcheson and his moral sense doctrines and, moreover, that Channing never really abandoned that philosophical archenemy of Transcendentalist epistemology, John Locke. This leaves Channing with the Protestant majority of "supernatural rationalists," committed to reason as a supporter of revealed religion, including the miracles that Emerson and Parker found such a stumbling block.

Despite his commitment to scripture, Channing refused to side with Norton in his attack on George Ripley and the Transcendentalists' evaluation of miracles, as William R. Hutchison recounts (*The Transcendentalist Ministers*). Daniel Walker Howe takes up both Ahlstrom and Wright in *The Unitarian Conscience*, the definitive study of early-nineteenth-century Unitarianism, which discusses Channing with lesser-known Unitarian colleagues. Channing is treated as a representative for Unitarian views of nature as moral symbol by Conrad Cherry, *Nature and Religious Imagination*, who emphasizes that Channing was a moral philosopher primarily. David Robinson discusses Channing's influence on Emerson in terms of their shared commitment to the idea of the growth of the soul ("The Legacy of Channing"). Bernhard Fabian's review of Channing scholarship is a useful assessment of the Channing revival.

Several other studies add to this picture of Channing's religious development. Thomas Wentworth Higginson ("Two New England Heretics") finds evidence in a letter from Channing's son that he was moving toward a Transcendentalist Christology in his late years. Francis Greenwood Peabody measures Channing against trends of nontheistic humanism but finds that Channing's humanism was theistic in origin. Neal F. Doubleday posits that Channing's literary influence was tied to his theological optimism about human nature and draws several helpful connections between Channing and Emerson. Perry Miller (*The Transcendentalists*), Alexander Kern ("The Rise of Transcendentalism"), and Claude Welch (*Protestant Thought in the Nineteenth Century*) have contributed important brief surveys of Channing's theology. Most recently, Conrad Wright has studied the evangelical and Christian aspects of "The Channing We Don't Know."

Sydney Ahlstrom's sense of Channing's influence is confirmed in Siegfried B. Puknat's two studies of his complicated relation to German philosophy. Ernest Renan's brilliant critique is the best evidence of his impact in France; it is discussed by Adrian Jaffe and translated and abridged with a discerning introduction by Warner Berthoff. Renan understood Channing's limitations ("religion without mystery, rationalism without criticism, intellectual cultivation without poetry") but also saw that, as a moral philosopher, he could be "praised unreservedly" for his originality. Other studies of Channing and French culture are Hester Hastings, *William Ellery Channing and l'Academie des Sciences Morales et Politiques 1870*, and Reino Virtanen's argument that Channing influenced Tocqueville. For a sense of Channing's reputation a century ago, see Russell Nevins Bellows, *The Channing Centenary in America, Great Britain, and Ireland*.

Robert E. Spiller's essay, a forthright attempt at "revision of a literary reputation," is the most thorough study of Channing's literary career, reminding us that, in British eyes, Channing was equalled only by Washington Irving and James Fenimore Cooper as American writers of the early nineteenth century. Spiller details the reception of Channing's works in the British quarterlies, noting attacks by William Hazlitt (1829) and Lord Brougham (1839) that ironically confirmed his importance, as violent reviews sometimes will. Contemporary reviews are listed in David Edgell's biography and in Clarence Gohdes, *American Literature in Nineteenth Century England*. Van Wyck Brooks builds on Spiller by stressing Channing's international literary reputation as "the great awakener," the opening wedge into New England's stifled intellectual atmosphere. Lyons works in Brooks's tradition, finding Channing's power not in his style or his ideas but in his "character," which helped "to establish a climate of ideas" that made Transcendentalism possible.

Lawrence Buell's *Literary Transcendentalism* forcefully reminds us that the most salient characteristic of Transcendentalism was the way it collapsed the convenient but ultimately false distinction between literature and religion, making literature a devotional act and religion a poetic effusion. Buell traces this tendency to its roots in Unitarianism, using Channing as a key example of the literary potential of the movement. Buell comments on Channing's style here and in a brief later essay ("Channing's Contribution to American Literature"), but there are few other detailed literary analyses of Channing. Marie Hochmuth stresses his conversational power, and Mary Worden Edrich finds that "The Channing Rhetoric" was limited by a rigid adherence to Hugh Blair's *Rhetoric*, with its conservative view of metaphoric language, even though some of Channing's remarks on the power of language may have encouraged Emerson's bolder style of expression ("The Rhetoric of Apostacy"). The influence of Channing's Milton essay is further explored by Phyllis Cole ("The Purity of Puritanism"), who believes that Channing shares the Transcendentalists' literary concerns.

Channing's other influential essay is "Remarks on National Literature" (1830), which has been variously described by literary historians as an early expression of nationalism and as a forerunner of Emerson's "The American Scholar." Harry Hayden Clark singles out Channing's insistence on inward and natural standards of taste rather than outer and mechanical ones (in *The Development of American Literary Criticism*, ed. Floyd Stovall), and Robert S. Ward finds the essay an important contribution to American literary independence.

Channing is hard to place on the spectrum of social reform movements. Anne Holt raises some question about the adequacy of his political views, but the attack of Arthur M. Schlesinger, Jr. (*The Age of Jackson*), has been most influential. He declares that Channing's doctrine of self-culture, which stressed individual rather than collective change, was an evasion of economic reality and a stumbling block for the poor. The argument echoes that of Orestes A. Brownson in "The Laboring Classes" (1840). Andrew Delbanco's reading of Channing is the most persuasive response to Schlesinger, pointing to the issue of slavery as "the test of his life." Delbanco's Channing is a divided man and in many senses a tragic figure, profoundly disturbed by the abuse of slavery but also too honest to accept the "easy externalization of evil" that he perceived in the abolitionist movement. Other details of the slavery issue can be found in an essay by Fulmer Mood and Granville Hicks and one by Thomas F. Harwood, and the general background of the issue is treated in Douglas C. Stange, *Patterns of Antislavery among American Unitarians*. Channing's contribution to the "ministry-at-large," an early attempt at urban social work, is discussed by Daniel Walker Howe (*The Unitarian Conscience*), Daniel T. McColgan (*Joseph Tuckerman*), and David Robinson ("Channing and the Problem of Social Reform"). Finally, John E. Reinhardt has surveyed the development of Channing's political ideas, rightly stressing the need to view them genetically and informatively placing them in the context of the politics of the period.

Channing's relation to Transcendentalism rests finally on those few contemporary documents in which he comments on the movement or its members comment on him. Elizabeth Palmer Peabody, in *Reminiscences*, reports one conversation in which Channing admits no major differences with Emerson's position in the Divinity School Address (though we have to accept Channing's doubtful sense of what that position is) and expresses sympathy with Ripley in his controversy with Norton. Important letters on the Theodore Parker controversy and on the "new movement" generally are partially reproduced in W. H. Channing's *Memoir*, where we find Channing vigorously dissenting from Parker on the existence of miracles and on the nature of Christ. But he also warmly commends Parker's views on the immutable truths of Christianity and encourages him to continue to speak and publish. Significantly, Channing calls abolitionism, not Transcendentalism, the great contemporary manifestation of practical religion.

Among Transcendentalist pronouncements on Channing, Emerson's "Historic Notes of Life and Letters in New England" (1884) is important, but the scattered references to him in his *Journals and Miscellaneous Notebooks* are also notable, especially his use of Channing's preaching as his vocational model (2: 237–42) and his entry on Channing's death in 1842 (7: 469–70). Henry F. Pommer has published Charles Chauncy Emerson's summary of "A Sermon by William Ellery Channing," and Lenthiel H. Downs reviews the points of biographical connection between Emerson and Channing.

Margaret Fuller's scattered comments amount to the most incisive critique of Channing among the Transcendentalists. She found in him a "true. . . respect for woman," without "one grain of masculine assumption," though she noted his temperamental caution in thought. She named him an ethical leader in her essay on American literature (1846), but she pointed out that his ignorance of man's "impulsive and passionate side" produced "narrow" but "noble" views of human character.

Theodore Parker's fervent eulogy, *An Humble Tribute to the Memory of William Ellery Channing, D. D.* (1842), is the most intense adulation of Channing by any of the Transcendentalists. The embattled Parker claimed Channing as the father of his undogmatic and morally-centered Unitarianism, stressing Channing's moral earnestness as the source of his influence. Parker also berated those Unitarians who had accepted Channing's leadership out of "a sectarian Zeal, a social clannishness, a political bigotry." Thus began the long war between liberal Free Religionists and conservative Unitarians for Channing's mantle; curiously, the latter group acquired the name "Channing Unitarians," a fact lamented by Minot J. Savage (in Bellows, *The Channing Centenary*). Channing's influence as a reformer is stressed in James Freeman Clarke's eulogy (*A Sermon Preached in Amory Hall* . . ., 1864) and in a later tribute by Clarke and Frederic Henry Hedge (*Services in Memory of Rev. William E. Channing* . . ., 1867). Hedge paints a paradoxical figure of no great intellectual power but with a compensating intensity of "spirituality" that gave him "more searching force than all the orators of his time."

There are other scattered testaments to Channing's influence. On Ripley, who called himself a "child of Channing," see Octavius Brooks Frothingham, *George Ripley*. On William Henry Channing, see Frothingham, *Memoir of William Henry Channing*. On Orestes Brownson, see Arthur M. Schlesinger, Jr., *Orestes A. Brownson*. On Cyrus A. Bartol, see his *Principles and Portraits*. On Jones Very, who found Channing "nearer to the kingdom of heaven than any body he had yet seen," see Edwin Gittleman, *Jones Very*. Channing, in fact, had an impact on almost all the Transcendentalists (except Thoreau, the most secular of them), and he rivaled Coleridge as the most important influence on the movement.

GEORGE WILLIAM CURTIS

W. Gordon Milne

At the age of eleven, George William Curtis heard Emerson lecture on the "over-soul." He remembered it later as the "cardinal event of our youth," instilling a faith in Transcendentalism that never left him: "How much of the wise and universal liberalizing of all views and methods is due to it! . . . The transcendental or spiritual philosophy has been strenuously questioned and assailed. But the life and character it fostered are its sufficient vindication." The practical idealism and moral enthusiasm that Curtis found embodied in the movement served as a constant guide in his political and literary careers.

The doctrine had its strongest impact on Curtis during the period 1842 to 1846, which he spent for the most part at Brook Farm and in Concord. He was drawn to the former primarily by its educational opportunities, the chance to learn from men like George Ripley, George Bradford, Charles Dana, and John Sullivan Dwight. He also enjoyed, during his eighteen-month sojourn, the community's social activities and collective labor, and he responded enthusiastically to its idealism and individualism. "One should examine himself to find the reflection of the ideal," he forthrightly proclaimed. "Every soul is necessary to my soul, but mine is not ripe and matured till it has naturally separated from every other and stands cool and alone." The "wiser man lends himself to no organization." Society is "but the shadow of the single man behind it." Such were the Emersonian notes resounding in his letters to a fellow Brook Farmer, Isaac Hecker (see Gordon Milne, *George William Curtis and the Genteel Tradition*).

These assertions of independence clearly did not harmonize altogether with the "associationist" nature of the Brook Farm experiment, and it is not surprising that

Curtis left the farm in the spring of 1844 to settle in Concord, with only his brother Burrill as his "community." To be sure, he continued to enjoy communal experiences in the congenial circle of Concord residents, developing friendships with Ralph Waldo Emerson, Henry David Thoreau, Nathaniel Hawthorne, Margaret Fuller, and others in the town's orbit, and he shared with them a faith in human perfectibility and in the importance of moral insight. As he helped Thoreau build his cabin and listened to the members of "The Club" converse in Emerson's library, he absorbed their key ideas: the importance of nature, the scholar as a man of action, the need for nativism in literature, the value of an intuitive and individualistic approach to literary art. Curtis stored all of these away in his mind and used them later in his writings.

Curtis afterwards spoke of the Brook Farm stay and its Concord sequel as "the most unique episode" of his life, and his career demonstrates how assiduously he employed the lessons learned during those formative years. On the lecture platform and in magazine pieces he argued for abolition, the extension of higher education, the elimination of child labor, the rights of Indians, and suffrage for women, exemplifying the "practical Transcendentalist" that Emerson and his friends had taught him to be. Transcendentalist strains—an assertion of the individual will, a demand for the ideal, an insistence on the right of private judgment in the face of orthodoxy and authority—echo throughout Curtis' works, suggesting the staying power of what he called the "purifying and elevating and liberalizing" influence of Emerson ("Mr. Emerson and the *Dial*"). In his political speeches and his *Harper's Magazine* "Easy Chair" column, Curtis affirmed the inherent goodness of the individual, the existence of an inward guide that permits one to know God and to recognize the moral law. With what Walt Whitman called a perpetually "large swing," Curtis went about reminding his contemporaries of that "light which God has kindled in you to walk by." We may safely conclude that the Transcendentalist movement did indeed permanently affect his "ideals of character and culture and modes of living."

Curtis once described the Transcendentalists in disparaging terms, as sitting pompously at their "meetings" seemingly ready to ask, "Who will now proceed to say the finest thing that has ever been said?" As a general rule, however, he displayed sympathy and affection for Sophia and George Ripley, Dana, and Bradford, for Brook Farm visitors like Emerson, Fuller, William Henry Channing, and Theodore Parker, and for correspondents like Dwight, Hecker, Charles King Newcomb, and Christopher Pearse Cranch. His remarks make one fact abundantly clear: Emerson impressed him the most and Amos Bronson Alcott the least. Curtis' reflections fall into the category of charming recollection rather than that of analysis or evaluation, but they nicely reproduce the impressions of a youthful idealist caught up in an idyllic community where unselfish cooperation was pursued in a lively intellectual climate. Even prickly Margaret Fuller seemed, to Curtis, "the noblest and truest of human beings."

Books on Transcendentalism mention Curtis fleetingly, if at all, and are apt to concentrate on a special aspect of his relationship. Lawrence Buell, for example, talks of Curtis' travel books, declaring that, in their focus on a self-portrayal of the traveler himself rather than on an objective account of the countries he visited, Curtis revealed himself to be "the child of Transcendentalism" (*Literary Transcendentalism*). The Brook Farm accounts mention such matters as Curtis' preference for discussions of belles lettres rather than Fourierism, and works on his political career simply suggest in general terms his abiding commitment to the principles of Brook Farm and Concord.

Curtis material on the Transcendentalists is to be found first in his letter collections, located primarily in the Houghton Library of Harvard University but also in the Abernethy Library of Middlebury College, Boston Athenæum, Boston Public Library, Library of Congress, Longfellow House (in Cambridge, Mass.), Brown University Library, Fruitlands Museums, Henry E. Huntington Library, Massachusetts Historical Society, New York Public Library, Paulist Fathers Archives (New York City), Rutherford B. Hayes Memorial Library, and Staten Island Institute of Arts and Sciences.

Other sources include his essays: "Ralph Waldo Emerson" (1852); "Mr. Emerson and the *Dial*"; "Emerson" (1893); two articles entitled "Hawthorne" (1852, 1864); and "Editor's Easy Chair" (*Har*, Jan. 1869). His "Easy Chair" columns in *Harper's New Monthly Magazine* and the volumes collected from them (*From the Easy Chair*, 1893; *Other Essays from the Easy Chair*, 1893; *From the Easy Chair, Third Series*, 1894) occasionally provide material as well, as do *Orations and Addresses of George William Curtis*, ed. Charles Eliot Norton (1894), and the unpublished "Notes of George William Curtis" (in the New York Public Library).

Two unpublished works on Curtis—Sheldon L. Berens, "The Emergence of a Moralist in Politics, George William Curtis: 1824–1849," and Florence Becker Lennon, "The Influence of Brook Farm on George William Curtis, 1842–1872"—are sources of information. See also Edward Cary, *George William Curtis*; John White Chadwick, *George William Curtis*; *Early Letters of George Wm. Curtis to John S. Dwight*; Edward H. Madden, *Civil Disobedience and Moral Law in Nineteenth-Century American Philosophy*; Gordon Milne, *George William Curtis and the Genteel Tradition*; and Joel Myerson, *The New England Transcendentalists and the* Dial. Helpful articles are George Willis Cooke, "George William Curtis at Concord"; Caroline Ticknor, "Some Early Letters of George William Curtis"; Edward H. Madden, "George William Curtis: Practical Transcendentalist"; and Milne, "George William Curtis — Inheritor of the Transcendental Mantle."

The following accounts of Brook Farm provide relevant information: George P. Bradford, "Reminiscences of Brook Farm"; Katherine Burton, *Paradise Planters*; John Thomas Codman, *Brook Farm*; Edith Roelker Curtis, *A Season in Utopia*; Zoltán Haraszti, *The Idyll of Brook Farm*; Marianne Dwight, *Letters from Brook Farm 1844–1847*, ed. Amy L. Reed; Myerson, "James Burrill Curtis and Brook Farm"; Amelia Russell, "Home Life of the Brook Farm Association"; Ora Gannett Sedgwick, "A Girl of Sixteen at Brook Farm"; and Lindsay Swift, *Brook Farm*.

For Curtis' relations with the *Dial*, see Myerson's book. For the *Harbinger*, see Sterling F. Delano, "The *Harbinger*."

EMILY DICKINSON

Paul J. Ferlazzo

What Emily Dickinson knew about Transcendentalism came to her primarily through the works of a single Transcendentalist, Ralph Waldo Emerson. She owned and read the works of Henry David Thoreau, but she never made specific mention of any of them. Her marked copies of Thoreau are in the Houghton Library of Harvard University. Of other Transcendentalist writings, it is believed she read only Margaret Fuller's translation of *Günderode* and a volume by Theodore Parker. Her comment on Parker is brief and uninformative: "I never read before what Mr. Parker wrote. I heard he was 'poison.' Then I like poison very well" (Letter 213).

There is no evidence that she ever heard Emerson on the several occasions that he lectured in Amherst or that she met him when he was the guest next door in her brother's home in December 1857. She was familiar with Emerson's writings when, in 1850, Benjamin F. Newton, an apprentice in her father's law firm who became for her a "gentle, yet grave Preceptor" (Letter 153), gave her the 1847 edition of Emerson's *Poems*. According to Jack L. Capps, *Emily Dickinson's Reading*, she certainly read the following poems by Emerson—"Each and All," "The Problem," "Woodnotes I," "Dirge," "The Sphinx," "To Rhea," "The Visit," and "The Snow Storm"—as well as "Nature" and "The Poet" from *Essays: First and Second Series*; *Representative Men*, which she called a "little Granite Book you can lean upon" (Letter 481); and Emerson's sketch of Thoreau in the *Atlantic Monthly Magazine* (1862). No doubt she read other poems and essays by Emerson—"Circles" and "Compensation," for example—evidence for which has been a continuing element of scholarly research and critical interpretation. In the *Handlist of Books Found in the Home of Emily Dickinson* are listed eight other titles by Emerson, as well as Thoreau's *Walden*,

A Week on the Concord and Merrimack Rivers, and *Letters to Various Persons*. All, or portions of them, it would seem safe to assume, were also read by Dickinson.

Dickinson's comments about the Transcendentalists and issues relating to Transcendentalism can be found in her poems and letters and in miscellaneous comments attributed to her. The definitive collections of her writings are Thomas H. Johnson, *The Poems of Emily Dickinson* (1955) and, with Theodora Ward, *The Letters of Emily Dickinson* (1958). Jay Leyda, *The Years and Hours of Emily Dickinson*, is a compilation of biographical materials and documents that supplements the letters and poems. The indexes of these works will direct the reader to relevant passages.

Bibliographic work on Emily Dickinson has been extensive. Of primary importance is Willis J. Buckingham, *Emily Dickinson, an Annotated Bibliography*. This volume has been supplemented with two addenda published in the *Emily Dickinson Bulletin*. Annual checklists appear in the *Emily Dickinson Bulletin*, renamed *Dickinson Studies* in 1978.

For explications of Dickinson's poetry, see Joseph Duchac, *The Poems of Emily Dickinson*. This is a massive and useful collection of brief excerpts from criticism relating to individual poems. It does not include theses, dissertations, microform, or foreign language items. Over 1,300 poems are listed alphabetically, and over 750 books, chapters, and articles of commentary and explication are listed.

Although scholars and critics generally agree that Transcendentalism contributed to the development of Emily Dickinson as a poet, there is some disagreement as to the extent and nature of the contribution. Between the extreme positions of arguing that she was a pure, committed Emersonian Transcendentalist on the one hand, and on the other that Transcendentalism is an overrated subject as far as Dickinson is concerned, lies a middle position that sees Transcendentalism as important but not all-important, as influential in her life but not dominant, as a philosophy from which she borrowed but borrowed selectively.

Elizabeth L. Reinke, "Puritan and Transcendental Influence on Emily Dickinson's Philosophy," says that Transcendentalism reached Dickinson through the New England atmosphere of the time, through friends, and through her reading. Benjamin F. Newton, Leonard Humphrey, Helen Hunt Jackson, and Thomas Wentworth Higginson were friends whose liberal Transcendentalist notions rubbed off on her. Her reading of Thoreau, Nathaniel Hawthorne, and James Russell Lowell probably had some slight educational value for her, but it was mainly from Emerson that she learned about Transcendentalism and formed her notions of poetic form and expression. Reinke attributes a very great deal to Emerson's influence, including Dickinson's ideas about friendship, nature, beauty, the role of the poet, self-reliance, and individualism. The differences between the two stem from the fact that Emerson was a "theological mystic" and Dickinson was not. Reinke states that, unlike Emerson, Dickinson was not a reformer, had no zeal to save the world, was not an optimist, and was never so completely transplanted out of Puritanism as the other Transcendentalists were.

Sister Mary Michelle Reney, "Transcendentalism in Emily Dickinson's Poetry," argues that Dickinson's poetry captured the Transcendentalist spirit and represented the "dynamic fulfillment" of Emerson's ideas. Reney sees Dickinson accepting all the basic principles of Transcendentalism, including the theory of innate ideas, self-reliance, denial of evil, the oversoul, and the theory of compensation. A significant bit of evidence for Reney is the fact that when Dickinson's poem "Success" appeared anonymously in *A Masque of Poets* (1878), reviewers thought it was written by Emerson.

In "Seeing New Englandly," Mary Ann Shubert plays down the influence of Emerson on Dickinson. She begins by outlining the numerous similarities between the two, suggesting that, "In many ways . . . the self Emily Dickinson portrayed in her poems seems the epitome of Emerson's intuitively knowing, self-reliant man." But Shubert goes on to note that the Transcendentalist individual was a potentially perfect creature in harmony with nature, whereas Dickinson saw human beings as helplessly in the grasp of ambivalent forces beyond their control. Shubert offers a clear summary of the differences: "Her preoccupation with the inner world, her philosophic use of the outer world of nature as a clue to inner truth, her poetic use of nature metaphors, and her preference for intuitive knowledge are all characteristic of Transcendentalism. . . . But overshadowing these affinities with Transcendentalism is her inability to believe fully in the Emersonian promise: that by achieving harmony with nature one may blend his soul with the soul of the universe, overcoming the pains of life and death by perceiving them an illusion."

Donna Cherno, "Emily Dickinson and Transcendentalism," analyzes and compares extensive quotations from Emerson, Dickinson, and Thoreau to point out similar attitudes toward nature, God, self-reliance, and formal religious practice. Cherno concludes that although Dickinson was not, strictly speaking, a Transcendentalist, "in some instances, Dickinsonian and Transcendental thought are so similar that they become indistinguishable."

In "Emily Dickinson: Viable Transcendentalist," B. R. McElderry, Jr., incautiously affirms and categorizes what he calls "obvious" parallels between Dickinson and Emerson and "easy to demonstrate" Emersonian influences. A thorough documentation of his claims is, however, lacking. His assertion that "a viable transcendentalism accounted in large part for the sale of Emily's poems between 1890 and 1920" is without substance.

Hisashi Noda, "Emily Dickinson and Transcendentalism," summarizes the positions of several leading Dickinson scholars who have analyzed Transcendentalist influences upon her poetry. Noda acknowledges the importance of Transcendentalism for Dickinson and quotes a number of poems that echo Emerson, but he concludes that these poems are her least interesting and important. "In point of fact," he writes, "most of the poems that have established Emily Dickinson as one of the greatest poets in the English language are those that show in one way or another aspects of deviation and break from the transcendental influences of her formative years. In them she shows herself to be a poet of doubt, anxiety and despair, passionately aware of her role as an individual existing in time with care and concern, talking about the separation of men from nature and inevitable revolt from tradition." Noda concludes by questioning the validity of calling her a Transcendentalist and by affirming that she "transcended Transcendentalism in many respects."

In "This Consciousness," Frank Davidson contends that Dickinson's dedication to the inner life of the soul identifies her with Transcendentalist thought. He then focuses on those ideas of Dickinson's that were not demonstrably borrowed from Emerson but are clearly analogous to Emerson's own thinking—the nature and function of the poet, the equation of truth and beauty, the use of the material world as symbol, and the idea of "double consciousness." This last concept enabled both Emerson and Dickinson to perceive the world on two levels at once—on a sensory level and a mystical suprasensory level.

James E. Mulqueen answers negatively his question, "Is Emerson's Work Central to the Poetry of Emily Dickinson?" Mulqueen points out the differences between the two on a number of significant points. Unlike Emerson, Dickinson never equated God with the oversoul and never viewed the poet as a prophet and lawgiver. Her term "circumference," Mulqueen argues, cannot be equated with Emerson's use of "circle," as some critics have held. Finally, where Emerson stressed the need for the poet to "disindividualize" the self, Dickinson focused on the unique, individual "I" in countless poems.

Joanne Feit Diehl, "Emerson, Dickinson, and the Abyss," examines those points on which Dickinson and Emerson are not in agreement. Emerson perceived a moral universe where compensation and benevolence allow man to escape discouraging circumstances. Dickinson, on the other hand, felt that the universe is indifferent toward man and does not necessarily permit release from suffering. Emerson had a conception of the self that is fluid, evolving, and boundless in its potency. Dickinson saw only two selves—herself and a strange masculine inner consciousness that she must ceaselessly confront.

Roland Hagenbuchle investigates further differences between Emerson and Dickinson with particular reference to their assumptions about the nature of language. In "Sign and Process," he points out that, for Emerson, language depends on nature for its meaning and substance, whereas Dickinson viewed language as "an autonomous symbolic realm" separate from nature. Emerson's poet, therefore, is a "namer" who "links words to things, man to nature." Dickinson's poet, on the other hand, is a lover of words who "links man to the eternal through language rather than via natural objects." Dickinson's poetry, therefore, is largely antimimetic and nonrepresentational, whereas Emerson's is predominantly presentational.

In "Dickinson, Emerson and the Abstract Concrete," Brian Attebery traces a dozen of Dickinson's abstract nouns to what he believes to be their source in Emerson's essay "Circles." He enhances the meaning given by Dickinson to "circumference," "circumscription," "circumstance," "divinity," "generation," "innocency," "omnipotence," "omnipresence," "perfect," "permanence," "possibility," and "principle" by discussing each word with reference to Emerson's definition. He suggests that other problematic words in Dickinson's poetry might benefit from similar analysis.

Several shorter articles attempt to explicate Dickinson's poems in the light of an Emersonian principle, source, or similarity, including Lee J. Richmond, "Emersonian Echoes in Dickinson's 'These Are the Signs' "; and Mario L. D'Avanzo, "Emily Dickinson's and Emerson's 'Presentiment,' " "The Emersonian Context of Three Poems by Emily Dickinson," "Dickinson's 'The Reticent Volcano' and Emerson," " 'Unto the White Creator,' " and "Emersonian Revelation in 'The way I read a letter's—this—.' "

Other articles consider the relation between Dickinson and Thoreau. Nathalia Wright, "Emily Dickinson's Boanerges and Thoreau's Atropos," admits that there is no evidence that Dickinson ever read *Walden* but attempts to show imagistic similarities between Dickinson's poem, "I like to see it lap the miles," and a section from Thoreau's chapter on "Sounds" about the Fitchburg Railroad. Thomas W. Ford, on the other hand, in "Thoreau's Cosmic Mosquito and Dickinson's Terrestrial Fly," seems to conclude that Dickinson must have read *Walden*. Ford claims the source for the image of the fly in "I heard a fly buzz—when I died" is a section from *Walden* in which Thoreau seems to hear celestial harmonies in the hum of a mosquito. Ford aligns portions of *Walden* with the Dickinson poem, enumerating Dickinson's ironical use of her possible source. Rhoda Nathan, "The Slanted Truth," emphasizes an important similarity between Dickinson and Thoreau in their commitment to seeking the truth and speaking it out clearly. Both tested the moral climate of their communities and paid the price of separation from their contemporaries. Both were nonconformists, intensely self-critical, and repelled by the glib opinion expressed by the preachers and lecturers of their day.

Although there is not a single published book on the relation between Dickinson and Transcendentalism, the debate has proceeded among scholars within larger published studies of Dickinson, American poetry, and Transcendentalism. George Frisbie Whicher, who is generally considered the first reliable biographer of Dickinson, holds that she was simply responding to the tenor of the times and owed no specific debt to a single Transcendentalist. He writes in *This Was a Poet*:

> Echoes of Emersonian ideas, if one chooses to call them that, may be detected in Emily Dickinson's poems as easily as in Whitman, but it is not profitable to single them out. The implication that Emerson created a point of view which other writers adopted is simply untrue. The resemblances that may be noted in Emerson, Parker, Thoreau, Emily Dickinson and several other New England authors were due to the fact that all were responsive to the spirit of the time. Their work was in various ways a fulfillment of the finer energies of a Puritanism that was discarding the husks of dogma.

All these writers, Whicher asserts, had "a single master thought" in common, "the conviction of self-sufficiency."

F. O. Matthiessen, *American Renaissance*, argues that Dickinson's poems were "more authentically in the metaphysical tradition than Emerson's." Henry Wells, writing in his *Introduction to Emily Dickinson*, does not sufficiently explain his belief that Dickinson was "the only person in America who really made Transcendentalism practical." Richard Chase, in *Emily Dickinson*, plays down the influence of Transcendentalism and emphasizes the importance of Calvinism: "The appeal of the Calvinist ideology was stronger for her than the appeal of Emerson's ethical spiritualism" because it had "the quality of exclusion and finality and rigorous limitation which characterized the profounder motions of Emily Dickinson's mind."

Thomas H. Johnson, the editor of Dickinson's poems and letters, holds much the same opinion as Chase. In *Emily Dickinson*, Johnson maintains that, borrowing from Romantic and Transcendentalist doctrines available in her youth, Dickinson affirmed the primacy of spiritual over material values, rejected traditional authority and logical demonstration for the freedom to follow her intuitions and personal revelations, and concluded that self-reliant individuals might improve their nature through effort. But in the final analysis, Johnson believes, she held on to her traditional values.

In *Emily Dickinson's Poetry*, Charles R. Anderson bluntly asserts it is "folly to try to make her into a Transcendentalist . . . on the evidence of [her] poems." Anderson finds no "evidence that she accepted the mystical bases of Emerson's transcendental esthetic: that the poet can absorb the spirit that energizes nature and so achieve merger with the Oversoul." Her poetic practice, Anderson adds, is "at the opposite pole from the theory of composition of the Transcendentalists. Emerson epitomized this concept of organicism by declaring that poems should grow like corn or melons in the sun, and Whitman boasted that he put the theory into practice. Dickinson was nearer to Poe in her emphasis on craftsmanship."

Clark Griffith, *The Long Shadow*, admits that Dickinson was too deeply involved with Emersonianism to be a willing critic of it, but he notes that some of her poems amount to contradictions of Emerson. To Griffith, Dickinson is "at best conceived of as a post-Emersonian, or, still more accurately perhaps, as a sort of Emersonian-in-reverse." She used Emersonian means to pursue her ends, but her poetry sometimes reflects the "shock of recognition" that those ends could have cruel and tragic opposites.

The chapter "Seeing New Englandly" in Albert J. Gelpi's *Emily Dickinson* presents a comprehensive discussion of the complex cultural milieu of the period and shows "how clearly she had absorbed, as early as 1850, the essential features of Transcendentalism—the optimism, the emphasis on experimentation and originality, the sense of social purpose, the metaphysical speculations, the pulse of rhythm and imagery." In a later review essay, Gelpi reaffirms the centrality of Emerson for Dickinson:

> In headier moments Dickinson believed with Emerson in the influx of the infinite into the finite mind, because like Emerson she had experienced it fleetingly; but the lesson of Emerson which sustained her in moments desperate as well as ecstatic was his conviction that the activity of life was the cultivation of the individual consciousness. Against the vicissitudes of time and the uncertainty of destiny she held to Emerson's famous axiom that "nothing is at last sacred but the integrity of your own mind."

In his study of American poetry, *The Tenth Muse*, Gelpi states that Emerson's description of the Transcendentalist in his essay of that title is an accurate depiction of Dickinson's temperament. Gelpi affirms that "Emerson was an inspiration and model—perhaps the inspiration and model—for Dickinson when she was choosing to be a poet."

Glauco Cambon, "Emily Dickinson and the Crisis of Self-Reliance," names "Self-Reliance," "Circles," and "Experience" as the central cluster of Emersonian sources. Cambon states that Dickinson shared Emerson's openness to experience but not his sense of oneness with the universe. Threatened with cosmic alienation, she resorted to self-reliance out of desperation.

Thomas W. Ford, *Heaven Beguiles the Tired*, believes that Dickinson turned to Transcendentalism in reaction to the darker side of her Puritan upbringing, particularly after her stay at Mount Holyoke. Transcendentalism briefly bolstered her shaken ego, but in the end she would endorse neither Puritanism nor Transcendentalism. Each served to highlight what in the other was unacceptable to her.

In *Circumference and Circumstance*, William R. Sherwood categorically states that Dickinson "rejected the tone, the taste, and the assumptions of transcendentalism." He holds that the Transcendentalist equation of God, man, and nature was to her "inane, blasphemous, and naive."

The chapter entitled "Proud Ephemeral: Emily Dickinson" in Hyatt H. Waggoner, *American Poets from the Puritans to the Present* (an earlier version appeared as "Emily Dickinson: The Transcendent Self"), is a strong argument for the importance of Emersonian Transcendentalism to Dickinson. Waggoner considers her admiration for Emerson of such magnitude that he speaks of her dual parentage: "Emily Dickinson could be said to have had two fathers and to have been deeply attached to both of them, though they pulled her in opposite directions." Her spiritual growth, Waggoner hypothesizes, consisted of private, lifelong debates with both Emerson and her father, questioning the two distinct faiths, Transcendentalism and Calvinism, that sustained these two very different men. Emerson, eventually, offered her not only a spiritual alternative to Calvinism but a conception of the proper role of the poet as well. He provided her with symbols and imagery, and her notion of circumference, Waggoner argues, came directly from Emerson's essay "Circles." Emerson became her rock, her church, and (along with nature and the Bible) one of the three resources she leaned upon for consolation in life.

Inder Nath Kher qualifies the importance of Emerson for Dickinson in *The Landscape of Absence*. He admits similarities in style and philosophy but maintains that they do not necessarily reflect the influence of Emerson. Kher emphasizes Dickinson's often quoted claim that, as an artist, she "never consciously touches a paint mixed by another." He upholds her uniqueness and sees the self in her poetry as quite distinct from the transcendent self or the oversoul of Emerson.

Robert Weisbuch calls Dickinson "transcendental" only in the general and broadest sense of the term, without reference to a specific philosophy or a set of fixed ideas. In *Emily Dickinson's Poetry* he further suggests that Emerson may have begun to doubt his initial exuberant visions of life by the time Dickinson might have been influenced by him. Nevertheless, Weisbuch sees Emerson's essay "Circles" as central to an understanding of Dickinson's poetic technique and her use of the term "circumference."

In the chapter "The Unused Universe," Karl Keller, *The Only Kangaroo among the Beauty*, analyzes all the evidence in her life and poetry concerning her relation with Emerson and comes to the conclusion that much scholarly opinion on the subject is conjecture. Keller believes that her abrasive skepticism severely limited the influence of Transcendentalist ideas. He sees the spirit of Emerson, rather than his ideas, as having an important influence upon her. She turned to him as an aid and encouragement to her own spiritual growth, the development of her will, and the exercise of her linguistic extravagances. She responded to Emerson not as the great teacher of Transcendentalist ideology but "as push, as stimulus, as prophet—as motivator, as prime mover, as provocateur." She was moved by Emerson to become herself rather than to become his student or disciple. Beyond this, Keller describes how she learned from Emerson the power of the aphoristic style.

One of the most promising areas of future research has been brought to the attention of Dickinson scholars by the publication of Joseph Duchac's *The Poems of Emily Dickinson*. This compilation reveals that over four hundred poems of hers have received no critical attention at all. An analysis of these neglected poems may provide valuable insights into a number of her major themes, including Transcendentalism.

NATHANIEL HAWTHORNE

Joel Myerson

Studies that attempt to discuss Hawthorne and Transcendentalism are faced with an odd juxtaposition: of all the major American Renaissance authors not clearly a Transcendentalist, Hawthorne was probably the one most closely associated with the people in the movement, while, at the same time, expressing his objections to its tenets in his writings. Hawthorne, steeped in Puritan history and deeply concerned with the problem of evil as an active force in the world, was nevertheless a Brook Farmer and neighbor of Ralph Waldo Emerson, Henry David Thoreau, and Amos Bronson Alcott in Concord. The man whom Herman Melville described as saying "NO! in thunder" was married to Sophia Peabody, whose whole family had strong sympathies and ties with the Transcendentalists. These contradictory elements in Hawthorne's own life, combined with the essential ambiguity of his fiction, have produced no consensus of opinion on Hawthorne's relationship with Transcendentalism.

BIBLIOGRAPHIES

Hawthorne has been in the critical and public eye since the publication of *The Scarlet Letter* in 1850, yet we lack a good bibliography of writings about him. Partial but well-annotated bibliographies are Buford Jones, *Checklist of Hawthorne Criticism, 1951-1966*, and Theodore L. Gross and Stanley Wertheim, *Hawthorne, Melville, Stephen Crane*. Beatrice Ricks, Joseph D. Adams, and Jack O. Hazelrig combined to produce *Nathaniel Hawthorne: A Reference Bibliography*, a miserable collection of erroneous entries and misleading annotations. Jeanetta Boswell, *Nathaniel Hawthorne and the Critics*, lists materials published between 1900 and 1978, but it is incomplete, inaccurate, and unannotated, and it contains entries for works that barely mention Hawthorne. Until a good bibliography is published (Buford Jones has one in preparation), one must still rely on *AAL* supplemented by the *MLA International Bibliography*, *AmLS*, and the regular bibliographical checklists published in the *Nathaniel Hawthorne Society Newsletter* (1975–) and the now-defunct *Nathaniel Hawthorne Journal* (1971–78). Two useful bibliographical essays have been written by Walter Blair for *Eight American Authors*. Lea Bertani Vozar Newman, *A Reader's Guide to the Short Stories of Nathaniel Hawthorne*, is a masterful study of fifty-four stories. For each, Newman discusses the publication history, circumstances of composition, sources and influences, relationship with other Hawthorne works, and interpretation and criticism. David Kesterson is presently working on a similar study of all of Hawthorne's works.

For Hawthorne's own writings, the standard work is C. E. Frazer Clark, Jr., *Nathaniel Hawthorne: A Descriptive Bibliography*. Hawthorne's manuscripts are incompletely listed in *ALM*. Two useful adjuncts are Evangeline M. O'Connor, *Analytical Index to the Works of Nathaniel Hawthorne*, and John R. Bryers, Jr., and James J. Owen, *A Concordance to the Five Novels of Nathaniel Hawthorne*.

WRITINGS

The standard edition of Hawthorne's writings, *The Centenary Edition of the Works of Nathaniel Hawthorne*, ed. William Charvat et al., 14 vols. to date, has already published his *American Notebooks*, *French and Italian Notebooks*, and *Letters*. For Hawthorne's *English Notebooks*, the edition by Randall Stewart (1941) is standard until a reedited version is published in the Centenary Edition.

Hawthorne left numerous comments on Transcendentalism in his published and private writings, of which perhaps the best known is the sketch of the "Giant Transcendentalist" in "The Celestial Railroad" (1843):

> . . . as to his form, his features, his substance, and his nature generally, it is the chief peculiarity of this huge miscreant, that neither he for himself, nor anybody for him, has ever been able to describe them. As we rushed by the cavern's mouth, we caught a hasty glimpse of him, looking somewhat like an ill-proportioned figure, but considerably more like a heap of fog and duskiness. He shouted after us, but in so strange a phraseology that we knew not what he meant, or whether to be encouraged or affrighted.

Hawthorne's often acerbic comments on contemporaries in "The Hall of Fantasy" (1843), which were omitted when the story was collected in his *Mosses from an Old Manse*, are described in Harold P. Miller, "Hawthorne Surveys His Contemporaries," and incorporated into the Centenary Edition (1974). Included are remarks on Bronson Alcott (a "great mystic innovator"), Orestes Brownson (an "acute and powerful intellect"), Charles King Newcomb ("in a deep mist of metaphysical fantasies"), Jones Very ("alone, within a circle, which no other of mortal race could enter, nor himself escape from"), and, of course, Emerson ("No more earnest seeker after truth than he, and few more successful finders of it; although, sometimes, the truth assumes a mystic unreality and shadowyness in his grasp"). Hawthorne also comments on his contemporaries, though more favorably, in "The Old Manse" (1846). For possible Transcendentalist echoes in "The Artist of the Beautiful," "The Celestial Railroad," "Ethan Brand," "The Great Stone Face" (in which the character of Ernest is thought to be based on Emerson), "The Man of Adamant," and "Rappaccini's Daughter," see Lea Newman's guide to the short stories.

Along with Hawthorne's letters, the best place to go for his opinions on the Transcendentalists is his *American Notebooks*, which include some perceptive and blunt appraisals. First published in a bowdlerized version by his wife in 1868, they were correctly edited in 1932 by Randall Stewart (whose notes are still valuable) and again, as part of the Centenary Edition, in 1972 by Claude M. Simpson.

BIOGRAPHY

The first biographies of Hawthorne were written by people who knew both him and the Transcendentalists and could remember the relationship between them. Of particular use are James T. Fields, *Yesterdays with Authors*, George Parsons Lathrop, *A Study of Hawthorne*, Julian Hawthorne, *Nathaniel Hawthorne and His Wife*, Moncure D. Conway, *Life of Nathaniel Hawthorne*, Rose Hawthorne Lathrop, *Memories of Hawthorne*, Julian Hawthorne, *Hawthorne and His Circle*, and Caroline Ticknor, *Hawthorne and His Publisher*. Of the modern biographies, those particularly strong on Hawthorne's association with the Transcendentalists are Robert Cantwell, *Nathaniel Hawthorne*, Randall Stewart, *Nathaniel Hawthorne*, Hubert H. Hoeltje, *Inward Sky*, James R. Mellow, *Nathaniel Hawthorne in His Times*, and Arlin Turner, *Nathaniel Hawthorne*. Also of use is Maurice Bassan, *Hawthorne's Son: The Life and Literary Career of Julian Hawthorne*.

Two periods of Hawthorne's life are especially pertinent in discussing his relations with the Transcendentalists: the time he spent at the Brook Farm community (April-October 1841) and the years he spent residing in the Old Manse in Concord (1842-45).

Hawthorne went to Brook Farm to establish a life of work and study for himself, into which he could bring Sophia Peabody after their marriage, but he left disappointed with the community and its ideas. *Autobiography of Brook Farm*, ed. Henry W. Sams, collects most of Hawthorne's remarks on the community, and Joel Myerson, *Brook Farm*, lists and comments on writings about the community—and Hawthorne—by members, visitors, and later critics. Nearly every book on Hawthorne or Brook Farm mentions his stay there, usually drawing upon the same documents, and they may be supplemented for factual material by M. D. Conway, "Concerning Hawthorne and Brook Farm," Manning Hawthorne, "Hawthorne and Utopian Socialism," Robert F. Metzdorf, "Hawthorne's Suit against Ripley and Dana," and Joseph T. Gordon, "Nathaniel Hawthorne and Brook Farm." In more specific studies, Arlin Turner discusses "Hawthorne and Reform" and concludes that Hawthorne rejected Brook Farm out of a conviction that "man's efforts to improve society will accomplish nothing until the heart is purified." Lillian Beatty, in "Typee and

Blithedale," argues that both Melville and Hawthorne rejected their respective idealized communities because they believed that individuals should not isolate themselves from society, that it is folly to attempt to reform an evil world, and that the intellect should not be glorified at the expense of the heart. In "Art vs. Utopia: The Case of Nathaniel Hawthorne and Brook Farm," Taylor Stoehr shows how Hawthorne differed from Emerson and Thoreau on the subject. A good general study of Hawthorne and reform is Lawrence Sargent Hall, *Nathaniel Hawthorne, Critic of Society*.

The one tangible result of Hawthorne's stay at Brook Farm was *The Blithedale Romance* (1852), which has long been considered a roman à clef about his Brook Farm days. Although there is considerable evidence that Hawthorne partially based his account upon people and incidents at Brook Farm, it would be unwise to read the story as pure autobiography or to see the characters as having exact counterparts in the real people of the community, just as Hawthorne himself warned in his preface to the novel. Of the many studies that attempt to find Hawthorne's models at Brook Farm, the best are Arlin Turner, "Autobiographical Elements in Hawthorne's *The Blithedale Romance*," Lina Böhmer, *Brookfarm und Hawthornes* Blithedale Romance, Harrison Bounds, "Brook Farm and Hawthorne's *The Blithedale Romance*," George H. Bell, "Nathaniel Hawthorne, Brook Farm, and *The Blithedale Romance*," and Judith Müller Anderson, "Hawthorne's Use of Experience in *The Blithedale Romance*." Of the critical studies of the novel, two are particularly good in relating Hawthorne's art to his life: Darrel Abel, "Hawthorne's Skepticism about Social Reform with Especial Reference to *The Blithedale Romance*," and Hans-Joachim Lang, "*The Blithedale Romance*."

It was in Concord, where Hawthorne moved after marrying Sophia in July 1842, that he established his friendships with Emerson, Thoreau, and the Alcotts. The best study of this period is John Joseph McDonald, "Hawthorne at the Old Manse," which is the basis for several articles: "The Old Manse Period Canon," "A Sophia Hawthorne Journal, 1843–1844," and the essential "A Guide to Primary Source Materials for the Study of Hawthorne's Old Manse Period." A good firsthand account is Moncure Daniel Conway, "The Transcendentalists of Concord." In "The Concord Group," Randall Stewart concludes that Hawthorne's relationship with Emerson was "pleasant enough, despite divergences of opinion," and that his friendship with Thoreau was generally positive, with both Emerson and Hawthorne agreeing on the younger man's "merits and limitations." More information about Hawthorne's life in Concord can be found in biographies of him and his neighbors and in histories of the town.

Hawthorne's relationship with Emerson was an odd one: neither man was in particular sympathy with the other's philosophy, and, later, they differed sharply over Emerson's support of John Brown and Hawthorne's support of Franklin Pierce. Randall Stewart (in his edition of the *American Notebooks*) has characterized their relationship as "a one-sided one, Emerson making all the advances." Emerson's own writings show his fondness for Hawthorne the man ("It was easy to talk with him— there were no barriers"), his awareness of Hawthorne's "unwillingness and caprice," and his dislike of Hawthorne's writings ("not good for anything"). Hawthorne's notebooks depict Emerson as "the mystic, stretching his hand out of cloud-land, in vain search for something real; and the man of sturdy sense, all of whose ideas seem to be dug out of his mind, hard and substantial," resulting in his being "a great searcher for facts; but they seem to melt away and become unsubstantial in his grasp." As Hawthorne put it in the preface to *Mosses from an Old Manse*, he admired Emerson as "a poet of deep beauty and austere tenderness, but sought nothing from him as a philosopher."

An excellent survey of the two men's relationship while living together in Concord is Gay Wilson Allen, "Emerson and Hawthorne, Neighbors." Most general studies take the tone of Elisabeth Luther Cary, who sees "Hawthorne and Emerson" as representing "sombre melancholy" and "high serenity," respectively. This meeting of opposites is also the theme of James W. Davies, "The Vision of Evil," and James M. Cox, "Emerson and Hawthorne." In "Emerson, Hawthorne, and *The Blithedale Romance*," Gustaaf Van Cromphout sees the two men more in agreement (particularly on reform) than is usually supposed, and R. A. Yoder finds similarities in their artistic views in "Hawthorne and the Artist." Ralph L. Rusk, "Emerson in Salem," shows how Hawthorne arranged for Emerson to lecture in that city. Other articles deal specifically with Emerson as a source for Hawthorne's works: B. Bernard Cohen, "Emerson's 'The Young American' and Hawthorne's 'The Intelligence Office,' " which also offers a good summary of their relationship between 1842 and 1844; Clare R. Goldfarb, "*The Marble Faun* and Emersonian Self-Reliance"; and Mary Sue Schriber, "Emerson, Hawthorne, and 'The Artist of the Beautiful.' " A broad and generally uninformative study is Beatrice E. Marotte, "The Influence of Emerson on Hawthorne." A complete list of works on the Emerson-Hawthorne relationship can be found in Robert E. Burkholder and Joel Myerson, *Ralph Waldo Emerson*.

The relationship between Thoreau and Hawthorne was less prickly than that between Emerson and Hawthorne. Thoreau had not yet published his major works when Hawthorne moved to Concord—indeed, he was just beginning his career as a writer— and the two men came together more on social than on literary or philosophical grounds. Hawthorne appreciated Thoreau's knowledge of nature and spent many hours in his company, often rowing with Thoreau on the river in a boat he had purchased from him. Unlike Emerson, Thoreau respected Hawthorne's reticence with other people, possibly because he himself appreciated, if not adopted, this trait. Hawthorne called Thoreau "a healthy and wholesome man to know," and Thoreau described to Emerson a visit with Hawthorne in this manner: "We had nothing to say to one another, and therefore we said a great deal!" After Hawthorne left Concord he continued to support Thoreau, getting him lecture engagements, trying to place his work with publishers, and encouraging others to read his books; see Raymond Adams, "Hawthorne and a Glimpse of *Walden*," Edward C. Sampson, "Three Unpublished Letters by Hawthorne to Epes Sargent," and Raymona E. Hull, "Hawthorne's Effort to Help Thoreau." The best general study of the relationship is Edward Cronin Peple, Jr., "The Personal and Literary Relationship of Hawthorne and Thoreau," from which two general articles are drawn: "The Background of the Hawthorne-Thoreau Relationship" and "Hawthorne on Thoreau, 1853–1857." Thoreau's possible influence on specific works by Hawthorne has been suggested by Frank Davidson, "Thoreau's

Contribution to Hawthorne's *Mosses*"; Buford Jones, " 'The Hall of Fantasy' and the Early Hawthorne-Thoreau Relationship," who contends that the narrator's guide is a "thinly disguised fictional portrait of Thoreau"; Richard Fleck, "Hawthorne's Possible Use of Thoreau in *The Marble Faun*"; G. Thomas Couser, " 'The Old Manse,' *Walden*, and the Hawthorne-Thoreau Relationship"; Edward Cronin Peple, Jr., "Thoreau and Donatello"; and Richard Predmore, "Thoreau's Influence on Hawthorne's 'The Artist of the Beautiful.' " More generally, David B. Kesterson, "Hawthorne and Nature," argues that it was Sophia Hawthorne, not Thoreau, who shaped Hawthorne's thoughts on nature, and Donald Ross, Jr., discusses the comments of "Hawthorne and Thoreau on 'Cottage Architecture.' " In " 'Grace' in the Thought of Emerson, Thoreau, and Hawthorne," Hyatt H. Waggoner finds the three essentially in agreement, though Hawthorne was more conservative. On the other hand, the differences between the three are discussed in passing in Taylor Stoehr, *Nay-Saying in Concord*, and, in a more specialized study, G. Ferris Cronkhite, "The Transcendental Railroad."

Three women associated with the Transcendentalists were important in Hawthorne's life: Sophia Peabody Hawthorne, Elizabeth Palmer Peabody (his wife's sister), and Margaret Fuller. Hawthorne's relationship with Sophia, an ardent early enthusiast of Emerson and Transcendentalism, is discussed in all the biographies of Hawthorne. The literature on Elizabeth Peabody (as well as on her sisters) is described in the chapter on her in this volume, but see especially Norman Holmes Pearson, "Elizabeth Peabody on Hawthorne," *Hawthorne's Two "Engagements,"* and "A 'Good Thing' for Hawthorne"; John O. Rees, Jr., "Elizabeth Peabody and 'The Very ABC' "; Arlin Turner, "Elizabeth Peabody Reviews *Twice-Told Tales*"; and Wayne Allen Jones, "Sometimes Things Just Don't Work Out." It should be noted that because Hawthorne did not always appreciate Peabody's interest (he would later term it meddling) in his affairs, some critics think that his portrait of Hepzibah Pyncheon in *The House of the Seven Gables* (1851) is based on her.

Hawthorne's relationship with Margaret Fuller was a complex one. He was uneasy about her aggressiveness but tended to treat it lightly, as in his sketch to Sophia from Brook Farm of "a transcendental heifer, belonging to Miss Margaret Fuller," who was "very fractious, I believe, and apt to knock over the milk pail." And he asked Sophia, "Thou knowest best, whether, in these traits of character, she resembles her mistress." More seriously, he was not pleased by Fuller's attempts to get Ellery Channing and his wife (Fuller's sister) to board with him and Sophia in Concord. Hawthorne's overall attitude towards Fuller is generally characterized as negative because of what is supposed to be his portrait of her as Zenobia in *The Blithedale Romance* and his comments on her while in Italy. For her part, Fuller seemed to like Hawthorne but considered him too reserved. In print, she championed his writings, and in her essay "American Literature" (1846) she called him "the best writer of the day." (For a discussion of all her comments on Hawthorne, see Vivian C. Hopkins, "Margaret Fuller.") In her private writings, she was similarly favorable; see Joel Myerson, "Margaret Fuller's 1842 Journal." Two good general studies, both M.A. theses, are Anne Elizabeth Gushee, "Nathaniel Hawthorne and Margaret Fuller," and Veda

Bagwell Sprouse, "The Relationship of Nathaniel Hawthorne and Margaret Fuller."

The character of Zenobia in *The Blithedale Romance* has always been identified with Fuller. It would be fair to say that Fuller may have given Hawthorne ideas for some of Zenobia's characteristics, but the overall similarities are not such that the two can be equated. Besides the aforementioned general articles on *The Blithedale Romance*, see Kelly Thurman, "Margaret Fuller in Two American Novels," and Jessie A. Coffie, "Margaret Fuller as Zenobia in *The Blithedale Romance*." When Julian Hawthorne published *Nathaniel Hawthorne and His Wife* in 1884, he "definitely" identified Fuller with Zenobia and included a section from his father's Italian notebooks quoting disparaging remarks about Fuller's husband, Giovanni Ossoli, and describing Fuller as "a great humbug,—of course with much talent and moral reality, or else she could never have been so great a humbug." The response was immediate: Julian was blasted for lacking a sense of propriety in publishing these remarks, and Fuller's friends rushed to her defense, the best rebuttal being Frederick T. Fuller, "Hawthorne and Margaret Fuller Ossoli." In this century, Francis E. Kearns, "Margaret Fuller as a Model for Hester Prynne," has seen Hawthorne's negative view of Fuller's relationship with Ossoli as the basis for Hester's fictional relationship with Arthur Dimmesdale. The Hawthorne-Fuller controversy was begun anew by Oscar Cargill, who, in "Nemesis and Nathaniel Hawthorne," argued that Hawthorne disliked Fuller's influence over Sophia and her attempts to insinuate the Channings into their household. According to Cargill, Zenobia was his "devastating satire" of her, but when his own sister died—like Fuller— of drowning, he felt that this act was divine retribution for his treatment of Fuller in *The Blithedale Romance*, and his creative powers were stilled. Immediate refutations of Cargill's poorly substantiated guesswork appeared: William Peirce Randel, "Hawthorne, Channing, and Margaret Fuller," and Austin Warren, "Hawthorne, Margaret Fuller, and 'Nemesis.'" Recent critics have looked more positively on Hawthorne's relationship with Fuller: Darrel Abel, "Hawthorne on the Strong Dividing Lines in Nature," describes his feelings as ambivalent, and Paul John Eakin notes Hawthorne's sensitivity to Fuller's different public and private personae in "Margaret Fuller, Hawthorne, and Sexual Politics." A complete listing of the literature on the Hawthorne-Fuller relationship can be found in Joel Myerson, *Margaret Fuller* (1977).

Finally, there are the following discussions of Hawthorne and other Transcendentalists: Frederick Wagner, "All Pine and Apple Orchard: Hawthorne and the Alcotts"; Rita K. Gollin, "Louisa May Alcott's 'Hawthorne'"; and Robert D. Arner, "Hawthorne and Jones Very." For Ellery Channing, see the chapter on him in this book, his own comments in *Thoreau*, and his poems "Hawthorne at the Old Manse" and "Count Julian."

CRITICISM

Although most discussions of Hawthorne's relationship with Transcendentalism concentrate on Brook Farm and individual Transcendentalists, there are general critical studies of value. Unfortunately, the subject is not adequately dealt with in any long work, including these M.A. theses: Alice Cabell Curtis, "Hawthorne—His Relations to the Transcendental Movement," William Donald Jordan, "Hawthorne and New England Transcendentalism," and Marie T. Steele, "Nathaniel Hawthorne and Transcendentalism." Marjorie J. Elder, *Nathaniel Hawthorne*, is also disappointing: her conclusion that Hawthorne and the Transcendentalists employed similar aesthetics (such as using symbols to stand for particular natural facts) is not new, and her book is generally marred by excessive quotation and paraphrasing. Still of use is Roy R. Male, Jr., " 'From the Innermost Germ.' " Of mixed value is Nancy L. Bunge, "Beyond Transcendentalism." In *Hawthorne's View of the Artist*, Millicent Bell argues that although Hawthorne agreed with the transcendental view of art ("a presentation of that ideal of which the visible world is but an imperfect expression"), his "important judgments on life [were] anti-Romantic," leading him "ultimately" to criticize Transcendentalism.

Other critics have seen the issue as more clear-cut. Those who feel that Hawthorne was an anti-Transcendentalist include Mary V. Hillman, "Hawthorne and Transcendentalism"; Austin Warren in his edition of *Nathaniel Hawthorne: Representative Selections*; Roy R. Male, *Hawthorne's Tragic Vision*; Dell Landreth McKeithan, "Nathaniel Hawthorne's Satire of Transcendentalism in 'The Artist of the Beautiful' "; and Michael J. Hoffman, *The Subversive Vision*. Still others, like Hawthorne himself, prefer a more balanced view. Frank Preston Stearns, "Hawthorne and Transcendentalism," argues that he sympathized too much with the Transcendentalists to be negative about them and, possibly because of his wife's and sister-in-law's own friendships with them, he had "no malice in his satire." In *American Renaissance*, F. O. Matthiessen sees Hawthorne as having an intellectual kinship with the Transcendentalists but differing with them over the issue of reform. B. R. McElderry, Jr., "The Transcendental Hawthorne," shows that a positive stream of Transcendentalism balanced the Puritan side of Hawthorne's writings. In "Hawthorne and Hindu Literature," Jac Tharpe notes parallels between Hawthorne's writings and the Hindu texts being read at the same time by the Transcendentalists. R. A. Yoder, in an excellent discussion of "Transcendental Conservatism and *The House of the Seven Gables*," concludes that Hawthorne, like Emerson, infused his work "with a special, shared consciousness— an English heritage that mingled Burke's spirit of a gentleman and reverence for the historical imagination with the radical idealism of the young Romantic poets." Most recently, Alfred Rosa, in *Salem, Transcendentalism, and Hawthorne*, argues that "Transcendentalism, more than any other single influence on him, was instrumental . . . in developing his philosophy, shaping his writings, and creating the tensions on which any artist thrives."

There are still many avenues of research open on Hawthorne and Transcendentalism. We still do not have an accurate and complete portrait of his relations with all the Transcendentalists and especially with Emerson, despite the opportunities for research opened up by McDonald's studies. We still have no adequate study of Sophia's relations with Hawthorne and her influence on her husband. And we still lack a solid study that relates Hawthorne's intellectual, philosophical, and religious thought to what his Transcendentalist contemporaries were doing.

JAMES RUSSELL LOWELL

Thomas Wortham

Time and place made James Russell Lowell in many respects one with the Transcendentalists: intellectual temperament—he called it a "Toryism of the nerves"—kept him apart, but the personal associations still weighed heavily. Lowell's respect and admiration for Ralph Waldo Emerson in particular increased over the years until his praise in "Emerson the Lecturer" took on messianic dimensions: "Emerson awakened us," Lowell wrote in 1868; he "saved us from the body of this death." Several years later, out of a sense of irreparable debt, Lowell dedicated to Emerson his most distinguished and enduring collection of literary essays, *Among My Books: Second Series* (1876). None of the other men and women associated with the Transcendentalist movement fared nearly so well in Lowell's estimation, but he knew them all, both professionally and sometimes even as friends. Personal affection could, in Lowell's judgment, redeem the intellectual excesses of his Harvard friend and original Transcendentalist, Charles Stearns Wheeler, just as later it would in his friendly relations with George William Curtis and John Sullivan Dwight, but toward the likes of Thomas Wentworth Higginson, Moncure D. Conway, F. B. Sanborn, and Elizabeth Palmer Peabody, Lowell's cordiality was never untainted by an ill-disguised sense of amused superiority. With Henry David Thoreau, Margaret Fuller, and Ellery Channing, Lowell's lack of sympathy led him to misrepresent their work, ignore their lasting importance, and attack their character and motives. In short, Lowell's response to the Transcendentalists was as mixed and contradictory as were his attitudes towards most of the great issues and concerns of his times. Like other modern conservatives, he was forced to argue largely in terms of the enemy's formulations, and his ultimate defeat—as well as his intellectual stance—was not unlike that of the New Humanists, Irving Babbitt and Paul Elmer More, a generation after.

Lowell disliked the term "transcendental" when used to describe the philosophical climate in New England during the late 1830s and the 1840s, characterizing it as a "maid of all work for those who could not think." The general index to the ten-volume standard "Riverside Edition" of Lowell's *Writings* (1890) shows how rarely he addressed the subject of "Transcendentalism" in his published works. Only two of his essays deal with the movement in detail, and both reflect the response of a mature Lowell no longer impressed, as he once had been, by the vitality of philosophical idealism and romantic mysticism. "Emerson the Lecturer" first appeared as "Mr. Emerson's New Course of Lectures" in the *Nation* (1868); enlarged by the addition of the greater part of Lowell's review of Emerson's *The Conduct of Life* (1861), it was reprinted in his collection of essays, *My Study Windows*, in 1871. "Thoreau," also collected in *My Study Windows*, was written as a review of Thoreau's *Letters to Various Persons* (1865), but it is, in fact, Lowell's fullest discussion of the Transcendentalist movement. His earlier review of Thoreau's *A Week on the Concord and Merrimack Rivers* (1849) and his sympathetic essay on Sylvester Judd's poem, *Philo: An Evangeliad* (1850), Lowell's only other prose writings on the Transcendentalists, were never reprinted by him, but they have been edited by Graham H. Duncan in "James Russell Lowell's Reviews of American Belles-Lettres."

Although Transcendentalist principles inspired many of the poems Lowell wrote during the decade following his graduation from Harvard in 1838, he is better remembered for his satiric attacks on the movement in his *Class Poem* (1838) and *A Fable for Critics* (1848). A more balanced but still unsympatheic poem on Margaret Fuller and Amos Bronson Alcott, "Studies for Two Heads," was frequently reprinted by Lowell after its first appearance in *Poems: Second Series* in 1848. Except in his warm tribute to "Agassiz" (1874), Lowell left no poetic sketch of Emerson other than in his satiric verses. In an age that tended to memorialize itself in rhyme, this was a curious omission. Emerson, on his part, read some lines "To Lowell, on His Fortieth Birthday" in 1859 but deemed them unworthy of publication; Edward Waldo Emerson and Charles Eliot Norton did not share his misgivings and saw that they were printed (1893) after Emerson and Lowell died. One suspects—and Lowell's extant writings support the impression—that Lowell failed to grasp the fundamental meaning and the far-reaching significance of Emerson and the other Transcendentalists.

At first, this failure was largely deliberate. Lowell's Harvard preceptors had grown increasingly alarmed at his disrespectful attitude towards them, and finally in exasperation they rusticated him to Concord during the glorious final weeks of spring term of his senior year. Ostensibly he went there to read John Locke's *Essay Concerning Human Understanding* and James Mackintosh's *Review of Ethical Philosophy*, neither in any way transcendental, but Lowell thought his time better spent in hating Concord and its country ways and working on his graduation poem. Lowell's tutor in exile was the Reverend Barzillai Frost, a man so witless and self-centered as to prove no match for the worldly-wise adolescent. Emerson's kindly overtures were another matter. Invited by the older man to accompany him on walks and into his household, Lowell remembered ever afterward "the exquisite suavity of his demeanor toward me—

a boy of nineteen and very young for my age." But the pride of the moment overcame this favorable impression, especially when Lowell detected an element of
foolishness in Emerson's sayings and, worse, in those calling themselves disciples. Frequent reports went out to Cambridge of the curious amusements of Concord. Immediately after his introduction to Emerson's circle, Lowell wrote to his classmate
Nathan Hale:

> Emerson is a very pleasant man in private conversation but his "talk" did not increase
> my opinion of his powers. He seemed to try after effect &—fail. After all I'd heard of
> him, as an Eagle soaring in pride of place, I was surprised to see a poor little hawk stoop-
> ing at flies or at best sparrows & groundlings. The "elect" would have pleased you, or
> I'll lose my guess. There was E[dward]. A[ugustus]. R[enouf]. did naught but ogle.
> R[ufus]. E[llis]. sat wiping the perspiration off his visage which I came to the conclusion
> was heated by vicinity of nose. W[endell]. P[hillips]. M. P. scarce said a word, E[dward].
> A. W[ashburn]. & G[eorge]. W[arren]. L[ippitt]. did all the talking. I was amused to
> see that none of the company saving E[merson] & myself made any direct assertion, it
> was all ?'s—as "Wouldn't it?" & "Isn't it?" &c.   (8 July 1838)

Four days later Lowell reported having met Thoreau, and his first impression was never
corrected: "It is exquisitely amusing to see how he imitates Emerson's tone & manner. With my eyes shut I shouldn't kn[ow] them apart."

It was during Lowell's unhappy rural retreat that Emerson went down to Cambridge to address the youth of the Divinity College. Lowell did not hear Emerson's
attack on historical Christianity, and it would be some months before he could read
the words in print, but on the authority of hearsay Lowell entered the theological
"storm in a washbowl" intent on defending cloth and gown. Writing to Hale on
23 July 1834, he asked:

> Did you hear R. W. E.'s sermon (if it be not a sin to call it when our Saviour's admirable
> discourse on the mount goes by the same name). . . . ? I hear that it was an abomina-
> tion. Every divinity student that has crossed my path since have I fixed upon & questioned
> as to their opinion. . . . They have asked him to publish it—I hope he will, for if
> it excites any notice (which I very much doubt) it will put the man down—if not, why
> then—each of his disciples will be by 12½ cents the poorer. . . . They say (I don't
> know who, but they *do* say) that man sees himself in everything around him, if E. could
> see *him*self & it didn't drive him crazy (if indeed in that respect he isn't past mending)
> why—amen. I've talked more about the man than he deserves—but I never can help it.

Happily for Lowell the opportunity to set things right was at hand: his class poem
would be printed that year because a public reading was prohibited. In halting pentameters Lowell took after most of the follies of the day—abolitionism, women's rights,
temperance, and the new philosophy—but it was Emerson's recent Cambridge per-
formance that elicited his particular disgust:

> Alas! that *Christian ministers* should dare
> To preach the views of Gibbon and Voltaire!

Alas! that one whose life, and gentle ways,
E'en hate could find it in its heart to praise,
Whose intellect is equalled but by few,
Should strive for what he'd weep to find were true!

Lowell characterized Emerson's confederates in cant as "misty rhapsodists" who

having made a "universal soul,"
Forget their own in thinking of the whole;
Who, seeking nothing, wander on through space,
Flapping their half-fledged wings in Reason's face,
And if they chance the vestal flame to find,
That burns a beacon to the storm-tost mind,
Like senseless insects dish within the fire,
And sink forgotten in their funeral pyre.

During the following decade, however, Lowell repented of the reactionary heresies of his youth and penned on the cover of his *Class Poem*:

Behold the baby arrows of that wit
    Wherewith I dared assail the woundless Truth!
Love hath refilled the quiver, and with it
    The man shall win atonement for the youth

The abolition of slavery came to command Lowell's most ardent attention, but on other issues as well he chose the side of the true, good, and beautiful. No doubt Maria White, whom Lowell married in 1844, was a decisive force in his conversion. An earnest thinker and an adherent to Transcendentalism, White had been an early participant in Margaret Fuller's Boston Conversations, and her own poetry spoke to the Ideal in passionately familiar terms. After *A Year's Life* (1841), his first book of poems, Lowell's verse also reflected current fashion, both in its romantic phrasing and its idealistic outlook. "Prometheus" (1843), "A Glance behind the Curtain" (1843), "Columbus" (1848), and "The Present Crisis" (1845) are typical of the best of Lowell's committed verse of the 1840s, but the accent here is political, not transcendental. Even the several sonnets by Lowell that Emerson and Fuller printed in the *Dial* are, in the words of Leon Howard, "negatively anti-sensuous rather than positively transcendental, misty rather than visionary."

Nobody bothers much nowadays with Lowell's "serious" poetry, understandably. His real achievement was the satire and humor of *The Biglow Papers* and *A Fable for Critics*, both published in 1848, and the public poetry that occasionally appeared after the Civil War. *A Fable for Critics* spoofs Emerson, Fuller, Alcott, Thoreau, Channing, and Theodore Parker, as well as other leading literary figures who were then striving to forge an American literature. Lowell's criticisms are harsh but usually just, at least as just as humorous caricature can allow. Only Fuller is treated unfairly. Called

"Miranda" in the verses, she is lampooned by Lowell with the same lack of grace he claims to have found in her:

> She's been travelling now, and will be worse than ever;
> One would think, though, a sharp-sighted noter she'd be
> Of all that's worth mentioning over the sea,
> For a woman must surely see well, if she try,
> The whole of whose being's a capital I:
> She will take an old notion, and make it her own,
> By saying it o'er in her Sibylline tone,
> Or persuade you 'tis something tremendously deep,
> By repeating it so as to put you to sleep;
> And she well may defy any mortal to see through it,
> When once she has mixed up her infinite *me* through it.
> There is one thing she owns in her own single right,
> It is native and genuine—namely, her spite;
> Though, when acting as censor, she privately blows
> A censer of vanity 'neath her own nose.

No doubt Lowell had remembered what Fuller wrote of him two years before in her essay "American Literature" (1846):

> Lowell. . . is absolutely wanting in the true spirit and tone of poesy. His interest in the moral questions of the day has supplied the want of vitality in himself; his great facility at versification has enabled him to fill the ear with a copious stream of pleasant sound. But his verse is stereotyped; his thought sounds no depth, and posterity will not remember him.

All this was long past when the *Atlantic Monthly* was founded under Lowell's editorship in 1857. The "Newness" of the 1840s was by then historic and its proponents were published by Lowell on equal footing with those of other points of view. Thoreau objected to Lowell's unauthorized tampering with one of his essays and never afterward concerned himself with the journal, but the rest bravely bore Lowell's cavalier editing until he was succeeded by James T. Fields in 1861.

After that came time for recollection. Lowell's essays on "Thoreau" and "Emerson the Lecturer" are important historical documents, but in both he addresses himself to personal matters and not to ideas. Lowell had always fancied himself an idealist, but his idealism was based on the traditions of literature and history, not some transcendent and universal oversoul. He sought to turn the "penetrating ray" of the mind "upon what seemed the confused and wavering cloud-chaos of man's nature and man's experience, and find there the indication of a divine offer." The world of the imagination was not "the world of abstraction and nonentity, as some conceive, but a world formed out of chaos by a sense of the beauty that is in man and the earth on which he dwells." Emerson taught that man was divine; Lowell preferred to bring God down to the level of humanity. William Dean Howells, who came to Cambridge just after the Civil War, later remembered "a saying of Lowell's which he was fond of repeating at the menace of any form of the transcendental, and he liked to warn himself and others with his homely, 'Remember the dinner-bell.' "

Lowell's several biographers have all portrayed his association with the Transcendentalists, but few have considered the movement's powerful attraction on him during his youth. Horace Elisha Scudder writes with the authority of familiar acquaintance in his *James Russell Lowell*, a book that still contains much material of primary importance. Another "intimate" account of value is Edward Everett Hale, *James Russell Lowell and His Friends*. Of the more recent biographical studies, only Leon Howard, *Victorian Knight-Errant*, penetrates the attractive surface of Lowell's life to the complexities of mind and temperament that interest us today. Howard's assessment of Emerson's influence on Lowell is especially commendable, the best statement on the subject we shall probably ever have. Martin Duberman had access to a greater number of unpublished manuscripts and letters, but his reading of them in *James Russell Lowell*, though competent on Lowell's relations with the Transcendentalists, pales in comparison with Howard's earlier study. Austin Warren, "Lowell on Thoreau," is informed and judicious, though Warren confuses references to Channing and Thoreau in *A Fable for Critics*. E. J. Nichols is also uncertain about the "Identification of Characters in Lowell's *A Fable for Critics*." Fortunately, Lowell's holograph for this section of *A Fable* has been preserved (in the Henry E. Huntington Library), and it indicates that it is Ellery Channing who treads "in Emerson's tracks with legs painfully short" and Thoreau who "has picked up all the windfalls" from Emerson's orchards. Howard calls attention to this manuscript in a note to *Victorian Knight-Errant*, but it passed the notice of some: see *Toward the Making of Thoreau's Modern Reputation*, ed. Fritz Oehlschlaeger and George Hendrick, which mislocates the names.

Lowell's early venture in periodical literature, the *Pioneer*, briefly competed with Emerson's *Dial*, and for more than just readers, as Sculley Bradley points out in "Lowell, Emerson, and the *Pioneer*." In 1947 a facsimile reprint of Lowell's 1843 magazine was published, with a brief introduction by Bradley. Lowell's brief association with the *Dial* is told in interesting detail in Joel Myerson, *The New England Transcendentalists and the* Dial. Lowell's contribution to the *Harbinger*, an organ of the Brook Farm phalanx, provoked a response from John Sullivan Dwight (13 Aug. 1845), a letter ineptly edited by R. Baird Shuman.

Lowell's own letters are the great untapped resource for an understanding of his career and his times. Charles Eliot Norton's edition of the *Letters of James Russell Lowell* (1894) is limited by Norton's decorous hesitations. M. A. DeWolfe Howe's edition of *New Letters of James Russell Lowell* (1932) is limited by Howe's restricted access to the letters. The need for a much fuller and more faithfully edited volume of Lowell's correspondence is evidenced by the many recent articles that publish selected letters, two of which bear on his relations with the Transcendentalists. Joel Myerson, "Eight Lowell Letters from Concord in 1838," a series of highly amusing and revealing letters Lowell wrote to his Harvard classmate George B. Loring, is nicely complemented by Philip Graham, "Some Lowell Letters," which include letters Lowell wrote at the same time to Nathan Hale. Graham's omission of one of the best of the letters to Hale is corrected in Myerson, "Lowell on Emerson." "The Letters of James Russell Lowell to Robert Carter 1842–1876," replete with important references to various Transcendentalists and especially those who contributed to the *Pioneer*, were the subject of a worthy master's thesis by Quentin G. Johnson. Privately owned at the time of Johnson's work, the forty-seven letters are now in the Berg Collection of the New York Public Library. The valuable correspondence of Lowell's first wife is also more accessible than it was when Hope Jillson Vernon presented *The Poems of Maria Lowell with Unpublished Letters and a Biography*. It is to this area of primary documentation that scholarly attention now needs be turned.

JAMES MARSH

Douglas McCreary Greenwood

James Marsh's contribution to American Transcendentalism has always been seen in terms of his 1829 edition—the first American edition—of Samuel Taylor Coleridge's *Aids to Reflection*. That volume has been described by Perry Miller as "the most immediate force behind American Transcendentalism" and more recently by Michael West as "the hornbook of the Transcendental movement." Amos Bronson Alcott noted in his journal, "The perusal of *Aids to Reflection* . . . forms a new era in my mental and psychological life," and Ralph Waldo Emerson, who read Marsh's edition less than two months after it was published, later found the Transcendental Club an ideal place to discuss Coleridge's crucial distinction between Reason and Understanding.

What many critics have overlooked, however, is that the *Aids* the American Transcendentalists read was not simply Coleridge's 1825 London text but a new edition substantially different from the original, containing Marsh's famous "Preliminary Essay" as well as numerous footnotes intended to elucidate the more obscure passages. Marsh also had a hand in other works that influenced the Transcendentalists; he edited Coleridge's *The Statesman's Manual* and *The Friend* (the former, anonymously, in 1832; the latter, with a short introduction, the following year). In addition, Marsh translated several works from the German, including J. G. Herder's *The Spirit of Hebrew Poetry* (1833). Although George Ripley found "Prof. Marsh's Translation of Herder" too literal, lacking "the vivacity and animation" of the original, Stanley M. Vogel, with the perspective of more than a century, noted in *German Literary Influences on the American Transcendentalists* that the book "was popular with the Transcendentalists."

Marsh's Transcendentalist impulse was expressed in one other important area—

college education. As president of the University of Vermont, he instituted a curriculum based on Transcendental ideals Coleridge espoused in the *Encyclopedia Metropolitana*. In modified form, these ideas took shape as *An Exposition of the System of Instruction and Discipline Pursued at the University of Vermont* (1829), the bulk of which Marsh wrote. The small institution "optimistically called the University of Vermont" (the phrase is John J. Duffy's) thus became the showplace of Transcendentalism. In the *Selected Works of James Marsh*, ed. Peter C. Carafiol (1976), three of Marsh's most important but inaccessible publications ("Ancient and Modern Poetry," 1822, "[Review of] Stuart on the Epistle to the Hebrews," 1829, and *The System of Instruction*, 1831 ed.) and two of his German translations (Herder's *Spirit* and D. H. Hegewisch's *Introduction to Historical Chronology*, 1837) are collected along with Marsh's Vermont editions of Coleridge's *Aids* and *The Friend*.

CRITICISM AND BIOGRAPHY

The starting point for Marsh studies is still Joseph Torrey, *The Remains of the Rev. James Marsh, D.D. . . . with a Memoir of His Life*. A fairly standard nineteenth-century memoir, *The Remains* contains some ten letters; essays on subjects ranging from physiology and psychology to evangelism and the grounds of original sin; Marsh's 1826 inaugural address; and Torrey's brief "Memoir," which he rightly termed a "sketch." Torrey surely could have given us a fuller portrait of his friend. He had access to virtually all of Marsh's papers—his personal correspondence, his lectures, his unfinished essays, and his now-lost journal. Furthermore, Torrey, who succeeded Marsh as professor of moral and intellectual philosophy and, later, as president of the University of Vermont, had known Marsh since their student days at Dartmouth College and Andover Seminary. *The Remains* is indispensable, if only for suggesting the depth, diversity, and tentative nature of Marsh's unpublished writings. But John J. Duffy has pointed out the inadequacies of Torrey's "Memoir" in *Coleridge's American Disciples: The Selected Correspondence of James Marsh* (1975), and Douglas McCreary Greenwood has conjectured in "James Marsh and the Transcendental Temper" that the profound temperamental differences between Marsh and Torrey may have had a marked effect on the latter's objectivity.

The first book-length study of Marsh as a Transcendentalist, Ronald Vale Wells, *Three Christian Transcendentalists*, emphasizes the religious and philosophical dimensions of Marsh's Transcendentalism. Wells's 1972 reprint contains several previously unpublished letters, an informative scholarly introduction, and further documentation concerning John McVickar's 1839 publication of a rival American edition of *Aids*.

In *Tradition Looks Forward*, a history of the University of Vermont, Julian Ira Lindsay devotes one chapter to Marsh, which, in its very title, "Our Golden Day," reflects Lindsay's bias. One should bear in mind that much of the material now available in the James Marsh Collection at the University of Vermont was then in the hands of Marsh's descendants and other collectors. A more substantial assessment of Marsh's role in the Transcendentalist movement is Henry A. Pochmann's wide-ranging *German Culture in America*. Tracing Marsh's development as scholar, interpreter, and translator of German thought, Pochmann tries to determine what German idealism had to offer Marsh and, by extension, the American Transcendentalists. An earlier commentator on Marsh's German interests, René Wellek, concludes in "The Minor Transcendentalists and German Philosophy" that, as a belated Cambridge Platonist, Marsh developed an interest in German thought that outstripped Coleridge's understanding of Kant. A provocative and neglected area of Marsh's contribution to American intellectual history—his interest in language—is treated in some depth by Philip F. Gura, *The Wisdom of Words*. Although Gura downplays Marsh's Transcendentalism, seeing him as mediator between Puritanism and liberal evangelism, he adds a crucial dimension to Marsh's intellectual character by focusing on his sporadic attempts to postulate a new theory of language.

The most recent book-length contribution to Marsh studies is John J. Duffy's edition of Marsh's correspondence, *Coleridge's American Disciples*, which prints eighty-four letters out of a collection probably five times as large. Although the book does have minor flaws (see Douglas McCreary Greenwood's review in *RALS*, 1975), it brings together more material about Marsh and his correspondents than any other book. Duffy's introduction, which bears a similar relation to his book as Marsh's "Preliminary Essay" bore to *Aids*, deals perceptively and comprehensively with the major events of Marsh's literary life. A briefer introduction to Marsh is Douglas McCreary Greenwood's essay in *The American Renaissance in New England*, ed. Joel Myerson.

Three early accounts of Marsh are George B. Cheever, *Characteristics of the Christian Philosopher*; Evert A. Duyckinck and George L. Duyckinck, *Cyclopædia of American Literature*; and William B. Sprague, *Annals of the American Pulpit* (vol. 2). Cheever's review-essay should be read alongside Frederic Henry Hedge's "Coleridge" and Noah Porter's "Coleridge and His American Disciples" to see the shift in Coleridge's American reputation during the Transcendentalist era.

Several critical essays on Marsh deserve special mention. Marjorie H. Nicolson, in "James Marsh and the Vermont Transcendentalists," discusses the structure of his "Preliminary Essay" and comments on the early critical reception of *Aids*. John Dewey, "James Marsh and American Philosophy," emphasizes the need to see Marsh as social and political philosopher, as does Lewis Feuer in "James Marsh and the Conservative Transcendentalist Philosophy." Whereas Dewey deals with some of the finer points of Marsh's politics, Feuer treats Marsh's philosophy in a broader cultural context, dealing with such topics as the Horace Greeley–Henry Raymond feud, the Marsh Creed at the University of Vermont, and Marsh's views on slavery. Peter C. Carafiol, "James Marsh" (*ESQ*, 1975), attributes Marsh's philosophical distance from the Concord Transcendentalists to their religious liberalism and pantheistic tendencies.

Perhaps the most convincing recent essay is John J. Duffy's "Problems in Publishing Coleridge." Although Duffy was not the first to have access to Marsh's papers, he was the first to draw a coherent picture of Marsh's motives in publishing *Aids* and the obstacles he faced in satisfying the needs of a religiously diverse audience.

Duffy reveals that Marsh was well aware of the controversy *Aids* would generate, especially among conservative theologians; consequently, he chose to downplay German aspects of Coleridge's thought in the "Preliminary Essay" and to emphasize Coleridge's affinity with the seventeenth-century divines.

In "James Marsh's American *Aids to Reflection*," Peter C. Carafiol takes the position that Marsh vacillated between rationalism and dogmatism. He finds the "Preliminary Essay" ambiguous because Marsh attempted to appease liberal and conservative audiences at the same time. In a less compelling essay, "James Marsh to John Dewey," Carafiol sees a continuity between Marsh's educational philosophy and Dewey's in combating the evils of Scottish realism. An intelligent and amusing paper that locates Marsh's place in American intellectual history is Michael West, "Scatology and Eschatology."

One recent article that has escaped general notice is Arthur C. McGiffert, Jr., "James Marsh (1794–1842)," a well-documented, somewhat technical examination of Marsh's religious beliefs. Anthony John Harding, "James Marsh as Editor of Coleridge," tussles with Marsh's problems as a Calvinist Coleridgean and comes up with some interesting—though very questionable—conjectures.

There are three unpublished dissertations on Marsh, by Ruth Helen White, Peter C. Carafiol, and Douglas McCreary Greenwood. White considers Marsh's role as educator and discusses the Coleridgean curriculum he inaugurated at Vermont, but she leaves much territory unexplored. For Marsh's crucial earlier experiences as a tutor at Dartmouth, see Greenwood, "James Marsh, Dartmouth, and American Transcendentalism," and especially "The Hanover Years" in his dissertation. For Marsh's troubled period as college professor in the South, see David E. Swift, "Yankee in Virginia," an informative account that comments as well on Marsh's apprenticeship as writer and editor. Carafiol's dissertation examines the "conflicts and continuities between Marsh's personal orthodoxy and radicalism," describing Marsh as an intermediary between Calvinism and Puritanism. Greenwood views Marsh's lifelong quest for truth as an inconclusive intellectual foray into the realms of Kantian philosophy and introspective theology. From Greenwood's perspective, Marsh charted a middle course throughout his public career, remaining a man torn between the illiberal demands of orthodox Congregationalism, which he could not fully accept, and the excesses of a Transcendentalism that he helped to formulate.

FURTHER RESEARCH

Continued interest in Marsh was evidenced by a symposium at the University of Vermont in 1979 celebrating the sesquicentennial of the publication of *Aids*. Joel Myerson presented an overview of Marsh's role in the Transcendentalist movement and suggested that Marsh's broad-ranging interest made any dogma, including Transcendentalism, unpalatable to him. Peter C. Carafiol discussed Marsh's difficulties in reconciling his philosophical, psychological, and religious beliefs. John J. Duffy treated Marsh's reaction to the Patriot's War in Canada (1837–38), and Douglas McCreary Greenwood dealt with the early Transcendentalist stirring in "Ancient and Modern Poetry," Marsh's first published essay (1822).

There are several other topics that need to be more fully explored: Marsh's friend-ships among the Boston literati (including Washington Allston, Richard Henry Dana, Sr., and George Ticknor); his role in the Convention of Literary and Scientific Gentlemen held in New York City in 1830; the English reception of both the English and the American editions of *Aids to Reflection*; and an examination of Marsh's views on psychology and the fine arts. The place to begin research on Marsh, of course, is the James Marsh Collection at the University of Vermont, the major repository of Marshiana.

It is still not clear why Marsh never accepted invitations to attend meetings of the Transcendental Club or why he refused Ripley's offer to contribute to the *Dial*. Perhaps he gave the best answer himself when he wrote a former student in 1841:

> The whole of Boston Transcendentalism I take to be a rather superficial affair; and there is some source in the remark of a friend of mine that the "Dial" indicates rather the place of the moon than the sun.

It was a scathing indictment, to be sure, yet it reflected the practical and the idealistic dualities of Marsh's philosophy.

HERMAN MELVILLE

Brian Higgins

WRITINGS ABOUT THE TRANSCENDENTALISTS

There is no evidence that Herman Melville ever met Ralph Waldo Emerson or Henry David Thoreau or any other member of the American Transcendentalist movement, though with his contacts in the New England literary and social worlds it is not improbable that he was introduced to one or more of them. But even if he had no personal association with the Transcendentalists, Melville was well aware of their activities: he heard Emerson lecture and subsequently read many of his essays and poems; he borrowed Thoreau's *A Week on the Concord and Merrimack Rivers* from his friend Evert A. Duyckinck and apparently discussed the book with Nathaniel Hawthorne; and he had ample opportunity to learn about Transcendentalism from newspapers and periodicals and from literary friends, particularly Nathaniel Hawthorne, whose acquaintance with the movement and its members was extensive. Melville also read widely in authors who influenced the American Transcendentalists from Plato and Proclus (in translation) to Samuel Taylor Coleridge and Thomas Carlyle, and his contact with Transcendentalism in its ancient and modern varieties left a significant impression on several of his major works.

Melville's explicit comments on individual American Transcendentalists are limited, however, to remarks on Emerson in two letters he wrote to Duyckinck (on 24 Feb. and 3 March 1849) in the relatively early days of his career as a professional author, and to annotations in his copies of Emerson's essays, which he acquired long after that career was over. In the first letter Melville simply recorded that he had heard Emerson lecture (in Boston on 5 Feb.) and added, "Say what they will, he's a great man.'' The next letter clearly responded to the conservatively religious Duyckinck's fear that such praise meant that Melville was becoming a camp follower of Emerson: this much longer assessment of Emerson, by turns bantering and earnest, now reassuringly leavens praise with censure. Melville did not ''oscillate in Emerson's rainbow'' but thought him ''more than a brilliant fellow'' and had been ''very agreeably disappointed'' in him. He had ''only glanced at a book of his once in Putnam's store'' but had heard that Emerson was ''full of transcendentalisms, myths & oracular gibberish.'' To his surprise Melville had found him ''quite intelligible,'' though, ''to say truth,'' people told him that Emerson that night ''was unusually plain.'' If Emerson was a fool, then Melville would ''rather be a fool than a wise man.'' Melville loved ''all men who *dive*''—any fish ''can swim near the surface, but it takes a great whale to go down stairs five miles or more''—and Emerson, he implied, belonged to the ''corps of thought-divers.'' Yet Melville could readily see the ''gaping flaw'' of intellectual arrogance in Emerson, the ''insinuation, that had he lived in those days when the world was made, he might have offered some valuable suggestions''; such men, he thought, ''are all cracked right across the brow.'' Melville agreed, too, with a complaint of Duyckinck's: ''this Plato who talks thro' his nose'' could not fit in with a ''company of jolly fellows,'' for his belly was ''in his chest'' and his brains descended ''down into his neck,'' offering ''an obstacle to a draught of ale or a mouthful of cake.'' Despite such reservations, in late July or August 1850, after he had presumably looked further into the essays, Melville placed Emerson's name second, after Hawthorne's, in a list of eight leading American authors of the day in the manuscript of ''Hawthorne and His Mosses,'' a list deleted from the published essay.

Melville's annotations in Emerson's *Essays* and *Essays: Second Series*, which he bought in 1862, and *The Conduct of Life*, which he bought in 1870, provide as trenchant and ambivalent a commentary on Emerson as his correspondence with Duyckinck. Melville applauded the truth or the nobility of thought or expression in various passages on the function of poets, the nature of language, and the virtues of veracity, honesty, and self-trust; but elsewhere he remarks on Emerson's puritanical narrowness and lack of warmth, his too easy disposal of disagreeable facts and inadequate apprehension of evil, and, once again, his intellectual arrogance. Emerson's ''gross and astonishing errors & illusions,'' Melville wrote in the margins of ''The Poet,'' spring ''from a self-conceit so intensely intellectual and calm that at first one hesitates to call it by its right name. Another species of Mr. Emerson's errors, or rather blindness, proceeds from a defect in the region of the heart.'' Yet many of his thoughts were admirable, Melville acknowledged, and though Emerson had ''his Dardanelles for his every Marmora,'' in these essays he kept ''nobly on, for all that!''

Parts of *Mardi* (1849), *Moby-Dick* (1851), and his later works are of major importance in assessing Melville's response to Transcendentalism, but the only open reference to American Transcendentalists in his fiction occurs in *Pierre* (1852), where Melville mocks ''amiable philosophers of either the 'Compensation,' or 'Optimist' school,'' who ''deny that any misery is in the world, except for the purpose of throwing the fine *povertiresque* element into its general picture." The asceticism and dietary experiments of some of the Transcendentalists appear to be satirized in the Apostles, philosophical eccentrics who adhere to "the Transcendental Flesh-Brush Philosophy" and to "Pythagorean and Shellian dietings." Transcendentalists, particularly Carlyle and Emerson, are probably among the members of what Melville calls a "guild of self-impostors, with preposterous rabble of Muggletonian Scots and Yankees, whose vile brogue still the more bestreaks the stripedness of their Greek or German Neoplatonical originals." In Melville's later works there are no explicit remarks on Transcendentalists or Transcendentalism, but twentieth-century readers have seen some of his tales (1853–56) as oblique commentaries on Transcendentalist thought, and the characters Mark Winsome and Egbert in *The Confidence-Man* (1857) have been described as caricatures of Emerson and Thoreau, respectively.

TEXTS AND BIBLIOGRAPHIES

Full texts of Melville's letters to Duyckinck are printed in *The Letters of Herman Melville*, ed. Merrell R. Davis and William H. Gilman (1960), and his markings and annotations in Emerson's *The Conduct of Life, Essays, Essays: Second Series*, and *Poems* are reproduced in vol. 5 of Wilson Walker Cowen, "Melville's Marginalia." The deleted passage naming Emerson is restored in the text of "Hawthorne and His Mosses" in *The Piazza Tales and Other Prose Pieces, 1839–1860*, forthcoming as vol. 9 of *The Writings of Herman Melville*, ed. Harrison Hayford, Hershel Parker, and G. Thomas Tanselle (1968–), and in the text of the essay edited by Hershel Parker for *The Norton Anthology of American Literature*, ed. Ronald Gottesman et al. No bibliography of studies on Melville's response to Transcendentalism has been published, but Brian Higgins, *Herman Melville: An Annotated Bibliography*, is useful for locating comments by reviewers and later critics on Melville's own "Transcendentalism." Many of the reviews are reprinted in Moby-Dick *as Doubloon*, ed. Hershel Parker and Harrison Hayford, and *Melville: The Critical Heritage*, ed. Watson G. Branch.

CRITICISM BEFORE 1930

Melville's reputation was tarnished by his affinities with the Transcendentalists for at least seven decades. Reviewers in the later 1840s and 1850s were the first to discover—and invariably deplore—the "transcendental," "metaphysical," or "mystical" elements in his works, particularly *Mardi, Moby-Dick*, and *Pierre*, and critics continued to harp on this theme until at least 1920. An English admirer, Henry S. Salt, claimed that Melville was affected by the "transcendental tendency of the age," with the result that "his stories of what purported to be plain matter-of-fact life" were "gradually absorbed and swallowed up in the wildest mystical speculations." Melville was at his best when his "mystic element" was kept in check, as in *Typee* or parts of *Mardi* and *Moby-Dick*, whereas in *Pierre* he achieved "perhaps the *ne plus ultra* in the way to metaphysical absurdity" ("Herman Melville"). Later ("Marquesan Melville"), Salt referred to *Typee* as the masterpiece of Melville's earlier period, when his "artistic sense" still predominated over his "transcendental tendencies." By this time Salt considered *Moby-Dick* "the supreme production of a master mind," but he still thought Melville's "transcendental mood" led him into "turgid mannerisms" and "mere bombast and rhetoric." Even the novelist W. Clark Russell, one of the first to recognize *Moby-Dick* as Melville's finest work, objected that in parts it is too obscure and that the reader is frequently "harassed" by a "transcendental mysticism" that "ill-fits" the mouth of sailors ("Editor's Preface" in *Typee*, 1904). According to Ernest Rhys, author of the "Editor's Note" in the Everyman's Library edition (1907), *Moby-Dick* was the last book in which Melville maintained a balance between Transcendentalism and reality; and, in one of the otherwise more perceptive centennial tributes, F. C. Owlett claimed that *Mardi*, *Pierre*, *Israel Potter*, *The Piazza Tales*, and *The Confidence-Man* all fail because their artistry is obscured by Transcendentalism and metaphysics.

Neither of Melville's first two biographers, Raymond M. Weaver and John Freeman, discussed the impact of Transcendentalism on Melville, but one effect of the new interest in Melville's life in the 1920s was that scholars and critics began to redefine his relation to Transcendentalism. Carl Van Doren, Vernon Louis Parrington, and Harry Hayden Clark all described Melville, briefly and anachronistically, as a youthful Transcendentalist subsequently disillusioned by his experience in the world, and Lewis Mumford concluded that Melville felt no kinship with Emerson except as one "thought-diver" with another: "the blandness, the sunniness, the mildness, the absence of curses, shadows, shipwrecks in Emerson's philosophy" set Melville against it (Van Doren, "Lucifer from Nantucket"; Parrington, *The Romantic Revolution in America 1800–1860*; Clark, "American Literary History and American Literature"; Mumford, *Herman Melville*).

RESEARCH AND CRITICISM AFTER 1930

William Braswell's "Melville as a Critic of Emerson" was the first detailed study of Melville's response to Emerson. It remains the most convenient place to examine Melville's annotations of the essays, which Braswell quotes in full and discusses under three headings: Melville's comments on Emerson's conception of the poet, his praise of Emerson's views on life, and his criticism of Emerson's view of the problem of evil. The essay should be read with caution, however: Braswell concludes, for example, that Melville wrote "capriciously" about Emerson in his correspondence with Duyckinck and that his comments should not be taken very seriously since he was unfamiliar with Emerson's works and had heard only one of Emerson's lectures. Later scholars have pointed out that Melville's early reaction to Emerson was consonant with his annotations of the essays, and one needs to consult Merton M. Sealts, Jr., "Melville and Emerson's Rainbow," for the fullest and most thoughtful discussion of the letter. Braswell's assumption that Melville probably did not read some of the unmarked essays, such as "Compensation," "Self-Reliance," and "The Over-Soul," invites question too: as Sealts points out, the essays may be unmarked because Melville had read them earlier—"he is known to have given away other books he had owned and annotated, and then to have bought the same titles again in different editions." Later scholarship has also shown that Braswell dismissed too casually the possibility that *The Confidence-Man* satirizes Emerson and Transcendentalism. Despite these failings, Braswell's essay showed that Melville's reaction to Emerson was more complex than Mumford had assumed and made available essential evidence for further attempts to redefine Melville's relation to Transcendentalism.

Subsequent scholarship has usually focused on Melville's opposition to aspects of Transcendentalism, often expressed in short passages in articles and books not primarily devoted to the subject. Floyd Stovall briefly describes Melville's "instinctive antagonism to the transcendental philosophy" (*American Idealism*), and Milton R. Stern provides an intermittent but provocative commentary on the differences between Melville's "naturalism" and Transcendentalism (*The Fine Hammered Steel of Herman Melville*). Melville's affinities with certain Transcendentalists are also stressed, again briefly, in David Bowers, "Democratic Vistas," which notes that Melville, Hawthorne, Emerson, Thoreau, and Whitman were linked by a common concern with the "great problems" of human nature, destiny, and experience. Charles Feidelson, Jr., *Symbolism and American Literature*, sees Melville and Emerson as "the polar figures of the American symbolist movement" who between them ran "the gamut of possibilities created by the symbolistic point of view": Emerson was "the theorist and advocate" and Melville was "the practicing poet" who assumed "the ambient idea that Emerson made explicit."

Various critics have claimed that in *Mardi*, the first of Melville's books to reveal his acquaintance with Transcendentalism, much of Babbalanja's thinking is Emersonian, whereas his argument against an innate moral sense and the statement in the "scroll" that "evil is the chronic malady of the universe" seem anti-Emersonian. In "Melville and Emersonian Transcendentalism," Barbara Ruth Nieweg Blansett argues that Melville was most strongly attracted to Transcendentalist theories while he was writing *Mardi*. Blansett does not claim that Melville drew his ideas directly from Emerson but notes that Melville had "been reading many of the same works that had been read earlier by Emerson." Whether Melville "arrived at his like conclusions independently, or whether he paraphrased them from Emerson" is not of "vital concern" to her study, but, unlike many of the scholars cited in this chapter, Blansett shows genuine resemblances between Melville's thought and Emerson's. She demonstrates that, at the time he wrote *Mardi*, Melville was interested in such Emersonian ideas as the repetition of great thoughts throughout the centuries, the mystical revelation of truth, nature as theologian, the necessity for "aloneness" in the search for truth, the failure of Christian doctrine as practiced in the world, and the limitations of science in ascertaining metaphysical truth. Sealts observes, however, that though the parallels Blansett cites confirm the impression "that by 1848 Melville had soaked up a good deal of information about transcendental idealism," they "do not necessarily demonstrate that his teacher had been Emerson rather than Plato and Proclus among the ancients or Wordsworth and Coleridge among the moderns." Reminding us that Melville admitted to knowing little of Emerson at first hand until after he had finished *Mardi*, Sealts argues in "Melville and the Platonic Tradition" that the Transcendentalist passages in the book derive from non-Emersonian sources already familiar to Melville, particularly Plato, whose influence on Melville's works from *Mardi* to *Billy Budd* Sealts then traces in meticulous detail.

Critics have found little in *Redburn* and *White-Jacket* relating to Transcendentalism beyond the passage in which Redburn loses part of himself "in one delirious throb at the center of the All," the slighting reference to a "merely transcendental mood" in *Redburn* (chs. 13 and 49), and the satire on the "transcendental divine" in *White-Jacket* (ch. 38). Victor J. Vitanza, "Melville's *Redburn* and Emerson's 'General Education of the Eye,'" has more to do with eye imagery than with Emerson and provides no persuasive evidence that in *Redburn* Melville "was able to compromise with Transcendental idealism, as he could not in his mature works," or that *Redburn* is in any way concerned with Transcendentalist idealism. More plausibly, Theodore L. Gross has described the narrator in *White-Jacket* as Emersonian in his idealism and self-reliance, and he describes the passages about the future of America as "a curious mixture of Calvinistic predestination and Emersonian idealism" ("Herman Melville: The Nature of Authority").

F. O. Matthiessen anticipated many later commentators by noting that in *Moby-Dick* Melville shared "key positions" with the Transcendentalists, "especially the doctrine of 'linked analogies' between nature and man's mind, and that of the symbolical significance of every natural fact." But Melville, according to Matthiessen, also diverged from the Transcendentalists in many of the book's "condensed parables," such as that of the young sailor "with the Phædon instead of Bowditch in his head" who "loses his identity" at the masthead, taking "the mystic ocean at his feet for the visible image of that deep, blue, bottomless soul, pervading mankind and nature" (ch. 35). Critics have frequently echoed Matthiessen's interpretation of this passage as Melville's "instinctive critique of transcendentalism," his realization that the "beautiful fins" in the mystic ocean are "part of cruel forms." Matthiessen anticipated many critics, too, in seeing Ahab as part of Melville's reaction against Emerson: Ahab is Emersonian in his conviction that all visible objects are "but as pasteboard masks" (ch. 36), yet, unlike Emerson, he is tormented by the demonic element in the unseen and comes to represent the destructiveness of Emerson's "self-enclosed individualism" (*American Renaissance*). Howard P. Vincent's similar judgment that Ahab represents the "fatality of rampant self-reliance" has also been frequently echoed by later critics (*The Trying-Out of* Moby-Dick).

Subsequent discussion has added little to our understanding of Transcendentalism in *Moby-Dick*. Perry Miller never adequately substantiates his claim that Melville's fundamental premises in *Moby-Dick* and *Pierre* were those of Transcendentalism

("Melville and Transcendentalism"). Clark Griffith makes the attractive-sounding argument that *Moby-Dick* is about symbols and that Ahab's fiasco derives from a breakdown in Emersonian symbolic doctrine: instead of proving transparent, natural objects present either an impenetrable front or a polished surface, on which the observer glimpses not metaphysical truth but the mirrored reflection of his own abortive search ("'Emersonianism' and 'Poeism'"). But Griffith's thesis considerably oversimplifies the book, ignoring, for instance, Ahab's madness and Ishmael's role as symbol-making truth-seeker. According to Allen Austin, Melville satirizes "Self-Reliance" in *Moby-Dick* by insisting that "the joint-stock company" of which Emerson complains is the nature of human society and that mutuality, a "joint-stock world," is preferable to individuality ("The Three-Stranded Allegory of *Moby-Dick*"). But Austin never substantiates his theory, and his related claim that particular passages in *Moby-Dick* are satirical of Transcendentalist ideas is even less convincing. S. A. Cowan's reply to Austin, "In Praise of Self-Reliance," usefully distinguishes between evil self-reliance (Ahab) and virtuous self-reliance (Queequeg and Bulkington) and argues sensibly that Melville endorses both mutuality and the heroic, virtuous brand of self-reliance. But Cowan's belief that Bulkington's self-reliance is recognizably Transcendentalist, that of a truth-seeker, is based in part on a misreading of "The Lee Shore" (ch. 23), in which he concludes that Bulkington himself has "glimpses" of the "mortally intolerable truth" Ishmael metaphorically announces. Bulkington's only other tenuous link with Transcendentalism is his aloofness at the Spouter-Inn (ch. 3), which, according to Cowan, seems to supply "a conscious parallel" with Emerson's "great man," who "in the midst of the crowd keeps with perfect sweetness the independence of solitude." Michael J. Hoffman unconvincingly portrays Ahab as Melville's version, ultimately parodic, of Emerson's "great man," his quest and failure showing that all attempts to force meaning on the world are futile and destructive ("The Anti-Transcendentalism of *Moby-Dick*"). Hoffman's evidence that Ahab is Emersonian is not compelling (he feels limited by nothing, privileged to do anything) and, in arguing that Melville damns the attempt to see physical entities as symbols, Hoffman (like Griffith) ignores the fact that Ishmael, more than Ahab, is an inveterate symbolist. E. J. Rose compares Melville's chapter 70, "The Sphynx," with Emerson's poem "The Sphinx" ("Melville, Emerson, and the Sphinx") and argues reasonably enough that the beliefs Emerson expresses are antithetical to Ahab's musings, which reveal Melville's characteristic belief in the inexplicability of the "all" and skepticism of any inherent justice or goodness in what appears to be a hostile universe. The rest of the essay, however, is a strained attempt to find significant similarities and differences between poem and chapter.

The largest claim for Emerson's impact on *Moby-Dick* is made by Nina Baym in "Melville's Quarrel with Fiction." She holds that Emerson was the single most significant influence on the shape of the book, that it reflects an Emersonian view of fiction and reading, and that Emerson's concepts of truth and the divine authorship of nature and language, as expressed in the "Language" section of *Nature*, are wrought into its texture and form. Emerson's ideas, Baym contends, "are used playfully and seriously in *Moby-Dick*, providing in large degree the conceptual energy that gives the heterogeneous work its coherence and structure." The classification of whales as books; the introductory extracts and etymology; the reflections on the horrors of the half-known life, on the beguilements of pantheism, and on the dangers of looking too long in the face of the fire; the search for meanings in the dart or the line; and the anatomizing of the whale "rise from the connections Emerson finds among human language, nature, and absolute meaning." But Baym offers no evidence that Melville was familiar with *Nature*, either through a reading of the work or otherwise. Merton M. Sealts, Jr., supplies evidence that Melville had not read *Nature* by August 1850 and concludes that Carlyle's *Sartor Resartus* had at least as much to do with the symbolism of *Moby-Dick* as anything in the "Language" section of *Nature*. In his 1980 and 1982 essays, however, Sealts does find parallels between *Moby-Dick* and passages in "Intellect," "The Transcendentalist," and *Representative Men*.

John Brindley Williams tries to discover "transcendental ethics" and a "transcendental esthetic" in Melville's books from *Typee* to *Moby-Dick* ("The Impact of Transcendentalism on the Novels of Herman Melville"), but most of the links he finds between Melville and Transcendentalism are tenuous. The similarities he cites between passages in Melville and passages in Emerson and Thoreau are often very general and hard to discern, and he does not actually demonstrate the "shifting impact" of "transcendental thought" on Melville. Marjorie J. Elder's account of Melville's debt to Emerson's "Transcendental aesthetic" in *Nathaniel Hawthorne* is sketchy, and it does not prove that the "Transcendental reflections" in Melville's aesthetic necessarily derived from Emerson or any other Transcendentalist. Robert G. Waite, "Linked Analogies," illustrates similarities and differences in Melville's and Emerson's perception of reality without investigating the nature and extent of Emerson's influence on Melville.

In the last fifty years, critics have regularly interpreted the Apostles in *Pierre* as parodies of the New England Transcendentalists and the reference to "a preposterous rabble of Muggletonian Scots and Yankees" pretending to have got a Voice out of Silence (book 14) as an allusion to Transcendentalists in general and to Carlyle and Emerson in particular. A number of critics see Plotinus Plinlimmon, leader of the Apostles, and his pamphlet "Chronometricals and Horologicals" as a spoof on Emerson. Elizabeth S. Foster, in "Herman Melville's *The Confidence-Man*," compares Plinlimmon's thoughts, behavior, and appearance with Emerson's and notes their similar roles as lecturers and leaders of Transcendentalist movements. Foster also claims that Plinlimmon's pamphlet offers parallels to a number of passages in Emerson's works, including the central trope of the chronometer, used in "The Transcendentalist" to refer to "rare and gifted men." Later critics have neither convincingly challenged nor supported Foster's identification. Mildred K. Travis notes some of the same parallels, without citing Foster, in "Echoes of Emerson in Plinlimmon" but adds nothing of substance.

Foster sees *Pierre* as a rebuttal of Emerson's doctrine of self-reliance and many other "specific passages" in his works, and she raises the possibility that a reading

of Emerson precipitated the novel. Barbara Blansett examines *Pierre* at greater length
for evidence that Melville became an ardent anti-Transcendentalist during his association with Hawthorne, citing passages that seem to contradict Emerson's essays. She
also shows that, as a lover, hero, and worshipper of nature, Pierre is a besotted
Transcendentalist, and that Melville's refusal to acknowledge universal truths and their
mystic revelation is part of a profound reaction against Transcendentalist beliefs that
is central to the book. Several scholars have noted, however, that even while he mocks
the Transcendentalist Apostles, Melville honors them as "noble men often at bottom" in contrast to the "fools and pretenders of humanity"; and Merton M. Sealts,
Jr. (1980), warns that *Pierre* is too large and complex to be read simply as an anti-
Transcendentalist tract.

Other studies are less persuasive. Jane Ellin Rogers argues in "The Transcendental Quest in Emerson and Melville" that *Pierre* both endorses the Emersonian impulse toward transcendence and explores its great risks, particularly those moments
of stasis and passivity that, according to Emerson, should create a tolerable "double
consciousness" but that in Pierre's case precipitate self-destruction. Rogers, however,
produces no evidence, external or internal, that Melville was responding to Emerson's
Transcendentalism or that Pierre's two moments of "passivity" (when he reads Plinlimmon's pamphlet and has the Enceladus nightmare) have anything to do with Emerson. In the last chapter of "A Natural History of American Virtue," Joseph Paul Alaimo
relates the proclamation of Emerson's aspirant to virtue, "Virtue, I am thine: save
me: use me: thee will I serve day and night, in great, in small," to Pierre's quest
for virtue and truth, but it is difficult to discern the connection Alaimo seeks to establish
between *Pierre* and other passages from the Divinity School Address. Michael Herbert
Strelow, in "Emerson's Paradigm of the Self and its Manifestations in the Work of
Melville and Thoreau," claims that Melville "consciously uses" the "model for the
self" Emerson developed in "Circles," but his analysis of *Pierre* overvalues three of
Melville's circular images and does not bear out the contention that Melville's "in-
vestigations of the self" were "based on Emerson's graphic assumption of how that
self worked." Michael J. Colacurcio offers no external evidence and nothing conclusive
from the text in arguing that Pierre's acceptance of Isabel's claim to be his sister illustrates the Transcendentalist concept of faith as recognition, as defined by George
Ripley ("A Better Mode of Evidence"). James Duban exaggerates when he claims that
Pierre's "shortcomings as a moral absolutist" can only be fully appreciated in the
context of Emerson's Divinity School Address ("The Spenserian Maze of Melville's
Pierre"). Like Alaimo, Duban quotes the proclamation of Emerson's aspirant to virtue, which resembles Pierre's vow to be " 'all Virtue's and all Truth's,' " but otherwise he draws no significant connections between the two works.

Several critics have tried to demonstrate that Melville's later work contains his
response to Thoreau, among them Egbert S. Oliver, who argues that Bartleby is
Melville's picture of Thoreau "abstracted" from "Resistance to Civil Government"
("A Second Look at 'Bartleby' "). Oliver states correctly that Melville had ample opportunity to learn about Thoreau and borrowed *A Week* from Duyckinck in 1850,

but, as Hershel Parker notes in "Melville's Satire of Emerson and Thoreau," "no proof exists that Melville borrowed the book for himself (he had a large household) or that he read it after borrowing it." Oliver provides no solid evidence that Melville actually read any of Thoreau's works, though he arbitrarily identifies passages in "Resistance" that "suggested much to Melville" and cites a dozen or so unconvincing "parallels" between Bartleby and Thoreau. Neither Robert E. Morsberger, " 'I Prefer Not To,' " nor Frederick Busch, "Thoreau and Melville as Cellmates," makes reference to Oliver's study, and neither strengthens the case for the influence of "Resistance" on "Bartleby."

Three essays find the source of "Bartleby" in Emerson, two of them, John Seelye, "The Contemporary 'Bartleby,' " and Christopher W. Sten, "Bartleby the Transcendentalist," arguing specifically for the influence of "The Transcendentalist." In Seelye's reading, the story reflects the confrontation between the rational, Whig establishment of antebellum America (represented by the narrator) and the radical intellectuals of the idealistic, Transcendentalist camp (represented by Bartleby). But Seelye cites only a few parallels with Emerson's essay, the most telling of which is that Bartleby withdraws and dies, factors that scarcely make him a Transcendentalist. Sten argues that Emerson's idealist and materialist became Melville's Bartleby and narrator respectively, Bartleby's "I would prefer not to" representing the idealist's rejection of the monotonous and spiritually bankrupt world of the materialist. But Sten fails to show any direct connection between the two pairs of characters and he makes unjustifiably confident assertions about Bartleby's values and motives. Francine S. Puk has only marginally better material in "'Bartleby the Scrivener,'" where she argues that the story is a parody of "Self-Reliance" that reveals the disastrous consequences of Emersonian nonconformity in a "structured society . . . too powerful to be fought." Puk's claim that "Self-Reliance" acts as "the controlling mechanism throughout the entire story" is based on arbitrary connections between the two works.

Two rival claims for Thoreau's influence on "Cock-A-Doodle-Doo!" have been advanced and challenged. Egbert S. Oliver found the source of the story in the "Monday" chapter of A Week (" 'Cock-A-Doodle-Doo!' and Transcendental Hocus-Pocus"), and William Bysshe Stein discovered its inspiration in "Walking" ("Melville Roasts Thoreau's Cock"). But, as Sidney P. Moss points out in "'Cock-A-Doodle-Doo!' and Some Legends in Melville Scholarship," Stein failed to note that "Walking" was not published till June 1862 (though Thoreau lectured on the subject in 1851 and 1852) and that Melville's story was published in December 1853. Moss also attempts to refute Oliver by asking why a well-known author like Melville would "wish to satirize an obscure passage in an obscure book by an unknown writer" when scarcely anyone would understand the point of his satire. Hershel Parker (1970) answers effectively that the first question is anachronistic, since to Melville "and many in Massachusetts in the early and mid-1850's Thoreau may well have seemed eccentric and imitative enough but still one of the major Concord Transcendentalists," whereas the second question "ignores what Melville was habitually writing in the mid-1850's, when he was a man driven to writing at least as much for himself as for the public" and when being understood "might be irrelevant, as far as any immediate audience was concerned." Parker does not support Oliver's claim for the influence of *A Week* (Oliver's parallels are "so unconvincing that they resist repetition," he notes), but he points out that Oliver might still be right in concluding that the story is a *reductio ad absurdum* of the Transcendentalist disregard of materialism. Ray B. Browne, "Source and Satire of 'Cock-A-Doodle-Doo' " (in *Melville's Drive to Humanism*), is an extension of Oliver and Stein, a labored and unconvincing attempt to root the story more securely in both "Monday" and "Walking." Impressed by Stein's evidence, Allan Moore Emery, "The Cocks of Melville's 'Cock-A-Doodle-Doo!,' " speculates that Hawthorne showed Melville a manuscript of Thoreau's lecture on "Walking" when he visited the Hawthornes at Concord in December 1852. The possibility exists, but Emery is able to supply no evidence that Hawthorne actually had such a manuscript in his possession at the time and does not improve on Stein's account of the connections between the two works, certainly not enough to warrant his own assertion that Melville had "detailed knowledge" of the essay and made "careful reference" to it in the story. Emery usefully alerts us to the possibility that Melville saw parts of *Walden* in draft form prior to the book's publication (Sidney Moss dismisses the possibility that *Walden* influenced "Cock-A-Doodle-Doo!" on the basis of their publication dates), but his attempts to link "Cock-A-Doodle-Doo!" to "A Winter Walk," "The Iron Horse," "Resistance to Civil Government," and *Walden* amount to little.

The influence of Transcendentalism on Melville's other works prior to *The Confidence-Man* has received slight attention. "Poor Man's Pudding," perhaps surprisingly, has attracted only passing references to its anti-Transcendentalist thrust, with both Martin Leonard Pops (*The Melville Archetype*) and Ray B. Browne reading the story as an attempt, in part, to refute some of the arguments of *Walden*. Clinton Keeler illustrates Amasa Delano's Emersonian optimism and self-trust in "Benito Cereno," quoting apposite sentences from *Nature*, "Prudence," and "Spiritual Laws" ("Melville's Delano"); but Beryl Rowland's claim that "The Two Temples" tests assertions in *Nature*, the Divinity School Address, and "The Over-Soul" ("Melville Answers the Theologians") depends on a strained reading of the protagonist's experience. The most telling similarity Frank Davidson cites between the last paragraphs of *Walden* and "The Apple-Tree Table" is that both Melville and Thoreau link the hatching of the insects to the resurrection of the spirit ("Melville, Thoreau, and 'The Apple-Tree Table'"). The other resemblances Davidson finds are not compelling, nor are the connections Helmbrecht Breinig seeks to establish in support of his view that the story comments ironically on both *Walden*'s Transcendentalist metaphysics and its "Transcendental theory of communication" ("Symbol, Satire, and the Will to Communicate in Melville's 'The Apple-Tree Table'"). In "The Piazza," Breinig finds echoes of Thoreau's *A Week* ("The Destruction of Fairyland"), but the images he cites are so commonplace that it seems special-pleading to claim Thoreau's work as their source. Marvin Fisher usefully locates the origin of the second part of the sentence "Whoever built the house, he builded better than he knew" in Emerson's poem "The Problem" (*Going Under*), but he exaggerates the significance of Emerson's lines in interpreting the story.

Carl Van Vechten was the first critic to recognize the satire of Emerson and Transcendentalism in *The Confidence-Man* ("A Belated Biography"). In "The Later Work of Herman Melville," Van Vechten hailed the book as a "great transcendental satire" in which "Emerson is the confidence man," his "fatuous essay on Friendship" being "required preparatory reading" for the book. Yvor Winters later specified the "incident" of Winsome and his disciple as "a very biting commentary on Emerson and on the practical implications of Emersonian philososophy" (*Maule's Curse*), and F. O. Matthiessen thought it "quite possible" that Melville "may have remembered his impression of Emerson" in his sketch of Winsome. Elizabeth S. Foster was the first, however, to make a detailed identification of Winsome with Emerson, persuasively listing similarities in their appearance, age, and remarks, parallels that are "even more explicit" than those between Emerson and Plinlimmon. According to Foster, Melville split Emerson into a philosopher and a working reformer to create Winsome and Egbert, who also represent respectively Emerson's metaphysics and ethics. The satiric portraits of Plinlimmon, Winsome, and Egbert, she notes, embody only Emerson's faults, Winsome and Egbert amplifying what was only hinted at in Plinlimmon's pamphlet, that Emerson's doctrine of self-reliance results in a heartless "egoistic, individualistic, competitive, fish-eat-fish, and might-is-right system."

Using some of the same evidence as Foster, Egbert S. Oliver independently identifies Winsome with Emerson in "Melville's Picture of Emerson and Thoreau in 'The Confidence-Man,'" but he is not able to demonstrate convincingly that Winsome's conversation "bears a relationship, in general and in many particulars, to the ideas and phrasing of Emerson's *Nature*." Oliver also argues that Egbert is "explicitly based" on Thoreau, pointing out that Egbert is fifteen years younger than Winsome, whereas Thoreau was fourteen years younger than Emerson; but the quality of the rest of his external evidence is suggested by his confusion of Thoreau and Channing in James Russell Lowell's *A Fable for Critics*. In discussing Melville's "caricature of transcendental friendship," however, Oliver introduces two quotations from *A Week* similiar in spirit to Egbert's views.

The identification of Winsome with Emerson is bolstered by Merton M. Sealts, Jr., who suggests that Melville may have been aware of Emerson's fondness for Proclus, whom Winsome quotes in chapter 36 ("Melville's 'Neoplatonical Originals'"). Elizabeth S. Foster's "Introduction" and "Explanatory Notes" to her edition of *The Confidence-Man* (1954) reproduce much of her dissertation material on the Winsome-Egbert-Emerson connection. Foster also plausibly interprets the activities of the herb-doctor as a satire on "the nature cult of the eighteenth and nineteenth centuries, from its deistic through its romantic and transcendental phases," and on the "Emersonian doctrines of the issuance of good from evil and of compensation." Most valuably, Foster places Melville's criticism of Emerson in the context of his satire on optimistic philosophies throughout *The Confidence-Man*, whether it be Shaftesburyan optimism, utilitarian optimism, the nature cult of the eighteenth and nineteenth centuries, modernist Christianity, or any ideology that assumes that "the universe is benevolent and human nature good." Less persuasively, Foster disputes Oliver's identification of Egbert with Thoreau, maintaining that Melville split Emerson's philosophy, "its metaphysics and its ethics respectively, or perhaps better the abstract philosophy and its practical effect," between Winsome and Egbert. As Hershel Parker (1970) notes, Foster's contention that Emerson was not Thoreau's "sublime master" in the 1850s is perhaps accurate, but it reflects the 1950s view of Thoreau rather than the 1850s view, and, in denying that Egbert is Winsome's disciple, Foster ignores a chapter title and a passage where Egbert is described as such. Parker strengthens the case for identifying Egbert with Thoreau by providing a brief survey of Melville's ample opportunities to learn about Thoreau and his ideas through Duyckinck, Horace Greeley, and Hawthorne, as well as through reviews and mentions of Thoreau in New York newspapers and magazines. Parker's edition of *The Confidence-Man* (1971) contains a number of footnotes further relating Winsome and Egbert to Emerson and Thoreau and to Melville's satire on Transcendentalism; otherwise, little more has been added to this debate. Parker's " 'The Story of China Aster,' " in the same edition, plausibly interprets Egbert's story as (on one of its levels) "satiric of the Transcendental respect for private impulses, best epitomized in 'Self-Reliance.' " Helen P. Trimpi notes correspondences between Melville's "man in gray" (chs. 6–8) and Theodore Parker in terms of appearance, personality, methods of argument, and "style," but the similarities are not close enough to identify the character specifically with Parker ("Three of Melville's Confidence Men").

There has been little exploration of the impact of the Transcendentalists on Melville's work after *The Confidence-Man*, despite Henry W. Wells's claim that *Clarel* "chiefly expresses the immense force of American transcendental idealism" (*The American Way of Poetry*), and Leon Howard's discovery of "evidence enough" in the shorter poems to indicate that they were affected by Emerson's "cryptic manner" (*Herman Melville*). Karl Keller, however, has plausibly suggested that Melville was indebted to Emerson's poetic theory and practice for the "metaphysical strain" in his poetry, citing similarities in the diction, imagery, and irony of the two poets ("The Metaphysical Strain in Nineteenth-Century American Poetry"). Merton M. Sealts, Jr. (1980), reminds us that, on the table of contents in his copy of the seventh edition of Emerson's *Poems*, Melville noted the omission of several of its poems in subsequent editions, "thus showing his continuing interest in Emerson's poetic output," and Sealts finds "good reason" to believe that "Emerson's versification and his individual tone as a poet strongly influenced Melville's own often rough poetic lines." Philip D. Beidler describes *Billy Budd* as Melville's "final definitive comment on the unworkability of Emersonian ideas of order" in a disordered world, in whch Billy and Claggart are "opposingly flawed versions of a single Emersonian model," distorted variations on "Emerson's model of the harmonious soul," and Vere is "a problematic, humanized version of Emersonian man" and an "Emersonian artificer"; but Beidler presents no compelling evidence from the text (and no external evidence) to suggest that Melville had Emerson in mind when writing the story ("*Billy Budd*: Melville's Valedictory to Emerson").

Few of the studies cited in this chapter make use of external evidence. Since William Braswell's study of the marginalia, attempts to increase our knowledge of what Melville actually knew of the Transcendentalists have been limited to Hershel Parker's 1970 essay, his "Melville and the Transcendentalists: A Chronology" in his edition of *The Confidence-Man*, and Merton M. Sealts, Jr., "Melville and Emerson's Rainbow." Using the format of Jay Leyda, *The Melville Log*, Parker's "Chronology" lists Melville's activities during the period 1847–62 that bear on his knowledge of the Transcendentalists. This chronology is "meant to be suggestive, not comprehensive," but it effectively demonstrates what most critics have merely assumed: that with "his contacts in the New York publishing world, with the Boston social world, and with Concord through Hawthorne, Melville heard and read much about Emerson, Thoreau, and other Transcendentalists." Sealts sets out "to assemble all the evidence concerning Melville's response to Emerson" and supplements the information already available with valuable new findings: that Melville, for instance, could have seen any or all of Emerson's first four books "in Putnam's store" or in Duyckinck's library before 1849 and heard Emerson lecture on either "Natural Aristocracy" or "The Superlative in Manners and Literature"—probably the former, in Sealts's view. Sealts also concludes that Melville probably became familiar with *Essays* and *Essays: Second Series* during 1849–50 and with *Nature; Addresses, and Lectures* and *Representative Men* during 1850–51 (though he may never have read *Nature*), and that *Representative Men* is "undoubtedly the source" of Melville's "repeated references to Plato as the fountainhead of modern knowledge."

Despite these studies by Parker and Sealts, large gaps clearly remain in our knowledge of Melville's familiarity with the Transcendentalists. We still cannot say with certainty, for instance, which of Emerson's essays he had read before he completed *Moby-Dick*, whether he ever read *Nature*, or how much of Thoreau's work he read. Yet Parker and Sealts provide a sturdy informative base for further exploration, and Sealts's two recent essays should counteract any lingering scholarly tendencies to portray Melville as Transcendentalist or anti-Transcendentalist, or exclusively preoccupied with American Transcendentalists at any stage of his career. They also indicate that an invaluable contribution to Melville research remains to be made by a scholar who is able to combine such factual information as is available with a comprehensive examination of Melville's works for all the evidence they yield about his response to American and European Transcendentalists and other philosophical idealists, including most notably Thoreau and Carlyle.

EDGAR ALLAN POE

Ottavio M. Casale

Had this essay been written fifty years ago, it probably would have been very brief and very sure in asserting that Edgar Allan Poe abhorred the Transcendentalists, shared few of the views of life and art held by the truly major writers of his day, and should not really be mentioned in the same breath with them. Often, these generalities seemed to merge causally in the minds of scholars, who concluded that Poe was unimportant because he was divorced from Transcendentalism and New England concerns, or vice versa. Poe was given short shrift in Vernon Louis Parrington, *The Romantic Revolution in America 1800–1860*, entirely overlooked in F. O. Matthiessen, *American Renaissance*, and generally neglected through the 1940s. As for Poe's cosmogony *Eureka*, a work that seems to beg for at least some assimilation to idealistic thought, most scholars used to ignore it or declare it an anomaly in Poe, perhaps even evidence of mental disintegration. In recent decades, however, Poe's serious reputation has grown, and as critical attention has focused on *Eureka*, *Pym*, and Poe's search for unity, his connection with American Romanticism and Transcendentalism has been highlighted.

AIDS FOR RESEARCH

Information on works about Poe appears in the standard general bibliographies on American literature, which may be supplemented by J. Lasley Dameron and Irby B. Cauthen, Jr., *Edgar Allan Poe*, and Esther F. Hyneman, *Edgar Allan Poe*. In addition to the current Poe listings appearing in *PMLA*, *AL*, and *AmLS*, the journal *Poe*

Studies (formerly *Poe Newsletter*) issues a checklist of recent scholarship at more or less regular intervals.

Readers must still rummage for reliable texts of Poe's works. James A. Harrison's Virginia Edition of *The Complete Works of Edgar Allan Poe* (1902), including letters and a biography in seventeen volumes, remains the most comprehensive source, but it should be checked against the *Collected Works of Edgar Allan Poe*, ed. Thomas Ollive Mabbott (1969–78), which includes one volume of *Poems* and two of *Tales and Sketches*. A fourth volume, *The Imaginary Voyages: The Narrative of Arthur Gordon Pym, The Unparalleled Adventure of One Hans Pfaall, The Journal of Julius Rodman*, has been edited by Burton R. Pollin (1981). Pollin has also provided a valuable *Word Index to Poe's Fiction*, which concords the previous four volumes. The letters are in excellent shape owing to the work of John Ward Ostrom, who published his two-volume edition *The Letters of Edgar Allan Poe* in 1948; followed up with a 1966 reprinting that included additional items first reported in *AL*; presented even more letters in *AL*; and then published a completely revised checklist of the correspondence in *SAR*.

For many years the complete text of *Eureka* was available only in the 1848 edition or as part of collected editions such as Harrison's or *The Works of Edgar Allan Poe*, ed. E. C. Stedman and George E. Woodberry (1893–95). In 1950, however, W. H. Auden included the work in his *Edgar Allan Poe: Selected Prose, Poetry, and Eureka*. More recently, Richard P. Benton has generated multiple (if confusing) publications. In 1974 he published a facsimile of the 1848 text simultaneously in *ATQ* and as a separate volume called *Eureka: A Prose Poem*; then in 1975 the same text was issued as part of a composite volume entitled *Poe as Literary Cosmologer in Eureka*, which included ten scholarly essays first published in *ATQ* (1975). Roland W. Nelson, "Apparatus for a Definitive Edition of Poe's *Eureka*," distills the author's 1975 dissertation on the subject. By incorporating Poe's holograph revisions in four copies of the first edition, Nelson allows us to construct a kind of master edition. Equally valuable is Nelson's commentary on the facts of *Eureka*'s publication, its reception, and its place in the literature of Poe and his times.

POE ON TRANSCENDENTALISM

Poe wrote few works exclusively or even chiefly about Transcendentalism or its advocates. He twitted Transcendentalist oracularity and faddishness in the satires "How to Write a Blackwood Article" (1845; originally "The Psyche Zenobia," 1838) and "Never Bet the Devil Your Head" (1841). There was also praise of Orestes A. Brownson's novel *Charles Elwood* in "Mesmeric Revelation" (1844); a sketch of Emerson in "An Appendix of Autographs" (1842); a review of Ellery Channing's poetry (1843); and the "Literati" description of Margaret Fuller (1846). Most of Poe's numerous references to Transcendentalism, however, are scattered throughout the canon, and to assess them one must scour the primary works and consult detailed secondary studies.

Most of Poe's explicit remarks about Transcendentalism support the conventional view that he hated nearly everything associated with New England and the "New Thought." In his "war to the knife" against New England, he mocked Emerson, scorned Alcottism, and scathingly reviewed Channing's poems. With an eye toward the European roots of the philosophy, he ridiculed Immanuel Kant, deplored Samuel Taylor Coleridge's "metaphysicianism," and seemed thoroughly repelled by Thomas Carlyle. Poe's animus against the *Dial* was as profound as his hatred of that journal's natural enemy, the *North American Review*. Boston was for him "the city of Smug," Henry Wadsworth Longfellow was a "plagiarist," and, in his battle with the Brahmin poet and his supporters, Poe created the swearwords "Frogpond" and "Frogpondians" to damn the entire Boston-Cambridge-Concord axis and the professors and writers therein. In his later criticism, he could barely mention didacticism without a wry reference to "the so called poetry of the so called transcendentalists," as in "The Philosophy of Composition" (1846). Even in *Eureka*, his explanation of the universe, Poe interrupted to satirize the Transcendentalists, those for whom "a tree can be a tree and not a tree" simultaneously.

These attacks, however, may have represented more than a simple intellectual response to Transcendentalism. Despite his Boston birth, Poe was very much a Southerner, sharing in the South's conservative resistance to New England liberalism and in its natural resentment of cultural exclusion and condescension. Poe was also a magazinist caught up in the personal and sectional literary skirmishes of his time: the frequency and acidity of his attacks on "Frogpondians" increased when he came to New York, where it was the fashion to ridicule Boston. Furthermore, there is evidence that Poe felt personally rejected by various New England groups, those who—as he once wrote to Sarah Whitman—"knew *me* least and are my enemies." This was near-paranoia, perhaps, but the nature of Poe's works and jobs and the realities of cultural power *did* make it difficult for him to be known and recognized in New England. It is striking that when we discuss the Poe-Transcendentalism connection, we almost exclusively cite Poe's comments about Transcendentalists, not theirs about him. Outside of Fuller's two reviews of Poe's tales and poems (1845), no leading Transcendentalist assessed (or felt the need to assess) Poe during the latter's lifetime.

In addition to the personal, sociopolitical, and even geocultural resentments expressed by Poe, he had a sharp sense of what literature and philosophy should be and do, and these distinctions consistently informed his scorn and praise of intellectuals. Thus he could assail Emerson's "mysticism" but appreciate some of his lyrics; lash out at the obscurity of Carlyle's writings and Amos Bronson Alcott's "Orphic Sayings" but deeply admire the elder Channing's lucid, convincing prose; accept the well-turned poems of Christopher Pearse Cranch but reject the badly crafted verse of Ellery Channing; chide Kant and Coleridge for deductive philosophizing but venerate Coleridge as a poet and hail Brownson for avoiding a priori abstractions in his search for belief.

What Transcendentalism precisely meant to Poe can only be guessed at, for Poe, the consummate definer, remained strangely indefinite on the question. Suffice it to say that from about 1844 on, he moved toward a vague distinction between two kinds of Transcendentalism—one the "cant" of insincere faddists professing an obscure mysticism, the other "a profound and ennobling philosophy" for approaching the sublime. The latter is reflected in two of his early stories: the heroine of "Morella" (1835) studies Fichte's pantheism and Schelling's doctrines of identity, and the lady "Ligeia" (1838)—Poe's own favorite tale—fastens on unspecified Transcendentalist writings.

This affirmation of a positive type of Transcendentalism may be connected to Poe's own development of metaphysic or myth not altogether different from that of the Transcendentalists, from the ambiguous early vision of supernal unity in the poem "Al Aaraaf" (1829) to the Shelleyan invocation of ideal beauty in the posthumously published "The Poetic Principle" (1850). In *Eureka*, Poe invoked both intuition and logic to suggest a vision of the unity that accounts for our origin and destiny; explained the difference between spirit and matter in terms of the apparently physical forces of attraction (gravity) and repulsion (electricity); and traced both poetry and science— the urges toward beauty and truth that he elsewhere thought irreconcilable—to the cosmic tug toward original oneness. As early as "The Fall of the House of Usher"(1839), Poe had used to Gothic effect the concept of the sentient interpenetration of all matter. He returned to that idea lyrically in "The Island of the Fay" (1841), where he saw the universe as "all within the Spirit Divine," and in "The Power of Words" (1845), where he used the notion that the connection among atoms is so tight that mere words can create new worlds. "The Colloquy of Monos and Una" (1841) carried a Thoreauvian distrust of materialism to apocalyptic extremes, attributing a projected destruction of the world to lust of intellect and the ravaging of nature. One of the major stepping-stones to the curiously scientific quasi-Transcendentalism of *Eureka* is "Mesmeric Revelation," which Poe summarized as his own philosophy in a 2 July 1844 letter to James Russell Lowell. In that work, Poe's persona Vankirk grounds physical phenomena in a unifying force, which he insists is "unparticled matter" but also calls "God."

In *Symbolism and American Literature*, Charles Feidelson, Jr., suggests that for Poe, as for Hawthorne and Melville, "ostentatious hostility to Transcendentalism was only one aspect of a real mixture of attraction and repulsion." On balance, this conclusion seems fair to the full evidence. Poe associated Transcendentalism with a complex of personal and cultural irritants, including social liberalism, literary didacticism, and affectation. He seldom criticized specific religious ideas of the Transcendentalists, but he did resent any "metaphysicianism" that built Edens on untenable a priori beliefs. At the purest level, much of his animus was aesthetic: Poe believed that the cause of good literature and clear thinking could only be damaged by the habits of so many of the Transcendentalists.

STUDIES ABOUT POE AND TRANSCENDENTALISM

Many lengthy studies offer material relevant to the nagging question of Poe's knowledge of European idealists, but a few works merit emphasis. Margaret Alterton,

The Origin of Poe's Critical Theory, is still basic to assessing the impact of Coleridgean and German aesthetic theory on Poe. Perhaps even more useful is Floyd Stovall, "Poe's Debt to Coleridge," which traces the strong, Coleridgean presence in Poe's works, linking specific passages of a "decided transcendental flavor" to the English writer. Henry A. Pochmann, *German Culture in America*, finds that German letters deeply influenced Poe and concludes that he preferred German Romanticism to "any other school." Glen A. Omans, "'Intellect, Taste, and the Moral Sense,'" rejects the notion that Poe learned his Kant mainly through Coleridge, arguing on admittedly circumstantial evidence that Poe's aesthetic debt to Kant was direct and extensive.

One of the first eminent scholars to stress the common ground Poe shared with his American contemporaries was Killis Campbell in *The Mind of Poe and Other Studies*, which collects earlier essays. Arguing that Poe drew much from current intellectual life, Campbell briefly notes some similarities between Poe and Emerson. Allan G. Halline, "Moral and Religious Concepts in Poe," reinforces Campbell by finding more moral and religious content in Poe than is usually recognized. In his *Cosmic Optimism*, Frederick W. Conner contends that Poe superimposed an uneasy Transcendentalism on a mechanistic philosophy and thus "pushed himself at least part way into the camp of the scorned transcendentalists."

In the 1950s two significant books emerged that connected Poe to Romantic and modern aesthetics and to Transcendentalism. Charles Feidelson, Jr., contends in his *Symbolism in American Literature* that Transcendentalism—in the sense of seeing the world as mind, of perceiving "psychophysically"—could not be avoided "even by writers like Melville, Hawthorne, and Poe, who were hostile to its superficial features." Poe created a "materialistic idealism" significantly like and unlike the "idealistic materialism" of the Transcendentalists. Edward H. Davidson, *Poe*, is dizzying in some of its generalizations; it is also, however, a milestone in the study of Poe as a serious philosophical writer. Davidson attempts to show that Poe's symbolic usage and quest for unity connect him to international aesthetics, both Romantic and modern; that Poe fused rationalistic epistemology with Coleridgean ontology in confronting the same metaphysical problems faced by Emerson and other romantics; and that he moved toward "a purposive monism." Junichi Nakamura, *Edgar Allan Poe's Relations with New England*, rather mechanically (and disappointingly) compiles statements made by Poe and various New Englanders.

In his somewhat overprotective *Edgar Allan Poe*, Vincent Buranelli finds Poe's aestheticism superior to the system-based Transcendentalist view of art. Sidney P. Moss's important *Poe's Literary Battles* not only captures the historical particulars and personalities of Poe's editorial conflicts but also describes the writer's steady campaign against "puffery" and for his own aesthetic principles, a crusade that at times brought him into conflicts with the Transcendentalist community. Of special interest are Moss's coverage of Poe's review of Ellery Channing, the Lowell relationship, the Longfellow "war," and the Boston Lyceum "hoax" so damaging to Poe's reputation.

By the time Edward Wagenknecht published his *Edgar Allan Poe*, attitudes toward *Eureka* and the Poe-Transcendentalism question had clearly shifted. Influenced by Conner and like-minded scholars, Wagenknecht stresses the merging of mechanism and Transcendentalism in *Eureka*, which for him shows Poe's passion for "a Sense of the Whole and a hunger for union with the Whole." Arnold Smithline, *"Eureka,"* boldly asserts the Transcendentalist nature of Poe's preference for intuition and his vision of unity; but this brief three-page article skims lightly over a rich subject and ignores or blurs the clear distinctions between the two views at issue. Ottavio M. Casale, "Poe on Transcendentalism," deriving from his dissertation, tries to strip away received opinions in analyzing Poe's complex remarks. Its coverage is more detailed than that of this chapter, but it makes essentially similar points. In a related article, "The Battle of Boston: A Revaluation of Poe's Lyceum Appearance," Casale suggests that Poe was probably not "hoaxing" his Boston listeners when he read "Al Aaraaf" to them in 1845, as he later claimed, but that he was apparently trying to impress by choosing his most philosophical, if unfortunately most obscure, poem. If there was any hoax, it was in his strident, unnecessary defense of his reading.

Robert D. Jacobs' modestly titled *Poe: Journalist and Critic*, one of the very best books on Poe, treats his growth as a journalist, practical critic, and "psychological aesthetician." Jacobs shows how Poe, influenced by the Scottish realists, at first distrusted metaphysical reasoning based on suprarational assumptions; how he vacillated between the neoclassical-rationalist and Romantic-Transcendentalist aesthetics; and how he increasingly sought to base his aesthetics on a metaphysical position of his own. *Eureka*, writes Jacobs, was "Poe's last attempt to formulate a consistent theory of the universe that would correlate with his aesthetics."

John F. Lynen's long essay in *The Design of the Present* focuses on *Eureka* and Poe's tendency to seek positive absolutes by way of opposites: beauty through terror or ugliness, life through death, existence through annihilation. Lynen notes a Transcendentalism in *Eureka* but argues that Poe, like Melville, appreciated that cosmic unity meant the obliteration of self, a realization lost on Emerson.

Harriet R. Holman, "Hog, Bacon, Ram and Other 'Savans' in *Eureka*," is a well-researched, textually sensitive article revealing the pervasive complexity of Poe's satiric usage in *Eureka* and the way he distorted the words and ideas of authorities in order to shore up his own cosmogonical theories. Holman finds many more references to Emerson and his group than meet the eye, although at times the reasoning is strained (e.g., "Moreover, Emerson's well-known dictum about a 'foolish consistency' is conversed in *Eureka*: '*A perfect consistency, I repeat, can be nothing but an absolute truth . . .* '"). Resuming her analysis of Poe's satire in "Splitting Poe's 'Epicurean Atoms,' " Holman dissects Poe's use of references to the discredited Epicurean theory of atoms to ridicule Emerson and others who, like the Epicureans, scorned logic and perched their cloudy systems on ego and feeling.

Stuart Levine's provocative *Edgar Poe* underlines Poe's ties to Romantic idealism and thus to Transcendentalism. In one chapter, Levine analyzes the similarities and "variables" that emerge when we compare Emerson and Poe as mystics or occultists: despite Poe's "nastiness" toward Emerson, they shared a "kinship in artistry" and a belief in "the interconnectedness of all things." Less convincing is Levine's assertion that the detective Dupin is a "transcendental hero." Starting from the positive comments of Poe on his own version of Transcendentalism, Eric W. Carlson, "Poe's

Vision of Man," contends that Poe's world view has three perspectives, the Neoplatonic, the existential, and the psychotranscendental, which correspond to Poe's sense of Man's past, present, and future, respectively. For Carlson the unifying and affirmative theme in Poe is "the quest for rebirth of mind and soul and thereby of a new unity of being," a quest that makes Poe "more transcendental even than Emerson." G. R. Thompson, "Poe and Romantic Irony," detects a dark, limited kind of Transcendentalism in Poe—a "transcendental irony" that Poe used to protect himself from an empty or perhaps malevolent universe. Roger Forclaz, *Le Monde d'Edgar Poe*, exhaustively treats all Poe's work and, it would appear, most of the extant scholarship. Judging Poe a key figure in American and international Romanticism, Forclaz argues that Poe's blend of pragmatic scientific traits and idealistic ones is essentially American, and that his spiritual tendencies resemble those of the Transcendentalists.

It is difficult to relate Poe to Transcendentalism without studying Emerson. Floyd Stovall, *American Idealism*, discusses Poe as a contemporary of Emerson who pursued idealistic goals, devotes several pages to comparing the two authors, and concludes that "It is odd that they should have been so totally incapable of understanding each other, since both were searching for perfection through ways transcendental." Jeremiah K. Durick's essay on Poe in *American Classics Reconsidered* notes metaphysical parallels between Poe and Emerson and ultimately disapproves of both writers, ostensibly for their similar and dangerous pantheisms. According to Clark Griffith, " 'Emersonianism' and 'Poeism,' " American Romanticism clusters around the poles of these two great authors. The Emersonian, including Herman Melville, broadens facts into symbols, ignores psychological realities, and aims at abstractions; the Poeist, including Hawthorne, tends to shun abstractions and to objectify inner or psychological forces. There may be some truth in this dichotomy, but it does violence to writers and works.

In 1963, Patrick F. Quinn published an influential article, "Poe's *Eureka* and Emerson's *Nature*." In a balanced manner, Quinn discusses the interesting likenesses in the two works but also shows how *Eureka* differs from *Nature* in its quest for logical proof and its ultimate fascination with death instead of life. Nevertheless, Quinn reaches the symmetrical conclusion "that *Nature* is Emerson's *Eureka* and that *Eureka* is Poe's *Nature*." A closely related article is that of D. Ramakrishna, "Poe's *Eureka* and Hindu Philosophy," which in effect suggests a three-way parallel, since Poe expressed "the essence of Emersonian Transcendentalism which is also the essence of Hindu philosophical thought." Ramakrishna admits that he is dealing with parallels rather than influences (since Poe probably did not know Hindu scriptures even if he may have known his Emerson), but the article suffers because the ideas chosen for comparison are so abstract that they resemble any number of monistic theories, not merely the ones convened by the author. After reviewing the growth of Poe's reputation, Louis Broussard's book *The Measure of Poe* settles down to rehearsing how *Eureka* fits into the Poe canon and how it reflects "basically the same pantheistic approach which had produced Emerson's 'The Over-Soul.' " In outline at least the book's conclusions are quite defensible, but as a whole it seems insulated from the work of earlier scholars, only some of whom are mentioned in an appended bibliography. In a fresh article, Barton Levi St. Armand, "Usher Unveiled," recognizes the "tantalizingly similar" idealisms of Emerson and Poe but submits that the two conflicted owing to the Gnostic source of Poe's vision as opposed to the Neoplatonic derivation of Emerson's. Gerald M. Garmon, "Emerson's 'Moral Sentiment' and Poe's 'Poetic Sentiment,' " seeks to identify the two faculties in question but does so at the expense of ignoring the incisive contrasts between them.

Although Poe's poetry is now out of critical fashion, several studies have compared it to Emerson's. Hyatt H. Waggoner, *American Poets from the Puritans to the Present*, contends that Poe's poems illustrate a paradoxical "destructive transcendence" based on negation and depair and resembling the doctrine of illusion in Emerson's essay "Experience." Waggoner uses Emerson's poetic practice and theory to minimize Poe, whom he evidently does not admire. Albert Gelpi, in an impressive psychological study of nineteenth-century poets, *The Tenth Muse*, also approaches Poe's poetry and aesthetic in the context of Emerson, but his conclusions are kinder to Poe. For Gelpi, Emerson's poems reflect his belief in natural and metaphysical order and unity, whereas Poe's are those of a formalist-mechanist whose sense of chaos and uncertainty led him (like Wallace Stevens) to seek in art the order unachievable in actual existence. This difference in metaphysical assumptions accounts for Poe's greater stress on craft and rational control in art. Between them, Emerson and Poe created the "two polar positions" from which modern American poetry subtly developed. David D. Anderson, "A Comparison of the Poetic Theories of Emerson and Poe," finds it "surprising" that the two authors arrived at antithetical aesthetic positions given certain similarities.

In his source study "Poe and Emerson," Thomas Ollive Mabbott observes that Poe's phrase "Out of Space, out of time" from his 1844 poem "Dreamland" may have been derived from Emerson's words "out of time, out of space" from the 1838 Divinity School Address. Burton R. Pollin, in "Poe's Use of D'Israeli's *Curiosities* to Belittle Emerson," cites Isaac D'Israeli as the source for Poe's comparison of Emerson and Carlyle to the ancients Arruntius and Sallust. The point is useful, but Pollin does not acknowledge that although Poe did "belittle" Emerson for aping Carlyle (as Arruntius had Sallust), Poe also praised Emerson for having so much "force" that imitation was unnecessary for him. Thoreau and Poe never mentioned each other, but E. Arthur Robinson, "Thoreau and the Deathwatch in Poe's 'The Tell-Tale Heart,' " suggests that Poe's curious phrase "death watches in the wall" echoes a similar one from Thoreau's "Natural History of Massachusetts," which appeared in an 1842 issue of the *Dial*.

Poe's satirical jabs in "How to Write a Blackwood Article" and "Never Bet the Devil Your Head" have occasioned some investigation. Walter F. Taylor, "Israfel in Motley," looks past the other targets Poe aimed at in his "Blackwood" piece and focuses on the anti-Transcendentalist satire. In "Poe's Zenobia," Thomas H. McNeal argues that Margaret Fuller's regal aggressiveness and manner of dress inspired the unflattering portrait of "Psyche Zenobia" and that Emerson was the prototype of "Dr. Moneypenny," her literary coach. McNeal is fairly undone by Burton R. Pollin, however, in "Poe's Tale of Psyche Zenobia." Pollin observes that the anti-*Dial* paragraph—like the *Dial* itself—did not exist in 1838, when the sketch was first published; moreover, Fuller had barely published at the time and was almost certainly unknown to Poe. Pollin convinces us that Poe was striking at various literary foibles ("using buckshot rather than a bullet") in the "Blackwood" article and its sister-piece "A Predicament," although one may balk at the assertion that the latter piece is "a masterly *tour de force*." In yet another article, "Poe on Margaret Fuller in 1845," Pollin identifies as Poe's a satirical notice accompanying a caricature of Fuller in the 8 March 1845 *Broadway Journal*. Eliot Glassheim, in "A Dogged Interpretation of 'Never Bet the Devil Your Head,' " contends that, with a densely wrought series of puns, Poe attempted to obliterate simultaneously the Transcendentalist idealist, the materialist, and the conventional social individual. Glassheim ingeniously notes that the simple Toby of the sketch is either a dog or at least an obedient, doglike Transcendentalist.

Since Poe's "Ligeia" immerses the heroine in Transcendentalist readings, critics have inevitably sought a link between the story and Transcendentalism. A stimulating treatment of the topic is E. Miller Budick, "Poe's Gothic Idea," which recognizes Poe's philosophical idealism but argues that he converted it into the stuff of terror in works like "Ligeia." Poe differed from the Transcendentalists, says Budick, in that he described a "Gothic" fall from Neoplatonic wholeness whereas they allegorized "the perfection of Nature and the perfectability of man." For Clark Griffith, "Poe's 'Ligeia' and the English Romantics," the tale is a veiled tongue-in-cheek attack on the Germanic "cant" so influential among English Romantics and American Transcendentalists. Joel Salzberg, "The Gothic Hero in Transcendental Quest: Poe's 'Ligeia' and James's 'The Beast in the Jungle,' " suggests that this improbable pair of authors created a new kind of "villain-hero" who was a Transcendentalist of sorts, as devoted to the realm of spirit as his Gothic predecessors had been to that of flesh.

ADDITIONAL SCHOLARSHIP ON *EUREKA*

In *AmLS* for 1969, Patrick F. Quinn correctly notes that "*Eureka* is more and more being thought of as perhaps the primal Poe text." Since Poe's cosmogony enriches our understanding of the intellectual character of Poe and his era, the efforts of certain scholars of *Eureka* who do not necessarily stress Transcendentalist connections deserve our attention.

By including *Eureka* in his 1950 anthology and by stressing in his introduction the significance of Poe's search for unity, W. H. Auden helped to energize and redirect the course of Poe study. An equally influential contribution is that of another poet-professor-critic, Richard Wilbur, who has published several pieces on Poe, including his 1959 Library of Congress lecture "The House of Poe," "The Poe Mystery Case," and—perhaps most comprehensive—the introduction to the Poe selections in *Major Writers of America*, ed. Perry Miller. Relying (perhaps too much) on *Eureka* and "Ligeia," the common thesis of Wilbur's brilliant, interlocking pieces is that Poe displays a Transcendentalist impulse to escape mundane reality and reachieve through imagination and dream (or the hypnagogic state) an ideal dimension otherwise lost to man.

Carol H. Maddison, "Poe's *Eureka*," is valuable for tracing the way Poe blended in *Eureka* his own aesthetic theory, recent natural theology and scientific theory, and spiritual doctrines he may have acquired from Leibnitz, the Hindus, and the Transcendentalists. Geoffrey Rans, *Edgar Allan Poe*, is a useful, compact, and intelligent introduction that stresses the value of the intuition-imagination to Poe and shows how basic *Eureka* and the criticism are to Poe's fiction and poetry. Joseph J. Moldenhauer, "Murder as a Fine Art," is the kind of criticism that makes more plodding scholars despair. Moldenhauer imaginatively and subtly argues that Poe creates a partly amoral ethic whereby all that tends toward unity is a "good" and all that tends toward division is "evil"; but "since the intensification of separateness provokes violent reactions like the urge to kill, even division can be understood as instrumental to goodness." A work that may be profitably read in conjunction with Moldenhauer's is David G. Halliburton, *Edgar Allan Poe*. Although the jargon here is more overwrought than is necessary, the book convincingly argues that Poe's myth of deliverance from destruction was inspired by his theory of unity, a theory that "is physical, aesthetic, religious, and even, though we do not often use the word in relation to Poe, moral."

At least two significant articles appear in Richard P. Benton's symposium *Poe as Literary Cosmologer in* Eureka. Burton R. Pollin, "Contemporary Reviews of *Eureka*," is far more than a checklist, covering as it does the facts regarding Poe's original lecture on the "Cosmogony of the Universe," the publication of *Eureka*, and the reception of both the lecture and the book. In light of later attacks, it is interesting to note how many of the first reactions were favorable. In the same symposium, Barton Levi St. Armand, " 'Seemingly Intuitive Leaps,' " insists that the work is neither anti-Christian nor an example of Coleridgean Romanticism but a later version of the natural theology advocated by William Paley and others, which found evidence of God in science and the working of nature.

One of the more solid articles on *Eureka* is Edward William Pitcher, "Poe's *Eureka* as a Prose Poem." Pitcher persuasively argues that Poe's work "was composed according to a philosophy of composition designed to stimulate 'poetic' effects in prose," and along the way he provides an admirable summary of the contents and design of *Eureka*.

SAMPSON REED

Elizabeth A. Meese

REED AND TRANSCENDENTALISM

During his lifetime, Sampson Reed's relation to Transcendentalism varied according to the changing definitions of that movement, particularly as it took shape in the mind of his friend Ralph Waldo Emerson. Initially, Reed's thought developed in a milieu similar to that of other Boston Transcendentalists. He attended Harvard College, graduating three years ahead of Emerson, and went on to study at Harvard Divinity School, where he turned to Swedenborgianism and abandoned his preparations for the Unitarian ministry. His principal role in the Transcendentalist circle was as a purveyor of Swedenborgian ideas, and as late as 1836 Emerson still regarded Reed as his "early oracle."

When Emerson received the baccalaureate in 1821, Reed delivered his "Oration on Genius" for the Master of Arts ceremony. The younger man treasured his copy of the address, which was not published until Elizabeth Palmer Peabody presented it under the title "Genius" in her *Aesthetic Papers* (1849). The remarkable compatibility of Reed's ideas with those of major Transcendentalists like Emerson diminished with the publication of Reed's preface to the 1838 edition of *Observations on the Growth of the Mind*. By this time, Emerson's own philosophical outlook had jelled somewhat, and Reed had grown more zealous in his Swedenborgianism. Reed, whom Emerson had once grouped with Madame de Staël, William Wordsworth, and Emanuel Swedenborg as representatives of their ages, now wrote that "*Transcendentalism* is the parasite of *sensualism*; and when it shall have done its work, it will be found to be itself a worm, and the offspring of a worm."

Reed's most notable work was a pamphlet entitled *Observations on the Growth of the Mind* (1826), first published a decade before Emerson's *Nature*. When the 1838 revised edition of *Observations* was issued, Reed noted in the preface that the book had already been through two editions in America and one in England; before the century was over, there would be six more editions (five in America and one in England)—testimonies to the popularity and importance of the book. To the 1838 edition, Reed added a preface and "Remarks on Some Other Subjects," a selection of his essays reprinted from the New Church periodical, *New Jerusalem Magazine* (1828–37): "Miracles," "Conscience," "Home," "Self-Love Essential Evil," "External Restraint," "Hereditary Evil," "Marriage in the Heavens," and "Children's Books." In addition to several letters written by Reed to his contemporaries, Kenneth Walter Cameron reprints two more of these essays—"The Free Agency of Man" (1827) and "On Animals" (1828)—in *Emerson the Essayist* (vol. 2). Of Reed's other works, the following are of secondary interest: *Address on Education* (1842), *Swedenborg and His Mission* (1859), *The Future of the New Church* (1875), and *A Biographical Sketch of Thomas Worcester* (1880). The two works most deserving of further consideration are the "Oration on Genius" and *Observations*. Selections from both may be found in *The Transcendentalists*, ed. Perry Miller, and *Selected Writings of the American Transcendentalists*, ed. George Hochfield.

Reed's brief address on genius signaled the collapse of eighteenth-century philosophy and pointed the way toward a new intellectual and spiritual optimism. Reed characterizes the individual as apprehending spiritual light through the agency of divine power; the finite and the infinite are linked by the genius of mind. Art is created from nature, which is itself unified with the spirit: "Thoughts fall to the earth with power, and make a language out of nature." In his final point, Reed predicts that "Locke's mind will not always be the standard of metaphysics. Had we a description of it in its present state, it would make a very different book from 'Locke on the Human Understanding.' "

Observations on the Growth of the Mind is important because it helped to establish the idea of correspondence as a significant feature of American Transcendentalism. In this work, which Emerson read and circulated among his friends, Reed stresses the power of the imagination in apprehending divine truth by means of the perfect relation of mind and matter. Ultimate, transcendent truth is accessible only through the mediation of objects in the visible world. Like others in his circle, Reed maintained that "Truth, all truth is practical." Through the agency of the eye, inner and outer realities are fused. Reed's view of art develops from his correspondential view of the interrelatedness of mind, matter, and spirit, with fact and mind struggling toward perfect reconciliation. Reed presents one of the clearest statements of the transcendental result of this perceptual process:

> The most perfect understanding of a subject is simply a perception of harmony existing between the subject and the mind itself. Indeed, the understanding which any individual possesses of a subject might be mathematically defined

The subject proposed,

---

the actual character of his mind;

and there is a constant struggle for the divisor and dividend to become the same by a change in the one or the other, that the result may be unity, and the understanding perfect.

Divine truth is embodied in nature, and the poet, employing "a language—not of words, but of things," bridges all illusions of separation and reveals participation in a higher order of being or meaning.

RESEARCH

Research on Reed's relation to Transcendentalism is preoccupied with the influence of his Swedenborgianism on Emerson's thought and art, as exemplified in Emerson Grant Sutcliffe, "Emerson's Theories of Literary Expression"; Clarence P. Hotson, "A Background for Emerson's Poem, 'Grace' " and "Sampson Reed, a Teacher of Emerson"; and Carl F. Strauch, "Emerson Rejects Reed and Hails Thoreau" and "The Mind's Voice." Several studies usefully differentiate the ideas of Swedenborg, Reed, and Emerson: Clarence P. Hotson, four articles on "Emerson and the Doctrine of Correspondence," and "Emerson and the Swedenborgians," which argues that "Emerson eagerly accepted and frequently repeated as his own Swedenborg's ideas of correspondence, influx, order, degrees, and ultimation, using the distinctive terminology of Swedenborg in doing so"; and Kenneth Walter Cameron, "Emerson and Swedenborgism," which presents a framework for the study of the interrelationship of ideas. Carl F. Strauch's "Introduction" to the reprint of *Observations* (1970) is the best general treatment of Reed's life, ideas, and work. Strauch contends that Reed contributed more than just "ideas and a vocabulary to Emerson." He presents useful bibliographical data for some of Reed's articles and provides a good discussion of responses made by some of Emerson's contemporaries. Also useful is Clarence P. Hotson's dissertation on Emerson and Swedenborg. In "Transcendentalism," Elizabeth A. Meese makes a case for Reed's essential place in the development of American Transcendental theory; the article, derived from her dissertation, "Transcendental Vision," concentrates on Reed's contribution to the doctrine of correspondence and the importance of that concept to the development of aesthetic theory in this period.

The accumulation of materials, documents, and perspectives on Reed's connections with Transcendentalists and Transcendentalism certainly deserves a full analysis. In particular, discussions of his relation to figures other than Emerson and to works other than "Oration" and *Observations* would be useful. Finally, Reed's contribution to the history of ideas in general warrants new research.

WALT WHITMAN

Jerome Loving

WHITMAN'S WRITINGS ABOUT THE TRANSCENDENTALISTS

"I was simmering, simmering, simmering; Emerson brought me to a boil," Walt Whitman is alleged to have told John Townsend Trowbridge in 1860. That Trowbridge, who clearly favored Emerson over Whitman, failed to report this confession until ten years after the poet's death suggests that the statement is an exaggeration at best, but it nevertheless initiated an ongoing inquiry into Whitman's indebtedness to Emerson and Transcendentalism. In the search for Transcendentalist origins and parallels in Whitman's work, critics have looked for more such outright admissions of debt—only to find Whitman "contradicting" himself, especially on the subject of Emerson.

Whitman's first recorded allusion to Emerson appears in the *New York Aurora* of 7 March 1842. After hearing "the Transcendentalist" deliver an early version of "The Poet," he described "Mr. Emerson's Lecture" as "one of the richest and most beautiful compositions . . . we have ever heard anywhere, at any time." The experience left an indelible mark on the future poet's mind, and in "Pictures"—a poem containing early drafts of lines found in the first *Leaves of Grass* (1855)—he wrote: "And there, tall and slender, stands Ralph Waldo Emerson, of New England, at the lecturer's desk lecturing." Although Whitman later denied *reading* Emerson until 1856 (see John Burroughs, *Notes on Walt Whitman as Poet and Person*), he revealed his familiarity with "Spiritual Laws" and perhaps other essays in the *Brooklyn Daily Eagle* of 15 December 1847. Whitman's marginalia in a copy of a review entitled "New Poetry in New England" (*USMDR*, 1847) suggests that he may also have read Emerson's *Poems* (1847) and compared it with his own ideas about poetry. Where the review remarks that Emerson communicates meaning without melody, Whitman wrote: "The perfect poet must be unimpeachable in *manner* as well as matter" (in *Complete Writings of Walt Whitman*, ed. Richard Maurice Bucke et al., vol. 9).

Whitman's "foreground" with regard to Emerson is otherwise obscure. Other than a few undated fragments, his next recorded comment was in a conversation with Moncure D. Conway sometime in September 1855 (*Autobiography Memories and Experiences*, vol. 1), which suggests that he did not receive Emerson's famous letter of 21 July 1855 until shortly after Conway's visit (see Jerome Loving, *Emerson, Whitman, and the American Muse*). This letter, which was published in the *New York Daily Tribune* of 10 October 1855 and in the appendix to the 1856 edition of *Leaves of Grass*, prompted Whitman to write an open reply (also printed in the edition) in which he hailed Emerson as "Master" and declared, "Those shores you found. I say you have led the States there—have led Me there." The letter reflects Whitman's euphoria over becoming the poet for whom Emerson had sought "in vain" back in the 1840s. It also reflects Whitman's anxiety, for later that year he wrote: "Walt Whitman stands to-day in the midst of the American people, a promise, a preface, an overture. . . . Will he justify the great prophecy of Emerson?" (*Daybooks and Notebooks*, ed. William White, vol. 3).

Whitman may have met Emerson by this time—the first of possibly "a dozen" meetings (*The Correspondence*, ed. Edwin Haviland Miller, vol. 4; and Horace Traubel, *With Walt Whitman in Camden*, vol. 2—cited below as *WWC*)—for Emerson's pocket diary for 11 December 1855 reads "Brooklyn" (Houghton Library, Harvard Univ.). If that was the day the New Englander finally struck his "tasks" and visited his "benefactor" (as he had promised in his letter of 21 July), the other details of the visit are less certain. In *The Life of Ralph Waldo Emerson*, Ralph L. Rusk places the meeting "at a New York hotel," basing his conjecture on the testimony of Edward Carpenter, an English disciple of both Emerson and Whitman (*Days with Walt Whitman*). In two statements to Horace Traubel, however, Whitman remembered first receiving the essayist at Mrs. Whitman's home in Brooklyn (*WWC*, vol. 2). Also in question is Carpenter's (and Rusk's) assertion that after dining at the New York hotel Whitman took Emerson to "a noisy fire-engine society" (see Jerome Loving, *Emerson, Whitman, and the American Muse*).

If Whitman and Emerson met again before 1860, there is no specific record of the meeting. Emerson may have been put off by the unauthorized publication of his letter; however, that did not stop him from persuading Amos Bronson Alcott and Henry David Thoreau to visit Brooklyn in the fall of 1856. Alcott first visited Whitman on 4 October and returned on 10 November with Thoreau. He thought Whitman a "nondescript . . . not so easily described" (*The Journals of Bronson Alcott*, ed. Odell Shepard), and Thoreau considered the poet "the most interesting fact to me at present" (*The Correspondence of Henry David Thoreau*, ed. Walter Harding and Carl Bode). Apparently, Whitman took to Alcott immediately and kept up the relationship, sending Alcott a copy of "Whispers of Heavenly Death" from the *Broadway Magazine* (*Letters of A. Bronson Alcott*, ed. Richard L. Herrnstadt). But he was not altogether pleased with Thoreau, though he presented him with a copy of the 1856 *Leaves of Grass*. Whitman thought it was not "so much a love of woods, streams, and hills that made [Thoreau] live in the country, as from a morbid dislike of humanity" (*Anne Gilchrist: Her Life and Writings*, ed. Herbert Harlakenden Gilchrist). For his part, Thoreau allegedly went back to Concord and championed *Leaves of Grass*, carrying it around Concord "like a red flag—defiantly, challenging the plentiful current opposition there" (*WWC*, vol. 3).

But Emerson was doubtless the primary reason for Whitman's interest in the Transcendentalists, and the two men met again in Boston in 1860. Whitman's third edition of *Leaves of Grass*—the first to find a commercial publisher—was being stereotyped at the firm of Thayer and Eldridge, and Emerson visited their offices on 17 March. Evidently, he had been allowed to look at the volume and learned that Whitman's intention to write songs of sex for his 1856 edition had developed into a "program" with the "Enfans d'Adam" poems ("Children of Adam" in 1867 and thereafter). That afternoon, as Whitman remembered twenty-one years later in *Specimen Days & Collect* (1882), the two poets walked on Boston Common. There Emerson urged Whitman to excise the "Adam" poems, but following Emerson's "argument-statement" Whitman felt more determined than ever "to adhere to [his own] theory, and exemplify it." Later Whitman insisted that the grounds for Emerson's criticisms had been practical, not moral or aesthetic (*WWC*, vol. 3).

Emerson had another reason for objecting to the sexual theme in the third *Leaves of Grass*: his letter had been published in the second edition (with a quotation from it stamped in gold on the spine), and thus he would be associated with future editions of the book as well. Whatever ridicule Whitman might receive would also fall upon Emerson—as in the case, for example, of a review published shortly after the appearance of the third edition in 1860. "The most charitable conclusion at which we can arrive," the *Boston Post* declared, "is that both Whitman's *Leaves* and Emerson's [letter of] laudation had a common origin in temporary insanity." Yet Whitman was apparently oblivious to any discomfort or embarrassment his actions might have caused Emerson, and when he found himself in Washington during the war without adequate employment, he did not hesitate to ask Emerson for letters of recommendation to the Secretaries of State and the Treasury—a favor Emerson granted with alacrity.

Whitman's interest in Emerson and the other Transcendentalists faded with the Civil War and the uproar caused by his dismissal in 1865 from the Department of the Interior for being the author of an obscene book. In *The Good Gray Poet* (1866), a pamphlet that was inspired by the firing, William Douglas O'Connor quoted from Emerson's "greeting" letter and the recently published letters of Thoreau (Jerome Loving, *Walt Whitman's Champion*). O'Connor sent a copy of the pamphlet to Emerson, but the man who found nothing in nature ultimately obscene never acknowledged it (perhaps recalling the fate of his 1855 letter to Whitman). Emerson also failed to speak out in Whitman's defense (few American literary men of consequence did) and this, coupled with the public silence Emerson had maintained on the subject of *Leaves of Grass* since 1855, left Whitman disappointed and even resentful (Kenneth M. Price, "Whitman on Other Writers"). It may also have jaundiced Whitman's view of Emerson's later work. In 1868, for example, Whitman called for an American culture that would outvie "all the rich pages of old-world Plutarch and Shakespeare, or our own Emerson" ("Personalism"), and in 1872, after hearing Emerson speak in Baltimore, Whitman commented that his former "Master" drew "on the same themes—as twenty-five years ago" (*Correspondence*, vol. 2). His complaints became more direct (and personal) in later years: shortly after he discovered that none of his work was included in *Parnassus* (1874), he remarked that Emerson's "constitutional distrust and doubt . . . have been too much for him—have not perhaps stopped him short of first-class genius, but have veiled it—have certainly clipped and pruned that free luxuriance of it which only satisfies the soul at last" (*Prose Works 1892*, vol. 2; see also *WWC*, vol. 2). In 1876, in an anonymous newspaper article ("Walt Whitman's Actual American Position"), he complained that the "still-born" reception of his poems was due in part to the "studious" apathy of established poets: "The *omnium gatherums* of poetry, by Emerson, Bryant, Whittier, and by lesser authorities, professing to include everybody of any note, carefully leave him out." For further commentary on Whitman's general reception in New England, see Sylvester Baxter, "Walt Whitman in Boston"; Clifton J. Furness, "Walt Whitman Looks at Boston"; and Portia Baker, "Walt Whitman and the *Atlantic Monthly*."

Whitman's attitude toward Emerson, it appears, began to sour in the mid-1860s. Indeed, this decade was the last in which he directly communicated with Emerson (see *Correspondence*, vol. 2, and *WWC*, vol. 2) until his visit to the Emerson homestead in 1881 (*Prose Works 1892*, vol. 1, and *Correspondence*, vol. 3). In "Emerson's Books (the Shadows of Them)" (1880), Whitman dismissed Emerson's "cold and bloodless intellectuality." In the same essay (in an issue honoring Emerson on his birthday) he attributed his 1856 "Master" letter to a touch of hero-worship—"of Emerson-on-the-brain"—and he concluded that "The best part of Emersonianism is, it breeds the giant that destroys itself." In its subtle ambivalence, the *Literary World* essay anticipates the numerous contradictory remarks made by Whitman and recorded by Horace Traubel in his *With Walt Whitman in Camden* volumes. Whenever the subject is Emerson the man, Whitman is decidedly enthusiastic, as he is in his eulogy "By Emerson's Grave" (1882). "I seem to have various feelings about Emerson but I am always loyal at last," he once remarked. "Emerson gratified me as a young man by what he did—he sometimes tantalized me as an old man by what he failed to do" (*WWC*, vol. 2). This observation more or less characterizes the poet's commentary on Emerson in *With Walt Whitman in Camden*, where there are approximately three hundred such references. They almost always focus on Emerson's character or his failure to champion *Leaves of Grass* after 1855, but Whitman's tone is usually affectionate. As he told Traubel in 1888, "We were like two Quakers together" (*WWC*, vol. 1). On the question of literary influence, however, Whitman was adamant to the end. A few years before his death he told William Sloane Kennedy: "It is of no importance whether I had read Emerson before starting L. of G. or not. The fact happens to be positively that I had *not*" (*Correspondence*, vol. 4).

WRITINGS ABOUT WHITMAN AND THE TRANSCENDENTALISTS

The commentary in this area can be divided between Whitman's personal and literary connections with the Transcendentalists, particularly Emerson. After Whitman's death in 1892, his disciples tried to keep their poet's reputation alive, mainly by reaffirming his originality and underscoring his denial of reading Emerson before 1856. Many of their polemics appeared in Traubel's magazine, *Conservator* (1890–1919). Typical of the arguments that appeared in its issues is William Sloane Kennedy's "Identities of Thought and Phrase in Emerson and Whitman." After citing more than a score of parallels, he concludes that they reflect nothing more than the fact that Emerson and Whitman were contemporaries. Yet Kennedy must have eventually discovered the weakness of his thesis, for when he reprinted the essay in his *An Autolycus Pack*, he titled it "Walt Whitman's Indebtedness to Emerson." Kennedy's confusion about the Emerson-Whitman question (as well as Whitman's opinion of Kennedy) is illuminated in George Hendrick, "Unpublished Notes on Whitman in William Sloan[e] Kennedy's Diary." A more general account of the Whitmaniacs' efforts is found in Charles B. Willard, *Whitman's American Fame*, and Gay Wilson Allen, *New Walt Whitman Handbook*.

The apotheosis of Whitman found its first real challenge in Bliss Perry, *Walt Whitman*, a biography that attempted to sort out the facts relating to Emerson and Whitman. The first comprehensive review of these facts, however, did not appear until 1929 with Clarence Gohdes, "Whitman and Emerson." Today one must still respect Gohdes' remarkable survey of evidence that was widely scattered at the time—though his assertion that Emerson later changed his opinion of the first *Leaves* must now be qualified. Many of the materials Gohdes describes can be conveniently found in "Emerson and Whitman: Documents on Their Relations (1855–88)," ed. Edmund Wilson. The most comprehensive collection to that date, Wilson's volume nevertheless merely lists Emerson's 1863 letters of introduction to Massachusetts Senator Sumner and Secretary of the Treasury Salmon P. Chase; it also fails to mention Emerson's letter in behalf of Whitman to Secretary of State William H. Seward. The letter to Sumner is not known; but the texts of the letters to Chase and Seward first became available in, respectively, Carlos Baker, "The Road to Concord," and Kenneth Walter Cameron, "Emerson's Recommendation of Whitman in 1863." The letters are also printed in *Correspondence* (vol. 1). Among the documents in Wilson's book are Emerson's famous letter to Whitman, Whitman's open letter to Emerson, and various letters by Emerson to Carlyle and others concerning *Leaves of Grass*. Other equally comprehensive surveys of the personal aspect of the Emerson-Whitman relationship can be found in Baker's introduction to the Chase letter; Joseph Jay Rubin, *The Historic Whitman*; and Floyd Stovall, *The Foreground of* Leaves of Grass. Both Rubin and Stovall present information not easily procured elsewhere.

Other attempts to shed light on the relationship depend on sources already cited. In "Trowbridge and Whitman," Rufus A. Coleman defends Trowbridge against the charge of discipleship; and J. V. Ridgely, "Whitman, Emerson and Friend," recounts some of Moncure D. Conway's efforts in behalf of Whitman. In two notes by William White, "Walt Whitman on New England Writers" and "Whitman on American Poets," further bits and pieces of the documentary puzzle are uncovered—information that suggests that Whitman lost faith in his mentor from time to time. Whitman's quarrel with Emerson is the subject of Jane Johnson, "Whitman's Changing Attitude towards Emerson," but her evidence appears to negate her conclusion. Noting that, in a special Emerson birthday issue of the Boston *Literary World*, Whitman was the only contributor "to criticize the Master," she claims that Whitman tried to hide his animosity after Emerson's death by removing the final two-and-a-half paragraphs of his essay when it was reprinted in *Specimen Days*; but this deleted material was—as Johnson herself observes—wholly favorable to Emerson. More puzzling is Kenneth Walter Cameron's "Rough Draft of Whitman's 'By Emerson's Grave.' " Offering no commentary on the manuscript, he directs the reader instead to Johnson's article, where the reader is exasperated to find nothing but a passing reference to Cameron's subject. The facts are also clouded by Edwin O. Grover ("The First Words of Warm Approval"), who claims that Edward Everett Hale's review of *Leaves of Grass* in the *North American Review* for January 1856 was the first favorable one. Yet Hale's remarks were as mixed as Charles A. Dana's in the *Tribune* of 23 July 1855, and if indeed we can find a favorable early review it has to be Charles Eliot Norton's in *Putnam's* for September 1855. On a grander scale of distortion, Lawrence Willson's attempt to make Whitman the "rough" and Emerson the "gentleman" of American literature is clearly indicated in his title "The 'Body Electric' Meets the Genteel Tradition."

Willson's assessment of Whitman recalls James Russell Lowell's denunciation of the poet as "a rowdy, a New York tough," and "a loafer" (*WWC*, vol. 3). According to Edward Emerson, his father's attitude toward Whitman was similar (*Emerson in Concord*). In fact, as a recently uncovered letter by F. B. Sanborn suggests, Emerson's opinion of Whitman's poetry was far more favorable (Jerome Loving, "Emerson's 'Constant Way of Looking at Whitman's Genius' "; for a garbled version of the letter, see *WWC*, vol. 6). Evidence in Gohdes and Willson, however, indicates that Emerson tired of Whitman's later creations (although he placed one of them in the *Atlantic* in 1869 [*Correspondence*, vol. 2]), and this evidence is updated in Allan B. Lefcowitz and Barbara F. Lefcowitz, "James Bryce's First Visit to America." As William M. Moss discovers in " 'So Many Promising Youths,' " Emerson's initial enthusiasm for Whitman and subsequent disillusionment followed the pattern of his discoveries of several New England poets, including Thoreau. See also Eleanor M. Tilton, "*Leaves of Grass*," and Jerome Loving, *Walt Whitman's Champion*, which contains William Douglas O'Connor's 1882 polemic "Emerson and Whitman." (With the exception of Alvin L. Rosenfeld, "Emerson and Whitman," no dissertation completed at this writing appears to deal with the connection between Whitman and the Transcendentalists in an original way.)

While the interest in Whitman and the Transcendentalists has focused for the most part on Emerson, Andrew Schiller speculates that Thoreau reacted ambivalently to Whitman after his 1856 visit because he found in the author of *Leaves* exactly what he (and Emerson) had sought in the Central Man; the discovery appears to have "set ajangle the inner conflict between Thoreau's self-conscious earthiness and his invincible gentility" ("Thoreau and Whitman"). Nevertheless, Emerson in his funeral oration is purported to have included Whitman among three persons who had "strongly impressed" Thoreau (see F. B. Sanborn, "Emerson and His Friends in Concord" and "The Emerson-Thoreau Correspondence"; and Joel Myerson, "Emerson's 'Thoreau.'"). Far less useful because of its flat abstractions is Charles R. Metzger, *Thoreau and Whitman*. Other essays dealing with Whitman and Transcendentalists other than Emerson are Lawrence Buell, "Whitman and Thoreau"; Larry J. Reynolds and Tibbie E. Lynch, "Sense and Transcendentalism in Emerson, Thoreau, and Whitman"; and Edwin Fussell, "*Leaves of Grass* and Brownson."

Perhaps in reaction to the generation of poets in this century who echoed Ezra Pound's declaration that Whitman had broken "the new wood" of American poetry, most critics have argued that the "new wood" was split by Emerson. "Not Whitman, but Emerson delivered the American literary declaration of independence," Emerson Grant Sutcliffe maintains in "Whitman, Emerson and the New Poetry." Whitman receives even less credit from Norman Foerster ("Whitman and the Cult of Confusion"), who compares "Emerson's love of distinctions, of gradations and contrasts of the Platonic sort, and Whitman's 'indiscriminate hurrahing for the Universe.'" In Foerster's opinion Whitman brought little more than "a fine body" to American literature—not a tradition of "humane culture" like Emerson. John B. Moore is as adamant in his belief that Whitman was more indebted to Emerson than to any other figure even in his earliest *Leaves* ("The Master of Whitman"). Less concerned with Emerson's influence is Leon Howard, who distinguishes between Emerson's and Whitman's Transcendentalism ("For a Critique of Whitman's Transcendentalism"). Howard was one of the earliest critics to see Whitman's art as something more than an echo of Emerson's, and indeed his essay is the only respite from a heavy anti-Whitman bias in criticism until the appearance of F. O. Matthiessen's *American Renaissance*. For example, Killis Campbell, "The Evolution of Whitman as Artist," sees Whitman as ultimately responding to Emerson's literary advice (after 1860) and finding as he ages "a better rhythm"—"a gain in picturesqueness and in comeliness of phrase." Clearly, Campbell has difficulty with the candor of Whitman's earlier images and is therefore more comfortable with the poetry that "gave up a number of words and allusions that violated good taste." Esther Shephard, *Walt Whitman's Pose*, is more annoyed by Whitman's lack of originality and uses evidence of his indebtedness to Emerson to dismiss Whitman as a fraud. Edward G. Bernard finds more evidence of Whitman's interest in Emerson in "Some New Whitman Manuscript Notes."

Matthiessen's *American Renaissance* lifts the Emerson-Whitman discussion out of bathos with a strikingly new thesis: "The whole question of the relation of Whitman's theory and practice of art to Emerson's is fascinating, since, starting so often from similar if not identical positions, they end up with very different results." Focusing on Whitman's use of language (or slang as "indirection"), Matthiessen suggests that Whitman expanded Emerson's proposition that natural facts are signs of spiritual facts "by launching from the word 'prophesy' into an enunciation of the transcendental view of the poet." In other words, through language itself, the poet's prophecy transcends mere prediction and becomes vision, for "the greater work [of the poet] is to reveal God." Matthiessen cites Trowbridge's claim that Emerson brought Whitman "to a boil" but does not see Whitman as Emerson's disciple: "The two share the same view of the poet as inspired seer."

Critics as profound as Matthiessen have taken Trowbridge's testimony at face value, probably because the quotation is so Whitmanesque in its phrasing. But Roger Asselineau, *The Evolution of Walt Whitman* (vol.1), doubts that "the lightning-stroke mentioned by Trowbridge" is consistent with the evidence that Whitman had read Emerson as early as 1847, and James E. Miller, Jr., *The American Quest for a Supreme Fiction*, suggests that if Whitman in fact made such statements, he meant that Emerson had brought him to *himself*—"an image that perhaps most fairly delineates the complex relationship without diminishing the genuine originality . . . of either writer."

Writing on the occasion of the centenary of *Leaves*, Richard P. Adams separates himself from the Emerson partisans by arguing that "Whitman is a more cautious thinker, and a more consistent writer" than Emerson ("Whitman"). Seeing both as organicists, he places Emerson with those who believe that the universe is perfect as it is and thus static. Whitman, on the other hand, celebrates variety and change. The dogma that Emerson was the master of Whitman is also challenged by the comprehensive biographies of Gay Wilson Allen, *The Solitary Singer*, and by Roger Asselineau. Most critics now view Whitman not so much as a disciple of Emerson but—in the words of Roy Harvey Pearce—as "the supremely realized Emersonian poet" (*The Continuity of American Poetry*). Lawrence Buell, for example, sees Whitman's use of catalogs as the culmination of the Transcendentalist faith in the endless expansion of the self ("Transcendentalist Catalogue Rhetoric"). This idea is incorporated in Buell's *Literary Transcendentalism*, where Whitman's poetry is regarded as "both the culmination and the epitaph of literary Transcendentalism."

The long shadow of Emerson returns, however, with Hyatt H. Waggoner, *American Poets from the Puritans to the Present*, where Whitman is censured for often restating Emersonian ideas in "flat, literal simplified journalistic terms." Waggoner sees "Self-Reliance" as a direct source for "Song of Myself" and does not believe there could have been a Whitman without an Emerson. Thomas Edward Crawley is also concerned with the question of influence in *The Structure of Leaves of Grass*; he credits both Emerson and Carlyle with giving Whitman his concept of the prophet-poet. Gene Bluestein, in two chapters on "The Emerson-Whitman Tradition" (in *The Voice of the Folk*), suggests that Whitman's nationalism was influenced by Emerson and J. G. Herder. In two books on poetic theory, Harold Bloom views Whitman as ultimately unable to overcome the "anxiety" of Emerson's influence. In *A Map of Misreading*, Whitman is Emerson's disciple because he failed to repress the Concordian's influence in writing *Leaves of Grass*, a hypothesis amplified in "Emerson and Whitman."

A number of parallel studies appeared between 1975 and 1980, beginning with Donald Ross, "Emerson's Stylistic Influence on Whitman." Transforming part of "The

Poet'' into free verse, Ross asserts that Whitman did not read the *Essays* for content alone but found Emerson's style useful as well. Suzanne Poirier, " 'A Song of the Rolling Earth' as Transcendental and Poetic Theory,'' applies the distinctions of Howard and Matthiessen to a comparison of Whitman's poem with the chapter on language in *Nature*. For Emerson, she concludes, the Real as opposed to the Apparent lies beyond the natural fact, whereas for Whitman it "resides within the earth.'' Michael Dressman, however, finds Whitman closer to Emerson on the subject of language—embarrassingly close. In "Another Whitman Debt to Emerson,'' he shows that a passage from Whitman's "Slang in America'' (1885) appears to have been taken almost verbatim from *Nature*. Not so lucid is G. Thomas Couser, "An Emerson-Whitman Parallel: 'The American Scholar' and 'A Song for Occupations,' '' which argues that the "crucial dichotomy in Emerson's essay is between men as they are and men as they should be,'' whereas in Whitman's poems it is between "men and their tools or creations.'' On slightly firmer ground is Jerome Loving's " 'A Well-Intended Halfness,' '' which maintains that Emerson sometimes found Whitman's poetic vision contrived rather than spontaneous—a part removed from the Whole and thus the object of humor. In "How Emerson, Thoreau, and Whitman Viewed the 'Frontier,' '' Gay Wilson Allen cites "Song of the Redwood-Tree'' as evidence that, of the three, Whitman was the least sensitive to ecological matters because of his faith in America as a symbol of endless expansion.

In " 'Half Song-Thrush, Half Alligator,' '' Justin Kaplan provides an overview of the Emerson-Whitman relationship. Some of the material was adapted from his *Walt Whitman: A Life*, where his observations on the friendship are also accurate but not new except in one particular—the speculation that Emerson did not object to the "Calamus'' poems because an undergraduate experience helped him to appreciate Whitman's homosexual theme. The salient facts and theories concerning the Emerson-Whitman question are also presented in Loving's "Emerson, Whitman, and the Paradox of Self-Reliance.'' Loving's argument is shaped from his larger study *Emerson, Whitman, and the American Muse*, which concludes that the two men shared a common apprenticeship, one in which each writer independently discovered "character'' and its relentless struggle to shape the individual from within. In doing so, it attempts to modify not only the notion that Emerson was the "master'' of Whitman but also our view of "The Poet''—which is now seen as desiderating rather than predicting a Whitman. The influence of the essay on Whitman, Loving believes, was much less direct than the critical consensus would have it.

BIBLIOGRAPHY

Full bibliographical information for essays in books may be found under the main entry for the book. For example, the complete reference for *The Genius and Character of Emerson* is given under Franklin Benjamin Sanborn, the book's editor, not under the authors of each of the essays that appear in it. Readers should consult the table of acronyms for abbreviated book and periodical titles.

Aaron, Daniel. *Men of Good Hope*. New York: Oxford Univ. Press, 1951.

——. *The Unwritten War*. New York: Oxford Univ. Press, 1973.

Abbot, Mabel, and Gail K. Schneider. "Return from Arcadia: The Journey of Christopher Pearse Cranch." *NewB* 13 (Feb. 1964): 63–70.

Abbott, A.W. Review of Sylvester Judd, *Richard Edney and the Governor's Family*. *NAR* 72 (April 1851): 493–505.

Abbott, Lawrence F. "A Transcendental Humorist." *Outlook* 136 (20 Feb. 1924): 299–300.

Abel, Darrel. "Hawthorne on the Strong Dividing Lines in Nature." *ATQ* no. 14 (Spr. 1972): 23–31.

——. "Hawthorne's Skepticism about Social Reform with Especial Reference to *The Blithedale Romance*." *UKCR* 19 (Spr. 1953): 181–93.

——, ed. *Critical Theory in the American Renaissance*. Hartford, Conn.: Transcendental Books, 1969.

Adams, Grace, and Edward Hutter. *The Mad Forties*. New York: Harpers, 1942.

Adams, Henry. "Frothingham's Transcendentalism." *NAR* 123 (Oct. 1876): 463–65.

Adams, John G. *Memoir of Thomas Whittemore*. Boston: Universalist Publishing House, 1878.

Adams, Mary Stroube. "Two Women Transcendentalists: Margaret Fuller and Elizabeth Palmer Peabody." M.A. thesis Univ. of Houston 1968.

Adams, Raymond. "The Bibliographical History of Thoreau's *A Week on the Concord and Merrimack Rivers*." *PBSA* 43 (1 Qtr. 1949): 39–47.

——. "'Civil Disobedience' Gets Printed." *TSB* no. 28 (Sum. 1949): 1–2.

——. "Hawthorne and a Glimpse of *Walden*." *EIHC* 94 (July 1958): 191–93.

——. "Henry Thoreau's Literary Theory and Criticism." Diss. Univ. of North Carolina 1928.

——. "Thoreau and Immortality." *SP* 26 (Jan. 1929): 58–66.

——. "Thoreau's Mock-Heroics and the American Natural History Writer." *SP* 52 (Jan. 1955): 86–97.

——. "Thoreau's Science." *SM* 60 (May 1945): 379–82.

——. "Thoreau's Sources for 'Resistance to Civil Government.'" *SP* 42 (July 1945): 640–53.

Adams, Richard P. "Emerson and the Organic Metaphor." *PMLA* 69 (March 1954): 117–30.

————. "Whitman: A Brief Revaluation." *TSE* 5 (1955) 111–49.

Adams, Sherman Hill. "The Influence of Emerson." *SNPL* 5 (1897): 23–39.

Adams, Stephen. "Thoreau Catching Cold: *A Yankee in Canada.*" *ESQ* 25 (4 Qtr. 1979): 224–34.

Adkins, Nelson Frederick. "Emerson and the Bardic Tradition." *PMLA* 63 (June 1948): 662–77.

————. *Fitz-Greene Halleck: An Early Knickerbocker Wit and Poet.* New Haven: Yale Univ. Press, 1930.

Adler, William. "Theodore Parker and D.F. Strauss's *Das Leben Jesu.*" *UUC* 30 (Aug. 1975): 19–30.

Ahearn, Kerry. "Thoreau and John Brown: What to Do about Evil." *TJQ* 6.3 (July 1974): 24–28.

Ahlstrom, Sydney E. "Francis Ellingwood Abbot and the Free Religious Association." *PUHS* 17.2 (1973–75): 1–21.

————. "The Interpretation of Channing." *NEQ* 30 (March 1957): 99–105.

————. "Introduction." In Octavius Brooks Frothingham, *Transcendentalism in New England: A History.* New York: Harpers,' 1959, ix–xxiii.

————. *A Religious History of the American People.* New Haven: Yale Univ. Press, 1972.

————. "The Scottish Philosophy and American Theology." *ChH* 24 (Sept. 1955): 257–72.

Alaimo, Joseph Paul. "A Natural History of American Virtue: Melville's Critique of the Transcendental Hero." Diss. Univ. of Minnesota 1974.

Albanese, Catherine L. *Corresponding Motion: Transcendental Religion and the New America.* Philadelphia: Temple Univ. Press, 1977.

————. "The Kinetic Revolution: Transformation in the Language of the Transcendentalists." *NEQ* 48 (Sept. 1975): 319–40. Incorporated into her *Corresponding Motion.*

Albee, John. *Remembrances of Emerson.* New York: Robert Grier Cooke, 1901.

Alberti, Charles Edward. "Brook Farm's Educational Philosophy (1841–1846): A Study into Its Methods, Axiology and Epistemology." Diss. Loyola Univ. of Chicago 1975.

Albrecht, Robert C. "Conflict and Resolution: 'Slavery in Massachusetts.' " *ESQ* 19 (3 Qtr. 1973): 179–88.

————. "The New England Transcendentalists' Response to the Civil War." Diss. Univ. of Minnesota 1962.

————. *Theodore Parker.* New York: Twayne, 1971.

————. "The Theological Response of the Transcendentalists to the Civil War." *NEQ* 38 (March 1965): 21–34.

————. "Thoreau and His Audience: 'A Plea for Captain John Brown.' " *AL* 32 (Jan. 1961): 393–402.

Alcott, Amos Bronson. *Concord Days.* Boston: Roberts, 1872.

————. *Conversations with Children on the Gospels.* 2 vols. Boston: James Munroe, 1836–37.

————. *The Doctrine and Discipline of Human Culture.* Boston: James Munroe, 1836.

————. *Essays on Education (1830–1862).* Ed. Walter Harding. Gainesville, Fla.: Scholars' Facsimiles & Reprints, 1960.

————. "Fuller, Thoreau, Emerson. Estimate by Bronson Alcott. The Substance of a 'Conversation.' " *BoCom,* 6 May 1871, 1–2.

————. "Has Mr. Emerson Changed His Views?" *Index* 12 (12 May 1881): 547.

————. *The Journals of Bronson Alcott.* Ed. Odell Shepard. Boston: Little, Brown, 1938.

————. *The Letters of A. Bronson Alcott.* Ed. Richard L. Herrnstadt. Ames: Iowa State Univ. Press, 1969.

————. *New Connecticut.* Boston: privately printed, 1881. 2nd ed., ed. F.B. Sanborn. Boston: Roberts, 1887.

————. *Orphic Sayings*. Ed. William Peirce Randel. Mt. Vernon, N.Y.: Golden Eagle Press, 1939.

————. *Ralph Waldo Emerson: An Estimate of His Genius and Character in Prose and Verse*. Boston: A. Williams, 1882.

————. *Ralph Waldo Emerson: Philosopher and Seer*. Boston: Cupples and Hurd, 1888.

————. "Reminiscences of the Transcendental Club." *BBB* 1 (Dec. 1877, March 1878): 3–5, 30.

————. *Tablets*. Boston: Roberts, 1868.

————. "The Transcendental Club and the *Dial*." *BoCom*, 24 April 1863, 1. Rpt. in Clarence Gohdes, "Alcott's 'Conversation' on the Transcendental Club and the *Dial*." *AL* 3 (March 1931): 14–27.

————, and Charles Lane. "Fruitlands." *Dial* 4 (July 1843): 135–36.

Alcott, Louisa May. "Reminiscences of Ralph Waldo Emerson." *YC* 55 (25 May 1882): 213–14. Rpt. in *Some Noted Princes, Authors, and Statesmen*. Ed. James Parton. New York: Crowell, 1885, 284–88.

————. "Transcendental Wild Oats." *Ind* 25 (18 Dec. 1873): 1569–71. Rpt. in her *Silver Pitchers*. Boston: William Gill, 1876, 79–101.

————. *Transcendental Wild Oats and Excerpts from the Fruitlands Diary*. Harvard, Mass.: Harvard Common Press, 1975; exp. ed., 1981.

Alexander, Colin Cuthbert. "Emerson and the Concord Lyceum." *StJ* 5 (Oct.–Dec. 1919): 206–16.

Alexander, Harriet C. B. "Emerson and Evolution." *PoSM* 54 (Feb. 1899): 555–56.

Alexander, J.W., A. Dod, and Charles Hodge. "Transcendentalism." *BRPR* 11 (Jan. 1839): 37–101.

Alger, William R. "Emerson, Spencer, and Martineau." *ChEx* 84 (May 1868): 257–87.

Allen, E. W., ed. *Memorial of Joseph and Lucy Clark Allen*. Boston: George H. Ellis, 1891.

Allen, Francis H. *A Bibliography of Henry David Thoreau*. Boston: Houghton Mifflin, 1908.

————. *Thoreau's Editors: History and Reminiscence*. Monroe, N.C.: Nocalore Press, 1950.

Allen, Gay Wilson. *American Prosody*. New York: American Book, 1935.

————. "Emerson and Hawthorne, Neighbors." *EIHC* 118 (Jan. 1982): 20–30.

————. "Emerson and the Establishment." *UWR* 9 (Fall 1973): 5–27.

————. "Emerson's Audiences: American and British." *Ariel* 7.3 (July 1976): 87–108.

————. "How Emerson, Thoreau, and Whitman Viewed the 'Frontier.'" In *Toward a New Literary History*. Ed. Louis J. Budd et al. Durham: Duke Univ. Press, 1980, 111–28.

————. "James's *Varieties of Religious Experience* as Introduction to American Transcendentalism." *ESQ* no. 39 (2 Qtr. 1965): 81–85.

————. "A New Look at Emerson and Science." In *Literature and Ideas in America*. Ed. Robert P. Falk. Athens: Ohio Univ. Press, 1975, 58–78.

————. *New Walt Whitman Handbook*. New York: New York Univ. Press, 1975.

————. *The Solitary Singer: A Critical Biography of Walt Whitman*. New York: Macmillan, 1955. Rev. ed., New York: New York Univ. Press, 1967.

————. *Waldo Emerson: A Biography*. New York: Viking, 1981.

————, Walter B. Rideout, and James K. Robinson, eds. *American Poetry*. New York: Harper and Row, 1965.

Allen, J. C. "The Two Phases of Emerson's Thought." *BapQR* 6 (Oct.–Dec. 1884): 432–45.

Allen, Joseph Henry. "The Contact of American Unitarianism and German Thought." In *Unitarianism: Its Origins and History*, 97–115.

————. "Frederic Henry Hedge." *UnitR* 34 (Oct. 1890): 281–301. Incorporated into his *Sequel to "Our Liberal Movement."*

————. "A Memory of Dr. Hedge." *UnitR* 34 (Oct. 1890): 266–70. Incorporated into his *Sequel to "Our Liberal Movement."*

————. *Our Liberal Movement in Theology.* Boston: Roberts, 1882.

————. *Sequel to "Our Liberal Movement."* Boston: Roberts, 1897.

————. "Weiss's Transcendentalism." *ChEx* 76 (Jan. 1864): 1–24.

————, and Richard Eddy. *A History of the Unitarians and Universalists in the United States.* New York: Christian Literature, 1894.

Allen, Margaret Vanderhaar. *The Achievement of Margaret Fuller.* University Park: Pennsylvania State Univ. Press, 1979.

Alstetter, Mabel Flick. "The Life and Work of Elizabeth Palmer Peabody." M.A. thesis George Peabody Coll. 1935.

Alterton, Margaret. *The Origin of Poe's Critical Theory.* Iowa City: Univ. of Iowa Press, 1925.

Ames, Charles G. "Cyrus Augustus Bartol." In *Heralds of a Liberal Faith*, ed. Samuel A. Eliot, 3: 17–22.

Ames, Van Meter. *Zen and American Thought.* Honolulu: Univ. of Hawaii Press, 1962.

Amory, Cleveland. *The Proper Bostonians.* New York: Dutton, 1947.

Anagnos, Julia R. *Philosophiæ Quæstor; or, Days in Concord.* Boston: D. Lothrop, 1885.

Anderson, Carl L. *The Swedish Acceptance of American Literature.* Philadelphia: Univ. of Pennsylvania Press, 1957.

Anderson, Charles R. *Emily Dickinson's Poetry: Stairway of Surprise.* New York: Holt, Rinehart, and Winston, 1960.

————. *The Magic Circle of* Walden. New York: Holt, Rinehart, and Winston, 1968.

————. "Thoreau and the *Dial*: The Apprentice Years." In *Essays Mostly on Periodical Publishing in America.* Ed. James Woodress. Durham: Duke Univ. Press, 1973, 92–120.

Anderson, David D. "A Comparison of the Poetic Theories of Emerson and Poe." *Person* 41 (Aut. 1960): 471–83.

Anderson, John Q. "Emerson and the Language of the Folk." In *Folk Travelers.* Ed. Mody C. Boatright et al. Dallas: Southern Methodist Univ. Press, 1953, 152–59.

————. "Emerson and the 'Moral Sentiment.'" *ESQ* no. 19 (2 Qtr. 1960): 13–15.

————. "Emerson on Texas and the Mexican War." *WHR* 13 (Sept. 1959): 191–99.

————. "Emerson's 'Eternal Pan': The Re-Creation of a Myth." *ATQ* no. 25 (Wtr. 1975): 2–6.

————. *The Liberating Gods: Emerson on Poets and Poetry.* Coral Gables, Fla.: Univ. of Miami Press, 1971.

Anderson, Judith Müller. "Hawthorne's Use of Experience in *The Blithdale Romance*." M.A. thesis Texas A&M Univ. 1967.

Anderson, Paul Russell. *Platonism in the Midwest.* New York: Temple Univ. Publications, 1963.

————, and Max Harold Fisch. *Philosophy in America.* New York: D. Appleton-Century, 1939.

Anderson, Quentin. *The Imperial Self: An Essay in American Literary and Cultural History.* New York: Knopf, 1971.

Andô, Shôei. *Zen and American Transcendenatlism.* Tokyo: Hokuseido, 1970.

Andrews, William P. "An Inspired Life." *CM* 2 (Oct. 1892): 859–62.

————. "Jones Very." *HaR* 3 (March 1881): 131–36.

————. "Memoir." In *Poems by Jones Very.* Ed. Andrews. Boston: Houghton, Mifflin, 1883, 3–31.

Angoff, Charles. "Theodore Parker." *AmM* 10 (Jan. 1927): 81–88.

Anhorn, Judy Schaaf. "Thoreau in the Beanfield: The Curious Language of *Walden*." *ESQ* 24 (4 Qtr. 1978): 179–96.

Anthony, Katharine. *Margaret Fuller: A Psychological Biography.* New York: Harcourt, Brace, and Howe, 1920.

Anzilotti, Rolando. "Emerson in Italia." *RLMC* 11 (March 1958): 3–14.

Applebee, John H. "The First Parish of West Roxbury: An Historic Sketch." In *West Roxbury Magazine*. Hudson, Mass.: E. F. Worcester, 1900, 5–29.

Apthorp, William. *Musicians and Music-Lovers*. New York: Scribners, 1894.

Arieli, Yehoshua. *Individualism and Nationalism in American Ideology*. Cambridge: Harvard Univ. Press, 1964.

Arms, George. "Emerson's 'Ode Inscribed to W. H. Channing.' " *CE* 22 (March 1961): 407–09.

Armstrong, James. "Thoreau as Philospher of Love." In *Henry David Thoreau: A Profile*, ed. Walter Harding, 222–43.

Arner, Robert D. "Hawthorne and Jones Very: Two Dimensions of Satire in 'Egotism; or, the Bosom Serpent.' " *NEQ* 42 (June 1969): 267–75.

Arnold, Matthew. "Emerson." *MacM* 50 (May 1884): 1–13. Rpt. in his *Discourses in America*. London: Macmillan, 1885, 138–207.

———. "Theodore Parker." *PMG* 6 (24 Aug. 1867): 11–12. Rpt. in *Complete Prose Works of Matthew Arnold*. Ed. R. H. Super. 11 vols. Ann Arbor: Univ. of Michigan Press, 1960–77, 5: 76–84.

Arvin, Newton. "The House of Pain: Emerson and the Tragic Sense." *HudR* 12 (Spr. 1959): 37–53. Rpt. in his *American Pantheon*. Ed. Daniel Aaron and Sylvan Schendler. New York: Delacorte, 1966, 16–38.

Ash, Lee. *Subject Collections*. Rev. ed. New York: Bowker, 1978.

Aspinwall, Bernard. "Orestes Brownson, critique cohérent." *RHE* 71 (1976): 5–30.

Asselineau, Roger. " 'Dreaming on the Grass,' or the Transcendentalist Constant in American Literature." *ForumH* 14.1 (Spr. 1976): 31–37. Rpt. in his *The Transcendentalist Constant in American Literature*. New York: New York Univ. Press, 1980, 1–16.

———. *The Evolution of Walt Whitman: The Creation of a Book*. Cambridge: Harvard Univ. Press, 1962.

———. *The Evolution of Walt Whitman: The Creation of a Personality*. Cambridge: Harvard Univ. Press, 1960.

Atkinson, Brooks. *Henry Thoreau: The Cosmic Yankee*. New York: Knopf, 1927.

Aton, James M. " 'Sons and Daughters of Thoreau': The Spiritual Quest in Three Contemporary Writers." Diss. Ohio Univ. 1981.

Atteberry, Brian. "Dickinson, Emerson and the Abstract Concrete." *DicS* no. 35 (1 Half 1979): 17–22.

Auden, W. H. "Introduction." In *Edgar Allan Poe: Selected Prose, Poetry, and Eureka*. Ed. Auden. New York: Rinehart, 1950, v–xvii. Rpt. in *The Recognition of Edgar Allan Poe*. Ed. Eric W. Carlson. Ann Arbor: Univ. of Michigan Press, 1966, 220–30.

Austin, Allen. "The Three-Stranded Allegory of *Moby-Dick*." *CE* 26 (Feb. 1965): 344–49.

B., J. H. "Ralph Waldo Emerson—History." *SLM* 18 (April 1852): 247–55.

B., L. W. "Ralph Waldo Emerson." *YLM* 5 (March 1850): 203–06.

Bacon, Edwin M. *Literary Pilgrimages in New England*. New York: Silver, Burdett, 1902.

Badger, Henry C. "Emerson's Agnosticism." *UnitR* 33 (April 1890): 331–45.

Baer, Helene G. *The Heart Is like Heaven: The Biography of Lydia Maria Child*. Philadelphia: Univ. of Pennsylvania Press, 1964.

———. "Mrs. Child and Miss Fuller." *NEQ* 26 (June 1953): 249–55.

Bagchee, Shyamal. "Echoes from *Walden* in Eliot's 'Portrait of a Lady.' " *RS* 47 (June 1979): 115–18.

Bailey, Elmer James. *Religious Thought in the Greater American Poets*. Boston: Pilgrim Press, 1922.

Baim, Joseph. "The Vision of the Child and the Romantic Dilemma: A Note on the Child-Motif in Emerson." *Thoth* 7 (Wtr. 1966): 22–30.

Baker, Carlos A. "Emerson and Jones Very." *NEQ* 7 (March 1934): 90–99.

———. "Jones Very." In *DAB*, 19: 256–57.

———. "The Road to Concord: Another Milestone in the Emerson-Whitman Friendship." *PULC* 7 (April 1946): 100–17.

Baker, Gail. "The Organic Unity of Henry David Thoreau's *A Week on the Concord and Merrimack Rivers*." Diss. Univ. of New Mexico 1970.

Baker, Portia. "Walt Whitman and the *Atlantic Monthly*." *AL* 6 (Nov. 1934): 283–301.

Baldwin, David. "Puritan Aristocrat in the Age of Emerson: A Study of Samuel Gray Ward." Diss. Univ. of Pennsylvania 1961.

Baldwin, Marilyn. "The Transcendental Phase of William Dean Howells." *ESQ* no. 57 (4 Qtr. 1969): 57–61.

Baldwin, Raymond. "Franklin B. Sanborn." In *Memoirs of Members of the Social Circle in Concord, Sixth Series*. Clinton, Mass.: Colonial Press, 1975, 1–19.

Barbour, Brian M. "Emerson's Poetic Prose." *MLQ* 35 (June 1974): 157–72.

———, ed. *American Transcendentalism: An Anthology of Criticism*. Notre Dame: Univ. of Notre Dame Press, 1973.

Barcus, Nancy. "Emerson, Calvinism, and Aunt Mary Moody Emerson: An Irrepressible Defender of New England Orthodoxy." *CSR* 7 (1977): 146–52.

Barish, Evelyn. "Emerson and 'The Magician': An Early Prose Fantasy." *ATQ* no. 31, suppl. (Sum. 1976): 13–18.

———. "The Moonless Night: Emerson's Crisis of Health, 1825–1827." In *Emerson Centenary Essays*, ed. Joel Myerson, 1–16.

Baritz, Loren. *City on a Hill: A History of Ideas and Myths in America*. New York: John Wiley, 1964.

Barker, Charles A. *American Convictions: Cycles of Public Thought*. Philadelphia: Lippincott, 1973.

Barmby, Goodwyn. "Emerson and His Writings." *HoJ* 2 (13 Nov. 1847): 315–16.

Barnes, Daniel R. "An Edition of the Early Letters of Orestes Brownson." Diss. Univ. of Kentucky 1970.

———. "Orestes Brownson and Hawthorne's Holgrave." *AL* 45 (May 1973): 271–78.

Barnes, Homer F. *Charles Fenno Hoffman*. New York: Columbia Univ. Press, 1930.

Barnes, James J. *Authors, Publishers, and Politicians: The Quest for an Anglo-American Copyright Agreement, 1815–1854*. Columbus: Ohio State Univ. Press, 1974.

Barrows, Samuel J. "Editorial." *ChReg* 61 (25 May 1882): 81.

Barrus, Clara. *John Burroughs: Boy and Man*. Garden City, N.Y.: Doubleday, Page, 1920.

———. *The Life and Letters of John Burroughs*. 2 vols. Boston: Houghton Mifflin, 1925.

Bartlett, George B. "Ralph Waldo Emerson." In *Poets' Homes*. Ed. Arthur Gilman et al. Boston: D. Lothrop, 1879, 140–71.

Bartlett, Irving. *The American Mind in the Mid-Nineteenth Century*. New York: Crowell, 1967.

Barlett, William Irving. "Early Years of Jones Very—Emerson's 'Brave Saint.'" *EIHC* 73 (Jan. 1937): 1–23.

———. *Jones Very: Emerson's "Brave Saint."* Durham: Duke Univ. Press, 1942.

———. "Jones Very—The Harvard Years." *EIHC* 74 (July 1938): 213–38.

Bartol, Cyrus Augustus. *Discourse on the Christian Spirit and Life*. Boston: Crosby, Nichols, 1850. Rpt. New York: Arno, 1972.

———. "Dr. Bartol on Dr. Hedge." *ChReg* 69 (Sept. 1890): 567.

———. "Emerson's Religion." In *The Genius and Character of Emerson*, ed. F. B. Sanborn, 109–45. Rpt. in *Concord Harvest*, ed. Kenneth Walter Cameron, 121–30.

——. "The Genius of Weiss." In his *Principles and Portraits*, 386–412.

——. "Goethe and Schiller." In *The Life and Genius of Goethe*. Ed. F. B. Sanborn. Boston: Ticknor, 1886, 107–34. Rpt. in *Concord Harvest*, ed. Kenneth Walter Cameron, 461–68.

——. "John Weiss." *BDA*, 10 March 1879, 3.

——. "John Weiss." *UnitR* 11 (April 1879): 410–19.

——. "The Nature of Knowledge: Emerson's Way." *UnitR* 18 (Oct. 1882): 289–312.

——. *On Spirit and Personality*. Ed. William G. Heath. St. Paul, Minn.: John Colet Press, 1977.

——. "Poetry and Imagination." *ChEx* 43 (March 1847): 250–70.

——. *Principles and Portraits*. Boston: Roberts, 1880.

——. *Radical Problems*. Boston: Roberts, 1872.

——. *The Rising Faith*. Boston: Roberts, 1874.

——. "Sermons by Frederic Henry Hedge." *UnitR* 36 (Nov. 1891): 325–37.

——. "Transcendentalism." In his *Radical Problems*, 61–97.

——. "William Ellery Channing." In his *Principles and Portraits*, 342–65.

Barton, William B., Jr. *A Calendar of the Complete Edition of the Sermons of Ralph Waldo Emerson*. Memphis: Bee Books, 1977.

——. "Emerson's Method as a Philosopher." *ATQ* no. 9 (Wtr. 1971): 20–28.

Basile, Joseph Lawrence. "The Crisis of Consciousness in Montaigne and Emerson." *CS* 11.1 (March 1976): 10–18.

——. "Man and Machine in Thoreau." Diss. Louisiana State Univ. 1972.

——. "Narcissus in the World of Machines." *SoR* 12 (Jan. 1976): 122–32.

——. "Technology and the Artist in *A Week*." *ATQ* no. 11 (Sum. 1971): 87–91.

Bassan, Maurice. *Hawthorne's Son: The Life and Literary Career of Julian Hawthorne*. Columbus: Ohio State Univ. Press, 1970.

Bassett, John Spencer. "An Exile from the South." *SAQ* 4 (Jan. 1905): 82–90.

Batchelor, George. "A Poet of Transcendentalism." *Dial* [Chicago] 4 (July 1883): 58–59.

——. "Unitarianism: The Transcendental Period." *ChReg* 73 (1 Feb. 1894): 72–73.

Baumgarten, Eduard. *Der Pragmatismus: R. W. Emerson, W. James, J. Dewey*. Frankfurt: Vittorio Klostermann, 1938.

Baumgartner, A. M. " 'The Lyceum is My Pulpit': Homiletics in Emerson's Early Lectures." *AL* 34 (Jan. 1963): 477–86.

Baxter, Sylvester. "Walt Whitman in Boston." *NEMag* n.s. 6 (Aug. 1892): 714–21.

Bayless, Joy. *Rufus Wilmot Griswold*. Nashville: Vanderbilt Univ. Press, 1943.

Baylor, Ruth M. *Elizabeth Palmer Peabody: Kindergarten Pioneer*. Philadelphia: Univ. of Pennsylvania Press, 1965.

Baym, Max I. *A History of Literary Aesthetics in America*. New York: Ungar, 1973.

Baym, Nina. "From Metaphysics to Metaphor: The Image of Water in Emerson and Thoreau." *SIR* 5 (Sum. 1966): 231–43.

——. "Melville's Quarrel with Fiction." *PMLA* 94 (Oct. 1979): 909–23.

——. "Thoreau's View of Science." *JHI* 26 (April–June 1965): 221–34.

——. "The Transcendentalism of Wallace Stevens." *ESQ* no. 57 (4 Qtr. 1969): 66–72.

Beach, Joseph Warren. *The Concept of Nature in Nineteenth-Century English Poetry*. New York: Macmillan, 1936.

——. "Emerson and Evolution." *UTQ* 3 (July 1934): 474–97. Rpt. in his *The Concept of Nature in Nineteenth-Century English Poetry*, 346–69, 601–02.

Beach, Walter E. "The Hall and the Man: Conway." *DiA* 43 (Wtr. 1965): 4–6.

Beasley, Clara Bancroft, comp. *Treasures New and Old*. Boston: American Unitarian Assn., 1910.

Beatty, Lillian. "Typee and Blithedale: Rejected Ideal Communities." *Person* 37 (Aut. 1956): 367–78.

Beaver, John. "Thoreau's Stylistic Use of the Negative." *ATQ* no. 32 (Fall 1976): 21.

Bedell, Madelon. *The Alcotts.* New York: Clarkson N. Potter, 1980.

Beers, Henry A. "Emerson's Transcendentalism." *BL* no. 18 (May–June 1903): 111–18. Rpt. in his *Points at Issue and Some Other Points.* New York: Macmillan, 1904, 91–118.

———. "A Pilgrim in Concord." *YR* 3 (July 1914): 673–88. Rpt. in his *Four Americans.* New Haven: Yale Univ. Press, 1919, 59–84.

Beer, Thomas. " 'An Irritating Archangel.' " *Bookman* 66 (Dec. 1927): 357–66.

Beidler, Philip D. "*Billy Budd*: Melville's Valedictory to Emerson." *ESQ* 24 (4 Qtr. 1978): 215–28.

Beirne, Charles J. "The Theology of Theodore Parker and the War with Mexico." *EIHC* 104 (April 1968): 130–37.

Bell, George H. "Nathaniel Hawthorne, Brook Farm, and *The Blithedale Romance*." M.A. thesis Univ. of Oregon 1957.

Bell, Margaret. *Margaret Fuller.* New York: Charles Boni, 1930.

Bell, Millicent. *Hawthorne's View of the Artist.* Albany: State Univ. of New York Press, 1962.

Belleisle, René de Poyen. "A French View of Emerson." In *The Genius and Character of Emerson,* ed. F. B. Sanborn, 92–108.

Bellows, Russell Nevins. *The Channing Centenary in America, Great Britain, and Ireland.* Boston: George H. Ellis, 1881.

Bennett, Fordyce Richard. "Alcott's Earliest Extant Writings on Education." *ATQ* no. 31 (Sum. 1976): 25–26.

———. "Bronson Alcott and Free Religion." *SAR* 1981: 407–21.

———. "Sources for Alcott's Fruitlands." *ATQ* no. 32, pt. 1 (Fall 1976): 19–20.

Benoit, Ray. "Emerson on Plato: The Fire's Center." *AL* 34 (Jan. 1963): 487–98. Rpt. in his *Single Nature's Double Vision.* The Hague: Mouton, 1973, 57–67.

Bensen, Adolph B. "Scandinavian Influences in the Writings of Thoreau." *SS* 16 (May, Aug. 1941): 201–11, 241–56.

Benton, Gayle T. "Moncure Daniel Conway of Stafford County." *NNVHM* 28 (Dec. 1978): 3152–55.

Benton, Joel. *Emerson as a Poet.* New York: M. L. Holbrook, 1883.

———. "The New Poems of Emerson." *CWM* 5 (6 Feb. 1884): 175–77.

Bentzon, Th. [pseud. for Marie Thérèsa Blanc]. *A Typical American: Thomas Wentworth Higginson.* Trans. E. M. Waller. London: Howard Wilford Bell, 1902.

Bercovitch, Sacvan. *The American Jeremiad.* Madison: Univ. of Wisconsin Press, 1978.

———. *The Puritan Origins of the American Self.* New Haven: Yale Univ. Press, 1975.

Berens, Sheldon L. "The Emergence of a Moralist in Politics, George William Curtis: 1824–1869." Undergraduate honors thesis Harvard 1951.

Bernard, Edward G. "Some New Whitman Manuscript Notes." *AL* 8 (March 1936): 59–63.

Bernath, Mary G. "Substance and Process in Thoreau's Universe." Diss. Univ. of Pittsburgh 1974.

Berry, Edmund G. "Bronson Alcott: Educational Reformer." *QQ* 52 (Spr. 1945): 44–52.

———. "Thoreau in Canada." *DR* 23 (April 1943): 68–74.

Berryman, Charles. "The Artist-Prophet: Emerson and Thoreau." *ESQ* no. 43 (2 Qtr. 1966): 81–86.

Berthoff, Warner. "Jones Very: New England Mystic." *BPLQ* 2 (Jan. 1950): 63–75.

———. "Remarks on W. E. Channing and American Unitarianism." *NEQ* 35 (March 1962): 71–92.

Bestor, Arthur E., Jr. *Brook Farm 1841-1847: An Exhibition to Commemorate the Centenary of Its Founding*. New York: Columbia Univ. Libraries, 1941.

———. "Fourierism in Northampton: A Critical Note." *NEQ* 13 (March 1940): 110–22.

Bethell, John T. "The Magnificent Activist." *HaAB* 70 (13 April 1968): 12–18.

Bhata, Karmala. *The Mysticism of Thoreau and Its Affinity with Indian Thought*. New Delhi: New India, 1966.

Bickman, Martin. *The Unsounded Centre: Jungian Studies in American Romanticism*. Chapel Hill: Univ. of North Carolina Press, 1980.

Biddle, Edward N. *Moncure Daniel Conway and Conway Hall; Historical Address*. Carlisle, Pa.: Hamilton Library Assn., 1919.

Bier, Jesse. "The Romantic Coordinates of American Literature." *BuR* 18 (Fall 1980): 16–33.

———. "Weberism, Franklin, and the Transcendental Style." *NEQ* 43 (June 1970): 179–92.

Bilbo, Queenie. "Elizabeth Palmer Peabody, Transcendentalist." Diss. New York Univ. 1932.

Billy, Ted. "A Checklist of Wordplays in Thoreau's *Week*." *CS* 14.3 (Fall 1979): 14–19.

Birdsall, Richard D. "Emerson and the Church of Rome." *AL* 31 (Nov. 1959): 273–81.

Bishop, Jonathan. *Emerson on the Soul*. Cambridge: Harvard Univ. Press, 1964.

———. "The Experience of the Sacred in Thoreau's *Week*." *ELH* 33 (March 1966): 68–91.

Blackburn, Charles E. "James Freeman Clarke: An Interpretation of the Western Years (1833–1840)." Diss. Yale 1952.

———. "Some New Light on the *Western Messenger*." *AL* 26 (Nov. 1954): 320–36.

Blackwelder, James Ray. "Ralph Waldo Emerson's Contributions to the *Dial*." M.A. thesis Wake Forest Coll. 1964.

Blair, John G. "Thoreau on Ktaadn." *AQ* 12 (Wtr. 1960): 508–17.

Blair, Walter. "Nathaniel Hawthorne." In *Eight American Authors*. Ed. Floyd Stovall. New York: Modern Language Association, 1956, 100–52. Rev. ed., ed. James Woodress, New York: Norton, 1971, 85–128.

———, and Clarence Faust. "Emerson's Literary Method." *MP* 42 (Nov. 1944): 79–95.

Blanchard, Paula. *Margaret Fuller: From Transcendentalism to Revolution*. New York: Delacorte, 1978.

Blanding, Thomas. "Walton and *Walden*." *TSB* no. 107 (Spr. 1969): 3.

———, and Walter Harding. "A Thoreau Iconography." *SAR* 1980: 1–35.

Blankenship, Russell. *American Literature as an Expression of the National Mind*. New York: Henry Holt, 1931.

Blansett, Barbara Ruth Nieweg. "Melville and Emersonian Transcendentalism." Diss. Univ. of Texas 1963.

Blasing, Mutlu K. *The Art of Life: Studies in American Autobiographical Literature*. Austin: Univ. of Texas Press, 1977.

Blau, Joseph L. "Kant in America." *JP* 54 (11 Nov. 1954): 874–80.

———. *Men and Movements in American Philosophy*. Englewood Cliffs, N.J.: Prentice-Hall, 1952.

Blinderman, Abraham. *American Writers on Education before 1865*. Boston: Twayne, 1975.

Block, Louis James. "Thoughts on the Transcendental Movement in New England." *NEMag* 15 (Jan. 1897): 564–70.

Bloom, Harold. "American Poetic Stances: Emerson to Stevens." In his *Wallace Stevens*. Ithaca: Cornell Univ. Press, 1977, 1–26.

———. "Bacchus and Merlin: The Dialectic of Romantic Poetry in America." In his *Ringers in the Tower*. Chicago: Univ. of Chicago Press, 1971, 291–321.

———. "Emerson and Influence." In his *A Map of Misreading*. New York: Oxford Univ. Press, 1975, 160–76.

————. "Emerson and Whitman: The American Sublime." In his *Poetry and Repression*. New Haven: Yale Univ. Press, 1976, 235–56.

————. "Emerson: The Glory and Sorrows of American Romanticism." *VQR* 47 (Aut. 1971): 546–63. Rpt. in *Romanticism: Vistas, Instances, Continuities*. Ed. Donald Thorburn and Geoffrey Hartman. Ithaca: Cornell Univ. Press, 1973, 155–73.

————. "Emerson: The Self-Reliance of American Romanticism." In his *Figures of Capable Imagination*. New York: Seabury, 1976, 46–64.

————. "In the Shadow of Emerson." In his *A Map of Misreading*, 177–92.

————. "The Native Strain: American Orphism." In his *Figures of Capable Imagination*, 67–88.

————. "The New Transcendentalism: The Visionary Strain in Merwin, Ashbery, and Ammons." In his *Figures of Capable Imagination*, 123–49.

————. "Wallace Stevens: The Transcendental Strain." In his *Poetry and Repression*, 267–93.

Blouin, Francis X., Jr. *The Boston Region, 1810–1850: A Study of Urbanization*. Ann Arbor, Mich.: UMI Research Press, 1980.

Bluestein, Gene. "Emerson's Epiphanies." *NEQ* 39 (Dec. 1966): 447–60.

————. "The Emerson-Whitman Tradition." In his *The Voice of the Folk: Folklore and American Literary Theory*. Amherst: Univ. of Massachusetts Press, 1972, 16–64, 160–62.

Blumenthal, Henry. *American and French Culture, 1800–1900*. Baton Rouge: Louisiana State Univ. Press, 1975.

Bode, Carl. *The American Lyceum: Town Meeting of the Mind*. New York: Oxford Univ. Press, 1956.

————. "The Half-Hidden Thoreau." *MR* 4 (Aut. 1962): 68–80. Rpt. in *Thoreau in Our Season*, ed. John Hicks, 104–16.

————, ed. *American Life in the 1840s*. Garden City, N.Y.: Doubleday, 1967.

————, ed. *Ralph Waldo Emerson: A Profile*. New York: Hill and Wang, 1969.

Böhmer, Lina. *Brookfarm und Hawthornes Blithedale Romance*. Jena: Universitäts-Buchdruckerei Gustav Neuenhahn, 1936.

Boies, J. J. "Circular Imagery in Thoreau's *Week*." *CE* 26 (Feb. 1965): 350–55.

Boller, Paul F., Jr. *American Transcendentalism, 1830–1860: An Intellectual Inquiry*. New York: Putnam's, 1974.

Bolster, Arthur S., Jr. *James Freeman Clarke: Disciple to Advancing Truth*. Boston: Beacon, 1954.

————. "The Life of James Freeman Clarke." Diss. Harvard 1953.

Bonner, Willard H. "Captain Thoreau: Gubernator to a Piece of Wood." *NEQ* 39 (March 1966): 24–46.

————. "The Harvest of Thought in Thoreau's 'Autumnal Tints.'" *ESQ* 22 (2 Qtr. 1976): 78–84.

————. "Mariners and Terreners: Some Aspects of Nautical Imagery in Thoreau." *AL* 34 (Jan. 1963): 507–19.

————, and Mary Alice Budge. "Thoreau and Robinson Crusoe: An Overview." *TJQ* 5.2 (April 1973): 16–18.

Boone, Joseph Allen. "Delving and Diving for Truth: Breaking Through to Bottom in Thoreau's *Week*." *ESQ* 27 (3 Qtr. 1981): 135–46.

Boorstin, Daniel. *The Americans: The National Experience*. New York: Random House, 1965.

Booth, Douglas Allen. "Words, Sounds, and the Over-Soul: A Study of the Aesthetic Philosophies of Ralph Waldo Emerson, Henry David Thoreau, John Sullivan Dwight, and Charles Edward Ives." Honors thesis Harvard 1975.

Booth, Earl Walter. "Beethoven and the American Transcendentalists." M.A. thesis Univ. of Utah 1970.

Booth, R. A., and Roland Stromberg. "Bibliography of Ralph Waldo Emerson, 1908–1920." *BB* 19 (Dec. 1948): 180–83.

Borck, Jim Springer, and Herbert B. Rothschild, Jr., "Meditative Discoveries in Thoreau's 'The Pond in Winter.' " *TSLL* 20 (Spr. 1978): 93–106.

Borges, Jorge Luis. *An Introduction to American Literature*. Trans. L. Clark Keating and Robert O. Evans. Lexington: Univ. Press of Kentucky, 1971.

Borst, Raymond R. *Henry David Thoreau: A Descriptive Bibliography*. Pittsburgh: Univ. of Pittsburgh Press, 1982.

Boswell, Jeanetta. *Nathaniel Hawthorne and the Critics*. Metuchen, N.J.: Scarecrow, 1982.

———. *Ralph Waldo Emerson and the Critics*. Metuchen, N.J.: Scarecrow, 1979.

———, and Sarah Crouch. *Henry David Thoreau and the Critics*. Metuchen, N.J.: Scarecrow, 1981.

Botta, Vincenzo, ed. *Memoirs of Anne C. L. Botta*. New York: J. Selwin Tait, 1894.

Bottorff, William K. " 'Compensation,' Emerson's Ebb and Flow." *AmerST* 9 (March 1979): 1–9.

———. " 'Whatever Inly Rejoices Me': The Paradox of 'Self-Reliance.' " *ESQ* 18 (4 Qtr. 1972): 207–17.

Boudreau, Gordon V. " 'Remember Thy Creator': Thoreau and St. Augustine." *ESQ* 19 (3 Qtr. 1973): 149–60.

Bounds, Harrison. "Brook Farm and Hawthorne's *The Blithedale Romance*." M.A. thesis Columbia 1949.

Bowen, Francis. "Locke and the Transcendentalists." *ChEx* 23 (Nov. 1837): 170–94.

———. "Nine New Poets." *NAR* 64 (April 1847): 402–34.

———. "Transcendentalism." *ChEx* 21 (Jan. 1837): 371–85.

Bowers, David. "Democratic Vistas." In *Literary History of the United States*, ed. Robert E. Spiller et al., 345–56.

Bowling, Lawrence. "Thoreau's Social Criticism as Poetry." *YR* 55 (Wtr. 1966): 255–64.

Boynton, Percy H. "Emerson in His Period." *IJE* 39 (Jan. 1929): 177–89.

Bradford, Alden. *An Address Delivered before the Society of Phi Beta Kappa in Bowdoin College*. Boston: S. G. Simpkins, 1841.

Bradford, Gamaliel. "Jones Very." *UnitR* 27 (Feb. 1887): 111–18. Rev. and rpt. in his *Biography and the Human Heart*. Boston: Houghton Mifflin, 1932, 185–212.

Bradford, George P. "Reminiscences of Brook Farm." *CM* 45 (Nov. 1892): 141–48.

Bradford, Samuel, Jr. *Some Incidents in the Life of Samuel Bradford, Senior*. Philadelphia: n.p., 1880.

Bradley, Lawrence J. *A Guide to the Microfilm Edition of the Orestes A. Brownson Papers*. Notre Dame: Univ. of Notre Dame Archives, 1966.

Bradley, Sculley. "Lowell, Emerson, and the *Pioneer*." *AL* 19 (Nov. 1947): 231–44.

Branch, E. Douglas. *The Sentimental Years 1836–1850*. New York: D. Appleton-Century, 1934.

Branch, Watson G., ed. *Melville: The Critical Heritage*. London: Routledge and Kegan Paul, 1974.

Brann, Henry A. "Free Thought in New England." *ACQR* 19 (Jan. 1885): 95–115.

———. "Hegel and His New England Echo." *CathW* 41 (April 1885): 56–61.

———. "The Rationalism of O. B. Frothingham and Felix Adler." In his *The Age of Unreason*. New York: Brown, 1881, 96–115.

Brashers, Charles. "Franklin, Thoreau, and the Decline of Pleasure." *RecL* 6 (Wtr. 1977): 31–42.

Braswell, William. "Melville as a Critic of Emerson." *AL* 9 (Nov. 1937): 317–34.

Braun, Frederick Augustus. "Goethe as Viewed by Emerson." *JEGP* 15 (Jan. 1916): 23–34.

———. *Margaret Fuller and Goethe*. New York: Henry Holt, 1910.

———. "Margaret Fuller's Translation and Criticism of Goethe's *Tasso.*" *JEGP* 13 (April 1914): 202–13.

Brawner, James P. "Emerson's Debt to Italian Art." *WVUPP* 8 (Oct. 1951): 49–58.

———. "Thoreau as Wit and Humorist." *SAQ* 44 (April 1945):170–94.

Breinig, Helmbrecht. "The Destruction of Fairyland: Melville's 'Piazza' in the Tradition of the American Imagination." *ELH* 35 (June 1968): 254–83.

———. "Symbol, Satire, and the Will to Communicate in Melville's 'The Apple–Tree Table.' " *Amst* 22.2 (1977): 269–85.

Breitwiesser, Mitchell R. "Thoreau and the Wrecks on Cape Cod." *SIR* 20 (Spr. 1981): 3–20.

Bremer, Fredrika. *The Homes of the New World.* Trans. Mary Howitt. New York: Harpers, 1853.

Brennan, Sister Thomas C. "Thomas Wentworth Higginson: Reformer and Man of Letters." Diss. Michigan State Univ. 1958.

Brennan, William. "An Index to Quotations in Thoreau's *A Week on the Concord and Merrimack Rivers.*" *SAR* 1980: 259–90.

Brewer, Edward V. "The New England Interest in Jean Paul Friedrich Richter." *UCPMP* 27 (1943): 1–25.

Brewer, Priscilla J. "Emerson, Lane, and the Shakers: A Case of Converging Ideologies." *NEQ* 55 (June 1982): 254–75.

Brickett, Elsie Furbush. "Studies in the Poets and Poetry of New England Transcendentalism." Diss. Yale 1937.

Bridges, William E. "Transcendentalism and Psychotherapy: Another Look at Emerson." *AL* 41 (May 1969): 157–77.

Bridgman, Raymond L., ed. *Concord Lectures on Philosophy: Comprising Outlines of All the Lectures at the Concord Summer School of Philosophy in 1882.* Cambridge, Mass.: Moses King, 1883.

Bridgman, Richard. *Dark Thoreau.* Lincoln: Univ. of Nebraska Press, 1981.

Brill, Leonard. "Thomas Wentworth Higginson and the *Atlantic Monthly.*" Diss. Univ. of Minnesota 1968.

Brittan, C. H. "John S. Dwight as I Knew Him." *Music* 10 (July 1896): 229–31.

Brittin, Norman A. "Emerson and the Metaphysical Poets." *AL* 8 (March 1936): 1–15.

Brock, Peter. *Pacifism in the United States from the Colonial Era to the First World War.* Princeton: Princeton Univ. Press, 1968.

Brockway, Beman. *Fifty Years in Journalism.* Watertown, N.Y.: Daily Times, 1891.

Brockway, Phillip Judd. *Sylvester Judd (1813-1853): Novelist of Transcendentalism.* Orono: Univ. of Maine Press, 1941.

Broderick, John C. "Bronson Alcott's 'Concord Book.' " *NEQ* 29 (Sept. 1956): 265–80.

———. "The Movement of Thoreau's Prose." *AL* 33 (May 1961): 133–42.

———. "The Problems of the Literary Executor: The Case of Theodore Parker." *QJLC* 23 (Oct. 1966): 260–73.

———. "Thoreau, Alcott and the Poll Tax." *SP* 53 (Oct. 1956): 612–26.

———. "Thoreau and *My Prisons.*" *BPLQ* 7 (Jan. 1955): 48–50.

———. "Thoreau's Proposals for Legislation." *AQ* 7 (Fall 1955): 285–90.

Brodwin, Stanley. "Emerson's Version of Plotinus: The Flight of Beauty." *JHI* 35 (July 1974): 465–83.

Brooks, Charles Timothy. *Aquidneck.* Providence, R.I.: Charles Burnett, 1848.

———. *Poems.* Ed. W. P. Andrews. Boston: Roberts, 1885.

———. *Remarks on Europe, Relating to Education, Peace, and Labor.* New York: C. S. Francis, 1846.

———. *Roman Rhymes.* Cambridge, Mass.: John Wilson, 1869.

———. *The Simplicity of Christ's Teachings.* Boston: Crosby, Nichols, 1859.

———. *Songs of Field and Flood.* Boston: John Wilson, 1853.

———. *William Ellery Channing: A Centennial Memory.* Boston: Roberts, 1880.

———, trans. *German Lyrics.* Boston: Ticknor and Fields, 1853.

———, trans. Johann Wolfgang von Goethe, *Faust*, part 1. Boston: Ticknor and Fields, 1856.

———, trans. John Paul Friedrich Richter, *Hesperus.* 2 vols. Boston: Ticknor and Fields, 1865.

———, trans. John Paul Friedrich Richter, *Titan.* 2 vols. Boston: Ticknor and Fields, 1862.

———, trans. Johann Christof Friedrich von Schiller, *Homage of the Arts.* Boston: James Munroe, 1847.

———, trans. Johann Christof Friedrich von Schiller, *William Tell.* Providence, R.I.: B. Cranston, 1838.

———, trans. *Songs and Ballads: Translated from Uhland, Körner, Bürger and Other German Lyric Poets.* Boston: James Munroe, 1842.

Brooks, Elbridge Streeter. *The Life-Work of Elbridge Gerry Brooks.* Boston: Universalist Publishing House, 1881.

Brooks, Gladys. *Three Wise Virgins.* New York: Dutton, 1957.

Brooks, Van Wyck. *Emerson and Others.* New York: Dutton, 1927.

———. *The Flowering of New England 1815–1865.* New York: Dutton, 1936.

———. *The Life of Emerson.* New York: Dutton, 1932.

———. *New England: Indian Summer, 1865–1915.* New York: Dutton, 1940.

———. Review of *Letters and Journals of Thomas Wentworth Higginson*, ed. Mary Thacher Higginson. Rpt. as "The Twilight of New England" in his *Sketches in Criticism.* New York: Dutton, 1932, 211–17.

Brougham, Henry. Review of William Ellery Channing, *Remarks on the Character and Writings of John Milton. EdR* 69 (April 1839): 214–30.

Broussard, Louis. *The Measure of Poe.* Norman: Univ. of Oklahoma Press, 1969.

Brown, Abram English. *Beneath Old Roof Trees.* Boston: Lee and Shepard, 1896.

Brown, Arthur W. *Always Young for Liberty: A Biography of William Ellery Channing.* Syracuse: Syracuse Univ. Press, 1956.

———. *Margaret Fuller.* New York: Twayne, 1964.

Brown, Charles H. *William Cullen Bryant.* New York: Scribners, 1971.

Brown, Florence Whiting. *Alcott and the Concord School of Philosophy.* N.p.: privately printed, 1926.

Brown, Howard N. "Frederic Henry Hedge." In *Heralds of a Liberal Faith*, ed. Samuel A. Eliot, 3: 158–67.

———. "Frederic Henry Hedge." *UnitR* 34 (Oct. 1890): 281–301.

———. *Frederic Henry Hedge: A Memorial Discourse.* Boston: George H. Ellis, 1891.

Brown, Jerry Wayne. *The Rise of Biblical Criticism in America, 1800–1870: The New England Scholars.* Middletown, Conn.: Wesleyan Univ. Press, 1969.

Brown, Mary Hosmer. *Memories of Concord.* Boston: Four Seas, 1926.

Brown, Percy Whiting. "Emerson's Philosophy of Aesthetics." *JAAC* 15 (March 1957): 350–54.

———. *Middlesex Monographs.* Cleveland: Rowfant Club, 1941.

Brown, Sarah Theo. *Letters of Theo. Brown.* Worcester, Mass.: Putnam, Davis, 1898.

Brown, Stuart Gerry. "Emerson's Platonism." *NEQ* 18 (Sept. 1945): 325–45.

Brown, Theodore M. "Greenough, Paine, Emerson and the Organic Aesthetic." *JAAC* 14 (March 1956): 304–17.

———. "Thoreau's Prophetic Architectural Program." *NEQ* 38 (March 1965): 3–20.

Browne, Ray B. "Source and Satire of 'Cock-A-Doodle-Doo.'" In his *Melville's Drive to Humanism.* Lafayette, Ind.: Purdue Univ. Studies, 1971, 189–200.

Brownell, William Cary. "Emerson." *SMM* 46 (Nov. 1909): 608–24. Rpt. in his *American Prose Masters*. New York: Scribners, 1909, 133–204.

Brownson, Henry F. *Orestes A. Brownson's Early Life: From 1803 to 1844*. Detroit: H. F. Brownson, 1898.

————. *Orestes A. Brownson's Life*. 3 vols. Detroit: H. F. Brownson, 1898–1900.

Brownson, Orestes Augustus. *The American Republic: Its Constitution, Tendencies, and Destiny*. New York: P. O'Shea, 1865.

————. "Brook Farm." *USMDR* 11 (Nov. 1842): 481–96.

————. *The Convert; or, Leaves from My Experience*. New York: D. and J. Sadlier, 1857.

————. "Emerson's *Essays*." *BoQR* 4 (July 1841): 291–308.

————. "Emerson's Prose Works." *CathW* 11 (May 1870): 202–11.

————. "Free Religion." *CathW* 10 (Nov. 1869): 195–206.

————. "Introductory Remarks." *BoQR* 1 (Jan. 1838): 1–8.

————. "The Laboring Classes." *BoQR* 3 (July, Oct. 1840): 358–95, 420–512. Rpt. as *The Laboring Classes* and *Brownson's Defense: Defense of the Article on the Laboring Classes*. Both, Boston: Benjamin H. Greene, 1840.

————. "Leroux on Humanity." *BoQR* 5 (July 1842): 257–322.

————. "Liberalism and Socialism." *BrQR* 17 (April 1855): 183–209.

————. *The Mediatorial Life of Jesus*. Boston: Charles C. Little and James Brown, 1842.

————. "Miss Fuller and Reformers." *BrQR* 2 (April 1845): 249–57.

————. "Mr. Emerson's Address." *BoQR* 1 (Oct. 1838): 500–14.

————. *New Views of Christianity, Society, and the Church*. Boston: James Munroe, 1836.

————. "Protestantism Ends in Transcendentalism." *BrQR* 2 (July 1846): 369–99.

————. Review of the *Dial*. *BoQR* 4 (Jan. 1841): 131–32.

————. Review of Margaret Fuller, *Summer on the Lakes, in 1843*. *BrQR* 1 (Oct. 1844): 546–47.

————. Review of Nathaniel Hawthorne, *The Blithedale Romance*. *BrQR* n.s. 6 (Oct. 1852): 561–64.

————. "R. W. Emerson's Poems." *BrQR* 4 (April 1847): 262–76.

————. *The Spirit-Rapper: An Autobiography*. Boston: Little, Brown, 1854.

————. "Transcendentalism, or Latest Form of Infidelity." *BrQR* 7 (July, Oct. 1845): 273–323, 409–42.

————. "Transient and Permanent in Christianity." *BoQR* 4 (Oct. 1841): 436–74. Rpt. as *A Review of Mr. Parker's Discourse on the Transient and Permanent in Christianity*. Boston: Benjamin H. Greene, 1842.

————. *The Works of Orestes A. Brownson*. Ed. H. F. Brownson. 20 vols. Detroit: Thorndike Nourse; H. F. Brownson, 1882–87.

————, and Issac Hecker. *The Brownson-Hecker Correspondence*. Ed. Joseph F. Gower and Richard M. Leliaert. Notre Dame: Univ. of Notre Dame Press, 1979.

Brumm, Ursula. *American Thought and Religious Typology*. Trans. John Hoaglund. New Brunswick: Rutgers Univ. Press, 1970.

Bryant, William Cullen. *The Letters of William Cullen Bryant*. Ed. William Cullen Bryant II and Thomas G. Voss. 3 vols. to date. New York: Fordham Univ. Press, 1975–   .

Bryer, Jackson R., and Robert A. Rees. "A Checklist of Emerson Criticism 1951–1961." *ESQ* no. 37 (4 Qtr. 1964): 1–50. Rpt. as *A Checklist of Emerson Criticism 1951–1961*. Hartford, Conn.: Transcendental Books, 1964.

Bryers, John R., Jr., and James J. Owen. *A Concordance to the Five Novels of Nathaniel Hawthorne*. 2 vols. New York: Garland, 1979.

Buchanan, Robert. "Free Thought in America." *NAR* 140 (April 1885): 316–28.

———. "Octavius Frothingham." In his *A Look around Literature*. London: Ward and Downey, 1887, 140–47.

Buck, Francis I. "Thomas Wentworth Higginson 1823–1911: A Selected Bibliography." Library school thesis Univ. of Wisconsin 1938.

Buck, Whitney W. "Warren Burton: Classmate of Emerson and Kindly Reformer-at-Large." Diss. Univ. of Michigan 1964.

Buckingham, Joseph T. *Personal Memories and Recollections of Editorial Life*. 2 vols. Boston: Ticknor, Reed, and Fields, 1852.

Buckingham, Willis J. "1880–1968 Addenda to the Buckingham Bibliography." *EDB* no. 26 (2 Half 1974): 103–28.

———. *Emily Dickinson, an Annotated Bibliography: Writings, Scholarship, Criticism, and Ana 1850-1968*. Bloomington: Indiana Univ. Press, 1970.

———. "Second Addendum to the Buckingham Bibliography." *EDB* no. 33 (1 Half 1978): 61–75.

Budick, E. Miller. "Poe's Gothic Idea: The Cosmic Geniture of Horror." *ELWIU* 3 (Spr. 1976): 73–85.

———. " 'Visible Images' and the 'Still Voice': Transcendental Vision in Bryant's 'Thanatopsis.' " *ESQ* 22 (2 Qtr. 1976): 71–77.

Buell, Lawrence. "Channing's Contribution to American Literature." *Kairos* 16 (Aut. 1979): 6.

———. "First Person Superlative: The Speaker in Emerson's Essays." *ATQ* no. 9 (Wtr. 1971): 28–35. Incorporated into his *Literary Transcendentalism*.

———. "Identification of Contributors to the *Monthly Anthology and Boston Review*, 1804–1811." *ESQ* 23 (2 Qtr. 1977): 99–105.

———. "Joseph Stevens Buckminster: The Making of a New England Saint." *CRevAS* 10 (Spr. 1979): 1–29.

———. *Literary Transcendentalism: Style and Vision in the American Renaissance*. Ithaca: Cornell Univ. Press, 1973.

———. "Ralph Waldo Emerson." In *The American Renaissance in New England*, ed. Joel Myerson, 48–60.

———. "Reading Emerson for the Structures: The Coherence of the Essays." *QJS* 58 (Feb. 1972): 58–69.

———. "Transcendentalist Catalogue Rhetoric: Vision versus Form." *AL* 40 (Nov. 1968): 325–39. Incorporated into his *Literary Transcendentalism*.

———. "Unitarian Aesthetics and Emerson's Poet-Priest." *AQ* 20 (Spr. 1968): 3–20. Incorporated into his *Literary Transcendentalism*.

———. "The Unitarian Movement and the Art of Preaching in Nineteenth Century America." *AQ* 24 (May 1972): 166–90.

———. "Whitman and Thoreau." *Calamus* 8 (Fall 1973): 18–28.

Buitenhuis, Peter. "The Stoic Strain in American Literature." In *The Stoic Strain in American Literature*. Ed. Duane J. MacMillan. Toronto: Univ. of Toronto Press, 1979, 3–16.

Bunge, Nancy L. "Beyond Transcendentalism: Hawthorne on Perspective and Reality." *NDQ* 45 (Wtr. 1977): 43–49.

Buranelli, Vincent. "The Case against Thoreau." *Ethics* 67 (July 1957): 257–68.

———. *Edgar Allan Poe*. New York: Twayne, 1971. Rev. ed., Boston: Twayne, 1977.

Burke, Kenneth. "I, Eye, Aye—Emerson's Early Essay 'Nature': Thoughts on the Machinery of Transcendence." In *Transcendentalism and Its Legacy*, ed. Myron Simon and Thornton H. Parsons, 3–24.

Burkholder, Robert E. "The Contemporary Reception of *English Traits*." In *Emerson Centenary Essays*, ed. Joel Myerson, 156–72.

———. "Ralph Waldo Emerson." In *FPAA*, 2: 143–60.

———. "Ralph Waldo Emerson's Reputation, 1831–1861. With a Secondary Bibliography." Diss. Univ. of South Carolina 1979.

———, and Joel Myerson. *Ralph Waldo Emerson: An Annotated Secondary Bibliography*. Pittsburgh: Univ. of Pittsburgh Press, forthcoming.

———, and Joel Myerson, eds. *Critical Essays on Ralph Waldo Emerson*. Boston: G. K. Hall, 1983.

Burnap, George W. "Transcendentalism." *MRM* 3 (Feb. 1846): 66–71.

Burnham, Philip E., and Carvel Collins. "Contributions toward a Bibliography of Thoreau, 1938–1945." *BB* 19 (Sept.–Dec. 1946, Jan.–April 1947): 16–19, 37–39.

Burns, John R. "Thoreau's Use of the Bible." Diss. Univ. of Notre Dame 1966.

Burns, Percy P. "Jones Very." *HCB* 80 (June 1922): 42–66.

Burrage, A. A. "Theodore Parker's Society." *ChReg* 68 (14 Feb. 1889): 5–6.

Burroughs, John. *The Last Harvest*. Boston: Houghton Mifflin, 1922.

———. *Notes on Walt Whitman as Poet and Person*. New York: American News, 1867.

———. "A Word or Two on Emerson." *Galaxy* 21 (Feb. 1876): 254.

Burtis, Mary Elizabeth. *Moncure Conway 1832–1907*. New Brunswick: Rutgers Univ. Press, 1952.

Burton, Katherine. *In No Strange Land: Some American Catholic Converts*. Philadelphia: Longmans, Green, 1942.

———. *Paradise Planters: The Story of Brook Farm*. London: Longmans, Green, 1939.

———. "Sophia Dana Ripley." *Missionary* 53 (Feb. 1939): 40–42.

Burton, Roland Crozier. "Margaret Fuller's Criticism of the Fine Arts." *CE* 6 (Oct. 1944): 18–23.

Busch, Frederick. "Thoreau and Melville as Cellmates." *MFS* 23 (Sum. 1977): 239–42.

Bush, George. *Prof. Bush's Reply to Ralph Waldo Emerson on Swedenborg*. New York: John Allen, 1846.

Butcher, Philip. "Emerson and the South." *Phylon* 17 (3 Qtr. 1956): 279–85.

Butler, Gerald J. "Comment on Brashers' Reappraisal of Franklin and Thoreau." *RecL* 6 (Wtr. 1977): 43–45.

Butterfield, L. H. "Come with Me to the Feast; or, Transcendentalism in Action." *MHSM* no. 6 (Dec. 1960): 1–5.

C. "Theosophy and Secular Literature." *TheosQ* 9 (April 1912): 351–58.

Cabot, James Elliot. *A Memoir of Ralph Waldo Emerson*. 2 vols. Boston: Houghton, Mifflin, 1887.

Cady, Edwin Harrison. *The Gentleman in America*. Syracuse: Syracuse Univ. Press, 1949.

Cady, Lyman V. "Thoreau's Quotations from the Confucian Books in *Walden*." *AL* 33 (March 1961): 20–32.

Cairns, William B. *A History of American Literature*. New York: Oxford Univ. Press, 1912.

———. Review of Clarence L. F. Gohdes, *The Periodicals of American Transcendentalism*. *AL* 4 (May 1932): 219–20.

Callow, James T., and Robert J. Reilly. *A Guide to American Literature from Its Beginnings through Walt Whitman*. New York: Barnes and Noble, 1976.

Calvert, George Henry. "Ralph Waldo Emerson." *NYQ* 1 (Jan. 1853): 439–46.

Calverton, V. F. *The Liberation of American Literature*. New York: Scribners, 1932.

———. *Where Angels Dared to Tread*. Indianapolis: Bobbs-Merrill, 1941.

Cambon, Glauco. "Emily Dickinson and the Crisis of Self-Reliance." In *Transcendentalism and Its Legacy*, ed. Myron Simon and Thornton H. Parsons, 123–33.

Cameron, Kenneth Walter. "American and British Authors in F. B. Sanborn's Papers." *ATQ* no. 6 (2 Qtr. 1970): 2–53.

——. *Bibliography on Transcendentalism or the American Renaissance*. Hartford, Conn.: Transcendental Books, n.d.

——. "Coleridge and the Genesis of Emerson's 'Uriel.' " *PQ* 30 (April 1951): 212–17.

——. "A College Poem by Jones Very." *ESQ* no. 5 (4 Qtr. 1956): 12–13.

——. *A Commentary on Emerson's Early Lectures (1833–1836) with an Index-Concordance*. Hartford, Conn.: Transcendental Books, 1962.

——. *Companion to Thoreau's Correspondence*. Hartford, Conn.: Transcendental Books, 1964.

——. "Dwight's Translation of Schiller's Bell Song before 1837." *ESQ* no. 51 (2 Qtr. 1968): 147–54.

——. "Emerson and Swedenborgism: A Study Outline and Analysis." *ESQ* no. 10 (1 Qtr. 1958): 14–20.

——. *Emerson the Essayist*. 2 vols. Raleigh, N.C.: Thistle Press, 1945.

——. "Emerson, Thoreau, and the Town and Country Club." *ESQ* no. 8 (3 Qtr. 1957): 2–17.

——. "Emerson, Transcendentalism, and Literary Notes in the Stearns Wheeler Papers." *ATQ* no. 20, suppl. (Fall 1973): 69–98.

——. "Emerson's Early Reading List (1819–1824)." *BNYPL* 55 (July 1951): 315–24.

——. "Emerson's Recommendation of Whitman in 1863: The Remainder of the Evidence." *ESQ* no. 3 (2 Qtr. 1956): 14–20.

——. "The Episcopal Church in the Romances of Sylvester Judd." *ESQ* no. 35 (2 Qtr. 1964): 100–01.

——. "Harvard Rules and Certificates of Thoreau's Day." *ESQ* no. 52 (3 Qtr. 1968): 86–87.

——. "History and Biography in Emerson's Unpublished Sermons." *PAAS* 66 (Oct. 1956): 103–18.

——. "Jones Very's Academic Standing at Harvard." *ESQ* no. 19 (2 Qtr. 1960): 52–60.

——. "Junius J. Alcott, Poet and Transcendentalist." *ESQ* no. 14 (1 Qtr. 1959): 57–76.

——. "The Library of George Ripley." In his *The Transcendentalists and Minerva*, 3: 808–17.

——. "Manuscript Diary of Franklin B. Sanborn." In his *Transcendental Climate*, 1: 205–43.

——. *Massachusetts Lyceum during the American Renaissance*. Hartford, Conn.: Transcendental Books, 1970.

——. "Notes on Emerson in Japan." *ESQ* no. 51 (2 Qtr. 1968): 102–07.

——. "Notes on the *Early Lectures*." *ESQ* no. 20 (3 Qtr. 1960): 25–123. Rev. and enl. as *A Commentary on Emerson's Early Lectures*.

——. *Over Thoreau's Desk*. Hartford, Conn.: Transcendental Books, 1965.

——. "*The Radical*: A Monthly Magazine Devoted to Religion." *ESQ* no. 47 (2 Qtr. 1967): 128.

——. *Ralph Waldo Emerson's Reading*. Raleigh, N.C.: Thistle Press, 1941.

——. "The Recent Sale of Thoreau Manuscripts." *ESQ* no. 13 (4 Qtr. 1958): 98–114.

——. "Rough Draft of Whitman's 'By Emerson's Grave.' " *ESQ* no. 13 (4 Qtr. 1958): 32–34.

——. "Sophomore Thoreau and Religious Improvement." *ESQ* no. 48 (3 Qtr. 1967): 82–85.

——. "Thoreau and Orestes Brownson." *ESQ* no. 51 (2 Qtr. 1968): 53–65.

——. "Thoreau and Stearns Wheeler: Four Letters and a Reading Record." *ESQ* no. 48 (3 Qtr. 1967): 73–81. Partially rpt. in his *Transcendental Reading Patterns*.

——. "Thoreau Discovers Emerson: A College Reading Record." *BNYPL* 57 (June 1953): 319–34. Rpt. as *Thoreau Discovers Emerson: A College Reading Record*. New York: New York Public Library, 1953.

——. "Thoreau's Lecture on 'Misspent Lives' and the Evolution of 'Life without Principle.' " *ATQ* no. 36, pt. 2 (Fall 1977): 75–79.

————. "Thoreau's Notes from Dubuat's *Principles*." *ESQ* no. 22 (1 Qtr. 1961): 68–76.

————. "Thoreau's Schoolmate, Alfred Munroe, Remembers Concord." *ATQ* no. 36, pt. 1 (Fall 1977): 10–38.

————. *Transcendental Apprenticeship: Notes on Young Henry Thoreau's Reading: A Contexture with a Researcher's Index*. Hartford, Conn.: Transcendental Books, 1976.

————. *Transcendental Climate*. 3 vols. Hartford, Conn.: Transcendental Books, 1963.

————. *Transcendental Epilogue*. 3 vols. Hartford, Conn.: Transcendental Books, 1965–82.

————. *Transcendental Log*. Hartford, Conn.: Transcendental Books, 1973.

————. *Transcendental Reading Patterns*. Hartford, Conn.: Transcendental Books, 1970.

————. *Transcendentalism and American Renaissance Bibliography*. Hartford, Conn.: Transcendental Books, 1977.

————. *The Transcendentalists and Minerva*. 3 vols. Hartford, Conn.: Transcendental Books, 1958.

————. "Two Harvard Essays by Jones Very." *ESQ* no. 29 (4 Qtr. 1962): 32–40.

————. *Young Emerson's Transcendental Vision*. Hartford, Conn.: Transcendental Books, 1971. Rpt. of his *Emerson the Essayist*, vol. 1.

————. "Young Thoreau and the Classics: A Review." *ATQ* no. 35 (Sum. 1977): 1–128.

————, ed. *Concord Harvest*. 2 vols. Hartford, Conn.: Transcendental Books, 1970.

————, ed. *Contemporary Dimension*. Hartford, Conn.: Transcendental Books, 1970.

————, ed. *Emerson, Thoreau, and Concord in Early Newspapers*. Hartford, Conn.: Transcendental Books, 1958.

————, ed. *Literary Comment in American Renaissance Newspapers*. Hartford, Conn.: Transcendental Books, 1977.

————, ed. *Lowell, Whittier, Very and the Alcotts among Their Contemporaries*. Hartford, Conn.: Transcendental Books, 1978.

————, ed. *Responses to Transcendental Concord*. Hartford, Conn.: Transcendental Books, 1974.

————, ed. *Romanticism and the American Renaissance*. Hartford, Conn.: Transcendental Books, 1977.

————, ed. *Thoreau's Harvard Years*. Hartford, Conn.: Transcendental Books, 1966.

Campbell, Killis. "The Evolution of Whitman as Artist." *AL* 6 (Nov. 1934): 254–63.

————. *The Mind of Poe and Other Studies*. Cambridge: Harvard Univ. Press, 1933.

Canby, Henry Seidel. *Thoreau*. Boston: Houghton Mifflin, 1939.

Cantwell, Robert. *Nathaniel Hawthorne: The American Years*. New York: Rinehart, 1948.

Caponigri, A. Robert. "Brownson and Emerson: Nature and History." *NEQ* 18 (Sept. 1945): 368–90.

————. "European Influences on the Thought of Orestes Brownson: Pierre Leroux and Vincenzo Gioberti." In *No Divided Allegiance: Essays in Brownson's Thought*, ed. Leonard Gilhooley, 100–24.

————. "Individual, Civil Society, and State in American Transcendentalism." In *American Philosophy from Edwards to Quine*. Ed. Robert W. Shahan and Kenneth R. Merrill. Norman: Univ. of Oklahoma Press, 1977, 49–77.

Capps, Jack L. *Emily Dickinson's Reading 1836–1886*. Cambridge: Harvard Univ. Press, 1966.

Carafiol, Peter C. "James Marsh to John Dewey: The Fate of Transcendentalist Philosophy in American Education." *ESQ* 24 (1 Qtr. 1978): 1–11.

————. "James Marsh: Transcendental Puritan." Diss. Claremont Graduate School 1974.

————. "James Marsh: Transcendental Puritan." *ESQ* 21 (3 Qtr. 1975): 127–36.

————. "James Marsh's American *Aids to Reflection*: Influence through Ambiguity." *NEQ* 49 (March 1976): 27–45.

Carew, Harold D. "F. B. Sanborn, the Last of the Abolitionists." *GrM* 44 (May 1912): 151–54.

Cargill, Oscar. "Nemesis and Nathaniel Hawthorne." *PMLA* 52 (Sept. 1937): 848–62.

Carlet, Yves. " 'Respectables Iniquités': Le Transcendentalisme et l'ordre social." *RFEA* 3 (April 1978): 19–31.

Carley, Peter. "The Early Life and Thought of Frederic Henry Hedge." Diss. Syracuse Univ. 1973.

Carlson, Eric W. "Poe's Vision of Man." In *Papers on Poe*. Ed. Richard P. Veler. Springfield, Ohio: Chantry Music Press, 1972, 7–20.

———, and J. Lasley Dameron, eds. *Emerson's Relevance Today: A Symposium*. Hartford, Conn.: Transcendental Books, 1971. Rpt. from *ATQ* no. 9 (Wtr. 1971): 1–59.

Carlson, Larry A. "Bronson Alcott's 'Journal for 1837.' " *SAR* 1980, 1981: 27–132, 53–168.

Carlson, Patricia Ann. "Sarah Alden Ripley—Emerson's *Other* Aunt." *ATQ* no. 40 (Fall 1978): 309–22.

Carpenter, Edward. *Days with Walt Whitman*. London: George Allen, 1906.

Carpenter, Frederic Ives. *American Literature and the Dream*. New York: Philosophical Library, 1955.

———. " 'The American Myth': Paradise (to Be) Regained." *PMLA* 74 (Dec. 1959): 599–606.

———. "American Transcendentalism in India." *ESQ* no. 31 (2 Qtr. 1963): 59–62.

———. "Bronson Alcott: Genteel Transcendentalist—An Essay in Definition." *NEQ* 13 (March 1940): 34–38.

———. *Emerson and Asia*. Cambridge: Harvard Univ. Press, 1930.

———. *Emerson Handbook*. New York: Hendricks House, 1953.

———. "Eugene O'Neill, the Orient, and American Transcendentalism." In *Transcendentalism and Its Legacy*, ed. Myron Simon and Thornton H. Parsons, 204–14.

———. "Introduction." In *Ralph Waldo Emerson: Representative Selections*. Ed. Carpenter. New York: American Book, 1934, xi–lvii. Rpt. in his *American Literature and the Dream*, 19–29, 208.

———. Review of Clarence L. F. Gohdes, *The Periodicals of American Transcendentalism*. *NEQ* 5 (July 1932): 632–33.

Carpenter, Hazen C. "Emerson and Christopher Pearse Cranch." *NEQ* 37 (March 1964): 18–42.

———. "Emerson, Eliot, and the Elective System." *NEQ* 24 (March 1951): 13–34.

Carpenter, Richard V. "Margaret Fuller in Northern Illinois." *JISHS* 2 (Jan. 1910): 7–22.

Carroll, Mary Suzanne. "Symbolic Patterns in Henry David Thoreau's *A Week on the Concord and Merrimack Rivers*." Diss. Indiana Univ. 1975.

Carson, Barbara Harrell. "Orpheus in New England: Alcott, Emerson, and Thoreau." Diss. Johns Hopkins 1968.

———. "Proclus' Sunflower and the *Dial*." *ELN* 11 (March 1974): 200–02.

Carter, Everett. *The American Idea: The Literary Response to American Optimism*. Chapel Hill: Univ. of North Carolina Press, 1977.

Carter, George E. "Martin Luther King: Incipient Transcendentalist." *Phylon* 40 (Dec. 1979): 318–24.

———. "Theodore Parker and John P. Hale." *DCLB* n.s. 13 (Nov. 1972): 13–33.

Carter, George F. "Democrat in Heaven—Whig on Earth—The Politics of Ralph Waldo Emerson." *HNH* 27 (Fall 1972): 123–40.

Caruthers, J. Wade. "John Weiss." In *The American Renaissance in New England*, ed. Joel Myerson, 188–89.

———. *Octavius Brooks Frothingham: Gentle Radical*. University: Univ. of Alabama Press, 1977.

———. "Thomas Wentworth Higginson." In *The American Renaissance in New England*, ed. Joel Myerson, 104–05.

———. "Who Was Octavius Brooks Frothingham?" *NEQ* 43 (Dec. 1970): 631–37.

Cary, Edward. *George William Curtis.* Boston: Houghton, Mifflin, 1894.

Cary, Elisabeth Luther. *Emerson: Poet and Thinker.* New York: Putnam's, 1904.

————. "Hawthorne and Emerson." *CriticNY* 45 (July 1904): 25–27.

Casale, Ottavio M. "The Battle of Boston: A Revaluation of Poe's Lyceum Appearance." *AL* 45 (Nov. 1973): 423–27.

————. "Edgar Allan Poe and Transcendentalism: Conflict and Affinity." Diss. Univ. of Michigan 1965.

————. "Poe on Transcendentalism." *ESQ* no. 50 (1 Qtr. 1968): 85–97.

Cashdollar, Charles D. "European Positivism and the American Unitarians." *ChH* 45 (Dec. 1976): 490–506.

Cavell, Stanley. *The Senses of* Walden. New York: Viking, 1972. Exp. ed. as *The Senses of Walden: An Expanded Edition.* San Francisco: North Point Press, 1981.

————. "Thinking of Emerson." *NLH* 11 (Aut. 1979): 167–76. Rpt. in his *The Senses of Walden: An Expanded Edition.*

Cawelti, John G. *Apostles of the Self-Made Man.* Chicago: Univ. of Chicago Press, 1965.

Cayton, Mary K. " 'Sympathy's Electric Chain' and the American Democracy: Emerson's First Vocational Crisis." *NEQ* 55 (March 1982): 3–24.

Celieres, Andre. *The Prose Style of Emerson.* Paris: Pierre Andre, 1936.

The Centenary of the Birth of Ralph Waldo Emerson. Cambridge, Mass.: Riverside Press, 1903.

Chable, Eugene R. "A Study of the Interpretation of the New Testament in New England Unitarianism." Diss. Columbia 1955.

Chadwick, John White. "Channing, Emerson, and Parker." *EthR* 4 (June–July 1903): 177–81.

————. "Emerson: The Patriot." *Index* 16 (19 March 1885): 451–54.

————. "Frederic Henry Hedge." *Nation* 51 (28 Aug. 1890): 165–66.

————. *Frederic Henry Hedge: A Sermon.* Boston: George H. Ellis, 1891.

————. "Funeral Address for Octavius Brooks Frothingham." *FrCR* 4.1 (Feb. 1896): 3–8.

————. *George William Curtis.* New York: Harper's, 1893.

————. *Old and New Unitarian Belief.* Boston: George H. Ellis, 1894.

————. *Theodore Parker: Preacher and Reformer.* Boston: Houghton, Mifflin, 1901.

————. *William Ellery Channing: Minister of Religion.* Boston: Houghton, Mifflin, 1903.

Channing, William Ellery. *Dr. Channing's Notebook.* Ed. Grace Ellery Channing. Boston: Houghton, Mifflin, 1887.

————. "The Importance and Means of a National Literature." *ChEx* 7 (Jan. 1830): 269–95. Rpt. in his *Works,* rev. ed. (1886).

————. *The Perfect Life.* Ed. William Henry Channing. Boston: Roberts, 1873. Rpt. in his *Works,* rev. ed. (1886).

————. *The Works of William E. Channing, D.D.* 6 vols. Boston: James Munroe, 1841–43.

————. *The Works of William E. Channing, D.D.* Boston: American Unitarian Assn., 1875; rev. ed., 1886.

————, and Lucy Aiken. *Correspondence of William Ellery Channing, D.D., and Lucy Aiken.* Ed. Anna Letitia Le Breton. Boston: Roberts, 1874.

Channing, William Ellery, II. *The Collected Poems of William Ellery Channing the Younger, 1817–1901.* Ed. Walter Harding. Gainesville, Fla.: Scholars' Facsimiles & Reprints, 1967.

————. *Conversations in Rome: Between an Artist, a Catholic, and a Critic.* Boston: William Crosby and H. P. Nichols, 1847.

————. "Count Julian." In his *Poems of Sixty-Five Years,* ed. F. B. Sanborn, 113–14.

————. *Eliot. A Poem.* Boston: Cupples, Upham, 1885.

————. "Hawthorne at the Old Manse." In his *Poems of Sixty-Five Years,* ed. F. B. Sanborn, 111–12.

——. *John Brown, and the Heroes of Harper's Ferry.* Boston: Cupples, Upham, 1886.

——. *Near Home.* Boston: James Munroe, 1858.

——. *Poems.* Boston: Charles C. Little and James Brown, 1843.

——. *Poems of Sixty-Five Years.* Ed. F. B. Sanborn. Philadelphia and Concord, Mass.: James H. Bentley, 1902.

——. *Poems: Second Series.* Boston: James Munroe, 1847.

——. *Thoreau: The Poet-Naturalist. With Memorial Verses.* Boston: Roberts, 1873. Enl. ed., ed. F. B. Sanborn, Boston: Charles E. Goodspeed, 1902.

——. *The Wanderer. A Colloquial Poem.* Boston: James R. Osgood, 1871.

——. *The Woodman, and Other Poems.* Boston: James Munroe, 1849.

Channing, William Henry. "Editor's Introduction." *WM* 8 (Oct. 1839): 1–8. Rpt. as "An Ideal of Humanity" in *The Transcendentalists: An Anthology,* ed. Perry Miller, 429–31.

——. "Emerson's *Phi Beta Kappa* Oration." *BoQR* 1 (Jan. 1838): 106–20.

——. *The Memoir and Writings of James Handasyd Perkins.* Cincinnati: Trueman and Spofford, 1851.

——. *Memoir of William Ellery Channing.* 3 vols. Boston: William Crosby and H. P. Nichols, 1848. Rpt. as *The Life of William Ellery Channing.* Boston: American Unitarian Assn., 1880.

——. "Poems of William Ellery Channing." *Present* 1 (Sept. 1843): 30–32.

——, trans. Théodore Joufroy, *Introduction to Ethics.* 2 vols. Boston: Hilliard, Gray, 1840–41.

Chapman, John Jay. "Emerson, Sixty Years After." *Atl* 79 (Jan., Feb. 1897): 27–41, 222–40. Rpt. in his *Emerson and Other Essays.* New York: Scribners, 1898, 3–108.

Charvat, William. "A Chronological List of Emerson's American Lecture Engagements." *BNYPL* 64 (Sept.–Dec. 1960): 492–507, 551–59, 606–10, 657–63; 65 (Jan. 1961): 40–46. Rpt. as *Emerson's American Lecture Engagements: A Chronological List.* New York: New York Public Library, 1961.

——. *Literary Publishing in America 1790–1850.* Philadelphia: Univ. of Pennsylvania Press, 1936.

——. *The Origins of American Critical Thought, 1810–1835.* Philadelphia: Univ. of Pennsylvania Press, 1936.

——. *The Profession of Authorship in America, 1800–1870.* Ed. Matthew J. Bruccoli. Columbus: Ohio State Univ. Press, 1968.

Chase, Harry. "Henry Thoreau, Surveyor." *S&Map* 25 (June 1965): 219–22.

Chase, Richard. *Emily Dickinson.* New York: William Sloane, 1951.

Chazin, Maurice. "Quinet, an Early Discoverer of Emerson." *PMLA* 48 (March 1933): 147–63.

Cheever, George B. *Characteristics of the Christian Philosopher: A Description of . . . James Marsh.* New York: Wiley and Putnam, 1843.

Chen, David T. Y. "Thoreau and Taoism." In *Asian Responses to American Literature.* Ed. C. D. Narasimhaiah. New York: Barnes and Noble, 1972, 406–16.

Cheney, Ednah Dow. "Emerson and Boston." In *The Genius and Character of Emerson,* ed. F. B. Sanborn, 1–35.

——. *Louisa May Alcott: Her Life, Letters, and Journals.* Boston: Roberts, 1889.

——. *Reminiscences of Ednah Dow Cheney.* Boston: Lee and Shepard, 1902.

——. "Reminiscences of Mr. Alcott's Conversations." *OC* 2 (2, 9 Aug. 1888): 1131–33, 1142–44.

——. "Theodore Parker, the Pastor." In *West Roxbury Magazine.* Hudson, Mass.: E. F. Worcester, 1900, 52–56.

Cherno, Donna. "Emily Dickinson and Transcendentalism." M.A. thesis Adelphi Univ. 1968.

Cherry, Conrad. *Nature and Religious Imagination from Edwards to Bushnell.* Philadelphia: Fortress Press, 1980.

Chevigny, Bell Gale. "Growing Out of New England: The Emergence of Margaret Fuller's Radicalism." *WS* 5 (1977): 65–100.

———. "The Long Arm of Censorship: Mythmaking in Margaret Fuller's Time and Our Own." *Signs* 2 (Wtr. 1976): 450–60.

———, ed. *The Woman and the Myth: Margaret Fuller's Life and Writings.* Old Westbury, N.Y.: Feminist Press, 1976.

Chew, Samuel C. "Byron in America." *AmM* 1 (March 1924): 335–44.

Cheyfitz, Eric. *The Trans-parent: Sexual Politics in the Language of Emerson.* Baltimore: Johns Hopkins Univ. Press, 1981.

Chielens, Edward E. *The Literary Journal in America to 1900.* Detroit: Gale, 1975.

Child, Francis J., ed. *War-Songs for Freemen.* Boston: Ticknor and Fields, 1862.

Child, Lydia Maria. *The Collected Correspondence of Lydia Maria Child.* Ed. Patricia G. Holland and Milton Meltzer. Millwood, N.Y.: KTO, 1980.

———. *Letters of Lydia Maria Child.* Ed. Harriet Winslow Sewall. Boston: Houghton, Mifflin, 1883.

———. "Letter XIII." In her *Letters from New-York. Second Series.* New York: C. S. Francis, 1845, 125–30.

Childs, George W. *Recollections.* Philadelphia: Lippincott, 1890.

Chipperfield, Faith. *In Quest of Love: The Life and Death of Margaret Fuller.* New York: Coward-McCann, 1957.

Chittick, V. L. O. "Emerson's 'Frolic Health.' " *NEQ* 30 (June 1957): 209–34.

Chivers, Thomas Holley. *The Correspondence of Thomas Holley Chivers.* Ed. Emma Lester Chase and Lois Ferry Parks. Providence: Brown Univ. Press, 1957.

Christadler, Martin. "Ralph Waldo Emerson in Modern Germany." *ESQ* no. 38 (1 Qtr. 1965): 112–30.

Christie, Francis A. "Theodore Parker." In *DAB*, 14: 238–41.

———. "Theodore Parker and Modern Theology." *MeadJ* 25 (Oct. 1930): 3–17.

Christie, John Aldrich. *Thoreau as World Traveler.* New York: Columbia Univ. Press, 1965.

———. "Thoreau on Civil Disobedience." *ESQ* no. 54 (1 Qtr. 1969): 5–12.

"Christopher Pearse Cranch." In *The Library of Southern Literature.* Ed. Edwin Anderson Alderman et al. 17 vols. Atlanta: Martin and Hoyt, 1907–23, 15: 99.

Christy, Arthur. *The Orient in American Transcendentalism.* New York: Columbia Univ. Press, 1932.

Church of the Disciples: Seventieth Birthday of James Freeman Clarke. Boston: The Committee, 1880.

Clapp, Dexter. Review of Sylvester Judd, *Margaret. SoQR* 9 (April 1846): 507–22.

Clapper, Ronald. "The Development of *Walden*: A Genetic Text." Diss. Univ. of California at Los Angeles 1967.

Clark, Allen R. "Andrews Norton: A Conservative Unitarian." Honors thesis Harvard 1942.

Clark, Annie M. L. "The Alcotts in Harvard." *NEMag* n.s. 22 (April 1900): 173–80. Rpt. as *The Alcotts in Harvard.* Lancaster, Mass.: J. C. L. Clark, 1902.

Clark, C. E. Frazer, Jr. "Elizabeth Peabody Identifies the 'Original' Judge Pyncheon." *NHJ* 1971: 70.

———. "Elizabeth P. Peabody to Mrs. Harriet K. Lothrop." *NHJ* 1972: 7–9.

———. *Nathaniel Hawthorne: A Descriptive Bibliography.* Pittsburgh: Univ. of Pittsburgh Press, 1978.

Clark, Clifford E., Jr. "Religious Beliefs and Social Reforms in the Gilded Age: The Case of Henry Whitney Bellows." *NEQ* 43 (March 1970): 59–78.

Clark, Harry Hayden. "American Literary History and American Literature." In *The Reinterpretation of American Literature*. Ed. Norman Foerster. New York: Harcourt, Brace, 1928, 207–12.

———. "Changing Attitudes in Early American Literary Criticism: 1800–1840." In *The Development of American Literary Criticism*. Ed. Floyd Stovall. Chapel Hill: Univ. of North Carolina Press, 1955, 15–73.

———. "Conservative and Mediatory Emphases in Emerson's Thought." In *Transcendentalism and Its Legacy*, ed. Myron Simon and Thornton H. Parsons, 25–62.

———. "Emerson and Science." *PQ* 10 (July 1931): 225–60.

Clark, Jerome L. *1844*. 3 vols. Nashville: Southern Publishing Assn., 1968.

Clark, Neal. "A Utopian Relic Worth Saving." *BoM* 73 (July 1981): 68, 70–71.

Clarke, James Freeman. *Anti-Slavery Days*. New York: J. W. Lovell, 1883.

———. *Autobiography, Diary and Correspondence*. Ed. Edward Everett Hale. Boston: Houghton, Mifflin, 1891.

———. *Common-Sense in Religion*. Boston: James R. Osgood, 1874.

———. "Dr. Hedge and His Critics." *MRM* 34 (Nov. 1865): 268–73.

———. *Events and Epochs in Religious History*. Boston: James R. Osgood, 1881.

———. *The Letters of James Freeman Clarke to Margaret Fuller*. Ed. John Wesley Thomas. Hamburg: Cram, de Gruyter, 1957.

———. "Memoir of Ralph Waldo Emerson, LL.D." *PMHS* 18 (June 1885): 329–30.

———. *Memorial and Biographical Sketches*. Boston: Houghton, Osgood, 1878.

———. *Natural and Artificial Methods in Education*. Boston: Ticknor and Fields, 1864.

———. "Religious Sonnets: By Jones Very." *WM* 6 (March 1839): 308–14.

———. "R. W. Emerson and the New School." *WM* 6 (Nov. 1838): 37–47.

———. *A Sermon Preached in Amory Hall* . . . . Boston: Benjamin H. Greene, 1842.

———. *Theodore Parker and His Theology*. Boston: Walker, Wise, 1859.

———. "William Henry Channing." *UnitR* 23 (March 1885): 211–16.

Clarke, Lilian Freeman. "James Freeman Clarke." In *Heralds of a Liberal Faith*, ed. Samuel A. Eliot, 3: 67–74.

Clarke, Samuel C. *Records of Some of the Descendants of Richard Hull, New Haven, 1639–1662*. Boston: D. Clapp, 1869.

———. *Records of Some of the Descendants of Thomas Clarke, Plymouth, 1623–1697*. Boston: D. Clapp, 1869.

Clarkson, John W., Jr. "An Annotated Checklist of the Letters of F. B. Sanborn (1831–1917)." Diss. Columbia 1971.

———. "A Bibliography of Franklin Benjamin Sanborn." *PBSA* 60 (1 Qtr. 1966): 73–85.

———. "Mentions of Emerson and Thoreau in the Letters of Franklin Benjamin Sanborn." *SAR* 1978: 387–420.

Clebsch, William A. *American Religious Thought: A History*. Chicago: Univ. of Chicago Press, 1973.

Clements, Richard. "Moncure Daniel Conway." *EthR* 73 (Feb. 1968): 5–8.

Clendenning, John. "Emerson's 'Days': A Psychoanalytic Study." *ATQ* no. 25 (Wtr. 1975): 6–11.

Clifford, J. H. "Emerson Explained." *Index* 13 (18 May 1882): 544–45.

Clough, Wilson O. *The Necessary Earth: Nature and Solitude in American Literature*. Austin: Univ. of Texas Press, 1964.

Coburn, Frederick. "Christopher Pearse Cranch." In *DAB*, 4: 501–02.

Codman, John Thomas. *Brook Farm: Historic and Personal Memoirs*. Boston: Arena, 1894.

———. "The Men and Thought That Made the Boston of the Forties Famous." *ComA* 2 (Sept. 1899): 239–47.

Coffie, Jessie A. "Margaret Fuller as Zenobia in *The Blithedale Romance*." *CCTEP* 38 (Sept. 1973): 23–27.

Coffin, Theron E. "Henry D. Thoreau—Quaker?" *CS* 10.1 (March 1975): 4–9.

Cohen, B. Bernard. "Emerson's 'The Young American' and Hawthorne's 'The Intelligence Office.' " *AL* 26 (March 1954): 32–43.

Cohen, Emanuel. "The Philosophy of Emerson." *PAM* 19 (Aug. 1882): 164–70.

Colacurcio, Michael J. "A Better Mode of Evidence—The Transcendental Problem of Faith and Spirit." *ESQ* no. 54 (1 Qtr. 1969): 12–22.

Cole, Phyllis. " Emerson, England, and Fate." In *Emerson: Prophecy, Metamorphosis, Influence*, ed. David Levin, 83–106.

———. "Jones Very's 'Epistles to the Unborn' " *SAR* 1982: 169–83.

———. "The Purity of Puritanism: Transcendentalist Readings of Milton." *SIR* 17 (Spr. 1978): 129–48.

Coleman, Caryl. "A Forgotten Convert." *CathW* 122 (Nov. 1925): 192–203.

Coleman, Rufus A. "Trowbridge and Whitman." *PMLA* 63 (March 1948): 262–73.

Coleman, William E., Jr. "The Role of the Prophet in the Abolition Rhetoric of the Reverend Theodore Parker, 1845–1860." Diss. Ohio Univ. 1975.

Collie, George L., and Robert K. Richardson. "A 'Conversation' of A. Bronson Alcott." *WMH* 32 (Sept. 1948): 85–88.

Collins, Christopher. *The Uses of Observation: A Study of the Correspondential Vision in the Writings of Emerson, Thoreau, and Whitman*. The Hague: Mouton, 1971.

Collins, Hildegard Plotzer, and Phillip Allison Shelley. "The Reception in England and America of Bettina von Arnim's *Goethe's Correspondence with a Child*." In *Anglo-German and American-German Crosscurrents*. Ed. Shelley and Arthur O. Lewis, Jr. Chapel Hill: Univ. of North Carolina Press, 1962, 2: 97–174.

Collison, Gary L. "A Calendar of the Letters of Theodore Parker." *SAR* 1979, 1980: 159–229, 317–408.

———. "A Critical Edition of the Correspondence of Theodore Parker and Convers Francis, 1836–1859." Diss. Pennsylvania State Univ. 1979.

Colquitt, Betsy F. "Thoreau's Poetics." *ATQ* no. 11 (Sum. 1971): 74–81.

Colton, Delia M. "Ralph Waldo Emerson." *CoM* 1 (Jan. 1862): 49–62.

Colville, Derek K. "James Freeman Clarke: A Practical Transcendentalist and His Writings." Diss. Washington Univ. 1953.

———. "The Transcendental Friends: Clarke and Margaret Fuller." *NEQ* 30 (Sept. 1957): 378–82.

Colyer, Richard. "Thoreau's Color Symbols." *PMLA* 86 (Oct. 1971): 999–1008.

Commager, Henry Steele. "The Dilemma of Theodore Parker." *NEQ* 6 (June 1933): 257–77.

———. "Tempest in a Boston Teacup." *NEQ* 6 (Dec. 1933): 651–75.

———. *Theodore Parker*. Boston: Little, Brown, 1936.

———. "Theodore Parker, Intellectual Gourmand." *ASch* 3 (Sum. 1934): 257–65.

Comprehensive Dissertation Index, 1861–1972. 37 vols. Ann Arbor, Mich.: University Microfilms International, 1973.

Conant, Wallace B. *Paper on Franklin Benjamin Sanborn*. Concord, Mass.: Concord Free Public Library, 1945.

Condry, William. "Thoreau's Influence in Britain." *TSB* no. 157 (Fall 1981): 1–5.

Congdon, Charles T. *Reminiscences of a Journalist*. Boston: James R. Osgood, 1880.

Conkin, Paul F. *Puritans and Pragmatists*. New York: Dodd, Mead, 1968.

Connelley, William E. "Personal Reminiscences of F. B. Sanborn." *CKSHS* 14 (1915–18): 63–70.

Conner, Frederick W. *Cosmic Optimism: A Study of the Interpretation of Evolution by American Poets from Emerson to Robinson*. Gainesville: Univ. of Florida Press, 1949.

Conrad, Susan P. " 'The Beauty of a Stricter Method': Margaret Fuller, Interpreter of Romanticism." In her *Perish the Thought: Intellectual Women in Romantic America, 1830–1860*. New York: Oxford Univ. Press, 1976, 45–92, 251–57.

Conron, John. " 'Bright American Rivers': The Luminist Landscapes of Thoreau's *A Week*." *AQ* 32 (Sum. 1980): 144–66.

Conroy, Stephen S. "Emerson and Phrenology." *AQ* 16 (Sum. 1964): 215–17.

"Convers Francis." *ChReg* 42 (2 May 1863): 70.

Conway, Katherine E. *In the Footprints of the Good Shepherd*. 2nd ed. New York: Convent of the Good Shepherd, 1907.

Conway, Moncure Daniel. *Addresses and Reprints 1850–1907*. Boston: Houghton Mifflin, 1909.

———. *Autobiography Memories and Experiences*. 2 vols. Boston: Houghton, Mifflin, 1904.

———. "Concerning Hawthorne and Brook Farm." *ESJ* 7 (2 Jan. 1869): 13–18.

———. *Demonology and Devil-Lore*. 2 vols. New York: Henry Holt, 1879.

———. *The Earthward Pilgrimage*. London: J. C. Hotten, 1870.

———. *Emerson and His Views of Nature*. London: Royal Inst. of Great Britain, 1883.

———. *Emerson at Home and Abroad*. Boston: James R. Osgood, 1882.

———. *The Golden Hour*. Boston: Ticknor and Fields, 1862.

———. *Life of Nathaniel Hawthorne*. London: Walter Scott, 1890.

———. *The Life of Thomas Paine with a History of His Literary, Political, and Religious Career in America, France, and England*. 2 vols. New York: Putnam's, 1892.

———. *My Pilgrimage to the Wise Men of the East*. Boston: Houghton Mifflin, 1906.

———. *Pine and Palm*. New York: Henry Holt, 1887.

———. *Prisons of Air*. New York: J. W. Lovell, 1891.

———. "Ralph Waldo Emerson." *FoR* 37 (1 June 1882): 747–70.

———. "Recent Lectures and Writings of Emerson." *FrM* 75 (May 1867): 586–600.

———. *The Rejected Stone: or Insurrection vs. Resurrection in America*. Boston: Walker, Wise, 1861.

———. Review of Mark Twain, *Tom Sawyer*. *Ath* no. 2539 (24 June 1876): 851.

———. *Solomon and Solomonic Literature*. Chicago: Open Court, 1899.

———. "Sylvester Judd." *FrM* 76 (July 1867): 45–60.

———. *Thomas Carlyle*. New York: Harpers, 1881.

———. "The Transcendentalists of Concord." *FrM* 70 (Aug. 1864): 245–64. Rpt. in *LLA* 83 (8 Oct. 1864): 99–115.

———, and William Dean Howells. "Venice Come True." *BoCom*, 28 Aug. 1863, 4.

Cook, Hugh. "Thoreau and the King James Bible." In *Hearing and Doing: Philosophical Essays Dedicated to H. Evan Runner*. Ed. John Kraay and Anthony Tol. Toronto: Wedge, 1979, 87–96.

Cook, Joseph. "Emerson's Theism." *Ind* 32 (18 March 1880): 8.

———. *Orthodoxy, with Preludes on Current Events*. Glasgow: David Bryce, 1878.

———. *Transcendentalism, with Preludes on Current Events*. Boston: James R. Osgood, 1878.

Cook, Reginald L. "Emerson and the American Joke." *ESQ* no. 54 (1 Qtr. 1969): 22–27.

———. "Looking for America: A Binocular Vision." *TJQ* 8.3 (July 1976): 10–17.

———. *Passage to Walden*. Boston: Houghton Mifflin, 1942. 2nd ed., New York: Russell and Russell, 1966.

————, ed. *Themes, Tones and Motifs in the American Renaissance*. Hartford, Conn.: Transcendental Books, 1968.

Cook, Richard C. "Thoreau and His Imagery: The Anatomy of an Imagination." *TSB* no. 70 (Wtr. 1960): 1–3.

Cooke, George Willis. *A Bibliography of Ralph Waldo Emerson*. Boston: Houghton Mifflin, 1908.

————. "Brook Farm." *NEMag* n.s. 17 (Dec. 1897): 391–407.

————. "The *Dial* and Corrigenda." *JSP* 19 (July 1885): 322–23.

————. "The *Dial*: An Historical and Biographical Introduction, with a List of the Contributors." *JSP* 19 (July 1885): 225–65.

————. "Emerson and Thoreau in the Index to the *Dial*." *ESQ* no. 18 (1 Qtr. 1960): 44–49. Rpt. from his *An Historical and Biographical Introduction to Accompany the* Dial.

————. "Emerson and Transcendentalism." *NEMag* n.s. 28 (May 1903): 264–80.

————. "Emerson's Attitude toward Religion." *Index* 11 (18 March 1880): 134–36.

————. "Emerson's View of Nationality." In *The Genius and Character of Emerson*, ed. F. B. Sanborn, 310–38.

————. "The Free Religious Association." *NEMag* n.s. 28 (June 1903): 484–99.

————. "George Ripley." In *Heralds of a Liberal Faith*, ed. Samuel A. Eliot, 3: 330–35.

————. "George William Curtis at Concord." *Har* 96 (Dec. 1897): 137–49. Rpt. in *Early Letters of George Wm. Curtis to John S. Dwight*, ed. Cooke.

————. *An Historical and Biographical Introduction to Accompany the* Dial. 2 vols. Cleveland: Rowfant Club, 1902.

————. *John Sullivan Dwight: Brook-Farmer, Editor, and Critic of Music*. Boston: Small, Maynard, 1898.

————. *Memorabilia of the Transcendentalists in New England*. Ed. Kenneth Walter Cameron. Hartford, Conn.: Transcendental Books, 1973. Rpt. in *ATQ* no. 27 (Sum. 1975): 1–122. Rpt. from his *An Historical and Biographical Introduciton to Accompany the* Dial.

————. *Ralph Waldo Emerson: His Life, Writings, and Philosophy*. Boston: James R. Osgood, 1881.

————. "Saturday Club." *NEMag* n.s. 19 (Sept. 1898): 24–34.

————. "Thomas Wentworth Higginson." In *Authors at Home*. Ed. J. L. and J. B. Gilder. New York: Cassell, 1889, 119–62.

————. *Unitarianism in America*. Boston: American Unitarian Assn., 1902.

————, ed. *The Poets of Transcendentalism*. Boston: Houghton, Mifflin, 1903.

Cory, Arthur M. "Humor in Emerson's Journals." *TxSE* 34 (1955): 114–24.

Cosbey, Robert C. "Thoreau at Work: The Writing of 'Ktaadn.'" *BNYPL* 65 (Jan. 1961): 21–30.

Courtney, W. L. "Emerson." *FoR* 44 (Sept. 1885): 319–31.

————. "Emerson's Philosophy." *Time* n.s. 3 (June 1886): 653–61.

Couser, G. Thomas. *American Autobiography: The Prophetic Mode*. Amherst: Univ. of Massachusetts Press, 1979.

————. "An Emerson-Whitman Parallel: 'The American Scholar' and 'A Song for Occupations.'" *WWR* 22 (Sept. 1976): 115–18.

————. "'The Old Manse,' *Walden*, and the Hawthorne-Thoreau Relationship." *ESQ* 21 (1 Qtr. 1975): 11–20.

————. "Thoreau's Cape Cod Pilgrimage." *ATQ* no. 26, suppl. (Spr. 1975): 31–37.

Cowan, Michael H. *City of the West: Emerson, America, and Urban Metaphor*. New Haven: Yale Univ. Press, 1967.

―――. "The Loving Proteus: Metamorphosis in Emerson's Poetry." *ATQ* no. 25 (Wtr. 1975): 11–22.

Cowan, S.A. "In Praise of Self-Reliance: The Role of Bulkington in *Moby-Dick*" *AL* 38 (Jan. 1967): 547–66.

Cowen, Wilson Walker. "Melville's Marginalia." Diss. Harvard 1965.

Cox, James M. "Emerson and Hawthorne: Trust and Doubt." *VQR* 45 (Wtr. 1969): 88–107.

―――. "Ralph Waldo Emerson: The Circles of the Eye." In *Emerson: Prophecy, Metamorphosis, Influence*, ed. David Levin, 57–81.

Craig, George D. "Literary Criticism in the Works of Henry David Thoreau." Diss. Univ. of Utah 1951.

Cranch, Christopher Pearse. *Address Delivered before the Harvard Musical Association*. Boston: S. N. Dickinson, 1845.

―――. *Ariel and Caliban with Other Poems*. Boston: Houghton, Mifflin, 1887.

―――. *The Bird and the Bell, with Other Poems*. Boston: James R. Osgood, 1875.

―――. *Collected Poems of Christopher Pearse Cranch*. Ed. Joseph M. De Falco. Gainesville, Fla.: Scholars' Facsimiles & Reprints, 1971.

―――. "Emerson's Limitations as a Poet." *CriticNY* n.s. 17 (27 Feb. 1892): 129.

―――. *Kobboltozo: A Sequel to the Last of the Huggermuggers*. Boston: Phillips, Sampson, 1857.

―――. *The Last of the Huggermuggers, a Giant Story*. Boston: Phillips, Sampson, 1856.

―――. "Personal Reminiscences." In *In Memoriam. Memorial to Robert Browning*. Cambridge, Mass.: Browning Soc., 1890, 48–53.

―――. *A Poem Delivered in the First Congregational Church in the Town of Quincy, May 25, 1840, the Two Hundredth Anniversary of the Incorporation of the Town*. Boston: James Munroe, 1840.

―――. *Poems*. Philadelphia: Carey and Hart, 1844.

―――. "The Poetical Picnic." In Mary E. Sargent, *Sketches and Reminiscences of the Radical Club*, 405–07.

―――. "Ralph Waldo Emerson." *UnitR* 20 (July 1883): 1–19.

―――. *Satan: A Libretto*. Boston: Roberts, 1874.

―――. "To my Sister M., with Wordsworth's Poems." *WM* 4 (Feb. 1838): 375–76.

―――. "Transcendentalism." *WM* 8 (Jan. 1841): 405–09.

―――, trans. *The* Aeneid *of Virgil Translated into English Blank Verse*. Boston: James R. Osgood, 1872.

Crawley, Thomas Edward. *The Structure of* Leaves of Grass. Austin: Univ. of Texas Press, 1970.

Cressey, George. *Frederic Henry Hedge: Pastor of the Society 1835-1850*. Bangor, Me.: J. H. Bacon, 1890.

―――. *Sketch of Frederic Henry Hedge*. Bangor, Me.: n.p., 1880.

Cromphout, Gustaaf Van. "Emerson and the Dialectics of History." *PMLA* 91 (Jan. 1976): 54–65.

―――. "Emerson, Hawthorne, and *The Blithedale Romance*." *GaR* 25 (Wtr. 1971): 471–80.

Cronin, Morton. "Some Notes on Emerson's Prose Diction." *AS* 29 (May 1954): 105–13.

Cronkhite, G. Ferris. "The Transcendental Railroad." *NEQ* 24 (Sept. 1951): 306–28.

Crothers, Samuel McChord. *Emerson: How to Know Him*. Indianapolis: Bobbs-Merrill, 1921.

Crowe, Charles R. "Christian Socialism and the First Church of Humanity." *ChH* 35 (March 1966): 93–106.

―――. "Fourierism and the Founding of Brook Farm." *BPLQ* 12 (April 1960): 79–88.

―――. "The Genesis of a Nineteenth Century Reformer as Seen in the Letters of George Ripley." *Manuscripts* 11 (Spr. 1959): 11–13, 38.

——. "George Ripley: Transcendentalist and Utopian Socialist." Diss. Brown 1955.

——. *George Ripley: Transcendentalist and Utopian Socialist.* Athens: Univ. of Georgia Press, 1967.

——. " 'This Unnatural Union of Phalansteries and Transcendentalists.' " *JHI* 20 (Oct.–Dec. 1959): 495–502.

——. "Transcendentalism and 'The Newness' in Rhode Island." *RIH* 14 (April 1955): 33–46.

——. "Transcendentalism and the Providence Literati." *RIH* 14 (July 1955): 65–78.

——. "Transcendentalist Support of Brook Farm: A Paradox?" *Historian* 21 (May 1959): 281–95.

——. "Utopian Socialism in Rhode Island 1845–1850." *RIH* 18 (Jan. 1959): 20–26.

Crozier, John Beattie. "Emerson." In his *The Religion of the Future.* London: Kegan Paul, 1880, 105–56.

——. "Emerson, Cicero, the Stoics, and Myself." *ContempR* 112 (Sept. 1917): 293–99.

Cruder, Maude Ethel. "An Examination of the Bibliophile Edition of Thoreau's *Walden.*" M.A. thesis Univ. of Chicago 1920.

Cummings, Charles A. "The Press and Literature of the Last Hundred Years." In *The Memorial History of Boston*, ed. Justin Winsor, 3: 617–82.

Cummins, Roger William. "The Second Eden: Charles Lane and American Transcendentalism." Diss. Univ. of Minnesota 1967.

Cupples, George. "Emerson and His Visit to Scotland." *DSJM* 7 (April 1848): 322–31.

Curti, Merle. "The Great Mr. Locke: America's Philosopher, 1783–1861." *HuLB* no. 11 (April 1937): 107–51.

Curtis, Alice Cabell. "Hawthorne—His Relations to the Transcendental Movement." M.A. thesis Cornell 1931.

Curtis, Edith Roelker. *A Season in Utopia: The Story of Brook Farm.* New York: Thomas Nelson, 1961.

Curtis, George William. *Early Letters of George Wm. Curtis to John S. Dwight: Brook Farm and Concord.* Ed. George Willis Cooke. New York: Harper's, 1898.

——. "Editor's Easy Chair." *Har* 30 (Feb. 1865): 395–96. Rpt. in his *From the Easy Chair*, 21–26.

——. "Editor's Easy Chair." *Har* 38 (Jan. 1869): 268–71. Rpt. in his *Essays from the Easy Chair, Third Series*, 1–19.

——. "Editor's Easy Chair." *Har* 43 (Nov. 1871): 929–33.

——. "Editor's Easy Chair." *Har* 84 (April 1892): 800–01.

——. "Emerson." In his *Other Essays from the Easy Chair*, 94–106.

——. *Essays from the Easy Chair, Third Series.* New York: Harper's, 1894.

——. *From the Easy Chair.* New York: Harper's, 1893.

——. "Hawthorne." In *Homes of American Authors.* New York: G. P. Putnam, 1852, 289–313. Rpt. in his *Literary and Social Essays.* New York: Harper's, 1895, 33–60.

——. "Hawthorne." *NAR* 99 (Oct. 1864): 539–57. Rpt. as "The Works of Nathaniel Hawthorne" in his *Literary and Social Essays*, 66–93.

——. "Mr. Emerson and the *Dial.*" *LW* 11 (22 May 1880): 178. Rpt. as "A Reprint of the *Dial.*" *JSP* 16 (July 1882): 329–31.

——. *Orations and Addresses of George William Curtis.* Ed. Charles Eliot Norton. 3 vols. New York: Harper's, 1894.

——. *Other Essays from the Easy Chair.* New York: Harper's, 1893.

——. "Ralph Waldo Emerson." In *Homes of American Authors.* New York: G. P. Putnam, 1852, 233–54. Rpt. in his *Literary and Social Essays*, 1–30.

Curtis, Georgianna Pell. *Some Roads to Rome in America*. St. Louis: B. Herder, 1909.
[Cyrus Augustus Bartol]. *BHJ*, 5 Oct. 1895.
"Cyrus Augustus Bartol." *HGM* 10 (March 1901): 421.
[Cyrus Augustus Bartol]. *TH* 9.23 (13 May 1899): 7–8.

Dahl, Curtis. "New England Unitarianism in Fictional Antiquity: The Romances of William Ware." *NEQ* 48 (March 1975): 104–15.
Dahlstrand, Frederick C. *Amos Bronson Alcott: An Intellectual Biography*. Rutherford, N.J.: Fairleigh Dickinson Univ. Press, 1982.
Dall, Caroline H. *"Alongside." Being Notes Suggested by "A New England Boyhood" of Doctor Edward Everett Hale*. Boston: Thomas Todd, 1900.
———. "The Late Lawsuit. Men and Women vs. Custom and Tradition." *Dial* [Cincinnati] 1 (May 1860): 286–293. Rpt. in her *Historical Pictures Retouched*. Boston: Walker, Wise, 1860, 249–64.
———. *Margaret and Her Friends*. Boston: Roberts, 1895.
———. "Margaret Fuller Ossoli." *NAR* 91 (July 1860): 119–29. Rpt. in her *Historical Pictures Retouched*, 226–48.
———. *Transcendentalism in New England: A Lecture*. Boston: Roberts, 1897.
Daly, John E. "Orestes Augustus Brownson and Transcendentalism." Diss. Fordham 1955.
Dameron, J. Lasley, and Irby B. Cauthen, Jr. *Edgar Allan Poe: A Bibliography of Criticism, 1827–1967*. Charlottesville: Univ. Press of Virginia, 1974.
Dana, Charles A. Review of Walt Whitman, *Leaves of Grass*. *NYDT*, 23 July 1855, 3.
Dana, Henry W. L. *The Dana Saga*. Cambridge, Mass.: Cambridge Historical Soc., 1941.
Dana, William F. *The Optimism of Ralph Waldo Emerson*. Boston: Cupples, Upham, 1886.
Daniels, George H. "An American Defense of Bacon: A Study of the Relations of Scientific Thought, 1840–1855." *HLQ* 28 (Aug. 1965): 321–39.
Darby, John Custis. "Ralph Waldo Emerson." *QRMECS* 6 (Jan. 1852): 31–42.
Darrow, F. S. "The Transcendentalists and Theosophy." *NO* 11 (March 1958): 9–18.
Das, S. P. "Beginnings of American Transcendentalism." *IJAS* 1 (July 1970): 15–22.
D'Avanzo, Mario L. "Dickinson's 'The Reticent Volcano' and Emerson." *ATQ* no. 16 (Spr. 1972): 11–13.
———. "The Emersonian Context of Three Poems by Emily Dickinson." *EDB* no. 16 (March 1971): 2–7.
———. "Emersonian Revelation in 'The way I read a letter's—this—.' " *ATQ* no. 17 (Wtr. 1973): 14–15.
———. "Emily Dickinson's and Emerson's 'Presentiment.' " *ESQ* no. 58 (1 Qtr. 1970): 157–59.
———. "Fortitude and Nature in Thoreau's *Cape Cod*." *ESQ* 20 (2 Qtr. 1974): 131–38.
———. "Frost's 'Sand Dunes' and Thoreau's *Cape Cod*." *NConL* 10.5 (Nov. 1980): 2–4.
———. " 'Unto the White Creator': The Snow of Dickinson and Emerson." *NEQ* 45 (June 1972): 278–80.
Davidson, Edward H. *Poe: A Critical Study*. Cambridge: Harvard Univ. Press, 1957.
Davidson, Frank. "Emerson and the Double Consciousness." *EarlR* 3 (April 1960): 1–15.
———. "Melville, Thoreau, and 'The Apple-Tree Table.' " *AL* 25 (Jan. 1954): 479–88.
———. " 'This Consciousness': Emerson and Dickinson." *ESQ* no. 44 (3 Qtr. 1966): 2–7.
———. "Thoreau's Contribution to Hawthorne's *Mosses*." *NEQ* 20 (Dec. 1947): 535–42.
Davidson, John Morrison. *Eminent English Liberals in and out of Parliament*. Boston: James R. Osgood, 1880.
Davies, Barrie. "Sam Quixote in Lower Canada: A Reading of Thoreau's *A Yankee in Canada*." *HAB* 20 (Fall 1969): 67–77.

Davies, James W. "The Vision of Evil: An Enquiry into the Dialogue between Emerson, Melville, and Hawthorne and the Nineteenth Century." Diss. Union Theological Seminary 1958.

Davis, Ada E. "Emerson's Thought on Education." *Education* 45 (Feb. 1925): 253–72.

Davis, Andrew McFarland. "Thomas Wentworth Higginson." *PAAAS* 47 (1912): 1–15.

Davis, Joe Lee. "Santayana as a Critic of Emerson." In *Transcendentalism and Its Legacy*, ed. Myron Simon and Thornton H. Parsons, 150–84.

Davis, Merrell R. "Emerson's 'Reason' and the Scottish Philosophers." *NEQ* 17 (June 1944): 209–28.

Davis, Richard Beale. "Moncure D. Conway Looks at Edgar Poe—Through Dr. Griswold." *MissQ* 18 (Wtr. 1964–65): 12–18.

————. "Moncure Daniel Conway: Radical Southern Intellectual." *Interpretations* 9 (1977): 1–6.

Davis, William Augustus. *Biographical Notice of Charles Stearns Wheeler*. Boston: James Munroe, 1843. Rpt. in C. C. Felton, "Notices of Mr. Wheeler," 232–44.

Dawson, W. J. "Emerson." In his *The Makers of Modern Prose*. New York: T. Whittaker, 1899, 208–22.

Deamer, Robert C. *The Westering Experience in American Literature*. Bellingham: Western Washington Univ. Press, 1977.

"The Death of Dr. Francis." *ChReg* 42 (11 April 1863): 10.

Dedmond, Francis B. "Channing's Unfinished Autobiographical Novel." *ESQ* 24 (1 Qtr. 1978): 42–55.

————. "A Checklist of Manuscripts Relating to Thoreau in the Huntington Library, the Houghton Library of Harvard University, and the Berg Collection of the New York Public Library." *TSB* no. 43 (Spr. 1953): 3–4.

————. "Economic Protest in Thoreau's Journal." *SN* 26 (1954): 65–76.

————. "Ellery Channing's 'Major Leviticus: His Three Days in Town': An Unpublished Satire." *SAR* 1979: 409–56.

————. "Emerson and the Concord Libraries." *BPLQ* 2 (Oct. 1951): 318–19.

————. "A Further Note on Emerson's Interest in Concord Libraries." *N&Q* 197 (Aug. 1952): 367–68.

————. *Sylvester Judd*. Boston: Twayne, 1980.

Deevey, Edward S., Jr. "A Re-Examination of Thoreau's *Walden*." *QRB* 17 (March 1942): 1–11.

DeFalco, Joseph. "From 'Civil Disobedience' to 'A Plea for Captain John Brown.' " *Topic* 6 (Fall 1966): 43–49.

————. " 'The Landlord': Thoreau's Emblematic Technique." *ESQ* no. 56 (3 Qtr. 1969): 23–32.

Deiss, Joseph Jay. *The Roman Years of Margaret Fuller*. New York: Crowell, 1969.

Delano, Sterling F. "The *Harbinger*: A Portrait of Associationism in America." Diss. Southern Illinois Univ. 1973.

————. "A Rediscovered Transcendental Poem by Frederic Hedge." *ATQ* no. 29 (Wtr. 1976): 35–36.

————, and Rita Colanzi. "An Index to Volume VIII of the *Harbinger*." *RALS* 10 (Aut. 1980): 173–86.

Delbanco, Andrew. *William Ellery Channing: An Essay on the Liberal Spirit in America*. Cambridge: Harvard Univ. Press, 1981.

Delizia, Michael. "Dr. Nabokov and Mr. Thoreau." *TSB* no. 142 (Wtr. 1977): 1–2.

De Majo, Maria Teresa. "La fortuna di Ralph Waldo Emerson in Italia (1847–1963)." *SA* 12 (1966): 45–87.

"The Democratic Review and O. A. Brownson." *Present* 1 (15 Oct. 1843): 72.

DeMott, Robert J. " 'The Eccentric Orbit': Dimensions of the Aesthetic Process in Henry David Thoreau's Major Writings." Diss. Kent State Univ. 1969.

Dennis, Carl. "Correspondence in Thoreau's Nature Poetry." *ESQ* no. 58 (1 Qtr. 1970): 101–09.

———. "Emerson's Poetics of Inspiration." *ATQ* no. 25 (Wtr. 1975): 22–28.

———. "Emerson's Poetry of Mind and Matter." *ESQ* no. 58 (1 Qtr. 1970): 139–53.

Derby, J. C. *Fifty Years among Authors, Books and Publishers.* Hartford, Conn.: M. A. Winter, 1885.

Detti, Emma. *Margaret Fuller Ossoli e i suoi corrispondenti.* Firenze: Felice Le Monnier, 1942.

Detweiler, Robert. "Emerson and Zen." *AQ* 14 (Fall 1972): 422–38.

———. "The Over-Rated 'Over-Soul.' " *AL* 36 (March 1964): 65–68.

Devlin, James E. "A Transcendental Cranch Poem Rebuking Dana." *ESQ* no. 22 (1 Qtr. 1961): 35–38.

DeVries, F. C. "The Influence of Parker on European Thought." *PUHS* 13.1 (1960): 84–86.

Dewey, Amy E., ed. *Autobiography and Letters of Orville Dewey.* Boston: Roberts, 1884.

Dewey, John. "James Marsh and American Philosophy." *JHI* 2 (April 1941): 131–50.

———. "The Philosopher of Democracy." *IJE* 13 (July 1903): 405–13. Rpt. in his *Characters and Events.* 2 vols. New York: Henry Holt, 1929, 1: 69–77.

Dickens, Charles. *American Notes for General Circulation.* 2 vols. London: Chapman and Hall, 1842.

Dickinson, Emily. *The Letters of Emily Dickinson.* Ed. Thomas H. Johnson with Theodora Ward. 3 vols. Cambridge: Harvard Univ. Press, 1958.

———. *The Poems of Emily Dicksinon.* Ed. Thomas H. Johnson. 3 vols. Cambridge: Harvard Univ. Press, 1955.

Diehl, Carl. *Americans and German Scholarship 1770-1870.* New Haven: Yale Univ. Press, 1978.

Diehl, Joanne Feit. "Emerson, Dickinson, and the Abyss." *ELH* 44 (Wtr. 1977): 683–700.

Diggins, John P. "Thoreau, Marx, and the 'Riddle' of Alienation." *SoRes* 39 (Wtr. 1972): 571–98.

Dillman, Richard H. "Resources for the Study of Transcendental Rhetoric: Emerson and Thoreau." *RSQ* 8 (Fall 1978): 165–75.

———. "Thoreau's Human Economy: A Reflection of Jean-Baptiste Say's Economic Philosophy." *ESQ* 25 (1 Qtr. 1979): 20–25.

———. "Thoreau's Psychological Rhetoric." Diss. Univ. of Oregon 1978.

Dillon, Patrick. "The Non-Sequaciousness of Ralph Waldo Emerson." *IM* 28 (July 1900): 415–21.

Dinwiddie, Shirley W., and Richard L. Herrnstadt. "Amos Bronson Alcott: A Bibliography." *BB* 21 (Jan.–Apr., May–Aug. 1954): 64–67, 92–96.

Dirks, John Edward. *The Critical Theology of Theodore Parker.* New York: Columbia Univ. Press, 1948.

"A Disciple." "Emerson's Essays." *USMDR* 16 (June 1845): 589–602.

Dobson, Eleanore Robinette. "John Sullivan Dwight." In *DAB*, 5: 567–68.

Doherty, Joseph F. "Emerson and the Loneliness of the Gods." *TSLL* 16 (Spr. 1974): 65–75.

Domina, Lyle. "Thoreau and Frost: The Search for Reality." *BSUF* 19 (Aut. 1978): 67–72.

Donadio, Stephen. "Emerson, Christian Identity, and the Dissolution of the Social Order." In *Art, Politics, and Will.* Ed. Quentin Anderson et al. New York: Basic Books, 1977, 99–123.

Donoghue, Lorraine. "The Musical Criticisms of John Sullivan Dwight in the *Harbinger* 1845-1849." M.A. thesis Univ. of Washington 1946.

Dorn, Minda Ruth. "Literary Criticism in the *Boston Quarterly Review*, the *Present*, and the *Massachusetts Quarterly Review*." Diss. Southern Illinois Univ. 1975.

Doten, Lizzie. *A Review of a Lecture by Jas. Freeman Clarke on the Philosophy of Ralph Waldo Emerson.* Boston: William White, 1865.

Doubleday, Neal F. "Channing on the Nature of Man." *JR* 23 (Oct. 1943): 245–57.

Doudna, Martin. "Echoes of Milton, Donne, and Carlyle in 'Civil Disobedience.'" *TJQ* 12.3 (July 1980): 5–7.

Douglas, Ann. *The Feminization of American Culture*. New York: Knopf, 1977.

———. "Margaret Fuller and the Disavowal of Fiction." In her *The Feminization of American Culture*, 259–88, 381–85.

Dowden, Edward. "The Transcendentalist Movement and Literature." *ContempR* 30 (July 1877): 297–318. Rpt. in his *Studies in Literature, 1799-1877*. London: Kegan Paul, Trench, Trübner, 1909, 44–84.

Downs, Lenthiel H. "Emerson and Dr. Channing: Two Men from Boston." *NEQ* 20 (Dec. 1947): 516–34.

Drake, William. "The Depth of *Walden*: Thoreau's Symbolism of the Divine in Nature." Diss. Univ. of Arizona 1967.

Dressman, Michael. "Another Whitman Debt to Emerson." *N&Q* 26 (Aug. 1979): 305–06.

Drinnon, Richard. "Thoreau's Politics of the Upright Man." *MR* 4 (Aut. 1962): 126–38. Rpt. in *Thoreau in Our Season*, ed. John Hicks, 154–68.

Duban, James. "The Spenserian Maze of Melville's *Pierre*." *ESQ* 23 (4 Qtr. 1977): 217–25.

Duberman, Martin. *James Russell Lowell*. Boston: Houghton Mifflin, 1966.

Duchac, Joseph. *The Poems of Emily Dickinson: An Annotated Guide to Commentary Published in English, 1890-1977*. Boston: G. K. Hall, 1979.

Duffey, Bernard. *Poetry in America*. Durham: Duke Univ. Press, 1968.

Duffy, John J. "Problems in Publishing Coleridge: James Marsh's First American Edition of *Aids to Reflection*." *NEQ* 43 (June 1970): 193–208.

———. "Transcendental Letters from George Ripley to James Marsh." *ESQ* no. 50, suppl. (1 Qtr. 1968): 210–24.

———, ed. *Coleridge's American Disciples: The Selected Correspondence of James Marsh*. Amherst: Univ. of Massachusetts Press, 1973.

Duncan, Graham H. "James Russell Lowell's Reviews of American Belles-Lettres: An Annotated Anthology." Diss. Cornell 1953.

Duncan, Jeffrey L. *The Power and Form of Emerson's Thought*. Charlottesville: Univ. Press of Virginia, 1973.

———. "Words and the Word in Emerson." *BMMLA* 9 (Spr.–Fall 1976): 25–31.

Dunn, Esther Cloudman. *Shakespeare in America*. 3 vols. New York: Macmillan, 1939.

Dunton, Edith Kellogg. "An Old and New Estimate of Thoreau." *Dial* [Chicago] 33 (16 Dec. 1902): 464–66.

Dupree, Robert. "From Analogy to Metaphor to Wordplay: Thoreau's Shifting View of the Relationship between Man and Nature." Diss. Auburn Univ. 1975.

Durick, Jeremiah K. "The Incorporate Silence and the Heart Divine." In *American Classics Reconsidered: A Christian Appraisal*. Ed. Harold C. Gardiner. New York: Scribners, 1958, 179–92.

Durning, Russell E. *Margaret Fuller, Citizen of the World. An Intermediary between European and American Literatures*. Heidelberg: Carl Winter, 1969.

———. "Margaret Fuller's Translation of Goethe's 'Prometheus.'" *JA* 12 (1967): 240–45.

Durocher, Aurele P. "The Story of Fruitlands: Transcendental Wild Oats." *MichA* 1 (Spr. 1969): 37–45.

Dutton, Frederic J. "Emerson's Optimism." *UnitR* 35 (Feb. 1891): 127–37.

Duyckinck, Evert A., and George L. Duyckinck. *Cyclopædia of American Literature*. 2 vols. New York: Charles Scribner, 1855.

Dwight, B. W. *The History of the Descendants of John Dwight, of Dedham, Mass.* 2 vols. New York: The Author, 1874.

Dwight, John Sullivan. "Music." In *Aesthetic Papers*, ed. Elizabeth Palmer Peabody, 25–36. Rpt. in *The Transcendentalists: An Anthology*, ed. Perry Miller, 410–14.

———. "The Religion of Beauty." *Dial* 1 (July 1840): 17–22. Rpt. in *Selected Writings of the American Transcendentalists*, ed. George Hochfield, 304–07.

———. Review of Christopher Pearse Cranch, *Poems. Harbinger* 1 (26 July 1845): 105–07.

———. Review of Ralph Waldo Emerson, *Poems. Harbinger* 4 (23, 30 Jan. 1847): 91–94, 106–90.

Dwight, Marianne. *Letters from Brook Farm 1844-1847.* Ed. Amy L. Reed. Poughkeepsie, N.Y.: Vassar Coll., 1928.

Eakin, Paul John. "Margaret Fuller, Hawthorne, and Sexual Politics." *SAQ* 75 (Sum. 1976): 323–38. Incorporated into his *The New England Girl: Cultural Ideals in Hawthorne, Stowe, Howells, and James*. Athens: Univ. of Georgia Press, 1976.

Early, James. *Romanticism and American Architecture.* New York: A. S. Barnes, 1965.

Easton, Loyd D. "German Philosophy in Nineteenth Century Cincinnati—Stallo, Conway, Nast and Willich." *BHPSO* 20 (Jan. 1962): 15–28.

———. "Hegelianism in Nineteenth-Century Ohio." *JHI* 23 (July–Sept. 1962): 355–78.

———. *Hegel's First American Followers: The Ohio Hegelians.* Athens: Ohio Univ. Press, 1966.

———. "Religious Naturalism and Reform in the Thought of Moncure Conway." In his *Hegel's First American Followers*, 123–58, 340–43.

Ebbitt, Wilma Robb. "The Critical Essays of Margaret Fuller from the New York *Tribune*." Diss. Brown 1943.

———. "Margaret Fuller's Ideas on Criticism." *BPLQ* 3 (July 1951): 171–87.

Eckstorm, Fanny Hardy. "Thoreau's *Maine Woods*." *Atl* 102 (July, Aug. 1908): 16–18, 242–50.

Edel, Leon. *Henry D. Thoreau.* Minneapolis: Univ. of Minnesota Press, 1970.

———. *Henry James: The Untried Years.* Philadelphia: Lippincott, 1953.

———. "*Walden*: The Myth and the Mystery." *ASch* 44 (Spr. 1975): 272–81.

Edelstein, Tilden G. *Strange Enthusiasm: A Life of Thomas Wentworth Higginson.* New Haven: Yale Univ. Press, 1968.

———. "Thomas Wentworth Higginson: The Ante-Bellum Years." *PCHS* 36 (1959): 73–89.

Edgell, David Palmer. "Bronson Alcott's 'Autobiographical Index.'" *NEQ* 14 (Dec. 1941): 704–15.

———. "Bronson Alcott's 'Gentility.'" *NEQ* 13 (Dec. 1940): 699–705.

———. "Charles Lane at Fruitlands." *NEQ* 33 (Sept. 1960): 374–77.

———. "The New Eden: A Study of Bronson Alcott's Fruitlands." M.A. thesis Wesleyan Univ. 1938.

———. "A Note on Channing's Transcendentalism." *NEQ* 22 (Sept. 1949): 394–97.

———. *William Ellery Channing: An Intellectual Portrait.* Boston: Beacon, 1955.

Edrich, Mary Worden. "The Channing Rhetoric and 'Splendid Confusion.'" *ESQ* no. 57 (4 Qtr. 1969): 5–12. Rpt. in *The Minor and Later Transcendentalists*, ed. Edwin Gittleman, 5–12.

———. "The Rhetoric of Apostasy." *TSLL* 8 (Wtr. 1967): 547–60.

Edwards, Jonathan. *Images or Shadows of Divine Things.* Ed. Perry Miller. New Haven: Yale Univ. Press, 1948.

Eells, James. "Theodore Parker and the Naturalization of Religion." In *Pioneers of Religious Liberty in Amerca.* Boston: American Unitarian Assn., 1903, 341–66.

Ehrlich, Heyward Bruce. "A Study of the Literary Activity in New York City during the 1840-Decade." Diss. New York Univ. 1963.

Eidson, John Olin. "Charles Stearns Wheeler: Emerson's 'Good Grecian.'" NEQ 27 (Dec. 1954): 472–83.

———. Charles Stearns Wheeler: Friend of Emerson. Athens: Univ. of Georgia Press, 1951.

———. Tennyson in America: His Reputation and Influence from 1827 to 1858. Athens: Univ. of Georgia Press, 1943.

Eiseley, Loren. The Unexpected Universe. New York: Harcourt, Brace, and World, 1964.

Eisenlohr, Herman L. "The Development of Thoreau's Prose." Diss. Univ. of Pennsylvania 1966.

Eisinger, Chester E. "Transcendentalism." In The American Renaissance. Ed. George Hendrick. Berlin: Moritz Diesterweg, 1961, 22–38.

Ekhtian, Mansur. Emerson and Persia: Emerson's Developing Interest in Persian Mysticism. Tehran: Tehran Univ. Press, 1976.

Ekirch, Arthur Alphonse. The Idea of Progress in America, 1815-1860. New York: Columbia Univ. Press, 1944.

Elder, Marjorie J. Nathaniel Hawthorne: Transcendental Symbolist. Athens: Ohio Univ. Press, 1969.

Eleanor, Sister Mary. "Hedge's Prose Writers of Germany as a Source of Whitman's Knowledge of German Philosophy." MLN 61 (June 1946): 381–88.

Eliot, Charlotte C. Walter Greenleaf Eliot. Boston: Houghton, Mifflin, 1904.

Eliot, Samuel A. "Cyrus Augustus Bartol." In DAB, 2: 17.

———, ed. Heralds of A Liberal Faith. 3 vols. Boston: American Unitarian Assn., 1910.

[Elizabeth Palmer Peabody number]. KindN 4 (Feb. 1894).

[Elizabeth Palmer Peabody number]. KindR 14 (May 1904).

Elkins, Stanley. Slavery. 3rd ed. Chicago: Univ. of Chicago Press, 1976.

Elliott, Fannie Mae, and Lucy Clark. Charles Timothy Brooks: A Checklist of Printed and Manuscript Works of Charles Timothy Brooks in the Library of the University of Virginia. Charlottesville: Univ. of Virginia Press, 1960.

Elliott, G. R. "Emerson as Diarist." UTQ 6 (April 1937): 299–308.

Elliott, Maud Howe. Three Generations. Boston: Little, Brown, 1923.

———. Uncle Sam Ward and His Circle. New York: Macmillan, 1938.

Elliott, Walter. The Life of Father Hecker. New York: Columbus Press, 1891.

Ellis, Arthur B. Memoir of Rufus Ellis. Boston: William B. Clarke, 1891.

Ellis, Charles Mayo. An Essay on Transcendentalism. Boston: Crocker and Ruggles, 1842.

Ellis, George E. "Parker at Cambridge." ChReg 71 (7 Jan. 1892): 4.

Els, Rüdiger. Ralph Waldo Emerson und "Die Natur" in Goethes Werken. Frankfurt: Peter Lang, 1977.

Emanuel, James A. "Emersonian Virtue: A Definition." AS 36 (May 1961): 117–32.

"Emerson." PoSM 54 (Feb. 1899): 558–59.

[Emerson as Lecturer]. BoP, 25 Jan. 1849, 2.

Emerson, Edward Waldo. The Early Years of the Saturday Club 1855-1870. Boston: Houghton Mifflin, 1918.

———. Emerson in Concord: A Memoir. Boston: Houghton, Mifflin, 1889.

———. "Frederick [sic] Henry Hedge." In his The Early Years of the Saturday Club, 277–81.

———. Henry Thoreau as Remembered by a Young Friend. Boston: Houghton Mifflin, 1917.

———. "Samuel Gray Ward." In his The Early Years of the Saturday Club, 109–16.

Emerson, Ellen Louisa Tucker. One First Love: Letters of Ellen Louisa Tucker to Ralph Waldo Emerson. Ed. Edith W. Gregg. Cambridge: Harvard Univ. Press, 1962.

Emerson, Ellen Tucker. *The Letters of Ellen Tucker Emerson*. Ed. Edith E. W. Gregg. 2 vols. Kent, Ohio: Kent State Univ. Press, 1982.

———. *The Life of Lidian Jackson Emerson*. Ed. Delores Bird Carpenter. Boston: Twayne, 1981.

Emerson, George B. *Reminiscences of an Old Teacher*. Boston: Alfred Mudge, 1878.

"The Emerson Mania." *EngRevL* 12 (Sept. 1849): 139–52.

Emerson, Ralph Waldo. "Amos Bronson Alcott." *The New American Cyclopædia*, ed. George Ripley and Charles A. Dana, 1: 301–02. Rpt. in Kenneth Walter Cameron, "Emerson on Bronson Alcott, Conversationalist." *ESQ* no. 18 (1 Qtr. 1960): 50.

———. *The Collected Works of Ralph Waldo Emerson*. Ed. Alfred R. Ferguson et al. 2 vols. to date. Cambridge: Harvard Univ. Press, 1971–

———. *The Complete Works of Ralph Waldo Emerson* [Centenary Edition]. Ed. Edward Waldo Emerson. 12 vols. Boston: Houghton, Mifflin, 1903–04.

———. *The Early Lectures of Ralph Waldo Emerson*. Ed. Robert E. Spiller, Stephen E. Whicher, and Wallace E. Williams. 3 vols. Cambridge: Harvard Univ. Press, 1959–72.

———. *Emerson in His Journals*. Ed. Joel Porte. Cambridge: Harvard Univ. Press, 1982.

———. *Emerson on Education*. Ed. Howard Mumford Jones. New York: Teachers Coll. Press, 1966.

———. *Emerson's Literary Criticism*. Ed. Eric W. Carlson. Lincoln: Univ. of Nebraska Press, 1979.

———. "English Reformers." *Dial* 3 (Oct. 1842): 227–47.

———. *Essais de philosophie américain*. Ed. Émile Montégut. Paris: Charpentier, 1851.

———. "Historic Notes of Life and Letters in Massachusetts." *Atl* 52 (Oct. 1883): 529–43. Rpt. as "Historic Notes of Life and Letters in New England" in his *Lectures and Biographical Sketches*. Boston: Houghton, Mifflin, 1884, 307–47.

———. *Indian Superstition*. Ed. Kenneth Walter Cameron. Hanover, N.H.: Friends of the Dartmouth Library, 1954.

———. *The Journals and Miscellaneous Notebooks of Ralph Waldo Emerson*. Ed. William H. Gilman, Ralph H. Orth, et al. 16 vols. Cambridge: Harvard Univ. Press, 1960–82.

———. *Journals of Ralph Waldo Emerson*. Ed. Edward Waldo Emerson and Waldo Emerson Forbes. 10 vols. Boston: Houghton Mifflin, 1909–14.

———. "Leaves of Grass." *NYDT*, 10 Oct. 1855, 7. Rpt. in Walt Whitman, *Leaves of Grass*. Brooklyn, N.Y.: n.p., 1856, 345–46.

———. *Letters from Ralph Waldo Emerson to a Friend*. Ed. Charles Eliot Norton. Boston: Houghton, Mifflin, 1899.

———. *The Letters of Ralph Waldo Emerson*. Ed. Ralph L. Rusk. 6 vols. New York: Columbia Univ. Press, 1939.

———. "Mr. Channing's Poems." *USMDR* 13 (Sept. 1843): 309–14.

———. *Nature*. Ed. Warner Berthoff. San Francisco: Chandler, 1968.

———. *Nature*. Ed. Kenneth Walter Cameron. New York: Scholars' Facsimiles & Reprints, 1940.

———. "New Poetry." *Dial* 1 (Oct. 1840): 220–32.

———. "Ode, Inscribed to W. H. Channing." In his *Poems*. Boston: James Munroe, 1847, 117–22.

———. "Preface." In William Ellery Channing, *The Wanderer. A Colloquial Poem*. Boston: James R. Osgood, 1871, v–viii.

———. Review of Jones Very, *Essays and Poems*. *Dial* 2 (July 1841): 130–31.

———. *Selected Writings of Ralph Waldo Emerson*. Ed. William H. Gilman. New York: New American Library, 1965.

———. *Selections from Ralph Waldo Emerson*. Ed. Stephen E. Whicher. Boston: Houghton Mifflin, 1957.

————. "Thoreau." *Atl* 10 (Aug. 1862): 239–49.

————. "To Lowell, on His Fortieth Birthday." *CM* 47 (Nov. 1893): 3–4.

————. "The Transcendentalist." In his *Nature; Addresses, and Lectures*. Boston: James Munroe, 1849, 319–48.

————. *Two Unpublished Essays*. Ed. Edward Everett Hale. Boston: Lamson, Wolffe, 1896.

————. *Uncollected Lectures*. Ed. Clarence Gohdes. New York: William Edwin Rudge, 1932.

————. *Uncollected Writings*. Ed. Charles C. Bigelow. New York: Lamb, 1912.

————. "Worship." In his *The Conduct of Life*. Boston: Ticknor and Fields, 1860, 175–211.

————. *Young Emerson Speaks*. Ed. Arthur Cushman McGiffert, Jr. Boston: Houghton Mifflin, 1938.

————, and Thomas Carlyle. *The Correspondence of Emerson and Carlyle*. Ed. Joseph Slater. New York: Columbia Univ. Press, 1964.

————, William Henry Channing, and James Freeman Clarke. *Memoirs of Margaret Fuller Ossoli*. 2 vols. Boston: Phillips, Sampson, 1852.

————, and Arthur Hugh Clough. *Emerson-Clough Letters*. Ed. Howard F. Lowry and Ralph Leslie Rusk. Cleveland: Rowfant Club, 1934.

————, and William Henry Furness. *Records of a Lifelong Friendship*. Ed. Horace Howard Furness. Boston: Houghton Mifflin, 1910.

————, and Herman Grimm. *Correspondence between Ralph Waldo Emerson and Herman Grimm*. Ed. Frederick William Holls. Boston: Houghton, Mifflin, 1903.

————, and John Sterling. *A Correspondence between John Sterling and Ralph Waldo Emerson*. Ed. Edward Waldo Emerson. Boston: Houghton, Mifflin, 1897.

Emerson, William. *Diary and Letters of William Emerson 1743-1776*. Ed. Amelia Forbes Emerson. Boston: Thomas Todd, 1972.

"Emerson's Addresses." *LWNY* 5 (3 Nov. 1849): 374–76.

"Emerson's Essays." *TUM* 13 (8 May 1841): 182.

"Emerson's Queer Movements in Literature." *NYHer*, 24 Mar. 1850, 2.

"Emerson's Social Philosophy." *ScR* 2 (Sept. 1883): 222–34.

Emery, Allan Moore. "The Cocks of Melville's 'Cock-A-Doodle-Doo!'" *ESQ* 28 (2 Qtr. 1982): 89–111.

Engel, Mary Miller. *I Remember the Emersons*. Los Angeles: Times-Mirror, 1941.

Englekirk, John E. "Notes on Emerson in Latin America." *PMLA* 74 (June 1961): 227–32.

d'Entremont, John. *Moncure Conway, 1832-1907: American Abolitionist, Spiritual Architect of "South Place," Author of* The Life of Thomas Paine. London: South Place Ethical Soc., 1977.

————. "Moncure Conway: The American Years." Diss. Johns Hopkins 1981.

Eppard, Philip B., and Alan Seaburg. "American Literary Manuscripts in the Andover-Harvard Theological Library: A Checklist." *RALS* 10 (Aut. 1980): 146–53.

Erlich, Michael. "Thoreau's 'Civil Disobedience': Strategy for Reform." *ConnR* 7 (Oct. 1973): 100–10.

Eulau, Heinz. "Wayside Challenger—Some Remarks on the Politics of Henry David Thoreau." *AR* 9 (Wtr. 1949): 509–22.

Eulert, Donald D. "Matter and Method: Emerson and the Way of Zen." *EWR* 3 (Wtr. 1966): 48–65.

Evans, Charles M. "The Political Theory of Henry David Thoreau: An Exposition and Criticism." Diss. Univ. of Oklahoma 1973.

Evans, Francis E. B. "The Genuine Word, the Unfolding Sentence: Thoreau's Paths to Truths." Diss. Purdue 1976.

Evans, Robert O. "Thoreau's Poetry and Prose Works." *ESQ* no. 56 (Aut. 1969): 40–52.

Everett, C. C. "The Poems of Emerson." *AndR* 7 (March 1887): 229–48. Rpt. in his *Essays Theological and Literary*. Boston: Houghton, Mifflin, 1901, 219–47.

Everson, Ida Gertrude. *George Henry Calvert: American Literary Pioneer*. New York: Columbia Univ. Press, 1944.

Fabian, Bernhard. "The Channing Revival: Remarks on Recent Publications." *JA* 2 (1957): 197–212.

Fairbanks, Henry G. "Theocracy to Transcendentalism in America." *ESQ* no. 44 (3 Qtr. 1966): 45–58.

Fairbanks, Jonathan. "Thoreau: Speaker for Wildness." *SAQ* 70 (Aut. 1971): 487–506.

"Famous People at Home. VIII. Franklin Benjamin Sanborn." *TH* 5 (10 April 1897): 5–6.

Faust, C. H. "The Background of the Unitarian Opposition to Transcendentalism." *MP* 35 (Feb. 1938): 297–324.

Feidelson, Charles, Jr. *Symbolism and American Literature*. Chicago: Univ. of Chicago Press, 1953.

Fellman, Michael. "Theodore Parker and the Abolitionist Role in the 1850's." *JAH* 61 (Dec. 1974): 666–84.

Feltenstein, Rosalie. "Mary Moody Emerson: The Gadfly of Concord." *AQ* 5 (Fall 1953): 231–46.

Felton, C. C. "Emerson's *Essays*." *ChEx* 30 (May 1841): 253–62.

———. "Notices of Mr. Wheeler." *ChEx* 35 (Nov. 1843): 232–44.

Fenn, William W. "Theodore Parker." In *Heralds of a Liberal Faith*, ed. Samuel A. Eliot, 3: 278–87.

Fergenson, Laraine R. "Thoreau, Daniel Berrigan, and the Problem of Transcendental Politics." *Soundings* 65 (Spr. 1982): 103–22.

———. "Was Thoreau Re-Reading Wordsworth in 1851?" *TJQ* 5.3 (July 1973): 20–23.

———. "Wordsworth and Thoreau: A Study of the Relationship between Man and Nature." Diss. Columbia 1973.

Ferguson, Alfred R. "Sill's Poems Wrongly Ascribed to Sanborn." *ESQ* no. 43 (1 Qtr. 1970): 131.

Ferguson, John De Lancey. *American Literature in Spain*. New York: Columbia Univ. Press, 1916.

Fertig, Walter L. "John Sullivan Dwight's Pre-Publication Notice of *Walden*." *NEQ* 30 (March 1957): 84–90.

———. "John Sullivan Dwight: Transcendentalist and Literary Amateur of Music." Diss. Univ. of Maryland 1952.

Feuer, Lewis. "James Marsh and the Conservative Transcendental Philosophy: A Political Interpretation." *NEQ* 31 (March 1958): 3–31.

Fiedler, Leslie A. *The Return of the Vanishing American*. New York: Stein and Day, 1968.

Field, Maunsell B. *Memories of Many Men and of Some Women*. New York: Harper's, 1874.

Fields, Annie. *Memories of a Hostess*. Ed. M. A. DeWolfe Howe. Boston: Atlantic Monthly Press, 1922.

———. "Mr. Emerson in the Lecture Room." *Atl* 51 (June 1883): 818–32. Rpt. in her *Authors and Friends*. Boston: Houghton, Mifflin, 1896, 65–106.

Fields, James T. *Biographical Notes and Personal Sketches*. Boston: Houghton, Mifflin, 1882.

———. *Yesterdays with Authors*. Boston: James R. Osgood, 1872.

Filler, Louis. *The Crusade against Slavery 1830-1860*. New York: Harper and Row, 1960.

Fink, Steven. "Variations on the Self: Thoreau's Personae in *A Week on the Concord and Merrimack Rivers*." *ESQ* 28 (1 Qtr. 1982): 24–35.

Finnegan, David F. "The Man Himself: Emerson's Prose Style." *ESQ* no. 39 (2 Qtr. 1965): 13–15.

Firkins, O. W. *Ralph Waldo Emerson*. Boston: Houghton Mifflin, 1915.

Fish, Carl Russell. *The Rise of the Common Man 1830–1850.* New York: Macmillan, 1927.

Fisher, Hersha Sue. "The Education of Elizabeth Palmer Peabody." Diss. Harvard 1980.

Fisher, Marvin. *Going Under: Melville's Short Fiction and the American 1850s.* Baton Rouge: Louisiana State Univ. Press, 1977.

Fitzgerald, Gabrielle. "In Time of War: The Context of Emerson's 'Thoreau.' " *ATQ* no. 41 (Wtr. 1979): 5–12.

Fitzsimmons, M. A. "Brownson's Search for the Kingdom of God: The Social Thought of an American Radical." *RP* 16 (Jan. 1954): 22–36.

Flanagan, John T. "Emerson and Communism." *NEQ* 10 (June 1937): 243–61.

———. "Emerson as a Critic of Fiction." *PQ* 15 (Jan. 1936): 30–45.

Fleck, Richard F. "Evidence for Thoreau's 'Indian' Notebooks as Being a Source for His Journal." *TJQ* 1.4 (Oct. 1969): 17–19.

———. "Hawthorne's Possible Use of Thoreau in *The Marble Faun.*" *TJQ* 6.2 (April 1974): 8–11.

———. "Henry David Thoreau's Interest in Myth, Fable and Legend." Diss. Univ. of New Mexico 1970.

———. "Jones Very—Another White Indian." *CS* 9.3 (Sept. 1974): 6–12.

———. "Thoreau as Mythologist." *RS* 40 (Sept. 1972): 195–206.

Flewelling, R. T. "Emerson and the Middle Border." *Person* 16 (Sept. 1935): 295–309.

Flint, Robert W. "The Boston Book Trade, 1835–1845: A Directory." Library school thesis Simmons Coll. n.d.

Floan, Howard R. *The South in Northern Eyes 1831 to 1861.* Austin: Univ. of Texas Press, 1958.

Flower, Elizabeth, and Murray G. Murphey. *A History of Philosophy in America.* 2 vols. New York: Putnam's, 1977.

Flynn, Kathleen. "The Literary Importance of the *Western Messenger* under the Editorship of James Freeman Clarke and Others." M.A. thesis Wagner Coll. 1969.

Fobes, Charles S. "Robert Bartlett, a Forgotten Transcendentalist." *NEMag* n.s. 23 (Oct. 1900): 211–19.

Foerster, Norman. *American Criticism.* Boston: Houghton Mifflin, 1928.

———. "Emerson as Poet of Nature." *PMLA* 37 (Sept. 1922): 599–614.

———. "Emerson on the Organic Principle in Art." *PMLA* 41 (March 1926): 193–208.

———. "The Intellectual Heritage of Thoreau." *TR* 2 (Jan. 1917): 192–212. Rpt. in *Twentieth Century Interpretations of* Walden, ed. Richard Ruland, 34–49.

———. *Nature in American Literature.* New York: Macmillan, 1923.

———. "Whitman and the Cult of Confusion." *NAR* 213 (June 1921): 799–812.

Fogle, Richard H. "Organic Form in American Criticism: 1840–1870." In *The Development of American Literary Criticism.* Ed. Floyd Stovall. Chapel Hill: Univ. of North Carolina Press, 1955, 75–111.

Fone, Byrne R. S. "A Note on the Very Editions." *AN&Q* 6 (Jan., Feb. 1968): 67–69, 88–89.

Forbes, Waldo Emerson. *The Letters and Journals of Waldo Emerson Forbes.* Ed. Amelia Forbes Thomas. Philadelphia: Dorrance, 1977.

Forclaz, Roger. *Le Monde d'Edgar Poe.* Berne: Herbert Lang, 1974.

Ford, Arthur Lewis, Jr. "The Poetry of Henry David Thoreau." *ESQ* no. 61 (4 Qtr. 1970): 1–26. Rpt. as *The Poetry of Henry David Thoreau.* Hartford, Conn.: Transcendental Books, 1970.

Ford, Nick Aaron. "Henry David Thoreau, Abolitionist." *NEQ* 19 (Sept. 1946): 359–71.

Ford, Thomas W. *Heaven Beguiles the Tired: Death in the Poetry of Emily Dickinson.* University: Univ. of Alabama Press, 1966.

———. "Thoreau's Cosmic Mosquito and Dickinson's Terrestial Fly." *NEQ* 48 (Dec. 1975): 487–504.

Forster, Joseph. "Ralph Waldo Emerson." In his *Four Great Teachers*. London: George Allen, 1890, 71–102. Rpt. in his *Great Teachers*. London: George Redway, 1898, 266–305.

Foster, Charles H. "Elizabeth Palmer Peabody." In *Notable American Women*. Ed. Edward T. James et al. 3 vols. Cambridge: Harvard Univ. Press, 3: 31–34.

Foster, Charles Howell. "Emerson as American Scripture." *NEQ* 16 (March 1943): 91–105.

———. *Emerson's Theory of Poetry*. Iowa City, Iowa: Midland House, 1939.

Foster, Edward Halsey. *The Civilized Wilderness: Backgrounds to American Romantic Literature*. New York: Macmillan, 1975.

Foster, Elizabeth S. "Herman Melville's *The Confidence-Man*: Its Origins and Meaning." Diss. Yale 1942.

Francis, Convers. *An Historical Sketch of Watertown*. Cambridge, Mass.: E. W. Metcalf, 1830.

Francis, Elamanamadathil V. *Emerson and Hindu Scriptures*. Cochin, India: Academic Publications, 1972.

Francis, Richard. "Circumstances and Salvation: The Ideology of the Fruitlands Utopia." *AQ* 25 (May 1973): 202–34.

———. "The Ideology of Brook Farm." *SAR* 1977: 1–48.

Francis, Richard Lee. "Archangel in the Pleached Garden: Emerson's Poetry." *ELH* 33 (Dec. 1966): 461–72.

———. "The Architectonics of Emerson's *Nature*." *AQ* 19 (Spr. 1967): 39–52.

———. "Charles King Newcomb: Transcendental Hamlet." *ESQ* no. 57 (4 Qtr. 1969): 46–52. Rpt. in *The Minor and Later Transcendentalists*, ed. Edwin Gittleman, 46–52.

———. " 'Morn at Mid Noon': The Emerging Emersonian Method." *PCP* 15.2 (Dec. 1980): 1–8.

———. "The Poet and Experience: *Essays: Second Series*." In *Emerson Centenary Essays*, ed. Joel Myerson, 93–106.

Francke, Kuno. "Emerson and German Personality." *IntQ* 8 (Sept.–Dec. 1903): 93–107. Rpt. in his *German Ideals of Today*. Boston: Houghton Mifflin, 1907, 93–126.

"Franklin Benjamin Sanborn." *GrM* 19 (Nov. 1895): 389–91.

"Frederic Henry Hedge: Unitarian Theologian of the Broad Church." *UUC* 36 (Spr.–Sum. 1981): 1–78.

Frederick, John T. "American Literary Nationalism: The Process of Definition, 1825–1850." *RP* 21 (Jan. 1959): 224–38.

Fredrickson, George M. *The Inner Civil War*. New York: Harper's, 1965.

Free Religious Association. *Freedom and Fellowship in Religion*. Boston: Roberts, 1875.

———. *Proceedings of the Forty-third Annual Meeting Held in Boston Mass., Thursday and Friday, May 26 and 27, 1910*. Boston: Free Religious Assn., 1910.

———. *Prophets of Liberalism*. Boston: James West, 1900.

Freeman, John. *Herman Melville*. London: Macmillan, 1926.

Freidel, Frank, ed. *Harvard Guide to American History*. Rev. ed. 2 vols. Cambridge: Harvard Univ. Press, 1974.

French, Allen. *Old Concord*. Boston: Little, Brown, 1915.

Freniere, Emile A. "Emerson and Parker." *ESQ* no. 22 (1 Qtr. 1961): 46–48.

Friden, Georg. "Transcendental Idealism in New England." *NM* 69 (June 1968): 256–71.

Fromm, Harold. "Emerson and Kierkegaard: The Problem of Historical Christianity." *MR* 9 (Aut. 1968): 741–52.

Frothingham, Octavius Brooks. *Boston Unitarianism 1820-1850: A Study of the Life and Work of Nathaniel Langdon Frothingham*. New York: Putnam's, 1890.

———. "Drift Period in Theology." *ChEx* 79 (July 1865): 1-27.

———. *Duties and Dreams*. New York: n.p., 1877.

———. *George Ripley*. Boston: Houghton, Mifflin, 1882.

———. "Imagination in Theology." *ChEx* 66 (Jan. 1859): 47-78.

———. "Introduction." In Samuel Johnson, *Oriental Religions and Their Relation to Universal Religion. Persia*, vii–xxix.

———. "John Weiss." *UnitR* 29 (May 1888): 417-29. Incorporated into his *Recollections and Impressions*.

———. "Manuscript Notes of Sunday School Lectures Delivered on the Gospels of Matthew and John, the Book of David, and the Apocalypse (1846-1847)," comp. Eliza David Bradlee. MS. Andover-Harvard Theological School.

———. "Memoir." In David A. Wasson, *Essays: Religious, Social, Political*. Boston: Lee and Shepard, 1889, 1-123.

———. "Memoir of Rev. James Walker, D.D., LL.D." *PMHS* 2nd ser. 6 (May 1891): 443-68.

———. *Memoir of William Henry Channing*. Boston: Houghton, Mifflin, 1886.

———. "Mill's Review of Hamilton." *ChEx* 79 (July 1865): 301-27.

———. *The Ministry of Reconciliation*. Cambridge, Mass.: John Wilson, 1868.

———. "The Philosophy of Conversion." *NAR* 139 (Oct. 1884): 324-34.

———. *Recollections and Impressions 1822-1890*. New York: Putnam's, 1891.

———. "Some Phases of Idealism in New England." *Atl* 52 (July 1883): 13-23.

———. "Theodore Parker." *NAR* 98 (April 1864): 305-42.

———. *Theodore Parker: A Biography*. Boston: James R. Osgood, 1874.

———. *Theodore Parker: A Sermon*. Boston: Walker, Wise, 1860.

———. *Transcendentalism in New England: A History*. New York: Putnam's, 1876.

———. "Why I Am a Free Religionist." *NAR* 145 (July 1887): 8-16.

Frothingham, Paul Revere. "Octavius Brooks Frothingham." In *Heralds of a Liberal Faith*, ed. Samuel A. Eliot, 3: 120-27.

Fryckstedt, Olov M. "Howells and Conway in Venice." *SN* 30 (1958): 165-74.

Frye, Hall. *Literary Reviews and Criticisms*. New York: Putnam's, 1908.

Fuller, Frederick T. "Hawthorne and Margaret Fuller Ossoli." *LW* 16 (10 Jan. 1885): 11-15.

Fuller, Richard Frederick. *Chaplain Fuller: Being a Life Study of a New England Clergyman and Army Chaplain*. Boston: Walker, Wise, 1863.

———. *Recollections of Richard F. Fuller*. Boston: privately printed, 1936.

———. "The Younger Generation in 1840: From the Diary of a New England Boy." *Atl* 136 (Aug. 1925): 216-24.

Fuller, [Sarah] Margaret. "American Literature; Its Position in the Present Time, and Prospects for the Future." In her *Papers on Literature and Art*, 2: 160-65.

———. *Art, Literature, and the Drama*. Boston: Brown, Taggard, and Chase, 1860.

———. *At Home and Abroad*. Ed. Arthur B. Fuller. Boston: Crosby, Nichols, 1856.

———. "Chat in Boston Bookstores.—No. I." *BoQR* 3 (Jan. 1840): 127-34.

———. *Life Without and Life Within*. Ed. Arthur B. Fuller. Boston: Brown, Taggard, and Chase, 1860.

———. *Love-Letters of Margaret Fuller 1845-1846*. New York: D. Appleton, 1903.

———. *Margaret Fuller: American Romantic*. Ed. Perry Miller. Garden City, N.Y.: Doubleday, 1963.

———. *Margaret Fuller: Essays on American Life and Letters*. Ed. Joel Myerson. New Haven: Coll. and Univ. Press, 1978.

————. *Papers on Literature and Art.* 2 vols. New York: Wiley and Putnam, 1846.

————. Review of Sylvester Judd, *Margaret. NYDT,* 1 Sept. 1845, 1.

————. Review of Edgar Allan Poe, *The Raven and Other Poems. NYDT,* 26 Nov. 1845, 1.

————. Review of Edgar Allan Poe, *Tales. NYDT,* 11 July 1845, 1.

————. *Summer on the Lakes, in 1843.* Boston: Charles C. Little and James Brown, 1844.

————. *Woman in the Nineteenth Century.* New York: Greeley and McElrath, 1845. Facs. rpt. with intro. by Madeleine B. Stern and textual note by Joel Myerson, Columbia: Univ. of South Carolina Press, 1980.

————. *Woman in the Nineteenth Century, and Kindred Papers.* Ed. Arthur B. Fuller. Boston: John P. Jewett, 1855.

————. *The Writings of Margaret Fuller.* Ed. Mason Wade. New York: Viking, 1941.

Furness, Clifton J. "Walt Whitman Looks at Boston." *NEQ* 1 (July 1928): 353–70.

Fussell, Edwin. *Frontier: American Literature and the American West.* Princeton: Princeton Univ. Press, 1965.

————. "*Leaves of Grass* and Brownson." *AL* 31 (March 1959): 77–78.

————. "The Meter-Making Argument." In *Aspects of American Poetry.* Ed. Richard M. Ludwig. Columbus: Ohio State Univ. Press, 1962, 3–31. Inc. into his *Lucifer in Harness.* Princeton: Princeton Univ. Press, 1973.

————. "Thoreau in His Time—The First Installment." *RLV* 42.6 (1976): 157–69.

G. "Dr. Channing as a Defender of Christianity." *NEMag* 4 (March 1833): 241.

Gabriel, Ralph Henry. *The Course of American Democratic Thought: An Intellectual History since 1815.* New York: Ronald Press, 1940.

————. "Evangelical Religion and Popular Romanticism in Early Nineteenth-Century America." *ChH* 19 (March 1950): 34–47.

Gafford, Lucile. "Transcendentalist Attitudes toward Drama and the Theatre." *NEQ* 13 (Sept. 1940): 442–66.

Galgan, Gerald J. "The Self and Society in the Thought of Henry David Thoreau." Diss. Fordham 1971.

Gallagher, G. W. *Were Emerson and Longfellow Christians?* New York: James Miller, 1882.

Gallagher, William D., ed. *Selections from the Poetical Literature of the West.* Cincinnati: U. P. James, 1841.

Gallaher, Helen. "Moncure Daniel Conway: Author and Preacher: A Bibliography." Library school thesis Univ. of Wisconsin 1938.

Gallant, Barbara Gans. "The New England Transcendentalists and the European Revolutions of 1848." M.A. thesis Univ. of Florida 1966.

Galligan, Edward L. "The Comedian at Walden Pond." *SAQ* 69 (Wtr. 1970): 20–37.

Gannett, William C. *Ezra Stiles Gannett.* Boston: Roberts, 1875.

Garate, Justo. *Thoreau and the Spanish Language: A Bibliography.* Geneseo, N.Y.: Thoreau Soc., 1970.

Garber, Frederick. *Thoreau's Redemptive Imagination.* New York: New York Univ. Press, 1977.

————. "Unity and Diversity in 'Walking.' " *ESQ* 56 (3 Qtr. 1969): 35–40.

Gardella, Raymond. "The Tenets and Limitations of Emerson's All-Conscious Man." *ABR* 21 (Sept. 1970): 375–88.

Garland, Mary. *A Sketch of the Life of Elizabeth Palmer Peabody.* Boston: Thomas Todd, 1901.

Garlitz, Barbara. "The Immortality Ode: Its Cultural Progeny." *SEL* 6 (Aut. 1966): 639–49.

Garmon, Gerald M. "Emerson's 'Moral Sentiment' and Poe's 'Poetic Sentiment': A Reconsideration." *PoeS* 6 (June 1973): 19–21.

Garnett, Richard. *Life of Ralph Waldo Emerson.* London: Walter Scott, 1885.

————. "Ralph Waldo Emerson." In his *Essays of an Ex-Librarian*. New York: Dodd, Mead, 1901, 303–28.

Garrison, Stephen, and Joel Myerson. "Elizabeth Curson's Letters from Brook Farm." *RALS* 12 (Spr. 1982).

Garrison, Wendell Phillips. "The Isms of Forty Years Ago." *Har* 60 (Jan. 1880): 182–92.

Gates, Michael. "*Walden*: Yantra above Yantras." *ESQ* 22 (1 Qtr. 1976): 14–23.

Gattell, Frank Otto. *John Gorham Palfrey and the New England Conscience*. Cambridge: Harvard Univ. Press, 1963.

Gawronski, Donald Vincent. "Transcendentalism: An Ideological Basis for Manifest Destiny." Diss. St. Louis Univ. 1964.

Gay, Carol McIntyre. "Bronson Alcott and 'His Little Critics': A Study in Reputation." Diss. Kent State Univ. 1972.

Gay, Robert M. *Ralph Waldo Emerson: A Study of the Poet as Seer*. Garden City, N.Y.: Doubleday, Doran, 1928.

Geffen, Elizabeth M. *Philadelphia Unitarianism, 1796–1861*. Philadelphia: Univ. of Pennsylvania Press, 1961.

Geller, L. D. *Between Concord and Plymouth: The Transcendentalists and the Watsons*. Concord, Mass.: Thoreau Lyceum, 1973.

Gelpi, Albert J. *Emily Dickinson: The Mind of the Poet*. Cambridge: Harvard Univ. Press, 1965.

————. Review of William R. Sherwood, *Circumference and Circumstance: Stages in the Mind and Art of Emily Dickinson*. *AL* 40 (Jan. 1969): 557–59.

————. *The Tenth Muse: The Psyche of the American Poet*. Cambridge: Harvard Univ. Press, 1975.

————. "White Light in the Wilderness: Landscape and Self in Nature's Nation." In *American Light*. Ed. John Wilmerding. Washington, D.C.: National Gallery of Art, 1980, 291–311.

Genzmer, George Harvey. "John Weiss." In *DAB*, 19: 615–16.

"George Ripley and the Brook Farm Association." *LLA* 67 (1 Dec. 1860): 571–73.

Gerbaud, Colette. "Jones Very, 1838–1880: Poète mystique de la Nouvelle Angleterre." Diss. Univ. de Paris 1974.

Gerber, John C. "Emerson and the Political Economists." *NEQ* 22 (Sept. 1949): 336–57.

Gerdts, William H., and Theodore E. Stebbins, Jr. *"A Man of Genius": The Art of Washington Allston (1779–1843)*. Boston: Museum of Fine Arts, 1979.

Geselbracht, Raymond H. "Transcendental Renaissance in the Arts: 1890–1920." *NEQ* 48 (Dec. 1975): 463–86.

Gierasch, Walter. "Bishop Hall and Thoreau." *TSB* no. 31 (April 1950): 3.

————. "Thoreau and Willa Cather." *TSB* no. 20 (Sum. 1947): 4.

Gilchrist, Herbert Harlakenden, ed. *Anne Gilchrist: Her Life and Writings*. London: T. Fisher Unwin, 1887.

Gilfillan, George. *Christianity and Our Era*. Edinburgh: James Hogg, 1857.

————. *The History of a Man*. London: Arthur Hall, 1856.

————. "Ralph Waldo Emerson." In his *Gallery of Literary Portraits*. Edinburgh: William Tait, 1845, 288–306.

————. "Ralph Waldo Emerson; or, the 'Coming Man.'" *TEM* 15 (Jan. 1848): 17–23. Rpt. in his *Modern Literature and Literary Men*. Edinburgh: William Tait, 1850, 158–77.

————. Review of the writings of Ralph Waldo Emerson. *CriticE* n.s. 10 (15 July 1851): 326–28. Rpt. as "Emerson" in his *A Third Gallery of Literary Portraits*. New York: Sheldon, Lamport, and Blakeman, 1855, 281–99. Rpt. as "Complete Works of Emerson" in his *Galleries of Literary Portraits*. Edinburgh: James Hogg, 1857, 177–82.

Gilhooley, Leonard. *Contradiction and Dilemma: Orestes Brownson and the American Idea*. New York: Fordham Univ. Press, 1972.

———. "Orestes Augustus Brownson." In *The American Renaissance in New England*, ed. Joel Myerson, 13–20.

———, ed. *No Divided Allegiance: Essays in Brownson's Thought*. New York: Fordham Univ. Press, 1980.

Gilman, Albert, and Roger Brown. "Personality and Style in Concord." In *Transcendentalism and Its Legacy*, ed. Myron Simon and Thornton H. Parsons, 87–122.

Gilman, Owen W., Jr. "John Dos Passos' *Three Soldiers* and *Walden*." *MFS* 26 (Aut. 1980): 470–81.

Gilman, Samuel. "Ralph Waldo Emerson." *SoRose* 7 (24 Nov. 1838): 100–06.

Gilmore, William J. "Orestes Brownson and New England Religious Culture, 1803–1827." Diss. Univ. of Virginia 1971.

Gimlin, Joan S. "Henry Thoreau and the American Indian." Diss. George Washington Univ. 1974.

Girard, William. "Du Transcendentalism consideré essentiellement dans sa definition et ses origines françaises." *UCPMP* 4 (18 Oct. 1916): 351–498.

———. "Du Transcendentalism consideré sous son aspect social." *UCPMP* 8 (6 Aug. 1918): 153–226.

Girgus, Sam B. *The Law of the Heart: Individualism and the Modern Self in American Literature*. Austin: Univ. of Texas Press, 1979.

———. "The Mechanical Mind: Thoreau and McLuhan on Freedom, Technology, and the Media." *TJQ* 9.4 (Oct. 1977): 3–9.

———. "The Scholar as Prophet: Brownson vs. Emerson and the Modern Need for a Moral Humanism." *MQ* 17 (Jan. 1975): 88–99. Rpt. as "Emerson and Brownson: The Scholar, the Self, and Society" in his *The Law of the Heart*, 37–51.

Gittleman, Edwin. *Jones Very: The Effective Years 1833–1840*. Hartford, Conn.: Transcendental Books, 1969.

———, ed. *The Minor and Later Transcendentalists*. Hartford, Conn.: Transcendental Books, 1969.

Glascheim, Eliot. "A Dogged Interpretation of 'Never Bet the Devil Your Head.'" *PoeN* 2 (Oct. 1969): 44–45.

Glick, Wendell. "Bishop Paley in America." *NEQ* 27 (Sept. 1954): 347–54.

———. "'Civil Disobedience': Thoreau's Attack upon Relativism." *WHR* 7 (Wtr. 1952): 35–42.

———. "Go Tell It on the Mountain: Thoreau's Vocation as a Writer." *ESQ* 19 (3 Qtr. 1973): 161–69.

———. "The Moral and Ethical Dimensions of Emerson's Aesthetics." *ESQ* 55 (2 Qtr. 1969): 13–14.

———. "Scholarly Editing and Dealing with Uncertainties: Thoreau's 'Resistance to Civil Government.'" *AEB* 2 (Spr. 1978): 103–15.

———. "Thoreau and Radical Abolitionism." Diss. Northwestern Univ. 1950.

———. "Thoreau and the 'Herald of Freedom.'" *NEQ* 22 (June 1949): 193–204.

———. "Thoreau's Use of His Sources." *NEQ* 44 (March 1971): 101–09.

———. "Yeats' Early Reading of *Walden*." *BPLQ* 5 (July 1953): 164–66.

———, ed. *The Recognition of Henry David Thoreau*. Ann Arbor: Univ. of Michigan Press, 1969.

Goblet D'Alviella, Count. "The Transcendental Movement." In his *The Contemporary Evolution of Religious Thought in England, America, and India*. Trans. J. Moden. New York: Putnam's, 1886, 167–81.

Goddard, Harold Clarke. *Studies in New England Transcendentalism*. New York: Columbia Univ. Press, 1908.

———. "Transcendentalism." In *Cambridge History of American Literature*. Ed. William Peterfield Trent et al. 3 vols. New York: Putnam's, 1917–21, 1: 326–48.

Goddard, John. " 'Swedenborg the Mystic': Is Emerson's Characterization Correct?" *NCR* 21 (July 1914): 321–37.

Godwin, Parke. *A Biography of William Cullen Bryant*. 2 vols. New York: D. Appleton, 1883.

Goetzmann, William H., ed. *The American Hegelians: An Intellectual Episode in the History of Western America*. New York: Knopf, 1973.

Gohdes, Clarence L. F. *American Literature in Nineteenth Century England*. New York: Columbia Univ. Press, 1944.

———. "Getting Ready for Brook Farm." *MLN* 49 (Jan. 1934): 36–39.

———. *The Periodicals of American Transcendentalism*. Durham: Duke Univ. Press, 1931.

———. "The *Western Messenger* and the *Dial*." *SP* 26 (Jan. 1929): 67–84. Rpt. in his *The Periodicals of American Transcendentalism*, 17–37.

———. "Whitman and Emerson." *SR* 37 (Jan. 1929): 79–93.

Goldfarb, Clare R. "*The Marble Faun* and Emersonian Self-Reliance." *ATQ* no. 1 (1 Qtr. 1969): 19–29.

Goldfarb, Russell M., and Clare R. Goldfarb. *Spiritualism and Nineteenth-Century Letters*. Rutherford, N.J.: Fairleigh Dickinson Univ. Press, 1978.

Golemba, Henry L. "The Balanced View in Margaret Fuller's Literary Criticism." Diss. Univ. of Washington 1971.

———. *George Ripley*. Boston: Twayne, 1977.

Gollin, Rita K. "Louisa May Alcott's 'Hawthorne.' " *EHIC* 118 (Jan. 1982): 42–48.

Gonnaud, Maurice. "Emerson and the Imperial Self: A European Critique." In *Emerson: Prophecy, Metamorphosis, Influence*, ed. David Levin, 107–28.

———. *Individu et société dans l'œuvre de Ralph Waldo Emerson: Essai de biographie spirituelle*. Paris: Didier, 1964.

Goodman, Paul. "Ethics and Enterprise: The Values of a Boston Elite, 1800–1860." *AQ* 18 (Fall 1966): 437–51.

Goodnight, S. H. *German Literature in American Magazines Prior to 1846*. Madison: Univ. of Wisconsin, 1907.

Goodrich, S. G. *Recollections of a Lifetime*. 2 vols. New York and Auburn, N.Y.: Miller, Orton, and Mulligan, 1856.

Goodwin, James. "Thoreau and John Brown: Transcendental Politics." *ESQ* 25 (3 Qtr. 1979): 156–68.

Gordon, George Stuart. *Anglo-American Literary Relations*. London: Oxford Univ. Press, 1942.

Gordon, Joseph T. "Nathaniel Hawthorne and Brook Farm." *ESQ* no. 33 (4 Qtr. 1963): 51–61.

Gorely, Jean. "Emerson's Theory of Poetry." *PoR* 22 (July–Aug. 1931): 263–73.

Gosse, Edmund. "Has America Produced a Poet?" *Forum* 6 (Oct. 1888): 176–86.

Gougeon, Len. "Abolition, the Emersons, and 1837." *NEQ* 54 (Sept. 1981): 345–64.

———. "Emerson and the New Bedford Affair." *SAR* 1981: 257–64.

Goyder, David George. "Advertisement." In *The Biblical Assistant, and Book of Practical Piety*. London: J. S. Hodson; Boston: Otis Clapp, 1841, v–ix.

Gozzi, Raymond. "The Meaning of the 'Complemental' Verses in *Walden*." *ESQ* no. 35 (2 Qtr. 1964): 79–82.

———. "Some Aspects of Thoreau's Personality" and "Mother-Nature." In *Henry David Thoreau: A Profile*, ed. Walter Harding, 150–71, 172–87.

———. "Tropes and Figures: A Psychological Study of David Henry Thoreau." Diss. New York Univ. 1957.

Grady, Charles. "Frederic Henry Hedge: A Forgotten Transcendentalist." *Kairos* 19 (Sum. 1980): 3, 19.

Graham, Philip. "Some Lowell Letters." *TSLL* 3 (Wtr. 1962): 557–82.

Grannis, Joseph C. "Henry Ware, Sr., Hollis Professor of Divinity at Harvard, 1805–1840." Undergraduate honors thesis Harvard 1954.

Gray, Henry David. *Emerson: A Statement of New England Transcendentalism as Expressed in the Philosophy of Its Chief Exponent.* Stanford: Stanford Univ., 1917.

Greeley, Horace. *Recollections of a Busy Life.* New York: J. B. Ford, 1869.

———[?]. Review of Henry David Thoreau, *A Week on the Concord and Merrimack Rivers.* *NYDT*, 12 June 1849, 1.

Green, Eugene. "Reading Local History: Shattuck's *History*, Emerson's 'Discourse,' and Thoreau's *Walden.*" *NEQ* 50 (June 1977): 303–14.

Green, Judith A. "Religion, Life, and Literature in the *Western Messenger.*" Diss. Univ. of Wisconsin 1981.

Green, Martin. *The Problem of Boston: Some Readings in Cultural History.* New York: Norton, 1966.

———. *Re-Appraisals: Some Commonsense Readings in American Literature.* New York: Norton, 1963.

Green, Sue Ellen. "Women in Fourierist Theory and Associationist Thought." M.A. thesis Univ. of Georgia 1977.

Greenberger, Evelyn Barish. "The Phoenix on the Wall: Consciousness in Emerson's Early and Late Journals." *ATQ* no. 21 (Wtr. 1974): 45–56.

Greene, Henry L. "The Greene-St. School, of Providence, and Its Teachers." *PRIHS* n.s. 6 (Jan. 1899): 199–219.

Greene, John G. "The *Western Messenger.*" *JLR* 4 (Sum. 1942): 49–54.

Greene, William B. *Transcendentalism.* West Brookfield, Mass.: Oliver S. Cooke, 1849. Rev. and rpt. as "New England Transcendentalism" in his *The Blazing Star.* Boston: A. Williams, 1872, 145–80.

Greenough, Horatio. *The Letters of Horatio Greenough.* Ed. Nathalia Wright. Madison: Univ. of Wisconsin Press, 1972.

Greenwood, Douglas McCreary. "James Marsh." In *The American Renaissance in New England*, ed. Joel Myerson, 134–36.

———. "James Marsh and the Transcendental Temper." Diss. Univ. of North Carolina 1979.

———. "James Marsh, Dartmouth and American Transcendentalism." *DAM* 61 (March 1969): 23–25.

———. Review of *Coleridge's American Disciples*, ed. John J. Duffy. *RALS* 5 (Aut. 1975): 258–61.

Gregg, Edith Emerson Webster. "Emerson and His Children: Their Childhood Memories." *HLB* 28 (Oct. 1980): 407–30.

Gregory, Winifred. *American Newspapers, 1821–1936.* New York: H. W. Wilson, 1937.

Greiner, Donald J. *Robert Frost: The Poet and His Critics.* Chicago: American Library Assn., 1974.

Griffin, C. S. *The Ferment of Reform, 1830–1860.* New York: Crowell, 1967.

Griffin, William J. "Thoreau's Reactions to Horatio Greenough." *NEQ* 30 (Dec. 1957): 509–12.

Griffith, Clark. " 'Emersonianism' and 'Poeism': Some Versions of the Romantic Sensibility." *MLQ* 22 (June 1961): 125–34.

———. *The Long Shadow: Emily Dickinson's Tragic Poetry.* Princeton: Princeton Univ. Press, 1964.

————. "Poe's 'Ligeia' and the English Romantics." *UTQ* 24 (Oct. 1954): 8–25.

Grimm, Herman. "Emerson." In his *Emerson über Goethe and Shakespeare*. Hannover: Carl Rümpler, 1857.

Griswold, Rufus W. *Passages from the Correspondence and Other Papers of Rufus W. Griswold*. Ed. W. M. Griswold. Cambridge, Mass.: W. M. Griswold, 1898.

————, ed. *The Poets and Poetry of America*. Philadelphia: Carey and Hart, 1842.

Grob, Gerald N. *American Social History before 1860*. New York: Appleton-Century-Crofts, 1970.

Gross, Robert A. "Culture and Cultivation: Agriculture and Society in Thoreau's Concord." *JAH* 69 (June 1982): 42–61.

————. " 'The Most Estimable Place in All the World': A Debate on Progress in Nineteenth-Century Concord." *SAR* 1978: 1–15.

Gross, Seymour L. "Emerson and Poetry." *SAQ* 54 (Jan. 1955): 82–94.

Gross, Theodore L. "Herman Melville: The Nature of Authority." *ColQ* 16 (Spr. 1968): 397–412. Rpt. in his *The Heroic Ideal in American Literature*. New York: Free Press, 1971, 34–50.

————. "Under the Shadow of Our Swords: Emerson and The Heroic Ideal." *BuR* 17 (March 1969): 22–34. Rpt. in his *The Heroic Ideal in American Literature*, 3–17.

————, and Stanley Wertheim. *Hawthorne, Melville, Stephen Crane: A Critical Bibliography*. New York: Free Press, 1971.

Grover, Edwin O. "The First Words of Warm Approval." *WWR* 5 (June 1959): 30–33.

Gruber, Christian. "The Education of Henry David Thoreau, Harvard 1833–37." Diss. Princeton 1953.

Gruenert, Charles F. "Henry David Thoreau's Humor in Theory and Practice." Diss. Univ. of Chicago 1957.

Guernsey, Alfred. *Ralph Waldo Emerson: Philosopher and Poet*. New York: D. Appleton, 1881.

Gura, Philip F. "Elizabeth Palmer Peabody and the Philosophy of Language." *ESQ* 23 (3 Qtr. 1977): 154–63.

————. "Henry Thoreau and the Wisdom of Words." *NEQ* 52 (March 1979): 38–54. Incorporated into his *The Wisdom of Words*.

————. "Language and Meaning: An American Tradition." *AL* 53 (March 1981): 1–21.

————. "Thoreau and John Josselyn." *NEQ* 48 (Dec. 1975): 505–18.

————. "Thoreau's Maine Woods Indians: More Representative Men." *AL* 49 (Nov. 1977): 366–84.

————. *The Wisdom of Words: Language, Theology, and Literature in the New England Renaissance*. Middletown, Conn.: Wesleyan Univ. Press, 1981.

————, and Joel Myerson, eds. *Critical Essays on American Transcendentalism*. Boston: G. K. Hall, 1982.

Gurney, Richard C. "The Worst of Thoreau." *ConnR* 3 (April 1970): 68–71.

Gushee, Anne Elizabeth. "Nathaniel Hawthorne and Margaret Fuller." M.A. thesis Columbia 1955.

Guthrie, Harold N. "The Humor of Thoreau." Diss. Univ. of Iowa 1953.

H. "Lyceum Lectures." *NEPur*, 5 March 1846, 38–39.

————. "Mr. Emerson's Lyceum Lectures." *NEPur*, 12 Feb. 1846, 26.

————. "Ralph W. Emerson's Lyceum Lectures." *NEPur*, 26 Feb. 1846, 34.

————. "Ralph Waldo Emerson." *NEPur*, 5 Feb. 1846, 22.

————. "Ralph Waldo Emerson's Lectures Once More." *NEPur*, 19 Feb. 1846, 30.

Habich, Robert David. "The History and Achievement of the *Western Messenger*, 1835–1841." Diss. Pennsylvania State Univ. 1982.

––––––. "James Freeman Clarke's 1833 Letter-journal for Margaret Fuller." *ESQ* 27 (1 Qtr. 1981): 47–56.

Haddin, Theodore. "Fire and Fire Imagery in Thoreau's Journal and *Walden*." *SAB* 41 (May 1976): 78–79.

Haefner, George. *A Critical Estimate of the Educational Theories and Practices of A. Bronson Alcott*. New York: Columbia Univ. Press, 1937.

Haertel, Martin Henry. *German Literature in American Magazines 1846 to 1880*. Madison: Univ. of Wisconsin, 1908.

Hagenbüchle, Roland. "Sign and Process: The Concept of Language in Emerson and Dickinson." *ESQ* 25 (3 Qtr. 1979): 137–55.

Haig, Robert L. "Emerson and the 'Electric Word' of John Hunter." *NEQ* 28 (Spr. 1955): 394–97.

Hale, Edward. "Convers Francis." In *Heralds of a Liberal Faith*, ed. Samuel A. Eliot, 3: 117–20.

Hale, Edward Everett. "A Harvard Undergraduate in the Thirties." *Har* 132 (April 1916): 691–702.

––––––. *James Russell Lowell and His Friends*. Boston: Houghton, Mifflin, 1899.

––––––. *Memories of a Hundred Years*. Rev. ed. 2 vols. New York: Macmillan, 1904.

––––––. Review of Arethusa Hall, *Life and Character of the Rev. Sylvester Judd. ChEx* 58 (Jan. 1855): 63–75.

––––––. Review of Walt Whitman, *Leaves of Grass. NAR* 83 (Jan. 1856): 275–77.

Hale, Edward Everett, Jr. *The Life and Letters of Edward Everett Hale*. 2 vols. Boston: Little, Brown, 1917.

Hale, Susan. *Life and Letters of Thomas Gold Appleton*. New York: D. Appleton, 1895.

Hall, Arethusa. *Life and Character of the Rev. Sylvester Judd*. Boston: Crosby, Nichols, 1854.

Hall, Edward S. *Memoir of Mary L. Ware, Wife of Henry Ware, Jr*. Boston: Crosby, Nichols, 1853.

Hall, Lawrence Sargent. *Nathaniel Hawthorne, Critic of Society*. New Haven: Yale Univ. Press, 1944.

Hall, Theresa Layton. "A Bibliography of the New England Transcendentalist Movement." M.A. thesis Columbia 1929.

Halliburton, David G. *Edgar Allan Poe: A Phenomenological View*. Princeton: Princeton Univ. Press, 1973.

Halline, Allan G. "Moral and Religious Concepts in Poe." *BUS* 2 (Jan. 1951): 126–50.

Hallowell, Anna David, ed. *James and Lucretia Mott: Life and Letters*. Boston: Houghton, Mifflin, 1884.

Hammell, G. M. "Jones Very—A Son of the Spirit." *MethR* 83 (Jan.-Feb. 1901): 20–30.

"Handlist of Books Found in the Home of Emily Dickinson at Amherst, Mass., Spring 1950," TS. Harvard Univ.

Hansen, Arlene J. "Plotinus: An Early Source of Emerson's View of Otherworldliness." *ESQ* 18 (3 Qtr. 1972): 184–85.

Hansen-Taylor, Marie, and Horace Scudder. *The Life and Letters of Bayard Taylor*. 2 vols. Boston: Houghton, Mifflin, 1885.

Haraszti, Zoltán. "Brook Farm Letters." *MB* 12 (Feb., March 1937): 49–68, 93–114. Rpt. as *The Idyll of Brook Farm as Revealed by Unpublished Letters in the Boston Public Library*. Boston: Trustees of the Public Library, 1937; enl. ed., 1940.

Harding, Anthony John. "James Marsh as Editor of Coleridge." In *Reading Coleridge*. Ed. Walter B. Crawford. Ithaca: Cornell Univ. Press, 1979, 223–25.

––––––. "Thoreau and the Adequacy of Homer." *SIR* 20 (Fall 1981): 317–32.

Harding, Brian R. "Metaphoric Imagery in Emerson's Later Essays." *ATQ* no. 31, suppl. (Sum. 1976): 18–21.

———. "Swedenborgian Spirit and Thoreauvian Sense: Another Look at Correspondence." *JAmS* 8 (April 1974): 65–79.

———. "Transcendental Symbolism in the Works of Emerson, Thoreau, and Whitman." Diss. Brown 1971.

Harding, Walter. "A Bibliography of Thoreau in Poetry, Fiction, and Drama." *BB* 18 (May–Aug. 1943): 15–18.

———. *A Catalog of the Thoreau Society Archives in the Concord Free Public Library*. Geneseo N.Y.: Thoreau Soc., 1978.

———. "A Check List of Thoreau's Lectures." *BNYPL* 70 (Fall 1949): 78–87.

———. *The Days of Henry Thoreau*. New York: Knopf, 1965. Enl. ed., New York: Dover, 1982.

———. *Emerson's Library*. Charlottesville: Univ. Press of Virginia, 1967.

———. "Franklin B. Sanborn and Thoreau's Letters." *BPLQ* 3 (Oct. 1951): 288–94.

———. "Henry D. Thoreau, Instructor." *EdF* (Nov. 1964): 89–97.

———. "A New Checklist of the Books in Henry David Thoreau's Library." *SAR* 1983: 151–86.

———. "The Thoreau Collection of the Pierpont Morgan Library of New York City." *TSB* no. 19 (April 1947): 2–3.

———. *A Thoreau Handbook*. New York: New York Univ. Press, 1959.

———. "Thoreau on the Lecture Platform." *NEQ* 24 (Sept. 1951): 365–74.

———. *Thoreau's Library*. Charlottesville: Univ. Press of Virginia, 1957.

———. "Two F. B. Sanborn Letters." *AL* 25 (March 1953): 230–34.

———. "Walden's Man of Science." *VQR* 57 (Wtr. 1981): 45–61.

———. "Was It Legal? Thoreau in Jail." *AH* 26 (Aug. 1975): 36–37.

———, ed. *Henry David Thoreau: A Profile*. New York: Hill and Wang, 1971.

———, ed. *Thoreau: A Century of Criticism*. Dallas: Southern Methodist Univ. Press, 1954.

———, ed. *The Thoreau Centennial*. Albany: State Univ. of New York Press, 1964.

———, ed. *Thoreau: Man of Concord*. New York: Holt, Rinehart, and Winston, 1962.

———, and Jean Cameron Advena. *A Bibliography of the Thoreau Society Bibliographies, 1941–1969*. Troy, N.Y.: Whitston, 1971.

———, and Michael Meyer. *The New Thoreau Handbook*. New York: New York Univ. Press, 1980.

———, and George Brenner, and Paul A. Doyle, eds. *Henry David Thoreau: Studies and Commentaries*. Rutherford, N.J.: Fairleigh Dickinson Univ. Press, 1972.

Haroutunian, Joseph. *Piety versus Moralism: The Passing of the New England Theology*. New York: Henry Holt, 1932.

Harper, George Mills. "Thomas Taylor in America." In *Thomas Taylor the Platonist*. Ed. Kathleen Raine and Harper. Princeton: Princeton Univ. Press, 1969, 49–102.

———. "Toward the Holy Land: Platonism in the Middle West." *SAB* 32 (March 1967): 1–6.

Harris, Kenneth E. "Thoreau's 'The Service': A Review of the Scholarship." *ATQ* no. 11 (Sum. 1971): 60–63.

Harris, Neil. *The Artist in American Society: The Formative Years, 1790–1860*. New York: George Braziller, 1966.

Harris, William Torrey. "The Dialectic Unity of Emerson's Prose." *JSP* 18 (April 1884): 195–202.

———. "Emerson's Orientalism." In *The Genius and Character of Emerson*, ed. F.B. Sanborn, 372–85.

———. "Emerson's Philosophy of Nature." In *The Genius and Character of Emerson*, ed. F. B. Sanborn, 339–64.

————. "Emerson's Relationship to Goethe and Carlyle." In *The Genius and Character of Emerson*, ed. F. B. Sanborn, 386–419.

————. "Frederic Henry Hedge, D.D." *JSP* 11 (Jan. 1877): 107–08.

Harrison, John S. *The Teachers of Emerson*. New York: Sturgis and Walton, 1910.

Harwood, Thomas F. "Prejudice and Anti-Slavery: The Colloquy between William Ellery Channing and Edward Strutt Abdy, 1834." *AQ* 18 (Wtr. 1966): 697–700.

Haselmayer, Louis A. "Amos Bronson Alcott and Southeast Iowa." *AnI* 38 (April 1965): 121–52.

Haskell, Augustus Mellen, ed. *Samuel Johnson: A Memorial*. Cambridge, Mass.: Riverside Press, 1882.

Haskins, David Green. *Ralph Waldo Emerson: His Maternal Ancestors*. Boston: Cupples, Upham, 1886.

Hastings, Hester. *William Ellery Channing and l'Academie des Sciences Morales et Politiques 1870*. Providence: Brown Univ. Press, 1959.

Hathaway, Lillie V. *German Literature of the Mid-Nineteenth Century in England and America as Reflected in the Journals 1840-1914*. Boston: Chapman and Grimes, 1935.

Hathaway, Richard D. *Sylvester Judd's New England*. University Park: Pennsylvania State Univ. Press, 1981.

Hawthorne, Julian. "Emerson as an American." In *The Genius and Character of Emerson*, ed. F. B. Sanborn, 68–91.

————. *Hawthorne and His Circle*. New York: Harper's, 1903.

————. *Nathaniel Hawthorne and His Wife*. 2 vols. Boston: James R. Osgood, 1884.

Hawthorne, Manning. "Hawthorne and Utopian Socialism." *NEQ* 12 (Dec. 1939): 726–30.

Hawthorne, Nathaniel. *The American Notebooks*. Ed. Randall Stewart. New Haven: Yale Univ. Press, 1932. Rev. ed., ed. Claude M. Simpson, Columbus: Ohio State Univ. Press, 1972.

————. *The Blithedale Romance*. Boston: Ticknor, Reed, and Fields, 1852.

————. "The Celestial Railroad." *USMDR* 12 (May 1843): 512–23. Rpt. in his *Mosses from an Old Manse*. 2 vols. New York: Wiley and Putnam, 1846, 1: 173–92.

————. *The Centenary Edition of the Writings of Nathaniel Hawthorne*. Ed. William Charvat et al. 14 vols. to date. Columbus: Ohio State Univ. Press, 1962– .

————. *The English Notebooks*. Ed. Randall Stewart. New York: Modern Language Assn., 1941.

————. "The Hall of Fantasy." *Pioneer* 1 (Feb. 1843): 49–55.

————. *Love Letters of Nathaniel Hawthorne*. 2 vols. Chicago: Soc. of the Dofobs, 1907.

————. "The Old Manse." In his *Mosses from an Old Manse*, 1: 1–31.

————. *Passages from the American Note-Books*. Ed. Sophia Hawthorne. 2 vols. Boston: Ticknor and Fields, 1868.

————. "A Virtuoso's Collection." *BM* 1 (May 1842): 193–200.

Hayden, Brad. "Echoes of *Walden* in *Trout Fishing in America*." *TJQ* 8.3 (July 1976): 21–26.

Hazard, Lucy Lockwood. *The Frontier in American Literature*. New York: Crowell, 1927.

Hazewell, C. C. "Emerson as a Politician." *BoCom*, 13 May 1882, 4.

Hazlitt, William. Review of William Ellery Channing, *Sermons and Tracts*. *EdR* 50 (Oct. 1829): 125–44.

Heath, William G. "Cyrus Bartol, Transcendentalist: An Early Critic of Emerson." Diss. Univ. of Minnesota 1970.

————. "Cyrus Bartol's Transcendental Capitalism." *SAR* 1979: 399–408.

Hecker, Isaac T. "The Transcendental Movement in New England." *CathW* 23 (July 1876): 528–37.

————. "Two Prophets of Their Age." *CathW* 47 (Aug. 1888): 684–93.

Hedge, Frederic Henry. *An Address Delivered before the Graduating Class of the Divinity School in Cambridge, July 15, 1849.* Cambridge, Mass.: John Bartlett, 1849. Rpt. in *UUC* 36 (Spr.–Sum. 1981): 57–69.

———. "Coleridge." *ChEx* 14 (March 1833): 109–29.

———. *Conservatism and Reform.* Boston: Charles C. Little and James Brown, 1843.

———. "The Destinies of Ecclesiastical Religion." *ChEx* 82 (Jan. 1867): 1–15.

———. "The Late Rev. Convers Francis, D.D." *PMHS* 7 (1863): 4–5.

———. "Lecture on Natural Religion" (1851), MS. Houghton Library, Harvard Univ.

———. *Prose Writers of Germany.* Philadelphia: Carey and Hart, 1848.

———. *Reason in Religion.* Boston: Walker, Fuller, 1865.

———. *Sermons.* Boston: Roberts, 1891.

———, ed. *Recent Inquiries in Theology.* Boston: Walker, Wise, 1860.

———, and Annis Lee Wister. *Metrical Translations and Poems.* Boston: Houghton, Mifflin, 1888.

Hedges, William L. "From Franklin to Emerson." In *The Oldest Revolutionary: Essays on Benjamin Franklin.* Ed. J. A. Leo Lemay. Philadelphia: Univ. of Pennsylvania Press, 1976, 139–56.

———. "A Short Way around Emerson's *Nature*." *TWA* 44 (1955): 21–27.

Hellenbrand, Harold. " 'A True Integrity Day by Day': Thoreau's Organic Economics in *Walden*." *ESQ* 25 (2 Qtr. 1979): 71–78.

Hellman, George Sidney. "An Unpublished Concord Journal." *CM* 103 (April 1922): 825–35.

Hemming, Henry. "A Few Notes on Emerson and the Pantheists." *NDM* 8 (Aug. 1871): 65–70.

Hendrick, George. "Dr. J. J. G. Wilkinson's Letters to Emerson." *ATQ* no. 39 (Sum. 1978): 245–62.

———. "The Influence of Thoreau's 'Civil Disobedience' on Gandhi's *Satyagraha*." *NEQ* 29 (Dec. 1956): 462–71.

———. "Unpublished Notes on Whitman in W. Sloan[e] Kennedy's Diary." *AL* 34 (May 1962): 279–85.

Hennessy, Helen. "The *Dial*: Its Poetry and Poetic Criticism." *NEQ* 31 (March 1958): 66–87.

Heraud, J. A. "Continental Philosophy in America." *MoM* 3rd ser. 4 (July, Aug., Oct., Dec. 1840): 1–14, 112–28, 331–38, 628–37.

———. "A Response from America." *MoM* 3rd ser., 2 (Sept. 1839): 344–52.

Herbold, Anthony. "Nature as Concept and Technique in the Poetry of Jones Very." *NEQ* 40 (June 1967): 244–59.

Herbst, Jurgen. *The German Historical School in American Scholarship.* Ithaca: Cornell Univ. Press, 1965.

Herreshoff, David. *American Disciples of Marx.* Detroit: Wayne State Univ. Press, 1967. Rpt. as *The Origins of American Marxism.* New York: Pathfinder Press, 1973.

Herr, William A. "A More Perfect State: Thoreau's Concept of Civil Government." *MR* 16 (Sum. 1975): 470–87.

Hertz, Robert N. "English and American Romanticism." *Person* 46 (Wtr. 1965): 81–92.

Hewett-Thayer, Harvey W. *American Literature as Viewed in Germany, 1818–1861.* Chapel Hill: Univ. of North Carolina Press, 1958.

Hickock, Benjamin Blakely. "The Political and Literary Careers of F. B. Sanborn." Diss. Michigan State Univ. 1953.

Hicks, Granville. "A Conversation in Boston." *SR* 39 (April–June 1931): 129–43.

———. "Letters to William Francis Channing." *AL* 2 (Nov. 1930): 294–98.

Hicks, John, ed. *Thoreau in Our Season.* Amherst: Univ. of Massachusetts Press, 1966. Exp. ed. of "Thoreau: A Centennial Gathering." *MR* 4 (Fall 1962): 41–172.

Hicks, Philip Marshall. *The Development of the Natural History Essay in American Literature*. Philadelphia: Univ. of Pennsylvania, 1924.

Higgins, Brian. *Herman Melville: An Annotated Bibliography, Vol. 1: 1846-1930*. Boston: G. K. Hall, 1979.

Higginson, Mary Thacher. *Thomas Wentworth Higginson*. Boston: Houghton Mifflin, 1914.

Higginson, Thomas Wentworth. "Address of Thomas Wentworth Higginson." *Index* 14 (14 June 1883): 596-97.

————. *Army Life in a Black Regiment*. Boston: Fields, Osgood, 1870.

————. "The Birth of a Literature." In his *Cheerful Yesterdays*, 167-95.

————. "The Brook Farm Period in New England." *DMM* 18 (July 1882): 534-35.

————. *Carlyle's Laugh and Other Surprises*. Boston: Houghton Mifflin, 1909.

————. *Cheerful Yesterdays*. Boston: Houghton, Mifflin, 1898.

————. *Common Sense about Women*. Boston: Lee and Shepard, 1882. Rpt. as *Women and the Alphabet*. Boston: Houghton, Mifflin, 1900.

————. "The Concord Group." In Higginson and Boynton, *A Reader's History of American Literature*, 167-98.

————. *Contemporaries*. Boston: Houghton, Mifflin, 1899.

————. "Emerson's 'Foot-note Person.' " In his *Carlyle's Laugh and Other Surprises*, 77-91.

————. "Glimpses of Authors. IV.—The Transcendental Authors." *Brains* 1 (1 Dec. 1891): 103-06.

————. "Glimpses of Authors. V.—The Town and Country Club." *Brains* 1 (15 Dec. 1891): 115-17.

————. "Glimpses of Authors. VI—Mr. Alcott and His Friends." *Brains* 1 (1 Jan. 1892): 131-33.

————. *Letters and Journals of Thomas Wentworth Higginson 1846-1906*. Ed. Mary Thacher Higginson. Boston: Houghton Mifflin, 1921.

————. "Margaret Fuller Ossoli." In *Eminent Women of the Age*. Hartford, Conn.: S. M. Betts, 1868, 173-201.

————. *Margaret Fuller Ossoli*. Boston: Houghton, Mifflin, 1884.

————. "Octavius Brooks Frothingham." *NW* 5 (March 1896): 1-9.

————. *Old Cambridge*. New York: Macmillan, 1899.

————. "Old Cambridge in Three Literary Epochs." In his *Old Cambridge*, 47-71.

————. *Out-Door Papers*. Boston: Ticknor and Fields, 1863.

————. *Part of a Man's Life*. Boston: Houghton Mifflin, 1905.

————. "The Personality of Emerson." *Outlook* 74 (23 May 1903): 221-27.

————. "Recent Poetry." *Nation* 75 (11 Dec. 1902): 465.

————. "Remarks." In *Samuel Johnson: A Memorial*, ed. Augustus Mellen Haskell, 23-26.

————. "Report on the Parker Library." In *Thirty-First Annual Report of the Trustees of the [Boston] Public Library*. Boston: n.p., 1883, 19-25. Rpt. in [*The Centenary Edition of the Works of Theodore Parker*], 15: 1-10.

————. *Studies in History and Letters*. Boston: Houghton, Mifflin, 1900.

————. "The Sunny Side of the Transcendental Period." *Atl* 93 (Jan. 1904): 6-14. Rpt. in his *Part of a Man's Life*, 1-25.

————. "The Sympathy of Religions." *Radical* 8 (Feb. 1871): 1-23. Rpt. as *The Sympathy of Religions*. Boston: The Radical, 1871.

————. "Tested by Time." *WJ* 7 (1 Jan. 1876): 1.

————. "Theodore Parker." *Atl* 6 (Oct. 1860): 449-57. Rpt. in his *Contemporaries*, 34-59.

————. "Two New England Heretics: Channing and Parker." *Ind* 54 (22 May 1902): 1234-36.

————. "Unpublished Letters from Theodore Parker." *Radical* 8 (May 1871): 244-48.

————. "Walks with Ellery Channing." *Atl* 90 (July 1902): 27-34.

————. "William Henry Channing." In *Heralds of a Liberal Faith*, ed. Samuel A. Eliot, 3: 59–66.

————. *The Young Folks' History of the United States*. Boston: Lee and Shepard, 1875.

————, and Henry Walcott Boynton. *A Reader's History of American Literature*. Boston: Houghton, Mifflin, 1903.

Hilbrunner, Anthony. "Emerson: Democratic Equalitarian." *CSSJ* 10 (Wtr. 1959): 25–30.

Hildenbrand, Christopher A. *A Bibliography of Scholarship about Henry David Thoreau: 1940–1967*. Fort Hays, Kan.: Fort Hays State Coll., 1967.

Hill, David W. "Emerson's Eumenides: Textual Evidence and the Interpretation of 'Experience.'" In *Emerson Centenary Essays*, ed. Joel Myerson, 107–21.

Hill, J. Arthur. *Emerson and His Philosophy*. London: W. Rider, 1919.

Hillis, Newell Dwight. *Right Living as a Fine Art: A Study of Channing's Symphony as an Outline of the Ideal Life and Character*. New York: Fleming H. Revell, 1899.

Hillman, Mary V. "Hawthorne and Transcendentalism." *CathW* 93 (May 1911): 199–212.

Himelick, Raymond. "Thoreau and Samuel Daniel." *AL* 24 (May 1952): 177–85.

Hinding, Andrea, et al., eds. *Women's History Sources*. 2 vols. New York: Bowker, 1980.

Hinds, William A. *American Communities and Cooperative Colonies*. Chicago: C. H. Kerr, 1908.

————. "Fruitlands." *AmS* 1 (29 June 1876): 109–10.

Hintz, Howard W. *The Quaker Influence in American Literature*. New York: Fleming H. Revell, 1940.

————. "Thomas Wentworth Higginson: Disciple of the Newness." Diss. New York Univ. 1938.

————. *Thomas Wentworth Higginson: Disciple of the Newness*. New York: New York Univ., 1939.

Hirst, George C. "Emerson's Style in His Essays: A Defence." *HMo* 31 (Oct. 1900): 29–38.

Hoag, Ronald. "The Mark on the Wilderness: Thoreau's Contact with Ktaadn." *TSLL* 24 (Spr. 1982): 23–46.

Hoar, Elizabeth. *Mrs. Samuel Ripley*. Philadelphia: Lippincott, 1877.

Hoch, David C. "Annals and Perennials: A Study of Cosmogonic Imagery in Thoreau." Diss. Kent State Univ. 1969.

————. "*Walden*, Yoga, and Creation." In *Artful Thunder*. Ed. Robert J. DeMott and Sanford E. Marovitz. Kent, Ohio: Kent State Univ. Press, 1975, 85–102.

Hochfield, George. "New England Transcendentalism." In *American Literature to 1900*. Ed. Marcus Cunliffe. London: Barrie and Jenkins, 1973, 160–96.

————, ed. *Selected Writings of the American Transcendentalists*. New York: New American Library, 1966.

Hochmuth, Marie. "William Ellery Channing, New England Conversationalist." *QJS* 30 (Dec. 1944): 429–39.

Hodges, James R. "Christian Science and Transcendentalism: A Comparative Study." M.A. thesis Vanderbilt Univ. 1942.

Hodges, Maud de Leigh. *Crossroads on the Charles: A History of Watertown, Massachusetts*. Canaan, N.H.: Phoenix, 1980.

Hodges, Robert R. "The Functional Satire of Thoreau's Hermit and Poet." *SaN* 8 (Spr. 1971): 105–08.

Hodgin, Edwin Stanton. "John Weiss, Genius of the Pulpit: Brilliant, Brave, Scholarly, Whimsical." In his *One Hundred Years of Unitarianism in New Bedford*. New Bedford, Mass.: First Congregational Soc., 1924, 31–40.

Hoeltje, Hubert H. "Amos Bronson Alcott in Iowa." *IJHP* 29 (July 1931): 375–401.

————. "Emerson, Citizen of Concord." *AL* 11 (Jan. 1940): 367–78.

————. *Inward Sky: The Heart and Mind of Nathaniel Hawthorne*. Durham: Duke Univ. Press, 1962.

————. "Misconceptions in Current Thoreau Criticism." *PQ* 47 (Oct. 1968): 563–70.

————. *Sheltering Tree: A Story of the Friendship of Ralph Waldo Emerson and Amos Bronson Alcott*. Durham: Duke Univ. Press, 1943.

————. "Thoreau and the Concord Academy." *NEQ* 21 (March 1948): 103–09.

Hoffman, Michael J. "The Anti-Transcendentalism of *Moby-Dick*." *GaR* 23 (Spr. 1969): 3–16. Rpt. in his *The Subversive Vision*, 87–100.

————. *The Subversive Vision: American Romanticism in Literature*. Port Washington, N.Y.: Kennikat, 1972.

Holden, Vincent F. *The Early Years of Isaac Thomas Hecker (1819-1844)*. Washington, D.C.: Catholic Univ. of America Press, 1939.

————. *The Yankee Paul: Isaac Thomas Hecker*. Milwaukee: Bruce, 1948.

Holder, Alan. "The Writer as Loon: Witty Structure in *Walden*." *ESQ* no. 43 (2 Qtr. 1966): 73–77.

Holland, Frederick May. "Emerson as Moralist." *Index* 12 (17 Feb. 1881): 404–05.

————. *Liberty in the Nineteenth Century*. New York: Putnam's, 1899.

Holland, H. N. "Mr. Emerson's Philosophy." *Nation* 33 (17 Nov. 1881): 396.

Hollis, C. Carroll. "The Literary Criticism of Orestes Brownson." Diss. Univ. of Michigan 1954.

————. "Orestes Brownson, Jacksonian Literary Critic." In *No Divided Allegiance: Essays in Brownson's Thought*, ed. Leonard Gilhooley, 51–83.

————. "A New England Outpost, as Revealed in Some Unpublished Letters of Emerson, Parker, and Alcott to Ainsworth Spofford." *NEQ* 38 (March 1965): 65–85.

Holloway, Jean. *Edward Everett Hale*. Austin: Univ. of Texas Press, 1956.

Holman, Harriet R. "Hog, Bacon, Ram and Other 'Savans' in *Eureka*: Notes toward Decoding Poe's Encyclopedic Satire." *PoeN* 2 (Oct. 1969): 49–55.

————. "Splitting Poe's 'Epicurean Atoms': Further Speculation on the Literary Satire of *Eureka*." *PoeS* 5 (Dec. 1972): 33–37.

Holmes, John Haynes. "The Education of Theodore Parker." *Unity* 119 (17 May 1937): 110–14.

————. "Theodore Parker and the Work of Social Reform." *Survey* 24 (6 Aug. 1910): 678–84.

Holmes, Oliver Wendell. "Cinders from the Ashes." *Atl* 23 (Jan. 1869): 115–23.

————. *Ralph Waldo Emerson*. Boston: Houghton, Mifflin, 1884.

Holmes, Stewart H. "Phineas Parkhurst Quimby: Scientist of Transcendentalism." *NEQ* 17 (Sept. 1944): 356–80.

Holt, Anne. "William Ellery Channing, 1780-1842." *HJ* (Oct. 1942): 42–49.

Hoornstra, Jean, and Trudy Heath, eds. *American Periodicals 1741-1900*. Ann Arbor, Mich.: University Microfilms International, 1979.

Hoover, Merle M. *Park Benjamin: Poet & Editor*. New York: Columbia Univ. Press, 1948.

Hopkins, Vivian C. "Emerson and the World of Dreams." *ATQ* no. 9 (Wtr. 1971): 56–69.

————. "The Influence of Goethe on Emerson's Aesthetic Theory." *PQ* 27 (Oct. 1948): 325–44.

————. "Margaret Fuller: American Nationalist Critic." *ESQ* no. 55 (2 Qtr. 1969): 24–41.

————. *Spires of Form: A Study of Emerson's Aesthetic Theory*. Cambridge: Harvard Univ. Press, 1951.

Hornbrooke, Frances. "Unitarianism and Modern Literature." In *Unitarianism: Its Origins and History*, 245–71.

Horton, John T. "Millard Fillmore and the Things of God and Caesar." *NiagF* 2 (Sum. 1955): 1–7, 39–48.

Horton, Rod W., and Herbert W. Edwards. *Backgrounds of American Literary Thought*. 2nd ed. New York: Appleton-Century-Crofts, 1967.

Hosmer, Horace. *Remembrances of Concord and the Thoreaus: Letters of Horace Hosmer to Dr. Samuel Arthur Jones*. Ed. George Hendrick. Urbana: Univ. of Illinois Press, 1977.

Hosmer, J. K., ed. *Memorial of George Washington Hosmer*. N.p.: n.p., 1882.

Hotson, Clarence Paul. "A Background for Emerson's Poem 'Grace.'" *NEQ* 1 (April 1928): 124–32.

———. "The Christian Critics and Mr. Emerson." *NEQ* 11 (March 1938): 29–47.

———. "Coleridge's 'Hamlet' and Emerson's 'Swedenborg.'" *NCMag* 53 (April–June 1934): 99–112.

———. "Emerson and Swedenborg." *NCM* 160 (Sept. 1930): 274–77.

———. "Emerson and the Doctrine of Correspondence." *NCR* 46 (Jan., April, July, Oct. 1929): 47–59, 173–86, 304–16, 435–48.

———. "Emerson and the *New-Church Quarterly Review.*" *NCMag* 48 (July–Sept., Oct.–Dec. 1929): 169–83, 239–53.

———. "Emerson and the Swedenborgians." *SP* 27 (July 1930): 517–545.

———. "Emerson, Swedenborg, and B. F. Barrett." *NCMag* 50 (Oct.–Dec. 1931): 244–52; 51 (Jan.–March 1932): 33–43.

———. "Emerson's Biographical Sources for 'Swedenborg.'" *SP* 26 (Jan. 1929): 23–36.

———. "Emerson's Boston Lecture on Swedenborg." *NCMag* 51 (April–June 1932): 91–101.

———. "Emerson's Philosophical Sources for 'Swedenborg.'" *NewP* 21 (Oct. 1928): 482–516.

———. "Emerson's Sources for 'Swedenborg.'" *NCM* 162 (Feb. 1932): 89–94.

———. "Emerson's Title for 'Swedenborg.'" *NCL* 44 (July 1929): 390–98.

———. "George Bush and Emerson's 'Swedenborg.'" *NCMag* 50 (Jan.–March, Apr.–June 1931): 22–34, 98–108.

———. "George Bush: Teacher and Critic of Emerson." *PQ* 10 (Oct. 1931): 369–83.

———. "Ralph Waldo Emerson and Swedenborg." Diss. Harvard 1929.

———. Review of Clarence L. F. Gohdes, *The Periodicals of American Transcendentalism*. *NCR* 39 (Jan. 1932): 111–15.

———. "Sampson Reed, Teacher of Emerson." *NEQ* 2 (April 1929): 249–77.

Hounchell, Saul. "The Pioneer Literary Magazines of the Ohio Valley to 1840." Diss. George Peabody Coll. 1934.

Hourihan, Paul. "The Ambiguities in the Emerson Sage-Image: The Facts of His Novel Reading." *BACH* 22 (Spr. 1971): 44–55.

———. "The Inner Dynamics of the Emerson-Thoreau Relationship." Diss. Boston Univ. 1967.

Houston, Howard R. "Metaphors in Walden." Diss. Claremont Graduate School 1967.

Hovde, Carl. "Literary Materials in Thoreau's *A Week.*" *PMLA* 80 (Mar. 1965): 76–83.

———. "Nature into Art: Thoreau's Use of His *Journals* in *A Week.*" *AL* 30 (May 1958): 165–84.

Hovenkamp, Herbert. *Science and Religion in America 1800–1860*. Philadelphia: Univ. of Pennsylvania Press, 1978.

Howard, Leon. "For a Critique of Whitman's Transcendentalism." *MLN* 47 (Feb. 1932): 79–85.

———. *Herman Melville: A Biography*. Berkeley: Univ. of California Press, 1951.

———. *Literature and the American Tradition*. Garden City, N.Y.: Doubleday, 1960.

———. *Victorian Knight-Errant: A Study of the Early Literary Career of James Russell Lowell*. Berkeley: Univ. of California Press, 1952.

Howarth, William L. *The Book of Concord: Thoreau's Life as a Writer*. New York: Viking, 1982.

———. *The Literary Manuscripts of Henry David Thoreau*. Columbus: Ohio State Univ. Press, 1974.

———. "Successor to *Walden*? Thoreau's 'Moonlight'—An Intended Course of Lectures." *Proof* 2 (1972): 89–115.

Howe, Daniel Walker. "The Decline of Calvinism: An Approach to the Study." *CSSH* 14 (June 1972): 306–27.

———. "A Massachusetts Yankee in Senator Calhoun's Court: Samuel Gilman in South Carolina." *NEQ* 44 (June 1971): 197–220.

———. "Samuel Gilman: Unitarian Minister and Public Man." *PUHS* 17.2 (1973–75): 45–53.

———. *The Unitarian Conscience: Harvard Moral Philosophy, 1805–1861*. Cambridge: Harvard Univ. Press, 1970.

Howe, Julia Ward. "The Church of the Disciples: The Ministry of James Freeman Clarke." *ChReg* 70 (14 May 1891): 308–10.

———. "Emerson's Relation to Society." In *The Genius and Character of Emerson*, ed. F. B. Sanborn, 286–309.

———. *Margaret Fuller (Marchesa Ossoli)*. Boston: Roberts, 1883.

———. "Ralph Waldo Emerson." *WJ* 13 (6 May 1882): 140.

———. *Reminiscences 1819–1899*. Boston: Houghton, Mifflin, 1899.

Howe, M. A. DeWolfe. "The Boston Religion." *Atl* 91 (June 1903): 729–38.

———. "The 'Literary Centre.'" *Atl* 92 (Sept. 1903): 346–55.

———. "Thomas Wentworth Higginson." In *DAB*, 9: 16–18.

Howells, William Dean. "My First Visit to New England. Fourth Part." *Har* 89 (Aug. 1894): 441–51. Rpt. in his *Literary Friends and Acquaintance*. New York: Harper's, 1900, 60–66.

———. Review of Christopher Pearse Cranch, *Satan: A Libretto*. *Atl* 33 (March 1874): 370–71.

Hoyt, Edward A., and Loriman S. Brigham. "Glimpses of Margaret Fuller: The Green Street School and Florence." *NEQ* 29 (March 1956): 87–98.

Hubbell, George Shelton. *A Concordance to the Poems of Ralph Waldo Emerson*. New York: H. W. Wilson, 1932.

Hubbell, Jay B. "Ralph Waldo Emerson." In his *The South in American Literature 1607–1900*, 375–85. Rev. and rpt. as "Ralph Waldo Emerson and the South" in his *South and Southwest*. Durham: Duke Univ. Press, 1965, 123–52.

———. *The South in American Literature 1607–1900*. Durham: Duke Univ. Press, 1954.

Huber, J. Parker. *The Wildest Country: A Guide to Thoreau's Maine*. Boston: Appalachian Mountain Club, 1982.

Hudson, Charles. *History of the Town of Lexington*. Boston: Wiggin and Lunt, 1868.

Hudson, Herbert Edson. "The Paradox of Theodore Parker." *CraneR* 1 (Spr. 1959): 111–20.

———. "Recent Interpretations of Parker: An Evaluation of the Literature since 1936." *PUHS* 13.1 (1960): 1–38.

Hudson, Winthrop S. *Religion in America*. 2nd ed. New York: Scribners, 1973.

Hudspeth, Robert N. "A Calendar of the Letters of Margaret Fuller." *SAR* 1977: 49–143.

———. *Ellery Channing*. New York: Twayne, 1973.

———. "Ellery Channing's Paradoxical Muse." *ESQ* no. 57 (4 Qtr. 1969): 34–40. Rpt. in *The Minor and Later Transcendentalists*, ed. Edwin Gittleman, 34–40.

———. "Margaret Fuller's 1839 Journal: Trip to Bristol." *HLB* 27 (Oct. 1979): 445–70.

———. "A Perennial Springtime: Channing's Friendship with Emerson and Thoreau." *ESQ* no. 54 (1 Qtr. 1969): 30–36. Incorporated into his *Ellery Channing*.

Huffert, Anton M. "Thoreau as Teacher, Lecturer, and Educational Thinker." Diss. New York Univ. 1951.

Huggard, William Allen. "Emerson's Philosophy of War and Peace." *PQ* 22 (Oct. 1943): 370–75.

———. "Ralph Waldo Emerson and the Problem of War and Peace." *UIHS* 5 (1938): 1–76.

——. *The Religious Teachings of Ralph Waldo Emerson*. New York: Vantage Press, 1972.

Hull, Raymona E. "Some Further Notes on Hawthorne and Thoreau." *TSB* no. 121 (Fall 1972): 7–8.

Hunt, T. W. "Emerson's English Style." In his *Studies in Literature and Style*. New York: Armstrong, 1890, 246–77.

Hunter, Doreen. "America's First Romantics: Richard Henry Dana, Sr., and Washington Allston." *NEQ* 45 (March 1972): 3–30.

——. " 'Frederic Henry Hedge, What Say You?' " *AQ* 32 (Sum. 1980): 186–201.

Huntington, Arria S. *Memoir and Letters of Frederic Dan Huntington*. Boston: Houghton Mifflin, 1906.

Huntington, Frederic Dan. "Ralph Waldo Emerson." *Ind* 34 (18, 25 May 1882): 1–2, 1–2.

——. "Ralph Waldo Emerson." *SST* 24 (20 May 1882): 307–08.

——. Review of Sylvester Judd, *Margaret*. *ChEx* 39 (Nov. 1845): 418–20.

Hutch, Robert A. "Emerson and Incest." *PsyR* 62 (Sum. 1975): 320–32. Rpt. in *The Biographical Process*. Ed. Frank E. Reynolds and Ronald Capps. The Hague: Mouton, 1976, 187–200.

Hutchinson, Jamie. " 'The Lapse of the Current': Thoreau's Historical Vision in *A Week on the Concord and Merrimack Rivers*." *ESQ* 25 (4 Qtr. 1979): 211–23.

Hutchison, William R. *The Modernist Impulse in American Protestantism*. Cambridge: Harvard Univ. Press, 1976.

——. "To Heaven in a Swing: The Transcendentalism of Cyrus Bartol." *HTR* 56 (Oct. 1963): 275–95.

——. *The Transcendentalist Ministers: Church Reform in the New England Renaissance*. New Haven: Yale Univ. Press, 1959.

Hyman, Stanley Edgar. "Henry Thoreau in Our Time." *Atl* 178 (Nov. 1946): 137–46.

Hyneman, Esther F. *Edgar Allan Poe: An Annotated Bibliography of Books and Articles in English, 1827–1973*. Boston: G. K. Hall, 1974.

Ihrig, Mary Alice. *Emerson's Transcendental Vocabulary*. New York: Garland, 1982.

Index to Early American Periodical Literature 1728–1870. 4 parts. New York: Pamphlet Distributing, 1941–43.

Inge, M. Thomas. "Thoreau's Humor in *Walden*." *RMCM* 37 (March 1966): 34–44.

Ingersoll, Robert. "Creed vs. Character." *ChReg* 61 (25 May 1882): 81.

Ingraham, Charles A. "Transcendentalism." *Americana* 15 (April 1921): 169–81.

Ireland, Alexander. *In Memoriam. Ralph Waldo Emerson*. London: Simpkin, Marshall, 1882. Exp. ed. as *Ralph Waldo Emerson: His Life, Genius, and Writings*. London: Simpkin, Marshall, 1882.

Ireland, Robert E. "The Concept of Providence in the Thought of William Ellery Channing, Ralph Waldo Emerson, Theodore Parker, and Orestes Augustus Brownson." Diss. Univ. of Maine 1972.

Irey, Eugene F. *Concordance to Five Essays of Ralph Waldo Emerson*. New York: Garland, 1981.

Irie, Yukio. *Emerson and Quakerism*. Tokyo: Kenkyusha, 1967.

Irwin, John T. *American Hieroglyphics*. New Haven: Yale Univ. Press, 1980.

——. "The Symbol of the Hieroglyphic in the American Renaissance." *AQ* 26 (May 1974): 103–26. Incorporated into his *American Hieroglyphics*.

Isely, Jeter A., and Elizabeth R. Isely. "A Note on George Ripley and the Beginnings of New England Transcendentalism." *PUHS* 13.2 (1961): 75–85.

Ishikawa, Jesse. "Convers Francis to Theodore Parker: Boston in 1844." *ESQ* 24 (1 Qtr. 1978): 20–29.

Jackson, A. W. "Col. Thomas Wentworth Higginson." *NEMag* n.s. 25 (Dec. 1901): 446–63.

Jackson, Carl T. "Oriental Ideas in American Thought." In *Dictionary of the History of Ideas.* Ed. Philip P. Weiner. 4 vols. New York: Scribners, 1973, 3: 427–39.

———. *The Oriental Religions and American Thought: Nineteenth-Century Explorations.* Westport, Conn.: Greenwood, 1981.

———. "The Orient in Post-Bellum American Thought: Three Pioneer Popularizers." *AQ* 22 (Spr. 1970): 67–81.

Jacobs, Robert D. *Poe: Journalist and Critic.* Baton Rouge: Louisiana State Univ. Press, 1969.

Jacques, John. "The Discovery of 'Ktaadn': A Study of Thoreau's *The Maine Woods.*" Diss. Columbia 1971.

Jaffe, Adrian. "Ernest Renan's Analysis of Channing." *FR* 28 (Jan. 1955): 218–23.

James, David L. "Movement and Growth in 'Walking.'" *TJQ* 4.3 (July 1972): 16–21.

[James Freeman Clarke number]. *ChReg* 67 (14 June 1888).

[James Freeman Clarke number]. *OBW,* 15 July 1888.

James, Henry. *The American Scene.* New York: Harper's, 1907.

———. *The Bostonians.* New York: Macmillan, 1886.

———. *Hawthorne.* London: Macmillan, 1879.

———. "The Life of Emerson." *MacM* 57 (Dec. 1887): 87–98. Rpt. in his *Partial Portraits.* London: Macmillan, 1888, 1–33.

———. *William Wetmore Story and His Friends.* 2 vols. Boston: Houghton, Mifflin, 1903.

James, Lewis G. "Emerson, the Believer." *Index* 18 (29 July, 5 Aug. 1886): 55–57, 67–68.

James, William. *The Varieties of Religious Experience.* New York: Longmans, Green, 1902.

Jamieson, Paul F. "Emerson in the Adirondacks." *NYH* 39 (July 1958): 215–37.

Japp, Alexander H. "A Gift from Emerson." *GentM* 253 (Nov. 1882): 618–28.

Jeswine, Miriam A. "Henry David Thoreau: Apprentice to the Hindu Sages." Diss. Univ. of Oregon 1971.

John Hopkins Morison: A Memorial. Boston: Houghton, Mifflin, 1897.

Johnson, Alexander. "An Appreciation of Frank B. Sanborn." *Survey* 37 (10 March 1917): 656–57.

Johnson, Anthony P. "Friend, Brother, Teacher: The Images of Jesus of Nazareth in the Preaching of Theodore Parker." *UUC* 33 (Aut.–Wtr. 1978): 20–33.

Johnson, Charles F. "Emerson." In his *Three Americans and Three Englishmen.* New York: Whittaker, 1886, 174–212.

Johnson, Elwood. "Emerson's Psychology of Power." *Rendezvous* 5 (Spr. 1970): 13–25.

Johnson, Glen M. "Emerson on 'Making' in Literature: His Problem of Professionalism, 1836–1841." In *Emerson Centenary Essays,* ed. Joel Myerson, 65–73.

———. "Emerson's Craft of Revision: The Composition of *Essays* (1841)." *SAR* 1980: 51–72.

———. "The Making of Emerson's *Essays.*" Diss. Indiana Univ. 1977.

Johnson, Harriet Hall. "Margaret Fuller as Known by Her Scholars." *ChReg* 89 (21 April 1910): 426–29.

Johnson, Jane. "Whitman's Changing Attitude towards Emerson." *PMLA* 73 (Sept. 1958): 452.

Johnson, Jane Maloney. "Moral Life at Brook Farm." In her " 'Through Change and through Storm': A Study of Federalist-Unitarian Thought, 1800–1860." Diss. Radcliffe 1958, 217–86.

Johnson, Linck C. "Into History: Thoreau's Earliest 'Indian Book' and His First Trip to Cape Cod." *ESQ* 28 (2 Qtr. 1982): 74–88.

———. "Natural Harvest: The Writing of *A Week on the Concord and Merrimack Rivers,* with the Text of the First Draft." Diss. Princeton 1975.

Johnson, Paul David. "Thoreau's Redemptive *Week*." *AL* 49 (March 1977): 22–23.

Johnson, Quentin G. "The Letters of James Russell Lowell to Robert Carter 1842–1876." M.A. thesis Univ. of Oregon 1956.

Johnson, Samuel. *Hymns*. Andover, Mass.: Andover Press, 1899.

———. *Lectures, Essays, and Sermons*. Ed. Samuel Longfellow. Boston: Houghton, Mifflin, 1883.

———. *Oriental Religions and Their Relation to Universal Religion. China*. Boston: James R. Osgood, 1877.

———. *Oriental Religions and Their Relation to Universal Religion. India*. Boston: James R. Osgood, 1872.

———. *Oriental Religions and Their Relation to Universal Religion. Persia*. Boston: James R. Osgood, 1885.

———. *Selected Writings of Samuel Johnson*. Ed. Roger C. Mueller. Delmar, N.Y.: Scholars' Facsimiles & Reprints, 1977.

———. *Theodore Parker: A Lecture*. Ed. John H. Clifford and Horace L. Traubel. Chicago: Charles H. Kerr, 1890.

———. "Transcendentalism." *RadR* 1 (Nov. 1877): 447–78. Rpt. in his *Lectures, Essays, and Sermons*, ed. Samuel Longfellow, 416–60.

———, and Samuel Longfellow, eds. *A Book of Hymns for Public and Private Devotion*. Cambridge, Mass.: Metcalf, 1846.

———, and Samuel Longfellow, eds. *Hymns of the Spirit*. Boston: Ticknor and Fields, 1864.

Johnson, Thomas H. *Emily Dickinson: An Interpretive Biography*. Cambridge: Harvard Univ. Press, 1955.

Johnston, Carol. "The Journals of Theodore Parker: July–December 1840." Diss. Univ. of South Carolina 1980.

Jones, Alexander E. "Margaret Fuller's Attempt to Write Fiction." *BPLQ* 6 (April 1954): 67–73.

Jones, Buford. *Checklist of Hawthorne Criticism, 1951-1966*. Hartford, Conn.: Transcendental Books, 1967. Rpt. in *ESQ* no. 52, suppl. (3 Qtr. 1968): 1–90.

———. " 'The Hall of Fantasy' and the Early Hawthorne-Thoreau Relationship." *PMLA* 83 (Oct. 1968): 1429–38.

———. "A Thoreauvian Wordplay and *Paradise Lost*." *ESQ* no. 47 (2 Qtr. 1967): 65–66.

Jones, Harry L. "Symbolism in the Mystical Poetry of Jones Very." Diss. Catholic Univ. of America 1967.

———. "The Very Madness: A New Manuscript." *CLAJ* 10 (March 1967): 196–200.

Jones, Howard Mumford. *America and French Culture, 1750-1848*. Chapel Hill: Univ. of North Carolina Press, 1927.

———. "American Comment on George Sand, 1837–1848." *AL* 3 (Jan. 1932): 389–407.

———. *The Pursuit of Happiness*. Cambridge: Harvard Univ. Press, 1953.

———. "Transcendentalism and Emerson." In his *Belief and Disbelief in American Literature*. Chicago: Univ. of Chicago Press, 1967, 48–69.

Jones, John Dillon. "A Biographical Dictionary of Brook Farm." M.A. thesis Washington Univ. 1949.

Jones, Joseph. "Emerson and Bergson on the Comic." *CL* 1 (Wtr. 1949): 63–72.

———. "Emerson and Whitman 'Down Under.' " *ESQ* no. 42 (1 Qtr. 1966): 35–46. Incorporated into his *Radical Cousins: Nineteenth Century American and Australian Writers*. St. Lucia: Univ. of Queensland Press, 1976.

———. "Introduction." In *Aesthetic Papers*, ed. Elizabeth Palmer Peabody. Gainesville, Fla.: Scholars' Facsimiles & Reprints, 1957, v–xii.

———. "Villages as Universities: *Aesthetic Papers* and a Passage in *Walden*." *ESQ* no. 7 (2 Qtr. 1957): 40–42.

Jones, Samuel A., ed. *Pertaining to Thoreau*. Detroit: Edwin B. Hill, 1901.

"Jones Very." *BoH*, 16 May 1880. Rpt. in Kenneth Walter Cameron, "Jones Very's Academic Standing at Harvard," 52–57.

Jones, W. A. "Emerson." *Arcturus* 1 (April 1841): 278–84.

Jones, Wayne Allen. "Sometimes Things Just Don't Work Out: Hawthorne's Income from *Twice-Told Tales* (1837), and Another 'Good Thing' for Hawthorne." *NHJ* 1975: 11–23.

Jones, Wilson Clough. "The New England Transcendentalists and the Mexican War." Diss. Univ. of Minnesota 1970.

Joost, Nicholas. "The *Dial*: A Journalistic Emblem and Its Tradition." *SP* 64, extra ser. no. 4 (Jan. 1967): 167–81. Rpt. as "Introduction" in his *Years of Transition: The Dial 1912-1920*. Barre, Mass.: Barre, 1967, xiii–xxvii.

Jordan, William Donald. "Hawthorne and New England Transcendentalism." M.A. thesis Univ. of Texas 1952.

Jorgenson, Chester Eugene. "Emerson's 'Paradise under the Shadow of Swords.'" *PQ* 11 (July 1932): 274–92.

Joy, Neill R. "Two Possible Analogies for 'The Ponds' in *Walden*: Jonathan Carver and Wordsworth." *ESQ* 24 (4 Qtr. 1978): 197–205.

Joyaux, Georges Jules. "French Thought in American Magazines 1800-1848." Diss. Michigan State Univ. 1951.

———. "George Sand, Eugène Sue, and the *Harbinger*." *FR* 27 (Dec. 1953): 122–31.

———. "Victor Cousin and American Transcendentalism." *FR* 29 (Dec. 1955): 117–30.

Judd, Sylvester. *The Birthright Church: A Discourse*. Boston: Crosby, Nichols, 1853.

———. *The Church: In a Series of Discourses*. Boston: Crosby, Nichols, 1854.

———. *Margaret. A Tale of the Real and Ideal, Blight and Bloom; Including Sketches of a Place Not Before Described, Called Mons Christi*. Boston: Jordan and Wiley, 1845. Rev. ed., 2 vols., Boston: Phillips, Sampson, 1851; rpt. Boston: Roberts, 1871.

———. *Philo: An Evangeliad*. Boston: Phillips, Sampson, 1850.

———. *Richard Edney and the Governor's Family. A Rus-Urban Tale, Simple and Popular, Yet Cultured and Noble, of Morals, Sentiment, and Life, Practically Treated and Pleasantly Illustrated Containing, Also, Hints on Being Good and Doing Good*. Boston: Phillips, Sampson, 1850.

Jugaku, Bunshō. *A Bibliography of Ralph Waldo Emerson in Japan from 1878 to 1935*. Kyoto: Sunward Press, 1947.

Kaiser, Mary L. "'Conversing with the Sky': The Imagery of Celestial Bodies in Thoreau's Poetry." *TJQ* 9.3 (July 1977): 15–28.

Kamei, Shunsuke. "Emerson, Whitman, and the Japanese in the Meiji Era: 1868–1912." *ESQ* no. 29 (4 Qtr. 1962): 28–62.

Kaplan, Justin. "'Half Song-Thrush, Half Alligator.'" *AH* 31 (Oct.–Nov. 1980): 62–67.

———. *Walt Whitman: A Life*. New York: Simon and Schuster, 1980.

Kaplan, Nathaniel, and Thomas Katsaros. *Origins of American Transcendentalism in Philosophy and Mysticism*. New Haven: Coll. and Univ. Press, 1975.

Kappes, Carolyn, et al. "A Calendar of the Correspondence of Henry David Thoreau." *SAR* 1982: 325–99.

Karabatsos, James. "A Word Index to *A Week on the Concord and Merrimack Rivers*." *ATQ* no. 12, suppl. (Fall 1971): 1–99. Rpt. as *A Word Index to* A Week on the Concord and Merrimack Rivers. Hartford, Conn.: Transcendental Books, 1971.

Kassel, Charles. "Theodore Parker—A Study from the Life of Edwin Miller Wheelock." *OC* 37 (Dec. 1923): 741–50.

Katz, Jonathan. *Gay American History*. New York: Crowell, 1976.

Kaufman, Marjorie Ruth. "The Literary Reviews of the *Harbinger* during Its Brook Farm Period 1845–1847." M.A. thesis Univ. of Washington 1947.

Kavanaugh, James V. "Music and American Transcendentalism: A Study of Transcendental Pythagoreanism in the Works of Henry David Thoreau, Nathaniel Hawthorne and Charles Ives." Diss. Yale 1978.

Kazin, Alfred. "Thoreau and American Power." *Atl* 223 (May 1969): 60–68.

Kearns, Francis E. "Margaret Fuller and the Abolition Movement." *JHI* 25 (Jan.–March 1964): 120–27.

———. "Margaret Fuller as a Model for Hester Prynne." *JA* 10 (1965): 161–97.

———. "Margaret Fuller's Social Criticism." Diss. Univ. of North Carolina 1960.

Keeler, Clinton. "Melville's Delano: Our Cheerful Axiologist." *CLAJ* 10 (Sept. 1966): 49–55.

Keller, Hans. *Emerson in Frankreich: Wirkungen und Parallelen.* Frankfurt: Geissen, 1932.

Keller, Karl. "Alephs, Zahirs, and the Triumph of Ambiguity: Typology in Nineteenth-Century American Literature." In *Literary Uses of Typology from the Late Middle Ages to the Present.* Ed. Earl Miner. Princeton: Princeton Univ. Press, 1977, 274–314.

———. "From Christianity to Transcendentalism: A Note on Emerson's Use of Conceit." *AL* 39 (March 1967): 94–98.

———. "The Metaphysical Strain in Nineteenth-Century American Poetry." Diss. Univ. of Minnesota 1964.

———. *The Only Kangaroo among the Beauty: Emily Dickinson and America.* Baltimore: Johns Hopkins Univ. Press, 1979.

Kelley, Michael. "Henry David Thoreau: A Transpersonal View." *JTP* 9.1 (1977): 43–82.

Kennard, James, Jr. "What Is Transcendentalism?" *Knick* 23 (March 1844): 205–11.

Kennedy, William Sloane. "Clews to Emerson's Mystic Verse." *PoL* 11 (April–June 1899): 243–50; 12 (Jan.–March, April–June 1900): 71–79, 270–83. Rpt. in *AmA* 2 (June 1903): 194–230.

———. "Identities of Thought and Phrase in Emerson and Whitman." *Conservator* 8 (Aug. 1897): 88–91. Rpt. as "Walt Whitman's Indebtedness to Emerson" in his *An Autolycus Pack; or, What You Will.* West Yarmouth, Mass.: Stonecroft Press, 1927, 45–51.

Kernahan, Coulson. "A Half-Made Poet." *LQR* 73 (Oct. 1889): 27–35.

———. "Is Emerson a Poet?" *NRev* 36 (Dec. 1900): 523–36.

Kern, Alexander C. "Church, Scripture, Nature and Ethics in Henry Thoreau's Religious Thought." In *Literature and Ideas in America.* Ed. Robert P. Falk. Athens: Ohio Univ. Press, 1975, 79–95.

———. "Coleridge and American Romanticism: The Transcendentalists and Poe." In *New Approaches to Coleridge.* Ed. Donald Sultana. New York: Vision Press/Barnes and Noble, 1981, 113–36.

———. "Emerson and Economics." *NEQ* 13 (Dec. 1940): 678–96.

———. "The Rise of Transcendentalism, 1815–1860." In *Transitions in American Literary History.* Ed. Harry Hayden Clark. Durham: Duke Univ. Press, 1954, 245–314.

———. "Thoreau Manuscripts at Harvard." *TSB* no. 53 (Fall 1955): 1–2.

Kerstesz, Louise C. "A Study of Thoreau as Myth Theorist and Myth Maker." Diss. Univ. of Illinois 1970.

Kesterson, David B. "Hawthorne and Nature: Thoreauvian Influence?" *ELN* 4 (March 1967): 200–06.

Kher, Inder Nath. *The Landscape of Absence: Emily Dickinson's Poetry.* New Haven: Yale Univ. Press, 1974.

Kides, Kathryn. "Transcendentalism as Reflected in the *Dial* Magazine." M.A. thesis Columbia 1953.

Kilgour, Raymond L. *Messrs. Roberts Brothers, Publishers*. Ann Arbor: Univ. of Michigan Press, 1952.

Kim, Kichung. "Ow Chuang Tzu and Thoreau." *LE&W* 17 (3 Qtr. 1973): 275–81.

———. "Thoreau's Involvement with Nature: Thoreau and the Naturalist Tradition." Diss. Univ. of California at Berkeley 1969.

———. "Thoreau's Science and Teleology." *ESQ* 18 (3 Qtr. 1972): 125–33.

Kinoy, Arthur [pseud. for Channing Edwards]. " 'Arise and Depart; For This Is Not Your Rest': A Study of the Resignation of George Ripley from the Ministry of the Unitarian Church on Purchase Street, in Boston, in the Year 1841." Bowdoin Prize essay, Harvard Univ., 1941.

Kirby, Georgiana Bruce. *Years of Experience: An Autobiographical Narrative*. New York: Putnam's, 1887.

Kirkham, E. Bruce, and John M. Fink. *Indices to American Annuals and Gift Books*. New Haven: Research Publications, 1975.

Kirk, Russell. *The Conservative Mind from Burke to Santayana*. Chicago: Henry Regnery, 1953.

———. *The Roots of American Order*. LaSalle, Ill.: Open Court, 1975.

———. "Two Facets of the New England Mind: Emerson and Brownson." *Month* 8 (Oct. 1952): 208–17.

Kleinfield, H. L. "The Structure of Emerson's Death." *BNYPL* 65 (Jan. 1961): 47–64.

Kloeckner, Alfred J. "Intellect and Moral Sentiment in Emerson's Opinions of 'The Meaner Kinds' of Men." *AL* 30 (Nov. 1958): 322–38.

Kneeland, Stillman F. *Seven Centuries in the Kneeland Family*. Albany, N.Y.: Joel Munsell's Sons, 1897.

Knickerbocker, Frances W. "New England Seeker: Sarah Bradford Ripley." *NEQ* 30 (March 1957): 3–22.

Knight, Harriet Elizabeth. "Two Streams of Mysticism in America: Quakerism and Transcendentalism." M.A. thesis Columbia 1929.

Kolbenschlag, M. Claire. "Thoreau and Crusoe: The Reconstruction of an American Myth and Style." *AmerS* 22.2 (1977): 229–46.

Konvitz, Milton R., ed. *The Recognition of Ralph Waldo Emerson*. Ann Arbor: Univ. of Michigan Press, 1972.

———, and Stephen E. Whicher, eds. *Emerson: A Collection of Critical Essays*. Englewood Cliffs, N.J.: Prentice-Hall, 1962.

Kopp, Charles C. "The Mysticism of Henry David Thoreau." Diss. Pennsylvania State Univ. 1963.

Koster, Donald N. "Transcendental Journals and the Transcendentalist Aesthetic." In his *Transcendentalism in America*, 25–30.

———. *Transcendentalism in America*. Boston: Twayne, 1975.

Kraditor, Aileen S. *Means and Ends in American Abolitionism*. New York: Pantheon, 1969.

Kramer, Aaron. *The Prophetic Tradition in American Poetry, 1835–1900*. Rutherford, N.J.: Fairleigh Dickinson Univ. Press, 1968.

Kraus, W. Keith. "An Uncited Reply to Twain's Letter on the Foster Case with a Note on John Weiss." *ALR* 14 (Spr. 1981): 98–100.

Kribbs, Jayne K. *An Annotated Bibliography of American Literary Periodicals, 1741–1850*. Boston: G. K. Hall, 1977.

Kring, Walter Donald. *Henry Whitney Bellows*. Boston: Skinner House, 1979.

———. *Liberals among the Orthodox: Unitarian Beginnings in New York City, 1819–1839*. Boston: Beacon, 1974.

Krishnamachari, V. "Transcendentalism in America." *CalR* 116 (June 1950): 10–27.

Krutch, Joseph Wood. *Henry David Thoreau*. New York: William Sloane, 1949.

Kuklick, Bruce. *The Rise of American Philosophy*. New Haven: Yale Univ. Press, 1977.

Kurtz, Ernest, and William R. Hutchison. "Boston Area Resources for the Study of American Religious History." *RTR* 2 (Oct.–Dec. 1971): 1–13.

Kwiat, Joseph. "Thoreau's Philosophical Apprenticeship." *NEQ* 18 (March 1945): 51–69.

Kwon, Teck-Young. "A. Bronson Alcott's Literary Apprenticeship to Emerson: The Role of Harris's *Journal of Speculative Philosophy*." Diss. Univ. of Nebraska 1980.

Lacey, James F. "Henry David Thoreau in German Criticism 1881–1965." Diss. New York Univ. 1968.

Lader, Lawrence. *The Bold Brahmins: New England's War against Slavery 1831–1863*. New York: Dutton, 1961.

Ladu, Arthur I. "Channing and Transcendentalism." *AL* 11 (May 1939): 129–37.

———. "Emerson: Whig or Democrat." *NEQ* 13 (Sept. 1940): 419–41.

———. "The Political Ideas of Theodore Parker." *SP* 38 (Jan. 1941): 106–23.

Lambert, L. Gray. "Rousseau and Thoreau: Their Concept of Nature." Diss. Rice Univ. 1969.

Lane, Charles. "A. Bronson Alcott's Works." *Dial* 3 (April 1843): 417–54. Rpt. as *The Law and Method in Spirit-Culture*. Boston: James Munroe, 1843.

———. "Brook Farm." *Dial* 4 (Jan. 1844): 351–57.

———. "Catalogue of Books." *Dial* 3 (April 1843): 545–48.

———. "The Consociate Family Life." *NYDT*, 1 Sept. 1843, 1. Rpt. in *Liberator*, 22 Sept. 1843, 152.

———. "Interior or Hidden Life." *Dial* 4 (Jan. 1844): 373–78.

———. "Life in the Woods." *Dial* 4 (April 1844): 415–25.

———. "Literature." *Union* [England] 1 (1 Nov. 1842): 356–60.

———. "Social Tendencies." *Dial* 4 (July, Oct. 1843): 65–86, 188–204.

———. "The Third Dispensation." *Present* 1 (15 Nov. 1843): 110–21.

———. "Transatlantic Transcendentalism." *Union* [England] 1 (1 Aug. 1842): 166–68.

———. "A Voluntary Political Government." *Liberator*, 3 March–16 June 1843, 36, 48, 56, 68, 76, 84, 96. Rpt. in *A Voluntary Political Government: Letters from Charles Lane*. Ed. Carl Watner. St. Paul, Minn: Michael E. Coughlin, 1983.

Lane, Lauriat, Jr. "*Cape Cod*—Thoreau's Sandy Pastoral." *ATQ* no. 11 (Sum. 1971): 69–74.

———. "Finding a Voice: Thoreau's Pentameters." *ESQ* no. 60 (Sum. 1970): 67–72.

———. "Mountain Gloom and Yankee Poetry: Thoreau, Emerson, Frost." *DR* 55 (Wtr. 1976): 612–30.

———. "Thoreau at Work: Four Versions of 'A Walk to Wachusett.'" *BNYPL* 69 (Jan. 1965): 3–16.

———. "Thoreau's Autumnal Archetypal Hero: Captain John Brown." *Ariel* 6 (Jan. 1975): 41–49.

———. "Thoreau's Autumnal Indians." *CRevAS* 6 (Fall 1975): 228–36.

———. "Thoreau's Two Walks: Structure and Meaning." *TSB* no. 109 (Fall 1969): 1–3.

———, ed. *Approaches to* Walden. San Francisco: Wadsworth, 1961.

Lang, Hans-Joachim. "*The Blithedale Romance*: A History of Ideas Approach." In *Literatur und Sprache der Vereinigten Staaten: Aufsätze zu Ehren von Hans Galinsky*. Ed. Hans Helmcke. Heidelberg: Carl Winter, 1969, 88–106.

Lapati, Americo D. *Orestes A. Brownson*. New York: Twayne, 1965.

La Piana, Angelina. *Dante's American Pilgrimage: A Historical Survey of Dante Studies in the United States 1800–1914*. New Haven: Yale Univ. Press, 1948.

Larned, Augusta. "Impressions of Concord." *CAW*, 21 Aug. 1884.

LaRosa, Ralph C. "Bacon and the 'Organic Method' of Emerson's Early Lectures." *ELN* 8 (Dec. 1970): 107–14.

———. "David Henry Thoreau: His American Humor." *SR* 83 (Fall 1975): 602–22.

———. "Emerson's Search for Literary Form: The Early Journals." *MP* 69 (Aug. 1971): 25–35.

———. "Invention and Imitation in Emerson's Early Lectures." *AL* 44 (March 1972): 13–30.

———. "Necessary Truths: The Poetics of Emerson's Proverbs." *LMonog* 8 (1976): 129–92.

Laski, Harold. *The American Democracy: A Commentary and an Interpretation*. New York: Viking, 1948.

"The Last Eminent Survivor of the Great New England Age." *CuL* 51 (July 1911): 97–99.

Lathrop, George Parsons. "Literary and Social Boston." *Har* 62 (Feb. 1881): 381–98.

———. Review of Christopher Pearse Cranch, *The Bird and the Bell*. *Atl* 37 (Feb. 1876): 244.

———. *A Study of Hawthorne*. Boston: James R. Osgood, 1876.

Lathrop, Rose Hawthorne. *Memories of Hawthorne*. Boston: Houghton, Mifflin, 1897.

Lauter, Paul. "Emerson's Revisions of *Essays: First Series*." *AL* 33 (May 1961): 143–58.

———. "Truth and Nature: Emerson's Use of Two Complex Words." *ELH* 27 (March 1960): 66–85.

Lavan, Spencer. "Raja Rammohun Roy and the American Unitarians: New Worlds to Conquer (1821–1834)." In *West Bengal and Bangladesh: Perspectives from 1972*. Ed. Barbara Thomas and Lavan. East Lansing: Asian Studies Center of Michigan State Univ., 1973, 1–16.

———. "Rammohun Roy and the Rev. Jared Sparks." *BPP* 94 (Jan.–June 1975): 25–30.

———. *Unitarians and India: A Study in Encounter and Response*. Boston: Beacon, 1977.

Law, S. "The Theology of Emerson." In his *The Theology of Modern Literature*. Edinburgh: T. and T. Clark, 1899, 97–128.

Laws, John Wallace. "A Discourse of Matters Pertaining to Theodore Parker." *PUHS* 13. 1 (1960): 39–53.

Leary, Lewis. "Beyond the Brink of Fear: Thoreau's Wilderness." *SLitI* 7 (Spr. 1978): 67–76.

———. "Henry David Thoreau." In *Eight American Authors*. Rev. ed. Ed. James Woodress. New York: Norton, 1971, 129–71.

———. "The Maneuverings of a Transcendental Mind: Emerson's *Essays* of 1841." *Prospects* 3 (1977): 499–520.

———. *Ralph Waldo Emerson: An Interpretive Essay*. Boston: Twayne, 1980.

Lease, Benjamin. *That Wild Fellow John Neal and the American Literary Revolution*. Chicago: Univ. of Chicago Press, 1972.

LeBeau, Bryan F. "Frederic Henry Hedge: Portrait of an Enlightened Conservative." Diss. New York Univ. 1982.

LeBeaux, Richard. "Emerson's Young Adulthood: From Patienthood to Patiencehood." *ESQ* 25 (4 Qtr. 1979): 203–10.

———. " 'Sugar Maple Man': Middle-aged Thoreau's Generativity Crisis." *SAR* 1981: 359–78.

———. *Young Man Thoreau*. Amherst: Univ. of Massachusetts Press, 1977.

Lee, Roland F. "Emerson through Kierkegaard: Toward a Definition of Emerson's Theory of Communication." *ELH* 26 (Spr. 1957): 229–48.

———. "Emerson's 'Compensation' as Argument and Art." *NEQ* 37 (Sum. 1964): 291–305.

Lee, Vernon [pseud. for Violet Paget]. "Emerson: Transcendentalist and Utilitarian." *ContempR* 67 (March 1895): 345–60.

Lefcowitz, Allan B., and Barbara F. Lefcowitz. "James Bryce's First Visit to America: The New England Sections of His 1870 Journal and Related Correspondence." *NEQ* 50 (June 1977): 314–31.

Leidecker, Kurt F. "Amos Bronson Alcott and the Concord School of Philosophy." *Person* 33 (Sum. 1952): 242–56.

———. *Yankee Teacher: The Life of William Torrey Harris*. New York: Philosophical Library, 1946.

Leighton, Walter L. *French Philosophers and New-England Transcendentalism*. Charlottesville: Univ. of Virginia, 1908.

Leisy, Ernest. *American Literature*. New York: Crowell, 1929.

———. "Frances Quarles and Henry David Thoreau." *MLN* 60 (May 1945): 37–44.

———. "Thoreau and Ossian." *NEQ* 18 (March 1945): 96–98.

Leland, Charles Godfrey. *Memoir*. 2 vols. New York: D. Appleton, 1893.

Leliaert, Richard M. "Orestes Augustus Brownson: Theological Perspectives on His Search for the Meaning of God, Christology, and the Development of Doctrine." Diss. Univ. of California at Berkeley 1977.

Lemchen, Leo. "A Summary View of the Vogue of French Eclecticism in New England—1829-1844." M.A. thesis Columbia 1936.

Lemelin, Robert. *Pathway to the National Character 1830-1861*. Port Washington, N.Y.: Kennikat, 1974.

Lenhart, Charmenz S. "Music and the Transcendentalists." In her *Musical Influence in American Poetry*. Athens: Univ. of Georgia Press, 1956, 105–17.

Lennon, Florence Baker. "The Influence of Brook Farm on George William Curtis, 1842–1872." M.A. thesis Univ. of Colorado 1947.

Lentricchia, Frank. "Coleridge and Emerson: Prophets of Silence, Prophets of Language." *JAAC* 32 (Fall 1973): 37–46.

Lenz, Frederick P., III. "Henry David Thoreau: The Forgotten Poems." *CS* 11.1 (Mar. 1976): 1–10.

Leonard and Co. *Catalogue of the Private Library of the Late John Weiss* . . . . Boston: W. Richardson, 1879.

Lerch, Charles H. "Emerson's Prose." *RQR* 12 (Jan., April, July 1890): 94–104, 240–51, 379–93.

Lesley, Susan I. *Memoir of the Life of Mrs. Anne Jean Lyman*. Cambridge, Mass.: privately printed, 1876. Rpt. as *Recollections of My Mother: Mrs. Anne Jean Lyman of Northampton*. Boston: Houghton, Mifflin, 1899.

"Letters from America. Ralph Waldo Emerson." *PeJ* 4 (20 Nov. 1848): 305.

Levenson, J. C. "Christopher Pearse Cranch: The Case History of a Minor Artist in America." *AL* 21 (Jan. 1950): 415–26.

Levernier, James A. "Calvinism and Transcendentalism in the Poetry of Jones Very." *ESQ* 24 (1 Qtr. 1976): 30–41.

Levin, David, ed. *Emerson: Prophecy, Metamorphosis, Influence*. New York: Columbia Univ. Press, 1975.

Levine, Stuart. *Edgar Poe: Seer and Craftsman*. Deland, Fla.: Everett/Edwards, 1972.

Levy, Leonard W. "Sims' Case: The Fugitive Slave Law in Boston in 1851." *JNH* 35 (Jan. 1950): 39–74.

Lewin, Walter. "Emerson and the Transcendentalists." *PT* 2 (Aug. 1879): 119–28.

Lewis, Albert. "Words, Action, and Emerson." *CE* 7 (Oct. 1945): 20–25.

Lewis, R. W. B. *The American Adam*. Chicago: Univ. of Chicago Press, 1955.

Lewis, Suzanne S. "Thoreau and His Sources: A Reading of *Cape Cod*." Diss. Univ. of Texas 1974.

———. "Thoreau's Use of Sources in *Cape Cod*." *SAR* 1978: 421–28.

Lewisohn, Ludwig. *Expression in America*. New York: Harper's, 1932.

Leyda, Jay. *The Melville Log*. 2 vols. New York: Harcourt, Brace, 1951. Exp. ed., New York: Gordian Press, 1969.

———. *The Years and Hours of Emily Dickinson*. 2 vols. New Haven: Yale Univ. Press, 1960.

Libman, Valentina. *Russian Studies of American Literature: A Bibliography*. Trans. Robert V. Allen. Chapel Hill: Univ. of North Carolina Press, 1969.

Liebman, Sheldon W. "The Development of Emerson's Theory of Rhetoric, 1821–1836." *AL* 41 (May 1969): 178–206.

———. "Emerson's Discovery of the English Romantics, 1818–1836." *ATQ* no. 21 (Wtr. 1974): 36–44.

———. "Emerson's Transformation in the 1820's." *AL* 40 (May 1968): 133–54.

———. "Origins of Emerson's Early Poetics: His Reading of the Scottish Common Sense Critics." *AL* 45 (March 1973): 23–33.

"The Life and Services to Literature of Jones Very." *BEI* 13 (Jan.–June 1881).

Liggera, Joseph J. "Thoreau's Heroic Language." Diss. Tufts Univ. 1971.

Lind, Sidney E. "Christopher Pearse Cranch's 'Gnosis': An Error in Title." *MLN* 62 (Nov. 1947): 486–88.

Lindeman, Eduard C. "Emerson's Pragmatic Mood." *ASch* 16 (Wtr. 1946): 57–64.

Lindquist, Vernon R. "Emerson and Bangor: An Analysis and History of Their Reciprocal Influence." M.A. thesis Univ. of Maine 1968.

Lindsay, James. "Emerson as a Thinker." In his *Essays: Literary and Philosophical*. Edinburgh: William Blackwood, 1896, 123–58.

Lindsay, Julian Ira. *Tradition Looks Forward*. Burlington: Univ. of Vermont, 1954.

Linstromberg, Robin, and James Ballowe. "Thoreau and Etzler: Alternate Views of Economic Reform." *MASJ* 11 (Spr. 1970): 20–29.

Literary Writings in America: A Bibliography. 8 vols. Millwood, N.Y.: KTO, 1977.

Locher, Kaspar T. "The Reception of American Literature in German Literary Histories in the Nineteenth Century." Diss. Univ. of Chicago 1949.

Lombard, Charles M. "The American Attitude towards the French Romantics (1800–1861)." *RLC* 39 (July–Sept. 1965): 358–71.

———. *Thomas Holley Chivers*. Boston: Twayne, 1979.

London, Herbert. "American Romantics; Old and New." *ColQ* 18 (Sum. 1969): 5–20.

Longfellow, Henry Wadsworth. *The Letters of Henry Wadsworth Longfellow*. Ed. Andrew Hilen. 6 vols. Cambridge: Harvard Univ. Press, 1967–82.

Longfellow, Samuel. *Life of Henry Wadsworth Longfellow*. 2 vols. Boston: Houghton, Mifflin, 1886.

———, ed. *Final Memorials of Henry Wadsworth Longfellow*. Boston; Houghton, Mifflin, 1887.

Long, Larry R. "The Bible and the Composition of *Walden*." *SAR* 1979: 309–54.

———. "Thoreau's Portmanteau Biblical Allusions." *TJQ* 11.3–4 (July–Oct. 1979): 49–54.

Long, Orie William. *Frederic Henry Hedge: A Cosmopolitan Scholar*. Portland, Me.: Southworth-Anthoensen Press, 1940.

———. *Literary Pioneers: Early American Explorers of European Culture*. Cambridge: Harvard Univ. Press, 1935.

Loomis, C. Grant. "Emerson's Proverbs." *WF* 17 (Oct. 1958): 257–62.

———. "Sylvester Judd's New England Lore." *JAF* 60 (April–June 1947): 151–58.

Lorch, Fred W. "Thoreau and the Organic Principle in Poetry." *PMLA* 53 (March 1938): 286–302.

Lothrop, Samuel Kirkland. *Some Reminiscences of the Life of Samuel Kirkland Lothrop*. Ed. Thornton Kirkland Lothrop. Cambridge, Mass.: John Wilson, 1888.

Loving, Jerome. *Emerson, Whitman, and the American Muse*. Chapel Hill: Univ. of North Carolina Press, 1982.

———. "Emerson, Whitman, and the Paradox of Self-Reliance." In *Critical Essays on Walt Whitman*. Ed. James Woodress. Boston: G. K. Hall, 1983, 306–19.

———. "Emerson's 'Constant Way of Looking at Whitman's Genius.' " *AL* 51 (Nov. 1979): 399–403.

———. "Emerson's Foreground." In *Emerson Centenary Essays*, ed. Joel Myerson, 41–64.

———. *Walt Whitman's Champion: William Douglas O'Connor*. College Station: Texas A&M Univ. Press, 1978.

———. " 'A Well-Intended Halfness': Emerson's View of *Leaves of Grass.*" *SAH* 3 (Oct. 1979): 61–68.

Low, Alvah H. "The Concord Lyceum." *OTNE* 50 (Oct.–Dec. 1959): 29–42.

Lowance, Mason I., Jr. "From Edwards to Emerson to Thoreau: A Revaluation." *ATQ* no. 18 (Spr. 1973): 3–13.

———. *The Language of Canaan: Metaphor and Symbol in New England from the Puritans to the Transcendentalists*. Cambridge: Harvard Univ. Press, 1980.

Lowell, James Russell. "Agassiz." *Atl* 33 (May 1874): 586–96. Rpt. in his *Heartsease and Rue*. Boston: Houghton, Mifflin, 1888, 1–22.

———. *Class Poem*. Cambridge, Mass.: Metcalf, Torry, and Ballou, 1838. Rpt. in *Uncollected Poems of James Russell Lowell*. Ed. Thelma M. Smith. Philadelphia: Univ. of Pennsylvania Press, 1950, 217–48.

———. *A Fable for Critics*. New York: George P. Putnam, 1848.

———. *Letters of James Russell Lowell*. Ed. Charles Eliot Norton. 2 vols. New York: Harper's, 1894. Rpt. with additions in *The Complete Writings of James Russell Lowell* [Elmwood Edition]. 16 vols. Boston: Houghton Mifflin, 1904. Vols. 14–16.

———. "Mr. Emerson's New Course of Lectures." *Nation* 7 (12 Nov. 1868): 389. Rpt. in "Emerson the Lecturer" in his *My Study Windows*. Boston: James R. Osgood, 1871, 375–84.

———. *New Letters of James Russell Lowell*. Ed. M. A. DeWolfe Howe. New York: Harper's, 1932.

———. Review of Ralph Waldo Emerson, *The Conduct of Life*. *Atl* 7 (Feb. 1861): 254–55. Rpt. in "Emerson the Lecturer" in his *My Study Windows*, 375–84.

———. Review of Sylvester Judd, *Philo*. *NASS*, 24 Jan. 1850, 139.

———. Review of Henry Wadsworth Longfellow, *Kavanagh*. *Nar* 69 (July 1849): 196–215.

———. Review of Henry David Thoreau, *A Week on the Concord and Merrimack Rivers*. *MassQR* 3 (Dec. 1849): 40–51.

———. "Studies for Two Heads." In his *Poems: Second Series*. Cambridge, Mass.: George Nichols; Boston: B. B. Mussey, 1848, 135–41.

———. "Thoreau's Letters." *NAR* 101 (Oct. 1865): 597–608. Rpt. in his *My Study Windows*, 193–209.

———. *The Writings of James Russell Lowell* [Riverside Edition]. 10 vols. Boston: Houghton, Mifflin, 1890.

———, ed. *The Pioneer*. Intro. Sculley Bradley. New York: Scholars' Facsimiles & Reprints, 1947.

Lowell, Maria. *The Poems of Maria Lowell with Unpublished Letters and a Biography*. Ed. Hope Jillson Vernon. Providence: Brown Univ. Press, 1936.

Lowens, Irving. "Writings about Music in the Periodicals of American Transcendentalism (1835–50)." *JAMS* 10 (Sum. 1957): 71–85. Rpt. in his *Music and Musicians in Early America*. New York: Norton, 1964, 249–63, 311–21.

Lowery, Margaret Ruth. "John Burroughs in Relation to the New England Transcendentalists." M.A. thesis Univ. of Chicago 1920.

Lucas, Alec. "Thoreau, Field Naturalist." *UTQ* 23 (April 1954): 227–32.

Lucas, John A. "Thomas Wentworth Higginson: Early Apostle of Health and Fitness." *JHPER* 42 (Feb. 1971): 30–33.

Luce, William. *The Belle of Amherst*. Boston: Houghton Mifflin, 1976.

Ludwig, Richard, comp. *Literary History of the United States: Bibliography*. 4th ed. New York: Macmillan, 1971.

Luedtke, Luther S. "Emerson in Western Europe (1955–1975)." *ATQ* no. 31, suppl. (Sum. 1976): 24–42.

———. "German Criticism and Reception of Ralph Waldo Emerson." Diss. Brown 1971.

Lunt, George. *A Reviewer Reviewed*. Boston: William L. Kent, 1858.

Lydenberg, John. "Emerson and the Dark Tradition." *CritQ* 4 (Wtr. 1962): 352–58.

Lynen, John F. *The Design of the Present: Essays on Time and Form in American Literature*. New Haven: Yale Univ. Press, 1969.

Lyon, Melvin E. "Walden Pond as Symbol." *PMLA* 82 (May 1967): 289–300.

Lyon, William H. *The First Parish in Brookline; an Historical Sketch*. Brookline, Mass.: C. A. W. Spencer, Riverdale Press, 1898.

———. *Frederic Henry Hedge: A Sermon*. Brookline, Mass.: The Parish, 1906.

Lyons, Nathan. "The Figure of William Ellery Channing." *MQR* 7 (Spr. 1968): 120–26.

Lyttle, Charles H. *Freedom Moves West: A History of the Western Unitarian Conference 1852–1952*. Boston: Beacon, 1952.

Mabbott, Thomas Ollive. "Poe and Emerson." *N&Q* 197 (Dec. 1952): 566.

Mabie, Hamilton Wright. "Concord and Emerson." *Outlook* 74 (2 May 1903): 18–29. Rpt. in his *Backgrounds of Literature*. New York: Outlook, 1903, 56–96.

McAleer, John J. "Thoreau's Epic *Cape Cod*." *Thought* 43 (Sum. 1968): 227–46.

McAtee, W. L. "Adaptationist Naiveté." *SM* 48 (March 1939): 253–55.

McCall, Roy Clyde. "The Public Speaking Principles and Practice of Theodore Parker." Diss. Univ. of Iowa 1937.

———. "Theodore Parker." In *History and Criticism of American Public Address*. Ed. William Norwood Brigance. 2 vols. New York: McGraw-Hill, 1943, 1: 238–64.

McCart, Doris Louise. "Elizabeth Palmer Peabody: A Biographical Study." M.A. thesis Univ. of Chicago 1918.

McCarthy, Leonard J. "Rhetoric in the Works of Orestes Brownson." Diss. Fordham 1961.

McCarthy, Mr. "Emerson." *DuR* 26 (March 1849): 152–79.

McColgan, Daniel T. *Joseph Tuckerman: Pioneer in American Social Work*. Washington, D.C.: Catholic Univ. of America Press, 1940.

McCormick, Edgar L. "Thomas Wentworth Higginson as a Literary Critic." Diss. Univ. of Michigan 1950.

———. "Thomas Wentworth Higginson, Poetry Critic for the *Nation*, 1877–1903." *Serif* 2 (Sept. 1965): 14–19.

McCormick, John O. "Emerson's Theory of Human Greatness." *NEQ* 26 (Sum. 1953): 291–314.

McCosh, James. "The Concord School of Philosophy." *PrR* n.s. 9 (Jan. 1882): 49–71.

M'Cully, R. "Emerson." *IRNJM* 22 (1 Feb., 1 April 1875): 60–68, 158–66.

McCusker, Honor. "Fifty Years of Music in Boston." *MB* 12 (Oct. 1937): 341–57.

McCuskey, Dorothy. *Bronson Alcott, Teacher*. New York: Macmillan, 1940.

Macdonald, Joan. "The *Dial* and the Curtis Brothers of Brook Farm." *SCUL* 5 (June 1973): 46–48.

McDonald, John Joseph. "Emerson and John Brown." *NEQ* 44 (Sept. 1971): 377–96.

———. "A Guide to Primary Source Materials for the Study of Hawthorne's Old Manse Period." *SAR* 1977: 261–312.

———. "Hawthorne at the Old Manse." Diss. Princeton 1971.

———. "The Old Manse Period Canon." *NHJ* 1972: 13–39.

————. "A Sophia Hawthorne Journal, 1843–1844." *NHJ* 1974: 1–30.

McElderry, B. R., Jr. "Emily Dickinson: Viable Transcendentalist." *ESQ* no. 44 (3 Qtr. 1966): 17–21.

————. "The Transcendental Hawthorne." *MQ* 2 (July 1961): 307–23.

McElrath, Joseph R., Jr. "Practical Editions: Henry David Thoreau's *Walden*." *Proof* 4 (1975): 175–82.

McEuen, Kathryn Anderson. "Emerson's Rhymes." *AL* 20 (March 1948): 31–42.

McGiffert, Arthur Cushman, Jr. "Emerson and the Religion of the American Frontier." *AIB* 36 (April 1961): 13–20.

————. "James Marsh (1794–1842): Philosophical Theologian, Evangelical Liberal." *ChH* 38 (Dec. 1969): 437–58.

McGill, Frederick T., Jr. *Channing of Concord: A Life of William Ellery Channing II.* New Brunswick: Rutgers Univ. Press, 1967.

McGovern, James R. *Yankee Family.* New Orleans: Polyanthos, 1975.

McGuire, Errol M. "The Art of Growing Pure: Nature and Grace in Henry David Thoreau." Diss. Univ. of Chicago 1978.

McIntosh, James. *Thoreau as Romantic Naturalist: His Shifting Stance toward Nature.* Ithaca: Cornell Univ. Press, 1974.

McKay, Glen W. "Self-Definition, Conscience, and Growth: The Political Standpoint of Thoreau." Diss. Univ. of California at Berkeley 1976.

McKay, Mae Bernadine. "Margaret Fuller (Ossoli), the Gnomon of *The Dial*." M.A. thesis Ohio State Univ. 1942.

McKeehan, Irene P. "Carlyle, Hitler, and Emerson: A Comparison of Political Theories." *UCS* 2.1 (May 1943): 1–29.

McKeithan, Dell Landreth. "Nathaniel Hawthorne's Satire of Transcendentalism in 'The Artist of the Beautiful.' " M.A. thesis Univ. of North Carolina at Greensboro 1965.

McKinsey, Elizabeth R. *The Western Experiment: New England Transcendentalists in the Ohio Valley.* Cambridge: Harvard Univ. Press, 1973.

Mackintosh, Charles G. *Some Recollections of the Pastors and People of the Second Church of Old Roxbury.* Salem, Mass.: Newcomb and Gauss, 1901.

McLean, Albert. "Thoreau's True Meridian: Natural Fact and Metaphor." *AQ* 20 (Fall 1968): 567–79.

McLean, Andrew M. "Emerson's 'Brahma' as an Expression of Brahman." *NEQ* 42 (March 1969): 115–22.

McMaster, Helen Neill. "Margaret Fuller as a Literary Critic." *UBS* 7 (Dec. 1928): 35–100.

McNamee, Lawrence Francis. *Dissertations in English and American Literature: Theses Accepted by American, British, and German Universities, 1865–1964.* New York: Bowker, 1968.

McNeal, Thomas H. "Poe's Zenobia: An Early Satire on Margaret Fuller." *MLQ* 9 (June 1950): 215–16.

McNulty, John Bard. "Emerson's Friends and the Essay on Friendship." *NEQ* 19 (Sept. 1946): 390–94.

McQuiston, Raymer. "The Relation of Ralph Waldo Emerson to Public Affairs." *BUK* 3 (15 April 1923): 5–63.

McRae, Donald. "Emerson and the Arts." *ArtB* 20 (March 1938): 79–95.

MacShane, Frank. "*Walden* and Yoga." *NEQ* 37 (Sept. 1964): 322–42.

McWilliams, Wilson Carey. "The All and the One." In his *The Idea of Fraternity in America*, 280–300.

————. *The Idea of Fraternity in America.* Berkeley: Univ. of California Press, 1973.

Madden, Edward H. *Civil Disobedience and Moral Law in Nineteenth-Century American Philosophy.* Seattle: Univ. of Washington Press, 1968.

———. "George William Curtis: Practical Transcendentalist." *Person* 40 (Aut. 1959): 369–79.

———. "The Transcendentalists." In his *Civil Disobedience and Moral Law in Nineteenth-Century American Philosophy,* 85–102.

Maddison, Carol H. "Poe's *Eureka.*" *TSLL* 2 (Aut. 1960): 350–67.

Magat, J. A. "Emerson's Aesthetics of Fiction." *ESQ* 23 (3 Qtr. 1977): 139–53.

Maginnes, David R. "The Case of the Court House Rioters in the Rendition of the Fugitive Slave Anthony Burns, 1854." *JNH* 56 (Jan. 1971): 31–42.

Magnus, Philip. "Emerson's Thoughts on Education." *NCent* 80 (Dec. 1916): 1198–1211.

Male, Roy R., Jr. " 'From the Innermost Germ': The Organic Principle in Hawthorne's Fiction." *ELH* 20 (Sept. 1953): 218–36.

———. *Hawthorne's Tragic Vision.* Austin: Univ. of Texas Press, 1957.

Malloy, Charles. [Emerson's poems]. *Arena* 31 (Feb.–June 1904): 138–52, 272–83, 370–80, 494–507, 592–602; 32 (July–Sept., Nov. 1904): 39–48, 145–51, 278–83, 504–13; 33 (Jan.–March 1905): 65–87, 182–87, 289–95. Rpt. in his *A Study of Emerson's Major Poems.*

———. "Emerson's Poems." *PrI* 5 (May 1903): 8–10. Rpt. in his *A Study of Emerson's Major Poems.*

———. "The Poems of Emerson." *ComA* 1 (Feb.–June 1899): 177–80, 295–99, 413–17, 535–43, 629–34; 2 (July–Sept., Nov.–Dec. 1899): 28–32, 159–64, 285–91, 479–85, 612–17; 3 (Jan.–June 1900): 59–64, 149–54, 250–74, 374–82, 495–99, 585–89; 4 (July 1900): 55–58. Rpt. in his *A Study of Emerson's Major Poems.*

———. *A Study of Emerson's Major Poems.* Ed. Kenneth Walter Cameron. Hartford, Conn.: Transcendental Books, 1973.

———. "What Bearing upon Emerson's Poems Have Their Titles?" *PoL* 14 (July 1903): 65–79. Rpt. in his *A Study of Emerson's Major Poems.*

Manning, J. H. *Half Truths and the Truth.* Boston: Lee and Shepard, 1872.

Mansfield, Luther S. "The Emersonian Idiom and the Romantic Period in American Literature." *ESQ* no. 35 (1 Qtr. 1964): 23–28.

Marble, Annie Russell. "Alcott as a Pioneer Educator." *Education* 24 (Nov. 1903): 153–66.

———. "Margaret Fuller as Teacher." *CriticNY* 43 (Oct. 1903): 334–45.

———. *Thoreau: His Home, Friends, and Books.* New York: Crowell, 1902.

Marchand, Ernest. "Emerson and the Frontier." *AL* 3 (May 1931): 149–74.

Marks, Barry A. "Civil Disobedience in Retrospect: Henry Thoreau and Norman Mailer." *Soundings* 62 (1979): 144–65.

Marks, Emerson R. "Victor Cousin and Emerson." In *Transcendentalism and Its Legacy,* ed. Myron Simon and Thornton H. Parsons, 63–86.

Marotte, Beatrice E. "The Influence of Emerson on Hawthorne." M.A. thesis Rutgers Univ. 1934.

Marovitz, Sanford E. "Emerson's Shakespeare: From Scorn to Apotheosis." In *Emerson Centenary Essays,* ed. Joel Myerson, 122–55.

Marsh, James. "Ancient and Modern Poetry." *NAR* 22 (July 1822): 94–131.

——— [as anonymous author]. *An Exposition of the System of Instruction and Discipline Pursued at the University of Vermont.* Burlington, Vt.: Chauncey Goodrich, 1829; 2nd ed., 1831.

———. *Selected Works of James Marsh.* Ed. Peter C. Carafiol. 3 vols. Delmar, N.Y.: Scholars' Facsimiles & Reprints, 1976.

———. "Stuart on the Epistle to the Hebrews." *QCS* 1 (March 1829): 112–49.

———, ed. Samuel Taylor Coleridge, *Aids to Reflection.* Burlington, Vt.: Chauncey Goodrich, 1829.

————, ed. Samuel Taylor Coleridge, *The Friend*. Burlington, Vt.: Chauncey Goodrich, 1833.

————, ed. Samuel Taylor Coleridge, *The Statesman's Manual* . . . . Burlington, Vt.: Chauncey Goodrich, 1832.

————, trans. Dietrich Hermann Hegewisch, *Introduction to Historical Chronology*. Burlington, Vt.: Chauncey Goodrich, 1837.

————, trans. Johann Gottfried von Herder, *The Spirit of Hebrew Poetry*. Burlington, Vt.: E. Smith, 1833.

Marshall, Helen E. "The Story of the *Dial*, 1840–44." *NMQ* 1 (May 1931): 147–65.

Marshall, James M. "The Heroic Adventure in 'A Winter Walk.' " *ESQ* no. 56 (Aut. 1969): 16–23.

Marshall, Margaret Wiley. "Emerson and the Psychological Origin of Scepticism." *RBUP* 31 (1960): 7–18.

Martin, Jay. *Harvests of Change: American Literature 1865–1914*. Englewood Cliffs, N.J.: Prentice-Hall, 1967.

Martin, John H. "Theodore Parker." Diss. Univ. of Chicago 1955.

Martin, John Stephen. "Finding a Usable Past: Emerson's Response to the Predicament of Early American Writers." In *Romantic Reassessment*. Ed. Erwin A. Stürzl. Salzburg: Inst. für Englische Sprache und Literatur, 1977, 159–90.

Martin, Terrence. *The Instructed Vision: Scottish Common Sense Philosophy and the Origins of American Fiction*. Bloomington: Indiana Univ. Press, 1961.

Marx, Leo. *The Machine in the Garden: Technology and the Pastoral Ideal in America*. New York: Oxford Univ. Press, 1964.

Massachusetts Historical Society. *Catalog Guide to the Microfilm Edition of the Theodore Parker Papers*. Boston: Massachusetts Historical Soc., 1979.

Mather, Winifred. *A Bibliography of Thomas Wentworth Higginson*. Cambridge, Mass.: Cambridge Public Library, 1906.

Mathews, J. Chesley. "Emerson's Translation of Dante's *Vita nuova*." *HLB* 11 (Spr., Aut. 1957): 208–44, 346–52. Rpt. as *Dante's* Vita nuova. N.p.: Ralph Waldo Emerson Memorial Assn., 1957. Enl. ed., Chapel Hill: Univ. of North Carolina Press, 1960.

————. "Thoreau's Reading of Dante." *Italica* 27 (June 1950): 77–81.

Mathews, James M. "An Early Brook Farm Letter." *NEQ* 53 (June 1980): 226–30.

————. "George Partridge Bradford: Friend of Transcendentalists." *SAR* 1981: 133–56.

Mathewson, Rufus, Jr. "Thoreau and Chekhov: A Note on 'The Steppe.' " *UR* 1 (Fall 1977): 28–40.

Mathis, Gerald Ray. "The *Dial*: A Religious Philosophy of Knowing." M.A. thesis Univ. of Georgia 1963.

Matthews, W. S. B. "John Sullivan Dwight." *Music* 4 (Sept. 1893): 553–57.

————. "John Sullivan Dwight, Editor, Critic, and Man." *Music* 15 (March 1899): 523–40.

Matthiessen, F. O. *American Renaissance: Art and Expression in the Age of Emerson and Whitman*. New York: Oxford Univ. Press, 1941.

————. *The James Family*. New York: Knopf, 1947.

Maulsby, David Lee. *The Contribution of Emerson to Literature*. Medford: Tufts Coll. Press, 1911.

Maurer, Armand. "Orestes Brownson: Philosopher of Freedom." In *No Divided Allegiance: Essays in Brownson's Thought*, ed. Leonard Gilhooley, 84–99.

Maxfield-Miller, Elizabeth. "Emerson and Elizabeth of Concord." *HLB* 19 (July 1971): 290–306.

May, Samuel J. *Some Recollections of Our Antislavery Conflict*. Boston: Fields, Osgood, 1869.

Mayer, Frederick. *A History of American Thought*. Dubuque, Iowa: W. C. Brown, 1951.

Maynard, Theodore. *Orestes Brownson: Yankee, Radical, Catholic*. New York: Macmillan, 1943.

Mead, C. David, ed. *"The American Scholar" Today: Emerson's Essay and Some Critical Views.* New York: Dodd, Mead, 1970.

Mead, David. "Some Ohio Conversations of Amos Bronson Alcott." *NEQ* 22 (Sept. 1949): 358–72. Rpt. in his *Yankee Eloquence in the Middle West: The Ohio Lyceum 1850-1870.* East Lansing: Michigan State Coll. Press, 1951, 78–91.

——. "Theodore Parker: Scholarly Divine." *NOQ* 21 (Wtr. 1949): 18–23. Rpt. in his *Yankee Eloquence in the Middle West*, 142–48.

Mead, Edwin D. "Emerson and Plato." *Index* 14 (7 Dec. 1882): 272–73.

——. "Emerson and Theodore Parker." In his *The Influence of Emerson*, 91–153.

——. "Emerson's Ethics." In *The Genius and Character of Emerson*, ed. F. B. Sanborn, 233–85.

——. *The Influence of Emerson.* Boston: American Unitarian Assn., 1903.

——. "Thomas Wentworth Higginson." *NEMag* n.s. 44 (May 1911): 397–412.

Meese, Elizabeth A. "Transcendentalism: The Metaphysics of the Theme." *AL* 47 (March 1975): 1–20.

——. "Transcendental Vision: A History of the Doctrine of Correspondence and Its Role in American Transcendentalism." Diss. Wayne State Univ. 1972.

Mellow, James R. *Nathaniel Hawthorne in His Times.* Boston: Houghton Mifflin, 1980.

Meltzer, Milton, and Walter Harding. *A Thoreau Profile.* New York: Crowell, 1962.

Melville, Herman. "The Apple-Tree Table." *PMM* 7 (May 1856): 465–75.

——. "Bartleby, the Scrivener." *PMM* 2 (Nov., Dec. 1853): 546–57, 609–15.

——. "Benito Cereno." *PMM* 6 (Oct.–Dec. 1855): 353–67, 459–73, 633–44.

——. *Billy Budd, Sailor: An Inside Narrative.* Ed. Harrison Hayford and Merton M. Sealts, Jr. Chicago: Univ. of Chicago Press, 1962.

——. "Cock-A-Doodle-Doo!" *Har* 8 (Dec. 1853): 77–86.

——. *The Confidence-Man.* New York: Dix and Edwards, 1857. New ed., ed. Elizabeth S. Foster, New York: Hendricks House, 1954. New ed., ed. Hershel Parker, New York: Norton, 1971.

——. "Hawthorne and His Mosses." *LWNY* 7 (17, 24 Aug. 1850): 125–27, 145–47. New ed., ed. Hershel Parker, in *The Norton Anthology of American Literature*. Ed. Ronald Gottesman et al. 2 vols. New York: Norton, 1979, 2: 2056–70.

——. *The Letters of Herman Melville.* Ed. Merrell R. Davis and William H. Gilman. New Haven: Yale Univ. Press, 1960.

——. *Mardi.* New York: Harper's, 1849.

——. *Moby-Dick.* New York: Harper's, 1851. New ed., ed. Harrison Hayford and Hershel Parker, New York: Norton, 1967.

——. "The Piazza." In his *The Piazza Tales.* New York: Dix and Edwards, 1856, 1–29.

——. *Pierre.* New York: Harper's, 1852.

——. "Poor Man's Pudding and Rich Man's Crumbs." *Har* 9 (June 1854): 95–101.

——. *Redburn.* New York: Harper's, 1849.

——. "The Two Temples." In his *Billy Budd and Other Prose Pieces.* Ed. Raymond W. [sic] Weaver. London: Constable, 1924, 173–91.

——. *Typee.* New York: Wiley and Putnam, 1846.

Memorial of the Commemoration by the Church of the Disciples. Boston: Prentiss and Deland, 1860.

Memorial of the Reverend George Putnam. Boston: First Religious Soc. of Roxbury, 1878.

Mendelsohn, Jack. *Channing: The Reluctant Radical.* Boston: Little, Brown, 1971.

Mendenhall, Lawrence. "Early Literature of the Ohio Valley." *MidM* 8 (Aug. 1897): 144–51.

Menzi, Marjorie Jean. "Women's Rights: An Aspect of Transcendentalism as Exhibited by Brook Farm." M.A. thesis Columbia 1967.

Mettke, Edith. *Der Dichter Ralph Waldo Emerson: Mystiches Denken und Poetischer Ausdruck.* Heidelberg: Carl Winter, 1963.

Metzdorf, Robert F. "Hawthorne's Suit against Ripley and Dana." *AL* 12 (May 1940): 235–41.

Metzger, Charles R. *Emerson and Greenough: Transcendental Pioneers of an American Aesthetic.* Berkeley: Univ. of California Press, 1954.

———. "Emerson's Religious Conception of Beauty." *JACC* 11 (Sept. 1952): 62–74. Incorporated into his *Emerson and Greenough.*

———. *Thoreau and Whitman: A Study of Their Esthetics.* Seattle: Univ. of Washington Press, 1971.

Meyer, Donald H. *The Instructed Conscience: The Shaping of the American National Ethic.* Philadelphia: Univ. of Pennsylvania Press, 1972.

Meyer, Howard N. *Colonel of the Black Regiment: The Life of Thomas Wentworth Higginson.* New York: Norton, 1967.

———. "Disciple of the Newness: Higginson." *HigJ* no. 32 (June 1982): 3–30.

———. "Higginson, Thoreau, and the Equation of Fame." *TJQ* 11.3–4 (July–Oct. 1979): 5–11.

Meyer, Michael. "An Advertisement for the *Dial* and Obscurity for Thoreau." *CS* 15.1 (Spr. 1980): 6–8.

———. "The Case for Greeley's *Tribune* Review of *A Week.*" *ESQ* 25 (2 Qtr. 1979): 92–94.

———. "The 1970s: The Question of Thoreau's Declining Reputation." *TSB* no. 151 (Spr. 1980): 1–3.

———. *Several More Lives to Live: Thoreau's Political Reputation in America.* Westport, Conn.: Greenwood, 1977.

———. "Thoreau and Black Emigration." *AL* 53 (Nov. 1981): 380–96.

———. "Thoreau's Rescue of John Brown from History." *SAR* 1980: 301–16.

Michaels, Walter B. "Walden's False Bottoms." *Glyph* 1 (1977): 132–49.

Michaels, William P. "The Good and the Wild: A Dichotomy in the Works of Henry David Thoreau." Diss. Univ. of California at Berkeley 1981.

Michaud, Régis. *Emerson the Enraptured Yankee.* Trans. George Boas. New York: Harper's, 1930.

———. "Emerson's Transcendentalism." *AJP* 30 (Jan. 1919): 73–82.

Mickle, Isaac. *A Gentleman of Much Promise: The Diary of Isaac Mickle 1837–1845.* Ed. Philip English Mackay. 2 vols. Philadelphia: Univ. of Pennsylvania Press, 1977.

Microfilm Edition of the Orestes Augustus Brownson Papers. 20 reels. Notre Dame: Univ. of Notre Dame, 1966.

Miles, Josephine. "Emerson's Wise Universe." *MinnR* 2 (Spr. 1962): 305–13.

———. *Ralph Waldo Emerson.* Minneapolis: Univ. of Minnesota Press, 1964. Rev. and rpt. in her *Style and Proportion: The Language of Prose and Poetry.* Boston: Little, Brown, 1967, 67–78.

Miller, Frederick De Wolfe. *Christopher Pearse Cranch and His Caricatures of New England Transcendentalism.* Cambridge: Harvard Univ. Press, 1951.

———. "Christopher Pearse Cranch: New England Transcendentalist." Diss. Univ. of Virginia 1942.

Miller, Harold P. "Hawthorne Surveys His Contemporaries." *AL* 12 (May 1940): 228–34.

Miller, James E., Jr. *The American Quest for a Supreme Fiction: Whitman's Legacy in the Personal Epic.* Chicago: Univ. of Chicago Press, 1979.

Miller, Lewis H., Jr. "Thoreau's Telegraphy." *ATQ* no. 26, suppl. (Spr. 1975): 14–18.

Miller, Norman. "Emerson's 'Each and All' Concept: A Re-Examination." *NEQ* 41 (Sept. 1968): 381–92.

Miller, Perry. "Emersonian Genius and American Democracy." *NEQ* 26 (March 1953): 27–44. Rpt. in his *Nature's Nation*. Cambridge: Harvard Univ. Press, 1967, 163–74.

———. "Jonathan Edwards to Emerson." *NEQ* 13 (Dec. 1940): 589–617. Rpt. as "From Edwards to Emerson," with new material, in his *Errand into the Wilderness*. Cambridge: Harvard Univ. Press, 1956, 184–203.

———. *The Life of the Mind in America from the Revolution to the Civil War*. New York: Harcourt, Brace, and World, 1965.

———. "Melville and Transcendentalism." *VQR* 29 (Aut. 1953): 556–75. Rpt. in his *Nature's Nation*, 184–96. Exp. version in *Moby-Dick Centennial Essays*. Ed. Tyrus Hillway and Luther S. Mansfield. Dallas: Southern Methodist Univ. Press, 1953, 123–52.

———. "Nature and the National Ego." In his *Errand into the Wilderness*, 204–16.

———. "New England's Transcendentalism: Native or Imported?" In *Literary Views*. Ed. Carroll Camden. Chicago: Univ. of Chicago Press, 1964, 115–30.

———. *The Raven and the Whale: The War of Words and Wits in the Era of Poe and Melville*. New York: Harcourt, Brace, and World, 1956.

———. "Theodore Parker: Apostasy within Liberalism." *HTR* 54 (Oct. 1961): 275–95. Rpt. in his *Nature's Nation*, 134–49.

———, ed. *The American Transcendentalists: Their Prose and Poetry*. Garden City, N.Y.: Doubleday, 1957.

———. *The Transcendentalists: An Anthology*. Cambridge: Harvard Univ. Press, 1950.

Millichap, Joseph R. "Plato's Allegory of the Cave and the Vision of *Walden*." *ELN* 7 (June 1970): 274–82.

Milne, Gordon. *George William Curtis and the Genteel Tradition*. Bloomington: Indiana Univ. Press, 1956.

———. "George William Curtis—Inheritor of the Transcendental Mantle." *ATQ* no. 18 (Spr. 1973): 35–40.

Milnes, Richard Monckton. "American Philosophy—Emerson's Works." *L&WR* 33 (March 1840): 345–72.

Minnegerode, Meade. *The Fabulous Forties 1840-1850*. Garden City, N.Y.: Garden City Publishing, 1924.

Minot, William. *Private Letters of William Minot*. N.p.: n.p., 1895.

Mishra, Vishwa Mohan. "Ralph Waldo Emerson: The Leading Spirit of the *Dial*." M.A. thesis Univ. of Georgia 1958.

"Mr. Emerson as a Lecturer." In *Radicalism in Religion, Philosophy and Social Life*. Boston: Little, Brown, 1858, 23–37.

"Mr. Emerson's Poems." *Nation* 4 (30 May 1867): 430–31.

"Mr. William Ellery Channing's 'Thoreau.'" *Nation* 18 (8 Jan. 1874): 29–30.

Mitchell, Donald G. *American Lands and Letters: From Leather-Stocking to Poe's "Raven."* New York: Scribners, 1899.

Mitterling, Philip I. *U.S. Cultural History*. Detroit: Gale, 1980.

Mize, George Edwin. "The Contribution of Evert A. Duyckinck to the Cultural Development of Nineteenth-Century America." Diss. New York Univ. 1954.

"Modern Transcendentalism." *ChOb* 1 (Jan. 1847): 18–21.

Moffit, Robert E. "Metaphysics and Constitutionalism: The Political Thought of Orestes Brownson." Diss. Univ. of Arizona 1975.

Moldenhauer, Joseph J. "Images of Circularity in Thoreau's Prose." *TSLL* 1 (Sum. 1959): 245–63.

———. "Murder as a Fine Art: Basic Connections between Poe's Aesthetics, Psychology, and Moral Vision." *PMLA* 83 (May 1968): 284–97.

———. "Paradox in *Walden*." *GrJ* 6 (Wtr. 1964): 132–46. Rpt. in *Twentieth Century Interpretations of* Walden, ed. Richard Ruland, 73–84.

————. "The Rhetorical Function of Proverbs in *Walden.*" *JAF* 80 (April–June 1967): 151–59.

————. "The Rhetoric of *Walden.*" Diss. Columbia 1964.

————, ed. *The Merrill Studies in* Walden. Columbus, Ohio: Charles E. Merrill, 1971.

Moller, Mary Elkins. *Thoreau and the Human Community.* Amherst: Univ. of Massachusetts Press, 1980.

————. " 'You Must First Have Lived': Thoreau and the Problem of Death." *ESQ* 23 (4 Qtr. 1977): 226–39.

[Moncure Daniel Conway number]. *SPM* 13.4 (1907).

Mondale, Lester. "The Practical Mysticism of Ralph Waldo Emerson." In *Mysticism and the Modern Mind.* Ed. Alfred P. Stiernotte. New York: Liberal Arts Press, 1959, 43–59.

Mood, Fulmer, and Granville Hicks. "Letters to Dr. Channing on Slavery and the Annexation of Texas, 1837." *NEQ* 5 (July 1932): 587–601.

Moody, Marjory M. "The Evolution of Emerson as an Abolitionist." *AL* 17 (March 1945): 1–21.

Moore, George F. "James Freeman Clarke." In *The Later Years of the Saturday Club 1870-1920.* Ed. M. A. DeWolfe Howe. Boston: Houghton Mifflin, 1927, 107–16.

Moore, John B. "The Master of Whitman." *SP* 23 (Jan. 1926): 77–89.

Moran, John Michael, Jr. "More F. B. Sanborn Poems." *ESQ* no. 43 (2 Qtr. 1966): 109–13.

Moran, Virginia. "Circle and Dialectic: A Study of Emerson's Interest in Hegel." *NR* 1.5 (Spr. 1969): 32–42.

Moravsky, Maria. "The Idol of Compensation." *Nation* 108 (28 June 1919): 1004–05.

More, Paul Elmer. "The Influence of Emerson." *Ind* 55 (21 May 1903): 1183–88. Rpt. in his *Shelburne Essays.* New York: Putnam's, 1904, 71–84.

————. "Thoreau's Journal." In his *Shelburne Essays: Fifth Series.* Boston: Houghton Mifflin, 1908, 106–31.

Morison, John Hopkins. Review of Arethusa Hall, *Life and Character of the Rev. Sylvester Judd. NAR* 80 (April 1855): 420–39.

Morison, Samuel Eliot. "The Great Rebellion in Harvard." *PCSM* 142 (1934): 54–112.

————. *The Oxford History of the American People.* New York: Oxford Univ. Press, 1965.

Morley, John. "Introductory." In Ralph Waldo Emerson, *Miscellanies.* London: Macmillan, 1884, vii–ix. Rpt. as *Ralph Waldo Emerson: An Essay.* New York: Macmillan, 1884.

Moro-oka, Aiko. "Margaret Fuller and the *Dial* of July, 1840." *SEAL* no. 9 (1974): 1–16.

Morrow, Honoré Willsie. *The Father of Little Women.* Boston: Little, Brown, 1927.

Morsberger, Robert E. " 'I Prefer Not To': Melville and the Theme of Withdrawal." *UCQ* 10 (Jan. 1965): 24–29.

Morse, John T., Jr. *Life and Letters of Oliver Wendell Holmes.* 2 vols. Boston: Houghton, Mifflin, 1896.

Morse, Jonathan. "Emily Dickinson and the Spasmodic School: A Note on Thomas Wentworth Higginson's Esthetics." *NEQ* 50 (Sept. 1977): 505–09.

Morton, Doris. "Ralph Waldo Emerson and the *Dial*: A Study in Literary Criticism." *ESRS* 18 (Dec. 1969): 5–51.

Moseley, Caroline. "Henry D. Thoreau and His Favorite Popular Song." *JPC* 12 (Spr. 1979): 624–29.

Mosher, Harold F., Jr. "The Absurd in Thoreau's *Walden.*" *TJQ* 3.4 (Oct. 1971): 1–9.

Mosier, Richard D. *The American Temper.* Berkeley: Univ. of California Press, 1952.

Moss, Marcia, ed. *A Catalog of Thoreau's Surveys in the Concord Free Public Library.* Geneseo, N.Y.: Thoreau Soc., 1976.

Moss, Sidney P. "Analogy: The Heart of Emerson's Style." *ESQ* no. 39 (2 Qtr. 1965): 21–24.

————. " 'Cock-A-Doodle-Doo!' and Some Legends in Melville Scholarship." *AL* 40 (May 1968): 192–210.

————. *Poe's Literary Battles: The Critic in the Context of His Historical Milieu*. Durham: Duke Univ. Press, 1963.

Moss, William M. " 'So Many Promising Youths': Emerson's Disappointing Discoveries of New England Poet-Seers." *NEQ* 49 (March 1976): 46–64.

Mott, Frank Luther. "The *Christian Disciple* and the *Christian Examiner*." *NEQ* 1 (April 1928): 197–207.

————. *Golden Multitudes: A History of Best Sellers in the United States*. New York: Macmillan, 1947.

————. *A History of American Magazines 1850–1865*. Cambridge: Harvard Univ. Press, 1938.

————. *A History of American Magazines 1865–1885*. Cambridge: Harvard Univ. Press, 1938.

————. *A History of American Magazines 1741–1850*. New York: D. Appleton–Century, 1930.

Mott, Wesley T. " 'Christ Crucified': Christology, Identity, and Emerson's Sermon No. 5." In *Emerson Centenary Essays*, ed. Joel Myerson, 17–40.

————. "Emerson and Antinomianism: The Legacy of the Sermons." *AL* 50 (Nov. 1978): 369–97.

————. "Emerson and Thoreau as Heirs to the Tradition of New England Puritanism." Diss. Boston Univ. 1975.

Mozoomdar, Protap Chunder. "Emerson as Seen from India." In *The Genius and Character of Emerson*, ed. F. B. Sanborn, 365–71.

Mueller, Roger Chester. "The Orient in American Transcendental Periodicals (1835–1886)." Diss. Univ. of Minnesota 1968.

————. "Samuel Johnson, American Transcendentalist: A Short Biography." *EIHC* 115 (Jan. 1979): 1–67.

————. "A Significant Buddhist Translation by Thoreau." *TSB* no. 138 (Wtr. 1977): 1–2.

————. "Thoreau and the Art of Motorcycle Maintenance: Transcendentalism in Our Time." *TJQ* 9.4 (Oct. 1977): 10–17.

————. "Thoreau's Selection from *Chinese Four Books* for the *Dial*." *TJQ* 4.4 (15 Oct. 1972): 1–8.

————. "Transcendental Periodicals and the Orient." *ESQ* no. 57 (4 Qtr. 1969): 52–57. Rpt. in *The Minor and Later Transcendentalists*, ed. Edwin Gittleman, 52–57.

Muir, John. "The Forests of Yosemite Park." *Atl* 85 (April 1900): 493–507.

Muirhead, John H. "How Hegel Came to America." *PhR* 37 (May 1928): 226–40.

————. *The Platonic Tradition in Anglo-Saxon Philosophy*. New York: Macmillan, 1931.

Mulqueen, James E. "Emersonian Transcendentalism: Over-Soul or Over-Self?" *TSL* 21 (1976): 21–27.

————. "Is Emerson's Work Central to the Poetry of Emily Dickinson?" *EDB* no. 24 (2 Half 1973): 211–20.

Mumford, Lewis. *The Golden Day: A Study in American Experience and Culture*. New York: Boni and Liveright, 1926.

————. *Herman Melville*. New York: Harcourt, Brace, 1929.

Murdock, James. "American Transcendentalism." In his *Sketches of Modern Philosophy*. Hartford, Conn.: John C. Wells, 1842, 167–88.

————. "German Philosophy in America." In his *Sketches of Modern Philosophy*, 156–66.

Murphey, Murray G. "Amos Bronson Alcott: The Origin and Development of His Philosophy." Undergraduate honors thesis Harvard 1949.

Murray, Donald M. "Emerson's Language as 'Fossil Poetry.' " *NEQ* 29 (June 1956): 204–15.
——. "Thoreau and Hemingway." *TJQ* 11.3–4 (July–Oct. 1979): 13–34.
——. "Thoreau's Indians and His Developing Art of Characterization." *ESQ* 21 (4 Qtr. 1975): 222–29.
Murray, James G. *Henry David Thoreau.* New York: Washington Square Press, 1968.
Myers, Richard E. "Two Unpublished Sermons by W. E. Channing." *UUC* 35 (Spr. 1980): 24–47.
Myerson, Joel. "Additions to Bronson Alcott's Bibliography: Letters and 'Orphic Sayings' in the *Plain Speaker.*" *NEQ* 49 (June 1976): 283–92.
——. "An Annotated List of Contributions to the Boston *Dial.*" *SB* 26 (1973): 133–66.
——. "Bronson Alcott's 'Journal for 1836.' " *SAR* 1978: 17–104.
——. "Bronson Alcott's 'Scripture for 1840.' " *ESQ* 20 (4 Qtr. 1974): 236–59.
——. *Brook Farm: An Annotated Bibliography and Resources Guide.* New York: Garland, 1978.
——. "A Calendar of Transcendental Club Meetings." *AL* 44 (May 1972): 197–207.
——. "Caroline Dall's Reminiscences of Margaret Fuller." *HLB* 22 (Oct. 1974): 414–28.
——. "Christopher Pearse Cranch." In *The American Renaissance in New England*, ed. Myerson, 29–30.
——. "The Contemporary Reception of the Boston *Dial.*" *RALS* 3 (Aut. 1973): 203–20.
——. "Convers Francis and Emerson." *AL* 50 (March 1978): 17–36.
——. "The Death of Charles Stearns Wheeler." *CS* 7.3 (Sept. 1972): 6–7.
——. "Eight Lowell Letters from Concord in 1838." *IllQ* 38 (Wtr. 1975): 20–42.
——. "Elizabeth Palmer Peabody." In *FPAA*, 3: 279–84.
——. "Emerson Additions to Thoreau's Library." *CS* 13.2 (Sum. 1978): 17.
——. "Emerson's 'Thoreau': A New Edition from Manuscript." *SAR* 1979: 17–92.
——. "Franklin Benjamin Sanborn." In *FPAA*, 4: 327–33.
——. "Frederic Henry Hedge." In *FPAA*, 3: 145–51.
——. "Frederic Henry Hedge and the Failure of Transcendentalism." *HLB* 23 (Oct. 1975): 396–410.
——. "George Ripley." In *FPAA*, 3: 287–89.
——. "Historic Notes on Life and Letters in Transcendental New England." In *American Literature: The New England Heritage*. Ed. James Nagel and Richard Astro. New York: Garland, 1981, 51–63.
——. "A History of the *Dial* (1840–1844)." Diss. Northwestern Univ. 1971.
——. "A History of the Transcendental Club." *ESQ* 23 (1 Qtr. 1977): 27–35.
——. " 'In the Transcendental Emporium': Bronson Alcott's 'Orphic Sayings' in the *Dial.*" *ELN* 10 (Sept. 1972): 31–38.
——. "Introduction." In *The Complete Works of Ralph Waldo Emerson* ["Centenary Edition"]. 12 vols. New York: AMS Press, 1979, 1: v–xli.
——. "James Burrill Curtis and Brook Farm." *NEQ* 51 (Sept. 1978): 396–423.
——. "James Freeman Clarke." In *FPAA*, 4: 93–107.
——. "Jones Very." In *FPAA*, 3: 319–20.
——. "Lowell on Emerson: A New Letter from Concord in 1838." *NEQ* 44 (Dec. 1971): 649–52.
——. *Margaret Fuller: A Descriptive Bibliography.* Pittsburgh: Univ. of Pittsburgh Press, 1978.
——. *Margaret Fuller: An Annotated Secondary Bibliography.* New York: Burt Franklin, 1977.
——. "Margaret Fuller's 1842 Journal: At Concord with the Emersons." *HLB* 21 (July 1973): 320–40.
——. "Mrs. Dall Edits Miss Fuller: The Story of *Margaret and Her Friends.*" *PBSA* 72 (2 Qtr. 1978): 187–200.

————. *The New England Transcendentalists and the* Dial: *A History of the Magazine and Its Contributors.* Rutherford: Fairleigh Dickinson Univ. Press, 1980.

————. "Orestes Augustus Brownson." In *FPAA*, 4: 45–51.

————. *Ralph Waldo Emerson: A Descriptive Bibliography.* Pittsburgh: Univ. of Pittsburgh Press, 1982.

————. "Samuel Johnson." In *FPAA*, 3: 197–200.

————. "Sarah Clarke's Reminiscences of the Peabodys and Hawthorne." *NHJ* 1973: 130–33.

————. "Theodore Parker." In *FPAA*, 4: 295–312.

————. *Theodore Parker: A Descriptive Bibliography.* New York: Garland, 1981.

————. "Thoreau and the *Dial*: A Survey of the Contemporary Press." *TJQ* 5.1 (Jan. 1973): 4–7.

————. "Transcendentalism and Unitarianism in 1840: A New Letter by C. P. Cranch." *CLAJ* 16 (March 1973): 366–68.

————. " 'A True & High Minded Person': Transcendentalist Sarah Clarke." *SWR* 59 (Spr. 1974): 163–72.

————. "An Ungathered Sanborn Lecture on Brook Farm." *ATQ* no. 26, suppl. (Spr. 1975): 1–11.

————. "A Union List of the *Dial* (1840–1844) and Some Information about Its Sales." *PBSA* 67 (3 Qtr. 1973): 322–28.

————. "William Ellery Channing." In *FPAA*, 4: 77–90.

————. "William Harry Harland's 'Bronson Alcott's English Friends.' " *RALS* 8 (Spr. 1978): 24–60.

————, ed. *The American Renaissance in New England.* Detroit: Gale, 1978.

————, ed. *Antebellum Writers in New York and the South.* Detroit: Gale, 1979.

————, ed. *Critical Essays on Margaret Fuller.* Boston: G. K. Hall, 1980.

————, ed. *Emerson Centenary Essays.* Carbondale: Southern Illinois Univ. Press, 1982.

N. "Emerson as a Poet." *HM* 1 (Oct. 1855): 422–33.

Nachlas, Morton deCorcey. "A Study and Transcription of William Ellery Channing's Unfinished Treatise on Man." B.D. thesis Meadville Theological School 1942.

Nagley, Winfield E. "Thoreau on Attachment, Detachment, and Non-Attachment." *PE&W* 3 (Jan. 1954): 307–20.

Nakamura, Junichi. *Edgar Allan Poe's Relations with New England.* Tokyo: Hokuseido, 1957.

Nash, Roderick. *Wilderness and the American Mind.* New Haven: Yale Univ. Press, 1964; rev. ed., 1973.

Nathan, Rhoda. "The Slanted Truth: Thoreau's and Dickinson's Roles." *TJQ* 11.3–4 (July–Oct. 1979): 35–40.

National Academy of Design Exhibition Record, 1826–1861. 2 vols. New York: New-York Historical Soc., 1943.

Neal, Valerie S. "Transcendental Optics: Science, Vision, and Imagination in the Works of Emerson and Thoreau." Diss. Univ. of Minnesota 1979.

Nelson, Roland W. "Apparatus for a Definitive Edition of Poe's *Eureka*." *SAR* 1978: 161–205.

————. "The Definitive Edition of Edgar Allan Poe's *Eureka: A Prose Poem*." Diss. Bowling Green State Univ. 1975.

Nelson, Truman. *The Passion by the Brook.* Garden City, N.Y.: Doubleday, 1953.

————. *The Sin of the Prophet.* Boston: Little, Brown, 1952.

————. "Theodore Parker as Revolutionary Moralist: From Divinity Hall to Harpers Ferry." *PUHS* 13.1 (1960): 71–83.

————. "Thoreau and John Brown." In *Thoreau in Our Season*, ed. John Hicks, 134–53.

Nettels, Elsa. " 'A Frugal Splendour': Thoreau and James and the Principles of Economy." *CLQ* 12 (March 1976): 5–13.

Neufeldt, Leonard. "Emerson and the Civil War." *JEGP* 71 (Oct. 1972): 502–13.

———. "Emerson, Thoreau, and Daniel Webster." *ESQ* 26 (1 Qtr. 1980): 26–37.

———. " 'The Fields of My Fathers' and Emerson's Literary Vocation." *ATQ* no. 31, suppl. (Sum. 1976): 3–9.

———. *The House of Emerson*. Lincoln: Univ. of Nebraska Press, 1982.

———. "James Freeman Clarke: Notes toward a Comprehensive Bibliography." *SAR* 1982: 209–26.

———. "The Law of Permutation: Emerson's Mode." *ATQ* no. 21 (Wtr. 1974): 20–30.

———. "The Science of Power: Emerson's Views of Science and Technology in America." *JHI* 38 (April 1977): 329–44.

———. "The Severity of the Ideal: Emerson's 'Thoreau.' " *ESQ* no. 58 (1 Qtr. 1970): 77–84.

———. "The Vital Mind: Emerson's Epistemology." *PQ* 50 (April 1971): 253–70.

———. "The Wild Apple Tree: Possibilities of the Self in Thoreau." Diss. Univ. of Illinois 1966.

Neussendorfer, Margaret. "Elizabeth Palmer Peabody." In *The American Renaissance in New England*, ed. Joel Myerson, 152–56.

"New Poetry in New England." *USMDR* 20 (May 1847): 294–300.

Newbrough, George F. "Reason and Understanding in the Works of Theodore Parker." *SAQ* 47 (Jan. 1948): 64–75.

Newcomb, Charles King. *The Journals of Charles King Newcomb*. Ed. Judith Kennedy Johnson. Providence: Brown Univ. Press, 1946.

———. "The Two Dolons." *Dial* 3 (July 1842): 112–23.

Newell, William. "Memoir of the Rev. Convers Francis, D.D." *PMHS* 8 (March 1865): 223–53.

Newman, Josephine K. "Changing Perspectives in Brownson's Philosophical Thought." Diss. Univ. of Toronto 1971.

Newman, Lea Bertani Vozar. *A Reader's Guide to the Short Stories of Nathaniel Hawthorne*. Boston: G. K. Hall, 1979.

Newton, Joseph Fort. *Lincoln and Herndon*. Cedar Rapids, Iowa: Torch Press, 1910.

Nichol, John. "Ralph Waldo Emerson." *NBR* 47 (Dec. 1867): 319–58.

———. "The Transcendentalist Movement." In his *American Literature*. Edinburgh: Adam and Charles Black, 1882, 254–86.

Nichols, Charles H. "Theodore Parker and the Transcendental Rhetoric: The Liberal Tradition and America's Debate on the Eve of Succession (1832–1861)." *JA* 13 (1968): 69–83.

Nichols, E. J. "Identification of Characters in Lowell's *A Fable for Critics*." *AL* 4 (May 1932): 191–94.

Nichols, Mary Gove. *Mary Lyndon*. New York: Stringer and Townsend, 1855.

Nichols, Thomas Low. *Forty Years of American Life 1841–1861*. London: J. Maxwell, 1864.

Nicoloff, Philip L. *Emerson on Race and History: An Examination of* English Traits. New York: Columbia Univ. Press, 1961.

Nicolson, Marjorie H. "James Marsh and the Vermont Transcendentalists." *PhR* 34 (Jan. 1925): 28–50.

Nicoson, Marilyn R. "Christopher Cranch and His Three Muses." *CS* 9.4 (Dec. 1974): 1–11.

———. "The Inworld and the Outworld in the Poetry of Christopher Pearse Cranch." Diss. Univ. of Pittsburgh 1974.

Nilon, Charles H. *Bibliography of Bibliographies in American Literature*. New York: Bowker, 1970.

Nissenbaum, Stephen. *Sex, Diet, and Debility in Jacksonian America: Sylvester Graham and Health Reform*. Westport, Conn.: Greenwood, 1980.

Noda, Hisashi. "Emily Dickinson and Transcendentalism." *KAL* 11 (1968): 44–58.

Norman, Henry. "Ralph Waldo Emerson: An Ethical Study." *FoR* 40 (1 Sept. 1883): 422–32.

Norton, Andrews. *A Discourse on the Latest Form of Infidelity.* Cambridge, Mass.: John Owen, 1839.

——. "The New School of Literature and Religion." *BDA*, 27 Aug. 1838, 2.

Norton, Charles Eliot. *Letters of Charles Eliot Norton.* Ed. Sara Norton and M. A. DeWolfe Howe. 2 vols. Boston: Houghton Mifflin, 1913.

——. "Walt Whitman's *Leaves of Grass.*" *PMM* 6 (Sept. 1855): 321–23. Rpt. in *A Leaf of Grass from Shady Hill, with a Review of Walt Whitman's* Leaves of Grass. Ed. Kenneth Ballard Murdock. Cambridge: Harvard Univ. Press, 1928, 27–31. Rpt. in *A Century of Whitman Criticism.* Ed. Edwin Haviland Miller. Bloomington: Indiana Univ. Press, 1969, 2–4.

Notopoulos, James A. "Emerson in Greece." *ESQ* no. 22 (1 Qtr. 1961): 42–43.

Novak, Barbara. *American Painting of the Nineteenth Century.* New York: Praeger, 1969.

——. "Americans in Italy: Arcady Revisited." *ArtA* 61 (Jan.–Feb. 1973): 56–69. Incorporated into her *Nature and Culture.*

——. *Nature and Culture: American Landscape Painting, 1825-1875.* New York: Oxford Univ. Press, 1980.

Noverr, Douglas A. "A Note on Wendell Glick's 'Thoreau's Use of His Sources.'" *NEQ* 44 (Sept. 1971): 475–77.

Noyes, D. P. "Theodore Parker." *BibS* 18 (Jan. 1861): 1–53.

Noyes, John Humphrey. *History of American Socialisms.* Philadelphia: Lippincott, 1870.

Nye, Russel Blaine. *George Bancroft: Brahmin Rebel.* New York: Knopf, 1944.

——. "The Literary Theory of Theodore Parker." *PMASAL* 32 (1946): 457–70.

——. "The Religion of George Bancroft." *JR* 19 (July 1939): 216–33.

——. *Society and Culture in America 1830-1860.* New York: Harper's, 1974.

——. *The Unembarrassed Muse: The Popular Arts in America.* New York: Dial, 1970.

Oates, Stephen B. *To Purge This Land with Blood: A Biography of John Brown.* New York: Harper and Row, 1970.

"Obituaries" [Convers Francis]. *BDA*, 15 July 1863, 2.

[Obituary of John Weiss]. *ChReg* 58 (29 March 1879): 2.

O'Brien, Harriet E. *Lost Utopias.* Boston: Walton, 1929.

Obuchowski, Peter A. "Emerson's Science: An Analysis." *PQ* 54 (Sum. 1975): 624–32.

O'Connor, Evangeline M. *Analytical Index to the Works of Nathaniel Hawthorne.* Boston: Houghton, Mifflin, 1882.

O'Connor, John Francis. "Ralph Waldo Emerson." *CathW* 27 (April 1878): 90–97.

O'Connor, William Douglas. "Emerson and Whitman." In Jerome Loving, *Walt Whitman's Champion: William Douglas O'Connor,* 226–32.

——. *The Good Gray Poet.* New York: Bunce and Huntington, 1866.

O'Daniel, Therman B. "Emerson as a Literary Critic." *CLAJ* 8 (Sept., Dec. 1964, March 1965): 21–43, 157–89, 246–72.

Odell, Alfred Taylor. *La Doctrine sociale d'Emerson.* Paris: Presses Modernes, 1931.

Oehlschlaeger, Fritz, and George Hendrick, eds. *Toward the Making of Thoreau's Modern Reputation: Selected Correspondence of S. A. Jones, A. W. Hosmer, H. S. Salt, H. G. O. Blake, and D. Ricketson.* Urbana: Univ. of Illinois Press, 1979.

Oliver, Egbert S. "'Cock-A-Doodle-Doo!' and Transcendental Hocus Pocus." *NEQ* 21 (June 1948): 204–16.

——. "Melville's Picture of Emerson and Thoreau in 'The Confidence-Man.'" *CE* 8 (Nov. 1946): 61–72.

———. "A Second Look at 'Bartleby.' " *CE* 6 (May 1945): 431–39.

———. "Thoreau and the Puritan Tradition." *ESQ* no. 44 (3 Qtr. 1966): 79–86.

Oliver, Robert T. *History of Public Speaking in America*. Boston: Allyn and Bacon, 1965.

Olmert, K. Michael. "Cranch on Emerson: A Letter Re-Edited." *ATQ* no. 13 (Wtr. 1972): 31–32.

Omans, Glen A. " 'Intellect, Taste, and the Moral Sense': Poe's Debt to Immanuel Kant." *SAR* 1980: 123–68.

Orians, G. Harrison. "The Rise of Romanticism, 1805–1855." In *Transitions in American Literary History*. Ed. Harry Hayden Clark. Durham: Duke Univ. Press, 1954, 161–244.

Orr, John. "The Transcendentalism of New England." *IntR* 13 (Oct. 1882): 381–98.

Orth, Michael. "The Prose Style of Henry Thoreau." *Lang&S* 7 (Wtr. 1974): 36–52.

Orvis, Helen D. "First Parish, West Roxbury." In *Sketches of Some Historic Churches of Greater Boston*. Ed. Katherine Gibbs Allen. Boston: Beacon, 1918, 165–91.

Osgood, Samuel. *Mile Stones in Our Life-Journey*. New York: D. Appleton, 1860.

———. "The Real and Ideal in New England." *NAR* 84 (April 1857): 535–59.

———. "Transcendentalism in New England." *IntR* 3 (Nov. 1876): 742–63.

Ostrander, Gilbert. "Emerson, Thoreau, and John Brown." *MVHR* 39 (March 1953): 713–26.

Ostrom, John Ward. "Fourth Supplement to *The Letters of Poe*." *AL* 45 (Jan. 1974): 513–36. Incorporated into his "Revised Checklist of the Correspondence of Edgar Allan Poe."

———. "Revised Checklist of the Correspondence of Edgar Allan Poe." *SAR* 1981: 169–255.

———. "Second Supplement to *The Letters of Poe*." *AL* 29 (March 1957): 69–86. Incorporated into *The Letters of Edgar Allan Poe* (1966).

———. "Supplement to *The Letters of Poe*." *AL* 24 (Nov. 1952): 358–66. Incorporated into *The Letters of Edgar Allan Poe* (1966).

"Our Weekly Gossip." *Ath* no. 1387 (27 May 1854): 655.

Owlett, F. C. "Herman Melville (1819–1891): A Centenary Tribute." *Bookman* [London] 56 (Aug. 1919): 164–67.

Pachori, Satya S. "Emerson and Slavery." *KAL* 16 (May 1975): 1–12.

Packer, Barbara L. *Emerson's Fall*. New York: Continuum, 1982.

———. "The Instructed Eye: Emerson's Cosmogony in 'Prospects.' " In *Emerson's* Nature— Origin, Growth, Meaning, ed. Merton M. Sealts, Jr., and Alfred R. Ferguson, 2nd ed., 209–21.

———. "Uriel's Cloud: Emerson's Rhetoric." *GaR* 31 (Sum. 1977): 322–42.

Page, H. A. [pseud. for A. H. Japp]. *Thoreau: His Life and Aims*. London: Chatto and Windus, 1877.

Paramananda, Swami. *Emerson and Vedanta*. 2nd ed. Boston: Vedanta Centre, 1918.

Parker, Gail Thain. *Mind Cure in New England*. Hanover, N.H.: Univ. Press of New England, 1973.

Parker, Hershel. "Melville and the Transcendentalists: A Chronology." In Melville, *The Confidence-Man*, ed. Parker, 254–63.

———. "Melville's Satire of Emerson and Thoreau: An Evaluation of the Evidence." *ATQ* no. 7 (Sum. 1970): 61–67. See also corrections in *ATQ*, no. 9 (Wtr. 1971): 70.

———. " 'The Story of China Aster': A Tentative Explication." In Melville, *The Confidence-Man*, ed. Parker, 353–56.

———, and Harrison Hayford, eds. Moby-Dick *as Doubloon*. New York: Norton, 1970.

Parker, Jane Marsh. "Elizabeth Peabody: A Reminiscence." *Outlook* 49 (3 Feb. 1894): 214–15.

Parker, Theodore. [*The Centenary Edition of the Works of Theodore Parker*]. 15 vols. Boston: American Unitarian Assn., 1907–12.

———. *The Collected Works of Theodore Parker*. Ed. Frances Power Cobbe. 14 vols. London: Trübner, 1863–71.

———. *A Discourse on the Transient and Permanent in Christianity*. Boston: The Author, 1841. Rpt. in *Three Prophets of Religious Liberalism*, ed. Conrad Wright, 113–49.

———. *Historic Americans*. Boston: Horace B. Fuller, 1870.

———. *An Humble Tribute to the Memory of William Ellery Channing, D. D.* Boston: Charles C. Little and James Brown, 1842.

——— [as "Levi Blodgett"]. *The Previous Question between Mr. Andrews Norton and His Alumni Moved and Handled, in a Letter to All Those Gentlemen*. Boston: Weeks, Jordan, 1840. Rpt. in John Edward Dirks, *The Critical Theology of Theodore Parker*, 137–60.

———. *The Revival of Religion Which We Need*. Boston: W. L. Kent, 1858. Rpt. in *ESQ* no. 59 (Spr. 1970): 87–94.

———. *Saemtliche Werke*. Trans. Johannes Ziethen. 5 vols. Leipzig: Voight and Guenther, 1854–61.

———. *Theodore Parker, American Transcendentalist: A Critical Essay and a Collection of His Writings*. Ed. Robert E. Collins. Metuchen, N.J.: Scarecrow, 1973.

———. *Theodore Parker: An Anthology*. Ed. Henry Steele Commager. Boston: Beacon, 1960.

———. *Theodore Parker's Experience as a Minister*. Boston: Rufus Leighton, Jr., 1859.

———. *Transcendentalism: A Lecture*. Boston: Free Religious Assn., 1876. Rpt. in *The World of Matter and the Spirit of Man*. Ed. George Willis Cooke. Vol. 6 of [*The Centenary Edition*]. Boston: American Unitarian Assn., 1907, 1–38.

———. *The Trial of Theodore Parker, for the "Misdemeanor" of a Speech in Faneuil Hall against Kidnapping . . . with the Defence, April 3, 1855*. Boston: The Author, 1855.

———. *West Roxbury Sermons 1837–1848*. Ed. Samuel J. Barrows. Boston: Roberts, 1892.

———. "The Writings of Ralph Waldo Emerson." *MassQR* 3 (March 1850): 200–55.

———, trans. Wilhelm M. L. DeWette, *A Critical and Historical Introduction to the Canonical Scriptures of the Old Testament*. 2 vols. Boston: Charles C. Little and James Brown, 1843.

Parker, Theodore (b. 1869). *Genealogy and Biographical Notes of John Parker of Lexington and His Descendants*. Worcester, Mass.: Charles Hamilton, 1893.

Parkes, Henry Bamford. "Emerson." *H&H* 5 (July–Sept. 1932): 581–601. Rpt. in his *The Pragmatic Test*. San Francisco: Colt Press, 1941, 39–62.

Parrington, Vernon Louis. *The Romantic Revolution in America 1800–1860*. New York: Harcourt, Brace, 1927.

Parsons, Theophilus. "Transcendentalism." *NJM* 14 (Dec. 1840, June 1841): 137–40, 380–88.

Parsons, Thornton H. "Thoreau, Frost, and the American Humorist Tradition." *ESQ* no. 33 (4 Qtr. 1963): 33–43.

Parsons, Vesta M. "Thoreau's *The Maine Woods*: An Essay in Appreciation." *HusR* 1 (Fall 1967): 17–27.

Patmore, Coventry. "Emerson." In his *Principle in Art, Etc.* London: George Bell, 1889, 125–33.

Pattee, Fred Lewis. "Critical Studies in American Literature. III. An Essay on Emerson's 'Self-Reliance.' " *Chautauquan* 30 (March 1900): 628–33.

———. *The Feminine Fifties*. New York: D. Appleton-Century, 1940.

———. *The First Century of American Literature*. New York: D. Appleton-Century, 1935.

———. "The Transcendentalists." In his *A History of American Literature*. New York: Silver, Burdett, 1896, 208–38.

Patterson, Robert Leet. *The Philosophy of William Ellery Channing*. New York: Bookman Associates, 1952.

Paul, Lucian. "Notable Contemporaries. No. II. Ralph Waldo Emerson." *CriticE* n.s. 10 (1 Aug. 1851): 347–48.

Paul, Sherman. "Alcott's Search for the Child." *BPLQ* 4 (April 1952): 88–96.

————. *Emerson's Angle of Vision: Man and Nature in American Experience*. Cambridge: Harvard Univ. Press, 1952.

————. "The Identities of John Jay Chapman." In *Transcendentalism and Its Legacy*, ed. Myron Simon and Thornton H. Parsons, 137–49. Rpt. in his *Repossessing and Renewing*. Baton Rouge: Louisiana State Univ. Press, 1976, 57–70.

————. *The Shores of America: Thoreau's Inward Explorations*. Urbana: Univ. of Illinois Press, 1958.

————. "Thoreau's 'The Landlord': 'Sublimely Trivial for the Good of Men.' " *JEGP* 54 (Oct. 1955): 587–90.

————. "Wise Silence: Sound as the Agency of Correspondence in Thoreau." *NEQ* 22 (Dec. 1949): 511–27.

————, ed. *Thoreau: A Collection of Critical Essays*. Englewood Cliffs, N.J.: Prentice-Hall, 1962.

Payne, William Donald. "Pressing the Seed: Thoreau's Rhetorical Strategies." Diss. Univ. of Illinois 1980.

Peabody, Andrew Preston. *Harvard Reminiscences*. Boston: Ticknor, 1888.

————. "Memoir of James Freeman Clarke." *PMHS* 2nd ser. 4 (March 1889): 320–35.

————. Review of Sylvester Judd, *Philo*. *NAR* 70 (April 1850): 433–43.

Peabody, Elizabeth Palmer. "Childhood." In *Concord Lectures on Philosophy*, ed. Raymond L. Bridgman, 119–23.

————. "The Dorian Measure." In *Aesthetic Papers*, ed. Peabody, 64–110. Rpt. in her *Last Evening with Allston*, 73–135.

————. "Emerson and the Abolitionists." *Index* 17 (17 Dec. 1885): 297.

————. "Emerson as Preacher." In *The Genius and Character of Emerson*, ed. F. B. Sanborn, 146–72.

————. "Exhibition of Allston's Paintings in Boston in 1839." In her *Last Evening with Allston*, 30–61.

————. *First Lessons in Grammar, on the Plan of Pestalozzi*. Boston: Carter and Hendee, 1830.

————. "Fourierism." *Dial* 4 (April 1844): 473–83. Rpt. in her *Last Evening with Allston*, 202–16.

————. "A Glimpse of Christ's Idea of Society." *Dial* 2 (Oct. 1841): 214–28. Rpt. as "Brook Farm Interpretation of Christ's Idea of Society" in her *Last Evening with Allston*, 181–201.

————. *The Hebrews*. Boston: Marsh, Capen, and Lyon, 1833.

————. *Kindergarten Culture*. Washington, D.C.: J.H. Holmes, 1870.

————. *Last Evening with Allston, and Other Papers*. Boston: D. Lothrop, 1886.

————. *Lectures in the Teaching Schools for Kindergartners*. Boston: D. C. Heath, 1886. Rpt. as *Education in the Home, the Kindergarten, and the Primary School*. London: Swan, Sonnenschein, Lowrey, 1887.

————. *Memorial of Mad. Susanne Kossuth Meszlenyi*. Boston: N. C. Peabody, 1856.

————. *Method of Spiritual Culture*. Boston: James Munroe, 1836.

————. "Nature—A Prose Poem." *USMDR* 1 (Feb. 1838): 319–27.

————. "Plan of the West Roxbury Community." *Dial* 2 (Jan. 1842): 361–72.

————. *The Polish-American System of Chronology, Reproduced, with Some Modifications, from General Bem's Franco-Polish Method*. Boston: E. P. Peabody, 1850. Rev. ed. as *Universal History*. New York: Sheldon, 1859.

————. *Record of a School*. Boston: James Munroe, 1835. Rev. ed., Boston: Russell and Shattuck, 1836. New ed., Boston: Roberts, 1874.

————. *Reminiscences of Rev. Wm. Ellery Channing. D.D.* Boston: Roberts, 1880.

————. "A Vision." *Pioneer* 1 (March 1843): 97–100. Rpt. in her *Last Evening with Allston*, 62–72.

————, ed. *Aesthetic Papers*. Boston: E. P. Peabody, 1849.

————, trans. Joseph Marie de Gerando, *Self-Education*. Boston: Carter and Hendee, 1830.

————, trans. Joseph Marie de Gerando, *The Visitor to the Poor*. Boston: Hilliard, Gray, Little, and Wilkins, 1832.

————, trans. La Motte-Fouqué, *The Water-Spirit*. Boston: Stimpson and Clapp, 1833.

————, trans. G. Oegger, *The True Messiah*. Boston: E. P. Peabody, 1842.

————, trans. "The Preaching of Buddha." *Dial* 4 (Jan. 1844): 391–401.

————, and Mary P. Mann. *Moral Culture of Infancy and Kindergarten Guide*. Boston: T. O. H. P. Burnham, 1863.

Peabody, Francis Greenwood. "The Humanism of William Ellery Channing." *ChReg* 109 (15 May 1930): 407–09.

————. *Reminiscences of Present-Day Saints*. Boston: Houghton Mifflin, 1927.

Peabody, W. B. O. Review of Sylvester Judd, *Margaret*. *NAR* 62 (Jan. 1846): 102–41.

Peacock, Leishman A. "Edwin Percy Whipple: A Biography." Diss. Pennsylvania State Univ. 1942.

Peairs, Edith. "The Hound, the Bay Horse, and the Turtle Dove: A Study of Thoreau and Voltaire." *PMLA* 52 (Sept. 1937): 863–69.

Pearce, Roy Harvey. *The Continuity of American Poetry*. Princeton: Princeton Univ. Press, 1961.

Pearson, Henry Greenleaf. *The Life of John A. Andrew*. 2 vols. Boston: Houghton Mifflin, 1904.

Pearson, Norman Holmes. "Elizabeth Peabody on Hawthorne." *EIHC* 94 (July 1958): 256–76.

————. "A 'Good Thing' for Hawthorne." *EIHC* 100 (Oct. 1964): 300–05.

————. *Hawthorne's Two "Engagements."* Northampton, Mass.: Smith Coll., 1963.

Pease, Jane H., and William H. Pease. *Bound with Them in Chains: A Biographical History of the Antislavery Movement*. Westport, Conn.: Greenwood, 1972.

Pease, William H. "Doctrine and Fellowship: William Channing Gannett and the Unitarian Credal Issue." *ChH* 25 (Sept. 1956): 210–38.

————, and Jane H. Pease. "Freedom and Peace: A Nineteenth Century Dilemma." *MQ* 9 (Oct. 1967): 23–40.

————. "Samuel J. May: Civil Libertarian." *CLJ* no. 3 (Aut. 1967): 7–25. Incorporated into their *Bound with Them in Chains*.

————, eds. *The Antislavery Argument*. Indianapolis: Bobbs-Merrill, 1965.

Pederson, Lee H. "Americanisms in Thoreau's Journal." *AL* 37 (May 1965): 167–84.

Peirce, Ann-Mari. "The Transcendentalists and Fiction." M.A. thesis Univ. of Utah 1969.

Pennell, Elizabeth Robins. *Charles Godfrey Leland: A Biography*. 2 vols. Boston: Houghton Mifflin, 1906.

Peple, Edward Cronin, Jr. "The Background of the Hawthorne-Thoreau Relationship." *RALS* 1 (Spr. 1971): 104–12.

————. "Hawthorne on Thoreau, 1853–1857." *TSB* no. 119 (Spr. 1972): 1–3.

————. "The Personal and Literary Relationship of Hawthorne and Thoreau." Diss. Univ. of Virginia 1970.

————. "Thoreau and Donatello." *TJQ* 5.3 (Oct. 1973): 22–25.

"A Pepysian Letter." *HDM* 3 (June 1849): 380–82.

Perkins, James H. "The *Western Messenger*: Devoted to Religion and Literature." *ChEx* 25 (Sept. 1838): 37–42.

Perkins, Norman C. "The Original *Dial*." *Dial* [Chicago] 1 (May 1880): 9–11.

Perry, Bliss. *The American Spirit in Literature*. New Haven: Yale Univ. Press, 1918.

————. *Emerson Today*. Princeton: Princeton Univ. Press, 1931.

————. "John Sullivan Dwight." In Edward Waldo Emerson, *The Early Years of the Saturday Club*, 46–52.

————. *The Praise of Folly and Other Papers*. Boston: Houghton Mifflin, 1923.

————. *Walt Whitman*. Boston: Houghton Mifflin, 1906; rev. ed., 1908.

Perry, Lewis. *Radical Abolitionism*. Ithaca: Cornell Univ. Press, 1973.

————. " 'We Have Had No Conversation in the World': The Abolitionists and Spontaneity." *CRevAS* 6 (Spr. 1975): 3–26.

Perry, Ralph Barton. *The Thought and Character of William James*. 2 vols. Boston: Little, Brown, 1936.

Perry, Thomas Sargent. *The Life and Letters of Francis Lieber*. Boston: James R. Osgood, 1882.

Persons, Stow. *American Minds: A History of Ideas*. 2nd ed. Huntington, N.Y.: Robert E. Krieger, 1975.

————. *The Decline of American Gentility*. New York: Columbia Univ. Press, 1973.

————. *Free Religion: An American Faith*. New Haven: Yale Univ. Press, 1947.

Pessen, Edward. *Jacksonian Democracy: Society, Personality, and Politics*. Homewood, Ill.: Dorsey, 1969.

Peterfreund, Sheldon P. "George Ripley: Forerunner of Twentieth Century Ethical Intuitionism." *Person* 55 (Sum. 1974): 298–302.

Peterson, Richard J. "Scottish Common Sense Philosophy in America, 1768–1850." Diss. American Univ. 1963.

Petre, Maud. "The Emersonian Creed." *CathW* 46 (Dec. 1887): 376–89.

Phillips, George Searle. "An Etching of Emerson." In his *Transatlantic Tracings and Popular Pictures from American Subjects*. London: W. Tweedie, 1853, 123–33.

Phillips, Mary E. *Reminiscences of William Wetmore Story*. Chicago: Rand, McNally, 1897.

"The Philosophy of Emerson." *Index* 14 (1 Feb. 1883): 369.

Pierce, Edward L. *Memoir and Letters of Charles Sumner*. 2 vols. Boston: Roberts, 1877.

Pietras, Thomas P. "Amos Bronson Alcott: A Transcendental Philosophy of Education." *EdT* 21 (Wtr. 1971): 105–11.

Pingel, Martha M. *An American Utilitarian: Richard Hildreth as a Philosopher*. New York: Columbia Univ. Press, 1948.

Pitcher, Edward William. "Poe's *Eureka* as a Prose Poem." *ATQ* no. 29 (Wtr. 1976): 61–71.

Pitman, Ursula Wall. "Moncure Daniel Conway: The Development and Career of a Southern Abolitionist." Diss. Boston Coll. 1978.

Pochmann, Henry A. *German Culture in America: Philosophical and Literary Influences 1600–1900*. Madison: Univ. of Wisconsin Press, 1957.

————. *New England Transcendentalism and St. Louis Hegelianism*. Philadelphia: Carl Schurz Foundation, 1948.

————. "Plato and Hegel Contend for the West." *AGR* 9 (Aug. 1943): 8–13. Incorporated into his *New England Transcendentalism and St. Louis Hegelianism*.

Poe, Edgar Allan. *Al Aaraaf. Tamerlane, and Minor Poems*. Baltimore: Hatch and Dunning, 1829.

————. "An Appendix of Autographs." *GrMag* 20 (Jan. 1842): 48.

————. *Collected Works of Edgar Allan Poe*. Ed. Thomas Ollive Mabbott. 3 vols. Cambridge: Harvard Univ. Press, 1969–78.

————. "The Colloquy of Monos and Una." *GrMag* 19 (Aug. 1841): 52–55.

————. *The Complete Works of Edgar Allan Poe* ["Virginia Edition"]. Ed. James A. Harrison. 17 vols. New York: Crowell, 1902.

————. "Editorial Miscellany." *BJ* 2 (13 Dec. 1845): 357–58. Rpt. in his *Complete Works*, 13: 27–32.

————. *Eureka: A Prose Poem*. New York: George P. Putnam, 1848. Rpt., ed. Richard P. Benton. *ATQ* no. 22 (Apr. 1974): 7–77. Rpt., ed. Benton. Hartford, Conn.: Transcendental Books, 1974. Rpt. in *Poe as Literary Cosmologer in* Eureka, ed. Benton, Hartford, Conn.: Transcendental Books, 1975. [All are facsimile rpts.]

———. "The Fall of the House of Usher." *BGM* 5 (Sept. 1839): 145–52.

———. *The Imaginary Voyages: The Narrative of Arthur Gordon Pym, The Unparalleled Adventure of One Hans Pfaall, The Journal of Julius Rodman*. Ed. Burton R. Pollin. Boston: Twayne, 1981.

———. "The Island of the Fay." *GrMag* 18 (June 1841): 253–55.

———. *The Letters of Edgar Allan Poe*. Ed. John Ward Ostrom. 2 vols. Cambridge: Harvard Univ. Press, 1948. Enl. ed., New York: Gordian Press, 1966.

———. "Ligeia." *AMLA* 1 (Sept. 1838): 25–37.

———. "The Literati of New York City—No. III." *GLB* 33 (July 1846): 13–19.

———. "The Literati of New York City—No. IV. Sarah Margaret Fuller." *GLB* 33 (Aug. 1846): 72–75.

———. "Mesmeric Revelation." *ColM* 2 (Aug. 1844): 67–70.

———. "Morella." *SLM* 1 (April 1835): 448–50.

———. "Never Bet the Devil Your Head." *GrMag* 19 (Sept. 1841): 124–27.

———. "Our Amateur Poets. No. III.—William Ellery Channing." *GrMag* 23 (Aug. 1843): 113–17.

———. "The Philosophy of Composition." *GrMag* 28 (April 1846): 163–67.

———. "The Poetic Principle." *SUM* 7 (Oct. 1850): 231–39.

———. "The Power of Words." *USMDR* 16 (June 1845): 602–04.

———. "The Psyche Zenobia." *AMLA* 1 (Nov. 1838): 301–10. Rev. and rpt. as "How to Write a Blackwood Article." *BJ* 2 (12 July 1845): 1–4.

———. "The Rationale of Verse." *SLM* 14 (Oct., Nov. 1848): 577–85, 673–82.

———. *The Works of Edgar Allan Poe*. Ed. E. C. Stedman and George E. Woodberry. 10 vols. Chicago: Stone and Kimball, 1894–95.

Poger, Sidney. "The Critical Stance of the *Dial*." *ESQ* no. 57 (4 Qtr. 1969): 22–27. Rpt. in *The Minor and Later Transcendentalists*, ed. Edwin Gittleman, 22–27.

———. "Thoreau as Yankee in Canada." *ATQ* no. 14 (Spr. 1972): 174–77.

———. "Yeats as Azed: A Possible Source in Thoreau." *TJQ* 5.4 (Fall 1973): 13–15.

Poirier, Richard. "Is There an I for an Eye? The Visionary Possession of America." In his *A World Elsewhere: The Place of Style in American Literature*. New York: Oxford Univ. Press, 1966, 50–92.

Poirier, Suzanne. " 'A Song of the Rolling Earth' as Transcendental and Poetic Theory." *WWR* 22 (June 1976): 67–74.

Pokrovsky, Nikita. "Basic Bibliography of Russian Translations, Publications and Studies of Thoreau." *TSB* no. 150 (Wtr. 1980): 1–3.

Pollin, Burton R. "Contemporary Reviews of *Eureka*: A Checklist." *ATQ* no. 26 (Spr. 1975): 26–30. Rpt. in *Poe as Literary Cosmologer in* Eureka, ed. Richard P. Benton. Hartford, Conn.: Transcendental Books, 1975, 26–30.

———. "Emerson's Annotations in the British Museum Copy of the *Dial*." *SB* 24 (1971): 187–95.

———. "Poe on Margaret Fuller in 1845: An Unknown Caricature and Lampoon." *W&L* 5.1 (Spr. 1977): 47–50.

———. "Poe's Tale of Psyche Zenobia: A Reading for Humor and Ingenious Construction." In *Papers on Poe*. Ed. Richard P. Veler. Springfield, Ohio: Chantry Music Press, 1972, 92–103.

———. "Poe's Use of D'Israeli's *Curiosities* to Belittle Emerson." *PoeN* 3 (Dec. 1970): 38.

———. *Word Index to Poe's Fiction*. New York: Gordian Press, 1982.

Pollack, Robert C. "A Reappraisal of Emerson." *Thought* 32 (Spr. 1957): 86–132. Rpt. as "Ralph Waldo Emerson: The Single Vision" in *American Classics Reconsidered: A Christian Appraisal*. Ed. Harold C. Gardiner. New York: Scribners, 1958, 15–58.

Pommer, Henry F. "The Contents and Basis of Emerson's Belief in Compensation." *PMLA* 77 (June 1962): 248–53.

———. *Emerson's First Marriage*. Carbondale: Southern Illinois Univ. Press, 1967.

———. "A Sermon by William Ellery Channing." *NEQ* 36 (March 1963): 77–79.

Pond, Enoch. "Pantheism." *ABiR* 3rd ser. 6 (April 1850): 243–72.

Pops, Martin Leonard. "An Analysis of Thoreau's *Cape Cod*." *BNYPL* 67 (Sept. 1963): 419–30.

———. *The Melville Archetype*. Kent, Ohio: Kent State Univ. Press, 1970.

Porte, Joel. *Emerson and Thoreau: Transcendentalists in Conflict*. Middletown, Conn.: Wesleyan Univ. Press, 1966.

———. "Emerson, Luther and the American Character." *ForumH* 13.3 (Wtr. 1976): 8–13. Incorporated into his *Representative Man*.

———. "Emerson, Thoreau, and the Double Consciousness." *NEQ* 41 (June 1968): 40–50.

———. " 'God Himself Culminates in the Present Moment': Thoughts on Thoreau's Faith." *TSB* no. 144 (Sum. 1978): 1–4.

———. "Henry Thoreau: Society and Solitude." *ESQ* 19 (3 Qtr. 1973): 131–40.

———. "Nature as Symbol: Emerson's Noble Doubt." *NEQ* 37 (Dec. 1964): 453–76. Incorporated into his *Emerson and Thoreau*.

———. "The Problem of Emerson." In *Uses of Literature*. Ed. Monroe Engel. Cambridge: Harvard Univ. Press, 1973, 85–114.

———. *Representative Man: Ralph Waldo Emerson in His Time*. New York: Oxford Univ. Press, 1979.

———. "Thoreau on Love: A Lexicon of Hate." *UKCR* 31 (Dec. 1964, March 1965): 111–16, 191–94.

———. "Transcendental Antics." In *Veins of Humor*. Ed. Harry Levin. Cambridge: Harvard Univ. Press, 1972, 167–84.

Porter, David. *Emerson and Literary Change*. Cambridge: Harvard Univ. Press, 1978.

Porter, James. *Three Lectures . . . on Come-out-ism*. Boston: Reid and Rand, 1844. Rpt. as *Modern Infidelity*. Boston: Waite, Peirce, 1845.

Porter, Lawrence Charles. "New England Transcendentalism: A Self-Portrait." Diss. Univ. of Michigan 1964.

———. "Transcendentalism: A Self-Portrait." *NEQ* 35 (March 1962): 27–47.

Porter, Maria S. "Elizabeth Palmer Peabody." *Bostonian* 3 (Jan. 1896): 340–50.

Porter, Noah, "Coleridge and His American Disciples." *BibS* 4 (Feb. 1847): 117–71.

———. "Transcendentalism." *ABiR* n.s. 8 (July 1842): 195–218.

Potter, William J. "Emerson's View of Ethics." *Index* 18 (22 July 1886): 38.

———. "Mr. Frothingham and His Alleged Change of Views." *Index* 13 (1 Dec. 1881): 254.

———. "Mr. O. B. Frothingham's Theological Position Past and Present." *Index* 13 (15 Dec. 1881): 278.

Powell, Janette Chilton. "A Study of the *Harbinger*." M.A. thesis Univ. of Chicago 1925.

Powell, Thomas. "Ralph Waldo Emerson." In his *The Living Authors of America. First Series*. New York: Stringer and Townsend, 1850, 49–77.

Power, Julia. *Shelley in America in the Nineteenth Century*. Lincoln: Univ. of Nebraska Press, 1940.

Predmore, Richard. "Thoreau's Influence on Hawthorne's 'The Artist of the Beautiful.' " *ATQ* no. 40 (Fall 1978): 329–34.

———. "Unamuno and Thoreau." *CLS* 6 (March 1969): 33–44.

Prentiss, G. "Theodore Parker." *MethQR* 33 (Jan., July, Oct. 1873): 5–42, 383–408, 533–62.

Price, Kenneth M. "Whitman on Other Writers: Controlled 'Graciousness' in *Specimen Days*." *ESQ* 26 (2 Qtr. 1980): 78–87.

Pritchard, John Paul. *Criticism in America*. Norman: Univ. of Oklahoma Press, 1956.

———. *Literary Wise Men of Gotham: Criticism in New York 1815–1860*. Baton Rouge: Louisiana State Univ. Press, 1963.

———. *Return to the Fountains: Some Classical Sources of American Criticism*. Durham: Duke Univ. Press, 1942.

Proceedings at a Reception Given in Honor of the Rev. O. B. Frothingham. New York: Putnam's, 1879.

Puk, Francine S. " 'Bartleby the Scrivener': A Study in Self-Reliance." *DeltaES* 7 (Nov. 1978): 7–20.

Puknat, Siegfried B. "Auerbach and Channing." *PMLA* 72 (Dec. 1957): 962–76.

———. "Channing and German Thought." *PAPS* 101 (Apr. 1957): 195–203.

———. "De Wette in New England." *PAPS* 102 (Aug. 1958): 376–95.

Putnam, Alfred P., ed. *Singers and Songs of the Liberal Faith*. Boston: Roberts, 1875.

Putnam, George Haven. *A Memoir of George Palmer Putnam*. 2 vols. New York: Putnam's, 1903. Rev. ed. as *George Palmer Putnam: A Memoir*. New York: Putnam's, 1912.

Pyre, J. F. A. "The *Dial* of 1840–45." *Dial* [Chicago] 26 (1 May 1899): 297–300.

Quade, Willie Vale Oldham. "Christopher Pearse Cranch and John Cranch: Nineteenth Century Artists." M.A. thesis George Washington Univ. 1969.

Quick, Donald G. "Thoreau as Limnologist." *TJQ* 4.2 (April 1972): 13–20.

Quincy, Edmund. "Parker's Historic Americans." *Nation* 12 (2 Feb. 1871): 76–77.

Quincy, Josiah P. "Memoir of Octavius B. Frothingham." *PMHS* 10 (March 1896): 500–01.

Quinn, Arthur Hobson. "American Literature and American Politics." *PAAS* 54 (April 1944): 59–112.

———. "Intuition and Independence." In *The Literature of the American People*, ed. Quinn, 276–91.

———, ed. *The Literature of the American People*. New York: Appleton-Century-Crofts, 1951.

Quinn, Joseph L. "Unrepresentative Man: The Significance of Orestes Brownson's Year of Self-Assessment." Diss. Harvard 1976.

Quinn, Patrick F. "Emerson and Mysticism." *AL* 21 (Jan. 1950): 397–414.

———. "Poe's *Eureka* and Emerson's *Nature*."*ESQ* no. 31 (2 Qtr. 1963): 4–7.

Rabinovitz, Albert L. "Criticism of French Novels in Boston Magazines, 1830–1860." *NEQ* 14 (Sept. 1941): 488–504.

Raghaven, Ellen, and Barry Wood. "Thoreau's Hindu Quotations in *A Week*." *AL* 51 (March 1979): 94–98.

"Ralph Waldo Emerson." *Knick* 65 (June 1865): 545–47.

"Ralph Waldo Emerson." *MEEJLR* 15 (Feb. 1848): 30–53.

Ramakrishna, D. "Poe's *Eureka* and Hindu Philosophy. " *ESQ* no. 47 (2 Qtr. 1967): 28–32.

Ramsey, Robert H. "Theodore Parker and the Gettysburg Phrase." *ABC* 9 (Feb. 1959): 5–7.

Randall, Randolph C. *James Hall: Spokesman of the New West*. Columbus: Ohio State Univ. Press, 1964.

Randel, William Peirce. "Hawthorne, Channing and Margaret Fuller." *AL* 10 (Jan. 1939): 472–76.

Rans, Geoffrey. *Edgar Allan Poe*. Edinburgh: Oliver and Boyd, 1965.

Rao, Adapa Ramakrishna. *Emerson and Social Reform*. Atlantic Highlands, N. J.: Humanities Press, 1980.

———. "Emerson and the American Negro." *OJES* 8.2 (1971): 79–88.

———. "Emerson and the Feminists." *IJAS* 4 (June-Dec. 1974): 13–20.

Ratcliffe, S. K. *The Story of South Place*. London: Watts, 1955.

Rathbun, John W. *American Literary Criticism, 1800-1860*. Boston: Twayne, 1979.

———. "George Bancroft on Man and History." *TWA* 43 (1954): 51–73.

Ray, Roberta K. "The Role of the Orator in the Philosophy of Ralph Waldo Emerson." *SpMonog* 41 (Aut. 1974): 215–25.

Rayapati, J. P. Rao. "Early Vedic Readings by American Transcendentalists." In his *Early American Interest in Vedanta*. London: Asia Publishing House, 1973, 93–106.

Raymond, Henrietta Raymond. "Sophia Willard Dana Ripley: Co-Founder of Brook Farm." M.A. thesis Columbia 1949.

Reaver, J. Russell. *Emerson as Mythmaker*. Gainesville: Univ. of Florida Press, 1954.

———. "Emerson's Use of Proverbs." *SFQ* 27 (Dec. 1963): 280–99.

———. "Mythology in Emerson's Poems." *ESQ* no. 39 (2 Qtr. 1965): 56–63.

Reccord, Augustus P. "Charles Timothy Brooks." In *Heralds of a Liberal Faith*, ed. Samuel A. Eliot, 3: 46–48.

Redding, Mary Edrich. "Emerson's 'Instant Eternity': An Existential Approach." *ATQ* no. 9 (Wtr. 1971): 43–52.

Reeck, Stephanie Ann. "Transcendentalism and Quakerism." M.A. thesis Univ. of Washington 1970.

Reed, Kenneth T. "Thoreauvian Echo in *Uncle Tom's Cabin?*" *ATQ* no. 11 (Sum. 1971): 37–38.

Reed, Sampson. *Address on Education*. Boston: Otis Clapp, 1842.

———. *A Biographical Sketch of Thomas Worcester*. Boston: Massachusetts New Church Union, 1880.

———. *The Future of the New Church*. Boston: Otis Clapp, 1875.

———. "Genius." In *Aesthetic Papers*, ed. Elizabeth Palmer Peabody, 59–65.

———. *Observations on the Growth of the Mind*. Boston: Cummings, Hilliard, 1826. Rev. ed., Boston: Otis Clapp, 1838.

———. *Swedenborg and His Mission*. Boston: Phinney, 1859.

Rees, John O. "Elizabeth Peabody and the Very ABC—A Note on *The House of the Seven Gables*." *AL* 38 (Jan. 1967): 537–40.

Reeves, Paschal. "Jones Very as Preacher: The Extant Sermons." *ESQ* no. 57 (4 Qtr. 1969): 16–22. Rpt. in *The Minor and Later Transcendentalists*, ed. Edwin Gittleman, 16–22.

———. "The Making of a Mystic: A Reconsideration of the Life of Jones Very." *EIHC* 103 (Jan. 1967): 3–30.

Reid, Alfred S. "Emerson and Bushnell as Forerunners of Jamesian Pragmatism." *FurmS* 13 (Nov. 1965): 18–30.

———. "Emersonian Ideas in the Youth Movement of the 1960s." *ATQ* no. 9 (Wtr. 1971): 12–16.

Reid, John T. *Indian Influences in American Literature and Thought*. N.p.: Indian Council for Cultural Relations, 1965.

Rein, Irving. "The New England Transcendentalists: Philosophy and Rhetoric." *P&R* 1 (Wtr. 1968): 103–17.

Reinhardt, John E. "The Evolution of William Ellery Channing's Sociopolitical Ideas." *AL* 26 (May 1954): 154–65.

Reinke, Elizabeth L. "Puritan and Transcendental Influences on Emily Dickinson's Philosophy." Diss. Columbia 1935.

Renan, Ernest. "Channing et le mouvement unitaire aux États-Unis." *RDM* 8 (15 Dec. 1854): 1085–1107.

Reney, Sister Mary Michelle. "Transcendentalism in Emily Dickinson's Poetry." M.A. thesis Boston Coll. 1962.

"A Reprint of the *Dial*." *JSP* 16 (July 1881): 329–31.

Reuben, Paul Purushottam. "Dynamics of New England Transcendentalism in Benjamin Orange Flower's *Arena* (1889–1909)." Diss. Bowling Green State Univ. 1970.

"Rev. George Ripley." *MMRL* 4 (May 1841): 293–95.

"The Rev. John Weiss." *BDA*, 10 March 1879, 1. Rpt. in *Index* 10 (20 March 1879): 136.

Review of William Ellery Channing, *Conversations in Rome*. *GrMag* 31 (Sept. 1847): 155–56.

Review of William Ellery Channing, *Thoreau*. *BQR* 59 (Jan. 1874): 181–94.

Review of William Ellery Channing, *Thoreau*. *MRM* 50 (Oct. 1873): 383–84.

Review of William Ellery Channing, *Thoreau*. *Nation* 75 (20 Nov. 1902): 403.

Review of Wilhelm M. L. De Wette, *A Critical and Historical Introduction to the Canonical Scriptures of the Old Testament*, trans. Theodore Parker. *NBR* 47 (Aug. 1847): 355–67.

Review of Ralph Waldo Emerson, *Essays [First Series]*. *NYR* 8 (April 1841): 509–12.

Review of Ralph Waldo Emerson, *May-Day*. *NAR* 105 (July 1867): 325–27.

Review of Ralph Waldo Emerson, *An Oration Delivered before the Phi Beta Kappa Society . . . . IRNJM* 11 (Oct. 1837): 67–72.

Review of Ralph Waldo Emerson, *Poems*. *Daguerreotype* 1 (4 Sept. 1847): 142–43.

Review of Samuel Johnson, *Oriental Religions and Their Relation to Universal Religion. India*. *Nation* 15 (21 Nov. 1872): 338.

Review of Walt Whitman, *Leaves of Grass*. *BoP*, ca. May 1860. Rpt. in Richard Maurice Bucke, *Walt Whitman*. Philadelphia: David McKay, 1883, 201.

Reynolds, Larry J., and Tibbie E. Lynch. "Sense and Transcendentalism in Emerson, Thoreau, and Whitman." *SCB* 39 (Wtr. 1979): 148–49.

Rhoads, Kenneth W. "Thoreau: The Ear and the Music." *AL* 46 (Nov. 1974): 313–28.

Riback, William. "Theodore Parker of Boston: Social Reformer (1840–1860)." *SSR* 22 (Dec. 1948): 451–60.

Rice, Madeline Hook. *Federal Street Pastor: The Life of William Ellery Channing*. New York: Bookman Associates, 1961.

Richards, Laura E., and Maud Howe Elliott. *Julia Ward Howe 1819–1910*. 2 vols. Boston: Houghton Mifflin, 1916.

Richardson, Charles F. *American Literature 1607–1885*. 2 vols. New York: Putnam's, 1887–89.

Richardson, E. P. *Washington Allston: A Study of the Romantic Artist in America*. Chicago: Univ. of Chicago Press, 1948.

Richardson, Merrill. "A Plain Discussion with a Transcendentalist." *NewE* 1 (Oct. 1843): 502–16.

Richardson, Robert D., Jr. "Margaret Fuller and Myth." *Prospects* 4 (1979): 169–84.

———. *Myth and Literature in the American Renaissance*. Bloomington: Indiana Univ. Press, 1978.

———. "A Perfect Piece of Stoicism." *TSB* no. 153 (Fall 1980): 1–5.

Richmond, Lee J. "Emersonian Echoes in Dickinson's 'These are the signs.'" *ATQ* no. 29 (Wtr. 1976): 2–3.

Ricks, Beatrice, Joseph D. Adams, and Jack O. Hazelrig. *Nathaniel Hawthorne: A Reference Bibliography*. Boston: G. K. Hall, 1972.

Rider, Daniel Edgar. "The Musical Thought and Activities of the New England Transcendentalists." Diss. Univ. of Minnesota 1964.

Ridgely, J. V. "Whitman, Emerson and Friend." *CLC* 10 (Nov. 1960): 15–19.

Riegel, Robert E. *Young America 1830–1840*. Norman: Univ. of Oklahoma Press, 1949.

Rieger, Wolfgang. "The *Dial*: Geschichte and Wetung Einer Zeitschrift (Boston 1840–1844)." Diss. Univ. Bonn 1955.

Riggs, Lisette. "George and Sophia Ripley." Diss. Univ. of Maryland 1942.

Riley, Woodbridge. *American Thought from Puritanism to Pragmatism and Beyond*. New York: Henry Holt, 1915.

———. "La Philosophie française en Amérique." *RPhil* 84 (Nov. 1917): 393–428.

Ripley, George. "The Angels of the Past." *ChEx* 42 (May 1847): 343–44.

———. "Articles of Association of the Subscribers to the Brook Farm Institute of Agriculture and Education" (1841). In Octavius Brooks Frothingham, *George Ripley*, 112–17.

———. "Benjamin Constant on Religion." *ChEx* 17 (Sept. 1824): 63–77.

———. "Brownson's Writings." *Dial* 1 (July 1840): 22–46.

———. "Channing's Works." *Dial* 1 (Oct. 1840): 246–47.

———. *The Claims of the Age on the Work on the Evangelist*. Boston: Weeks, Jordan, 1840.

———. "Cobb on Slavery." *NYDT*, 5 Nov. 1858, 3.

———. *Constitution of the Brook Farm Association for Industry and Education*. Boston: I. R. Butts, 1844; 2nd ed., 1844.

———. *Constitution of the Brook Farm Phalanx*. Boston: n.p., 1845.

———. "Cousin's Philosophy." *ChEx* 21 (Sept. 1836): 33–64.

———. "Cousin's Plato." *Dial* 1 (Oct. 1840): 271–72.

———. *Defence of "The Latest Form of Infidelity" Examined. A Second Letter to Mr. Andrews Norton . . . .* Boston: James Munroe, 1840.

———. *Defence of "The Latest Form of Infidelity" Examined. A Third Letter to Mr. Andrews Norton . . . .* Boston: James Munroe, 1840.

———. "Degerando on Self-Education." *ChEx* 9 (Sept. 1830): 70–107.

———. *Discourses on the Philosophy of Religion. Addressed to Doubters Who Wish to Believe*. Boston: James Munroe, 1836.

———. *The Divinity of Jesus Christ*. Boston: Gray and Bowen, 1831.

———. "Edward Palmer's 'A Letter to Those Who Think.' " *Dial* 1 (Oct. 1840): 251–56.

———. *A Farewell Discourse, Delivered to the Congregational Church in Purchase Street, March 28, 1841*. Boston: Freeman and Bowles, 1841. Rpt. in Octavius Brooks Frothingham, *George Ripley*, 84–86.

———. "Fitzgerald's Rubaiyat." *NYDT*, 22 Dec. 1877, 6.

———. "Forms of Guarantyism." *Harbinger* 3 (31 Oct. 1846): 335.

———. "Greeley's American Conflict." *Atl* 14 (July 1864): 133–35.

———. "The *Harbinger*." *Phalanx* 1 (3 May 1845): 340.

———. "Harwood's Materialism in Religion." *Dial* 1 (Oct. 1840): 267–71.

———. "Hawthorne's *The House of the Seven Gables*." *Har* 2 (May 1851): 855.

———. "Hawthorne's *The Scarlet Letter*." *NYDT*, suppl., 1 April 1850, 2.

———. "Heine's Work." *PMM* 8 (Nov. 1856): 517–26.

———. "Infidelity of Modern Society." *Harbinger* 1 (14 June 1845): 12.

———. "Influence of Machinery." *Harbinger* 1 (14 June 1845): 16.

———. "Influence of Social Circumstances." *Harbinger* 5 (26 July 1847): 146.

———. "Introductory Notice." *Harbinger* 1 (14 June 1845): 8–10.

———. "Jouffroy's Contributions to Philosophy." *ChEx* 22 (May 1837): 196–217.

———. *"The Latest Form of Infidelity" Examined. A Letter to Mr. Andrews Norton . . . .* Boston: James Munroe, 1839.

———. *A Letter Addressed to the Congregational Church in Purchase Street*. Boston: Freeman and Bowles, 1840.

———. "Letter to a Theological Student." *Dial* 1 (Oct. 1840): 183–87.
———. "A Letter to a Trinitarian Friend." *TAUA* 6 (March 1833): 193–204. Rpt. as *The Doctrines of the Trinity and Transubstantiation Compared*. Boston: Charles Bowen, 1833.
———. Letter to Andrews Norton. *BDA*, 9 Nov. 1836, 1.
———. "Mackintosh's Ethical Philosophy." *ChEx* 13 (Jan. 1833): 311–32.
———. "Martineau." *ChEx* 21 (Nov. 1836): 226–54.
———. "Martineau's Rationale." *ChEx* 11 (Jan. 1832): 255–64.
———. "Melville's *Moby Dick*." *Har* 4 (Dec. 1851): 137.
———. "Our Predicament." *Harbinger* 2 (20 Dec. 1845): 30.
———. "Pestalozzi." *ChEx* 11 (Jan. 1832): 347–73.
———. "The Philosophy of Herbert Spencer." *NYDT*, 26 March 1869, 2.
———. "Professor Follen's Inaugural." *ChEx* 11 (Jan. 1832): 373–80.
———. "Professor Marsh's Translation of Herder." *ChEx* 18 (May 1835): 167–221.
———. "Professor Walker's Vindication of Philosophy." *Dial* 1 (Oct. 1840): 256–360.
———. "Religion in France." *ChEx* 10 (July 1831): 273–93.
———. "Schleiermacher as a Theologian." *ChEx* 20 (March 1836): 1–46.
———. *The Temptations of the Times*. Boston: Hilliard, Gray, 1837.
———. "Tendencies of Modern Civilization." *Harbinger* 1 (28 June 1845): 47–48.
———. "Thackeray's *History of Pendennis*." *Har* 2 (Feb. 1851): 428.
———. "Theological Aphorisms." *ChEx* 21 (Jan. 1839): 385–98.
———. "Two Sermons on the Kind Treatment and on the Emancipation of Slaves." *Dial* 1 (Oct. 1840): 248–51.
———. "The War in Europe." *NYDT*, 22 July 1870, 1.
———. "War to the Knife." *Harbinger* 3 (12 Sept. 1845): 221–22.
———. "Waste! Waste! Waste!" *Harbinger* 5 (31 July 1847): 125.
———. "What Do You Propose?" *Harbinger* 1 (28 June 1845): 46.
———. "Where Are We?" *Harbinger* 3 (12 Sept. 1845): 222.
———, ed. *Specimens of Foreign Standard Literature*. 14 vols. Boston: Hilliard, Gray, 1838–41; Boston; James Munroe, 1842.
———, trans. *Philosophical Miscellanies, Translated from the French of Cousin, Jouffroy, and B. Constant*. 2 vols. Boston: Hilliard, Gray, 1838.
———, and George P. Bradford. "Philosophic Thought in Boston." In *The Memorial History of Boston*, ed. Justin Winsor, 4: 295–330.
———, and Charles A. Dana, eds. *The New American Cyclopædia*. 16 vols. New York: D. Appleton, 1858–63.
———, and Bayard Taylor, eds. *Hand-Book of Literature and the Fine Arts*. New York: George P. Putnam, 1852.
———, et al. *Report on a Union of Churches for Benevolent Purposes*. Boston: Tuttle and Weeks, 1834.
Ripley, Sophia. "Letter." *Dial* 2 (July 1841): 122–29.
———. "Painting and Sculpture." *Dial* 2 (July 1841): 78–81.
———. "Woman." *Dial* 1 (Jan. 1841): 362–66.
Rittenhouse, Caroline Smith. "The Testimony of Man's Inward Nature: A Study of George Ripley's Transcendentalism." Diss. Harvard 1965.
Robbins, J. Albert. "Fees Paid to Authors by Certain American Periodicals, 1840–1850." *SB* 2 (1949–50): 95–104.
Roberts, J. Russell. "Emerson's Debt to the Seventeenth Century." *AL* 21 (Nov. 1949): 298–310.
Roberts, Josephine Elizabeth. "Elizabeth Peabody and the Temple School." *NEQ* 15 (Sept. 1942): 497–508.

————. "A New England Family: Elizabeth Palmer Peabody, 1804–1894, Mary Tyler Peabody (Mrs. Horace Mann), 1806–1887, Sophia Amelia Peabody (Mrs. Nathaniel Hawthorne), 1809–1871." Diss. Western Reserve Univ. 1937.

Robertson, John M. *Modern Humanists*. London: Swan Sonnenschein, 1891.

————. *Ralph Waldo Emerson: Man and Teacher*. Edinburgh: William Brown, 1884.

Robinson, David M. *Apostle of Culture: Emerson as Preacher and Lecturer*. Philadelphia: Univ. of Pennsylvania Press, 1982.

————. "The Career and Reputation of Christopher Pearse Cranch: An Essay in Biography and Bibliography." *SAR* 1978: 453–72.

————. "Channing and the Problem of Social Reform." *Kairos* 16 (Aut. 1979): 7.

————. "Christopher Pearse Cranch, Robert Browning, and the Problem of Transcendental Friendship." *SAR* 1977: 145–53.

————. "Emerson and the Challenge of the Future: The Paradox of the Unachieved in 'Circles.'" *PQ* 57 (Spr. 1978): 243–53.

————. "Emerson's Natural Theology and the Paris Naturalists: Toward a Theory of Animated Nature." *JHI* 41 (Jan.–March 1980): 69–88.

————. "The Exemplary Self and the Transcendent Self in the Poetry of Jones Very." *ESQ* 24 (4 Qtr. 1978): 206–14.

————. "Four Early Poems of Jones Very." *HLB* 28 (April 1980): 146–51.

————. "Jones Very." In *The American Renaissance in New England*, ed. Joel Myerson, 184–85.

————. "Jones Very: An Essay in Bibliography." *RALS* 5 (Aut. 1975): 131–46.

————. "Jones Very, the Transcendentalists, and the Unitarian Tradition." *HTR* 68 (April 1975): 105–24.

————. "The Legacy of Channing: Culture as a Religious Category in New England Thought." *HTR* 74 (April 1981): 221–39.

————. "Margaret Fuller and the Transcendental Echos: *Woman in the Nineteenth Century*." *PMLA* 97 (Jan. 1982): 83–98.

————. "*The Method of Nature* and Emerson's Period of Crisis." In *Emerson Centenary Essays*, ed. Joel Myerson, 74–92.

————. "The Political Odyssey of William Henry Channing." *AQ* 34 (Sum. 1982): 165–84.

————. "Unitarian Historiography and the American Renaissance." *ESQ* 23 (2 Qtr. 1977): 130–37.

Robinson, E. Arthur. "Thoreau and the Deathwatch in Poe's 'The Tell-Tale Heart.'" *PoeS* 4 (June 1971): 14–16.

Robinson, George Frederick, and Ruth Robinson Wheeler. *Great Little Watertown*. Watertown, Mass.: Watertown Historial Soc., 1930.

Roemer, Lawrence. *Brownson, Democracy, and the Trend toward Socialism*. New York: Philosophical Library, 1953.

Rogers, C. A. "God, Nature and Personhood: Thoreau's Alternative to Inanity." *RinL* 48 (Spr. 1979): 101–13.

Rogers, Jane Ellin. "The Transcendental Quest in Emerson and Melville." Diss. Univ. of Pittsburgh 1973.

Rollins, Hyder Edward. *Keats' Reputation in America to 1884*. Cambridge: Harvard Univ. Press, 1946.

Ronda, Bruce A. "Sylvester Judd's *Margaret*: Open Spirits and Hidden Heart." *ATQ* no. 39 (Sum. 1978): 217–29.

————. "The Transcendental Child: Images and Concepts of the Child in American Transcendentalism." Diss. Yale 1975.

Rosa, Alfred F. "Charles Ives: Music, Transcendentalism, and Politics." *NEQ* 44 (Sept. 1971): 433–43.

———. *Salem, Transcendentalism, and Hawthorne*. Rutherford, N. J.: Fairleigh Dickinson Univ. Press, 1980.

Rose, Anne C. *Transcendentalism as a Social Movement, 1830-1850*. New Haven: Yale Univ. Press, 1981.

Rose, Edward J. "The American Scholar Incarnate." *ESQ* 19 (Fall 1973): 170–78.

———. "Melville, Emerson, and the Sphinx." *NEQ* 36 (June 1963): 249–58.

Rosenfeld, Alvin L. "Emerson and Whitman: Their Personal and Literary Relationship." Diss. Brown 1967.

Rosenfeld, William. "The Divided Burden: Common Elements in the Search for a Religious Synthesis in the Works of Theodore Parker, Horace Bushnell, Nathaniel Hawthorne, and Herman Melville." Diss. Univ. of Minnesota 1961.

Rosenthal, Bernard. *City of Nature: Journeys to Nature in the Age of American Romanticism*. Newark: Univ. of Delaware Press, 1980.

———. "The *Dial*, Transcendentalism, and Margaret Fuller." *ELN* 8 (Sept. 1970): 28–36.

———. "Thoreau's Book of Leaves." *ESQ* no. 56 (3 Qtr. 1969): 7–11.

Ross, Donald, Jr. "Composition as a Stylistic Feature." *Style* 4 (Wtr. 1970): 1–10.

———. "Emerson and Thoreau: A Comparison of Prose Styles." *Lang&S* 6 (Sum. 1973): 185–95.

———. "Emerson's Stylistic Influence on *Walden*." *ATQ* no. 25 (Wtr. 1975): 41–51.

———. "Hawthorne and Thoreau on 'Cottage Architecture.'" *ATQ* no. 1 (1 Qtr. 1969): 100–01.

———. "Verbal Wit and *Walden*." *ATQ* no. 11 (Sum. 1971): 38–44.

Rostenberg, Leona. "Margaret Fuller's Roman Diary." *JMH* 12 (June 1940): 209–20.

———. "Number Thirteen West Street." *BCP* 4 (Sept. 1945): 7–9.

Roundtree, Thomas J., ed. *Critics on Emerson*. Coral Gables, Fla.: Univ. of Miami Press, 1973.

Rowe, John Carlos. "'The Being of Language: The Language of Being' in *A Week on the Concord and Merrimack Rivers*." *Boundary* 7.3 (Spr. 1979): 91–115.

Rowland, Beryl. "Melville Answers the Theologians: The Ladder of Charity in 'The Two Temples.'" *Mosaic* 7 (Sum. 1974): 1–13.

Rubin, Joseph Jay. *The Historic Whitman*. University Park: Pennsylvania State Univ. Press, 1973.

Ruland, Richard. *The Rediscovery of American Literature: Premises of Critical Taste, 1900-1940*. Cambridge: Harvard Univ. Press, 1967.

———, ed. *Twentieth Century Interpretations of* Walden. Englewood Cliffs, N. J.: Prentice-Hall, 1968.

Rusk, Ralph Leslie. "Emerson and the Stream of Experience." *CE* 14 (April 1953): 373–79.

———. "Emerson in Salem." *EIHC* 4 (July 1958): 194–95.

———. *The Life of Ralph Waldo Emerson*. New York: Scribners, 1949.

———. *The Literature of the Middle Western Frontier*. 2 vols. New York: Columbia Univ. Press, 1925.

Russell, Amelia. "Home Life of the Brook Farm Association." *Atl* 42 (Oct., Nov. 1878): 458–66, 556–63.

Russell, Phillips. *Emerson: The Wisest American*. New York: Brentano's, 1929.

Russell, W. Clark. "Editor's Preface." In Herman Melville, *Typee*. London: John Lane, 1904, v–x.

Ryan, Alvan S. "Brownson's Significance for American Democracy Today." In *No Divided Allegiance: Essays in Brownson's Thought*, ed. Leonard Gilhooley, 175–93.

———. "Orestes Brownson: The Critique of Transcendentalism." In *American Classics Reconsidered: A Christian Appraisal*. Ed. Harold C. Gardiner. New York: Scribners, 1958, 98–120, 290–91.

Ryan, George E. "Shanties and Shiftlessness: The Immigrant Irish of Henry Thoreau." *Éire* 13 (Fall 1978): 54–78.

Ryan, Kevin. "Henry David Thoreau: Critic, Theorist, and Practitioner of Education." *SchR* 77 (March 1969): 54–63.

Ryan, Thomas R. *Orestes A. Brownson: A Definitive Biography*. Huntington, Ind.: Our Sunday Visitor, 1976.

St. Armand, Barton Levi. "Luminism in the Work of Henry David Thoreau: The Dark and the Light." *CRevAS* 11 (Spr. 1980): 13–30.

———. " 'Seemingly Intuitive Leaps': Belief and Unbelief in *Eureka*." *ATQ* no. 26 (Spr. 1975): 4–15. Rpt. in *Poe as Literary Cosmologer in* Eureka, ed. Richard P. Benton. Hartford, Conn.: Transcendental Books, 1975, 4–15.

———. "Usher Unveiled: Poe and the Metaphysics of Gnosticism." *PoeS* 5 (June 1972): 1–18.

Sakmann, Paul. *Ralph Waldo Emerson's Geisteswelt*. Stuttgart: Fr. Fromanns, 1927.

Salinas, Oscar. "Emerson's *Nature*: Oral Merger Fantasy." *AI* 35 (Wtr. 1978): 387–406.

Salomon, Louis B. "Practical Thoreau." *CE* 17 (Jan. 1956): 229–32.

———. "The Straight-Cut Ditch: Thoreau on Education." *AQ* 14 (Spr. 1962): 19–36.

———. "A Walk with Emerson on the Dark Side." *Costerus* 6 (1972): 121–35.

Salt, Henry S. "Herman Melville." *ScAR* 2 (Nov. 1889): 186–90.

———. *The Life of Henry David Thoreau*. London: Richard Bentley, 1890.

———. "Marquesan Melville." *GentM* 272 (March 1892): 248–57.

Salter, William. "The Christian Idealism of R. W. Emerson." *NewE* 45 (July 1886): 633–39.

———. "Emerson's Views on Reform." *NEMag* 4 (July 1891): 656–64.

Salzberg, Joel. "The Gothic Hero in Transcendental Quest: Poe's 'Ligeia' and James's 'The Beast in the Jungle.' " *ESQ* 18 (2 Qtr. 1972): 108–14.

Sampson, Edward C. "Three Unpublished Letters by Hawthorne to Epes Sargent." *AL* 34 (March 1962): 102–05.

Sampson, H. Grant. "Structure in the Poetry of Thoreau." *Costerus* 6 (1972): 137–54.

Sams, Henry W., ed. *Autobiography of Brook Farm*. Englewood Cliffs, N.J.: Prentice-Hall, 1958.

Sanborn, Franklin Benjamin. *Bronson Alcott at Alcott House, England, and Fruitlands, New England (1842–1844)*. Cedar Rapids, Iowa: Torch Press, 1908.

———. *Collected Poems of Franklin Benjamin Sanborn of Transcendental Concord*. Ed. John Michael Moran, Jr. Hartford, Conn.: Transcendental Books, 1964.

———. *The Correspondence of Franklin Benjamin Sanborn the Transcendentalist*. Ed. Kenneth Walter Cameron. Hartford, Conn.: Transcendental Books, 1982.

———. "The *Dial*: A Chapter for the Unwritten History of American Literature." *HM* 1 (April 1855): 153–59.

———. "Ellery Channing and His Table-Talk." *CriticNY* 47 (July–Sept. 1905): 76–81, 121–28, 267–72.

———. "Emerson among the Poets." In *The Genius and Character of Emerson*, ed. Sanborn, 173–214.

———. "Emerson and His Friends in Concord." *NEMag* 8 (Dec. 1890): 411–31.

———. *Hawthorne and His Friends: Reminiscence and Tribute*. Cedar Rapids, Iowa: Torch Press, 1908.

———. *Henry D. Thoreau*. Boston: Houghton, Mifflin, 1882.

———. "The Homes and Haunts of Emerson." *SMM* 17 (Feb. 1879): 496–511.

————. *Lectures on Literature and Philosophy: Reports of Transcendental, Biographical, and Historical Papers Read before the Concord School 1881-1888*. Ed. Kenneth Walter Cameron. Hartford, Conn.: Transcendental Books, 1975.

————. *The Life and Letters of John Brown*. Boston: Roberts, 1885.

————. *The Life of Henry David Thoreau*. Boston: Houghton Mifflin, 1917.

————. *Literary Sketches and Criticism: Evaluations of the Writers of the American Renaissance—With Fresh Approaches to Transcendentalism, Literary Influences, New England Cultural Patterns and the Creative Experience*. Ed. Kenneth Walter Cameron. Hartford, Conn.: Transcendental Books, 1980.

————. "The Maintenance of a Poet." *Atl* 86 (Dec. 1900): 819–25.

————. *Memorabilia of Hawthorne, Alcott and Concord*. Ed. Kenneth Walter Cameron. Hartford, Conn.: Transcendental Books, 1970.

————. "Mr. Channing's Wanderer." *Ind* 23 (23 Nov. 1871): 6.

————. *The Personality of Emerson*. Boston: Charles E. Goodspeed, 1903.

————. *The Personality of Thoreau*. Boston: Charles E. Goodspeed, 1901.

————. *Ralph Waldo Emerson*. Boston: Small, Maynard, 1901.

————. *Recollections of Seventy Years*. 2 vols. Boston: Richard G. Badger, 1909.

————[?]. Review of William Ellery Channing, *Near Home*. *BoCom*, 14 Aug. 1863, 1.

————. Review of William Ellery Channing, *Thoreau*. *Atl* 33 (Feb. 1874): 230–31.

————. *Sixty Years of Concord 1855-1915: Life, People, Institutions and Transcendental Philosophy in Massachusetts—With Memories of Emerson, Thoreau, Alcott, Channing and Others*. Ed. Kenneth Walter Cameron. Hartford, Conn.: Transcendental Books, 1976.

————. *Table Talk: A Transcendentalist's Opinions on American Life, Literature, Art and People from the Mid-Nineteenth Century through the First Decade of the Twentieth*. Ed. Kenneth Walter Cameron. Hartford, Conn.: Transcendental Books, 1981.

————. "Theodore Parker and R. W. Emerson." *CriticNY* 49 (Sept. 1906): 273–81. Rpt. in his *Recollections of Seventy Years*, 2: 539–67.

————. "Theodore Parker's Ecclesiastical Relations." In *West Roxbury Magazine*. Hudson, Mass.: E. F. Worcester, 1900, 41–46.

————. "Thoreau and Ellery Channing." *CriticNY* 47 (Nov. 1905): 441–51.

————. "Thoreau and Emerson." *Forum* 23 (April 1897): 218–27.

————. "Thoreau, Newcomb, Brook Farm." *SpR*, 2 Dec. 1896, 5.

————. *Transcendental and Literary New England: Emerson, Thoreau, Alcott, Bryant, Whittier, Lowell, Longfellow and Others*. Ed. Kenneth Walter Cameron, Hartford, Conn.: Transcendental Books, 1975.

————. *The Transcendental Eye: Historical Papers Concerning New England and Other Points on a Great Circle*. Ed. Kenneth Walter Cameron. Hartford, Conn.: Transcendental Books, 1980.

————. *Transcendental Writers and Heroes: Papers Chiefly on Emerson, Thoreau, Literary Friends and Contemporaries with Regional and Critical Backgrounds*. Ed. Kenneth Walter Cameron. Hartford, Conn.: Transcendental Books, 1978.

————. *Transcendental Youth and Age: Chapters in Biography and Autobiography*. Ed. Kenneth Walter Cameron. Hartford, Conn.: Transcendental Books, 1980.

————[?]. "Twelve Apostles of Heresy." *Ind* 22 (27 Jan. 1870): 1.

————. *Ungathered Poems and Transcendental Papers*. Ed. Kenneth Walter Cameron. Hartford, Conn.: Transcendental Books, 1981.

————. *Young Reporter of Concord: Extracts from Sanborn's Letters to Benjamin Lyman Smith, 1853-1867, Emphasizing Life and Literary Events in the World of Emerson*. Ed. Kenneth Walter Cameron. Hartford, Conn.: Transcendental Books, 1978.

————, ed. "The Emerson-Thoreau Correspondence." *Atl* 69 (May–June 1892): 577–96, 736–53.

————, ed. *The Genius and Character of Emerson*. Boston: James R. Osgood, 1885.

————, and William T. Harris. *A. Bronson Alcott: His Life and Philosophy*. 2 vols. Boston: Roberts, 1893.

Sanborn, John Newell. "Thoreau in Emerson's 'Forbearance.'" *TJQ* 9.4 (Oct. 1977): 22–23.

Sanborn, Victor Channing. "Franklin Benjamin Sanborn." In *History of Hampton Falls, New Hampshire*. Ed. Warren Brown. 2 vols. Concord, N.H.: Rumford Press, 1900–18, 2: 305–11.

————. "Franklin Benjamin Sanborn, A.B." In his *Genealogy of the Family of Sambourne and Sanborn in England and America, 1194–1898*. Concord, N.H.: privately printed, 1899, 465–74.

————. "Franklin Benjamin Sanborn, A.B., 1831–1917." *CKSHS* 14 (1915–18): 58–63.

————. "Memoir of Franklin Benjamin Sanborn, A.B." *NEHGR* 61 (Oct. 1917): 291–95.

Sandeen, Ernest E. "Emerson as an American." *UIHS* 6.1 (1942): 63–118.

Sanfillippo, Sister Mary Helena. "The New England Transcendentalists' Opinions of the Catholic Church." Diss. Univ. of Notre Dame 1972.

San Juan, Epifanio, Jr. "Symbolic Significance in the Poems of Emerson." *SLQ* 4 (March 1966): 37–54.

Santayana, George. "The Optimism of Emerson" (1886), MS. Harvard Univ. Archives.

————. "Ralph Waldo Emerson." In *American Prose*. Ed. George Rice Carpenter. New York: Macmillan, 1898, 187–93. Rpt. as "Emerson" in his *Interpretations of Poetry and Religion*. London: Adam and Charles Black, 1900, 217–33.

Sargent, George H. "Frank B. Sanborn's Jewels and Junk." *BET*, 19 Sept. 1917, pt. 2, 4.

Sargent, John T. "Theodore Parker in His Social Relations and Letters." *Radical* 8 (July 1871): 428–31.

Sargent, Mary E. *Sketches and Reminiscences of the Radical Club*. Boston: Roberts, 1880.

Sarma, Sreekrishna. "A Short Study of Oriental Influences on Henry David Thoreau." *JA* 1 (1956): 76–92.

Sartain, John. *The Reminiscences of a Very Old Man 1808–1897*. New York: D. Appleton, 1899.

Sattelmeyer, Robert, Jr. "Away from Concord: The Travel Writings of Henry David Thoreau." Diss. Univ. of New Mexico, 1975.

————. "Thoreau's Projected Work on the English Poets." *SAR* 1980: 239–58.

Saunders, Judith. "Economic Metaphor Redefined: The Transcendentalist Capitalist at Walden." *ATQ* no. 36, pt. 1 (Fall 1977): 4–7.

Saunders, Robert James. "The Contributions of Horace Mann, Mary Peabody Mann and Elizabeth Palmer Peabody to Art Education in the United States." Diss. Pennsylvania State Univ. 1961.

Savage, Minot J. *Bishop Huntington and Mr. Emerson*. Boston: George H. Ellis, 1882.

————. "John Weiss." In *Heralds of a Liberal Faith*, ed. Samuel A. Eliot, 3: 376–80.

————. "O. B. Frothingham and His Supposed Change of Base." *Index* 13 (22 Dec. 1881): 294–96.

————. *Ralph Waldo Emerson: The Preacher and What He Preached*. Boston: George H. Ellis, 1882.

Savage, W. H. "The Religion of Emerson." *Arena* 10 (Nov. 1894): 736–44.

Savary, John. "An Echo of the Past." *Index* 7 (6 Jan. 1876): 8.

Saxton, J. A. "Prophecy—Transcendentalism—Progress." *Dial* 2 (July 1841): 83–121.

Saxton, Martha. *Louisa May*. Boston: Houghton Mifflin, 1977.

Sayre, Robert F. *Thoreau and the American Indians*. Princeton: Princeton Univ. Press, 1977.

Schamberger, J. Edward. "The Influence of Dugald Stewart and Richard Price on Emerson's Concept of Reason: A Reassessment." *ESQ* 18 (3 Qtr. 1972): 179–83.

Scheick, William J. *The Slender Human Word: Emerson's Artistry in Prose*. Knoxville: Univ. of Tennessee Press, 1978.

Schiff, Martin. "Neo-Transcendentalism in the New Left Counter-Culture." *CSSH* 15 (March 1973): 130–42.

Schiller, Andrew. "Gnomic Structure in Emerson's Poetry." *PMASAL* 40 (1955): 313–20.

———. "Thoreau and Whitman: The Record of a Pilgrimage." *NEQ* 28 (June 1955): 186–97.

Schleiner, Louise. "Emerson's Orphic Poet and Messianic Bard." *ESQ* 25 (4 Qtr. 1979): 191–202.

Schlesinger, Arthur M., Jr. *The Age of Jackson*. Boston: Little, Brown, 1945.

———. *Orestes A. Brownson: A Pilgrim's Progress*. Boston: Little, Brown, 1939. Rpt. as *A Pilgrim's Progress: Orestes A. Brownson*. Boston: Little, Brown, 1966.

———. "Orestes Brownson. An American Marxist before Marx." *SR* 47 (July 1939): 317–23.

Schlicht, Rüdiger C. *Die pädagogischen Ansätze amerikanischer Transzendentalisten*. Frankfurt am Main: Peter Lang, 1977.

Schneider, Herbert W. "American Transcendentalism's Escape from Phenomenology." In *Transcendentalism and Its Legacy*, ed. Myron Simon and Thornton H. Parsons, 215–28.

———. *A History of American Philosophy*. New York: Columbia Univ. Press, 1946.

———. "The Intellectual Background of William Ellery Channing." *ChH* 7 (March 1938): 3–23. Rpt. in his *A History of American Philosophy*, 59–67.

———. "Spirituality among Christians." In his *History of American Philosophy*, 268–80.

Schneider, Richard J. "The Balanced Vision: Thoreau's Observations of Nature." Diss. Univ. of California at Santa Barbara 1973.

———. "*Cape Cod*: Thoreau's Wilderness of Illusion." *ESQ* no. 26 (4 Qtr. 1980): 184–96.

———. "Humanizing Henry David Thoreau." *ESQ* 27 (1 Qtr. 1981): 57–71.

———. "Reflection in Walden Pond: Thoreau's Optics." *ESQ* 21 (2 Qtr. 1975): 65–75.

Schneider, Valerie. "Parker's Assessment of Webster: Argumentative Synthesis through the Tragic Metaphor." *QJS* 59 (Oct. 1973): 330–36.

Schoenbaum, S. *Shakespeare's Lives*. New York: Oxford Univ. Press, 1970.

Schoenfeldt, Arthur. "Charles Timothy Brooks; Translator of German Literature." *AGR* 18 (Feb. 1952): 22–23.

Schorer, Jean. *Deux grands Américains: T. Parker, W. Channing*. Genève: Mileu du Monde, 1947.

Schriber, Mary Sue. "Emerson, Hawthorne, and 'The Artist of the Beautiful.'" *SSF* 8 (Fall 1971): 607–16.

Schroeder, Fred E. H. "Andrew Wyeth and the Transcendental Tradition." *SQ* 17 (Fall 1965): 559–67.

Schroeder, John H. *Mr. Polk's War: American Opposition and Dissent, 1846-48*. Madison: Univ. of Wisconsin Press, 1973.

Schultz, Arthur R. "Margaret Fuller—Transcendentalist Interpreter of German Literature." *MDU* 34 (April 1942): 169–82.

———, and Henry A. Pochmann. "George Ripley: Unitarian, Transcendentalist, or Infidel?" *AL* 14 (March 1942): 1–19.

Schuster, Eunice M. "Native American Anarchism." *SCSH* 17 (Oct. 1931–July 1932): 5–202.

Schwartz, Harold. "Fugitive Slave Days in Old Boston." *NEQ* 27 (June 1954): 191–212.

Scott, Leonora Cranch. *The Life and Letters of Christopher Pearse Cranch*. Boston: Houghton Mifflin, 1917.

Scott, Otto J. *The Secret Six: John Brown and the Abolitionist Movement*. New York: Times Books, 1979.

Scovel, Carl R. "Theodore Parker: The Man as a Minister." *PUHS* 13.1 (1960): 54–70.

Scudder, Horace Elisha. *James Russell Lowell: A Biography*. 2 vols. Boston: Houghton, Mifflin, 1901.

Scudder, Jennie W. *A Century of Unitarianism in the National Capital, 1821-1921*. Boston: Beacon, 1922.

Scudder, Townsend. *Concord: American Town*. Boston: Little, Brown, 1947.

———. "Emerson's British Lecture Tour, 1847–1848." *PMLA* 7 (March, May 1936): 15–36, 166–80.

———. *The Lonely Wayfaring Man: Emerson and Some Englishmen*. New York: Oxford Univ. Press, 1936.

Seaburg, Alan. "Some Unitarian Manuscripts at Andover-Harvard." *HLB* 26 (Jan. 1978): 112–20.

Sealts, Merton M., Jr. "The American Scholar and Public Issues: The Case of Emerson." *Ariel* 7.3 (July 1976): 109–21.

———. "The Composition of *Nature*." In *Emerson's* Nature—*Origin, Growth, Meaning*, ed. Sealts and Alfred R. Ferguson, 2nd ed., 175–93.

———. "Emerson as Teacher" In *Emerson Centenary Essays*, ed. Joel Myerson, 180–92.

———. "Emerson on the Scholar, 1838: A Study of 'Literary Ethics.' " In *Literature and Ideas in America*. Ed. Robert P. Falk. Athens: Ohio Univ. Press, 1975, 40–57.

———. "Emerson on the Scholar, 1833–1837." *PMLA* 85 (Mar. 1970): 185–95.

———. "Melville and Emerson's Rainbow." *ESQ* 26 (2 Qtr. 1980): 53–78. Rpt. in his *Pursuing Melville, 1940-1980*. Madison: Univ. of Wisconsin Press, 1982, 250–77, 377–86.

———. "Melville and the Platonic Tradition." In his *Pursuing Melville, 1940-1980*, 278–336, 386–96.

———. "Melville's 'Neoplatonical Originals.' " *MLN* 67 (Feb. 1952): 80–86.

———, and Alfred R. Ferguson, eds. *Emerson's* Nature—*Origin, Growth, Meaning*. New York: Dodd, Mead, 1969. 2nd ed., Carbondale: Southern Illinois Univ. Press, 1979.

Searle, January [pseud. for George Searle Phillips]. *Emerson: His Life and Writings*. London: Holyoake, 1855.

Sears, Clara Endicott. *Bronson Alcott's Fruitlands*. Boston: Houghton Mifflin, 1915.

———. *Revised Catalogue of "Fruitlands" at Harvard, Mass*. Harvard, Mass.: n.p., 1915.

Sears, John Van Der Zee. *My Friends at Brook Farm*. New York: Desmond FitzGerald, 1912.

Sedgwick, Ora Gannett. "A Girl of Sixteen at Brook Farm." *Atl* 85 (March 1900): 394–404.

Seeyle, John. "The Contemporary Bartleby." *ATQ* no. 7 (Sum. 1970): 12–18.

———. "Some Green Thoughts on a Green Theme." *TriQ* 24 (Spr. 1972): 576–638.

Seldes, Gilbert. *The Stammering Century*. New York: John Day, 1928.

Services in Memory of Rev. William E. Channing, D.D., at the Arlington-Street Church, Boston . . . . Boston: John Wilson, 1867.

Sewall, Frank. "The New Church and the New England Transcendentalists." *NCR* 10 (Oct. 1903): 535–39.

Sewell, Richard H. *John P. Hale and Politics of Abolition*. Cambridge: Harvard Univ. Press, 1965.

Seybold, Ethel. *Thoreau: The Quest and the Classics*. New Haven: Yale Univ. Press, 1951.

Shaffer, Robert B. "Emerson and His Circle: Advocates of Functionalism." *JSAH* 8 (July-Dec. 1948): 17–20.

Shanley, J. Lyndon. *The Making of* Walden. Chicago: Univ. of Chicago Press, 1957.

———. "Thoreau's Geese and Yeats' Swans." *AL* 30 (Nov. 1958): 361–64.

———. "Thoreau: Years of Decay and Disappointment?" In *The Thoreau Centennial*, ed. Walter Harding, 53–64.

Shapiro, Samuel. "The Rendition of Anthony Burns." *JNH* 44 (Jan. 1959): 34–51.

Sharma, Mohal Lal. "Cholmondeley's Gift for Thoreau: An Indian Pearl to the U. S." *JOFS* 3 (Sum. 1968): 61–89.

Shaw, Charles Gray. "Emerson, the Nihilist." *IJE* 25 (Oct. 1914): 68–86.

Shea, Daniel B. "Emerson and the American Metamorphosis." In *Emerson: Prophecy, Metamorphosis, Influence*, ed. David Levin, 29–56.

Shear, Walter L. "Thoreau's Imagery and Symbolism." Diss. Univ. of Wisconsin 1961.

Shelley, Phillip Allison. "A German Art of Life in America: The American Reception of the Goethean Doctrine of Self-Culture." In *Anglo-German and American-German Crosscurrents*. Ed. Shelley et al. Chapel Hill: Univ. of North Carolina Press, 1957, 241–92.

Shepard, Odell. *Pedlar's Progress, The Life of Bronson Alcott*. Boston: Little, Brown, 1937.

Shephard, Esther. *Walt Whitman's Pose*. New York: Harcourt, Brace, 1938.

Shepherd, Holley M. "Unitariana." *PUHS* 12.1 (1958): 27–46.

Sherman, Stuart P. "Introduction." In *Essays and Poems of Emerson*. Ed. Sherman. New York: Harcourt, Brace, 1921, vii–xlv. Rpt. as "The Emersonian Liberation" in his *Americans*. New York: Scribners, 1922, 62–121.

Sherwin, J. S., and R. C. Reynolds. *A Word Index to* Walden. Charlottesville: Univ. of Virginia Press, 1960. Rev. and rpt. in *ESQ* no. 57 (4 Qtr. 1969): 1–130.

Sherwin, Oscar. "Of Martyr Built: Theodore Parker." *Phylon* 20 (June 1959): 143–48.

Sherwood, M. E. W. *An Epistle to Posterity Being Rambling Recollections of Many Years of My Life*. New York: Harper's, 1897.

———. *Here & There & Everywhere*. Chicago: Herbert S. Stone, 1898.

Sherwood, Mary P. "Fanny Eckstorm's Bias." *MR* 4 (Aut. 1962): 139–47. Rpt. in *Thoreau in Our Season*, ed. John Hicks, 58–66.

Sherwood, William R. *Circumference and Circumstance: Stages in the Mind and Art of Emily Dickinson*. New York: Columbia Univ. Press, 1968.

Shivers, Frank R., Jr. "A Western Chapter in the History of American Transcendentalism." *BHPSO* 15 (April 1957): 117–30.

Shubert, Mary Ann. "Seeing New Englandly: Emily Dickinson and Transcendentalism." M.A. thesis Univ. of Wyoming 1967.

Shuman, R. Baird. "Dwight Writes Lowell from Brook Farm." *ESQ* no. 27 (2 Qtr. 1962): 24–25.

Shurr, William. "Typology and Historical Criticism of the American Renaissance." *ESQ* 20 (1 Qtr. 1974): 57–63.

Sidney, Margaret. *Old Concord: Her Highways and Byways*. Rev. ed. Boston: D. Lothrop, 1893.

Siebert, Wilbur H. "The Underground Railroad in Massachusetts." *NEQ* 9 (Sept. 1936): 447–67.

———. "The Underground Railroad in Massachusetts." *PAAS* n.s. 45 (April 1935): 25–100.

———. "The Vigilance Committee of Boston." *PBS* 1953: 23–45.

Silsbee, William. "The Transcendental Doctrine of Self-Reliance." *ChEx* 37 (Nov. 1844): 331–49.

Silver, Mildred. "Emerson and the Idea of Progress." *AL* 12 (March 1940): 1–19.

Simmons, Edward. *From Seven to Seventy: Memories of a Painter and a Yankee*. New York: Harper's, 1922.

Simmons, Nancy Craig. "Arranging the Sibylline Leaves: James Elliot Cabot's Work as Emerson's Literary Executor." *SAR* 1983: 335–89.

———. "The 'Autobiographical Sketch' of James Elliot Cabot." *HLB* 30 (April 1982): 117–52.

———. "Man without a Shadow: The Life and Work of James Elliot Cabot, Emerson's Biographer and Literary Executor." Diss. Princeton 1980.

Simms, William Gilmore. *The Letters of William Gilmore Simms*. Ed. Mary C. Simms Oliphant, Alfred Taylor Odell, and R. C. Duncan Eaves. 5 vols. Columbia: Univ. of South Carolina Press, 1952.

Simon, Julius. *Ralph Waldo Emerson in Deutschland (1851-1932)*. Giessen: Junker und Dunnhaupt Verlag, 1937.

Simon, Myron, and Thornton H. Parsons, eds. *Transcendentalism and Its Legacy*. Ann Arbor: Univ. of Michigan Press, 1966.

Simpson, Lewis P. " 'The Intercommunity of the Learned': Boston and Cambridge in 1800." *NEQ* 23 (Dec. 1950): 491–503.

———. "Joseph Stevens Buckminster: The Rise of the New England Clerisy." In his *The Man of Letters in New England and the South*. Baton Rouge: Louisiana State Univ. Press, 1973, 3–31.

———. "A Literary Adventure of the Early Republic: The Anthology Society and the *Monthly Anthology*." *NEQ* 27 (June 1954): 168–90.

———, ed. *The Federalist Literary Mind*. Baton Rouge: Louisiana State Univ. Press, 1962.

Siracusa, Carl. *A Mechanical People: Perceptions of the Industrial Order in Massachusetts, 1815-1880*. Middletown: Wesleyan Univ. Press, 1979.

Skwire, David. "A Checklist of Wordplays in *Walden*." *AL* 31 (Nov. 1959): 282–89.

Slater, Joseph. "George Ripley and Thomas Carlyle." *PMLA* 67 (June 1952): 341–49.

Slethaug, Gordon E. "Thoreau's Use of the Pastoral and Fable Traditions." Diss. Univ. of Nebraska 1968.

Sloan, John H. " 'The Miraculous Uplifting': Emerson's Relationship with His Audience." *QJS* 52 (Feb. 1966): 10–15.

Slochower, Harry. "Margaret Fuller and Goethe." *GR* 7 (April 1932): 130–44.

Slotkin, Richard. *Regeneration through Violence: The Mythology of the American Frontier, 1600-1860*. Middletown: Wesleyan Univ. Press, 1973.

Smart, George K. "A Note on *The Periodicals of American Transcendentalism*." *AL* 10 (Jan. 1939): 494–95.

Smith, Bernard. *Forces in American Criticism*. New York: Harcourt, Brace, 1930.

Smith, Duane E. "Romanticism in America: The Transcendentalists." *RP* 35 (July 1973): 302–25.

Smith, Elizabeth Oakes. *Selections from the Autobiography of Elizabeth Oakes Smith*. Ed. Mary Alice Wyman. Lewiston, Me.: Lewiston Journal, 1924.

Smith, Gayle L. "Style and Vision in Emerson's 'Experience.' " *ESQ* 27 (2 Qtr. 1981): 85–95.

Smith, George W. "Thoreau and Bacon: The Idols of the Theatre." *ATQ* no. 11 (Sum. 1971): 6–12.

Smith, H. Shelton. *Changing Conceptions of Original Sin: A Study of American Theology since 1750*. New York: Scribners, 1955.

———. "Was Theodore Parker a Transcendentalist?" *NEQ* 23 (Sept. 1950): 351–64.

———, Robert T. Handy, and Lefferts A. Loetscher, eds. *American Christianity*. Vol. 2. New York: Scribners, 1963.

Smith, Henry Nash. "Emerson's Problem of Vocation: A Note on 'The American Scholar.' " *NEQ* 12 (March 1939): 52–67.

Smith, Herbert F. "Thoreau among the Classical Economists." *ESQ* 23 (2 Qtr. 1977): 114–22.

Smith, Timothy L. *Revivalism and Social Reform in Mid-Nineteenth-Century America*. New York: Abingdon Press, 1957.

Smith, Warren Sylvester. " 'The Imperceptible Arrows of Quakerism': Moncure Conway at Sandy Spring." *QH* 52 (Spr. 1963): 19–26.

———. *The London Heretics 1870-1914*. New York: Dodd, Mead, 1968.

———. "Moncure Daniel Conway at South Place Chapel." *ChCent* 80 (16 Jan. 1963): 77–80.

Smith, William Henry. "Emerson." *BEM* 62 (Dec. 1947): 643–57.

Smith, Wilson. "John Locke in the Great Unitarian Controversy." In *Freedom and Reform: Essays for Henry Steele Commager*. Ed. Harold M. Hyman and Leonard W. Levy. New York: Harper and Row, 1967, 78–100, 324–27.

————. *Professors and Public Ethics: Studies of Northern Moral Philosophers before the Civil War*. Ithaca: Cornell Univ. Press, 1956.

Smithline, Arnold. *"Eureka*: Poe as Transcendentalist." *ESQ* no. 39 (2 Qtr. 1965): 25–28.

————. *Natural Religion in American Literature*. New Haven, Conn.: Coll. and Univ. Press, 1966.

Smith-Rosenberg, Carroll. "The Female World of Love and Ritual: Relations between Women in Nineteenth-Century America." *Signs* 1 (Aut. 1975): 1–29.

Snider, Denton J. *A Biography of Ralph Waldo Emerson*. St. Louis: William Harvey Miner, 1921.

————. *A Writer of Books in His Genesis*. St. Louis: Sigma, 1910.

Snodgrass, J. E. "Transcendentalism. A Miniature Essay." *Magnolia* 4 (April 1842): 214–15.

Soleta, Chester. "The Literary Criticism of O. A. Brownson." *RP* 16 (July 1954): 334–51.

Somkin, Fred. *Unquiet Eagle: Memory and Desire in the Idea of American Freedom, 1815-1860*. Ithaca: Cornell Univ. Press, 1967.

Southworth, James G. "Thoreau, Moralist of the Picturesque." *PMLA* 49 (Sept. 1934): 971–74.

Sowder, William J. "Emerson's Early Impact on England." *PMLA* 77 (Dec. 1962): 561–76. Incorporated into his *Emerson's Impact on the British Isles and Canada*.

————. *Emerson's Impact on the British Isles and Canada*. Charlottesville: Univ. Press of Virginia, 1966.

————. "Emerson's Rationalist Champions: A Study in the British Periodicals." *NEQ* 37 (June 1964): 147–70. Incorporated into his *Emerson's Impact on the British Isles and Canada*.

————. "Ralph Waldo Emerson's Reviewers and Commentators: Nineteenth-Century Periodical Criticism." *ESQ* no. 53 (4 Qtr. 1968): 1–51. Rpt. as *Emerson's Reviewers and Commentators*. Hartford, Conn.: Transcendental Books, 1968.

Spaulding, A. F. "Phases of American Liberal Theology." *ChRev* 27 (Oct. 1962): 618–29.

Spencer, Benjamin T. "A National Literature, 1837–1855." *AL* 8 (May 1936): 125–59.

————. *The Quest for Nationality: An American Literary Campaign*. Syracuse: Syracuse Univ. Press, 1957.

Spencer, Donald S. *Louis Kossuth and Young America: A Study of Sectionalism and Foreign Policy, 1848-1852*. Columbia: Univ. of Missouri Press, 1977.

Spender, Stephen. *Love-Hate Relationships: English and American Sensibilities*. New York: Random House, 1974.

Spiller, Robert E. "A Case for W. E. Channing." *NEQ* 3 (Jan. 1930): 55–81.

————. "The Four Faces of Emerson." In *Four Makers of the American Mind: Emerson, Thoreau, Whitman, and Melville*. Ed. Thomas Edward Crawley. Durham: Duke Univ. Press, 1976, 3–23.

————. "From Lecture to Essay: Emerson's Method of Composition." *LCrit* 5 (Wtr. 1962): 28–38. Rpt. in *Selected Essays, Poems, and Lectures of Ralph Waldo Emerson*. Ed. Spiller. New York: Washington Square Press, 1965, ix–xx. Rpt. in *The Mirror of American Life: Essays and Reviews in American Literature*. Tokyo: Eichosha, 1971, 61–74.

————. "Ralph Waldo Emerson." In *Literary History of the United States*, ed. Spiller et al., 358–387. Rpt. in his *The Oblique Light: Studies in Literary History and Biography*. New York: Macmillan, 1968, 111–47.

————, et al., eds. *Literary History of the United States*. New York: Macmillan, 1948.

Sprague, William B. "James Marsh, D.D." In his *Annals of the American Pulpit*. 9 vols. New York: R. Carter, 1859–69. Vol. 2, *Trinitarian Congregational*, 692–704.

Sprouse, Veda Bagwell. "The Relationship of Nathaniel Hawthorne and Margaret Fuller." M.A. thesis Duke Univ. 1965.

Spurgeon, Caroline. *Five Hundred Years of Chaucer Criticism and Allusion*. Cambridge: Cambridge Univ. Press, 1925.

Staebler, Warren. *Ralph Waldo Emerson*. New York: Twayne, 1973.

Stafford, John. *The Literary Criticism of "Young America": A Study in the Relationship of Politics and Literature 1837-1850*. Berkeley: Univ. of California Press, 1952.

Stange, Douglas C. "Abolitionism as Treason: The Unitarian Elite Defends Law, Order, and the Union." *HLB* 28 (April 1980): 152-70.

———. "From Treason to Antislavery Patriotism: Unitarian Conservatives and the Fugitive Slave Law." *HLB* 25 (Oct. 1977): 466-88.

———. "The Making of an Abolitionist Martyr: Harvard Professor Charles Theodore Christian Follen (1796-1840)." *HLB* 24 (Jan. 1976): 17-24.

———. *Patterns of Antislavery among American Unitarians, 1831-1860*. Rutherford, N.J.: Fairleigh Dickinson Univ. Press, 1977.

Stansberry, Gloria J. "Let Wild Birds Sing: A Study of the Bird Imagery in the Writings of Henry David Thoreau." Diss. Kent State Univ. 1973.

Stanton, Elizabeth Cady. *Eighty Years or More (1815-1897)*. London: T. Fisher Unwin, 1898.

Stanwood, Edward. "Memoir of Franklin Benjamin Sanborn." *PMHS* 51 (1917-18): 307-11.

Staples, Laurence C. *Washington Unitarianism: A Rich Heritage*. Washington, D.C.: All Souls Church, 1970.

Stapleton, Laurence. *The Elected Circle: Studies in the Art of Prose*. Princeton: Princeton Univ. Press, 1973.

Starr, Harris Elwood. "Charles Timothy Brooks." In *DAB*, 3: 75.

———. "Convers Francis." In *DAB*, 6: 577.

———. "Samuel Johnson." In *DAB*, 10: 119-20.

Stauffer, Donald B. *A Short History of American Poetry*. New York: Dutton, 1974.

Stearns, Frank Preston. *Cambridge Sketches*. Philadelphia: Lippincott, 1905.

———. "Concord Thirty-Odd Years Ago." In his *Sketches from Concord and Appledore*. New York: Putnams, 1895, 1-28.

———. "Emerson as a Poet." *UnitR* 36 (Oct. 1891): 259-70.

———. "Hawthorne and Transcendentalism." In *The Hawthorne Centenary Celebration at the Wayside*. Ed. Thomas Wentworth Higginson. Boston: Houghton Mifflin, 1905, 150-58. Incorporated into his *The Life and Genius of Nathaniel Hawthorne*. Boston: Richard G. Badger, 1906.

———. *The Life and Public Service of George Luther Stearns*. Philadelphia: Lippincott, 1907.

Stebbins, Giles. "Transcendentalism." In his *Upward Steps of Seventy Years*. New York: United States Book, 1890, 51-71.

Stedman, Edmund C. "Emerson." *CM* 25 (April 1883): 872-86.

———. "Octavius Brooks Frothingham: A Sketch." *Galaxy* 22 (Oct. 1876): 478-88. Rpt. as *Octavius Brooks Frothingham and the New Faith*. New York: Putnams, 1879.

———, ed. *The Poets of America*. Boston: Houghton, Mifflin, 1885.

Stedman, Laura, and George M. Gould. *Life and Letters of Edmund Clarence Stedman*. 2 vols. New York: Moffat, Yard, 1910.

Steele, Marie T. "Nathaniel Hawthorne and Transcendentalism." M.A. thesis Univ. of New Hampshire 1956.

Stein, William Bysshe. "A Bibliography of Hindu and Buddhist Literature Available to Thoreau through 1854." *ESQ* no. 47 (2 Qtr. 1967): 52-56.

———. "The Hindu Matrix of *Walden*: The King's Son." *CL* 22 (Fall 1970): 303-18.

———. "Melville Roasts Thoreau's Cock." *MLN* 74 (March 1959): 218-19.

———. "Thoreau's *A Week* and Om Cosmography." *ATQ* no. 11 (Sum. 1971): 15-37.

———. "Thoreau's First Book: A Spoor of Yoga." *ESQ* no. 41 (4 Qtr. 1965): 4-25.

————. "Thoreau's *Walden* and the *Bhagavad-Gita.*" *Topic* 6 (Fall 1963): 38–55.

————. "The Yoga of 'Reading' in *Walden.*" *TSLL* 13 (Fall 1971): 481–95.

————. "The Yoga of *Walden*: Chapter I, 'Economy.' " *LE&W* 13 (June 1969): 303–18.

————, ed. *New Approaches to Thoreau*. Hartford, Conn.: Transcendental Books, 1969. Rpt. from *ESQ* no. 56 (3 Qtr. 1969).

Steinbrink, Jeffrey. "Novels of Circumstance and Novels of Character." *ESQ* 20 (2 Qtr. 1974): 101–10.

Sten, Christopher W. "Bartleby the Transcendentalist: Melville's Dead Letter to Emerson." *MLQ* 35 (March 1974): 30–44.

Stenberg, Theodore T. "Emerson and Oral Discourse." In *Studies in Rhetoric and Public Speaking in Honor of John Albert Winans*. New York: Century, 1925.

Stenerson, Douglas C. "Emerson and the Agrarian Tradition." *JHI* 14 (Jan. 1953): 95–115.

Stern, Daniel [pseud. for Comtesse D'Agoult]. "Etudes contemporaires: Emerson." *ReI* 2nd ser. 4 (July 1846): 446–56.

Stern, Guy. "Blücher, Brooks, and August Kopisch." *GAS* 5 (1972): 8–11.

Stern, Madeleine B. "Elizabeth Peabody's Foreign Library (1840)." *ATQ* no. 20, suppl. (Fall 1973): 5–12. Rpt. in her *Books and Book People in Nineteenth-Century America*. New York: Bowker, 1978, 121–35.

————. "Four Letters from George Keats." *PMLA* 56 (March 1941): 207–18.

————. "The House of Expanding Doors: Anne Lynch's Soirees, 1846." *NYH* 23 (Jan. 1942): 42–51.

————. "James P. Walker and Horace B. Fuller: Transcendental Publishers." *BPLQ* 6 (July 1954): 123–40. Rpt. in her *Imprints on History: Book Publishers and American Frontiers*. Bloomington: Indiana Univ. Press, 1956, 45–59.

————. *The Life of Margaret Fuller*. New York: Dutton, 1942.

————. "Margaret Fuller and the *Dial.*" *SAQ* 40 (Jan. 1941): 11–21.

————. "Margaret Fuller and the Phrenologist Publishers." *SAR* 1980: 229–37.

————. "New England Artists in Italy, 1835–1855." *NEQ* 14 (June 1941): 243–71.

————. "William Henry Channing's Letters on 'Woman in Her Social Relations.' " *CLJ* no. 6 (Aut. 1968): 54–62.

Stern, Milton R. *The Fine Hammered Steel of Herman Melville*. Urbana: Univ. of Illinois Press, 1957.

Stevenson, Robert Louis. "Henry D. Thoreau: His Character and Opinions." *CoMag* 41 (June 1880): 664–82. Rpt. in his *Familiar Studies of Men and Books*. London: Chatto and Windus, 1882, 129–71.

Stewart, George, Jr. "Evenings in the Library. No. 2. Emerson." *BelMM* 1 (Jan. 1877): 222–34. Rpt. in his *Evenings in the Library*. Toronto: Belford Brothers, 1878, 24–51.

Stewart, Randall. "The Concord Group: A Study in Relationships." *SR* 44 (Oct.–Dec. 1936): 434–46.

————. "Emerson, Asset or Liability?" *TSL* 2 (1957): 33–40. Rpt. as "The Deification of Man" in his *American Literature and Christian Doctrine*. Baton Rouge: Louisiana State Univ. Press, 1958, 43–72.

————. *Nathaniel Hawthorne: A Biography*. New Haven: Yale Univ. Press, 1948.

Stewart, Samuel Barrett. "Theodore Parker." In *Unitarianism: Its Origins and History*, 220–44.

Stibitz, E. Earle. "Thoreau's Humanism and Ideas on Literature." *ESQ* no. 55 (Sum. 1969): 110–16.

Stiem, Marjorie. "The Beginnings of Modern Education: Bronson Alcott." *PJE* 38 (July 1960): 613–28.

Stillman, William J. "Autobiography of W. J. Stillman. V. Journalism." *Atl* 85 (May 1900): 613–28.

———. "The Philosophers' Camp." *CM* 46 (Aug. 1893): 598–606.

Stockton, Edwin, Jr. "Henry David Thoreau, Terrener or Mariner." *RadfR* 20 (Oct. 1966): 143–54.

Stoddard, Richard Henry. *Recollections: Personal and Literary.* Ed. Ripley Hitchcock. New York: A. S. Barnes, 1903.

Stoehr, Taylor. "Art vs. Utopia: The Case of Nathaniel Hawthorne and Brook Farm." *AR* 36 (Wtr. 1978): 89–102.

———. " 'Eloquence Needs No Constable'—Alcott, Emerson, and Thoreau on the State." *CRevAS* 2 (Fall 1974): 81–100. Incorporated into his *Nay-Saying in Concord.*

———. *Nay-Saying in Concord.* Hamden, Conn.: Archon Books, 1979.

———. "Transcendentalist Attitudes toward Communitism and Individualism." *ESQ* 20 (2 Qtr. 1974): 65–90. Incorporated into his *Nay-Saying in Concord.*

Stokes, Harry M. "Henry W. Bellows's Vision of the Christian Church." *PUHS* 15.2 (1965): 1–16.

Stoller, Leo. *After* Walden: *Thoreau's Changing Views on Economic Man.* Stanford: Stanford Univ. Press, 1957.

———. "Christopher A. Greene: Rhode Island Transcendentalist." *RIH* 22 (Oct. 1963): 97–111.

———. "A Note on Thoreau's Place in Phenology." *Isis* 47 (June 1956): 172–81.

Story, Ronald. *The Forging of an Aristocracy: Harvard and the Boston Upper Class, 1800–1870.* Middletown: Wesleyan Univ. Press, 1980.

Stovall, Floyd. *American Idealism.* Norman: Univ. of Oklahoma Press, 1943.

———. *The Foreground of* Leaves of Grass. Charlottesville: Univ. Press of Virginia, 1974.

———. "Poe's Debt to Coleridge." *UTSE* no. 10 (1930): 70–127. Rpt. in his *Edgar Poe the Poet.* Charlottesville: Univ. Press of Virginia, 1969, 126–74.

———. "Ralph Waldo Emerson." In *Eight American Authors.* Ed. Stovall. New York: Modern Language Assn., 1956, 47–99. Rev. ed., ed. James Woodress. New York: Norton, 1971, 37–83.

———. "The Value of Emerson Today." *CE* 3 (Feb. 1942): 442–54. Rpt. in his *American Idealism,* 37–54.

Stowell, Robert F. *A Thoreau Gazeteer.* Princeton: Princeton Univ. Press, 1970.

Strachner, Stephen D. "*Walden*: Thoreau's *Vānaprasthya.*" *TJQ* 5.1 (Jan. 1974): 8–12.

Straker, Robert Lincoln. "A Gloss upon Glosses" (1956), TS. Antioch Coll. Library.

Strauch, Carl F. "The Background and Meaning of the 'Ode Inscribed to W. H. Channing.' " *ESQ* no. 42, suppl. (2 Qtr. 1966): 4–14.

———. "A Critical and Variorum Edition of the Poems of Ralph Waldo Emerson." Diss. Yale 1946.

———. "The Daemonic and Experimental in Emerson." *Person* 33 (Wtr. 1952): 40–55.

———. "Emerson and the American Continuity." *ESQ* no. 61 (1 Qtr. 1957): 1–5.

———. "Emerson and the Doctrine of Sympathy." *SIR* 6 (Spr. 1967): 152–74.

———. "Emerson as Literary Middleman." *ESQ* no. 18 (2 Qtr. 1960): 2–9.

———. "Emerson Rejects Reed and Hails Thoreau." *HLB* 16 (July 1968): 257–73.

———. "Emerson's Sacred Science." *PMLA* 73 (June 1958): 237–50.

———. "Emerson's Use of the Organic Method." *ESQ* no. 55 (2 Qtr. 1969): 18–24.

———. "Hatred's Swift Repulsions: Emerson, Margaret Fuller, and Others." *SIR* 7 (Wtr. 1968): 65–103.

———. "The Importance of Emerson's Skeptical Mood." *HLB* 11 (Wtr. 1957): 117–39.

———. "Introduction." In Sampson Reed, *Observations on the Growth of the Mind*. Gainesville, Fla.: Scholars' Facsimiles & Reprints, 1970, v–xvi.

———. "The Mind's Voice: Emerson's Poetic Styles." *ESQ* no. 60 (Sum. 1970): 43–59.

———. "The Sources of Emerson's 'Song of Nature.'" *HLB* 9 (Aug. 1955): 300–34.

———, ed. *Characteristics of Emerson, Transcendental Poet: A Symposium*. Hartford, Conn.: Transcendental Books, 1975.

———, ed. *Style in the American Renaissance*. Hartford, Conn.: Transcendental Books, 1970.

Strelow, Michael Herbert. "Emerson's Paradigm of the Self and Its Manifestations in the Work of Melville and Thoreau." Diss. Univ. of Oregon 1979.

Strickland, Charles. "A Transcendentalist Father: The Child-Rearing Practices of Bronson Alcott." *PAH* 3 (1969): 5–73. Abridged rpt. in *HCQ* 1 (Sum. 1973): 4–51.

Stromberg, R. N. "Thoreau and Marx: A Century After." *SocS* 40 (Feb. 1949): 53–56.

Strong, Augustus Hopkins. *American Poets and Their Theology*. Philadelphia: Griffith and Rowland, 1916.

Strong, George Templeton. *The Diary of George Templeton Strong*. Ed. Allan Nevins and Milton Halsey Thomas. 4 vols. New York: Macmillan, 1952.

Sudol, Ronald A. "'The Adirondacs' and Technology." In *Emerson Centenary Essays*, ed. Joel Myerson, 173–79.

Summerlin, Charles T. "The Possible Oracle: Three Transcendental Poets." Diss. Yale 1973.

Sundquist, Eric. *Home as Found: Authority and Genealogy in Nineteenth-Century American Literature*. Baltimore: Johns Hopkins Univ. Press, 1979.

Sutcliffe, Emerson Grant. "Emerson's Theories of Literary Expression." *UISLL* 8 (Feb. 1923): 9–152.

———. "Whitman, Emerson and the New Poetry." *NRep* 19 (24 May 1919): 114–16.

Sveino, Per. *Orestes A. Brownson's Road to Catholicism*. New York: Humanities Press, 1971.

Swan, Michael Munson. *The Athenæum Gallery, 1827–1873*. Boston: Boston Athenæum, 1940.

Sweet, William W. *Religion in the Development of American Culture 1765–1840*. New York: Scribners, 1952.

Swift, David E. "Yankee in Virginia: James Marsh at Hampden-Sydney, 1823–1826." *VMHB* 80 (July 1972): 312–32.

Swift, Lindsay. *Brook Farm: Its Members, Scholars, and Visitors*. New York: Macmillan, 1900.

———. "Tribute to Franklin Benjamin Sanborn." *PMHS* 50 (March 1917): 209–13.

Swiniarski, Louise. "A Comparative Study of Elizabeth Palmer Peabody and Susan Blow by Examination of Their Work and Writings." Diss. Boston Coll. 1976.

Swisher, Walter Samuel. "William Henry Channing." *PUHS* 6 (1939): 1–12.

Szymanski, Karen Ann. "Margaret Fuller: The New York Years." Diss. Syracuse Univ. 1980.

Talmadge, John E. "Georgia Tests the Fugitive Slave Law." *GHQ* 49 (March 1965): 57–64.

Tanner, Tony. "Notes for a Comparison between American and European Romanticism." *JAmS* 2 (April 1968): 83–103.

———. *The Reign of Wonder: Naivety and Reality in American Literature*. Cambridge: Cambridge Univ. Press, 1965.

Tassin, Algernon. *The Magazine in America*. New York: Dodd, Mead, 1916.

Taylor, H. Leland. "Margaret Fuller: Commitment in Italy." *Carrell* 13 (Dec. 1972): 9–24.

Taylor, J. Golden. *Neighbor Thoreau's Critical Humor*. Logan: Utah State Univ. Press, 1958.

———. "Thoreau's Sour Grapes." *PUASAL* 42 (1965): 38–49.

———, ed. *The Western Thoreau Centenary*. Logan: Utah State Univ. Press, 1963.

Taylor, Walter Fuller. "Israfel in Motley: A Study of Poe's Humor." *SR* 42 (July 1934): 330–34.

————. *The Story of American Letters*. Chicago: Henry Regnery, 1956.

Temmer, M. J. "Rousseau and Thoreau." *YFS* 28 (1961–62): 112–21.

Templeman, William. "Thoreau, Moralist of the Picturesque." *PMLA* 47 (Sept. 1932): 864–89.

Thacher, A. G., Jr. "William Henry Channing and the *Spirit of the Age*." M.A. thesis Columbia 1941.

Tharp, Louise Hall. *The Peabody Sisters of Salem*. Boston: Little, Brown, 1950.

Tharpe, Jac. "Hawthorne and Hindu Literature." *SoQ* 10 (Jan. 1972): 107–15.

Thayer, James B. *Rev. Samuel Ripley of Waltham*. Cambridge, Mass.: John Wilson, 1897.

————. *A Western Journey with Mr. Emerson*. Boston: Little, Brown, 1884.

Thayer, William R. *The Influence of Emerson*. Boston: Cupples, Upham, 1886.

Theodore Parker: Anniversaries of Birth and Death Celebrated in Chicago, November 13–20, 1910. Chicago: Unity, 1910.

"Theodore Parker's Bettine." *BET*, 28 June, 12 July 1897, 6, 6.

Thomas, J. B. "Darwin, Emerson and the Gospel." *ChT* ser. 1 (1886): 193–224.

Thomas, John L. "Romantic Reform in America, 1815–1865." *AQ* 17 (Wtr. 1965): 656–81.

Thomas, John Wesley. *James Freeman Clarke: Apostle of German Culture to America*. Boston: John W. Luce, 1949.

————. "James Freeman Clarke as a Translator." *AGR* 10 (Dec. 1943): 31–33.

————. "John Sullivan Dwight: A Translator of German Romanticism." *AL* 21 (Jan. 1950): 427–41.

————. "New Light on Margaret Fuller's Projected 'Life of Goethe.' " *GR* 24 (Oct. 1949): 216–23.

————. "The *Western Messenger* and German Culture." *AGR* 11 (Oct. 1944): 17–18.

Thomas, Robert K. "The Tree and the Stone: Time and Space in the Works of Henry David Thoreau." Diss. Columbia 1967.

"Thomas Wentworth Higginson." *Dial* [Chicago] 50 (16 May 1911): 375–76.

Thomas, William S. "José Martí and Thoreau: Pioneers of Personal Freedom." *DosP* Aug. 1949: 1–3.

Thompson, Cameron. "John Locke and New England Transcendentalism." *NEQ* 35 (Dec. 1962): 435–57.

Thompson, Frank T. "Emerson's Indebtedness to Coleridge." *SP* 23 (Jan. 1926): 55–76.

————. "Emerson's Theory and Practice of Poetry." *PMLA* 43 (Dec. 1928): 1170–84.

Thompson, G. R. "Poe and Romantic Irony." In *Papers on Poe*. Ed. Richard P. Veler. Springfield, Ohio: Chantry Music Press, 1972, 28–41.

Thompson, Lawrance. *Young Longfellow, 1807–1843*. New York: Macmillan, 1938.

Thompson, Wade. "The Impractical Thoreau: A Rebuttal." *CE* 19 (Nov. 1957): 67–70.

Thoreau, Henry David. *The Annotated Walden*. Ed. Philip Van Doren Stern. New York: Clarkson N. Potter, 1970.

————. *Collected Poems of Henry Thoreau*. Ed. Carl Bode. Chicago: Packard, 1943. Enl. ed., Baltimore: Johns Hopkins Univ. Press, 1964.

————. *Consciousness in Concord: The Text of Thoreau's Hitherto "Lost Journal" (1840–41), Together with Notes and a Commentary*. Ed. Perry Miller. Boston: Houghton Mifflin, 1958.

————. *The Correspondence of Henry David Thoreau*. Ed. Walter Harding and Carl Bode. New York: New York Univ. Press, 1958.

————. *Early Essays and Miscellanies*. Ed. Joseph J. Moldenhauer. Princeton: Princeton Univ. Press, 1975.

————. *Familiar Letters of Henry David Thoreau*. Ed. F. B. Sanborn. Boston: Houghton, Mifflin, 1894.

————. *The First and Last Journeys of Thoreau*. Ed. F. B. Sanborn. 2 vols. Boston: Bibliophile Soc., 1905.

——. *H. D. Thoreau: A Writer's Journal*. Ed. Laurence Stapleton. New York: Dover, 1960.

——. *The Illustrated Maine Woods*. Ed. Joseph J. Moldenhauer. Princeton: Princeton Univ. Press, 1974.

——. *The Illustrated Walden*. Ed. J. Lyndon Shanley. Princeton: Princeton Univ. Press, 1973.

——. *The Indians of Thoreau: Selections from the Indian Notebooks*. Ed. Richard F. Fleck. Albuquerque, N.M.: Hummingbird Press, 1974.

——. *Journal*. Ed. Bradford Torrey [and Francis H. Allen]. Vols. 7–20 of *The Writings of Henry David Thoreau*. Rpt. as *The Journals of Henry David Thoreau*. 2 vols. New York: Dover, 1962.

——. *Journal, Volume 1: 1837–1844*. Ed. John C. Broderick et al. Princeton: Princeton Univ. Press, 1981.

——. *The Maine Woods*. Boston: Ticknor and Fields, 1864. New ed., ed. Joseph J. Moldenhauer. Princeton: Princeton Univ. Press, 1972.

——. *Poems of Nature*. Ed. H. S. Salt and F. B. Sanborn. London: John Lane, 1895.

——. *Reform Papers*. Ed. Wendell Glick. Princeton: Princeton Univ. Press, 1973.

——. *Thoreau in the Mountains*. Ed. William Howarth. New York: Farrar, Straus & Giroux, 1982.

——. *Thoreau on the Art of Writing*. Ed. Franklin W. Hamilton. Flint, Mich.: Walden Press, 1967.

——. *Thoreau's Bird-Lore*. Ed. Francis H. Allen. Boston: Houghton Mifflin, 1925.

——. *Thoreau's Literary Notebooks in the Library of Congress*. Ed. Kenneth Walter Cameron. Hartford, Conn.: Transcendental Books, 1964.

——. *The Variorum Walden*. Ed. Walter Harding. New York: Twayne, 1962.

——. *Walden*. Boston: Ticknor and Fields, 1854. New ed., ed. J. Lyndon Shanley. Princeton: Princeton Univ. Press, 1971.

——. *Walden*. Ed. F. B. Sanborn. 2 vols. Boston: Bibliophile Soc., 1909.

——. *A Week on the Concord and Merrimack Rivers*. Boston: James Munroe, 1849. New ed., ed. Carl Hovde et al. Princeton: Princeton Univ. Press, 1980.

——. *The Writings of Henry David Thoreau*. 20 vols. Boston: Houghton Mifflin, 1906.

——. *The Writings of Henry D. Thoreau*. Ed. Walter Harding et al. 6 vols. to date. Princeton: Princeton Univ. Press, 1971–

Thundyil, Zacharias. "Emerson and the Problem of Evil: Paradox and Solution." *HTR* 62 (Jan. 1969): 51–61.

Thurin, Erik Ingvar. *Emerson as Priest of Pan*. Lincoln: Univ. of Nebraska Press, 1981.

——. *The Universal Autobiography of Ralph Waldo Emerson*. Lund, Sweden: C. W. K. Gleerup, 1974.

Thurman, Kelly. "Margaret Fuller in Two American Novels: *The Blithedale Romance* and *Elsie Venner*." M.A. thesis Univ. of Kentucky 1945.

Thurow, Waldemar A. "Amos Bronson Alcott, 1799–1888: An Annotated Bibliography." Library school thesis Univ. of Wisconsin 1938.

Thwing, Charles W. "Education According to Emerson." *SchS* 2 (16 Oct. 1915): 551–53. Rpt. in his *Education According to Some Modern Masters*. New York: Platt and Peck, 1916, 1–37.

Tichi, Cecelia. *New World, New Earth: Environmental Reform in American Literature from the Puritans through Whitman*. New Haven: Yale Univ. Press, 1979.

Ticknor, Anna, and G. S. Hillard, ed. *Life, Letters, and Journal of George Ticknor*. 2 vols. Boston: James R. Osgood, 1876.

Ticknor, Caroline. *Hawthorne and His Publisher*. Boston: Houghton Mifflin, 1913.

——. *Poe's Helen*. New York: Scribners, 1916.

——. "Some Early Letters of George William Curtis." *Atl* 114 (Sept. 1914): 363–76.

Tiffany, Frances. "Transcendentalism: The New England Renaissance." *UnitR* 31 (Feb. 1889): 97–117. Rpt. in *Unitarianism: Its Origins and History*, 196–219.

Tiffany, Nina Moore. *Samuel E. Sewall: A Memoir*. Boston: Houghton, Mifflin, 1898.

———, and Frances Tiffany. *Harm Jan Huidekoper*. Cambridge, Mass.: Riverside Press, 1904.

Tileston, Mary Wilder, ed. *Caleb and Mary Wilder Foote: Reminiscences and Letters*. Boston: Houghton Mifflin, 1918.

Tillinghast, C.A. "The West of Thoreau's Imagination: The Development of a Symbol." *Thoth* 6 (Wtr. 1965): 42–50.

Tillman, James S. "The Transcendental Georgic in *Walden*." *ESQ* 21 (3 Qtr. 1975): 137–41.

Tilton, Eleanor M. *Amiable Autocrat: A Biography of Oliver Wendell Holmes*. New York: Henry Schuman, 1947.

———. "Emerson's Lecture Schedule—1837–1838—Revised." *HLB* 21 (Oct. 1973): 382–99.

———. "*Leaves of Grass*: Four Letters to Emerson." *HLB* 27 (July 1979): 336–41.

Timpe, Eugene F. *American Literature in Germany 1861–1872*. Chapel Hill: Univ. of North Carolina Press, 1964.

———, ed. *Thoreau Abroad: Twelve Bibliographical Essays*. Hamden, Conn.: Shoe String Press, 1971.

Tingley, Donald F. *Social History of the United States*. Detroit: Gale, 1979.

Todd, Edgeley Woodman. "Philosophical Ideas at Harvard College, 1817–1837." *NEQ* 16 (March 1943): 63–90.

Tolles, Frederick B. "Emerson and Quakerism." *AL* 10 (May 1938): 142–65.

Tolman, George. *Mary Moody Emerson*. N.p.: n.p., 1929.

Tompkins, Philip K. "On 'Paradoxes' in the Rhetoric of the New England Transcendentalists." *QJS* 62 (Feb. 1976): 40–48.

Torrey, Joseph. *The Remains of the Rev. James Marsh, D.D. . . . with a Memoir of His Life*. Boston: Crocker and Brewster, 1843.

Touloumtzis, Michael. "The Influence of Thomas Carlyle on Henry D. Thoreau's Art and Thought." Diss. Brandeis 1981.

Townsend, Harvey Gates. *Philosophical Ideas in the United States*. New York: American Book, 1934.

Traubel, Horace. *With Walt Whitman in Camden*. 6 vols. to date. Vol. 1: Boston: Small, Maynard, 1906. Vol. 2: New York: D. Appleton, 1908. Vol. 3: New York: Mitchell, Kennerley, 1914. Vols. 4 (ed. Sculley Bradley), 5 (ed. Gertrude Traubel), 6 (ed. Gertrude Traubel and William White): Carbondale: Southern Illinois Univ. Press, 1953, 1964, 1982.

Travelers in Arcadia: American Artists in Italy, 1830–1875. Detroit: Detroit Museum of Arts, 1951.

Travis, Mildred K. "Echoes of Emerson in Plinlimmon." *ATQ* no. 14 (Apr. 1972): 47–48.

Treat, Robert, and Betty Treat. "Thoreau and Institutional Christianity." *ATQ* no. 1 (1 Qtr. 1969): 44–47.

Trent, William P. *A History of American Literature*. New York: D. Appleton, 1903.

Trimpi, Helen P. "Three of Melville's Confidence Men: William Cullen Bryant, Theodore Parker, and Horace Greeley." *TSLL* 21 (Fall 1979): 36–95.

Trowbridge, John Townsend. *My Own Story*. Boston: Houghton, Mifflin, 1903.

———. "Reminiscences of Walt Whitman." *Atl* 89 (Feb. 1902): 163–75. Incorporated into his *My Own Story*.

Trueblood, D. Elton. "The Influence of Emerson's 'Divinity School Address.'" *HTR* 32 (Jan. 1939): 41–56.

Tryon, W. S. *Parnassus Corner: A Life of James T. Fields*. Boston: Houghton Mifflin, 1963.

Tucker, Louis L. "The Semi-Colon Club of Cincinnati." *OhH* 73 (Wtr. 1964): 13–26, 57–58.

Tuckerman, Henry T. *Book of the Artists: American Artist Life*. New York: Putnams, 1867.

Tuerk, Richard. *Central Still: Circle and Sphere in Thoreau's Prose*. The Hague: Mouton, 1975.

———. "Emerson's Darker Vision: 'Hamatreya' and 'Days.' " *ATQ* no. 25 (Wtr. 1975): 28–33.

———. "Man and Nature in 'Slavery in Massachusetts.' " *CS* 7.1 (March 1972): 7–8.

———. "Thoreau's Early Versions of a Myth." *ATQ* no. 10 (Spr. 1971): 32–38.

Tuomi, Martha Ilona. "Dr. Frederic Henry Hedge: His Life and Works to the End of His Bangor Pastorate: 1805–1850." M.A. thesis Univ. of Maine 1935.

Turco, Lewis. "The Pro-Am Tournament." *MQR* 14 (Wtr. 1975): 84–91.

Turner, Arlin. "Autobiographical Elements in Hawthorne's *The Blithedale Romance*." *UTSE* no. 15 (8 July 1935): 39–62.

———. "Elizabeth Peabody Reviews *Twice-Told Tales*." *NHJ* 1974: 75–84.

———. "Hawthorne and Reform." *NEQ* 15 (Dec. 1942): 700–14.

———. *Nathaniel Hawthorne: A Biography*. New York: Oxford Univ. Press, 1980.

Turpie, Marcy C. "A Quaker Source for Emerson's Sermon on the Lord's Supper." *NEQ* 17 (March 1944): 95–101.

Tuttleton, James W. *Thomas Wentworth Higginson*. Boston: Twayne, 1978.

The Twenty-Eighth Congregational Society of Boston: Its Services, Organization, Officers, and Principles. Boston: n.p., 1883.

Tyack, David B. *George Ticknor and the Boston Brahmins*. Cambridge: Harvard Univ. Press, 1967.

Tyler, Alice Felt. *Freedom's Ferment*. Minneapolis: Univ. of Minnesota Press, 1944.

Uhlig, Herbert. "Improved Means to an Unimproved End." *TSB* no. 128 (Sum. 1974): 1–3.

Underwood, Francis H. "Ralph Waldo Emerson." *NAR* 130 (May 1880): 479–98.

Underwood, Sarah A. "Sketches of Concord Philosophers." *BelMM* 10 (April 1893): 675–88.

Underwood, W. J. *Emerson and Swedenborg: A Review of Emerson's Lecture on Swedenborg*. London: James Speirs, 1896.

Unitarianism: Its Origins and History. Boston: American Unitarian Assn., 1890.

Unrue, Darlene. "John Smith and Thoreau: A-Fishing in the Same Stream." *TJQ* 8.3 (July 1976): 3–9.

Urbanski, Marie Mitchell Olesen. "The Ambivalence of Ralph Waldo Emerson towards Margaret Fuller." *TJQ* 10.3 (July 1978): 26–36.

———. "Henry David Thoreau and Margaret Fuller." *TJQ* 8.4 (Oct. 1976): 24–30.

———. *Margaret Fuller's* Woman in the Nineteenth Century: *A Literary Study of Form and Content, of Sources and Influence*. Westport, Conn.: Greenwood, 1980.

Ustick, W. Lee. "Emerson's Debt to Montaigne." *WUS* 9 (April 1922): 245–62.

Van Anglen, Kevin P. "A Paradise Regained: Thoreau's *Wild Apples* and the Myth of the American Adam." *ESQ* 27 (1 Qtr. 1981): 28–37.

———. "The Sources for Thoreau's Greek Translations." *SAR* 1980: 291–300.

Vance, William Silas. "Carlyle and the American Transcendentalists." Diss. Univ. of Chicago 1941.

———. "Carlyle in America before *Sartor Resartus*." *AL* 7 (Jan 1936): 363–75.

Vanderbilt, Kermit. *Charles Eliot Norton: Apostle of Culture in a Democracy*. Cambridge: Harvard Univ. Press, 1959.

Van Deusen, Glyndon G. *Horace Greeley: Nineteenth-Century Crusader*. Philadelphia: Univ. of Pennsylvania Press, 1953.

Van Deusen, Marshall. *A Metaphor for the History of American Criticism*. Uppsala, Sweden: A-B Lundequiska Bokhandeln, 1961.

Van Doren, Carl. *The American Novel, 1789-1939*. New York: Macmillan, 1949.
———. "Lucifer from Nantucket: An Introduction to *Moby Dick.*" *CM* 110 (Aug. 1925): 494–501.
Van Doren, Mark. *Henry David Thoreau: A Critical Study*. Boston: Houghton Mifflin, 1916.
Van Nostrand, A. D. *Everyman His Own Poet: Romantic Gospels in American Literature*. New York: McGraw-Hill, 1968.
Van Vechten, Carl. "A Belated Biography." *LitRev* 2 (31 Dec. 1921): 316.
———. "The Later Work of Herman Melville." *DD* 3 (Jan. 1922): 9–20. Rpt. in his *Excavations: A Book of Advocacies*. New York: Knopf, 1926, 65–88.
Varner, John Grier. "Sarah Helen Whitman: Seeress of Providence." Diss. Univ. of Virginia 1940.
Vaughan, Mosetta I. *Sketch of the Life and Work of Convers Francis, D.D.* Watertown, Mass.: Historical Soc. of Watertown, 1944.
Venable, W. H. *Beginnings of Literary Culture in the Ohio Valley*. Cincinnati: Robert Clarke, 1891.
———. "Early Periodical Literature of the Ohio Valley: II." *MWH* 8 (July 1888): 197–203. Incorporated into his *Beginnings of Literary Culture in the Ohio Valley*.
———. "Early Periodical Literature of the Ohio Valley: VI." *MWH* 9 (Nov. 1888): 35–40. Incorporated into his *Beginnings of Literary Culture in the Ohio Valley*.
Very, Jones. *Essays and Poems*. Boston: Charles C. Little and James Brown, 1839.
———. "Influence of Christianity on Epic Poetry." *ChEx* 24 (May 1838): 201–21.
———. *Jones Very, der Dichter des Christentums*. Trans. Albert Ritter. Linz, Wien, Leipzig: Oesterreichische Verlag Sanstatt, 1903.
———. *Jones Very: Selected Poems*. Ed. Nathan Lyons. New Brunswick, N. J.: Rutgers Univ. Press, 1966.
———. *Poems and Essays by Jones Very: Complete and Revised Edition*. Ed. James Freeman Clarke. Boston: Houghton, Mifflin, 1886.
———. *Poems by Jones Very: James Freeman Clarke's Enlarged Collection of 1886 Re-edited with a Thematic and Topical Index*. Ed. Kenneth Walter Cameron. Hartford, Conn.: Transcendental Books, 1965. Rpt. in *ATQ* no. 21 (Wtr. 1974): 1–143.
———. *Poems by Jones Very with a Introductory Memoir by William P. Andrews*. Boston: Houghton, Mifflin, 1883.
———. "The Very Family." *EIHC* 1 (July 1859): 116; 2 (Feb. 1860): 33–38.
———. "What Reasons Are There for Not Expecting Another Great Epic Poem." Ed. Kenneth Walter Cameron. *ESQ* no. 12 (3 Qtr. 1958): 25–32.
Very, Lydia. "Jones Very Again." *BoH*, 6 June 1880.
Veysey, Laurence, ed. *The Perfectionists: Radical Social Thought in the North, 1815-1860*. New York: John Wiley, 1973.
Vincent, Howard P. *The Trying Out of* Moby-Dick. Boston: Houghton Mifflin, 1949.
Vitanen, Reino. "Tocqueville and William Ellery Channing." *AL* 22 (March 1950): 21–28.
Vitanza, Victor J. "Melville's *Redburn* and Emerson's 'General Education of the Eye.'" *ESQ* 21 (1 Qtr. 1975): 40–45.
Vogel, Stanley M. *German Literary Influences on the American Transcendentalists*. New Haven: Yale Univ. Press, 1955.
Volkman, Arthur G. "Henry David Thoreau, Physicist." *TSB* no. 123 (Spr. 1973): 4.
von Frank, Albert J. "Emerson's Unpublished Boyhood and Collegiate Verse." *SAR* 1983: 1–56.
———. "Life as Art in America: The Case of Margaret Fuller." *SAR* 1981: 1–26.
von Klenze, Camillo. *Charles Timothy Brooks: Translator from the German and the Genteel Tradition*. New York: Modern Language Assn., 1937.

Wade, Joseph S. "A Contribution to a Bibliography from 1909 to 1939 of Henry David Thoreau." *JNYES* 47 (June 1939): 163–203.

———. "Some Insects of Thoreau's Writings." *JNYES* 35 (March 1927): 1–21.

Wade, Mason. *Margaret Fuller: Whetstone of Genius*. New York: Viking, 1940.

Wagenknecht, Edward. *Edgar Allan Poe*. New York: Oxford Univ. Press, 1963.

———. *Henry David Thoreau: What Manner of Man?* Amherst: Univ. of Massachusetts Press, 1981.

———. *Ralph Waldo Emerson: Portrait of a Balanced Soul*. New York: Oxford Univ. Press, 1974.

Waggoner, Hyatt H. *American Poets from the Puritans to the Present*. Boston: Houghton Mifflin, 1968.

———. *Emerson as Poet*. Princeton: Princeton Univ. Press, 1974.

———. "Emily Dickinson: The Transcendent Self." *Criticism* 7 (Fall 1965): 297–334. Rpt. as "Proud Ephemeral: Emily Dickinson" in his *American Poets from the Puritans to the Present*, 181–222.

———. " 'Grace' in the Thought of Emerson, Thoreau, and Hawthorne." *ESQ* no. 54 (1 Qtr. 1969): 68–72.

Wagner, Frederick. "All Pine and Apple Orchard: Hawthorne and the Alcotts." *EIHC* 118 (Jan. 1982): 31–41.

———. "Eighty-Six Letters (1814–1882) of A. Bronson Alcott." *SAR* 1979, 1980: 239–308, 183–228.

Wagner, Roland C. "Lucky Fox at Walden." In *Thoreau in Our Season*, ed. John Hicks, 117–33.

Wahr, Frederic B. *Emerson and Goethe*. Ann Arbor, Mich: George Wahr, 1915.

———. "Emerson and the Germans." *MDU* 33 (Feb. 1941): 49–63.

Waite, Robert G. " 'Linked Analogies': The Symbolic Mode of Perception and Expression in Emerson and Melville." Diss. Univ. of Kentucky 1973.

Walcutt, Charles Child. *American Literary Naturalism*. Minneapolis: Univ. of Minnesota Press, 1956.

———. "*Walden* as a Response to 'The American Scholar.' " *ArQ* 34 (Spr. 1978): 5–30.

Walker, C. S. "Emerson's Relation to Christ and Christianity." *NewE* 41 (Nov. 1882): 742–50.

Walker, Edwin C. *A Sketch and Appreciation of Moncure Daniel Conway*. New York: Edwin C. Walker, 1908.

Walker, Peter. "Moncure Conway: Apostate Slave Master." In his *Moral Choices: Memory, Desire, and Imagination in Nineteenth-Century American Abolition*. Baton Rouge: Louisiana State Univ. Press, 1978, 1–86.

Walker, Robert Howard. "Charles Lane and the Fruitlands Utopia." Diss. Univ. of Texas 1967.

Walters, Ronald G. *American Reformers, 1815–1860*. New York: Hill and Wang, 1978.

Ward, Annie J. "Transcendental Wild Oats." *SpR*, 15 Dec. 1895, 5. Rpt. in Thomas Blanding, "Beans, Baked and Half-Baked (II)." *CS* 14.2 (Sum. 1979): 23–24.

Ward, J. A. "Emerson and 'The Educated Will': Notes on the Process of Conversion." *ELH* 35 (Dec. 1967): 495–517.

Ward, Robert S. "The American System in Literature." *NEQ* 38 (Sept. 1965): 363–74.

Ward, Robert Stafford. "Still 'Christians,' Still Infidels." *SHR* 2 (Sum. 1978): 365–74.

Ward, Samuel Gray, comp. *Ward Family Papers*. Boston: Merrymount Press, 1900.

Ward, Theodora V. W. "Emily Dickinson and Thomas Wentworth Higginson." *BPLQ* 5 (Jan. 1953): 3–18.

Warders, Donald F. " 'The Progress of the Hour and the Day': A Critical Study of the *Dial* (1840–1844)." Diss. Univ. of Kansas 1973.

Ware, John. *Memoir of the Life of Henry Ware, Jr*. Boston: James Munroe, 1846.

Warfel, Harry R. "Margaret Fuller and Ralph Waldo Emerson." *PMLA* 50 (June 1935): 576–94.

Warren, Austin. "The Concord School of Philosophy." *NEQ* 2 (April 1929): 199–233.

——. *The Elder Henry James*. New York: Macmillan, 1934.

——. "Hawthorne, Margaret Fuller, and 'Nemesis.' " *PMLA* 54 (June 1939): 613–15.

——. "Introduction." In *Nathaniel Hawthorne: Representative Selections*. Ed. Warren. New York: American Book, 1934, xi–xci.

——. "Lowell on Thoreau." *SP* 27 (July 1930): 442–61.

——. "The Orphic Sage: Bronson Alcott." *AL* 3 (March 1931): 3–13. Rpt. as "Neo-Platonic Alcott" in his *New England Saints*. Ann Arbor: Univ. of Michigan Press, 1956, 35–45.

Washburn, W. E. "The Oriental 'Roots' of American Transcendentalism." *SWJ* 4 (Fall 1949): 141–55.

Wasson, David Atwood. *Beyond Concord: Selected Writings of David Atwood Wasson*. Ed. Charles H. Foster. Bloomington: Indiana Univ. Press, 1965.

——. Review of Ralph Waldo Emerson, *May-Day*. *Radical* 2 (Aug. 1867): 760–62.

Waters, Edward. "John Sullivan Dwight, First American Critic of Music." *MuQ* 21 (Jan. 1935): 69–88.

Weaver, Raymond M. *Herman Melville: Mariner and Mystic*. Garden City, N.Y.: George H. Doran, 1921.

Webber, Everett. *Escape to Utopia: The Communal Movement in America*. New York: Hastings House, 1959.

Weber, Ralph Emil. "The *Dial*: A Transcendental Journal 1840–1844." M.A. thesis Fairleigh Dickinson Univ. 1961.

Webster, Frank Martindale. "Transcendental Points of View: A Survey of the Criticism of Music, Art, and Letters in the *Dial*, 1840–1844." *WUA* 7 (April 1920): 187–203.

Weeks, Louis B., III. "Theodore Parker: The Minister as Revolutionary." Diss. Duke 1970.

Weidman, Bette S. "Charles Frederick Briggs." Diss. Columbia 1968.

Weisbuch, Robert. *Emily Dickinson's Poetry*. Chicago: Univ. of Chicago Press, 1975.

Weiss, John. *American Religion*. Boston: Roberts, 1871.

——. *Discourse Occasioned by the Death of Convers Francis, D.D.* Cambridge, Mass.: privately printed, 1863.

——. *The Immortal Life*. Boston: Lockwood, Brooks, 1880.

——. *The Life and Correspondence of Theodore Parker*. 2 vols. New York: D. Appleton, 1864.

——. *Wit, Humor, and Shakspeare. Twelve Essays*. Boston: Roberts, 1876.

——, ed. William Smith, *Memoir of J. G. Fichte*. Boston: James Munroe, 1846.

Welch, Claude. *Protestant Thought in the Nineteenth Century*. New Haven: Yale Univ. Press, 1972.

Welch, Donovan L. "A Chronological Study of the Poetry of Henry David Thoreau." Diss. Univ. of Nebraska 1966.

Welker, R. H. *Birds and Men*. Cambridge: Harvard Univ. Press, 1955.

Welland, Dennis. "John Camden Hotten and Emerson's Uncollected Essays." *YES* 6 (1976): 156–75.

——. *Mark Twain in England*. Atlantic Highlands, N.J.: Humanities Press, 1978.

——. "Moncure Daniel Conway and Anglo-American Relations." *EthR* 81 (Sept. 1976): 4–7.

Wellek, René. "Emerson and German Philosophy." *NEQ* 16 (March 1943): 41–62. Rpt. in his *Confrontations*. Princeton: Princeton Univ. Press, 1965, 187–212.

——. "Emerson's Literary Theory and Criticism." In *Worte and Werte*. Ed. Gustav Erdman and Alfons Eichstaedt. Berlin: Walter de Gruyter, 1961, 444–56. Rpt. as "Ralph Waldo Emerson" in his *A History of Modern Criticism: 1750-1950. The Age of Transition*, 163–76.

——. *A History of Modern Criticism: 1750-1950. The Age of Transition*. New Haven: Yale Univ. Press, 1965.

——. "Irving Bartlett, Paul More and Transcendentalism." In *Transcendentalism and Its Legacy*, ed. Myron Simon and Thornton H. Parsons, 185-203.

——. "The Minor Transcendentalists and German Philosophy." *NEQ* 15 (Dec. 1942): 652-80. Rpt. in his *Confrontations*, 153-86.

Wellisz, Leopold. *The Friendship of Margaret Fuller D'Ossoli and Adam Mickiewicz*. New York: Polish Book Importing, 1947.

Wells, Anna Mary. *Dear Preceptor: The Life and Times of Thomas Wentworth Higginson*. Boston: Houghton Mifflin, 1963.

——. "Early Criticism of Emily Dickinson." *AL* 1 (Nov. 1929): 243-59.

——, and Howard N. Meyer. "The *Atlantic*'s Mr. Higginson." *Hig J* no. 24 (1 Half 1980): 1-11.

Wells, Daniel A. *The Literary Index to American Magazines, 1815-1865*. Metuchen, N.J.: Scarecrow Press, 1980.

Wells, Henry W. *The American Way of Poetry*. New York: Columbia Univ. Press, 1943.

——. "An Evaluation of Thoreau's Poetry." *AL* 16 (May 1944): 99-109.

——. *Introduction to Emily Dickinson*. Chicago: Hendricks House, 1947.

Wells, Ronald Vale. *Three Christian Transcendentalists: James Marsh, Caleb Sprague Henry, and Frederic Henry Hedge*. New York: Columbia Univ. Press, 1943. Exp. ed., New York: Octagon Books, 1972.

Welter, Barbara. "The Merchant's Daughter: A Tale from Life." *NEQ* 42 (March 1969): 3-22. Rpt. in her *Dimity Convictions: The American Woman in the Nineteenth Century*. Athens: Ohio Univ. Press, 1976. 42-56, 211-14.

——. "Mystical Feminist: Margaret Fuller, a Woman of the Nineteenth Century." In her *Dimity Convictions*, 145-98.

Welter, Rush. *The Mind of America 1820-1869*. New York: Columbia Univ. Press, 1975.

Wendell, Barrett. *A Literary History of America*. New York: Scribners, 1900.

Wendell, Julia. "An Examination of the Emerson-Thoreau Friendship." *CS* 14.1 (Sept. 1979): 3-11.

Wendte, Charles William. "Bibliography." In [*The Centenary Edition of the Works of Theodore Parker*], 15: 13-50.

——. "Memoir." In Charles Timothy Brooks, *Poems*, ed. W. P. Andrews, 3-114.

——. *The Wider Fellowship: Memories, Friendships, and Endeavors for Religious Unity*. 2 vols. Boston: Beacon, 1927.

Werge, Thomas. "The Idea and Significance of 'Economy' before *Walden*." *ESQ* 20 (4 Qtr. 1974): 270-74.

Werkmeister, W. H. *A History of Philosophical Ideas in America*. New York: Ronald Press, 1949.

The West Church, Boston, Commemorative Services. Boston: Damrell and Upham, 1887.

West, Michael. "Charles Kraitsir's Influence upon Thoreau's Theory of Language." *ESQ* 19 (4 Qtr. 1973): 262-74.

——. "Scatology and Eschatology: The Heroic Dimensions of Thoreau's Wordplay." *PMLA* 89 (Oct. 1974): 1043-64.

——. "Versifying Thoreau: Frost's 'The Quest of the Purple Fringed' and 'Fire and Ice.' " *ELN* 16 (Sept. 1978): 40-47.

——. "*Walden*'s Dirty Language: Thoreau and Walter Whiter's Geocentric Etymological Theories." *HLB* 22 (April 1974): 117-28.

Westall, John. Review of Ralph Waldo Emerson, *Nature*. *NJM* 15 (Oct. 1841): 48-52.

Westbrook, Perry D. *John Burroughs*. Boston: Twayne, 1974.

Whaling, Anne. "Studies in Thoreau's Reading of English Poetry and Prose, 1340–1660." Diss. Yale 1946.

"What Is Talked About." *LWNY* 4 (12, 19 May 1849): 417–18, 435–36.

Wheeler, Charles Stearns. "Letters from Germany." *Pioneer* 1 (March 1843): 143–44.

———. "Literary Intelligence." *Dial* 3 (Jan., April 1843): 388–97, 541–44.

———. Review of James Russell Lowell, *A Year's Life*. *ChEx* 30 (March 1841): 131–34.

———. "What Reasons Are There for Not Expecting Another Great Epic Poem." Ed. Kenneth Walter Cameron. *ESQ* no. 12 (3 Qtr. 1958): 10–18.

Wheeler, Otis B. "Emerson's Political Quandary." In *Studies in American Literature*. Ed. Waldo McNeir and Leo B. Levy. Baton Rouge: Louisiana State Univ. Press, 1960, 22–32.

Wheeler, Ruth Robinson. *Concord: Climate for Freedom*. Concord, Mass.: Concord Antiquarian Soc., 1967.

Wheelock, Lucy. "Miss Peabody and the Kindergarten." *Education* 15 (Sept. 1894): 27–31.

———. "Miss Peabody as I Knew Her." In *Pioneers of the Kindergarten in America*. New York: Century, 1924, 26–38.

Whicher, George Frisbie. *This Was a Poet: A Critical Biography of Emily Dickinson*. New York: Scribners, 1938.

———, ed. *Poetry of the New England Renaissance, 1790–1890*. New York: Rinehart, 1950.

———, ed. *The Transcendentalist Revolt against Materialism*. Boston: D. C. Heath, 1949. Rev. ed., with Gail Kennedy, as *The Transcendentalist Revolt*. Boston: D. C. Heath, 1968.

Whicher, Stephen E. "Emerson's Tragic Sense." *ASch* 22 (Sum. 1953): 285–92.

———. *Freedom and Fate: An Inner Life of Ralph Waldo Emerson*. Philadelphia: Univ. of Pennsylvania Press, 1953.

Whipple, Edwin Percy. *Recollections of Eminent Men*. Boston: Ticknor, 1887.

Whitaker, Daniel K. "Transcendentalism." *SoQR* 2 (Oct. 1842): 437–71.

Whitaker, Rosemary. "*A Week on the Concord and Merrimack Rivers*: An Experiment in the Communication of the Transcendental Experience." Diss. Univ. of Oklahoma 1970.

White, Morton. "Transcendentalism: 'Hallelujah to the Reason Forevermore.' " In his *Science and Sentiment in America*. New York: Oxford Univ. Press, 1972, 71–96, 317–22.

White, Peter. "Reason and Intuition in the Theology of Theodore Parker." *JRH* 11 (June 1980): 111–20.

White, Ruth Helen. "James Marsh: Educator." Diss. Univ. of Southern Mississippi 1963.

White, Viola C. *Check List: Abernethy Library of American Literature*. Middlebury, Vt.: Middlebury Coll., 1940.

White, William. "Emerson as Editor: A Letter to Benjamin F. Presbury." *AN&Q* 12 (Dec. 1973): 59–61.

———. "A Henry David Thoreau Bibliography, 1908–37." *BB* 16 (Jan.–April, May–Aug., Sept.–Dec. 1938, Jan.–April, May–Aug., Sept.–Dec. 1939): 90–92, 111–13, 131–32, 163, 181–82, 199–202. Rpt. as *A Henry David Thoreau Bibliography, 1908–37*. Boston: Faxon, 1939.

———. "Walt Whitman on New England Writers: An Uncollected Fragment." *NEQ* 27 (Sept. 1954): 395–96.

———. "Whitman on American Poets: An Uncollected Piece." *ELN* 1 (Sept. 1963): 42–43.

Whitfield, Francis J. "Mickiewicz and American Literature." In *Adam Mickiewicz in World Literature*. Ed. Waclaw Lednicki. Berkeley: Univ. of California Press, 1956, 339–52.

Whitford, Kathryn. "Thoreau and the Woodlots of Concord." *NEQ* 23 (Sept. 1950): 291–306.

———. "Water, Wind, and Light Imagery in Emerson's Essay 'The Over-Soul.' " *WSL* no. 6 (1969): 100–05.

Whitford, Philip, and Kathryn Whitford. "Thoreau: Pioneer Ecologist and Conservationist." *SM* 73 (Nov. 1951): 291–96.

Whiting, Lilian. *Boston Days*. Boston: Little, Brown, 1911.

Whitman, Walt. "By Emerson's Grave." *CriticNY* 2 (6 May 1882): 123. Rpt. in his *Prose Works 1892*, ed. Floyd Stovall, 1: 290–91.

———. Comment on Compensation. *BDE*, 15 Dec. 1847. Rpt. in his *The Gathering of the Forces*. Ed. Cleveland Rodgers and John Black. 2 vols. New York: Putnams, 1920, 2: 270–71.

———. *Complete Writings of Walt Whitman*. Ed. Richard Maurice Bucke et al. 10 vols. New York: Putnams, 1902.

———. *The Correspondence*. Ed. Edwin Haviland Miller. 6 vols. New York: New York Univ. Press, 1961–77.

———. *Daybooks and Notebooks*. Ed. William White. 3 vols. New York: New York Univ. Press, 1978.

———. "Emerson's Books (The Shadows of Them)." *LW* 11 (22 May 1880): 177. Rpt. in his *Prose Works 1892*, ed. Floyd Stovall, 2: 514–18.

———. *Leaves of Grass: Comprehensive Reader's Edition*. Ed. Harold Blodgett and Sculley Bradley. New York: New York Univ. Press, 1965.

———. "Mr. Emerson's Lecture." *NYA*, 7 March 1842. Rpt. in *Walt Whitman of the* New York Aurora. Ed. Joseph Jay Rubin and Charles H. Brown. State College, Pa.: Bald Eagle Press, 1950, 105.

———. "Personalism." *Galaxy* 5 (April 1868): 540–47.

———. "Pictures." In Emory Holloway, "Whitman's Embryonic Verse." *SWR* 10 (July 1925): 28–40. Rpt. as *Pictures: An Unpublished Poem*. Ed. Holloway. New York: June House, 1927. Rpt. in *Leaves of Grass: Comprehensive Reader's Edition*, ed. Harold Blodgett and Sculley Bradley, 642–49.

———. *Prose Works 1892*. Ed. Floyd Stovall. 2 vols. New York: New York Univ. Press, 1963–64.

———. *Specimen Days & Collect*. Philadelphia: Rees, Welsh, 1882. Rpt. in his *Prose Works 1892*, ed. Floyd Stovall.

———. "Walt Whitman's Actual American Position." *WJP*, 26 Jan. 1876. Rpt. in *Walt Whitman's Workshop*. Ed. Clifton J. Furness. Cambridge: Harvard Univ. Press, 1928, 245–48.

Whitney, Solon F. *Historical Sketches of Watertown, Massachusetts*. Watertown, Mass.: n.p., 1893.

Whittier, John Greenleaf. *The Letters of John Greenleaf Whittier*. Ed. John B. Pickard. 3 vols. Cambridge: Harvard Univ. Press, 1975.

Wichelns, Herbert A. "Ralph Waldo Emerson." In *A History and Criticism of American Public Address*. Ed. William Norwood Brigance. 2 vols. New York: McGraw-Hill, 1943, 2: 501–25.

Wiggin, Kate Douglas. *My Garden of Memory: An Autobiography*. Boston: Houghton Mifflin, 1923.

Wilbur, Earl Morse, *A History of Unitarianism in Transylvania, England, and America*. Cambridge: Harvard Univ. Press, 1952.

Wilbur, Richard. "Edgar Allan Poe." In *Major Writers of America*. Ed. Perry Miller. 2 vols. New York: Harcourt, Brace, and World, 1962, 1: 369–82. Rpt. in his *Responses*. New York: Harcourt Brace Jovanovich, 1976. 39–66.

———. "The House of Poe." In *Anniversary Lectures 1959*. Washington, D.C.: Reference Dept. Library of Congress, 1959, 21–38. Rpt. in *The Recognition of Edgar Allan Poe*. Ed. Eric W. Carlson. Ann Arbor: Univ. of Michigan Press, 1966, 255–77.

———. "The Poe Mystery Case." *NYRB* 13 (13 July 1967): 16, 25–28. Rpt. in his *Responses*, 127–38.

Wild, Paul H. "Flower Power: A Student's Guide to Pre-Hippie Transcendentalism." *EJ* 58 (Jan. 1969): 62–68.

Willard, Abbie F. *Wallace Stevens: The Poet and His Critics*. Chicago: American Library Assn., 1978.

Willard, Charles B. *Whitman's American Fame: The Growth of His Reputation in America after 1892*. Providence: Brown Univ. Press, 1950.

Williams, George Huntston. "The Attitude of Liberals in New England toward Non-Christian Religions, 1784–1885." *CraneR* 9 (Wtr. 1967): 59–89.

———. *Rethinking the Unitarian Relationship with Protestantism: An Examination of the Thought of Frederic Henry Hedge (1805–47)*. Boston: Beacon, 1949. Rpt. in *UUC* 36 (Spr.–Sum. 1981): 7–47.

———, ed. *The Harvard Divinity School: Its Place in Harvard University and in American Culture*. Boston: Beacon, 1954.

Williams, Henry. "Charles Stearns Wheeler." In his *Memorials of the Class of 1837 of Harvard University*. Boston: George H. Ellis, 1887, 23–24. Rpt. as *Thoreau and His Harvard Classmates*. Ed. Kenneth Walter Cameron. Hartford, Conn.: Transcendental Books, 1965.

———. "John Weiss." In his *Memorials of the Class of 1837 of Harvard University*, 58–63.

Williams, John Brindley. "The Impact of Transcendentalism on the Novels of Herman Melville." Diss. Univ. of Southern California 1965.

Williams, Mentor L. " 'Why Nature Loves the Number Five': Emerson Toys with the Occult." *PMASAL* 30 (1944): 639–49.

Williams, Paul O. "The Concept of Inspiration in Thoreau's Poetry." *PMLA* 79 (Sept. 1964): 466–68.

———. "Emerson Guided: Walks with Thoreau and Channing." *ESQ* no. 35 (2 Qtr. 1964): 66–68.

———. "The Influence of Thoreau on the American Nature Essay." *TSB* no. 145 (Fall 1978): 1–5.

———. "The Persistence of Cranch's 'Enosis.' " *ESQ* no. 57 (4 Qtr. 1969): 41–46. Rpt. in *The Minor and Later Transcendentalists*, ed. Edwin Gittleman, 41–46.

———. "Thoreau's Growth as a Transcendental Poet." *ESQ* 19 (3 Qtr. 1973): 189–98.

———. "The Transcendental Movement in American Poetry." Diss. Univ. of Pennsylvania 1962.

Williams, Stanley T. "The Poet of Philosophic Thought." In his *The Beginnings of American Poetry*. Upsala, Sweden: Almquist and Wiksells, 1951, 95–123, 141–48.

———. *The Spanish Background of American Literature*. 2 vols. New Haven: Yale Univ. Press, 1955.

Willingham, Robert Marion, Jr. "The Poetic Theory of Thomas Holley Chivers and Its Relationship to Transcendentalism." M.A. thesis Univ. of Georgia 1972.

Willis, Frederick L. H. *Alcott Memoirs*. Boston: Richard G. Badger, 1915.

Willis, Lonnie. "Folklore in the Published Writings of Henry David Thoreau: A Study and a Compendium Index." Diss. Univ. of Colorado 1966.

Willson, E. B., C. W. Wendte, R. S. Rantoul, and W. P. Andrews. *Brooks Memorial. Communications on the Death of Charles Timothy Brooks*. Salem, Mass.: Essex Inst., 1884.

Willson, Lawrence. "The 'Body Electric' Meets the Genteel Tradition." *NMQ* 26 (Wtr. 1956–57): 369–86.

———. "The Influence of Early North American History and Legend in the Writings of Henry David Thoreau." Diss. Yale 1949.

———. "Thoreau and New England's Weather." *Weatherwise* 12 (June 1959): 91–94, 118–24.

———. "Thoreau and Roman Catholicism." *CHR* 42 (July 1956): 157–72.

———. "Thoreau and the French in Canada." *RUO* 29 (July–Sept. 1959): 281–97.

————. "The Transcendentalist View of the West." *WHR* 14 (Spr. 1960): 183–91.

Wilmes, D. R. "F. B. Sanborn and the Lost New England World of Transcendentalism." *CLQ* 16 (Dec. 1980): 237–47.

Wilson, Edmund, ed. "Emerson and Whitman: Documents on Their Relations (1855–88)." In *The Shock of Recognition*. Ed. Wilson. Garden City, N.Y.: Doubleday, Doran, 1943. 245–95.

Wilson, Howard. "George Ripley, Social and Literary Critic." Diss. Univ. of Wisconsin 1941.

Wilson, James Grant. *The Life and Letters of Fitz-Greene Halleck*. New York: D. Appleton, 1869.

Wilson, Janice Elizabeth. "An Inquiry into Selected Writings of Margaret Fuller as They Appeared in the *Dial* Magazine, 1840–1844." M.A. thesis San Jose State Coll. 1966.

Wilson, John Byron. "Activities of the New England Transcendentalists in the Dissemination of Culture." Diss. Univ. of North Carolina 1941.

————. "The Aesthetics of Transcendentalism." *ESQ* no. 57 (4 Qtr. 1969): 27–34. Rpt. in *The Minor and Later Transcendentalists*, ed. Edwin Gittleman, 27–34.

————. "Bronson Alcott, Platonist or Pestalozzian." *SchS* 81 (Feb. 1955): 49–53.

————. "Darwin and the Transcendentalists." *JHI* 26 (April–June 1965): 286–90.

————. "Elizabeth Peabody and Other Transcendentalists on History and Historians." *Historian* 30 (Nov. 1967): 72–86.

————. "Emerson and the 'Rochester Rappings.'" *NEQ* 41 (June 1968): 248–58.

————. "Grimm's Law and the Brahmins." *NEQ* 16 (March 1943): 106–09.

————. "Grimm's Law and the Brahmins." *NEQ* 38 (June 1965): 234–39.

————. "Phrenology and the Transcendentalists." *AL* 28 (May 1956): 220–25.

————. "Pythagoras Crosses the Merrimack (Fruitlands Revisited)." *EdF* 30 (Jan. 1966): 209–15.

————. "A Transcendental Minority Report." *NEQ* 29 (June 1956): 147–58.

————. "The Transcendentalists and Women's Education." *AAUWJ* 59 (March 1966): 118, 121–24.

————. "The Transcendentalists' 'Idea of a University.'" *EdF* 33 (March 1969): 343–54.

Wilson, R. Jackson. *In Quest of Community: Social Philosophy in the United States, 1860–1920*. New York: John Wiley, 1968.

Winslow, Helen M. *Literary Boston of To-Day*. Boston: L. C. Page, 1903

Winsor, Justin, ed. *The Memorial History of Boston*. 4 vols. Boston: James R. Osgood, 1881.

Winston, George P. "Washington Allston and the Objective Correlative." *BuR* 11 (Dec. 1962): 95–108.

Winters, Yvor. "Foreword." In *The Complete Poems of Frederick Goddard Tuckerman*. Ed. N. Scott Momaday. New York: Oxford Univ. Press, 1965, ix–xvi.

————. "Jones Very: A New England Mystic." *AmR* 7 (May 1936): 159–78. Rpt. as "Jones Very and R. W. Emerson: Aspects of New England Mysticism" in his *Maule's Curse*, 125–36.

————. *Maule's Curse*. Norfolk, Conn.: New Directions, 1938.

Wintersteen, Prescott Browning, ed. *Christology in American Unitarianism: An Anthology of Outstanding Nineteenth and Twentieth Century Unitarians, with Commentary and Background*. Boston: Unitarian Universalist Christian Fellowship, 1977.

Wiseman, James. "The Meaning of God for Emerson." *Month* 212 (Sept. 1961): 133–40.

Wish, Harvey. *Science and Thought in Early America*. New York: Longmans, Green, 1950.

Witherell, Elizabeth Hall. "The Poetry of Henry David Thoreau: A Selected Critical Edition." Diss. Univ. of Wisconsin 1979.

Wolf, William J. *Thoreau: Mystic, Prophet, Ecologist*. Philadelphia: Pilgrim Press, 1974.

Wolff, Cynthia Griffin. "The Reality of Emily Dickinson." *HM* 83 (Nov.–Dec. 1980): 48–53.

Wood, Barry. "The Growth of the Soul: Coleridge's Dialectical Method and the Strategy of Emerson's *Nature*." *PMLA* 91 (May 1976): 385–97.

————. "Thoreau's Narrative Art in 'Civil Disobedience.'" *PQ* 60 (Wtr. 1981): 105–15.

Woodall, Guy R. "The Journals of Convers Francis." *SAR* 1981, 1982: 265–343, 227–84.

Woodberry, George Edward. *Ralph Waldo Emerson*. New York: Macmillan, 1907.

————. Review of Christopher Pearse Cranch, *Ariel and Caliban*. *Atl* 59 (March 1887): 417–18.

————, ed. *A Troutbeck Letter-Book (1861–1867)*. Amenia, N.Y.: Troutbeck Press, 1925.

Woodbury, Charles J. "Emerson Talks with a College Boy." *CM* 39 (Feb. 1890): 621–27. Exp. as *Talks with Ralph Waldo Emerson*. New York: Baker and Taylor, 1890.

Woodlief, Annette M. "Emerson's Prose: An Annotated Checklist of Literary Criticism through 1976." *SAR* 1978: 105–60.

————. "The Influence of Theories of Rhetoric on Thoreau." *TJQ* 7.1 (Jan. 1975): 13–22.

————. "*Walden*: A Checklist of Literary Criticism through 1973." *RALS* 5 (Spr. 1975): 15–58.

Woodress, James. *Dissertations in American Literature, 1891–1966*. Durham: Duke Univ. Press, 1968.

Woodson, Thomas. "Thoreau on Poverty and Magnanimity." *PMLA* 85 (Jan. 1970): 21–34.

————. "The Title and Text of Thoreau's 'Civil Disobedience.'" *BRH* 81 (Spr. 1978): 103–12.

————. "The Two Beginnings of *Walden*: A Distinction of Styles." *ELH* 35 (Sept. 1968): 440–73.

Wright, Conrad. *The Beginnings of Unitarianism in America*. Boston: Starr King Press, 1955.

————. "A Channing Bibliography: 1929–1959." *PUHS* 12.2 (1959): 22–24.

————. "The Channing We Don't Know." *UUC* 35 (Wtr. 1980–81): 39–47.

————. "The Early Period (1811–40)." In *The Harvard Divinity School*, ed. George Huntston Williams, 21–77.

————. "Emerson, Barzillai Frost, and 'The Divinity School Address.'" *HTR* 49 (Jan. 1956): 19–43. Rpt. in his *The Liberal Christians*. Boston: Beacon, 1970, 41–61, 128–31.

————. "Henry W. Bellows and the Origin of the National Conference." *PUHS* 15.2 (1965): 17–46. Rpt. in his *The Liberal Christians*, 81–109.

————. "In Search of a Usable Past." *CP* 1 (1979): 115–36.

————. "Rational Religion in Eighteenth-Century America." In his *The Liberal Christians*, 1–21.

————. "The Rediscovery of Channing." *PUHS* 12.2 (1959): 8–25. Rpt. in his *The Liberal Christians*, 22–28.

————. "Theodore Parker." In *The American Renaissance in New England*, ed. Joel Myerson, 143–50.

————. "The Theological World of Samuel Gilman." *PUHS* 17.2 (1973–75): 54–72.

————, ed. *A Stream of Light: A Sesquicentennial History of American Unitarianism*. Boston: Beacon, 1975.

————, ed. *Three Prophets of Religious Liberalism: Channing, Emerson, Parker*. Boston: Beacon, 1961.

Wright, Nathalia. "Emily Dickinson's Boanerges and Thoreau's Atropos: Locomotives on the Same Line?" *MLN* 72 (Feb. 1957): 101–03.

Wyman, Mary A. *The Lure for Feeling in the Creative Process*. New York: Philosophical Library, 1960.

Wynkoop, William M. *Three Children of the Universe: Emerson's View of Shakespeare, Bacon, and Milton*. The Hague: Mouton, 1966.

Yannella, Donald Joseph, Jr. "Cornelius Mathews: Knickerbocker Satirist." Diss. Fordham 1971.

Yannella, Philip R. "Socio-Economic Disarray and Literary Response: Concord and *Walden*." *Mosaic* 14 (Wtr. 1981): 1–24.

Yoder, R. A. *Emerson and the Orphic Poet in America*. Berkeley: Univ. of California Press, 1978.

———. "Emerson's Dialectic." *Criticism* 11 (Aut. 1969): 313–28.

———. "The Equilibrist Perspective: Toward a Theory of American Romanticism." *SIR* 12 (Fall 1973): 705–40.

———. "Hawthorne and the Artist." *SIR* 7 (Sum. 1968): 193–206.

———. "Toward the 'Titmouse Dimension': The Development of Emerson's Poetic Style." *PMLA* 87 (March 1972): 255–70. Incorporated into his *Emerson and the Orphic Poet in America*.

———. "Transcendental Conservatism and *The House of the Seven Gables*." *GaR* 28 (Spr. 1974): 33–51.

Yohannan, J. D. "Emerson's Translations of Persian Poetry from German Sources." *AL* 14 (Jan. 1943): 407–20.

———. "The Influence of Persian Poetry upon Emerson's Work." *AL* 15 (March 1943): 25–41.

———. *Persian Poetry in England and America*. Delmar, N.Y.: Caravan Books, 1977.

York, Robert M. "George B. Cheever: Religious and Social Reformer, 1807–1890." *UMB* 57 (1 April 1955): 1–239.

Young, Charles Lowell. *Emerson's Montaigne*. New York: Macmillan, 1941.

Young, Edward. "Remarks [on the Death of O. B. Frothingham]." *PMHS* 10 (Nov. 1895): 363–67.

Young, Gloria. "The Fountainhead of All Forms: Poetry and the Unconscious in Emerson and Howard Nemerov." In *Artful Thunder*. Ed. Robert J. DeMott and Sanford E. Marovitz. Kent: Kent State Univ. Press, 1975, 241–67.

Ziff, Larzer, *Literary Democracy: The Declaration of Cultural Independence in America*. New York: Viking, 1981.

Zink, Harriet Rodgers. "Emerson's Use of the Bible." *UNSLLC* 14 (1935): 5–75.

Zonderman, David A. "George Ripley's Unpublished Lecture on Charles Fourier." *SAR* 1982: 185–208.

CONTRIBUTORS

LAWRENCE BUELL, Professor of English at Oberlin College, is the author of *Literary Transcendentalism: Style and Vision in the American Renaissance*.

ROBERT E. BURKHOLDER is Assistant Professor of English at Pennsylvania State University at Wilkes-Barre and coauthor of *Ralph Waldo Emerson: An Annotated Secondary Bibliography*.

J. WADE CARUTHERS, Professor Emeritus at Southern Connecticut State College, is the author of *Octavius Brooks Frothingham: Gentle Radical*.

OTTAVIO M. CASALE, Professor of English and Dean of the Honors College at Kent State University, has published articles on American and comparative literature in such journals as *American Literature* and *Comparative Literature Studies*.

GARY L. COLLISON, Assistant Professor of English at Pennsylvania State University at York, is editing Theodore Parker's letters.

CHARLES CROWE is Professor of History at the University of Georgia and author of *George Ripley: Transcendentalist and Utopian Socialist*.

FREDERICK C. DAHLSTRAND, Assistant Professor of History at Ohio State University at Mansfield, has written *Amos Bronson Alcott: An Intellectual Biography*.

FRANCIS B. DEDMOND, Professor of English at Catawba College, is the author of *Sylvester Judd*. He has edited Ellery Channing's unpublished fiction in *ESQ: A Journal of the American Renaissance* and *Studies in the American Renaissance*, and he is now preparing an edition of Channing's correspondence.

PAUL J. FERLAZZO, Professor and Head of English at Montana State University, is the author of *Emily Dickinson* and is currently editing *Critical Essays on Emily Dickinson*.

LEONARD GILHOOLEY is Professor of English at Fordham University, author of *Contradiction and Dilemma: Orestes Brownson and the American Idea*, and editor of *No Divided Allegiance: Essays in Brownson's Thought*.

DOUGLAS MCCREARY GREENWOOD works at Georgetown University and is writing a book on James Marsh.

WILLIAM G. HEATH, Associate Professor of English at Lakehead University, has published an edition of Cyrus Bartol's writings and articles on a number of Transcendentalists.

BRIAN HIGGINS is Associate Professor of English at the University of Illinois at Chicago and author of *Herman Melville: An Annotated Bibliography*.

ROBERT N. HUDSPETH, Professor of English at Pennsylvania State University, has written *Ellery Channing* and edited *The Letters of Margaret Fuller*.

CAROL JOHNSTON, Assistant Professor of English at Clemson University, has published on Ralph Waldo Emerson. She is a field editor for *The Writings of Henry D. Thoreau* and is preparing an edition of Theodore Parker's journals.

JEROME LOVING is Professor of English at Texas A&M University and the author of a number of studies in American literature, including *Emerson, Whitman, and the American Muse*.

ELIZABETH R. MCKINSEY, Associate Professor of English and American Literature at Harvard University, has written *The Western Experiment: New England Transcendentalists in the Ohio Valley*.

ELIZABETH A. MEESE, Associate Professor of English at the University of Alabama, has written studies on the doctrine of correspondence in American Transcendentalist theory.

HOWARD N. MEYER is an attorney and student of American human relations history and literature. He has written a number of biographies, including one on Thomas Wentworth Higginson, whose *Army Life in a Black Regiment* he has edited.

MICHAEL MEYER, Associate Professor of English at the University of Connecticut, is the author of *Several More Lives to Live: Thoreau's Political Reputation in America* and coauthor of *The New Thoreau Handbook*.

W. GORDON MILNE, Professor of English and Chairman of American Studies at Lake Forest College, is the author of *George William Curtis and the Genteel Tradition*.

ROGER C. MUELLER, Professor of English at the University of the Pacific, has written a biography of Samuel Johnson.

JOEL MYERSON, Professor of English at the University of South Carolina, is the author or editor of over two dozen books and fifty articles on American Transcendentalism. He edits the annual publication *Studies in the American Renaissance*.

LEONARD N. NEUFELDT, Professor of English and American Studies at Purdue University, has written extensively on American Transcendentalism and is an editor of *The Writings of Henry D. Thoreau*. His most recent publication is *The House of Emerson*.

MARGARET NEUSSENDORFER is Chairman of the Faculty of Literature at the University of Texas of the Permian Basin and is writing a biography of Elizabeth Palmer Peabody.

DAVID ROBINSON, Associate Professor of English and Director of American Studies at Oregon State University, has written *Apostle of Culture: Emerson as Preacher and Lecturer* and a number of essays on the American Transcendentalists.

DONALD F. WARDERS, Assistant Professor of English at the University of Kansas, is working on a book-length critical study of the *Dial*.

GUY R. WOODALL, Professor of English at Tennessee Technological University, has published many articles on American Renaissance authors, including an edition of Convers Francis' journal in *Studies in the American Renaissance*.

THOMAS WORTHAM is Professor of English at the University of California at Los Angeles and editor of James Russell Lowell's *The Biglow Papers, First Series*. He is currently editing the *Poems* volume in *The Collected Works of Ralph Waldo Emerson*.

CONRAD WRIGHT, Professor of American Church History at the Harvard Divinity School, is the author of *The Beginnings of Unitarianism in America*, *The Liberal Christians*, and other works in the field of Unitarian history.

INDEX

Aaron, Daniel, 23, 158, 225
Abbey, Edward, 284
Abbot, Francis Ellingwood, 54, 55, 82, 174, 231
Abbot, Mabel, 129
Abbott, A. W., 210
Abbott, Lawrence F., 161
Abel, Darrel, 7, 331, 334
Abernethy Library, 262, 319
Adam, William, 53
Adams, Grace, 38
Adams, Henry, 174
Adams, John G., 43
Adams, Joseph D., 328
Adams, Mary Stroube, 238
Adams, Raymond, 255, 273, 277, 279, 281, 282, 332
Adams, Richard P., 152, 382
Adams, Sherman Hill, 166
Adams, Stephen, 282
Addams, Jane, 231
"A Discipline," 143
Adkins, Nelson Frederick, 41, 163
Adler, Felix, 174
Adler, William, 229
Advena, Jean Cameron, 5, 260
Aesthetic Papers, 69, 70, 80–81, 233, 240, 372
Agassiz, Louis, 273, 337
Ahearn, Kerry, 276
Ahlstrom, Sydney E., 15, 31, 39, 48, 50, 54, 174, 248, 311–14
Aiken, Conrad, 166
Aiken, Lucy, 311
Alaimo, Joseph Paul, 356
Albanese, Catherine L., 22, 25, 96, 116, 159, 161, 170, 194, 249
Albee, John, 139
Alberti, Charles Edward, 66
Albrecht, Robert C., 23, 99, 116, 224, 282, 283
Alcott, Abigail, 58, 60, 61, 67, 68, 212
Alcott, Amos Bronson, 6–8, 10, 13, 16, 20, 23, 24, 31, 33, 34, 56–58, 60–62, 67, 68,

73, 77, 87–96, 103, 105, 106, 143, 154, 180, 197, 202, 211–13, 228, 229, 235, 236, 238, 239, 250, 252, 255–58, 264, 274, 276, 281, 289, 296, 304, 318, 328, 329, 331, 334, 337, 339, 343, 364, 376
Alcott, Anna, 58, 61
Alcott, Junius J., 44, 57
Alcott, Louisa May, 7, 10, 58, 60, 61, 67, 93, 141, 212, 236, 264, 331, 334
Alcott, W. A., 89
Alcott House, 58, 68
Alderman, Edwin Anderson, 125
Alexander, Colin Cuthbert, 141
Alexander, Harriet C. B., 153
Alexander, J. W., 12, 153
Alger, Horatio, 210
Alger, William R., 150
Allen, E. W., 42
Allen, Francis H., 259, 260, 263, 272
Allen, Gay Wilson, 42, 76, 140, 153, 158, 162, 163, 272, 288, 332, 379, 382, 383
Allen, J. C., 150
Allen, Joseph, 42
Allen, Joseph Henry, 10, 38, 40, 50, 53, 114, 190, 192, 231, 297, 298
Allen, Lucy Clark, 42
Allen, Margaret Vanderhaar, 75, 182, 186, 188
Allston, Washington, 42, 236, 238, 347
Alstetter, Mabel Flick, 237
Alterton, Margaret, 365, 366
American Annals of Education and Instruction, 89
American Antiquarian Society, 196, 235, 254
American Journal of Education, 89
American Literary Manuscripts, 3, 58, 87, 88, 98, 100, 102, 108, 113, 118, 123, 131, 132, 137, 167, 168, 171, 175, 189, 190, 196, 204, 207, 211, 214, 216, 217, 234, 235, 242, 250, 254, 262, 286, 287, 296, 299, 310, 329
American Literary Scholarship, 4, 329, 362, 370
American Literature, 362
American Monthly Review, 168
American Phrenological Journal, 181

American Socialist, 93
American Transcendental Quarterly, 5
American Union of Associationists, 79
American Unitarian Association, 49, 167, 168, 189, 193, 217, 311
Ames, Charles G., 97, 98
Ames, Van Meter, 166
Ammons, A. R., 28
Amory, Cleveland, 40
AMS Press, 137
Anagnos, Julia R., 40, 240
Anderson, Carl L., 136
Anderson, Charles R., 76, 83, 278, 279, 281, 282, 325
Anderson, David D., 369
Anderson, John Q., 157, 159, 161, 164
Anderson, Judith Müller, 331
Anderson, Paul Russell, 92, 94
Anderson, Quentin, 146, 158, 308
Anderson, Sherwood, 166
Andô, Shôei, 22, 166
Andover-Harvard Theological Library, 4, 49, 100, 108, 113, 118, 124, 176, 189, 190, 208, 217, 250, 287, 310
Andover-Harvard Theological School, 167, 171, 173, 243
Andover Theological Seminary, 287, 344
Andrew, John A., 42
Andrews, William P., 100, 101, 287, 290–92
Angoff, Charles, 223
Anhorn, Judy Schaaf, 283
Anthony, Katharine, 75, 178
Antioch College. *See* Olive Kettering Library
Antioch College Library, 234, 237
Anzilotti, Rolando, 136
Applebee, John H., 221
Appleton, Thomas Gold, 42
Apthorp, William, 133
Aquinas, Thomas, 308
Arconati, Costanza, 179
Arena, 83
Arieli, Yehoshua, 38
Arms, George, 158
Armstrong, James, 274
Arner, Robert D., 290, 334
Arnim, Bettina von, 183
Arnold, Matthew, 144, 154, 166, 223
Arruntius, 369
Articles in American Literature, 4, 87, 97, 100, 102, 108, 112, 118, 123, 131, 167, 171, 175, 189, 196, 204, 207, 211, 214, 216, 234, 242, 250, 254, 286, 296, 299, 310, 329
Arvin, Newton, 156
Ash, Lee, 57
Ashbery, John, 28
Aspinwall, Bernard, 308
Asselineau, Roger, 28, 35, 382

Astro, Richard, 141
Athenæum, 121, 165
Atkinson, Brooks, 265
Atlantic Monthly Magazine, 83, 106, 121, 122, 172, 195, 201, 202, 234, 246, 264, 295, 340, 378, 380
Aton, James M., 284
Attebery, Brian, 323
Auden, W. H., 363, 370
Audubon, John James, 273
Austin, Allen, 354
Ave Maria, 304

B., L. W., 143
Babbitt, Irving, 36, 146, 166, 309, 336
Bacon, Edwin M., 114
Bacon, Francis, 39, 148, 149, 183, 269
Badaracco, Claire, 241
Badger, Henry C., 154
Baer, Helene G., 44, 186
Bagchee, Shyamal, 284
Bailey, Elmer James, 163
Baim, Joseph, 151
Baker, Carlos, 290–92, 379
Baker, Gail, 282
Baker, Portia, 378
Baldwin, David, 44
Baldwin, Marilyn, 35
Baldwin, Raymond, 258
Ballou, Adin, 65
Ballowe, James, 274, 281
Balmes, Jaime, 306
Bancroft, George, 42, 234, 240, 243
Bangor Historical Society, 189
Barbour, Brian M., 4, 6, 147, 161
Barcus, Nancy, 140
Barish, Evelyn, 147
Baritz, Loren, 156
Barker, Charles A., 18, 38, 159
Barlow, Almira, 37
Barmby, Goodwyn, 142
Barnard, Henry, 234
Barnes, Daniel R., 304
Barnes, Homer F., 41
Barnes, James J., 39
Barrows, Samuel J., 154, 218
Barrus, Clara, 42
Bartlett, George B., 141
Bartlett, Irving H., 17, 38
Bartlett, Robert, 44, 203
Bartlett, William Irving, 286, 287, 289
Bartol, Cyrus A., 10, 97–99, 144, 150, 153, 154, 163, 190, 192, 194, 297, 316
Barton, William B., Jr., 137, 151
Bartrum, William, 273
Basile, Joseph Lawrence, 148, 275

Bassan, Maurice, 330
Bassett, John Spencer, 120
Batchelor, George, 114, 292
Baudelaire, Charles, 166
Baumgarten, Eduard, 151
Baumgartner, A. M., 162
Baxter, Sylvester, 378
Bayle, Pierre, 149
Bayless, Joy, 43
Baylor, Ruth M., 233, 234, 237
Baym, Max I., 152
Baym, Nina, 35, 273, 279, 354, 355
Beach, Joseph Warren, 148, 153
Beach, Mrs. Sylvester Judd, 207
Beach, Walter E., 120
Beasley, Clara Bancroft, 114
Beatty, Lillian, 330, 331
Beaver, John, 281
Bedell, Madelon, 90, 212, 239
Beer, Thomas, 91
Beers, Henry A., 13, 151
Beethoven, Ludwig van, 130, 133, 149
Beidler, Philip D., 360
Beirne, Charles J., 226
Bell, George H., 331
Bell, Margaret, 178, 179
Bell, Millicent, 335
Belleisle, René de Poyen, 144
Bellows, Henry Whitney, 42, 54, 97, 114,
   191, 290
Bellows, Russell Nevins, 314
Benjamin, Park, 41
Bennett, Fordyce Richard, 57, 68, 87, 90, 94
Benoit, Ray, 148
Benson, Adolph B., 269
Bentham, Jeremy, 13
Bentley Historical Library, 54
Benton, Gayle T., 122
Benton, Joel, 163
Benton, Myron P., 119
Benton, Richard P., 363, 371
Bentzon, Th. See Blanc, Marie Thérèsa
Bercovitch, Sacvan, 19, 30, 146, 210, 268
Berens, Sheldon L., 319
Berg Collection, 4, 235, 237, 238, 262, 342
Bernard, Edward G., 381
Bernath, Mary G., 272
Berrigan, Daniel, 281
Berry, Edmund G., 92, 282
Berryman, Charles, 267
Berthoff, Warner, 164, 293, 314
Bestor, Arthur E., Jr., 56, 57, 67
Bethell, John T., 200
Bhagavad Gita, 270
Bhata, Karmala, 270
Bibliography of American Literature, 3, 87, 100,
   102, 123, 135, 175, 195, 207
Bickman, Martin, 147

Biddle, Edward N., 120
Bier, Jesse, 19, 35, 161, 274
Bigelow, Charles C., 137
Bilbo, Queenie, 237
Billy, Ted, 281
Birdsall, Richard D., 155
Bishop, Jonathan, 26, 146, 282
Blackburn, Charles E., 70, 71, 115, 126, 181
Blackwelder, James Ray, 76
Blair, Hugh, 314
Blair, John G., 271
Blair, Walter, 161, 329
Blake, H. G. O., 274
Blake, William, 28
Blanc, Marie Thérèsa, 197
Blanchard, Paula, 75, 180, 186, 252
Blanding, Thomas, 264, 269
Blankenship, Russell, 14, 29, 91
Blansett, Barbara Ruth Nieweg, 352, 353, 356
Blasing, Mutlu K., 283
Blau, Joseph L., 16, 40
Blinderman, Abraham, 275
Block, Louis James, 13
Blodgett, Levi [Theodore Parker], 218
Bloom, Harold, 25, 28, 35, 146, 151, 164,
   382
Blouin, Francis X., Jr., 40
Blow, Susan, 238
Blücher, Gebhard Leberecht von, 101
Bluestein, Gene, 161, 382
Blumenthal, Henry, 33, 40, 136
Boatright, Mody C., 161
Bode, Carl, 38, 60, 140, 212, 259, 263, 265,
   300, 376
Boehme, Jacob, 34, 95, 149
Böhmer, Lina, 331
Boies, J. J., 279
Boller, Paul F., Jr., 4, 8, 18, 74, 92, 116,
   224, 247, 308
Bolster, Arthur S., Jr., 71, 112–14, 181
Bonner, Willard H., 269, 279, 284
Boone, Joseph Allen, 283
Boorstin, Daniel, 17
Booth, Douglas Allen, 133
Booth, Earl Walter, 133
Booth, R. A., 135
Borck, Jim Springer, 283
Borges, Jorge Luis, 14, 166
Borst, Raymond R., 260
Boston Association of Ministers, 219
Boston Athenæum, 171, 222, 234, 319
Boston Commonwealth, 103, 106, 119, 122, 253,
   254, 259
Boston Daily Advertiser, 245, 254, 295, 297
Boston Herald, 290
Boston Home Journal, 98
Boston Journal, 254
Boston Post, 162, 377

Boston Public Library, 4, 56, 57, 97, 108, 123, 131, 167, 175, 188, 196, 217, 235, 237, 242, 243, 250, 254, 296, 319
Boston Quarterly Review, 70, 72, 291, 303–06, 308
Boston Reformer, 304
Boston Religious Union of Associationists, 111
Boston Vigilance Committee, 219
Boswell, Jeanetta, 135, 261, 328
Botta, Anne C. Lynch, 41
Botta, Vincenzo, 41
Bottorff, William K., 159
Boudreau, Gordon V., 268
Bounds, Harrison, 331
Bowdoin College. *See* Hawthorne-Longfellow Library
Bowdoin Prize, 150, 243, 247, 288, 300
Bowen, Francis, 11, 50, 53, 106, 163
Bowers, David, 14, 352
Bowling, Lawrence, 276
Boyd Lee Spahr Library, 118
Boynton, Henry Walcott, 196
Boynton, Percy H., 165
Bradford, Alden, 12
Bradford, Gamaliel, 292
Bradford, George Partridge, 10, 12, 44, 59, 149, 246, 317–19
Bradford, Samuel, Jr., 42
Bradford, Samuel, Sr., 42
Bradlee, Eliza David, 173
Bradley, Lawrence, 304
Bradley, Sculley, 300, 341
Branch, E. Douglas, 38
Branch, Watson G., 350
Brann, Henry A., 40, 148, 150, 174
Brashers, Charles, 274
Braswell, William, 351, 352, 360
Braun, Frederick Augustus, 148, 182, 183
Brautigan, Richard, 284
Brawner, James P., 148, 278
Breinig, Helmbrecht, 358
Bremer, Fredrika, 12, 94
Brennan, Sister Thomas C., 200
Brennan, William, 281
Brenner, George, 266
Brewer, Edward V., 40
Brewer, Priscilla J., 149, 213
Brickett, Elsie Furbush, 96, 116
Bridges, William E., 147
Bridgman, Raymond L., 24, 89, 240
Bridgman, Richard, 280
Brietwiesser, Mitchell R., 283
Brigance, William Norwood, 162, 227
Briggs, Charles Frederick, 41
Brigham, Loriman S., 181
Brill, Leonard, 195, 201
Brisbane, Albert, 56, 65, 111
British Museum, 75
British Quarterly Review, 106

Brittan, C. H., 132
Brittin, Norman A., 148
Broadway Journal, 370
Broadway Magazine, 376
Brock, Peter, 53
Brockway, Beman, 42
Brockway, Phillip Judd, 208
Broderick, John C., 89, 94, 221, 263, 269, 276, 278, 281
Brodwin, Stanley, 149
Brooke, Roger, 121
Brook Farm, 1, 10, 11, 23, 24, 32, 44, 56–68, 77, 79, 109, 111, 125, 127, 131, 133, 157, 203, 212, 214, 215, 236, 242–48, 251, 252, 256, 303, 317–19, 328, 330, 331, 333, 341
Brooklyn Daily Eagle, 375
Brooks, Charles Timothy, 6, 100–01, 133
Brooks, Elbridge Gerry, 42
Brooks, Elbridge Streeter, 42
Brooks, Gladys, 237
Brooks, Van Wyck, 37, 91, 127, 140, 199, 200, 209, 215, 312, 314
Broughton, Lord, 314
Broussard, Louis, 368
Brown, Abram English, 220
Brown, Arthur W., 75, 179, 182, 311, 312
Brown, Charles H., 41
Brown, Florence Whiting, 241
Brown, Howard N., 190, 192–94
Brown, Jerry Wayne, 51, 228, 229, 232
Brown, John, 103, 158, 222, 254, 257, 258, 268, 276, 277, 283, 284, 331
Brown, Mary Hosmer, 40, 41
Brown, Percy Whiting, 152, 166
Brown, Roger, 25, 146, 278
Brown, Sarah Theo., 42
Brown, Stuart Gerry, 148
Brown, Theo., 42
Brown, Theodore M., 152, 277
Browne, Ray B., 358
Brownell, W. C., 160
Browning, Robert, 119, 125, 129
Brownson, Henry F., 72, 252, 304
Brownson, Orestes, Jr., 303
Brownson, Orestes Augustus, 10, 11, 19, 62–64, 72, 105, 148, 153, 154, 163, 209, 224, 229–31, 243, 245, 248, 252, 267, 303–09, 315, 316, 329, 363, 364, 381
Brownson's Quarterly Review, 295, 304, 306, 309
Brown University, 4. *See also* Harris Collection of American Poetry *and* John Hay Library
Brown University Library, 100, 214, 215, 287, 319
Brumm, Ursula, 30, 161
Bryant, William Cullen, 41, 378
Bryce, James, 380
Bryer, Jackson R., 135
Bryers, John R., Jr., 329
Buchanan, Robert, 174

Buck, Francis I., 195
Buck, Whitney W., 42
Bucke, Richard Maurice, 376
Buckingham, Joseph T., 42
Buckingham, Willis J., 321
Buckminster, Joseph Stevens, 51
Budd, Louis J., 272
Budge, Mary Alice, 269
Budick, E. Miller, 41, 370
Buell, Lawrence, 21, 25, 27, 49, 51, 94, 96,
    99, 105, 125, 147, 155, 160, 161, 186,
    227, 228, 280, 294, 314, 318, 319, 381,
    382
Buitenhuis, Peter, 274
Bunge, Nancy L., 335
Bunyan, John, 125
Buranelli, Vincent, 276, 366
Bureau of Indian Affairs, 235
Bürger, Gottfried August, 6, 101
Burke, Edmund, 335
Burke, Kenneth, 146
Burkholder, Robert E., 76, 135, 136, 142,
    147, 149, 163–66, 332
Burnap, George W., 12
Burnham, Philip E., 260
Burns, Anthony, 221, 222
Burns, John R., 268
Burns, Percy P., 290
Burrage, A. A., 222
Burroughs, John, 42, 160, 165, 272, 375
Burtis, Mary Elizabeth, 82, 117, 119
Burton, Katherine, 66, 127, 252, 319
Burton, Roland Crozier, 75, 184
Burton, Warren, 42
Busch, Frederick, 357
Bush, George, 149
Bushnell, Horace, 15, 30, 151, 231, 267
Butcher, Philip, 158
Butler, Gerald J., 274
Butler Library, 118
Butterfield, L. H., 290
Byron, George Gordon, Lord, 39, 149

C., 165
Cabot, James Elliot, 42, 76, 137, 139, 191,
    300
Cady, Edwin Harrison, 157
Cady, Lyman V., 270
Cairns, William B., 14, 69
Callow, James T., 14
Calvert, George Henry, 42, 143
Calverton, V. F., 18, 19, 29, 66, 68, 93, 147
Cambon, Glauco, 326
Cambridge Public Library, 195, 198
Cameron, Kenneth Walter, 4–7, 13, 20, 24,
    44, 76, 82, 89, 90, 98, 116, 133, 135–38,
    140, 141, 145, 148, 149, 155, 164, 166,

191, 210, 222, 248, 254–58, 263, 264, 266,
    267, 269, 276, 284, 287, 288, 290, 299,
    300, 373, 374, 379, 380
Campbell, Killis, 366, 381
Canby, Henry Seidel, 265, 271
Cantwell, Robert, 330
Caponigri, A. Robert, 19, 307
Capps, Jack L., 320
Carafiol, Peter C., 344–46
Carew, Harold D., 258
Cargill, Oscar, 104, 334
Carlet, Yves, 18
Carley, Peter, 191
Carlson, Eric W., 147, 162, 367, 368
Carlson, Larry A., 89, 180
Carlson, Patricia Ann, 140
Carlyle, Thomas, 28, 33, 39, 76, 118, 138,
    143, 144, 154, 157, 172, 180, 248, 263,
    269, 300, 348, 350, 355, 361, 364, 369,
    379, 382
Carman, Bliss, 166
Carnegie, Andrew, 120
Carpenter, Delores Bird, 140
Carpenter, Edward, 376
Carpenter, Frederick Ives, 9, 14, 34–36, 69,
    76, 92, 136, 147, 148, 281
Carpenter, George Rice, 160
Carpenter, Hazen C., 127, 158
Carpenter, Richard V., 181
Carroll, Mary Suzanne, 282
Carson, Barbara Harrell, 75, 95
Carter, Everett, 155
Carter, George E., 219, 284
Carter, George F., 157
Carter, Jimmy, 166
Carter, Robert, 342
Caruthers, J. Wade, 171, 174, 200, 297
Carver, Jonathan, 283
Cary, Edward, 319
Cary, Elisabeth Luther, 76, 144, 332
Casale, Ottavio M., 106, 367
Cashdollar, Charles D., 55, 231
Cass, Lewis, 179
Cathen, Irby B., Jr., 362
Cather, Willa, 284
Catholic World, 304
Cavell, Stanley, 151, 282
Cawelti, John G., 158
Cayton, Mary K., 158
Celieres, Andre, 161
The Centenary of the Birth of Ralph Waldo Emerson,
    144
Center for Research Libraries, 74
Chable, Eugene R., 51, 229
Chadwick, John White, 50, 157, 174, 190,
    216, 220, 230, 310, 311, 319
Champollion, Jean François, 279
Channing, Ellen Fuller, 104, 179, 333, 334
Channing, Grace Ellery, 311

Channing, William Ellery, 8, 21, 48, 51, 53, 101, 102, 108, 153, 172, 185, 209, 220, 221, 226, 230, 231, 236–38, 245, 306, 308, 310–16, 364

Channing, William Ellery, II, 5, 77, 102–07, 125, 179, 181, 202, 255, 256, 264, 267, 274, 291, 333, 334, 336, 339, 341, 359, 363, 364, 366

Channing, William Francis, 219

Channing, William Henry, 2, 6, 10, 21, 56, 65, 67, 70, 71, 75, 78, 80, 105, 108–11, 113, 114, 116, 126, 158, 172, 176, 178, 226, 239, 311, 315, 316, 318

Chapin Library, 234

Chapman, John Jay, 36, 144, 166

Charvat, William, 39, 50, 163, 329

Chase, Harry, 272

Chase, Maria, 235

Chase, Richard, 325

Chase, Salmon P., 379

Chatto, Andrew, 121

Chaucer, Geoffrey, 269

Chauncy, Charles, 47, 230

Chazin, Maurice, 136

Cheever, George B., 42, 345

Chekhov, Anton, 284

Chen, David T. Y., 270

Cheney, Ednah Dow, 44, 58, 60, 90, 94, 144, 180, 212, 222, 239

Cherno, Donna, 322

Cherry, Conrad, 30, 313

Chevigny, Bell Gale, 110, 116, 177, 179, 180, 186, 187

Chew, Samuel C., 39

Cheyfitz, Eric, 146, 147

Chielens, Edward E., 39, 70

Child, Francis J., 190

Child, Lydia Maria, 44, 61, 169, 186

Childs, George W., 42

Chipperfield, Faith, 179

Chittick, V. L. O., 162

Chivers, Thomas Holley, 42

Cholmondeley, Thomas, 270

Christadler, Martin, 136

Christian Disciple, 83, 168

Christian Examiner, 49, 83, 168, 172, 244, 246, 288, 295, 304

Christian Observatory, 12

Christian Register, 114, 153, 167, 243, 295, 297

Christie, Francis A., 220, 229

Christie, John Aldrich, 266, 281

Christy, Arthur, 34, 95, 148, 270

Church of the Disciples: Seventieth Birthday of James Freeman Clarke, 114

Clapp, Dexter, 209

Clapper, Ronald, 282

Clark, Allen R., 43

Clark, Annie M. L., 62

Clark, C. E. Frazer, Jr., 240, 329

Clark, Clifford E., Jr., 54

Clark, Harry Hayden, 146, 153, 315, 351

Clark, Jerome L., 38

Clark, Lucy, 100

Clark, Neal, 57

Clarke, James Freeman, 6, 21, 23, 34, 49, 54, 70, 71, 75, 108, 109, 112–16, 121, 126, 153, 176, 178, 180, 181, 183, 186, 191, 194, 205, 235, 239, 240, 287, 288, 290, 292, 316

Clarke, John L., 67

Clarke, Lilian Freeman, 114

Clarke, Samuel C., 114

Clarke, Sarah, 44, 181, 240

Clarkson, John W., Jr., 254, 256, 257

Clebsch, William A., 16, 165

Clements, Richard, 122

Clendenning, John, 147

Clifford, John H., 154, 223

Clifton Waller Barrett Collection, 4

Clough, Arthur Hugh, 138

Clough, Wilson O., 159

Cobb, Lyman, 246

Cobbe, Frances Power, 217, 218

Coburn, Frederick, 125

Codman, John Thomas, 42, 59, 64, 65, 79, 127, 248, 252, 319

Coffie, Jessie A., 334

Coffin, Theron E., 273

Cohen, B. Bernard, 332

Cohen, Emanuel, 149

Colacurcio, Michael J., 249, 356

Colanzi, Rita, 79

Cole, Phyllis, 30, 146, 158, 289, 294, 314

Coleman, Caryl, 252

Coleman, Rufus A., 379

Coleman, William E., 227

Coleridge, Samuel Taylor, 16, 33, 39, 47, 48, 148, 149, 190, 193, 248, 269, 316, 343–48, 353, 364, 366, 371

Collections of the Massachusetts Historical Society, 168

Collie, George L., 94

Collins, Carvel, 260

Collins, Christopher, 25, 159

Collins, Hildegard Platzer, 183

Collins, Robert E., 218, 230

Collison, Gary L., 169, 170, 216, 217, 219

Colquitt, Betsy F., 280

Colton, Delia M., 143

Columbia University. *See* Butler Library

Columbia University Library, 57, 137

Colville, Derek K., 113, 114, 186

Colyer, Richard, 279

Commager, Henry Steele, 81, 172, 173, 216, 218, 220, 227, 229

Comprehensive Dissertation Index, 1861–1972, 5

Comte, Auguste, 231

Conant, Wallace B., 258
Concord (Mass.), 7, 13, 40, 41, 89, 139, 141, 264, 283, 284, 317–19, 330, 331, 333, 337, 364
Concord Academy, 267, 269
Concord Freeman, 254
Concord Free Public Library, 4, 88, 103, 104, 234, 241, 254, 261, 272
Concord Lyceum, 141, 275
Concord Saunterer, 5, 261
Concord School of Philosophy, 12, 24, 40, 89–91, 94, 98, 99, 144, 240, 241, 255, 256
Condry, William, 261
Confucius, 270
Congdon, Charles T., 43
Conkin, Paul K., 16, 151
Connelley, William E., 258
Conner, Frederick W., 155, 366
Conrad, Susan P., 187
Conron, John, 26, 284
Conroy, Stephen S., 151
Conservator, 379
Constant, Benjamin, 6, 32, 244, 245, 305
Continent Weekly Magazine, 163
Convention of Literary and Scientific Gentlemen, 347
Conway, Katherine E., 252
Conway, Moncure Daniel, 82, 117–22, 139, 141, 153, 157, 162, 169, 205, 209, 239, 330, 331, 336, 376, 380
Cook, Hugh, 268
Cook, Joseph, 154, 223
Cook, Reginald L., 7, 162, 271, 274, 284
Cook, Richard C., 279
Cooke, Frances E., 220
Cooke, George Willis, 5, 10, 19, 21, 49, 59, 65, 70–76, 78–82, 89, 90, 99–101, 109–11, 113, 114, 116, 123, 124, 127, 129, 130, 132–35, 139, 141, 144, 151, 154, 155, 180, 181, 185, 190–92, 198, 212, 215, 221, 231, 239, 247, 249, 290, 296, 297, 300, 319
Cooke, Joseph J., 67
Cooper, James Fenimore, 314
Cornell University Press, 178
Cortés, Donoso, 306
Cory, Arthur M., 161
Cosebey, Robert, 283
Countway Library, 108
Courtney, W. L., 150, 160
Couser, G. Thomas, 27, 283, 333, 383
Cousin, Victor, 6, 32, 33, 146, 149, 244, 245, 305, 307
Cowan, Michael H., 146, 161
Cowan, S. A., 354
Cowen, Wilson Walker, 350
Cox, James M., 146, 161, 332
Craft, Ellen, 222
Craft, William, 222
Craig, George D., 277

Cranch, Christopher Pearse, 5, 10, 21, 70, 71, 105, 123–30, 163, 267, 291, 318, 364
Cranch, John, 130
Crawley, Thomas Edward, 382
Cressey, George, 190
Critic, 143, 165
Cromphout, Gustaaf Van, 158, 332
Cronin, Morton, 165
Cronkhite, G. Ferris, 275, 333
Crothers, Samuel McChord, 145
Crouch, Sarah, 261
Crowe, Charles R., 23, 41, 56, 62, 67, 76, 79, 111, 181, 185, 242, 247, 248, 250, 251
Crozier, John Beattie, 154, 159
Cryder, Maude Ethel, 258, 259
Cudworth, Ralph, 149
Cummings, Charles A., 73
Cummins, Roger William, 57, 68, 211, 212
Cunliffe, Marcus, 9
Cupples, George, 142
Current Literature, 199
Curson, Elizabeth, 59
Curti, Merle, 39
Curtis, Alice Cabell, 335
Curtis, Edith Roelker, 23, 66, 79, 111, 127, 319
Curtis, George William, 59, 73, 76, 77, 106, 127, 129, 132, 141, 162, 317–19, 336
Curtis, Georgianna Pell, 252
Curtis, James Burrill, 59, 77, 318, 319
Cushman, Charlotte, 234

D'Agoult, Comtesse, 142
Dahl, Curtis, 52
Dahlstrand, Frederick C., 90, 94–96, 212
Dall, Caroline Healey, 10, 20, 30, 44, 116, 181, 191, 235, 239
Daly, John E., 308
Dameron, J. Lasley, 147, 362
Dana, Charles A., 56, 65, 246, 317, 318, 330, 380
Dana, Charlotte, 250
Dana, Henry W. L., 252
Dana, Richard Henry, Sr., 347
Dana, William F., 150
Daniel, Samuel, 269
Daniels, George H., 39
Dante Alighieri, 40, 138, 149, 269
Darby, John Custis, 143
Darrow, F. S., 151
Dartmouth College, 344, 346
Dartmouth College Library, 217, 219
Darwin, Charles, 2, 22, 53, 152, 153, 172, 173, 273
Das, S. P., 31
D'Avanzo, Mario L., 283, 284, 324
Davidson, Edward H., 366
Davidson, Frank, 159, 323, 332, 358

Davidson, J. M., 121
Davies, Barrie, 282
Davies, James W., 332
Davis, Ada E., 158
Davis, Andrew McFarland, 199
Davis, George, 181
Davis, Harriet, 181
Davis, Joe Lee, 36, 146
Davis, Merrell R., 33, 149, 350
Davis, Richard Beale, 120, 122
Davis, William Augustus, 300
Dawes, Henry, 234, 235
Dawson, W. J., 160
Deamer, Robert C., 272
Dedmond, Francis B., 103–05, 141, 207–09,
    262, 274
Deevey, Edward S., Jr., 273
DeFalco, Joseph M., 124, 276, 281
Defoe, Daniel, 269
Deiss, Joseph Jay, 179
Delano, Amasa, 358
Delano, Sterling F., 79, 133, 194, 319
Delbanco, Andrew, 312, 315
Delizia, Michael, 284
De Majo, Maria Teresa, 136
DeMott, Robert J., 277
Dennis, Carl, 155, 163, 280
D'Entremont, John, 119, 120, 122
Derby, J. C., 43
Detti, Emma, 179
Detweiler, Robert, 159, 166
Devlin, James E., 124
DeVries, C. F., 232
De Wette, Wilhelm M. L., 6, 40, 218, 223,
    228, 229
Dewey, John, 66, 157, 345, 346
Dewey, Orville, 43, 51
Dial (Boston), 1, 3, 12, 20, 27, 44, 63, 70,
    73–78, 83, 94, 102–04, 109, 111, 114, 121,
    123–28, 133, 141, 142, 163, 181, 182, 184,
    185, 188, 191, 197, 199, 202, 203, 211,
    212, 215, 221, 239, 244, 245, 249, 251,
    270, 287, 291, 293, 300, 306, 319, 339,
    341, 347, 364, 369
Dial (Cincinnati), 82
Dickens, Charles, 12
Dickinson, Emily, 27, 196–201, 284, 292,
    320–27
Dickinson College, 120. *See also* Boyd Lee Spahr
    Library
Dickinson Studies, 321
Diehl, Carl, 50
Diehl, Joanne Feit, 323
Diggins, John P., 275
Dillard, Annie, 284
Dillman, Richard H., 161, 267, 275, 279
Dillon, Patrick, 160
Dinwiddie, Shirley W., 57, 87
Dirks, John Edward, 218, 229

D'Israeli, Isaac, 369
Dissertation Abstracts International, 5
Dix, Dorothea, 235
Dobson, Eleanore Robinette, 132
Dod, Albert, 12, 153
Doherty, Joseph F., 156
Domina, Lyle, 284
Domingo Faustino Sarmiento Museum, 235
Donadio, Stephen, 155
Donoghue, Lorraine, 80
Dorn, Minda Ruth, 72, 78, 81, 308
Dos Passos, John, 284
Doten, Lizzie, 116
Doubleday, Neal F., 313
Doudna, Martin, 281
Douglas, Ann, 38, 110, 186–88
Douglass, Frederick, 234
Dover Publications, 263, 265
Dowden, Edward, 33
Downs, Lenthiel H., 316
Doyle, Paul A., 266
Drake, William, 279
Dressman, Michael, 383
Drinnon, Richard, 276
Duban, James, 356
Duberman, Martin, 341
Dublin Review, 142
Dubuat Nançay, Comte Louis Gabriel, 269
Duchac, Joseph, 321, 327
Duffy, Bernard, 163
Duffy, John J., 248, 344–47
Duncan, Graham H., 337
Duncan, Isadora, 35
Duncan, Jeffrey L., 146, 161
Duncan, Rebecca L., 218
Duncan, Robert, 166
Dunn, Esther Cloudman, 269
Dunton, Edith Kellogg, 107
Dupree, Robert, 272
Durick, Jeremiah K., 368
Durning, Russell E., 182–84
Durocher, Aurele P., 68, 93
Dutton, Frederic J., 150
Duyckinck, Evert A., 41, 292, 345, 348–51,
    356, 360, 361
Duyckinck, George L., 292, 345
Dwight, B. W., 132
Dwight, Frank, 65
Dwight, John Sullivan, 6, 56, 65, 67, 77, 80,
    124, 125, 127–34, 163, 180, 226, 235, 243,
    244, 250, 317–19, 336, 341
Dwight, Marianne, 59, 60, 64, 65, 215, 248,
    252, 319
Dwight's Journal of Music, 124, 131, 132
Dylan, Bob, 225

Eakin, Paul John, 334
Early, James, 152

Easton, Loyd D., 82, 121
Eaton, John, 235
Ebbitt, Wilma Robb, 75, 177, 184
Eckermann, Johann Peter, 6
Eckstorm, Fanny Hardy, 272, 283
Eddy, Richard, 38
Edel, Leon, 42, 271, 274
Edelstein, Tilden G., 114, 195, 197, 198
Edgell, David Palmer, 58, 61, 68, 89, 92, 93, 212, 311–14
Edrich, Mary Worden, 21, 164, 314
Edwards, Channing, 247
Edwards, Herbert W., 14
Edwards, Jonathan, 15, 16, 29, 30, 47, 48, 95, 150, 165, 210, 268
Eells, James, 229
Ehrlich, Heyward Bruce, 41
Eidson, John Olin, 39, 290, 299, 300
Eiseley, Loren, 273
Eisenlohr, Herman L., 278
Eisinger, Chester E., 14
Ekhtiar, Mansur, 148
Ekirch, Arthur Alphonse, 158
Elder, Marjorie J., 335, 355
Eleanor, Sister Mary, 193
Elijah P. Grant Papers, 59
Eliot, Charlotte C., 43
Eliot, Samuel A., 20, 44, 98, 174, 190, 231, 247, 296
Eliot, T. S., 166, 182, 284
Eliot, Walter Greenleaf, 43
Elizabeth Peabody House Association, 239
Elkins, Stanley, 23, 226
Elliott, Fannie Mae, 100
Elliott, G. R., 165
Elliott, Maud Howe, 43, 114, 180
Elliott, Walter, 61, 252
Ellis, Arthur B., 43
Ellis, Charles Mayo, 11
Ellis, George E., 53, 220
Ellis, Rufus, 43, 338
Ellison, Ralph, 166
Els, Rüdiger, 148
Emanuel, James A., 159
Emerson, Amelia Forbes, 140
Emerson, Charles Chauncy, 140, 316
Emerson, Edward Waldo, 20, 44, 132, 137–39, 141, 169, 265, 337, 380
Emerson, Ellen Louisa Tucker, 140
Emerson, Ellen Tucker, 137, 140
Emerson, George B., 43
Emerson, Lidian Jackson, 140, 235, 274
Emerson, Mary Moody, 140, 235
Emerson, Ralph Waldo, 1, 2, 4–10, 12, 13, 15–25, 27–36, 40, 45–48, 55, 58–64, 67, 73, 75–77, 80–82, 90–93, 98, 103–06, 108, 109, 113, 114, 116, 118, 120, 121, 124–28, 130, 133, 135–66, 169, 172, 173, 176–78, 181, 182, 185, 186, 188, 191, 192, 193,

197, 201–03, 205, 208, 209, 211, 212, 214, 215, 217, 220, 221, 223–25, 227–31, 234, 236, 238–41, 243, 245, 248, 250–52, 255–57, 264, 267, 268, 272, 274–79, 282, 287–94, 296, 299, 300, 303–08, 312–33, 335–43, 348–61, 363, 364, 366–69, 372–83
Emerson, Waldo, 141
Emerson, William, 140
Emerson Society Quarterly, 5
Emery, Allan Moore, 358
Emily Dickinson Bulletin, 201, 321
Engel, Mary Miller, 141
Englekirk, John E., 136
Epicurus, 367
Eppard, Philip B., 4, 49
Erikson, Erik, 147, 215, 265
Erlich, Michael, 281
ESQ: A Journal of the American Renaissance, 5
Essex Institute, 101, 171, 204, 234, 287, 292
Ethical Culture Society, 172
Etzler, J. A., 274
Eulau, Heinz, 276
Eulert, Donald D., 166
Evans, Charles M., 276
Evans, Francis E. B., 278
Evans, Robert O., 281
Everett, C. C., 163
Everson, Ida Gertrude, 42

Fabian, Bernhard, 313
Fairbanks, Henry G., 16, 38
Fairbanks, Jonathan, 271
Fales Library, 234
Falk, Robert, 153
Faulkner, William, 155, 166
Faust, Clarence H., 21, 155, 161, 248
Feidelson, Charles, Jr., 25, 29, 160, 279, 352, 365, 366
Fellman, Michael, 226
Feltenstein, Rosalie, 140
Felton, C. C., 6, 12, 300
Fenn, William W., 43
Fergenson, Laraine R., 269, 281
Ferguson, Alfred R., 124, 137, 164, 256
Ferguson, John De Lancey, 136
Fertig, Walter L., 131–34
Feuer, Lewis, 345
Fichte, Johann Gottlieb, 296, 365
Fiedler, Leslie A., 275
Field, Maunsell B., 43
Fields, Annie, 42, 162
Fields, James T., 42, 235, 330, 340
Filler, Louis, 225
Fillmore, Millard, 222
Fink, John M., 3
Fink, Stephen, 282
Finney, Charles G., 2, 15
Finnigan, David F., 161

Firkins, O. W., 76, 139, 145
First Parish Congregational (Unitarian) Church (Watertown, Mass.), 168, 169
First Printings of American Authors, 3
Fisch, Max Harold, 92
Fish, Carl Russell, 37
Fisher, Hersha Sue, 234, 238
Fisher, Marvin, 358
Fitzgerald, Edward, 246
Fitzgerald, Gabrielle, 267
Fitzsimmons, Matthew A., 308
Flanagan, John T., 157, 162
Fleck, Richard F., 268, 279, 294, 333
Flewelling, R. T., 158
Flint, Robert W., 39
Floan, Howard R., 158
Flower, Benjamin Orange, 83
Flower, Elizabeth, 16, 24, 92, 151
Flynn, Kathleen, 71
Fobes, Charles S., 44
Foerster, Norman, 152, 162, 163, 267, 381
Fogle, Richard H., 78, 162
Follen, Charles Theodore Christian, 53, 244
Folsom, Charles, 234
Fone, Byrne R. S., 287
Foote, Caleb, 43
Foote, Mary Wilder, 43
Forbes, Edith Emerson, 255
Forbes, Waldo Emerson, 138, 141
Forclaz, Roger, 368
Ford, Arthur Lewis, Jr., 280
Ford, Nick Aaron, 276
Ford, Thomas W., 284, 324, 326
Forman, Charles C., 49
Forster, Joseph, 144
Foster, Charles Howell, 155, 164, 237
Foster, Edward Halsey, 151
Foster, Elizabeth S., 355, 359, 360
Fourier, Charles, 32, 33, 62–67, 78, 79, 111, 237, 246–48
Fowler, Orson, 181
Fowler and Wells (publishers), 181
Fox, George, 290
Francis, Convers, 167–70, 219
Francis, Elamanamadathil V., 148
Francis, Richard, 23, 62, 67, 68, 93, 111, 213
Francis, Richard Lee, 147, 151, 163, 164, 215
Francke, Kuno, 148
Franklin, Benjamin, 165, 274
Frederick, John T., 41
Fredrickson, George M., 23, 54, 111, 226
Free Church (Lynn, Mass.), 205
Free Inquirer, 304
Freeman, John 351
Free Religious Association, 12, 21, 22, 54, 55, 82, 83, 94, 99, 153–55, 172, 174, 197, 201–03, 205, 231, 296, 297, 316
Freidel, Frank, 37
French, Allen, 40

Freniere, Emile A., 219
Freud, Sigmund, 147, 265
Friden, Georg, 31
Froebel, Friedrich Wilhelm August, 236, 238
Fromm, Harold, 155
Frost, Barzillai, 48, 337
Frost, Robert, 35, 166, 284
Frothingham, Nathaniel Langdon, 46, 172
Frothingham, Octavius Brooks, 7–10, 12, 13, 31, 33, 34, 45, 46, 54, 59, 62, 73, 79, 81, 82, 91, 99, 108–10, 114, 116, 125, 150, 169, 170, 171–74, 184, 191, 201, 203, 206, 209, 219, 220, 223, 231, 243, 246–48, 251, 297, 298, 307, 316
Frothingham, Paul Revere, 174
Fruitlands, 1, 10, 11, 23, 24, 56–68, 77, 88, 89, 93, 94, 212, 213
Fruitlands Museums, 4, 57, 60, 88, 176, 211, 242, 319
Fryckstedt, Olov M., 122
Frye, Hall, 160
Fugitive Slave Law, 221, 222
Fuller, Arthur B., 44, 176, 177, 180, 183, 184
Fuller, Ellen. *See* Channing, Ellen Fuller
Fuller, Frederick T., 334
Fuller, Horace B., 39, 217
Fuller, Kenneth, 4
Fuller, Margaret, 6–8, 10, 20, 23, 25, 59, 62, 63, 65, 73, 75, 76, 103–05, 108, 110, 113–16, 130, 142, 143, 175–88, 191, 196, 203, 209, 215, 233, 238, 239, 250–52, 264, 291, 306, 316, 318, 320, 333, 334, 336, 337, 339, 340, 363, 364, 369, 370
Fuller, Margarett Crane, 176, 187
Fuller, Richard Frederick, 44, 175, 180
Fuller, Timothy, 187
Furness, Clifton J., 378
Furness, Horace Howard, 138
Furness, William Henry, 51, 52, 138, 304
Fussell, Edwin, 27, 29, 272, 282, 381

G., 153
Gabriel, Ralph Henry, 37, 38, 157, 173, 174
Gafford, Lucile, 25, 78, 79, 130
Gage, Ann Brewer Sargent, 235
Galaxy, 295
Galgan, Gerald J., 274
Gallagher, G. W., 154
Gallagher, William D., 113
Gallaher, Helen, 117, 118
Gallant, Barbara Gans, 72, 79–81, 248
Galligan, Edward L., 278
Gandhi, Mahatma, 36, 166, 284
Gannett, Ezra Stiles, 44, 51
Gannett, William Channing, 44, 54
Garate, Justo, 261

Garber, Frederick, 272, 281
Gardella, Raymond, 159
Garland, Mary, 239
Garlitz, Barbara, 93, 95
Garmon, Gerald M., 369
Garnett, Richard, 139, 157
Garrison, Stephen, 59
Garrison, Wendell Phillips, 38
Garrison, William Lloyd, 225, 235, 258
Gatell, Frank Otto, 43
Gates, Michael, 270
Gawronski, Donald Vincent, 41
Gay, Robert M., 145
Geffen, Elizabeth M., 52
Geller, L. D., 4, 41, 103, 104, 196
Gelpi, Albert J., 26, 146, 163, 325, 326, 369
Genesee Republican and Herald of Reform, 304
Genzmer, George Harvey, 296, 297
George, Henry, 225
Gerando, Joseph Marie, Baron de, 32, 149, 233, 236, 244
Gerbaud, Colette, 293
Gerber, John C., 157
Gerdts, William H., 42
Geselbracht, Raymond H., 35
Gierasch, Walter, 269, 284
Gilchrist, Herbert Harlakenden, 377
Gilfillan, George, 142, 143
Gilhooley, Leonard, 72, 304, 307
Gilman, Albert, 25, 146, 278
Gilman, Caroline Howard, 52
Gilman, Owen W., Jr., 284
Gilman, Samuel, 52, 142
Gilman, William H., 138, 212, 215, 350
Gilmore, William J., 304, 308
Gilpin, William, 269
Gimlin, Joan S., 275
Gioberti, Vincenzo, 306
Girard, William, 32, 33, 249
Girgus, Sam B., 19, 35, 275
Gittleman, Edwin, 7, 181, 286, 287, 289, 290, 293, 316
Glassheim, Eliot, 370
Gleason, Herbert W., 263
Glick, Wendell, 39, 152, 263, 266, 267, 276, 277, 281, 283, 285
Goblet d'Alviella, Count, 12, 232
Goddard, Harold Clarke, 8, 9, 14, 46, 48, 74, 91, 125, 151, 223, 313
Goddard, John, 149
Godwin, Parke, 41
Goethe, Johann Wolfgang von, 5, 6, 32, 40, 98, 101, 114, 144, 148, 153, 183, 184, 192, 272
Goetzmann, William H., 40
Gohdes, Clarence L. F., 3, 20, 34, 39, 69, 70, 72, 74, 78–83, 94, 99, 110, 115, 123, 126, 133, 136, 138, 201, 221, 240, 248, 298, 308, 314, 379, 380

Goldfarb, Clare R., 24, 151, 332
Goldfarb, Russell M., 24, 151
Golemba, Henry L., 76, 79, 184, 247
Gollin, Rita K., 334
Gonnaud, Maurice, 140, 146, 158
Goodman, Paul, 40
Goodnight, S. H., 115
Goodrich, S. G., 43
Goodwin, James, 276
Gordon, George Stuart, 39
Gordon, Joseph T., 63, 330
Gorely, Jean, 163
Gospel Advocate and Impartial Observer, 304
Gosse, Edmund, 163
Gottesman, Ronald, 350
Gougeon, Len, 158
Gould, George M., 43
Gower, Joseph F., 304
Gower, kichard F., 252
Goyder, David George, 149
Gozzi, Raymond, 265, 281
Grady, Charles, 191, 193
Graeter, Francis, 238
Graham, Philip, 342
Graham, Sylvester, 38
Graham's Magazine, 106
Grannis, Joseph C., 43
Gray, Henry David, 145, 150
Greaves, James Pierrepont, 57, 58, 61
Greeley, Horace, 41, 65, 67, 180, 246, 264, 345, 360
Green, Eugene, 283
Green, Judith A., 71, 110, 116, 126
Green, Martin, 40, 52, 155
Green, Sue Ellen, 252
Greenberger, Evelyn Barish, 165
Greene, Christopher A., 44
Greene, Henry L., 181
Greene, John G., 70
Greene, William B., 11
Greenough, Horatio, 44, 277
Greenwood, Douglas McCreary, 344–47
Greenwood, F. W. P., 51
Gregg, Edith Emerson Webster, 140
Gregory, Winifred, 3
Greiner, Donald J., 35
Griffin, C. S., 38
Griffin, William J., 277
Griffith, Clark, 161, 325, 354, 368, 370
Grimm, Herman, 138, 142
Griswold, Rufus W., 43, 113, 122, 128, 292
Grob, Gerald N., 37
Gross, Robert A., 41, 275, 283
Gross, Seymour L., 163
Gross, Theodore L., 158, 328, 353
Grover, Edwin O., 380
Gruber, Christian, 267
Gruenert, Charles F., 278
Guernsey, Alfred, 143

Gura, Philip F., 7, 26, 27, 32, 161, 240, 241, 267, 268, 275, 279, 345
Gurney, Richard C., 280
Gushee, Anne Elizabeth, 333
Guthrie, Harold N., 278

H., J. B., 143
Habich, Robert David, 71, 110, 113, 116, 126, 180
Haddin, Theodore, 279
Haefner, George, 92
Haertel, Martin Henry, 100
Hagenbüchle, Roland, 323
Haig, Robert L., 153
Hale, Edward, 169
Hale, Edward Everett, 42, 112, 137, 209, 341, 380
Hale, Edward Everett, Jr., 42
Hale, John Parker, 217, 219
Hale, Nathan, 338, 342
Hale, Susan, 42
Hall, Arethusa, 207
Hall, Bishop, 269
Hall, Edward S., 43
Hall, James, 114
Hall, Lawrence Sargent, 331
Hall, Theresa Layton, 97, 112, 195, 216, 295
Halleck, Fitz-Greene, 41
Halliburton, David G., 371
Halline, Allan G., 366
Hallowell, Anna Davis, 43
Hamilton, Franklin W., 277
Hamilton, William, 173
Hammell, G. M., 290
Handy, Robert T., 15
Hansen, Arlene J., 149
Hansen-Taylor, Marie, 41
Haraszti, Zoltán, 56, 60, 251, 319
Harbinger, 56, 59, 65, 70, 79–80, 109, 123–25, 127, 131, 133, 226, 246, 248, 319, 341
Harding, Anthony John, 269, 346
Harding, Brian R., 161, 269, 279
Harding, Walter, 5, 6, 60, 89, 103, 136, 148, 166, 181, 212, 254, 256, 259–66, 272, 273, 275, 276, 279, 281, 282, 284, 300, 376
Harland, William Harry, 58, 61, 88, 89, 212
Haroutunian, Joseph, 51
Harper, George Mills, 33, 94, 148
Harper's Magazine, 246, 318
Harper's New Monthly Magazine, 319
Harris, Kenneth E., 281
Harris, Neil, 26
Harris, William Torrey, 43, 61, 90, 95, 144, 148, 152, 160, 193, 194, 234
Harris Collection of American Poetry, 287
Harrison, James A., 363

Harrison, John S., 148
Harte, Bret, 166
Harvard Common Press, 60
Harvard Divinity School, 40, 48, 115, 167, 169, 170, 172, 173, 220, 243, 287, 338, 372
Harvard Graduate Magazine, 98
Harvardiana, 286
Harvard Magazine, 163
Harvard University, 24, 40, 52, 220, 265, 267, 289, 290, 299, 300, 307, 337, 372. See also Andover-Harvard Theological Library, Bowdoin Prize, Countway Library, and Houghton Library
Harvard University Archives, 132, 167
Harvard University Library, 75, 123, 222, 300
Harwood, Edward, 245
Harwood, Thomas F., 315
Haskell, Augustus Mellen, 203, 206
Haskins, David Green, 140
Hasselmayer, Louis A., 94
Hastings, Hester, 314
Hathaway, Lillie V., 78, 81
Hathaway, Richard D., 207, 208
Hawthorne, Julian, 144, 239, 330, 334
Hawthorne, Manning, 330
Hawthorne, Nathaniel, 10, 13, 59, 62, 63, 65, 66, 80, 103, 104, 106, 118, 121, 180, 183, 186, 199, 209, 215, 231, 234, 237, 239, 240, 246, 251, 252, 255, 264, 269, 275, 284, 290, 291, 293, 303, 318, 319, 321, 328–35, 348, 349, 352, 356, 358, 360, 361, 365, 366, 368
Hawthorne, Sophia Peabody, 59, 104, 235, 238, 240, 328, 330, 331, 333, 335
Hawthorne-Longfellow Library, 97
Hayden, Brad, 284
Hayes, Rutherford B., 166
Hayford, Harrison, 350
Hazard, Lucy Lockwood, 29, 158
Hazelrig, Jack O., 328
Hazewell, C. C., 157
Hazlitt, William, 314
Heath, Trudy, 3, 39, 69
Heath, William G., 97–99
Hecker, Isaac T., 11, 42, 58, 61, 154, 211, 252, 264, 304, 317, 318
Hedge, Frederic Henry, 11, 22, 114, 169, 170, 173, 181, 189–94, 231, 316, 345
Hedges, William L., 152, 165
Hegel, Georg Wilhelm Friedrich, 40, 94, 121, 148, 151, 183, 229
Hegewisch, D. H., 344
Heidegger, Martin, 151
Heine, Heinrich, 246
Hellenbrand, Harold, 275
Hellman, George Sidney, 256
Hemingway, Ernest, 166, 284

Hemming, Henry, 154
Hendrick, George, 14, 41, 149, 264, 284, 341, 379
Hennessy, Helen, 27, 78, 128, 129, 185
Henri, Robert, 166
Henry, Caleb Sprague, 2, 22, 194
Henry E. Huntington Library, 4, 59, 137, 196, 217, 254, 262, 319, 341
Herald of Freedom, 75, 281
Heraud, John A., 40, 142
Herbert, George, 149
Herbold, Anthony, 293, 294
Herbst, Jurgen, 50
Herder, Johann Gottfried von, 229, 240, 244, 343, 344, 382
Herndon, William, 218
Herr, William A., 276
Herreshoff, David, 19, 147
Herrnstadt, Richard L., 57, 61, 87, 89, 376
Hertz, Robert N., 151
Hewett-Thayer, Harvey W., 136
Hickock, Benjamin Blakely, 253, 254, 257, 258
Hicks, Granville, 219, 252, 315
Hicks, John, 266, 276
Hicks, Philip Marshall, 27, 152, 284
Higgins, Bryan, 350
Higginson, Mary Thacher, 180, 195–97, 199
Higginson, Thomas Wentworth, 13, 23, 59, 62, 64, 74, 75, 90, 104, 107, 109, 114, 141, 144, 153, 156, 169, 175, 178, 180, 191, 195–203, 217, 218, 239, 252, 254, 264, 296, 313, 321, 336
Higginson Journal, 201
Hilbrunner, Anthony, 158
Hildenbrand, Christopher A., 260, 261
Hildreth, Richard, 43
Hill, David W., 147, 160
Hill, J. Arthur, 145
Hillard, G. S., 43
Hillis, Newell Dwight, 110
Hillman, Mary V., 335
Himelick, Raymond, 269
Hinding, Andrea, 234
Hinds, William A., 93
Hintz, Howard W., 149, 195, 199, 200
Hirst, George C., 160
Historical Society of Pennsylvania, 254
Hitler, Adolf, 157
Hoag, Ronald, 271
Hoar, Elizabeth, 44, 140
Hoch, David G., 270
Hochfield, George, 5, 9, 14, 60, 75, 89, 132, 218, 246, 373
Hochmuth, Marie, 314
Hodge, Charles, 12, 153
Hodges, James R., 39
Hodges, Maud de Leigh, 169

Hodges, Robert R., 279
Hodgin, Edwin Stanton, 297
Hoeltje, Hubert H., 90, 91, 94, 141, 267, 330
Hoffman, Charles Fenno, 41
Hoffman, Michael J., 25, 335, 354
Hofstra University, 198
Holden, Vincent F., 42, 61
Holder, Alan, 279
Holland, Frederick May, 150, 159
Holland, H. N., 150
Hollis, C. Carroll, 94, 219, 308
Holloway, Jean, 42
Holls, Frederick William, 138
Holman, Harriet R., 367
Holmes, John Haynes, 220, 224
Holmes, Oliver Wendell, 43, 76, 139, 157, 160, 180
Holmes, Oliver Wendell, Jr., 309
Holmes, Stewart H., 36, 44
Holt, Anne, 315
Homer, 269
Hoornstra, Jean, 3, 39, 69
Hoover, Merle M., 41
Hopkins, Samuel, 313
Hopkins, Sarah Winnemucca, 235
Hopkins, Vivian C., 145, 147, 148, 152, 185, 333
Hornbrooke, Francis, 192
Horton, John T., 222
Horton, Rod W., 14
Hosmer, George Washington, 43
Hosmer, Horace, 41
Hosmer, J. K., 43
Hotson, Clarence Paul, 34, 69, 148, 149, 159, 374
Hotten, John Camden, 121, 122
Houghton Library, 3, 10, 57, 58, 87–89, 97, 100, 102, 108, 113, 131, 137, 167, 175, 188, 190, 196, 207, 211, 214, 217, 235, 242, 243, 250, 254, 262, 286, 287, 296, 299, 310, 319, 320, 376
Hounchell, Saul, 70
Hourihan, Paul, 162, 267
Houston, Howard R., 279
Hovde, Carl F., 262, 282
Hovenkamp, Herbert, 38, 51, 228
Howard, Leon, 14, 339, 341, 360, 381, 383
Howarth, William L., 262, 271, 277, 284
Howe, Daniel Walker, 40, 49–52, 293, 313, 315
Howe, Julia Ward, 43, 73, 75, 114, 144, 157, 177, 178, 180
Howe, M. A. DeWolfe, 40, 114, 199, 341
Howe, Samuel Gridley, 234
Howe, W. T. H., 237
Howells, William Dean, 13, 35, 122, 128, 130, 264, 340, 341
Hoyt, Edward A., 181

Hubbard, Elbert, 261
Hubbell, George Shelton, 136
Hubbell, Jay B., 41, 120, 158
Huber, J. Parker, 283
Hudson, Charles, 220
Hudson, Herbert Edson, 216, 217, 224
Hudson, Winthrop S., 15
Hudspeth, Robert N., 102, 104, 105, 176–78, 181, 186
Huffert, Anton M., 275
Huggard, William Allen, 146, 157, 158
Huidekoper, Harm Jan, 44
Hull, Raymona E., 332
Hume, David, 149, 244
Humphrey, Leonard, 321
Hunt, T. W., 160
Hunter, Doreen, 42, 192
Huntington, Arria S., 43
Huntington, Frederic Dan, 43, 154, 209
Hurlbut, William H., 180
Hutch, Robert A., 147
Hutcheson, Frances, 313
Hutchinson, Anne, 10
Hutchinson, Jamie, 282
Hutchison, William R., 21, 36, 48, 52, 99, 109, 116, 125, 155, 164, 170, 194, 221, 224, 249, 286, 313
Hutter, Edward, 38
Hyman, Stanley Edgar, 276
Hyneman, Esther F., 362

Ihrig, Mary Alice, 136
Independent, 103, 106
Index, 12, 70, 82, 157, 173
Index to Early American Periodical Literature, 70
Inge, M. Thomas, 278
Ingersoll, Robert, 154
Ingraham, Charles A., 16
Intellectual Repository and New Jerusalem Magazine, 149
Ireland, Alexander, 139
Ireland, Robert E., 231, 308
Irey, Eugene F., 136
Irie, Yukio, 149
Irving, Washington, 314
Irwin, John T., 161, 279
Isely, Jeter A., 248
Isely, Lisette Riggs, 247, 248, 252
Ishikawa, Jesse, 169
Ives, Charles Edward, 35, 134, 166

Jackson, A. W., 198, 199
Jackson, Carl T., 34, 35, 53, 95, 121, 206, 270
Jackson, Helen Hunt, 321
Jackson, Lydia. *See* Emerson, Lidian Jackson

Jackson, R. M. S., 219
Jacobi, Friedrich, 183, 231
Jacobs, Robert D., 367
Jacques, John, 271
Jaffe, Adrian, 314
James, David L., 281
James, Edward T., 237
James, Henry, 13, 42, 43, 129, 130, 144, 162, 166, 180, 251, 264, 274, 370
James, Henry, Sr., 17, 42, 309
James, William, 16, 36, 42, 144, 154, 166
Jamieson, Paul F., 141
Janes, Lewis G., 154
Japp, Alexander H., 149, 264
Jarvis, Edward, 275
Jefferson, Thomas, 149, 276, 312
Jeswine, Miriam A., 270
John Hay Library, 57
Johnson, Alexander, 258
Johnson, Alexander Bryan, 267
Johnson, Anthony P., 230
Johnson, Charles F., 144
Johnson, Ellwood, 159
Johnson, Glen M., 147, 165
Johnson, Harriet Hall, 181
Johnson, Jane, 380
Johnson, Jane Maloney, 66
Johnson, Judith Kennedy, 214, 215
Johnson, Linck C., 268, 282
Johnson, Paul David, 282
Johnson, Quentin G., 342
Johnson, Samuel, 10, 34, 82, 121, 172, 203, 204–06, 223, 234
Johnson, Thomas H., 321, 325
Johnston, Carol, 216, 219–21
Jones, Alexander E., 181
Jones, Buford, 269, 328, 333
Jones, Harry L., 290, 293
Jones, Howard Mumford, 16, 33, 39, 72, 78, 80, 151, 155, 158, 197, 307
Jones, John Dillon, 66
Jones, Joseph, 36, 80, 81, 136, 161, 240
Jones, Samuel Arthur, 41, 266
Jones, Wayne Allen, 240, 333
Jones, William A., 142
Jones, William Clough, 226
Joost, Nicholas, 74
Jordan, William Donald, 335
Jordan and Wiley (publishers), 208
Jorgenson, Chester Eugene, 156
Josselyn, John, 268
Jouffroy, Théodore, 6, 32, 109, 244, 245
Journal of Speculative Philosophy, 95, 103
Joy, Neill R., 283
Joyaux, Georges Jules, 32, 33, 40, 71, 72, 78, 80, 81
Judd, Sylvester, 2, 47, 207–10, 337
Judd, Sylvester, Sr., 207
Jugaku, Bunshō, 136

Jung, Carl, 147
Juvenile Miscellany, 168

Kaiser, Mary L., 279
Kamei, Shunsuke, 136
Kansas State Historical Society, 57, 254
Kant, Immanuel, 12, 16, 31, 32, 40, 45, 47, 148, 192, 193, 231, 345, 346, 364, 366
Kaplan, Justin, 383
Kaplan, Nathaniel, 31
Kappes, Carolyn, 262
Karabatsos, James, 281
Kassel, Charles, 222
Katsaros, Thomas, 31
Katz, Jonathan, 147, 274
Kaufman, Marjorie Ruth, 79
Kavanaugh, James V., 278
Kazin, Alfred, 281
Kearns, Francis E., 185, 334
Keats, George, 43
Keats, John, 39, 149
Keeler, Clinton, 358
Keller, Hans, 148
Keller, Karl, 30, 155, 198, 327, 360
Kelley, Michael, 273
Kennard, James, Jr., 12
Kennebec Historical Society, 207
Kennedy, John F., 227
Kennedy, William Sloane, 163, 378, 379
Kern, Alexander C., 8, 9, 14, 33, 48, 151, 157, 193, 201, 230, 262, 267–69, 307, 313
Kernahan, Coulson, 163
Kerstesz, Louise C., 280
Kesterson, David B., 329, 333
Kher, Inder Nath, 326
Kides, Kathryn, 77
Kierkegaard, Søren, 155, 161
Kilgour, Raymond L., 39
Kilshaw, Ellen, 187
Kim, Kichung, 270, 273
Kindergarten News, 239
Kindergarten Review, 239
King, Martin Luther, Jr., 284
Kinoy, Arthur. *See* Edwards, Channing
Kirby, Georgiana Bruce, 44, 59, 180, 215, 252
Kirk, Russell, 151, 307
Kirkham, E. Bruce, 3
Kleinfeld, H. L., 140
Kloeckner, Alfred J., 158
Kneeland, Stillman F., 191
Knickerbocker, Frances W., 140
Knight, Harriet Elizabeth, 38
Kolbenschlag, M. Claire, 274
Konvitz, Milton R., 147
Kopisch, August, 101
Kopp, Charles C., 273
Körner, Karl Theodor, 6, 101

Kossuth, Louis, 38
Koster, Donald N., 8, 74, 92, 224, 247
Kraditor, Aileen S., 23, 225
Kraitsir, Charles, 32, 234, 235, 238, 240, 267
Kramer, Aaron, 27, 163
Kraus, W. Keith, 298
Kribbs, Jayne K., 3, 39, 70
Kring, Walter Donald, 42, 52, 54, 110, 114, 191
Krishnamachari, V., 35
Krutch, Joseph Wood, 270, 271
Kuklick, Bruce, 16, 53
Kurtz, Ernest, 286
Kwiat, Joseph, 267

Lacey, James F., 261
Lader, Lawrence, 38, 222
Ladu, Arthur I., 157, 225, 313
Lambert, L. Gray, 269
La Motte-Fouqué, Friedrich, 233
Lane, Charles, 11, 24, 57, 58, 60–62, 64, 65, 67, 68, 93, 94, 211–13, 248
Lane, Lauriat, Jr., 266, 275, 280, 281, 283, 284
Lang, Hans-Joachim, 331
Lanier, Sidney, 166
Lapati, Americo D., 304
La Piana, Angelina, 40
Larned, Augusta, 241
LaRosa, Ralph C., 161, 162, 165, 278
Laski, Harold, 308
Lathrop, George Parsons, 128, 141, 330
Lathrop, Rose Hawthorne, 235, 239, 330
Lauter, Paul, 159, 165
Lavan, Spencer, 53
Law, S., 154
Lawrence, D. H., 166
Laws, John Wallace, 230
Leary, Lewis, 4, 146, 165, 261, 266, 271
Lease, Benjamin, 43
Lebeau, Bryan F., 194
Lebeaux, Richard, 147, 265, 271
Le Breton, Anna Letitia, 311
Lee, Roland F., 159, 161
Lee, Vernon. *See* Paget, Violet
Lefcowitz, Allan B., 380
Lefcowitz, Barbara F., 380
Leibnitz, Gottfried Wilhelm, 371
Leidecker, Kurt F., 43, 95
Leighton, Walter L., 32, 148, 249
Leisy, Ernest, 14, 269
Leland, Charles Godfrey, 43
Leliaert, Richard M., 252, 304, 308
Lemchen, Leo, 40
Lemelin, Robert, 41
Lenhart, Charmenz S., 26, 129
Lennon, Florence Becker, 319

Lentricchia, Frank, 148
Lenz, Frederick P., III, 280
Lerch, Charles H., 160
Leroux, Pierre, 306
Lesley, Susan I., 43
Levenson, J. C., 128
Levernier, James A., 294
Levertov, Denise, 166
Levin, David, 146
Levine, Stuart, 367
Levy, Leonard W., 221
Lewin, Walter, 150
Lewis, Albert, 161
Lewis, R. W. B., 29, 152, 229, 308
Lewis, Suzanne S., 283
Lewisohn, Ludwig, 18, 147
Leyda, Jay, 321, 361
Liberal Preacher, 168
Libman, Valentina, 136
Library of Congress, 97, 217, 234, 266, 319, 370
Lieber, Francis, 43
Liebman, Sheldon W., 148, 149, 155, 161
Liggera, Joseph J., 278
Lincoln, Abraham, 218, 227
Lincoln Public Library, 299
Lind, Sidney E., 129
Lindeman, Eduard C., 151
Lindquist, Vernon R., 193
Lindsay, Julian Ira, 344
Lindsey, James, 150
Linstromberg, Robin, 274, 281
Lippitt, George Warren, 338
Literary World (Boston), 378, 380
Literary Writings in America, 97, 102, 118, 254, 296
Locher, Kaspar T., 40
Locke, John, 2, 33, 39, 50, 244, 305, 313, 337, 373
Loetscher, Lefferts A., 15
Lombard, Charles M., 40, 42
London, Herbert, 36, 225
London and Westminster Review, 142
London Times, 119
Long, Governor, 235
Long, Larry R., 268
Long, Orie William, 50, 189, 190
Longfellow, Henry Wadsworth, 42, 154, 209, 235, 364, 366
Longfellow, Samuel, 42, 204, 205
Longfellow House, 319
Loomis, C. Grant, 161, 209
Lorch, Fred W., 278
Loring, George B., 341
Lothrop, Daniel, 235
Lothrop, Harriet K., 235, 240
Lothrop, Samuel Kirkland, 12, 43, 53
Lothrop, Thornton Kirkland, 43
Loving, Jerome, 147, 376, 377, 380, 383

Low, Alvah H., 141
Lowance, Mason I., Jr., 30, 161, 165, 268
Lowdermilk, W. H., 236, 237
Lowell, Anna Cabot Jackson, 238
Lowell, James Russell, 7, 10, 81, 122, 130, 133, 143, 162, 165, 209, 236, 251, 264, 278, 284, 299, 300, 321, 336–42, 359, 365, 366, 380
Lowell, Maria White, 339, 342
Lowens, Irving, 26, 71, 72, 78, 80, 81, 131, 133
Lowery, Margaret Ruth, 42
Lowry, Howard F., 138
Lucas, Alec, 272
Lucas, John A., 200
Luce, William, 198
Lucretius, 149
Ludwig, Richard, 4
Luedtke, Luther S., 136
Lunt, George, 162
Lutheran Gethsemane Cemetery, 57
Lydenberg, John, 155
Lyman, Anne Jean, 43
Lyman, Benjamin Smith, 257
Lynch, Anne. *See* Botta, Anne C. Lynch
Lynch, Tibbie E., 381
Lynen, John F., 367
Lyon, Melvin E., 279
Lyon, William H., 191
Lyons, Nathan, 288–90, 293, 314
Lyttle, Charles H., 155

Mabbott, Thomas Ollive, 363, 369
Mabie, Hamilton Wright, 141
McAleer, John J., 283
McAtee, W. L., 272
McCall, Roy C., 227
McCart, Doris Louise, 237
McCarthy, Leonard, 308
McCarthy, Mr., 142
McColgan, Daniel T., 315
McCormick, Edgar L., 200
McCormick, John O., 158
McCosh, James, 94
M'Cully, R., 149
McCusker, Honor, 133
McCuskey, Dorothy, 87, 92
Macdonald, Joan, 77
McDonald, John Joseph, 158, 331, 335
McElderry, B. R., Jr., 322, 335
McElrath, Joseph R., Jr., 263
McGiffert, Arthur Cushman, Jr., 137, 155, 158, 346
McGill, Frederick T., Jr., 102–04, 181
McGovern, James R., 191
McGuire, Errol M., 268
McIntosh, James, 271, 272, 280

McIntyre, Carol Gay, 91
McKay, Glen W., 276
McKay, Mae Bernardine, 75
McKeehan, Irene P., 157
McKeithan, Dell Landreth, 335
McKinsey, Elizabeth R., 21, 71, 110, 115, 116, 126
Mackintosh, Charles G., 221
Mackintosh, James, 244, 337
McKuen, Kathryn Anderson, 163
McLean, Albert, 272
McLean, Andrew M., 148
McLean Asylum, 289
McLuhan, Marshall, 166, 275
McMaster, Helen Neill, 184
Macmillan (publishers), 144
MacMillan, Duane J., 274
McNamee, Lawrence Francis, 4
McNeal, Thomas H., 369
McNulty, John Bard, 159, 186
McQuiston, Raymer, 157
MacRae, Donald, 152
MacShane, Frank, 270
McVickar, John, 344
McWilliams, Wilson Carey, 24, 158, 274
Madden, Edward H., 24, 157, 319
Maddison, Carol H., 371
Magat, J. A., 162
Maginnes, David R., 222
Magnus, Philip, 158
Mailer, Norman, 284
Male, Roy R., Jr., 335
Malloy, Charles, 163
Malthus, Thomas Robert, 275
Mann, Benjamin Pickman, 236
Mann, Horace, 238
Mann, Horace, III 237
Mann, Mary Peabody, 235, 236, 238
Manning, J. M., 12
Mansfield, Luther S., 166
Marble, Annie Russell, 92, 181, 265
Marchand, Ernest, 158
Marks, Barry A., 284
Marks, Emerson R., 33, 146
Marotte, Beatrice E., 332
Marovitz, Sanford E., 147
Marsh, James, 22, 33, 194, 244, 248, 343–47
Marshall, Helen E., 74, 185
Marshall, James M., 281
Marshall, Margaret Wiley, 155
Martí, José, 166, 284
Martin, Jay, 151
Martin, John H., 220
Martin, John Stephen, 151
Martin, Terrence, 39
Martineau, Harriet, 305
Martineau, James, 150, 244
Marx, Karl, 19, 147, 224, 275, 282, 284, 306
Marx, Leo, 29, 152, 275

Mason, John A., 119, 120, 122
Massachusetts Free-Soil Party, 257
Massachusetts Historical Society, 3, 57, 97, 98, 103, 108, 113, 123, 137, 167, 168, 176, 196, 217, 235, 237, 243, 250, 254, 296, 310, 319
Massachusetts Quarterly Review, 70, 81, 221, 295, 308
Mather, Cotton, 165, 210
Mather, Winifred, 195
Mathews, Cornelius, 41
Mathews, James M., 44, 59
Mathews, J. Chesley, 138, 269
Mathewson, Rufus, Jr., 284
Mathis, Gerald Ray, 77
Matthessen, Peter, 284
Matthews, W. S. B., 132
Matthiessen, F. O., 18, 25, 42, 160, 277, 278, 307, 324, 335, 353, 359, 362, 381–83
Maulsby, David Lee, 166
Maurer, Armand, 308
Maxfield-Miller, Elizabeth, 140
May, Samuel J., 44, 53
Mayer, Frederick, 17
Maynard, Theodore, 304
Mazzini, Guiseppe, 179
Mead, C. David, 164
Mead, David, 94, 221
Mead, Edwin D., 144, 150, 199, 223
Meadville Theological School, 310, 311
Meese, Elizabeth A., 25, 151, 374
Mellow, James R., 330
Meltzer, Milton, 264
Melville, Herman, 222, 223, 231, 246, 267, 269, 283, 328, 331, 348–61, 365–68
Memorial of the Commemoration by the Church of the Disciples, 114
Mendelsohn, Jack, 312
Mendenhall, Lawrence, 70
Menzel, Wolfgang, 6
Menzi, Marjorie Jean, 66
Merwin, W. S., 28
Meszlenyi, Susanne Kossuth, 233
Mettke, Edith, 155
Metzdorf, Robert F., 330
Metzger, Charles R., 25, 152, 277, 381
Meyer, Donald H., 53
Meyer, Howard N., 195–98, 201, 203
Meyer, Michael, 75, 246, 261–63, 266, 276, 277, 282, 284
Miami University Library, 234
Michaels, Walter B., 283
Michaels, William P., 272
Michaud, Régis, 140, 151
Michelangelo Buonarroti, 149
Mickiewicz, Adam, 40, 179–81
Mickle, Isaac, 43
Middlebury College Library, 57, 59, 88. See also Abernethy Library

Miles, Josephine, 147, 163
Mill, John Stuart, 173
Miller, Edward Haviland, 376
Miller, F. DeWolfe, 123–25, 129
Miller, Harold P., 329
Miller, Henry, 166
Miller, James E., Jr., 35, 382
Miller, Lewis H., Jr., 275
Miller, Norman, 160
Miller, Perry, 5, 10, 15–17, 21, 22, 29, 30,
   31, 41, 45–48, 75, 89, 95, 109, 124–26,
   128, 132, 151, 157, 165, 177, 186, 218,
   228, 246, 251, 263, 268, 271, 274, 288,
   292, 293, 304, 307, 308, 313, 343, 353,
   370, 373
Millichap, Joseph R., 270
Milne, Gordon, 317, 319
Milnes, Richard Monckton, 142
Milton, John, 28, 30, 144, 148, 149, 163,
   269, 294, 314
Minnegerode, Meade, 38
Minot, William, 43
Mishra, Vishwa Mohan, 76
Mitchell, Donald G., 14
Mitterling, Philip I., 37
Mize, George Edwin, 41
MLA International Bibliography, 4, 329
Moffit, Robert E., 308
Moldenhauer, Joseph J., 263, 266, 279, 371
Moller, Mary Elkins, 273, 274
Momaday, N. Scott, 292
Mondale, Lester, 155
Montaigne, Michel Eyquem de, 143, 148
Montégut, Émile, 142
Monthly Anthology, 51
Monthly Miscellany, 59
Monthly Religious Magazine, 106
Mood, Fulmer, 315
Moody, Marjory M., 158
Moore, George F., 114
Moore, John B., 381
Moran, John Michael, Jr., 256
Moran, Virginia, 151
Moravsky, Maria, 159
More, Paul Elmer, 36, 146, 147, 166, 269,
   309, 336
Morey, Frederick L., 201
Morison, John Hopkins, 43, 209
Morison, Samuel Eliot, 17, 248
Morley, John, 144
Moro-oka, Aiko, 75
Morrow, Honoré Willsie, 90, 91
Morsberger, Robert E., 357
Morse, John T., Jr., 43
Morse, Jonathan, 198
Morse, Sidney H., 82
Morton, Doris, 76, 83, 142
Moseley, Caroline, 278

Mosher, Harold F., Jr., 279
Mosier, Richard D., 17
Moss, Marcia, 272
Moss, Sidney P., 161, 357, 358, 366
Moss, William M., 105, 127, 159, 215, 267,
   291, 380
Mott, Frank Luther, 3, 39, 70, 72, 74, 79–83
Mott, James, 43
Mott, Lucretia, 43, 225
Mott, Wesley T., 147, 155, 268
Mozoomdar, Protap Chunder, 144
Mueller, Roger Chester, 34, 71, 76, 78–82,
   204, 205, 270, 284
Muir, John, 139, 166
Muirhead, John H., 33, 34, 40
Müller, Max, 205
Mulqueen, James E., 151, 323
Mumford, Lewis, 151, 351, 352
Murdock, James, 12, 40
Murdock, Kenneth, 307, 308
Murphey, Murray G., 16, 24, 92, 95, 151
Murray, Donald M., 148, 275, 284
Murray, James G., 271
Myers, Richard E., 311
Myerson, Joel, 3, 4, 7, 19, 20, 41, 44, 56, 57,
   59, 61, 62, 69, 70, 73, 74–77, 79, 89–91,
   96, 101, 102, 104, 109, 111, 112, 114,
   123–25, 127, 131, 133, 135–38, 141, 142,
   147, 149, 157, 163–66, 169, 175, 176, 178,
   180–82, 185, 186, 189, 191–93, 200, 204,
   212, 215, 216, 220, 221, 233, 237, 239,
   240, 242, 249, 250, 254, 256, 264, 267,
   281, 286, 290, 291, 297, 300, 304, 310,
   319, 330, 332–34, 341, 342, 345, 346, 381

Nabokov, Vladimir, 284
Nachlas, Morton deCorcey, 311
Nagel, James, 141
Nagley, Winfield E., 274
Nakamura, Junichi, 366
Nash, Roderick, 29, 272
Nathan, James, 175, 177, 187
Nathan, Rhoda, 284, 324
Nathaniel Hawthorne Journal, 329
Nathaniel Hawthorne Society Newsletter, 329
Nation, 106, 107, 163, 200
National Academy of Design, 130
National Anti-Slavery Standard, 82, 287
National Archives, 235
National Union Catalog of Pre-1956 Imprints, 3,
   100, 101, 108, 131, 171, 233, 295
National Union Catalogue of Manuscript Collections,
   108, 234
National Woman's Rights Convention, 157
Neal, John, 43
Neal, Valerie S., 273

Nehru, Jawaharlal, 36
Nelson, Roland W., 363
Nelson, Truman, 63, 222, 231, 276
Nettels, Elsa, 274
Neufeldt, Leonard, 23, 112, 113, 141, 147, 151, 153, 158, 161, 267, 274, 276
Neussendorfer, Margaret, 237, 241
New Bedford Public Library, 296
Newberry Library, 80, 111
Newbrough, George F., 230
New-Church Quarterly Review, 149
Newcomb, Charles King, 57, 105, 214–15, 252, 291, 318, 329
Newell, William, 167–69
New England Hospital, 235
New-England Magazine, 153
New England Puritan, 162
New England Women's Club, 239
New Hampshire Historical Society, 217, 219
New Jerusalem Magazine, 373
Newman, Josephine K., 308
Newman, Lea Bertani Vozar, 329, 330
Newton, Benjamin F., 320, 321
Newton, Isaac, 149
Newton, Joseph Fort, 219
New York Aurora, 375
New-York Daily Tribune, 103, 376, 380
New York Herald Tribune, 242
New-York Historical Society, 108
New York Public Library, 4, 88, 171, 319. See also Berg Collection
New-York Tribune, 177, 184, 246
New York University. See Fales Library
Nichol, John, 13, 143
Nichols, Charles H., 227
Nichols, E. J., 341
Nichols, Mary Gove, 212
Nichols, Thomas Low, 43
Nicholson, Marjorie H., 33
Nicoloff, Philip L., 153
Nicolson, Marjory H., 345
Nicoson, Marilyn R., 128
Nietzsche, Friedrich, 166
Nilon, Charles H., 4
Nissenbaum, Stephen, 38
Noda, Hisashi, 322, 323
Norman, Henry, 150
North American Review, 163, 172, 210, 364, 380
North Church (Salem, Mass.), 171
Norton, Andrews, 12, 43, 47, 48, 50, 51, 55, 153, 218, 244, 245, 313, 315
Norton, Charles Eliot, 43, 138, 235, 319, 337, 341, 380
Notopoulos, James A., 136
Novak, Barbara, 26, 129, 284
Novalis [Friedrich von Hardenberg], 296
Noverr, Douglas A., 267
Noyes, D. P., 223

Noyes, John Humphrey, 157
Nye, Russel Blaine, 38, 42, 228

Oates, Stephen B., 222
O'Brien, Harriet E., 58
Observer and Religious Intelligencer, 243
Obuchowski, Peter A., 153
O'Connor, Evangeline M., 329
O'Connor, John Francis Xavier, 143
O'Connor, William Douglas, 377, 380
O'Daniel, Therman B., 162
Odell, Alfred Taylor, 157
Oegger, Guillaume, 240
Oehlschlaeger, Fritz, 284, 341
Oken, Lorenz, 95
Oldham, William, 57, 61
Olive Kettering Library, 236
Oliver, Egbert S., 268, 356–59
Oliver, Robert T., 162, 227
Olmert, K. Michael, 124
Omans, Glen A., 366
O'Neill, Eugene, 35
Orians, G. Harrison, 151
Orr, John, 12
Orth, Michael, 279
Orth, Ralph H., 138
Orvis, Helen D., 221
Orvis, Marianne Dwight. See Dwight, Marianne
Osgood, Samuel, 6, 11, 12, 44, 209
Ossian, 269
Ossoli, Giovanni, 179, 334
Ossoli, Sarah Margaret Fuller. See Fuller, Margaret
Ostrander, Gilman, 277
Ostrom, John Ward, 363
O'Sullivan, John, 306
Our Best Words, 114
Owen, James J., 329
Owen, Robert, 69
Owlett, F. C., 351

Pabodie, William J., 182
Pachori, Satya S., 158
Packer, Barbara L., 147, 161, 164
Page, H. A. See Japp, Alexander H.
Paget, Violet, 150
Paine, Thomas, 118
Paley, William, 39, 371
Palfrey, John Gorham, 43, 47
Pall Mall Gazette, 223
Palmer, Edward, 245
Paramananda, Swami, 148
Parker, Gail Thain, 36, 38, 159
Parker, Hershel, 350, 357, 360, 361
Parker, Jane Marsh, 239

Parker, Lydia, 216, 219, 221, 224
Parker, Theodore, 7, 8, 10, 11, 15, 21, 23, 24,
   31, 48, 53, 54, 65, 81, 113, 120, 143, 144,
   169, 170–74, 197, 201, 202, 209, 216–32,
   235, 239, 240, 244, 250, 252, 254, 258,
   296–98, 306, 308, 312, 313, 315, 316,
   318, 320, 324, 339, 360
Parker, Theodore (b. 1869), 220
Parkes, Henry Bamford, 151
Parrington, Vernon Louis, 17, 18, 157, 223,
   247, 276, 312, 313, 351, 362
Parsons, Anna Q. T., 65
Parsons, Theophilus, 12
Parsons, Thornton H., 6, 146, 278, 284
Parsons, Vesta M., 283
Patmore, Coventry, 144
Pattee, Fred Lewis, 13, 14, 38, 159
Patterson, Robert Leet, 311
Paul, Lucian, 165
Paul, Sherman, 25, 36, 93, 145, 212, 266,
   269–71, 278, 279, 281
Paulist Fathers Archives, 58, 211, 319
Payne, William Donald, 279
Peabody, Andrew Preston, 40, 53, 114, 210
Peabody, Elizabeth Palmer, 24, 48, 56, 60, 62–
   65, 80, 81, 88, 116, 132, 144, 154, 157,
   211, 233–41, 248, 250, 251, 311, 315, 333,
   335, 336, 372
Peabody, Ephraim, 53, 70, 71
Peabody, Francis Greenwood, 114, 313
Peabody, Mary. See Mann, Mary Peabody
Peabody, Sophia. See Hawthorne, Sophia
   Peabody
Peabody, W. B. O., 209
Peacock, Leishman A., 44
Peairs, Edith, 269
Pearce, Roy Harvey, 27, 30, 35, 382
Pearson, Henry Greenleaf, 42
Pearson, Norman Holmes, 239, 240, 333
Pease, Jane H., 38, 53
Pease, William H., 38, 53, 54
Peckham, Morse, 25
Pederson, Lee H., 278
Peirce, Ann-Mari, 78
Peirce, Charles Santiago Sanders, 36, 309
Pellico, Silvio, 269
Pennell, Elizabeth Robins, 43
Peple, Edward Cronin, Jr., 332, 333
Perkins, James Handasyd, 108, 115, 126
Perkins, Norman C., 73
Perry, Bliss, 14, 132, 145, 147, 191, 199, 379
Perry, Lewis, 94
Perry, Ralph Barton, 42
Perry, Thomas Sargent, 43
Persons, Stow, 17, 21, 22, 38, 54, 82, 99,
   155, 173, 174, 200, 232
Pessen, Edward, 38
Pestalozzi, Johann Heinrich, 92, 233, 244

Peterfreund, Sheldon P., 248
Peterson, Richard J., 39
Petre, Maud, 154
Phalanx, 59
Philanthropist, 304
Phillips, George Searle, 143, 162
Phillips, Mary E., 43, 180
Phillips, Wendell, 217, 225, 338
Pierce, Edward L., 43
Pierce, Franklin, 331
Pierpont Morgan Library, 4, 137, 235, 240,
   262
Pietras, Thomas P., 92
Pilgrim Society, 4, 103, 196
Pingel, Martha M., 43
Pioneer, 133, 236, 300, 341, 342
Pirsig, Robert M., 284
Pitcher, Edward William, 371
Pitman, Ursula Wall, 117, 118, 120
Plain Speaker, 90
Plato, 34, 91, 94, 144, 148, 161, 183, 270,
   345, 348, 353, 361, 381
Plotinus, 143
Plutarch, 149, 160, 378
PMLA, 362
Pochmann, Henry A., 32, 33, 36, 40, 50, 72,
   78, 80, 81, 94, 99, 101, 115, 126, 130,
   133, 148, 183, 184, 193, 194, 231, 247,
   249, 345, 366
Poe, Edgar Allan, 42, 79, 105, 106, 122, 127,
   128, 143, 199, 326, 362–71
Poe Newsletter, 363
Poe Studies, 362
Poger, Sidney, 78, 282, 285
Poirier, Richard, 28, 161
Poirier, Suzanne, 383
Pokrovsky, Nikita, 261
Polis, Joe, 275
Pollin, Burton R., 75, 363, 369–71
Pollock, Robert C., 155
Pommer, Henry F., 140, 159, 316
Pond, Enoch, 12
Pops, Martin Leonard, 283, 358
Porte, Joel, 25, 29, 138, 146–48, 152, 162,
   267, 272–74
Porter, David, 146, 294
Porter, James, 12
Porter, Lawrence Charles, 26, 77, 126
Porter, Maria S., 239
Porter, Noah, 12, 33, 39, 345
Potter, William J., 150, 173
Pound, Ezra, 166, 381
Powell, Janette Chilton, 79
Powell, Thomas, 143
Power, Julia, 39
Pratt, Frederick Woolsey, 58
Pratt, Minot, 65
Predmore, Richard, 284, 285, 333

Prentiss, G., 223
Prescott, William Hickling, 228
Present, 70, 78, 103, 109, 308
Price, Kenneth M., 378
Princeton University Library, 176
Princeton University Press, 262, 263
Pritchard, John Paul, 41, 162, 185
Proceedings at a Reception Given in Honor of the Rev. O. B. Frothingham, 173
Proclus, 348, 353, 359
Proust, Marcel, 166
Puk, Francine S., 357
Puknat, Siegfried B., 40, 229, 314
Purchase Street Church, 243, 244, 247
Putnam, Alfred P., 5, 20, 100, 113, 190, 296, 297
Putnam, George, 43, 53
Putnam, George Haven, 41
Putnam, George Palmer, 41, 361
Putnam's Monthly Magazine, 246, 380
Pyre, J. F. A., 74

Quade, Willie Vale Oldham, 130
Quarles, Francis, 269
Queens Borough Public Library, 242
Quick, Donald G., 273
Quimby, Phineas Parkhurst, 36, 44
Quincy, Edmund, 223
Quincy, Josiah P., 174
Quinn, Arthur Hobson, 14, 38, 147, 157
Quinn, Joseph L., 308
Quinn, Patrick F., 155, 368, 370

Rabinovitz, Albert L., 72, 78, 80
Radcliffe College. *See* Schlesinger Library
Radical, 12, 82, 163, 205, 218, 256, 295, 298
Radical Club, 20, 173, 197, 202, 297, 298
Raghaven, Ellen, 270
Raleigh, Walter, 263, 269
Ramakrishna, D., 368
Ramsey, Robert H., 227
Randall, Randolph C., 114
Randel, William Peirce, 96, 104, 334
Rans, Geoffrey, 371
Rantoul, R. S., 101
Rao, Adapa Ramakrishna, 151, 157, 158
Ratcliffe, S. K., 121
Rathbun, John W., 42, 162
Ray, Roberta K., 162
Rayapati, J. P. Rao, 34, 148
Raymond, Henrietta Dana, 252
Raymond, Henry, 345
Reaver, J. Russell, 147, 161
Reccord, Augustus P., 101
Redding, Mary Edrich, 147

Reeck, Stephanie Ann, 38
Reed, Amy L., 248, 252, 319
Reed, Kenneth T., 285
Reed, Sampson, 34, 43, 149, 372–74
Rees, John O., Jr., 240, 333
Rees, Robert A., 135
Reeves, Paschal, 289, 294
Reid, Alfred S., 151, 166
Reid, John T., 34
Reid, Whitelaw, 235
Reilly, Robert J., 14
Rein, Irving, 26
Reinhardt, John E., 315
Reinke, Elizabeth L., 321
Renan, Ernest, 314
Reney, Sister Mary Michelle, 321, 322
Renouf, Augustus Edward, 338
Reuben, Paul Purushottam, 83
Reynolds, Larry J., 381
Reynolds, R. C., 282
Rhoads, Kenneth W., 278
Rhys, Ernest, 351
Riback, William, 224
Ricardo, David, 275
Rice, Madeleine Hooke, 310–12
Richards, Laura E., 43, 114, 180
Richardson, Charles F., 13
Richardson, E. P., 42
Richardson, Merrill, 12
Richardson, Robert D., Jr., 31, 32, 90, 96, 161, 186, 187, 228, 232, 269, 270, 274, 279
Richardson, Robert K., 94
Richmond, Lee J., 324
Richter, Jean Paul Friedrich, 40, 101
Ricketson, Daniel, 103, 264
Ricks, Beatrice, 328
Rideout, Walter B., 288
Rider, Daniel Edgar, 26
Ridgely, J. V., 121, 379
Riegel, Robert E., 38
Rieger, Wolfgang, 74, 77
Riggs, Lisette. *See* Isely, Lisette Riggs
Riley, Woodbridge, 17, 39, 152
Rilke, Rainer Maria, 166
Ripley, Ezra, 264
Ripley, George, 6, 7, 10, 12, 16, 56, 59, 60, 62, 65–67, 76, 79, 80, 109, 124, 133, 149, 171, 181, 219, 226, 236, 240, 242–49, 251, 304, 308, 313, 315–18, 330, 343, 347, 356
Ripley, Samuel, 43
Ripley, Sarah Alden Bradford, 44, 140
Ripley, Sophia, 56, 62, 247, 250–52, 318
Rittenhouse, Caroline Smith, 247
Ritter, Albert, 288
Robbins, Chandler, 153
Robbins, J. Albert, 39
Roberts, Josephine Elizabeth, 234, 238, 239

Roberts, J. Russell, 148
Roberts Brothers (publishers), 39, 73, 236
Robertson, John M., 122, 150, 154
Robinson, David M., 21, 47, 49, 109, 110, 111, 123, 129, 147, 152, 155, 185, 286, 288, 291, 293, 294, 313, 315
Robinson, E. Arthur, 369
Robinson, Edwin Arlington, 166
Robinson, George Frederick, 169
Robinson, James K., 288
Rochester Unitarian Church, 108
Rodgers, Jane Ellin, 356
Roemer, Lawrence, 308
Rogers, C. A., 273
Rollins, Hyder Edward, 39
Ronda, Bruce A., 210, 238, 241, 293
Rosa, Alfred F., 35, 41, 335
Rose, Anne C., 17, 20, 23, 24
Rose, Edward J., 267, 283, 354
Rosenfeld, Alvin L., 380
Rosenfeld, William, 230, 231
Rosenthal, Bernard, 29, 75, 142, 185, 284
Ross, Donald, Jr., 161, 278, 279, 333, 382, 383
Rossetti, William Michael, 121
Rostenberg, Leona, 178, 239
Rothschild, Herbert B., Jr., 283
Roundtree, Thomas J., 147
Rousseau, Jean-Jacques, 32, 33, 269
Rowe, John C., 282
Rowfant Club, 73
Rowland, Beryl, 358
Roy, Rammohun, 53
Rubin, Joseph Jay, 379
Ruland, Richard, 136, 266
Rusk, Ralph Leslie, 59, 70, 76, 115, 126, 137–40, 159, 169, 177, 180, 181, 186, 215, 218, 219, 332, 376
Ruskin, John, 132, 166
Russell, Amelia, 319
Russell, Phillips, 140
Russell, W. Clark, 351
Russell and Russell (publishers), 73
Rutherford B. Hayes Memorial Library, 319
Ryan, Alvan S., 307
Ryan, George E., 277
Ryan, Kevin, 275
Ryan, Thomas R., 72, 304

St. Armand, Barton Levi, 284, 369, 371
St. Augustine, 268
Saint-Simon, Louis de Rouvroy, Duc de, 32, 305
Sakmann, Paul, 148
Salem Observer, 286, 287
Salinas, Oscar, 147
Salinger, J. D., 166

Sallust, 369
Salomon, Louis B., 155, 271, 275
Salt, Henry S., 255, 259, 265, 350, 351
Salter, William, 154, 156
Salzberg, Joel, 370
Sampson, Edward C., 332
Sampson, H. Grant, 280
Sams, Henry W., 56, 59, 64, 65, 246, 251, 330
Sanborn, Francis, 254
Sanborn, Franklin Benjamin, 13, 24, 61, 67, 73, 89, 90, 93, 98, 103–07, 138, 139, 141, 144, 165, 203, 212, 214, 216, 217, 219, 222, 230, 239, 241, 253–59, 263, 264, 297, 336, 380, 381
Sanborn, John Newell, 166
Sanborn, Victor Channing, 254, 258
Sand, George, 32, 39, 72, 78, 80
Sandeen, Ernest E., 157
Sanfillippo, Sister Mary Helena, 39
San Juan, Epifanio, Jr., 163
Santayana, George, 36, 146, 150, 160, 166, 309
Sargent, Epes, 332
Sargent, George H., 258
Sargent, John T., 218
Sargent, Mary E., 20, 124, 173, 298
Sarma, Sreekrishna, 270
Sartain, John, 41
Sartre, Jean-Paul, 166
Sattelmeyer, Robert C., Jr., 269, 282, 283
Saturday Club, 20, 141
Saunders, Judith, 274
Saunders, Robert James, 238
Savage, Minot J., 154, 173, 296, 297, 316
Savage, W. H., 154
Savary, John, 153
Saxton, J. A., 11
Saxton, Martha, 93
Say, Jean-Baptiste, 275
Sayre, Robert F., 268, 275
Schamberger, J. Edward, 149
Scheick, William J., 146, 160, 161
Schelling, Friedrich Wilhelm Joseph von, 149, 192, 365
Schiff, Martin, 36
Schiller, Andrew, 163, 277, 380, 381
Schiller, Johann Christoph Friedrich von, 6, 98, 101, 133, 296
Schleiermacher, Friedrich, 231, 244
Schleiner, Louise, 163
Schlesinger, Arthur M., Jr., 18, 23, 37, 38, 72, 247, 303, 304, 306, 307, 315, 316
Schlesinger, Arthur M., Sr., 307
Schlesinger Library, 235, 250
Schlicht, Rüdiger C., 24, 92, 158
Schneider, Gail K., 129
Schneider, Herbert W., 16, 92, 192, 194, 230, 312, 313

Schneider, Richard J., 272, 273, 283
Schneider, Valerie, 227
Schoenbaum, S., 294
Schoenfeldt, Arthur, 101
Schopenhauer, Arthur, 194
Schorer, Jean, 220
Schriber, Mary Sue, 332
Schroeder, Fred E. H., 35
Schroeder, John H., 226
Schultz, Arthur R., 183, 247
Schurz, Carl, 235
Schuster, Eunice M., 276
Schwarz, Harold, 221
Scott, Leonora Cranch, 71, 124, 125, 127
Scott, Otto J., 222
Scott, Walter, 149
Scovel, Carl R., 224
Scriptural Interpreter, 168, 228
Scudder, Horace Elisha, 41, 341
Scudder, Jeanie W., 120
Scudder, Townsend, 40, 140, 141, 163, 264
Seaburg, Alan, 4, 49
Sealts, Merton M., Jr., 124, 147, 164, 351–53, 355, 356, 359–61
Searle, January. *See* Phillips, George Searle
Sears, Clara Endicott, 23, 57, 58, 60, 61, 67, 89, 93, 212
Sears, John Van Der Zee, 59, 63, 65, 66, 248
Sedgwick, Ora Gannett, 319
Seelye, John, 270, 275, 357
Seldes, Gilbert, 37, 151
Sewall, Frank, 34, 39
Sewall, Samuel E., 43
Seward, William Henry, 217, 379
Sewell, Richard H., 219
Seybold, Ethel, 269
Shaffer, Robert B., 152
Shaftesbury, Anthony Ashley-Cooper, Third Earl of, 359
Shakespeare, William, 147–49, 163, 215, 269, 287, 294, 296, 298, 378
Shaler, Nathan, 173
Shanley, J. Lyndon, 262, 271, 282, 285
Shapiro, Samuel, 222
Sharma, Mohan Lal, 270
Shattuck, Lemuel, 283
Shaw, Charles Gray, 155
Shea, Daniel B., 146, 161
Shear, Walter L., 279
Shelley, Percy Bysshe, 39, 365
Shelley, Philip Allison, 40, 148, 183
Shepard, Odell, 10, 56, 60, 61, 67, 68, 89–93, 95, 212, 239, 376
Shephard, Esther, 381
Shepherd, Holley M., 49
Sherman, Stuart P., 157
Sherwin, J. S., 282
Sherwin, Oscar, 222
Sherwood, Mary P., 272

Sherwood, M. E. W., 43
Sherwood, William R., 326
Shivers, Frank R., Jr., 21, 71, 110, 115, 126
Shubert, Mary Ann, 322
Shuman, R. Baird, 133, 341
Shurr, William, 30
Sidney, Margaret, 40
Siebert, Wilbur H., 222
Sill, Edward Rowland, 256
Silsbee, Edward A., 291, 292
Silsbee, William, 12
Silver, Mildred, 158
Simmons, Edward, 43
Simmons, Nancy Craig, 42, 137
Simms, William Gilmore, 43
Simon, Jules, 136
Simon, Myron, 6, 146, 278
Simpson, Claude M., 180, 330
Simpson, Lewis P., 51, 52
Sims, Thomas, 221
Siracusa, Carl, 225
Skwire, David, 279
Slater, Joseph, 76, 138, 180, 248, 300
Slethhaug, Gordon E., 270
Sloan, John H., 162
Slochower, Harry, 183
Slotkin, Richard, 29, 272
Smart, George K., 69
Smith, Adam, 275
Smith, Bernard, 14, 162
Smith, Duane E., 18, 308
Smith, Elizabeth Oakes, 43
Smith, Gayle L., 161
Smith, George W., 269
Smith, Henry Nash, 164
Smith, Herbert F., 274, 275
Smith, H. Shelton, 15, 51, 230
Smith, John, 269
Smith, Timothy L., 38
Smith, Warren Sylvester, 121
Smith, William, 296
Smith, William Henry, 142
Smith, Wilson, 50, 52
Smith College Library. *See* Sophia Smith Collection
Smithline, Arnold, 165, 229, 367
Smith-Rosenberg, Carrol, 182
Snider, Denton J., 43, 139
Snodgrass, J. E., 12
Social Circle of Concord, 141
Soleta, Chester, 308
Solger, Reinhold, 235
Somaj, Brahmo, 53
Somkin, Fred, 38
Sophia Smith Collection, 235
Southern Illinois University Library, 76
Southern Rose, 142
South Place Magazine, 122
South Place Society, 119, 121

Southworth, James G., 269
Sowder, William J., 135, 136
Sparks, Jared, 53, 168
Spaulding, A. F., 154
Specimens of Foreign Standard Literature, 6, 109, 245, 246, 251
Spencer, Benjamin T., 26, 41, 151, 185
Spencer, Donald S., 38
Spencer, Herbert, 150, 246
Spender, Stephen, 39
Spiller, Robert E., 14, 57, 92, 138, 147, 155, 161, 312, 314
Spirit of the Age, 69, 80, 109, 111
Sprague, William B., 345
Springfield Republican, 253
Sproude, Veda Bagwell, 333, 334
Spurgeon, Caroline, 269
Staebler, Warren, 146
Staël, Madame de, 32, 33, 372
Stafford, John, 41, 162
Stange, Douglas C., 23, 53, 116, 226, 315
Stansberry, Gloria J., 279
Stanton, Elizabeth Cady, 43
Stanwood, Edward, 258
Staples, Laurence C., 120
Stapleton, Laurence, 161, 277, 278
Starr, Harris Elwood, 101, 169, 205
State Historical Society of Wisconsin, 242
Staten Island Institute of Arts and Sciences, 129, 319
Stauffer, Donald B., 27, 129
Stearns, Frank Preston, 40, 43, 125, 129, 163, 335
Stearns, George Luther, 43
Stearns, Oliver, 53
Stearns, Sarah, 252
Stebbins, Giles, 13
Stebbins, Theodore E., Jr., 42
Stedman, Edmund Clarence, 43, 163, 173, 363
Stedman, Laura, 43
Steele, Marie T., 335
Stein, William Bysshe, 266, 270, 357, 358
Steinbrink, Jeffrey, 25, 162
Sten, Christopher W., 357
Stenberg, Theodore T., 162
Stenerson, Douglas C., 152
Sterling, John, 138
Stern, Daniel. *See* D'Agoult, Comtesse
Stern, Guy, 101
Stern, Madeleine B., 39, 41, 43, 75, 110, 129, 176, 179, 181, 239, 252
Stern, Milton R., 352
Stern, Philip Van Doren, 282
Stevens, Wallace, 28, 35, 166, 369
Stevenson, Robert Louis, 165, 284
Stewart, Dugald, 149
Stewart, George, Jr., 143
Stewart, Randall, 41, 155, 180, 329–31
Stewart, Samuel Barrett, 231

Stibitz, E. Earle, 267
Stiem, Marjorie, 92
Stillman, William J., 141
Stockton, Edwin, Jr., 279
Stoddard, Richard Henry, 41
Stoehr, Taylor, 18, 24, 41, 66, 67, 93, 94, 158, 213, 276, 331, 333
Stokes, Harry M., 54
Stoller, Leo, 44, 273, 274
Story, Emelyn, 180
Story, Ronald, 40, 52
Story, William Wetmore, 43, 129, 130, 180
Stovall, Floyd, 136, 155, 315, 352, 366, 368, 379
Stowe, Harriet Beecher, 285
Stowell, Robert F., 264
Strachner, Stephen D., 270
Straker, Robert Lincoln, 234, 236, 237
Strauch, Carl F., 7, 20, 136, 152, 153, 155, 156, 158–60, 164, 166, 186, 374
Strauss, David Friedrich, 121, 229
Strelow, Michael Herbert, 356
Strickland, Charles, 93
Stromberg, Roland N., 135, 284
Strong, Augustus Hopkins, 163
Strong, George Templeton, 41
Stuart, Moses, 344
Studies in the American Renaissance, 5
Sturgis, Caroline, 184, 186, 214
Stutler, Boyd B., 254
Sudol, Ronald A., 147
Sue, Eugène, 80
Sullivan, Louis, 277
Sultana, Donald, 269
Summerlin, Charles T., 293
Sumner, Charles, 43, 217, 219, 379
Sunderland, J. T., 54
Sundquist, Eric, 282
Sutcliffe, Emerson Grant, 161, 374, 381
Sveino, Per, 308
Swan, Mabel Munson, 130
Swedenborg, Emanuel, 12, 31, 34, 39, 69, 79, 149, 159, 269, 372–74
Sweet, William W., 15
Swift, David E., 346
Swift, Lindsay, 23, 44, 56, 64, 65, 79, 111, 127, 132, 157, 248, 252, 258, 319
Swinburn, Algernon, 166
Swiniarski, Louise, 238
Swisher, Walter Samuel, 109, 111
Synod of Dort, 305
Szymanski, Karen Ann, 184

Talmadge, John E., 222
Tanner, Tony, 25, 28, 35, 160, 161, 280
Tanselle, G. Thomas, 350
Tassin, Algernon, 70, 72, 74, 79, 81

Taylor, Bayard, 41, 199, 246
Taylor, Edward, 292
Taylor, H. Leland, 185
Taylor, J. Golden, 266, 278, 279
Taylor, Thomas, 33, 94
Taylor, Walter Fuller, 14, 369
Teck-Young, Kwon, 95
Temmer, M. J., 269
Templeman, William, 269
Tennyson, Alfred, Lord, 39, 300
Thacher, A. G., Jr., 111
Thackeray, William Makepeace, 246
Tharp, Louise Hall, 237
Tharpe, Jac, 335
Thayer, James B., 43, 139
Thayer, William R., 144
Thayer and Eldridge (publishers), 377
Theodore Parker: Anniversaries of Birth and Death Celebrated in Chicago, 231
Thomas, Amelia Forbes, 141
Thomas, J. B., 153
Thomas, John L., 18, 38
Thomas, John Wesley, 71, 77, 80, 113–15, 133, 180, 183, 186
Thomas, Robert K., 272
Thomas, William S., 284
Thompson, Cameron, 33, 50
Thompson, Frank T., 148, 163
Thompson, G. R., 368
Thompson, Lawrance, 42
Thompson, Wade, 271
Thoreau, Henry David, 1, 2, 4–8, 10, 13, 17–19, 22–27, 29, 31, 33, 34, 36, 40, 45, 60, 67, 76, 80, 92, 94, 103–07, 109, 120, 133, 134, 138, 143, 146, 165, 166, 181, 186, 197, 199, 203, 205, 212, 214, 234, 240, 246, 255–59, 260–285, 290, 291, 300, 305, 307, 316, 318, 320–22, 324, 328, 331–33, 336–41, 348, 350, 352, 355–61, 365, 369, 374, 376, 377, 380, 381, 383
Thoreau, John, 265
Thoreau Journal Quarterly, 5, 261
Thoreau Quarterly, 5, 261
Thoreau Society Bulletin, 5, 260, 261
Thundyil, Zacharias, 156
Thurin, Erik Ingvar, 146
Thurman, Kelly, 334
Thurow, Waldemar A., 87
Thwing, Charles W., 158
Tichi, Cecelia, 272
Ticknor, Anna, 43
Ticknor, Caroline, 44, 319, 330
Ticknor, George, 43, 52, 347
Tiffany, Francis, 10, 44, 192
Tiffany, Nina Moore, 43, 44
Tileston, Mary Wilder, 43
Tillinghast, C. A., 279
Tillman, James, 275
Tilton, Eleanor M., 43, 138, 163, 380

Time and the Hour, 98
Timpe, Eugene F., 136, 261, 284
Tingley, Donald F., 37
Tocqueville, Alexis de, 308, 314
Todd, Edgeley Woodman, 33, 40, 248, 267
Tolles, Frederick B., 149
Tolman, George, 140
Tolstoy, Lev, 166
Tompkins, Philip K., 26
Torrey, Bradford, 263
Torry, Joseph, 344
Touloumtzis, Michael, 269
Town and Country Club, 20, 88, 89, 141
Townsend, Harvey Gates, 17
Transcendental Books, 4
Transcendental Club, 1, 8, 11, 20, 49, 74, 91, 94, 141, 169, 170, 172, 181, 191, 193, 221, 249, 251, 290, 303, 305, 343, 347
Traubel, Horace, 223, 376, 378, 379
Travellers in Arcadia, 130
Travis, Mildred K., 355
Treat, Betty, 273
Treat, Robert, 273
Trent, William P., 14, 247
Trimpi, Helen P., 222, 360
Trinity College. *See* Watkinson Library
Trowbridge, John Townsend, 43, 94, 375, 379, 382
Trueblood, D. Elton, 164
Trumpet and Universalist Magazine, 159
Tryon, W. S., 42
Tucker, Louis L., 20, 115, 126
Tuckerman, Frederick Goddard, 292
Tuckerman, Henry T., 130
Tuckerman, Joseph, 315
Tuerk, Richard, 155, 279, 281, 282
Tuomi, Martha Ilona, 191
Turco, Lewis, 166, 292
Turner, Arlin, 63, 240, 330, 331, 333
Turpie, Marcy C., 149
Tuttleton, James W., 198, 201
Twain, Mark, 121, 298
Twenty-Eighth Congregational Society, 221, 222
The Twenty-Eighth Congregational Society of Boston, 222
Tyack, David B., 43, 52
Tyler, Alice Felt, 18, 37, 93, 224
Tyler, Moses Coit, 198
Tyndall, John, 166
Tzu, Chuang, 270

Uhland, Johann Ludwig, 6, 101
Uhlig, Herbert, 273
Unamuno, Miguel de, 166, 285
Underwood, Benjamin F., 82
Underwood, Francis H., 143

Underwood, Sarah A., 241
Underwood, W. J., 149
Union List of Serials, 3, 69
Unitarian Advocate, 168
Unitarian Review, 190
Unitarian Universalist Association, 171
Unitarian Universalist Christian, 190
United States Magazine, and Democratic Review, 72, 163, 304, 306
United States Office of Education, 235
United States Sanitary Commission, 111
University of Chicago Library. *See* Elijah P. Grant Papers
University of Illinois Library, 57
University of Michigan, 198. *See also* Bentley Historical Library
University of Notre Dame Library, 57, 304
University of Pennsylvania Library, 88
University of Rochester Library, 217
University of Vermont, 344–47
University of Virginia. *See* Clifton Waller Barrett Collection
University of Virginia Library, 88, 100, 137, 176, 196
University of Wyoming Library, 124
Unrue, Dorothy, 269
Updike, John, 166
Upham, Thomas, 290
Urbanski, Marie Mitchell Olesen, 182, 183, 186, 188
Ustick, W. Lee, 148

Van Anglen, Kevin P., 269, 284
Vance, William Silas, 39
Vanderbilt, Kermit, 43
Van Deusen, Glyndon G., 41
Van Deusen, Marshall, 165
Van Doren, Carl, 209, 351
Van Doren, Mark, 265, 271
Van Nostrand, A. D., 28, 156
Van Vechten, Carl, 359
Varner, John Grier, 44
Vassar College Library, 235
Vaughan, Mosetta I., 168, 169
Venable, William H., 70, 82, 110, 115, 126
Vernon, Hope Jillson, 342
Very, Jones, 5, 7, 25, 47, 105, 181, 267, 286–94, 316, 329, 334
Very, Lydia, 290
Veysey, Laurence, 38
Vico, Giovanni Battista, 149
Vincent, Howard P., 353
Virgil, 124
Vitanen, Reino, 314
Vitanza, Victor J., 353
Vogel, Stanley M., 32, 72, 78, 80, 101, 115, 126, 133, 148, 183, 192, 194, 231, 249, 269, 343

Volkman, Arthur G., 273
Voltaire, 269
von Frank, Albert J., 163, 184
von Klenze, Camillo, 101

Wade, Joseph, 273
Wade, J. S., 260
Wade, Mason, 75, 177, 179
Wagenknecht, Edward, 146, 271, 273, 366, 367
Waggoner, Hyatt H., 27, 28, 30, 35, 164, 165, 280, 293, 326, 333, 369, 382
Wagner, C. Roland, 276, 277
Wagner, Frederick, 61, 89, 334
Wahr, Frederic B., 148
Waite, Robert G., 355
Walcutt, Charles Child, 35, 283
Walker, Ariana, 255, 257
Walker, C. S., 154
Walker, Edwin C., 122
Walker, James, 49, 52, 173, 245
Walker, James P., 39
Walker, Peter, 120
Walker, Robert Howard, 68, 212
Wall, Annie, 13
Walters, Ronald G., 38
Walton, Isaak, 269
Ward, Anna Barker, 235
Ward, Annie J., 60
Ward, J. A., 158
Ward, Prudence, 60
Ward, Robert S., 315
Ward, Robert Stafford, 155
Ward, Sam, 43, 182
Ward, Samuel Gray, 44, 138, 179, 182, 186, 235, 290
Ward, Theodora V. W., 198, 321
Warders, Donald F., 8, 23, 77, 127, 142, 281, 293
Ware, Henry, Jr., 43, 51–53
Ware, Henry, Sr., 43
Ware, John, 43
Ware, Mary L., 43
Ware, William, 51, 52
Warfel, Harry R., 75, 76, 186
Warren, Austin, 24, 42, 91, 94, 95, 99, 334, 335, 341
Washburn, Edward A., 338
Washburn, W. E., 35
Wasson, David Atwood, 44, 82, 163, 172
Waters, Edward, 133
Watertown Free Public Library, 168
Watertown Public Library, 296
Watkinson Library, 254
Watner, Carl, 212
Watson, Marston, 103, 104
Watson, Mary, 103, 104
Weaver, Raymond W., 351

Webber, Everett, 66, 68
Weber, Max, 274
Weber, Ralph Emil, 77
Webster, Daniel, 23, 197, 227, 276
Webster, Frank Martindale, 77
Weeks, Louis B., III, 225
Weidman, Bette S., 41
Weisbuch, Robert, 326, 327
Weiss, John, 82, 168, 169, 219, 220, 295–98
Welch, Claude, 313
Welch, Donovan L., 280
Welker, R. H., 272
Welland, Dennis, 121, 122
Wellek, René, 25, 32, 36, 95, 146, 148, 162, 183, 194, 231, 249, 307, 345
Wellesley College Library, 287
Wellisz, Leopold, 180
Wells, Anna Mary, 195, 197, 198, 201
Wells, Daniel A., 3, 70
Wells, Henry W., 280, 324, 325, 360
Wells, Ronald Vale, 21, 22, 170, 189, 192, 193, 344
Welter, Barbara, 44, 187
Welter, Rush, 38
Wendell, Barrett, 13, 17, 91, 247
Wendell, Julia, 166
Wendte, Charles William, 44, 101, 216, 218, 220, 222
Werge, Thomas, 274
Werkmeister, W. H., 17
Wertheim, Stanley, 328
West, Michael, 267, 279, 284, 343, 346
Westall, John, 149
Westbrook, Perry D., 42
The West Church, Boston, Commemorative Services, 98
Western Messenger, 70–72, 109, 110, 115, 116, 124–26, 188, 286, 287, 290
Whaling, Anne, 268
Whately, Richard, 267
Wheeler, Charles Stearns, 287, 290, 299–300, 336
Wheeler, Otis B., 157
Wheeler, Ruth Robinson, 40, 169, 264
Wheelock, Edwin Miller, 222
Wheelock, Lucy, 239
Whicher, George Frisbie, 5, 6, 324
Whicher, Stephen E., 138, 140, 145, 147, 156
Whipple, Edwin Percy, 44
Whitaker, Daniel K., 12
Whitaker, Rosemary, 282
White, Maria. See Lowell, Maria White
White, Morton, 16, 17, 166
White, Peter, 230
White, Ruth Helen, 346
White, Viola C., 262
White, William, 76, 260, 376, 380
Whitehead, Alfred North, 116, 166
Whiter, Walter, 267

Whitfield, Francis J., 40
Whitford, Kathryn, 159, 272, 273
Whitford, Philip, 272
Whiting, Lilian, 40
Whitman, Mrs. Louisa Van Velsor, 376
Whitman, Sarah Helen, 44, 364
Whitman, Walt, 27, 28, 30, 35, 36, 121, 129, 166, 193, 223, 227, 264, 267, 269, 272, 277, 279, 291, 294, 318, 324, 325, 352, 375–83
Whitney, Solon F., 169
Whittemore, Thomas, 43
Whittier, John Greenleaf, 7, 43, 378
Wichelns, Herbert A., 162
Wiggin, Kate Douglas, 43, 239
Wilbur, Earl Morse, 49
Wilbur, Richard, 370, 371
Wild, Paul H., 36
Willard, Abbie F., 35
Willard, Charles B., 379
Williams, George Huntston, 40, 48, 51, 53, 155, 169, 194
Williams, Henry, 297, 300
Williams, John Brindley, 355
Williams, Mentor L., 155
Williams, Paul O., 27, 104, 105, 129, 280, 284, 293
Williams, Stanley T., 27, 148, 163
Williams, Wallace E., 138
Williams College. See Chapin Library
Willingham, Robert Marion, Jr., 42
Willis, Frederick L. H., 90
Willis, Lonnie, 268
Willson, E. B., 101
Willson, Lawrence, 268, 272, 273, 282, 380
Wilmes, D. R., 257
Wilson, Edmund, 379
Wilson, Howard, 247
Wilson, James Grant, 41
Wilson, Janice Elizabeth, 75
Wilson, John Byron, 22–24, 26, 32, 68, 77, 81, 92, 93, 116, 151, 185, 238, 240, 273
Wilson, Leslie P., 241
Wilson, R. Jackson, 157
Winslow, Helen M., 40
Winsor, Justin, 40
Winston, George P., 42
Winters, Yvor, 155, 292–94, 359
Wintersteen, Prescott Browning, 230
Wiseman, James, 155
Wish, Harvey, 38
Wister, Annis Lee, 190
Witherell, Elizabeth Hall, 263, 280
Wolf, William J., 272, 273
Wolfe, Thomas, 166
Wolff, Cynthia Griffin, 198
Wood, Barry, 148, 270, 281
Woodall, Guy R., 168

Woodberry, George Edward, 119, 128, 144,
    145, 363
Woodbury, Charles J., 139
Woodlief, Annette M., 136, 261, 267, 282,
    283
Woodress, James, 4
Woodson, Thomas, 263, 282, 283
Worcester, Thomas, 44, 373
Wordsworth, William, 33, 95, 126, 149, 269,
    272, 283, 292, 353, 372
Wordsworth Museum, 235
Wright, Conrad, 21, 48–52, 54, 116, 155,
    164, 191, 218, 220, 221, 248, 310, 312–14
Wright, Frank Lloyd, 35, 277
Wright, Henry Gardiner, 61
Wright, Nathalia, 324
Wyeth, Andrew, 35
Wyman, Mary A., 148
Wynkoop, William M., 148

Yale University Library, 196, 238, 288
Yannella, Donald Joseph, Jr., 41
Yannella, Philip, 283
Yeats, William Butler, 285
Yoder, R. A., 18, 19, 25, 146, 161, 164, 332,
    335
Yohannan, J. D., 148
York, Robert M., 42
Young, Charles Lowell, 148
Young, Edward, 149, 174
Young, Gloria, 147

Ziethen, Johannes, 217
Ziff, Larzer, 41
Zink, Harriet Rodgers, 148
Zonderman, David A., 246